COMPILATION OF SELECTED UNITED STATES INTELLIGENCE LAWS

VOLUME 1: FOUNDATIONAL NATIONAL SECURITY FRAMEWORK AND CIA AUTHORITIES

Prepared by M. TWINCHEK

2024

Forward

This Compilation of Selected United States Intelligence Laws is a resource for those interested in U.S. laws governing the Intelligence Community.

This volume includes the foundational statutes that shape the modern national security framework. It covers the creation of the national security apparatus in the National Security Act of 1947, the establishment and authorities of the National Security Agency and Central Intelligence Agency, and major structural reforms enacted through the Intelligence Reform and Terrorism Prevention Act of 2004.

The materials included come from publicly available, open-source information, prepared for the public by the Office of the Legislative Counsel of the U.S. House of Representatives and the Office of the Law Revision Counsel.

Items listed as a Statute Compilation do not appear in the U.S. Code or have been classified to a title of the U.S. Code that has not been enacted into positive law. Each Statute Compilation incorporates the amendments made to the underlying statute since it was originally enacted and is current as of the date noted.

This compilation is not an official document and should not be cited as evidence of any law. The official version of federal law is found in the United States Statutes at Large and in the U.S. Code, the legal effect of which is established in sections 112 and 204, respectively, of title 1, United States Code.

Questions and comments may be directed to:

M. Twinchek

Email: mtwinchek@outlook.com

Contents

Contents

Foundational National Security Framework

National Security Act of 1947

National Security Agency Act of 1959

Intelligence Reform and Terrorism Prevention Act of 2004

SELECTED PROVISIONS OF THE NATIONAL SECURITY ACT OF 1947

CHAPTER 343

AS AMENDED THROUGH P.L. 118–159

NATIONAL SECURITY ACT OF 1947

[Chapter 343; 61 Stat. 496; approved July 26, 1947]

[As Amended Through P.L. 118–159, Enacted December 23, 2024]

AN ACT To promote the national security by providing for a Secretary of Defense; for a National Military Establishment; for a Department of the Army, a Department of the Navy, and a Department of the Air Force; and for the coordination of the activities of the National Military Establishment with other departments and agencies of the Government concerned with the national security.

Be it enacted by the Senate and House of Representatives of the United States of America in Congress assembled,

SHORT TITLE

That [50 U.S.C. 3001] this Act may be cited as the "National Security Act of 1947".

TABLE OF CONTENTS

[1] The toc item of section 108B does not match the section heading. The toc item reads "world-wide" while the section heading reads "worldwide". See amendments made by section 617 of division W of Public Law 116-260.

* * * * * * *

DECLARATION OF POLICY

SEC. 2. [50 U.S.C. 3002] In enacting this legislation, it is the intent of Congress to provide a comprehensive program for the future security of the United States; to provide for the establishment of integrated policies and procedures for the departments, agencies, and functions of the Government relating to the national security; to provide a Department of Defense, including the three military Departments of the Army, the Navy (including naval aviation and the United States Marine Corps), and the Air Force under the direction, authority, and control of the Secretary of Defense; to provide that each military department shall be separately organized under its own Secretary and shall function under the direction, authority, and control of the Secretary of Defense; to provide for their unified direction under civilian control of the Secretary of Defense but not to merge these departments or services; to provide for the establishment of unified or specified combatant commands, and a clear and direct line of command to such commands; to eliminate unnecessary duplication in the Department of Defense, and particularly in the field of research and engineering by vesting its overall direction and control in the Secretary of Defense; to provide more effective, efficient, and economical administration in the Department of Defense; to provide for the unified strategic direction of the combatant forces, for their operation under unified command, and for their integration into an efficient team of land, naval, and air forces but not to establish a single Chief of Staff over the armed forces nor an overall armed forces general staff.

DEFINITIONS

SEC. 3. **[50 U.S.C. 3003]** As used in this Act:

(1) The term "intelligence" includes foreign intelligence and counterintelligence.

(2) The term "foreign intelligence" means information relating to the capabilities, intentions, or activities of foreign governments or elements thereof, foreign organizations, or foreign persons, or international terrorist activities.

(3) The term "counterintelligence" means information gathered, and activities conducted, to protect against espionage, other intelligence activities, sabotage, or assassinations conducted by or on behalf of foreign governments or elements thereof, foreign organizations, or foreign persons, or international terrorist activities.

(4) The term "intelligence community" includes the following:

(A) The Office of the Director of National Intelligence.

(B) The Central Intelligence Agency.

(C) The National Security Agency.

(D) The Defense Intelligence Agency.

(E) The National Geospatial-Intelligence Agency.

(F) The National Reconnaissance Office.

(G) Other offices within the Department of Defense for the collection of specialized national intelligence through reconnaissance programs.

(H) The intelligence elements of the Army, the Navy, the Air Force, the Marine Corps, the Space Force, the Coast Guard, the Federal Bureau of Investigation, the Drug Enforcement Administration, and the Department of Energy.

(I) The Bureau of Intelligence and Research of the Department of State.

(J) The Office of Intelligence and Analysis of the Department of the Treasury.

(K) The Office of Intelligence and Analysis of the Department of Homeland Security.

(L) Such other elements of any department or agency as may be designated by the President, or designated jointly by the Director of National Intelligence and the head of the department or agency concerned, as an element of the intelligence community.

(5) The terms "national intelligence" and "intelligence related to national security" refer to all intelligence, regardless of the source from which derived and including information gathered within or outside the United States, that—

(A) pertains, as determined consistent with any guidance issued by the President, to more than one United States Government agency; and

(B) that involves—

(i) threats to the United States, its people, property, or interests;

(ii) the development, proliferation, or use of weapons of mass destruction; or

(iii) any other matter bearing on United States national or homeland security.

(6) The term "National Intelligence Program" refers to all programs, projects, and activities of the intelligence community, as well as any other programs of the

intelligence community designated jointly by the Director of National Intelligence and the head of a United States department or agency or by the President. Such term does not include programs, projects, or activities of the military departments to acquire intelligence solely for the planning and conduct of tactical military operations by United States Armed Forces.

(7) The term "congressional intelligence committees" means—

(A) the Select Committee on Intelligence of the Senate; and

(B) the Permanent Select Committee on Intelligence of the House of Representatives.

TITLE I—COORDINATION FOR NATIONAL SECURITY

SEC. 101. [50 U.S.C. 3021] NATIONAL SECURITY COUNCIL.

(a) National Security Council.— There is a council known as the National Security Council (in this section referred to as the "Council").

(b) Functions.—Consistent with the direction of the President, the functions of the Council shall be to—

(1) advise the President with respect to the integration of domestic, foreign, and military policies relating to the national security so as to enable the Armed Forces and the other departments and agencies of the United States Government to cooperate more effectively in matters involving the national security;

(2) assess and appraise the objectives, commitments, and risks of the United States in relation to the actual and potential military power of the United States, and make recommendations thereon to the President;

(3) make recommendations to the President concerning policies on matters of common interest to the departments and agencies of the United States Government concerned with the national security; and

(4) coordinate, without assuming operational authority, the United States Government response to malign foreign influence operations and campaigns.

(c) Membership.—

(1) In general.— The Council consists of the President, the Vice President, the Secretary of State, the Secretary of Defense, the Secretary of Energy, the Secretary of the Treasury, the Director of the Office of Pandemic Preparedness and Response Policy and such other officers of the United States Government as the President may designate.

(2) Attendance and participation in meetings.— The President may designate such other officers of the United States Government as the President considers appropriate, including the Director of National Intelligence, the Director of National Drug Control Policy, the Chairman of the Joint Chiefs of Staff, and the National Cyber Director, to attend and participate in meetings of the Council.

(d) Presiding Officers.— At meetings of the Council, the President shall preside or, in the absence of the President, a member of the Council designated by the President shall preside.

(e) Staff.—

(1) IN GENERAL.— The Council shall have a staff headed by a civilian executive secretary appointed by the President.

(2) STAFF.— Consistent with the direction of the President and subject to paragraph (3), the executive secretary may, subject to the civil service laws and chapter 51 and subchapter III of chapter 53 of title 5, United States Code, appoint and fix the compensation of such personnel as may be necessary to perform such duties as may be prescribed by the President in connection with performance of the functions of the Council.

(3)[2] NUMBER OF PROFESSIONAL STAFF.— The professional staff for which this subsection provides shall not exceed 200 persons, including persons employed by, assigned to, detailed to, under contract to serve on, or otherwise serving or affiliated with the staff. The limitation in this paragraph does not apply to personnel serving substantially in support or administrative positions.

---

[2] Section 1085(b) of division A of Public Law 114-328 states "The limitation on the number of professional staff of the National Security Council specified in subsection (e)(3) of section 101 of the National Security Act of 1947, as amended by subsection (a) of this section, shall take effect on the date that is 18 months after the date of the enactment of this Act.".

(f) SPECIAL ADVISOR TO THE PRESIDENT ON INTERNATIONAL RELIGIOUS FREEDOM.— It is the sense of Congress that there should be within the staff of the Council a Special Adviser to the President on International Religious Freedom, whose position should be comparable to that of a director within the Executive Office of the President. The Special Adviser should serve as a resource for executive branch officials, compiling and maintaining information on the facts and circumstances of violations of religious freedom (as defined in section 3 of the International Religious Freedom Act of 1998 (22 U.S.C. 6402)), and making policy recommendations. The Special Adviser should serve as liaison with the Ambassador at Large for International Religious Freedom, the United States Commission on International Religious Freedom, Congress and, as advisable, religious nongovernmental organizations.

(g) COORDINATOR FOR COMBATING MALIGN FOREIGN INFLUENCE OPERATIONS AND CAMPAIGNS.—

(1) IN GENERAL.— The President shall designate an employee of the National Security Council to be responsible for the coordination of the interagency process for combating malign foreign influence operations and campaigns.

(2) CONGRESSIONAL BRIEFING.—

(A) IN GENERAL.— Not less frequently than twice each year, the employee designated under this subsection, or the employee's designee, shall provide to the congressional committees specified in subparagraph (B) a briefing on the responsibilities and activities of the employee designated under this subsection.

(B) COMMITTEES SPECIFIED.—The congressional committees specified in this subparagraph are the following:

(i) The Committees on Armed Services, Foreign Affairs, and Oversight and Government Reform, and the Permanent Select Committee on Intelligence of the House of Representatives.

(ii) The Committees on Armed Services, Foreign Relations, and Homeland Security and Governmental Affairs, and the Select Committee on

Intelligence of the Senate.

(h) Definition of Malign Foreign Influence Operations and Campaigns.— In this section, the term "malign foreign influence operations and campaigns" means the coordinated, direct or indirect application of national diplomatic, informational, military, economic, business, corruption, educational, and other capabilities by hostile foreign powers to affect attitudes, behaviors, decisions, or outcomes within the United States.

JOINT INTELLIGENCE COMMUNITY COUNCIL

Sec. 101A. [50 U.S.C. 3022] (a) Joint Intelligence Community Council.— There is a Joint Intelligence Community Council.

(b) Membership.—The Joint Intelligence Community Council shall consist of the following:

(1) The Director of National Intelligence, who shall chair the Council.

(2) The Secretary of State.

(3) The Secretary of the Treasury.

(4) The Secretary of Defense.

(5) The Attorney General.

(6) The Secretary of Energy.

(7) The Secretary of Homeland Security.

(8) Such other officers of the United States Government as the President may designate from time to time.

(c) Functions.—The Joint Intelligence Community Council shall assist the Director of National Intelligence in developing and implementing a joint, unified national intelligence effort to protect national security by—

(1) advising the Director on establishing requirements, developing budgets, financial management, and monitoring and evaluating the performance of the intelligence community, and on such other matters as the Director may request; and

(2) ensuring the timely execution of programs, policies, and directives established or developed by the Director.

(d) Meetings.— The Director of National Intelligence shall convene meetings of the Joint Intelligence Community Council as the Director considers appropriate.

(e) Advice and Opinions of Members Other Than Chairman.—(1) A member of the Joint Intelligence Community Council (other than the Chairman) may submit to the Chairman advice or an opinion in disagreement with, or advice or an opinion in addition to, the advice presented by the Director of National Intelligence to the President or the National Security Council, in the role of the Chairman as Chairman of the Joint Intelligence Community Council. If a member submits such advice or opinion, the Chairman shall present the advice or opinion of such member at the same time the Chairman presents the advice of the Chairman to the President or the National Security Council, as the case may be.

(2) The Chairman shall establish procedures to ensure that the presentation of the advice of the Chairman to the President or the National Security Council is not unduly delayed by reason of the submission of the individual advice or opinion of

another member of the Council.

(f) RECOMMENDATIONS TO CONGRESS.— Any member of the Joint Intelligence Community Council may make such recommendations to Congress relating to the intelligence community as such member considers appropriate.

DIRECTOR OF NATIONAL INTELLIGENCE

SEC. 102. [50 U.S.C. 3023] (a) DIRECTOR OF NATIONAL INTELLIGENCE.—(1) There is a Director of National Intelligence who shall be appointed by the President, by and with the advice and consent of the Senate. Any individual nominated for appointment as Director of National Intelligence shall have extensive national security expertise.

(2) The Director of National Intelligence shall not be located within the Executive Office of the President.

(b) PRINCIPAL RESPONSIBILITY.—Subject to the authority, direction, and control of the President, the Director of National Intelligence shall—

(1) serve as head of the intelligence community;

(2) act as the principal adviser to the President, to the National Security Council, and the Homeland Security Council for intelligence matters related to the national security; and

(3) consistent with section 1018 of the National Security Intelligence Reform Act of 2004, oversee and direct the implementation of the National Intelligence Program.

(c) PROHIBITION ON DUAL SERVICE.— The individual serving in the position of Director of National Intelligence shall not, while so serving, also serve as the Director of the Central Intelligence Agency or as the head of any other element of the intelligence community.

RESPONSIBILITIES AND AUTHORITIES OF THE DIRECTOR OF NATIONAL INTELLIGENCE

SEC. 102A. [50 U.S.C. 3024] (a) PROVISION OF INTELLIGENCE.—(1) The Director of National Intelligence shall be responsible for ensuring that national intelligence is provided—

(A) to the President;

(B) to the heads of departments and agencies of the executive branch;

(C) to the Chairman of the Joint Chiefs of Staff and senior military commanders;

(D) to the Senate and House of Representatives and the committees thereof; and

(E) to such other persons as the Director of National Intelligence determines to be appropriate.

(2) Such national intelligence should be timely, objective, independent of political considerations, and based upon all sources available to the intelligence community and other appropriate entities.

(b) ACCESS TO INTELLIGENCE.— Unless otherwise directed by the President, the Director of National Intelligence shall have access to all national intelligence and intelligence related to the national security which is collected by any Federal department, agency, or other entity, except as otherwise provided by law or, as appropriate, under guidelines agreed upon by the Attorney General and the Director of National Intelligence.

(c) BUDGET AUTHORITIES.—(1) With respect to budget requests and appropriations for the National Intelligence Program, the Director of National Intelligence shall—

(A) based on intelligence priorities set by the President, provide to the heads of departments containing agencies or organizations within the intelligence community, and to the heads of such agencies and organizations, guidance for developing the National Intelligence Program budget pertaining to such agencies and organizations;

(B) based on budget proposals provided to the Director of National Intelligence by the heads of agencies and organizations within the intelligence community and the heads of their respective departments and, as appropriate, after obtaining the advice of the Joint Intelligence Community Council, develop and determine an annual consolidated National Intelligence Program budget; and

(C) present such consolidated National Intelligence Program budget, together with any comments from the heads of departments containing agencies or organizations within the intelligence community, to the President for approval.

(2) In addition to the information provided under paragraph (1)(B), the heads of agencies and organizations within the intelligence community shall provide the Director of National Intelligence such other information as the Director shall request for the purpose of determining the annual consolidated National Intelligence Program budget under that paragraph.

(3)(A) The Director of National Intelligence shall participate in the development by the Secretary of Defense of the annual budget for the Military Intelligence Program or any successor program or programs.

(B) The Director of National Intelligence shall provide guidance for the development of the annual budget for each element of the intelligence community that is not within the National Intelligence Program.

(4) The Director of National Intelligence shall ensure the effective execution of the annual budget for intelligence and intelligence-related activities.

(5)(A) The Director of National Intelligence shall be responsible for managing appropriations for the National Intelligence Program by directing the allotment or allocation of such appropriations through the heads of the departments containing agencies or organizations within the intelligence community and the Director of the Central Intelligence Agency, with prior notice (including the provision of appropriate supporting information) to the head of the department containing an agency or organization receiving any such allocation or allotment or the Director of the Central Intelligence Agency.

(B) Notwithstanding any other provision of law, pursuant to relevant appropriations Acts for the National Intelligence Program, the Director of the Office of Management and Budget shall exercise the authority of the Director of the Office of Management and Budget to apportion funds, at the exclusive direction of the Director of National Intelligence, for allocation to the elements of the intelligence community through the relevant host executive departments and the Central Intelligence Agency. Department comptrollers or appropriate budget execution officers shall allot, allocate, reprogram, or transfer funds appropriated for the National Intelligence Program in an expeditious manner.

(C) The Director of National Intelligence shall monitor the implementation and execution of the National Intelligence Program by the heads of the elements of the intelligence community that manage programs and activities that are part of the National Intelligence Program, which shall include audits and evaluations.

(D) Consistent with subparagraph (C), the Director of National Intelligence shall ensure that the programs and activities that are part of the National Intelligence Program, including those of the Federal Bureau of Investigation, are structured and executed in a manner than enables budget traceability.

(6) Apportionment and allotment of funds under this subsection shall be subject to chapter 13 and section 1517 of title 31, United States Code, and the Congressional Budget and Impoundment Control Act of 1974 (2 U.S.C. 621 et seq.).

(7)(A) The Director of National Intelligence shall provide a semi-annual report, beginning April 1, 2005, and ending April 1, 2007, to the President and the Congress regarding implementation of this section.

(B) The Director of National Intelligence shall report to the President and the Congress not later than 15 days after learning of any instance in which a departmental comptroller acts in a manner inconsistent with the law (including permanent statutes, authorization Acts, and appropriations Acts), or the direction of the Director of National Intelligence, in carrying out the National Intelligence Program.

(d) ROLE OF DIRECTOR OF NATIONAL INTELLIGENCE IN TRANSFER AND REPROGRAMMING OF FUNDS.—(1)(A) No funds made available under the National Intelligence Program may be transferred or reprogrammed without the prior approval of the Director of National Intelligence, except in accordance with procedures prescribed by the Director of National Intelligence.

(B) The Secretary of Defense shall consult with the Director of National Intelligence before transferring or reprogramming funds made available under the Military Intelligence Program or any successor program or programs.

(2) Subject to the succeeding provisions of this subsection, the Director of National Intelligence may transfer or reprogram funds appropriated for a program within the National Intelligence Program—

(A) to another such program;

(B) to other departments or agencies of the United States Government for the development and fielding of systems of common concern related to the collection, processing, analysis, exploitation, and dissemination of intelligence information; or

(C) to a program funded by appropriations not within the National Intelligence Program to address critical gaps in intelligence information sharing or access capabilities.

(3) The Director of National Intelligence may only transfer or reprogram funds

referred to in paragraph (1)(A)—

(A) with the approval of the Director of the Office of Management and Budget; and

(B) after consultation with the heads of departments containing agencies or organizations within the intelligence community to the extent such agencies or organizations are affected, and, in the case of the Central Intelligence Agency, after consultation with the Director of the Central Intelligence Agency.

(4) The amounts available for transfer or reprogramming in the National Intelligence Program in any given fiscal year, and the terms and conditions governing such transfers and reprogrammings, are subject to the provisions of annual appropriations Acts and this subsection.

(5)(A) A transfer or reprogramming of funds may be made under this subsection only if—

(i) the funds are being transferred to an activity that is a higher priority intelligence activity;

(ii) the transfer or reprogramming supports an emergent need, improves program effectiveness, or increases efficiency;

(iii) the transfer or reprogramming does not involve a transfer or reprogramming of funds to a Reserve for Contingencies of the Director of National Intelligence or the Reserve for Contingencies of the Central Intelligence Agency;

(iv) the transfer or reprogramming results in a cumulative transfer or reprogramming of funds out of any department or agency, as appropriate, funded in the National Intelligence Program in a single fiscal year—

(I) that is less than $150,000,000, and

(II) that is less than 5 percent of amounts available to a department or agency under the National Intelligence Program; and

(v) the transfer or reprogramming does not terminate an acquisition program.

(B) A transfer or reprogramming may be made without regard to a limitation set forth in clause (iv) or (v) of subparagraph (A) if the transfer has the concurrence of the head of the department involved or the Director of the Central Intelligence Agency (in the case of the Central Intelligence Agency). The authority to provide such concurrence may only be delegated by the head of the department involved or the Director of the Central Intelligence Agency (in the case of the Central Intelligence Agency) to the deputy of such officer.

(6) Funds transferred or reprogrammed under this subsection shall remain available for the same period as the appropriations account to which transferred or reprogrammed.

(7) Any transfer or reprogramming of funds under this subsection shall be carried out in accordance with existing procedures applicable to reprogramming notifications for the appropriate congressional committees. Any proposed transfer or reprogramming for which notice is given to the appropriate congressional committees shall be accompanied by a report explaining the nature of the proposed transfer or reprogramming and how it satisfies the requirements of this subsection.

In addition, the congressional intelligence committees shall be promptly notified of any transfer or reprogramming of funds made pursuant to this subsection in any case in which the transfer or reprogramming would not have otherwise required reprogramming notification under procedures in effect as of the date of the enactment of this subsection.

(e) TRANSFER OF PERSONNEL.—(1)(A) In addition to any other authorities available under law for such purposes, in the first twelve months after establishment of a new national intelligence center, the Director of National Intelligence, with the approval of the Director of the Office of Management and Budget and in consultation with the congressional committees of jurisdiction referred to in subparagraph (B), may transfer not more than 100 personnel authorized for elements of the intelligence community to such center.

(B) The Director of National Intelligence shall promptly provide notice of any transfer of personnel made pursuant to this paragraph to—

(i) the congressional intelligence committees;

(ii) the Committees on Appropriations of the Senate and the House of Representatives;

(iii) in the case of the transfer of personnel to or from the Department of Defense, the Committees on Armed Services of the Senate and the House of Representatives; and

(iv) in the case of the transfer of personnel to or from the Department of Justice, to the Committees on the Judiciary of the Senate and the House of Representatives.

(C) The Director shall include in any notice under subparagraph (B) an explanation of the nature of the transfer and how it satisfies the requirements of this subsection.

(2)(A) The Director of National Intelligence, with the approval of the Director of the Office of Management and Budget and in accordance with procedures to be developed by the Director of National Intelligence and the heads of the departments and agencies concerned, may transfer personnel authorized for an element of the intelligence community to another such element for a period of not more than 2 years.

(B) A transfer of personnel may be made under this paragraph only if—

(i) the personnel are being transferred to an activity that is a higher priority intelligence activity; and

(ii) the transfer supports an emergent need, improves program effectiveness, or increases efficiency.

(C) The Director of National Intelligence shall promptly provide notice of any transfer of personnel made pursuant to this paragraph to—

(i) the congressional intelligence committees;

(ii) in the case of the transfer of personnel to or from the Department of Defense, the Committees on Armed Services of the Senate and the House of Representatives; and

(iii) in the case of the transfer of personnel to or from the Department of Justice, to the Committees on the Judiciary of the Senate and the House of

Representatives.

(D) The Director shall include in any notice under subparagraph (C) an explanation of the nature of the transfer and how it satisfies the requirements of this paragraph.

(3)(A) In addition to the number of full-time equivalent positions authorized for the Office of the Director of National Intelligence for a fiscal year, there is authorized for such Office for each fiscal year an additional 100 full-time equivalent positions that may be used only for the purposes described in subparagraph (B).

(B) Except as provided in subparagraph (C), the Director of National Intelligence may use a full-time equivalent position authorized under subparagraph (A) only for the purpose of providing a temporary transfer of personnel made in accordance with paragraph (2) to an element of the intelligence community to enable such element to increase the total number of personnel authorized for such element, on a temporary basis—

(i) during a period in which a permanent employee of such element is absent to participate in critical language training; or

(ii) to accept a permanent employee of another element of the intelligence community to provide language-capable services.

(C) Paragraph (2)(B) shall not apply with respect to a transfer of personnel made under subparagraph (B).

(D) For each of the fiscal years 2010, 2011, and 2012, the Director of National Intelligence shall submit to the congressional intelligence committees an annual report on the use of authorities under this paragraph. Each such report shall include a description of—

(i) the number of transfers of personnel made by the Director pursuant to subparagraph (B), disaggregated by each element of the intelligence community;

(ii) the critical language needs that were fulfilled or partially fulfilled through the use of such transfers; and

(iii) the cost to carry out subparagraph (B).

(4) It is the sense of Congress that—

(A) the nature of the national security threats facing the United States will continue to challenge the intelligence community to respond rapidly and flexibly to bring analytic resources to bear against emerging and unforeseen requirements;

(B) both the Office of the Director of National Intelligence and any analytic centers determined to be necessary should be fully and properly supported with appropriate levels of personnel resources and that the President's yearly budget requests adequately support those needs; and

(C) the President should utilize all legal and administrative discretion to ensure that the Director of National Intelligence and all other elements of the intelligence community have the necessary resources and procedures to respond promptly and effectively to emerging and unforeseen national security challenges.

(f) Tasking and Other Authorities.—(1)(A) The Director of National Intelligence shall—

(i) establish objectives, priorities, and guidance for the intelligence community to ensure timely and effective collection, processing, analysis, and dissemination (including access by users to collected data consistent with applicable law and, as appropriate, the guidelines referred to in subsection (b) and analytic products generated by or within the intelligence community) of national intelligence;

(ii) determine requirements and priorities for, and manage and direct the tasking of, collection, analysis, production, and dissemination of national intelligence by elements of the intelligence community, including—

(I) approving requirements (including those requirements responding to needs provided by consumers) for collection and analysis; and

(II) resolving conflicts in collection requirements and in the tasking of national collection assets of the elements of the intelligence community; and

(iii) provide advisory tasking to intelligence elements of those agencies and departments not within the National Intelligence Program.

(B) The authority of the Director of National Intelligence under subparagraph (A) shall not apply—

(i) insofar as the President so directs;

(ii) with respect to clause (ii) of subparagraph (A), insofar as the Secretary of Defense exercises tasking authority under plans or arrangements agreed upon by the Secretary of Defense and the Director of National Intelligence; or

(iii) to the direct dissemination of information to State government and local government officials and private sector entities pursuant to sections 201 and 892 of the Homeland Security Act of 2002 (6 U.S.C. 121, 482).

(2) The Director of National Intelligence shall oversee the National Counterterrorism Center, the National Counterproliferation Center, and the National Counterintelligence and Security Center and may establish such other national intelligence centers as the Director determines necessary.

(3)(A) The Director of National Intelligence shall prescribe, in consultation with the heads of other agencies or elements of the intelligence community, and the heads of their respective departments, binding personnel policies and programs applicable to the intelligence community that—

(i) require and facilitate assignments and details of personnel to national intelligence centers, and between elements of the intelligence community over the course of the careers of such personnel;

(ii) set standards for education, training, and career development of personnel of the intelligence community;

(iii) encourage and facilitate the recruitment and retention by the intelligence community of highly qualified individuals for the effective conduct of intelligence activities;

(iv) ensure that the personnel of the intelligence community are sufficiently diverse for purposes of the collection and analysis of intelligence through the recruitment and training of women, minorities, and individuals with diverse ethnic, cultural, and linguistic backgrounds;

(v) require service in more than one element of the intelligence community as a condition of promotion to such positions within the intelligence community as the Director shall specify, and take requisite steps to ensure compliance among elements of the intelligence community; and

(vi) ensure the effective management of intelligence community personnel who are responsible for intelligence community-wide matters.

(B) Policies prescribed under subparagraph (A) shall not be inconsistent with the personnel policies otherwise applicable to members of the uniformed services.

(4) The Director of National Intelligence shall ensure compliance with the Constitution and laws of the United States by the Central Intelligence Agency and shall ensure such compliance by other elements of the intelligence community through the host executive departments that manage the programs and activities that are part of the National Intelligence Program.

(5) The Director of National Intelligence shall ensure the elimination of waste and unnecessary duplication within the intelligence community.

(6) The Director of National Intelligence shall establish requirements and priorities for foreign intelligence information to be collected under the Foreign Intelligence Surveillance Act of 1978 (50 U.S.C. 1801 et seq.), and provide assistance to the Attorney General to ensure that information derived from electronic surveillance or physical searches under that Act is disseminated so it may be used efficiently and effectively for national intelligence purposes, except that the Director shall have no authority to direct or undertake electronic surveillance or physical search operations pursuant to that Act unless authorized by statute or Executive order.

(7)(A) The Director of National Intelligence shall, if the Director determines it is necessary, or may, if requested by a congressional intelligence committee, conduct an accountability review of an element of the intelligence community or the personnel of such element in relation to a failure or deficiency within the intelligence community.

(B) The Director of National Intelligence, in consultation with the Attorney General, shall establish guidelines and procedures for conducting an accountability review under subparagraph (A).

(C)(i) The Director of National Intelligence shall provide the findings of an accountability review conducted under subparagraph (A) and the Director's recommendations for corrective or punitive action, if any, to the head of the applicable element of the intelligence community. Such recommendations may include a recommendation for dismissal of personnel.

(ii) If the head of such element does not implement a recommendation made by the Director under clause (i), the head of such element shall submit to the congressional intelligence committees a notice of the determination not to implement the recommendation, including the reasons for the determination.

(D) The requirements of this paragraph shall not be construed to limit any authority of the Director of National Intelligence under subsection (m) or with respect to supervision of the Central Intelligence Agency.

(8) The Director of National Intelligence shall—

(A) conduct assessments and audits of the compliance of each element of the intelligence community with minimum insider threat policy;

(B) receive information from each element of the intelligence community regarding the collection, sharing, and use by such element of audit and monitoring data for insider threat detection across all classified and unclassified information technology systems within such element;

(C) provide guidance and oversight to Federal departments and agencies to fully implement automated records checks, consistent with personnel vetting reforms and the Trusted Workforce 2.0 initiative, or successor initiative, and ensure that information collected pursuant to such records checks is appropriately shared in support of intelligence community-wide insider threat initiatives;

(D) carry out evaluations of the effectiveness of counterintelligence, security, and insider threat program activities of each element of the intelligence community, including with respect to the lowest organizational unit of each such element, that include an identification of any gaps, shortfalls, or resource needs of each such element;

(E) identify gaps, shortfalls, resources needs, and recommendations for adjustments in allocations and additional resources and other remedies to strengthen counterintelligence, security, and insider threat detection programs;

(F) pursuant to final damage assessments facilitated by the National Counterintelligence and Security Center that have been undertaken as a result of an unauthorized disclosure, determine whether the heads of the elements of the intelligence community implement recommended mitigation, and notify the congressional intelligence committees of such determinations and notify the Committee on Armed Services of the Senate and the Committee on Armed Services of the House of Representatives in cases involving elements of the intelligence community within the Department of Defense; and

(G) study the data collected during the course of background investigations and adjudications for security clearances granted to individuals who subsequently commit unauthorized disclosures, and issue findings regarding the quality of such data as a predictor for insider threat activity, delineated by the severity of the unauthorized disclosure.

(9) The Director of National Intelligence shall ensure there is established a policy for minimum insider threat standards for the intelligence community and ensure compliance by the elements of the intelligence community with that policy.

(10) The Director of National Intelligence shall perform such other intelligence-related functions as the President may direct, and upon receiving any such direction, the Director shall notify the congressional intelligence committees immediately in writing with a description of such other intelligence-related functions directed by the President.

(11) Nothing in this title shall be construed as affecting the role of the Department of Justice or the Attorney General under the Foreign Intelligence Surveillance Act of 1978.

(g) Intelligence Information Sharing.—(1) The Director of National Intelligence shall have principal authority to ensure maximum availability of and access to intelligence information within the intelligence community consistent with national security requirements. The Director of National Intelligence shall—

(A) establish uniform security standards and procedures;

(B) establish common information technology standards, protocols, and interfaces;

(C) ensure development of information technology systems that include multi-level security and intelligence integration capabilities;

(D) establish policies and procedures to resolve conflicts between the need to share intelligence information and the need to protect intelligence sources and methods;

(E) develop an enterprise architecture for the intelligence community and ensure that elements of the intelligence community comply with such architecture;

(F) have procurement approval authority over all enterprise architecture-related information technology items funded in the National Intelligence Program; and

(G) in accordance with Executive Order No. 13526 (75 Fed. Reg. 707; relating to classified national security information) (or any subsequent corresponding executive order), and part 2001 of title 32, Code of Federal Regulations (or any subsequent corresponding regulation), establish—

(i) guidance to standardize, in appropriate cases, the formats for classified and unclassified intelligence products created by elements of the intelligence community for purposes of promoting the sharing of intelligence products; and

(ii) policies and procedures requiring the increased use, in appropriate cases, and including portion markings, of the classification of portions of information within one intelligence product.

(2) The President shall ensure that the Director of National Intelligence has all necessary support and authorities to fully and effectively implement paragraph (1).

(3) Except as otherwise directed by the President or with the specific written agreement of the head of the department or agency in question, a Federal agency or official shall not be considered to have met any obligation to provide any information, report, assessment, or other material (including unevaluated intelligence information) to that department or agency solely by virtue of having provided that information, report, assessment, or other material to the Director of National Intelligence or the National Counterterrorism Center.

(4) The Director of National Intelligence shall, in a timely manner, report to Congress any statute, regulation, policy, or practice that the Director believes impedes the ability of the Director to fully and effectively ensure maximum availability of access to intelligence information within the intelligence community consistent with the protection of the national security of the United States.

(h) Analysis.—To ensure the most accurate analysis of intelligence is derived from all sources to support national security needs, the Director of National Intelligence shall—

(1) implement policies and procedures—

(A) to require sound analytic methods and tradecraft, independent of political considerations, throughout the elements of the intelligence community;

(B) to ensure that analysis is based upon all sources available; and

(C) to ensure that the elements of the intelligence community regularly conduct competitive analysis of analytic products, whether such products are produced by or disseminated to such elements;

(2) ensure that resource allocation for intelligence analysis is appropriately proportional to resource allocation for intelligence collection systems and operations in order to maximize analysis of all collected data;

(3) ensure that substantial differences in analytic judgment are fully considered, brought to the attention of policymakers, and documented in analytic products; and

(4) ensure that sufficient relationships are established between intelligence collectors and analysts to facilitate greater understanding of the needs of analysts.

(i) PROTECTION OF INTELLIGENCE SOURCES AND METHODS.—(1) The Director of National Intelligence shall protect, and shall establish and enforce policies to protect, intelligence sources and methods from unauthorized disclosure.

(2) Consistent with paragraph (1), in order to maximize the dissemination of intelligence, the Director of National Intelligence shall establish and implement requirements for the intelligence community for the following purposes:

(A) Classification of information under applicable law, Executive orders, or other Presidential directives.

(B) Access to and dissemination of intelligence, both in final form and in the form when initially gathered.

(C) Preparation of intelligence products in such a way that source information is removed to allow for dissemination at the lowest level of classification possible or in unclassified form to the extent practicable.

(3) The Director may only delegate a duty or authority given the Director under this subsection to the Principal Deputy Director of National Intelligence.

(4)(A) Each head of an element of the intelligence community shall ensure that any congressionally mandated report submitted to Congress by the head, other than such a report submitted solely to the congressional intelligence committees, shall be consistent with the protection of intelligence sources and methods in accordance with the policies established by the Director under paragraph (1), regardless of whether the provision of law mandating the report explicitly requires such protection.

(B) Nothing in this paragraph shall be construed to alter any congressional leadership's or congressional committee's jurisdiction or access to information from any element of the intelligence community under the rules of either chamber of Congress.

(j) UNIFORM PROCEDURES FOR CLASSIFIED INFORMATION.—The Director of National Intelligence, subject to the direction of the President, shall—

(1) establish uniform standards and procedures for the grant of access to sensitive compartmented information to any officer or employee of any agency or department of the United States and to employees of contractors of those agencies

or departments;

(2) ensure the consistent implementation of those standards and procedures throughout such agencies and departments;

(3) ensure that security clearances granted by individual elements of the intelligence community are recognized by all elements of the intelligence community, and under contracts entered into by those agencies;

(4) ensure that the process for investigation and adjudication of an application for access to sensitive compartmented information is performed in the most expeditious manner possible consistent with applicable standards for national security;

(5) ensure that the background of each employee or officer of an element of the intelligence community, each contractor to an element of the intelligence community, and each individual employee of such a contractor who has been determined to be eligible for access to classified information is monitored on a continual basis under standards developed by the Director, including with respect to the frequency of evaluation, during the period of eligibility of such employee or officer of an element of the intelligence community, such contractor, or such individual employee to such a contractor to determine whether such employee or officer of an element of the intelligence community, such contractor, and such individual employee of such a contractor continues to meet the requirements for eligibility for access to classified information; and

(6) develop procedures to require information sharing between elements of the intelligence community concerning potentially derogatory security information regarding an employee or officer of an element of the intelligence community, a contractor to an element of the intelligence community, or an individual employee of such a contractor that may impact the eligibility of such employee or officer of an element of the intelligence community, such contractor, or such individual employee of such a contractor for a security clearance.

(k) Coordination With Foreign Governments.— Under the direction of the President and in a manner consistent with section 207 of the Foreign Service Act of 1980 (22 U.S.C. 3927), the Director of National Intelligence shall oversee the coordination of the relationships between elements of the intelligence community and the intelligence or security services of foreign governments or international organizations on all matters involving intelligence related to the national security or involving intelligence acquired through clandestine means.

(l) Enhanced Personnel Management.—(1)(A) The Director of National Intelligence shall, under regulations prescribed by the Director, provide incentives for personnel of elements of the intelligence community to serve—

(i) on the staff of the Director of National Intelligence;

(ii) on the staff of the national intelligence centers;

(iii) on the staff of the National Counterterrorism Center; and

(iv) in other positions in support of the intelligence community management functions of the Director.

(B) Incentives under subparagraph (A) may include financial incentives, bonuses, and such other awards and incentives as the Director considers appropriate.

(2)(A) Notwithstanding any other provision of law, the personnel of an element of the intelligence community who are assigned or detailed under paragraph (1)(A) to service under the Director of National Intelligence shall be promoted at rates equivalent to or better than personnel of such element who are not so assigned or detailed.

(B) The Director may prescribe regulations to carry out this paragraph.

(3)(A) The Director of National Intelligence shall prescribe mechanisms to facilitate the rotation of personnel of the intelligence community through various elements of the intelligence community in the course of their careers in order to facilitate the widest possible understanding by such personnel of the variety of intelligence requirements, methods, users, and capabilities.

(B) The mechanisms prescribed under subparagraph (A) may include the following:

(i) The establishment of special occupational categories involving service, over the course of a career, in more than one element of the intelligence community.

(ii) The provision of rewards for service in positions undertaking analysis and planning of operations involving two or more elements of the intelligence community.

(iii) The establishment of requirements for education, training, service, and evaluation for service involving more than one element of the intelligence community.

(C) It is the sense of Congress that the mechanisms prescribed under this subsection should, to the extent practical, seek to duplicate for civilian personnel within the intelligence community the joint officer management policies established by chapter 38 of title 10, United States Code, and the other amendments made by title IV of the Goldwater-Nichols Department of Defense Reorganization Act of 1986 (Public Law 99–433).

(D) The mechanisms prescribed under subparagraph (A) and any other policies of the Director—

(i) may not require an employee of an office of inspector general for an element of the intelligence community, including the Office of the Inspector General of the Intelligence Community, to rotate to a position in an office or organization of such an element over which such office of inspector general exercises jurisdiction; and

(ii) shall be implemented in a manner that exempts employees of an office of inspector general from a rotation that may impact the independence of such office.

(4)(A) Except as provided in subparagraph (B) and subparagraph (D), this subsection shall not apply with respect to personnel of the elements of the intelligence community who are members of the uniformed services.

(B) Mechanisms that establish requirements for education and training pursuant to paragraph (3)(B)(iii) may apply with respect to members of the uniformed services who are assigned to an element of the intelligence community funded through the National Intelligence Program, but such mechanisms shall not be inconsistent with personnel policies and education and training requirements otherwise applicable to members of the uniformed services.

(C) The personnel policies and programs developed and implemented under this subsection with respect to law enforcement officers (as that term is defined in section 5541(3) of title 5, United States Code) shall not affect the ability of law enforcement entities to conduct operations or, through the applicable chain of command, to control the activities of such law enforcement officers.

(D) Assignment to the Office of the Director of National Intelligence of commissioned officers of the Armed Forces shall be considered a joint-duty assignment for purposes of the joint officer management policies prescribed by chapter 38 of title 10, United States Code, and other provisions of that title.

(m) Additional Authority With Respect to Personnel.—(1) In addition to the authorities under subsection (f)(3), the Director of National Intelligence may exercise with respect to the personnel of the Office of the Director of National Intelligence any authority of the Director of the Central Intelligence Agency with respect to the personnel of the Central Intelligence Agency under the Central Intelligence Agency Act of 1949 (50 U.S.C. 403a et seq.), and other applicable provisions of law, as of the date of the enactment of this subsection to the same extent, and subject to the same conditions and limitations, that the Director of the Central Intelligence Agency may exercise such authority with respect to personnel of the Central Intelligence Agency, including with respect to the notification requirement under section 8(c) of such Act (50 U.S.C. 3510(c)).

(2) Employees and applicants for employment of the Office of the Director of National Intelligence shall have the same rights and protections under the Office of the Director of National Intelligence as employees of the Central Intelligence Agency have under the Central Intelligence Agency Act of 1949, and other applicable provisions of law, as of the date of the enactment of this subsection.

(n) Acquisition and Other Authorities.—(1) In carrying out the responsibilities and authorities under this section, the Director of National Intelligence may exercise the acquisition and appropriations authorities referred to in the Central Intelligence Agency Act of 1949 (50 U.S.C. 403a et seq.) other than the authorities referred to in section 8(b) of that Act (50 U.S.C. 403j(b)).

(2) For the purpose of the exercise of any authority referred to in paragraph (1), a reference to the head of an agency shall be deemed to be a reference to the Director of National Intelligence or the Principal Deputy Director of National Intelligence.

(3)(A) Any determination or decision to be made under an authority referred to in paragraph (1) by the head of an agency may be made with respect to individual purchases and contracts or with respect to classes of purchases or contracts, and shall be final.

(B) Except as provided in subparagraph (C), the Director of National Intelligence or the Principal Deputy Director of National Intelligence may, in such official's discretion, delegate to any officer or other official of the Office of the Director of National Intelligence any authority to make a determination or decision as the head of the agency under an authority referred to in paragraph

(1).

(C) The limitations and conditions set forth in section 3(d) of the Central Intelligence Agency Act of 1949 (50 U.S.C. 403c(d)) shall apply to the exercise by the Director of National Intelligence of an authority referred to in paragraph (1).

(D) Each determination or decision required by an authority referred to in the second sentence of section 3(d) of the Central Intelligence Agency Act of 1949 shall be based upon written findings made by the official making such determination or decision, which findings shall be final and shall be available within the Office of the Director of National Intelligence for a period of at least six years following the date of such determination or decision.

(4)(A) In addition to the authority referred to in paragraph (1), the Director of National Intelligence may authorize the head of an element of the intelligence community to exercise an acquisition authority referred to in section 3 or 8(a) of the Central Intelligence Agency Act of 1949 (50 U.S.C. 403c and 403j(a)) for an acquisition by such element that is more than 50 percent funded under the National Intelligence Program.

(B) The head of an element of the intelligence community may not exercise an authority referred to in subparagraph (A) until—

(i) the head of such element (without delegation) submits to the Director of National Intelligence a written request that includes—

(I) a description of such authority requested to be exercised;

(II) an explanation of the need for such authority, including an explanation of the reasons that other authorities are insufficient; and

(III) a certification that the mission of such element would be—

(aa) impaired if such authority is not exercised; or

(bb) significantly and measurably enhanced if such authority is exercised; and

(ii) the Director of National Intelligence issues a written authorization that includes—

(I) a description of the authority referred to in subparagraph (A) that is authorized to be exercised; and

(II) a justification to support the exercise of such authority.

(C) A request and authorization to exercise an authority referred to in subparagraph (A) may be made with respect to an individual acquisition or with respect to a specific class of acquisitions described in the request and authorization referred to in subparagraph (B).

(D)(i) A request from a head of an element of the intelligence community located within one of the departments described in clause (ii) to exercise an authority referred to in subparagraph (A) shall be submitted to the Director of National Intelligence in accordance with any procedures established by the head of such department.

(ii) The departments described in this clause are the Department of Defense, the Department of Energy, the Department of Homeland Security, the Department of Justice, the Department of State, and the Department of the Treasury.

(E)(i) The head of an element of the intelligence community may not be authorized to utilize an authority referred to in subparagraph (A) for a class of acquisitions for a period of more than 3 years, except that the Director of National Intelligence (without delegation) may authorize the use of such an authority for not more than 6 years.

(ii) Each authorization to utilize an authority referred to in subparagraph (A) may be extended in accordance with the requirements of subparagraph (B) for successive periods of not more than 3 years, except that the Director of National Intelligence (without delegation) may authorize an extension period of not more than 6 years.

(F) Subject to clauses (i) and (ii) of subparagraph (E), the Director of National Intelligence may only delegate the authority of the Director under subparagraphs (A) through (E) to the Principal Deputy Director of National Intelligence or a Deputy Director of National Intelligence.

(G) The Director of National Intelligence shall submit—

(i) to the congressional intelligence committees a notification of an authorization to exercise an authority referred to in subparagraph (A) or an extension of such authorization that includes the written authorization referred to in subparagraph (B)(ii); and

(ii) to the Director of the Office of Management and Budget a notification of an authorization to exercise an authority referred to in subparagraph (A) for an acquisition or class of acquisitions that will exceed $50,000,000 annually.

(H) Requests and authorizations to exercise an authority referred to in subparagraph (A) shall remain available within the Office of the Director of National Intelligence for a period of at least 6 years following the date of such request or authorization.

(I) Nothing in this paragraph may be construed to alter or otherwise limit the authority of the Central Intelligence Agency to independently exercise an authority under section 3 or 8(a) of the Central Intelligence Agency Act of 1949 (50 U.S.C. 403c and 403j(a)).

(5) Any authority provided to the Director of National Intelligence or the head of an element of the intelligence community pursuant to this subsection to make an expenditure referred to in subsection (a) of section 8 of the Central Intelligence Agency Act of 1949 (50 U.S.C. 3510) is subject to the notification requirement under subsection (c) of such section. If the Director of National Intelligence is required to make a notification for a specific expenditure pursuant to both this paragraph and paragraph (4)(G), the Director may make a single notification.

(6) Other transaction authority.—

(A) In general.— In addition to other acquisition authorities, the Director of National Intelligence may exercise the acquisition authorities referred to in sections 4021 and 4022 of title 10, United States Code, subject to the provisions of this paragraph.

(B) DELEGATION.—(i) The Director shall delegate the authorities provided by subparagraph (A) to the heads of elements of the intelligence community.

(ii) The heads of elements of the intelligence community shall, to the maximum extent practicable, delegate the authority delegated under clause (i) to the official of the respective element of the intelligence community responsible for decisions with respect to basic, applied, or advanced research activities or the adoption of such activities within such element.

(C) INTELLIGENCE COMMUNITY AUTHORITY.—(i) For purposes of this paragraph, the limitation in section 4022(a)(1) of title 10, United States Code, shall not apply to elements of the intelligence community.

(ii) Subject to section 4022(a)(2) of such title, the Director may enter into transactions and agreements (other than contracts, cooperative agreements, and grants) of amounts not to exceed $75,000,000 under this paragraph to carry out basic, applied, and advanced research projects and prototype projects in support of intelligence activities.

(iii) For purposes of this paragraph, the limitations specified in section 4022(a)(2) of such title shall apply to the intelligence community in lieu of the Department of Defense, and the Director shall—

(I) identify appropriate officials who can make the determinations required in subparagraph (B)(i) of such section for the intelligence community; and

(II) brief the congressional intelligence committees, the Subcommittee on Defense of the Committee on Appropriations of the Senate, and the Subcommittee on Defense of the Committee on Appropriations of the House of Representatives in lieu of the congressional defense committees, as specified in subparagraph (B)(ii) of such section.

(iv) For purposes of this paragraph, the limitation in section 4022(a)(3) of such title shall not apply to elements of the intelligence community.

(v) In carrying out this paragraph, section 4022(d)(1) of such title shall be applied by substituting "Director of National Intelligence" for "Secretary of Defense".

(vi) For purposes of this paragraph, the limitations in section 4022(d)(2) of such title shall not apply to elements of the intelligence community.

(vii) In addition to the follow-on production contract criteria in section 4022(f)(2) of such title, the following additional criteria shall apply:

(I) The authorizing official of the relevant element of the intelligence community determines that Government users of the proposed production product or production service have been consulted.

(II) In the case of a proposed production product that is software, there are mechanisms in place for Government users to provide ongoing feedback to participants to the follow-on production contract.

(III) In the case of a proposed production product that is software, there are mechanisms in place to promote the interoperability and accessibility with and between Government and commercial software providers, including by the promotion of open application programming interfaces and requirement of appropriate software documentation.

(IV) The award follows a documented market analysis as mandated by the Federal Acquisition Regulations surveying available and comparable products.

(V) In the case of a proposed production product that is software, the follow-on production contract includes a requirement that, for the duration of such contract (or such other period of time as may be agreed to as a term of such contract)—

(aa) the participants provide the most up-to-date version of the product that is available in the commercial marketplace and is consistent with security requirements;

(bb) there are mechanisms in place for the participants to provide timely updates to the production product; and

(cc) the authority specified in section 4022(f)(5) of such title shall be exercised by the Director in lieu of the Secretary of Defense.

(D) Implementation policy.—The Director, in consultation with the heads of the elements of the intelligence community, shall—

(i) not later than 180 days after the date of the enactment of the Intelligence Authorization Act for Fiscal Year 2023, establish and implement an intelligence community-wide policy prescribing the use and limitations of the authority under this paragraph, particularly with respect to the application of subparagraphs (B) and (C);

(ii) periodically review and update the policy established under clause (i); and

(iii) submit to the congressional intelligence committees, the Committee on Appropriations of the Senate, and the Committee on Appropriations of the House of Representatives the policy when established under clause (i) or updated under clause (ii).

(E) Annual report.—

(i) In general.— Not less frequently than annually, the Director shall submit to the congressional intelligence committees, the Committee on Appropriations of the Senate, and the Committee on Appropriations of the House of Representatives a report detailing the use by the intelligence community of the authority provided by this paragraph.

(ii) Elements.—

(I) Required elements.—Each report required by clause (i) shall detail the following:

(aa) The number of transactions.

(bb) The participants to such transactions.

(cc) The purpose of the transaction.

(dd) The amount of each transaction.

(ee) Concerns with the efficiency of the policy.

(ff) Any recommendations for how to improve the process.

(II) Other elements.— Each report required by clause (i) may describe such transactions which have been awarded follow-on production contracts either pursuant to the authority provided by this paragraph or another acquisition authority available to the intelligence community.

(o) Consideration of Views of Elements of Intelligence Community.— In carrying out the duties and responsibilities under this section, the Director of National Intelligence shall take into account the views of a head of a department containing an element of the intelligence community and of the Director of the Central Intelligence Agency.

(p) Certain Responsibilities of Director of National Intelligence Relating to National Intelligence Program.—(1) Subject to the direction of the President, the Director of National Intelligence shall, after consultation with the Secretary of Defense, ensure that the National Intelligence Program budgets for the elements of the intelligence community that are within the Department of Defense are adequate to satisfy the national intelligence needs of the Department of Defense, including the needs of the Chairman of the Joint Chiefs of Staff and the commanders of the unified and specified commands, and wherever such elements are performing Government-wide functions, the needs of other Federal departments and agencies.

(2) Consistent with subsection (c)(5)(C), the Director of National Intelligence shall, after consultation with the Director of the Federal Bureau of Investigation, ensure that the programs and activities of the Federal Bureau of Investigation that are part of the National Intelligence Program are executed in a manner that conforms with the requirements of the national intelligence strategy under section 108A of this Act and the National Intelligence Priorities Framework of the Office of the Director of National Intelligence (or any successor mechanism established for the prioritization of such programs and activities).

(3) Not later than March 1 of each year, the President, acting through the Director of National Intelligence, shall submit to the congressional intelligence committees, the Subcommittee on Defense of the Committee on Appropriations of the Senate, and the Subcommittee on Defense of the Committee on Appropriations of the House of Representatives a copy of the most recently updated National Intelligence Priorities Framework of the Office of the Director of National Intelligence (or any such successor mechanism).

(q) Acquisitions of Major Systems.—(1) For each intelligence program within the National Intelligence Program for the acquisition of a major system, the Director of National Intelligence shall—

(A) require the development and implementation of a program management plan that includes cost, schedule, security risks, and performance goals and program milestone criteria, except that with respect to Department of Defense programs the Director shall consult with the Secretary of Defense;

(B) serve as exclusive milestone decision authority, except that with respect to Department of Defense programs the Director shall serve as milestone decision authority jointly with the Secretary of Defense or the designee of the Secretary; and

(C) periodically—

(i) review and assess the progress made toward the achievement of the goals and milestones established in such plan; and

(ii) submit to Congress a report on the results of such review and assessment.

(2) If the Director of National Intelligence and the Secretary of Defense are unable to reach an agreement on a milestone decision under paragraph (1)(B), the President shall resolve the conflict.

(3) Nothing in this subsection may be construed to limit the authority of the Director of National Intelligence to delegate to any other official any authority to perform the responsibilities of the Director under this subsection.

(4) In this subsection:

(A) The term "intelligence program", with respect to the acquisition of a major system, means a program that—

(i) is carried out to acquire such major system for an element of the intelligence community; and

(ii) is funded in whole out of amounts available for the National Intelligence Program.

(B) The term "major system" has the meaning given such term in section 4(9) of the Federal Property and Administrative Services Act of 1949 (41 U.S.C. 403(9)).

(r) PERFORMANCE OF COMMON SERVICES.— The Director of National Intelligence shall, in consultation with the heads of departments and agencies of the United States Government containing elements within the intelligence community and with the Director of the Central Intelligence Agency, coordinate the performance by the elements of the intelligence community within the National Intelligence Program of such services as are of common concern to the intelligence community, which services the Director of National Intelligence determines can be more efficiently accomplished in a consolidated manner.

(s) PAY AUTHORITY FOR CRITICAL POSITIONS.—(1) Notwithstanding any pay limitation established under any other provision of law applicable to employees in elements of the intelligence community, the Director of National Intelligence may, in coordination with the Director of the Office of Personnel Management and the Director of the Office of Management and Budget, grant authority to the head of a department or agency to fix the rate of basic pay for one or more positions within the intelligence community at a rate in excess of any applicable limitation, subject to the provisions of this subsection. The exercise of authority so granted is at the discretion of the head of the department or agency employing the individual in a position covered by such authority, subject to the provisions of this subsection and any conditions established by the Director of National Intelligence when granting such authority.

(2) Authority under this subsection may be granted or exercised only—

(A) with respect to a position that requires an extremely high level of expertise and is critical to successful accomplishment of an important mission; and

(B) to the extent necessary to recruit or retain an individual exceptionally well qualified for the position.

(3) The head of a department or agency may not fix a rate of basic pay under this subsection at a rate greater than the rate payable for level II of the Executive Schedule under section 5313 of title 5, United States Code, except upon written approval of the Director of National Intelligence or as otherwise authorized by law.

(4) The head of a department or agency may not fix a rate of basic pay under this subsection at a rate greater than the rate payable for level I of the Executive Schedule under section 5312 of title 5, United States Code, except upon written approval of the President in response to a request by the Director of National Intelligence or as otherwise authorized by law.

(5) Any grant of authority under this subsection for a position shall terminate at the discretion of the Director of National Intelligence.

(6)(A) The Director of National Intelligence shall notify the congressional intelligence committees not later than 30 days after the date on which the Director grants authority to the head of a department or agency under this subsection.

(B) The head of a department or agency to which the Director of National Intelligence grants authority under this subsection shall notify the congressional intelligence committees and the Director of the exercise of such authority not later than 30 days after the date on which such head exercises such authority.

(t) Award of Rank to Members of the Senior National Intelligence Service.—(1) The President, based on the recommendation of the Director of National Intelligence, may award a rank to a member of the Senior National Intelligence Service or other intelligence community senior civilian officer not already covered by such a rank award program in the same manner in which a career appointee of an agency may be awarded a rank under section 4507 of title 5, United States Code.

(2) The President may establish procedures to award a rank under paragraph (1) to a member of the Senior National Intelligence Service or a senior civilian officer of the intelligence community whose identity as such a member or officer is classified information (as defined in section 606(1)).

(u) Conflict of Interest Regulations.— The Director of National Intelligence, in consultation with the Director of the Office of Government Ethics, shall issue regulations prohibiting an officer or employee of an element of the intelligence community from engaging in outside employment if such employment creates a conflict of interest or appearance thereof.

(v) Authority To Establish Positions in Excepted Service.—(1) The Director of National Intelligence, with the concurrence of the head of the covered department concerned and in consultation with the Director of the Office of Personnel Management, may—

(A) convert competitive service positions, and the incumbents of such positions, within an element of the intelligence community in such department, to excepted service positions as the Director of National Intelligence determines necessary to carry out the intelligence functions of such element; and

(B) establish new positions in the excepted service within an element of the intelligence community in such department, if the Director of National Intelligence determines such positions are necessary to carry out the intelligence functions of such element.

(2) An incumbent occupying a position on the date of the enactment of the Intelligence Authorization Act for Fiscal Year 2012 selected to be converted to the excepted service under this section shall have the right to refuse such conversion. Once such individual no longer occupies the position, the position may be converted to the excepted service.

(3) A covered department may appoint an individual to a position converted or established pursuant to this subsection without regard to the civil-service laws, including parts II and III of title 5, United States Code.

(4) In this subsection, the term "covered department" means the Department of Energy, the Department of Homeland Security, the Department of State, or the Department of the Treasury.

(w) NUCLEAR PROLIFERATION ASSESSMENT STATEMENTS INTELLIGENCE COMMUNITY ADDENDUM.— The Director of National Intelligence, in consultation with the heads of the appropriate elements of the intelligence community and the Secretary of State, shall provide to the President, the congressional intelligence committees, the Committee on Foreign Affairs of the House of Representatives, and the Committee on Foreign Relations of the Senate an addendum to each Nuclear Proliferation Assessment Statement accompanying a civilian nuclear cooperation agreement, containing a comprehensive analysis of the country's export control system with respect to nuclear-related matters, including interactions with other countries of proliferation concern and the actual or suspected nuclear, dual-use, or missile-related transfers to such countries.

(x) REQUIREMENTS FOR INTELLIGENCE COMMUNITY CONTRACTORS.—The Director of National Intelligence, in consultation with the heads of the elements of the intelligence community, shall—

(1) ensure that—

(A) any contractor to an element of the intelligence community with access to a classified network or classified information develops and operates a security plan that is consistent with standards established by the Director of National Intelligence for intelligence community networks; and

(B) each contract awarded by an element of the intelligence community includes provisions requiring the contractor comply with such plan and such standards;

(2) conduct periodic assessments of each security plan required under paragraph (1)(A) to ensure such security plan complies with the requirements of such paragraph; and

(3) ensure that the insider threat detection capabilities and insider threat policies of the intelligence community, including the policy under subsection (f)(8), apply to facilities of contractors with access to a classified network.

(y) FUNDRAISING.—(1) The Director of National Intelligence may engage in fundraising in an official capacity for the benefit of nonprofit organizations that—

(A) provide support to surviving family members of a deceased employee of an element of the intelligence community; or

(B) otherwise provide support for the welfare, education, or recreation of employees of an element of the intelligence community, former employees of an element of the intelligence community, or family members of such employees.

(2) In this subsection, the term "fundraising" means the raising of funds through the active participation in the promotion, production, or presentation of an event designed to raise funds and does not include the direct solicitation of money by any other means.

(3) Not later than 7 days after the date the Director engages in fundraising authorized by this subsection or at the time the decision is made to participate in such fundraising, the Director shall notify the congressional intelligence committees of such fundraising.

(4) The Director, in consultation with the Director of the Office of Government Ethics, shall issue regulations to carry out the authority provided in this subsection. Such regulations shall ensure that such authority is exercised in a manner that is consistent with all relevant ethical constraints and principles, including the avoidance of any prohibited conflict of interest or appearance of impropriety.

(z) Analyses and Impact Statements Regarding Proposed Investment Into the United States.—(1) Not later than 20 days after the completion of a review or an investigation of any proposed investment into the United States for which the Director has prepared analytic materials, the Director shall submit to the Select Committee on Intelligence of the Senate and the Permanent Select Committee on Intelligence of the House of Representative copies of such analytic materials, including any supplements or amendments to such analysis made by the Director.

(2) Not later than 60 days after the completion of consideration by the United States Government of any investment described in paragraph (1), the Director shall determine whether such investment will have an operational impact on the intelligence community, and, if so, shall submit a report on such impact to the Select Committee on Intelligence of the Senate and the Permanent Select Committee on Intelligence of the House of Representatives. Each such report shall—

(A) describe the operational impact of the investment on the intelligence community, including with respect to counterintelligence; and

(B) describe any actions that have been or will be taken to mitigate such impact.

(3) Definitions.—In this subsection:

(A) The term "a review or an investigation of any proposed investment into the United States for which the Director has prepared analytic materials" includes a review, investigation, assessment, or analysis conducted by the Director pursuant to section 7 or 10(g) of Executive Order 13913 (85 Fed. Reg. 19643; relating to Establishing the Committee for the Assessment of Foreign Participation in the United States Telecommunications Services Sector), or successor order.

(B) The term "investment" includes any activity reviewed, investigated, assessed, or analyzed by the Director pursuant to section 7 or 10(g) of Executive Order 13913, or successor order.

OFFICE OF THE DIRECTOR OF NATIONAL INTELLIGENCE

Sec. 103. [50 U.S.C. 3025] (a) Office of Director of National Intelligence.— There is an Office of the Director of National Intelligence.

(b) FUNCTION.— The function of the Office of the Director of National Intelligence is to assist the Director of National Intelligence in carrying out the duties and responsibilities of the Director under this Act and other applicable provisions of law, and to carry out such other duties as may be prescribed by the President or by law.

(c) COMPOSITION.—The Office of the Director of National Intelligence is composed of the following:

(1) The Director of National Intelligence.

(2) The Principal Deputy Director of National Intelligence.

(3) Any Deputy Director of National Intelligence appointed under section 103A.

(4) The National Intelligence Council.

(5) The National Intelligence Management Council.

(6) The General Counsel.

(7) The Civil Liberties Protection Officer.

(8) The Director of Science and Technology.

(9) The Director of the National Counterintelligence and Security Center.

(10) The Chief Information Officer of the Intelligence Community.

(11) The Inspector General of the Intelligence Community.

(12) The Director of the National Counterterrorism Center.

(13) The Director of the National Counter Proliferation Center.

(14) The Chief Financial Officer of the Intelligence Community.

(15) Such other offices and officials as may be established by law or the Director may establish or designate in the Office, including national intelligence centers.

(d) STAFF.—(1) To assist the Director of National Intelligence in fulfilling the duties and responsibilities of the Director, the Director shall employ and utilize in the Office of the Director of National Intelligence a professional staff having an expertise in matters relating to such duties and responsibilities, and may establish permanent positions and appropriate rates of pay with respect to that staff.

(2) The staff of the Office of the Director of National Intelligence under paragraph (1) shall include the staff of the Office of the Deputy Director of Central Intelligence for Community Management that is transferred to the Office of the Director of National Intelligence under section 1091 of the National Security Intelligence Reform Act of 2004.

(e) TEMPORARY FILLING OF VACANCIES.—With respect to filling temporarily a vacancy in an office within the Office of the Director of National Intelligence (other than that of the Director of National Intelligence), section 3345(a)(3) of title 5, United States Code, may be applied—

(1) in the matter preceding subparagraph (A), by substituting "an element of the intelligence community, as that term is defined in section 3(4) of the National Security Act of 1947 (50 U.S.C. 401a(4))," for "such Executive agency"; and

(2) in subparagraph (A), by substituting "the intelligence community" for "such agency".

(f) LOCATION OF THE OFFICE OF THE DIRECTOR OF NATIONAL INTELLIGENCE.— The headquarters of the Office of the Director of National Intelligence may be located in the Washington metropolitan region, as that term is defined in section 8301 of title 40, United States Code.

DEPUTY DIRECTORS OF NATIONAL INTELLIGENCE

SEC. 103A. [50 U.S.C. 3026] (a) PRINCIPAL DEPUTY DIRECTOR OF NATIONAL INTELLIGENCE.—(1) There is a Principal Deputy Director of National Intelligence who shall be appointed by the President, by and with the advice and consent of the Senate.

(2) In the event of a vacancy in the position of Principal Deputy Director of National Intelligence, the Director of National Intelligence shall recommend to the President an individual for appointment as Principal Deputy Director of National Intelligence.

(3) Any individual nominated for appointment as Principal Deputy Director of National Intelligence shall have extensive national security experience and management expertise.

(4) The individual serving as Principal Deputy Director of National Intelligence shall not, while so serving, serve in any capacity in any other element of the intelligence community.

(5) The Principal Deputy Director of National Intelligence shall assist the Director of National Intelligence in carrying out the duties and responsibilities of the Director.

(6) The Principal Deputy Director of National Intelligence shall act for, and exercise the powers of, the Director of National Intelligence during the absence or disability of the Director of National Intelligence or during a vacancy in the position of Director of National Intelligence.

(b) DEPUTY DIRECTORS OF NATIONAL INTELLIGENCE.—(1) There may be not more than four Deputy Directors of National Intelligence who shall be appointed by the Director of National Intelligence.

(2) Each Deputy Director of National Intelligence appointed under this subsection shall have such duties, responsibilities, and authorities as the Director of National Intelligence may assign or are specified by law.

(c) MILITARY STATUS OF DIRECTOR OF NATIONAL INTELLIGENCE AND PRINCIPAL DEPUTY DIRECTOR OF NATIONAL INTELLIGENCE.—(1) Not more than one of the individuals serving in the positions specified in paragraph (2) may be a commissioned officer of the Armed Forces in active status.

(2) The positions referred to in this paragraph are the following:

(A) The Director of National Intelligence.

(B) The Principal Deputy Director of National Intelligence.

(3) It is the sense of Congress that, under ordinary circumstances, it is desirable that one of the individuals serving in the positions specified in paragraph (2)—

(A) be a commissioned officer of the Armed Forces, in active status; or

(B) have, by training or experience, an appreciation of military intelligence activities and requirements.

(4) A commissioned officer of the Armed Forces, while serving in a position

specified in paragraph (2)—

(A) shall not be subject to supervision or control by the Secretary of Defense or by any officer or employee of the Department of Defense;

(B) shall not exercise, by reason of the officer's status as a commissioned officer, any supervision or control with respect to any of the military or civilian personnel of the Department of Defense except as otherwise authorized by law; and

(C) shall not be counted against the numbers and percentages of commissioned officers of the rank and grade of such officer authorized for the military department of that officer.

(5) Except as provided in subparagraph (A) or (B) of paragraph (4), the appointment of an officer of the Armed Forces to a position specified in paragraph (2) shall not affect the status, position, rank, or grade of such officer in the Armed Forces, or any emolument, perquisite, right, privilege, or benefit incident to or arising out of such status, position, rank, or grade.

(6) A commissioned officer of the Armed Forces on active duty who is appointed to a position specified in paragraph (2), while serving in such position and while remaining on active duty, shall continue to receive military pay and allowances and shall not receive the pay prescribed for such position. Funds from which such pay and allowances are paid shall be reimbursed from funds available to the Director of National Intelligence.

NATIONAL INTELLIGENCE COUNCIL

SEC. 103B. [50 U.S.C. 3027] (a) NATIONAL INTELLIGENCE COUNCIL.— There is a National Intelligence Council.

(b) COMPOSITION.—(1) The National Intelligence Council shall be composed of senior analysts within the intelligence community and substantive experts from the public and private sector, who shall be appointed by, report to, and serve at the pleasure of, the Director of National Intelligence.

(2) The Director shall prescribe appropriate security requirements for personnel appointed from the private sector as a condition of service on the Council, or as contractors of the Council or employees of such contractors, to ensure the protection of intelligence sources and methods while avoiding, wherever possible, unduly intrusive requirements which the Director considers to be unnecessary for this purpose.

(c) DUTIES AND RESPONSIBILITIES.—(1) The National Intelligence Council shall—

(A) produce national intelligence estimates for the United States Government, including alternative views held by elements of the intelligence community and other information as specified in paragraph (2);

(B) evaluate community-wide collection and production of intelligence by the intelligence community and the requirements and resources of such collection and production; and

(C) otherwise assist the Director of National Intelligence in carrying out the responsibilities of the Director under section 102A.

(2) The Director of National Intelligence shall ensure that the Council satisfies

the needs of policymakers and other consumers of intelligence.

(d) Service as Senior Intelligence Advisers.— Within their respective areas of expertise and under the direction of the Director of National Intelligence, the members of the National Intelligence Council shall constitute the senior intelligence advisers of the intelligence community for purposes of representing the views of the intelligence community within the United States Government.

(e) Authority To Contract.— Subject to the direction and control of the Director of National Intelligence, the National Intelligence Council may carry out its responsibilities under this section by contract, including contracts for substantive experts necessary to assist the Council with particular assessments under this section.

(f) Staff.— The Director of National Intelligence shall make available to the National Intelligence Council such staff as may be necessary to permit the Council to carry out its responsibilities under this section.

(g) Availability of Council and Staff.—(1) The Director of National Intelligence shall take appropriate measures to ensure that the National Intelligence Council and its staff satisfy the needs of policymaking officials and other consumers of intelligence.

(2) The Council shall be readily accessible to policymaking officials and other appropriate individuals not otherwise associated with the intelligence community.

(h) Support.— The heads of the elements of the intelligence community shall, as appropriate, furnish such support to the National Intelligence Council, including the preparation of intelligence analyses, as may be required by the Director of National Intelligence.

(i) National Intelligence Council Product.— For purposes of this section, the term "National Intelligence Council product" includes a National Intelligence Estimate and any other intelligence community assessment that sets forth the judgment of the intelligence community as a whole on a matter covered by such product.

GENERAL COUNSEL

Sec. 103C. [50 U.S.C. 3028] (a) General Counsel.— There is a General Counsel of the Office of the Director of National Intelligence who shall be appointed by the President, by and with the advice and consent of the Senate.

(b) Prohibition on Dual Service as General Counsel of Another Agency.— The individual serving in the position of General Counsel may not, while so serving, also serve as the General Counsel of any other department, agency, or element of the United States Government.

(c) Scope of Position.— The General Counsel is the chief legal officer of the Office of the Director of National Intelligence.

(d) Functions.— The General Counsel shall perform such functions as the Director of National Intelligence may prescribe.

CIVIL LIBERTIES PROTECTION OFFICER

Sec. 103D. [50 U.S.C. 3029] (a) Civil Liberties Protection Officer.—(1) Within the Office of the Director of National Intelligence, there is a Civil Liberties Protection Officer who shall be appointed by the Director of National Intelligence.

(2) The Civil Liberties Protection Officer shall report directly to the Director of National Intelligence.

(b) Duties.—The Civil Liberties Protection Officer shall—

(1) ensure that the protection of civil liberties and privacy is appropriately incorporated in the policies and procedures developed for and implemented by the Office of the Director of National Intelligence and the elements of the intelligence community within the National Intelligence Program;

(2) oversee compliance by the Office and the Director of National Intelligence with requirements under the Constitution and all laws, regulations, Executive orders, and implementing guidelines relating to civil liberties and privacy;

(3) review and assess complaints and other information indicating possible abuses of civil liberties and privacy in the administration of the programs and operations of the Office and the Director of National Intelligence and, as appropriate, investigate any such complaint or information;

(4) ensure that the use of technologies sustain, and do not erode, privacy protections relating to the use, collection, and disclosure of personal information;

(5) ensure that personal information contained in a system of records subject to section 552a of title 5, United States Code (popularly referred to as the "Privacy Act"), is handled in full compliance with fair information practices as set out in that section;

(6) conduct privacy impact assessments when appropriate or as required by law; and

(7) perform such other duties as may be prescribed by the Director of National Intelligence or specified by law.

(c) Use of Agency Inspectors General.— When appropriate, the Civil Liberties Protection Officer may refer complaints to the Office of Inspector General having responsibility for the affected element of the department or agency of the intelligence community to conduct an investigation under paragraph (3) of subsection (b).

Director of Science and Technology

Sec. 103E. [50 U.S.C. 3030] (a) Director of Science and Technology.— There is a Director of Science and Technology within the Office of the Director of National Intelligence who shall be appointed by the Director of National Intelligence.

(b) Requirement Relating to Appointment.— An individual appointed as Director of Science and Technology shall have a professional background and experience appropriate for the duties of the Director of Science and Technology. In making such appointment, the Director of National Intelligence may give preference to an individual with experience outside of the United States Government.

(c) Duties.—The Director of Science and Technology shall—

(1) act as the chief representative of the Director of National Intelligence for science and technology;

(2) chair the Director of National Intelligence Science and Technology Committee under subsection (d);

(3) assist the Director in formulating a long-term strategy for scientific advances

in the field of intelligence;

(4) assist the Director on the science and technology elements of the budget of the Office of the Director of National Intelligence; and

(5) perform other such duties as may be prescribed by the Director of National Intelligence or specified by law.

(d) Director of National Intelligence Science and Technology Committee.—(1) There is within the Office of the Director of Science and Technology a Director of National Intelligence Science and Technology Committee.

(2) The Committee shall be composed of the principal science officers of the National Intelligence Program.

(3) The Committee shall—

(A) coordinate advances in research and development related to intelligence; and

(B) perform such other functions as the Director of Science and Technology shall prescribe.

DIRECTOR OF THE NATIONAL COUNTERINTELLIGENCE AND SECURITY CENTER

Sec. 103F. [50 U.S.C. 3031] (a) Director of the National Counterintelligence and Security Center.— The Director of the National Counterintelligence and Security Center appointed under section 902 of the Counterintelligence Enhancement Act of 2002 (50 U.S.C. 3382) is a component of the Office of the Director of National Intelligence.

(b) Duties.— The Director of the National Counterintelligence and Security Center shall perform the duties provided in the Counterintelligence Enhancement Act of 2002 and such other duties as may be prescribed by the Director of National Intelligence or specified by law.

CHIEF INFORMATION OFFICER

Sec. 103G. [50 U.S.C. 3032] (a) Chief Information Officer.— To assist the Director of National Intelligence in carrying out the responsibilities of the Director under this Act and other applicable provisions of law, there shall be within the Office of the Director of National Intelligence a Chief Information Officer of the Intelligence Community who shall be appointed by the Director. The Chief Information Officer shall report directly to the Director of National Intelligence.

(b) Duties and Responsibilities.—Subject to the direction of the Director of National Intelligence, the Chief Information Officer of the Intelligence Community shall—

(1) manage activities relating to the information technology infrastructure and enterprise architecture requirements of the intelligence community;

(2) have procurement approval authority over all information technology items related to the enterprise architectures of all intelligence community components;

(3) direct and manage all information technology-related procurement for the intelligence community; and

(4) ensure that all expenditures for information technology and research and

development activities are consistent with the intelligence community enterprise architecture and the strategy of the Director for such architecture.

(c) PROHIBITION ON SIMULTANEOUS SERVICE AS OTHER CHIEF INFORMATION OFFICER.— An individual serving in the position of Chief Information Officer of the Intelligence Community may not, while so serving, serve as the chief information officer of any other department or agency, or component thereof, of the United States Government.

(d) PROHIBITION ON SIMULTANEOUS SERVICE AS CHIEF DATA OFFICER AND CHIEF INFORMATION OFFICER.— An individual serving in the position of Chief Information Officer of the Intelligence Community or chief information officer of any other element of the intelligence community shall not concurrently serve as the Intelligence Community Chief Data Officer under section 103K and as the chief data officer of any other element of the intelligence community.

INSPECTOR GENERAL OF THE INTELLIGENCE COMMUNITY

SEC. 103H. [50 U.S.C. 3033] (a) OFFICE OF INSPECTOR GENERAL OF THE INTELLIGENCE COMMUNITY.— There is within the Office of the Director of National Intelligence an Office of the Inspector General of the Intelligence Community.

(b) PURPOSE.—The purpose of the Office of the Inspector General of the Intelligence Community is—

(1) to create an objective and effective office, appropriately accountable to Congress, to initiate and conduct independent investigations, inspections, audits, and reviews on programs and activities within the responsibility and authority of the Director of National Intelligence;

(2) to provide leadership and coordination and recommend policies for activities designed—

(A) to promote economy, efficiency, and effectiveness in the administration and implementation of such programs and activities; and

(B) to prevent and detect fraud and abuse in such programs and activities;

(3) to provide a means for keeping the Director of National Intelligence fully and currently informed about—

(A) problems and deficiencies relating to the administration of programs and activities within the responsibility and authority of the Director of National Intelligence; and

(B) the necessity for, and the progress of, corrective actions; and

(4) in the manner prescribed by this section, to ensure that the congressional intelligence committees are kept similarly informed of—

(A) significant problems and deficiencies relating to programs and activities within the responsibility and authority of the Director of National Intelligence; and

(B) the necessity for, and the progress of, corrective actions.

(c) INSPECTOR GENERAL OF THE INTELLIGENCE COMMUNITY[3].—(1) There is an Inspector General of the Intelligence Community, who shall be the head of the Office of the Inspector General of the Intelligence Community, who shall be appointed by the

President, by and with the advice and consent of the Senate.

[3] Sections 5202(a)(3)(A)(i) and 5203(b) of division E of P.L. 117-263 provide for amendments to this subsection of the "National Security Act", but such amendments should have been made to the "National Security Act of 1947". Such amendments have been executed to show the probable intent of Congress.

(2) The nomination of an individual for appointment as Inspector General shall be made—

(A) without regard to political affiliation;

(B) on the basis of integrity, compliance with security standards of the intelligence community, and prior experience in the field of intelligence or national security; and

(C) on the basis of demonstrated ability in accounting, financial analysis, law, management analysis, public administration, or investigations.

(3) The Inspector General shall report directly to and be under the general supervision of the Director of National Intelligence.

(4)(A) The Inspector General may be removed from office only by the President. The President shall communicate in writing to the congressional intelligence committees the substantive rationale, including detailed and case-specific reasons, for the removal not later than 30 days prior to the effective date of such removal. Nothing in this paragraph shall be construed to prohibit a personnel action otherwise authorized by law, other than transfer or removal.

(B) If there is an open or completed inquiry into the Inspector General that relates to the removal or transfer of the Inspector General under subparagraph (A), the written communication required under that subparagraph shall—

(i) identify each entity that is conducting, or that conducted, the inquiry; and

(ii) in the case of a completed inquiry, contain the findings made during the inquiry.

(5)(A) Subject to the other provisions of this paragraph, only the President may place the Inspector General on nonduty status.

(B) If the President places the Inspector General on nonduty status, the President shall communicate in writing the substantive rationale, including detailed and case-specific reasons, for the change in status to the congressional intelligence committees not later than 15 days before the date on which the change in status takes effect, except that the President may submit that communication not later than the date on which the change in status takes effect if—

(i) the President has made a determination that the continued presence of the Inspector General in the workplace poses a threat described in any of clauses (i) through (iv) of section 6329b(b)(2)(A) of title 5, United States Code; and

(ii) in the communication, the President includes a report on the determination described in clause (i), which shall include—

(I) a specification of which clause of section 6329b(b)(2)(A) of title 5, United States Code, the President has determined applies under clause (i);

(II) the substantive rationale, including detailed and case-specific reasons, for the determination made under clause (i);

(III) an identification of each entity that is conducting, or that conducted, any inquiry upon which the determination under clause (i) was made; and

(IV) in the case of an inquiry described in subclause (III) that is completed, the findings made during that inquiry.

(C) The President may not place the Inspector General on nonduty status during the 30-day period preceding the date on which the Inspector General is removed or transferred under paragraph (4)(A) unless the President—

(i) has made a determination that the continued presence of the Inspector General in the workplace poses a threat described in any of clauses (i) through (iv) of section 6329b(b)(2)(A) of title 5, United States Code; and

(ii) not later than the date on which the change in status takes effect, submits to the congressional intelligence committees a written communication that contains the information required under subparagraph (B), including the report required under clause (ii) of that subparagraph.

(6)(A) In this subsection, the term "first assistant to the position of Inspector General" has the meaning given in section 3 of the Inspector General Act of 1978 (5 U.S.C. App.).

(B) If the Inspector General dies, resigns, or is otherwise unable to perform the functions and duties of the position—

(i) section 3345(a) of title 5, United States Code, and section 103(e) of the National Security Act of 1947 (50 U.S.C. 3025(e)) shall not apply;

(ii) subject to subparagraph (D), the first assistant to the position of Inspector General shall perform the functions and duties of the Inspector General temporarily in an acting capacity subject to the time limitations of section 3346 of title 5, United States Code; and

(iii) notwithstanding clause (ii), and subject to subparagraphs (D) and (E), the President (and only the President) may direct an officer or employee of any Office of an Inspector General to perform the functions and duties of the Inspector General temporarily in an acting capacity subject to the time limitations of section 3346 of title 5, United States Code, only if—

(I) during the 365-day period preceding the date of death, resignation, or beginning of inability to serve of the Inspector General, the officer or employee served in a position in an Office of an Inspector General for not less than 90 days, except that—

(aa) the requirement under this subclause shall not apply if the officer is an Inspector General; and

(bb) for the purposes of this clause, performing the functions and duties of an Inspector General temporarily in an acting capacity does not qualify as service in a position in an Office of an Inspector General;

(II) the rate of pay for the position of the officer or employee described in subclause (I) is equal to or greater than the minimum rate of pay payable for a position at GS–15 of the General Schedule;

(III) the officer or employee has demonstrated ability in accounting, auditing, financial analysis, law, management analysis, public administration, or investigations; and

(IV) not later than 30 days before the date on which the direction takes effect, the President communicates in writing to the congressional intelligence committees the substantive rationale, including the detailed and case-specific reasons, for such direction, including the reason for the direction that someone other than the individual who is performing the functions and duties of the Inspector General temporarily in an acting capacity (as of the date on which the President issues that direction) perform those functions and duties temporarily in an acting capacity.

(C) Notwithstanding section 3345(a) of title 5, United States Code, section 103(e) of the National Security Act of 1947 (50 U.S.C. 3025(e)), and clauses (ii) and (iii) of subparagraph (B), and subject to subparagraph (D), during any period in which the Inspector General is on nonduty status—

(i) the first assistant to the position of Inspector General shall perform the functions and duties of the position temporarily in an acting capacity subject to the time limitations of section 3346 of title 5, United States Code; and

(ii) if the first assistant described in clause (i) dies, resigns, or becomes otherwise unable to perform those functions and duties, the President (and only the President) may direct an officer or employee in the Office of Inspector General to perform those functions and duties temporarily in an acting capacity, subject to the time limitations of section 3346 of title 5, United States Code, if—

(I) that direction satisfies the requirements under subclauses (II), (III), and (IV) of subparagraph (B)(iii); and

(II) that officer or employee served in a position in that Office of Inspector General for not fewer than 90 of the 365 days preceding the date on which the President makes that direction.

(D) An individual may perform the functions and duties of the Inspector General temporarily and in an acting capacity under clause (ii) or (iii) of subparagraph (B), or under subparagraph (C), with respect to only 1 Inspector General position at any given time.

(E) If the President makes a direction under subparagraph (B)(iii), during the 30-day period preceding the date on which the direction of the President takes effect, the functions and duties of the position of the Inspector General shall be performed by—

(i) the first assistant to the position of Inspector General; or

(ii) the individual performing those functions and duties temporarily in an acting capacity, as of the date on which the President issues that direction, if that individual is an individual other than the first assistant to the position of Inspector General.

(d) Assistant Inspectors General.—Subject to the policies of the Director of National Intelligence, the Inspector General of the Intelligence Community shall—

(1) appoint an Assistant Inspector General for Audit who shall have the responsibility for supervising the performance of auditing activities relating to programs and activities within the responsibility and authority of the Director;

(2) appoint an Assistant Inspector General for Investigations who shall have the responsibility for supervising the performance of investigative activities relating to such programs and activities; and

(3) appoint other Assistant Inspectors General that, in the judgment of the Inspector General, are necessary to carry out the duties of the Inspector General.

(e) Duties and Responsibilities.—It shall be the duty and responsibility of the Inspector General of the Intelligence Community—

(1) to provide policy direction for, and to plan, conduct, supervise, and coordinate independently, the investigations, inspections, audits, and reviews relating to programs and activities within the responsibility and authority of the Director of National Intelligence;

(2) to keep the Director of National Intelligence fully and currently informed concerning violations of law and regulations, fraud, and other serious problems, abuses, and deficiencies relating to the programs and activities within the responsibility and authority of the Director, to recommend corrective action concerning such problems, and to report on the progress made in implementing such corrective action;

(3) to take due regard for the protection of intelligence sources and methods in the preparation of all reports issued by the Inspector General, and, to the extent consistent with the purpose and objective of such reports, take such measures as may be appropriate to minimize the disclosure of intelligence sources and methods described in such reports; and

(4) in the execution of the duties and responsibilities under this section, to comply with generally accepted government auditing.

(f) Limitations on Activities.—(1) The Director of National Intelligence may prohibit the Inspector General of the Intelligence Community from initiating, carrying out, or completing any investigation, inspection, audit, or review if the Director determines that such prohibition is necessary to protect vital national security interests of the United States.

(2) Not later than seven days after the date on which the Director exercises the authority under paragraph (1), the Director shall submit to the congressional intelligence committees an appropriately classified statement of the reasons for the exercise of such authority.

(3) The Director shall advise the Inspector General at the time a statement under paragraph (2) is submitted, and, to the extent consistent with the protection of intelligence sources and methods, provide the Inspector General with a copy of such statement.

(4) The Inspector General may submit to the congressional intelligence committees any comments on the statement of which the Inspector General has notice under paragraph (3) that the Inspector General considers appropriate.

(g) AUTHORITIES.—(1) The Inspector General of the Intelligence Community shall have direct and prompt access to the Director of National Intelligence when necessary for any purpose pertaining to the performance of the duties of the Inspector General.

(2)(A) The Inspector General shall, subject to the limitations in subsection (f), make such investigations and reports relating to the administration of the programs and activities within the authorities and responsibilities of the Director as are, in the judgment of the Inspector General, necessary or desirable.

(B) The Inspector General shall have access to any employee, or any employee of a contractor, of any element of the intelligence community needed for the performance of the duties of the Inspector General.

(C) The Inspector General shall have direct access to all records, reports, audits, reviews, documents, papers, recommendations, or other materials that relate to the programs and activities with respect to which the Inspector General has responsibilities under this section.

(D) The level of classification or compartmentation of information shall not, in and of itself, provide a sufficient rationale for denying the Inspector General access to any materials under subparagraph (C).

(E) The Director, or on the recommendation of the Director, another appropriate official of the intelligence community, shall take appropriate administrative actions against an employee, or an employee of a contractor, of an element of the intelligence community that fails to cooperate with the Inspector General. Such administrative action may include loss of employment or the termination of an existing contractual relationship.

(3)(A) The Inspector General is authorized to receive and investigate, pursuant to subsection (h), complaints or information from any person concerning the existence of an activity within the authorities and responsibilities of the Director of National Intelligence constituting a violation of laws, rules, or regulations, or mismanagement, gross waste of funds, abuse of authority, or a substantial and specific danger to the public health and safety. Once such complaint or information has been received from an employee of the intelligence community—

(i) the Inspector General shall not disclose the identity of the employee without the consent of the employee, unless the Inspector General determines that such disclosure is unavoidable during the course of the investigation or the disclosure is made to an official of the Department of Justice responsible for determining whether a prosecution should be undertaken, and this provision shall qualify as a withholding statute pursuant to subsection (b)(3) of section 552 of title 5, United States Code (commonly known as the "Freedom of Information Act"); and

(ii) no action constituting a reprisal, or threat of reprisal, for making such complaint or disclosing such information to the Inspector General may be taken by any employee in a position to take such actions, unless the complaint was made or the information was disclosed with the knowledge that it was false or with willful disregard for its truth or falsity.

(B)(i) An individual may disclose classified information to the Inspector General in accordance with the applicable security standards and procedures established under section 102A or 803 of this Act, chapter 12 of the Atomic

Energy Act of 1954 (42 U.S.C. 2161 et seq.), Executive Order 13526 (50 U.S.C. 3161 note; relating to Classified National Security Information), or any applicable provision of law.

(ii) A disclosure under clause (i) of classified information made by an individual without appropriate clearance or authority to access such classified information at the time of the disclosure, but that is otherwise made in accordance with applicable security standards and procedures, shall be treated as an authorized disclosure that does not violate a covered provision.

(iii) Nothing in clause (ii) may be construed to limit or modify the obligation of an individual to appropriately store, handle, or disseminate classified information in accordance with applicable security guidance and procedures, including with respect to the removal or retention of classified information.

(iv) In this subparagraph, the term "covered provision" means—

(I) any otherwise applicable nondisclosure agreement;

(II) any otherwise applicable regulation or order issued under the authority of chapter 18 of the Atomic Energy Act of 1954 (42 U.S.C. 2271 et seq.) or Executive Order 13526;

(III) section 798 of title 18, United States Code; or

(IV) any other provision of law with respect to the unauthorized disclosure of national security information.

(4) The Inspector General shall have the authority to administer to or take from any person an oath, affirmation, or affidavit, whenever necessary in the performance of the duties of the Inspector General, which oath, affirmation, or affidavit when administered or taken by or before an employee of the Office of the Inspector General of the Intelligence Community designated by the Inspector General shall have the same force and effect as if administered or taken by, or before, an officer having a seal.

(5)(A) Except as provided in subparagraph (B), the Inspector General is authorized to require by subpoena the production of all information, documents, reports, answers, records, accounts, papers, and other data in any medium (including electronically stored information, as well as any tangible thing) and documentary evidence necessary in the performance of the duties and responsibilities of the Inspector General.

(B) In the case of departments, agencies, and other elements of the United States Government, the Inspector General shall obtain information, documents, reports, answers, records, accounts, papers, and other data and evidence for the purpose specified in subparagraph (A) using procedures other than by subpoenas.

(C) The Inspector General may not issue a subpoena for, or on behalf of, any component of the Office of the Director of National Intelligence or any element of the intelligence community, including the Office of the Director of National Intelligence.

(D) In the case of contumacy or refusal to obey a subpoena issued under this paragraph, the subpoena shall be enforceable by order of any appropriate district court of the United States.

(6) The Inspector General may obtain services as authorized by section 3109 of title 5, United States Code, at rates for individuals not to exceed the daily equivalent of the maximum annual rate of basic pay payable for grade GS–15 of the General Schedule under section 5332 of title 5, United States Code.

(7) The Inspector General may, to the extent and in such amounts as may be provided in appropriations, enter into contracts and other arrangements for audits, studies, analyses, and other services with public agencies and with private persons, and to make such payments as may be necessary to carry out the provisions of this section.

(h) Coordination Among Inspectors General.—(1)(A) In the event of a matter within the jurisdiction of the Inspector General of the Intelligence Community that may be subject to an investigation, inspection, audit, or review by both the Inspector General of the Intelligence Community and an inspector general with oversight responsibility for an element of the intelligence community, the Inspector General of the Intelligence Community and such other inspector general shall expeditiously resolve the question of which inspector general shall conduct such investigation, inspection, audit, or review to avoid unnecessary duplication of the activities of the inspectors general.

(B) In attempting to resolve a question under subparagraph (A), the inspectors general concerned may request the assistance of the Intelligence Community Inspectors General Forum established under paragraph (2). In the event of a dispute between an inspector general within a department or agency of the United States Government and the Inspector General of the Intelligence Community that has not been resolved with the assistance of such Forum, the inspectors general shall submit the question to the Director of National Intelligence and the head of the affected department or agency for resolution.

(2)(A) There is established the Intelligence Community Inspectors General Forum, which shall consist of all statutory or administrative inspectors general with oversight responsibility for an element of the intelligence community.

(B) The Inspector General of the Intelligence Community shall serve as the Chair of the Forum established under subparagraph (A). The Forum shall have no administrative authority over any inspector general, but shall serve as a mechanism for informing its members of the work of individual members of the Forum that may be of common interest and discussing questions about jurisdiction or access to employees, employees of contract personnel, records, audits, reviews, documents, recommendations, or other materials that may involve or be of assistance to more than one of its members.

(3) The inspector general conducting an investigation, inspection, audit, or review covered by paragraph (1) shall submit the results of such investigation, inspection, audit, or review to any other inspector general, including the Inspector General of the Intelligence Community, with jurisdiction to conduct such investigation, inspection, audit, or review who did not conduct such investigation, inspection, audit, or review.

(i) Counsel to the Inspector General.—(1) The Inspector General of the Intelligence Community shall—

(A) appoint a Counsel to the Inspector General who shall report to the Inspector General; or

(B) obtain the services of a counsel appointed by and directly reporting to another inspector general or the Council of the Inspectors General on Integrity and Efficiency on a reimbursable basis.

(2) The counsel appointed or obtained under paragraph (1) shall perform such functions as the Inspector General may prescribe.

(j) Staff and Other Support.—(1) The Director of National Intelligence shall provide the Inspector General of the Intelligence Community with appropriate and adequate office space at central and field office locations, together with such equipment, office supplies, maintenance services, and communications facilities and services as may be necessary for the operation of such offices.

(2)(A) Subject to applicable law and the policies of the Director of National Intelligence, the Inspector General shall select, appoint, and employ such officers and employees as may be necessary to carry out the functions, powers, and duties of the Inspector General. The Inspector General shall ensure that any officer or employee so selected, appointed, or employed has security clearances appropriate for the assigned duties of such officer or employee.

(B) In making selections under subparagraph (A), the Inspector General shall ensure that such officers and employees have the requisite training and experience to enable the Inspector General to carry out the duties of the Inspector General effectively.

(C) In meeting the requirements of this paragraph, the Inspector General shall create within the Office of the Inspector General of the Intelligence Community a career cadre of sufficient size to provide appropriate continuity and objectivity needed for the effective performance of the duties of the Inspector General.

(3) Consistent with budgetary and personnel resources allocated by the Director of National Intelligence, the Inspector General has final approval of—

(A) the selection of internal and external candidates for employment with the Office of the Inspector General; and

(B) all other personnel decisions concerning personnel permanently assigned to the Office of the Inspector General, including selection and appointment to the Senior Intelligence Service, but excluding all security-based determinations that are not within the authority of a head of a component of the Office of the Director of National Intelligence.

(4)(A) Subject to the concurrence of the Director of National Intelligence, the Inspector General may request such information or assistance as may be necessary for carrying out the duties and responsibilities of the Inspector General from any Federal, State (as defined in section 805), or local governmental agency or unit thereof.

(B) Upon request of the Inspector General for information or assistance from a department, agency, or element of the Federal Government under subparagraph (A), the head of the department, agency, or element concerned shall, insofar as is practicable and not in contravention of any existing statutory restriction or regulation of the department, agency, or element, furnish to the Inspector General, such information or assistance.

(C) The Inspector General of the Intelligence Community may, upon reasonable notice to the head of any element of the intelligence community and in coordination with that element's inspector general pursuant to subsection (h), conduct, as authorized by this section, an investigation, inspection, audit, or review of such element and may enter into any place occupied by such element for purposes of the performance of the duties of the Inspector General.

(k) Reports.—(1)(A) The Inspector General of the Intelligence Community shall, not later than October 31 and April 30 of each year, prepare and submit to the Director of National Intelligence a classified, and, as appropriate, unclassified semiannual report summarizing the activities of the Office of the Inspector General of the Intelligence Community during the immediately preceding 6-month period ending September 30 and March 31, respectively. The Inspector General of the Intelligence Community shall provide any portion of the report involving a component of a department of the United States Government to the head of that department simultaneously with submission of the report to the Director of National Intelligence.

(B) Each report under this paragraph shall include, at a minimum, the following:

(i) A list of the title or subject of each investigation, inspection, audit, or review conducted during the period covered by such report.

(ii) A description of significant problems, abuses, and deficiencies relating to the administration of programs and activities of the intelligence community within the responsibility and authority of the Director of National Intelligence, and in the relationships between elements of the intelligence community, identified by the Inspector General during the period covered by such report.

(iii) A description of the recommendations for corrective action made by the Inspector General during the period covered by such report with respect to significant problems, abuses, or deficiencies identified in clause (ii).

(iv) A statement of whether or not corrective action has been completed on each significant recommendation described in previous semiannual reports, and, in a case where corrective action has been completed, a description of such corrective action.

(v) A certification of whether or not the Inspector General has had full and direct access to all information relevant to the performance of the functions of the Inspector General.

(vi) A description of the exercise of the subpoena authority under subsection (g)(5) by the Inspector General during the period covered by such report.

(vii) Such recommendations as the Inspector General considers appropriate for legislation to promote economy, efficiency, and effectiveness in the administration and implementation of programs and activities within the responsibility and authority of the Director of National Intelligence, and to detect and eliminate fraud and abuse in such programs and activities.

(C) Not later than 30 days after the date of receipt of a report under subparagraph (A), the Director shall transmit the report to the congressional intelligence committees together with any comments the Director considers appropriate. The

Director shall transmit to the committees of the Senate and of the House of Representatives with jurisdiction over a department of the United States Government any portion of the report involving a component of such department simultaneously with submission of the report to the congressional intelligence committees.

(2)(A) The Inspector General shall report immediately to the Director whenever the Inspector General becomes aware of particularly serious or flagrant problems, abuses, or deficiencies relating to programs and activities within the responsibility and authority of the Director of National Intelligence.

(B) The Director shall transmit to the congressional intelligence committees each report under subparagraph (A) within 7 calendar days of receipt of such report, together with such comments as the Director considers appropriate. The Director shall transmit to the committees of the Senate and of the House of Representatives with jurisdiction over a department of the United States Government any portion of each report under subparagraph (A) that involves a problem, abuse, or deficiency related to a component of such department simultaneously with transmission of the report to the congressional intelligence committees.

(3)(A) In the event that—

(i) the Inspector General is unable to resolve any differences with the Director affecting the execution of the duties or responsibilities of the Inspector General;

(ii) an investigation, inspection, audit, or review carried out by the Inspector General focuses on any current or former intelligence community official who—

(I) holds or held a position in an element of the intelligence community that is subject to appointment by the President, whether or not by and with the advice and consent of the Senate, including such a position held on an acting basis;

(II) holds or held a position in an element of the intelligence community, including a position held on an acting basis, that is appointed by the Director of National Intelligence; or

(III) holds or held a position as head of an element of the intelligence community or a position covered by subsection (b) or (c) of section 106;

(iii) a matter requires a report by the Inspector General to the Department of Justice on possible criminal conduct by a current or former official described in clause (ii);

(iv) the Inspector General receives notice from the Department of Justice declining or approving prosecution of possible criminal conduct of any current or former official described in clause (ii); or

(v) the Inspector General, after exhausting all possible alternatives, is unable to obtain significant documentary information in the course of an investigation, inspection, audit, or review,

the Inspector General shall immediately notify, and submit a report to, the congressional intelligence committees on such matter.

(B) The Inspector General shall submit to the committees of the Senate and of the House of Representatives with jurisdiction over a department of the United States Government any portion of each report under subparagraph (A) that involves an investigation, inspection, audit, or review carried out by the Inspector General focused on any current or former official of a component of such department simultaneously with submission of the report to the congressional intelligence committees.

(4) The Director shall submit to the congressional intelligence committees any report or findings and recommendations of an investigation, inspection, audit, or review conducted by the office which has been requested by the Chairman or Vice Chairman or ranking minority member of either committee.

(5)(A)(i) An employee of an element of the intelligence community, an employee assigned or detailed to an element of the intelligence community, or an employee of a contractor to the intelligence community who intends to report to Congress a complaint or information with respect to an urgent concern may report such complaint or information in writing to the Inspector General.

(ii) The Inspector General shall—

(I) provide reasonable support necessary to ensure that an employee can report a complaint or information under this subparagraph in writing; and

(II) if such submission is not feasible, create a written record of the employee's verbal complaint or information and treat such written record as a written submission.

(B)(i) In accordance with clause (ii), the Inspector General shall determine whether a complaint or information reported under subparagraph (A) appears credible. Upon making such a determination, the Inspector General shall transmit to the Director a notice of that determination, together with the complaint or information.

(ii) The Inspector General shall make the determination under clause (i) with respect to a complaint or information under subparagraph (A) by not later than the end of the 14-calendar-day period beginning on the date on which the employee who reported the complaint or information confirms to the Inspector General the intent of the employee to report to Congress that complaint or information.

(C) Upon receipt of a transmittal from the Inspector General under subparagraph (B), the Director shall, within 7 calendar days of such receipt, forward such transmittal to the congressional intelligence committees, together with any comments the Director considers appropriate.

(D)(i) If the Inspector General does not find credible under subparagraph (B) a complaint or information submitted under subparagraph (A), or does not transmit the complaint or information to the Director in accurate form under subparagraph (B), the employee (subject to clause (ii)) may submit the complaint or information to Congress by contacting either or both of the congressional intelligence committees directly.

(ii) An employee may contact the congressional intelligence committees directly as described in clause (i) only if the employee—

(I) before making such a contact, furnishes to the Director, through the Inspector General, a statement of the employee's complaint or information and notice of the employee's intent to contact the congressional intelligence committees directly; and

(II) obtains and follows from the Director, through the Inspector General, direction on how to contact the congressional intelligence committees in accordance with appropriate security practices.

(iii) A member or employee of one of the congressional intelligence committees who receives a complaint or information under this subparagraph does so in that member or employee's official capacity as a member or employee of such committee.

(E) The Inspector General shall notify an employee who reports a complaint or information to the Inspector General under this paragraph of each action taken under this paragraph with respect to the complaint or information. Such notice shall be provided not later than 3 days after any such action is taken.

(F) An action taken by the Director or the Inspector General under this paragraph shall not be subject to judicial review.

(G)(i) In this paragraph, the term "urgent concern" means any of the following:

(I) A serious or flagrant problem, abuse, violation of law or Executive order, or deficiency relating to the funding, administration, or operation of an intelligence activity of the Federal Government that is—

(aa)[4] a matter of national security; and

(bb) not a difference of opinion concerning public policy matters.

[4] The margins of items (aa) and (bb) are so in law. See amendment made by section 6609(a) of division F of Public Law 117–263 (136 Stat. 3559).

(II) A false statement to Congress, or a willful withholding from Congress, on an issue of material fact relating to the funding, administration, or operation of an intelligence activity.

(III) An action, including a personnel action described in section 2302(a)(2)(A) of title 5, United States Code, constituting reprisal or threat of reprisal prohibited under subsection (g)(3)(B) of this section in response to an employee's reporting an urgent concern in accordance with this paragraph.

(ii) Within the executive branch, the Inspector General shall have sole authority to determine whether any complaint or information reported to the Inspector General is a matter of urgent concern under this paragraph.

(H) Nothing in this section shall be construed to limit the protections afforded to an employee under section 17(d) of the Central Intelligence Agency Act of 1949 (50 U.S.C. 403q(d)) or section 416 of title 5, United States Code.

(I) An individual who has submitted a complaint or information to the Inspector General under this section may notify any member of either of the congressional intelligence committees, or a staff member of either of such committees, of the fact that such individual has made a submission to the Inspector General, and of the date on which such submission was made.

(J) In this paragraph, the term "employee" includes a former employee, if the complaint or information reported under subparagraph (A) arises from or relates to the period during which the former employee was an employee.

(6) In accordance with section 535 of title 28, United States Code, the Inspector General shall expeditiously report to the Attorney General any information, allegation, or complaint received by the Inspector General relating to violations of Federal criminal law that involve a program or operation of an element of the intelligence community, or in the relationships between the elements of the intelligence community, consistent with such guidelines as may be issued by the Attorney General pursuant to subsection (b)(2) of such section. A copy of each such report shall be furnished to the Director.

(l) CONSTRUCTION OF DUTIES REGARDING ELEMENTS OF INTELLIGENCE COMMUNITY.— Except as resolved pursuant to subsection (h), the performance by the Inspector General of the Intelligence Community of any duty, responsibility, or function regarding an element of the intelligence community shall not be construed to modify or affect the duties and responsibilities of any other inspector general having duties and responsibilities relating to such element.

(m) SEPARATE BUDGET ACCOUNT.— The Director of National Intelligence shall, in accordance with procedures issued by the Director in consultation with the congressional intelligence committees, include in the National Intelligence Program budget a separate account for the Office of the Inspector General of the Intelligence Community.

(n) BUDGET.—(1) For each fiscal year, the Inspector General of the Intelligence Community shall transmit a budget estimate and request to the Director of National Intelligence that specifies for such fiscal year—

(A) the aggregate amount requested for the operations of the Inspector General;

(B) the amount requested for all training requirements of the Inspector General, including a certification from the Inspector General that the amount requested is sufficient to fund all training requirements for the Office of the Inspector General; and

(C) the amount requested to support the Council of the Inspectors General on Integrity and Efficiency, including a justification for such amount.

(2) In transmitting a proposed budget to the President for a fiscal year, the Director of National Intelligence shall include for such fiscal year—

(A) the aggregate amount requested for the Inspector General of the Intelligence Community;

(B) the amount requested for Inspector General training;

(C) the amount requested to support the Council of the Inspectors General on Integrity and Efficiency; and

(D) the comments of the Inspector General, if any, with respect to such proposed budget.

(3) The Director of National Intelligence shall submit to the congressional intelligence committees, the Committee on Appropriations of the Senate, and the Committee on Appropriations of the House of Representatives for each fiscal year—

(A) a separate statement of the budget estimate transmitted pursuant to paragraph (1);

(B) the amount requested by the Director for the Inspector General pursuant to paragraph (2)(A);

(C) the amount requested by the Director for the training of personnel of the Office of the Inspector General pursuant to paragraph (2)(B);

(D) the amount requested by the Director for support for the Council of the Inspectors General on Integrity and Efficiency pursuant to paragraph (2)(C); and

(E) the comments of the Inspector General under paragraph (2)(D), if any, on the amounts requested pursuant to paragraph (2), including whether such amounts would substantially inhibit the Inspector General from performing the duties of the Office of the Inspector General.

(o) INFORMATION ON WEBSITE.—(1) The Director of National Intelligence shall establish and maintain on the homepage of the publicly accessible website of the Office of the Director of National Intelligence information relating to the Office of the Inspector General of the Intelligence Community including methods to contact the Inspector General.

(2) The information referred to in paragraph (1) shall be obvious and facilitate accessibility to the information related to the Office of the Inspector General of the Intelligence Community.

CHIEF FINANCIAL OFFICER OF THE INTELLIGENCE COMMUNITY

SEC. 103I. [50 U.S.C. 3034] (a) CHIEF FINANCIAL OFFICER OF THE INTELLIGENCE COMMUNITY.— To assist the Director of National Intelligence in carrying out the responsibilities of the Director under this Act and other applicable provisions of law, there is within the Office of the Director of National Intelligence a Chief Financial Officer of the Intelligence Community who shall be appointed by the Director. The Chief Financial Officer shall report directly to the Director of National Intelligence.

(b) DUTIES AND RESPONSIBILITIES.—Subject to the direction of the Director of National Intelligence, the Chief Financial Officer of the Intelligence Community shall—

(1) serve as the principal advisor to the Director of National Intelligence and the Principal Deputy Director of National Intelligence on the management and allocation of intelligence community budgetary resources;

(2) participate in overseeing a comprehensive and integrated strategic process for resource management within the intelligence community;

(3) ensure that the strategic plan of the Director of National Intelligence—

(A) is based on budgetary constraints as specified in the Future Year Intelligence Plans and Long-term Budget Projections required under section 506G; and

(B) contains specific goals and objectives to support a performance-based budget;

(4) prior to the obligation or expenditure of funds for the acquisition of any major system pursuant to a Milestone A or Milestone B decision, receive verification from appropriate authorities that the national requirements for meeting

the strategic plan of the Director have been established, and that such requirements are prioritized based on budgetary constraints as specified in the Future Year Intelligence Plans and the Long-term Budget Projections for such major system required under section 506G;

(5) ensure that the collection architectures of the Director are based on budgetary constraints as specified in the Future Year Intelligence Plans and the Long-term Budget Projections required under section 506G;

(6) coordinate or approve representations made to Congress by the intelligence community regarding National Intelligence Program budgetary resources;

(7) participate in key mission requirements, acquisitions, or architectural boards formed within or by the Office of the Director of National Intelligence; and

(8) perform such other duties as may be prescribed by the Director of National Intelligence.

(c) Other Law.— The Chief Financial Officer of the Intelligence Community shall serve as the Chief Financial Officer of the intelligence community and, to the extent applicable, shall have the duties, responsibilities, and authorities specified in chapter 9 of title 31, United States Code.

(d) Prohibition on Simultaneous Service as Other Chief Financial Officer.— An individual serving in the position of Chief Financial Officer of the Intelligence Community may not, while so serving, serve as the chief financial officer of any other department or agency, or component thereof, of the United States Government.

(e) Definitions.—In this section:

(1) The term "major system" has the meaning given that term in section 506A(e).

(2) The term "Milestone A" has the meaning given that term in section 506G(f).

(3) The term "Milestone B" has the meaning given that term in section 506C(e).

SEC. 103J. [50 U.S.C. 3034a] FUNCTIONAL MANAGERS FOR THE INTELLIGENCE COMMUNITY.

(a) Functional Managers Authorized.— The Director of National Intelligence may establish within the intelligence community one or more positions of manager of an intelligence function. Any position so established may be known as the "Functional Manager" of the intelligence function concerned.

(b) Personnel.— The Director shall designate individuals to serve as manager of intelligence functions established under subsection (a) from among officers and employees of elements of the intelligence community.

(c) Duties.—Each manager of an intelligence function established under subsection (a) shall have the duties as follows:

(1) To act as principal advisor to the Director on the intelligence function.

(2) To carry out such other responsibilities with respect to the intelligence function as the Director may specify for purposes of this section.

SEC. 103K. [U.S.C. 3034b] INTELLIGENCE COMMUNITY CHIEF DATA OFFICER.

(a) Intelligence community chief data officer .—There is an Intelligence Community Chief Data Officer within the Office of the Director of National Intelligence who shall be appointed by the Director of National Intelligence.

(b) Requirement relating to appointment.— An individual appointed as the Intelligence Community Chief Data Officer shall have a professional background and experience appropriate for the duties of the Intelligence Community Chief Data Officer. In making such appointment, the Director of National Intelligence may give preference to an individual with experience outside of the United States Government.

(c) Duties.—The Intelligence Community Chief Data Officer shall—

(1) act as the chief representative of the Director of National Intelligence for data issues within the intelligence community;

(2) coordinate, to the extent practicable and advisable, with the Chief Data Officer of the Department of Defense to ensure consistent data policies, standards, and procedures between the intelligence community and the Department of Defense;

(3) assist the Director of National Intelligence regarding data elements of the budget of the Office of the Director of National Intelligence; and

(4) perform other such duties relating to data as may be prescribed by the Director of National Intelligence or specified in law.

SEC. 103L. [U.S.C. 3034c] INTELLIGENCE COMMUNITY INNOVATION UNIT.

(a) Definitions .—In this section:

(1) Emerging technology .—the term "emerging technology" has the meaning given that term in section 6701 of the Intelligence Authorization Act for Fiscal Year 2023 (Public Law 117–263; 50 U.S.C. 3024 note).

(2) Unit .—The term "Unit" means the Intelligence Community Innovation Unit.

(b) Plan for implementation of Intelligence Community Innovation Unit.—

(1) Plan required .—Not later than 180 days after the date of the enactment of the Intelligence Authorization Act for Fiscal Year 2024, the Director of National Intelligence shall develop a plan for how to implement the Intelligence Community Innovation Unit within the intelligence community.

(2) Matters covered.—The plan developed pursuant to paragraph (1) shall cover how the Unit will—

(A) benefit heads of the elements of the intelligence community in identifying commercial emerging technologies and associated capabilities to address critical mission needs of elements of the intelligence community;

(B) provide to the heads of the elements of the intelligence community seeking to field commercial emerging technologies technical expertise with respect to such technologies.

(C) facilitate the transition of potential prototypes and solutions to critical mission needs of the intelligence community from research and prototype projects to production; and

(D) serve as a liaison between the intelligence community and the private sector, in which capacity such liaison shall focus on small- and medium-sized companies and other organizations that do not have significant experience engaging with the intelligence community.

(3) REQUIREMENTS.—The plan developed pursuant to paragraph (1) shall—

(A) plan for not more than 50 full-time equivalent personnel; and

(B) include an assessment as to how the establishment of the Unit would benefit the identification and evaluation of commercial emerging technologies for prototyping and potential adoption by the intelligence community to fulfill critical mission needs.

(4) SUBMISSION TO CONGRESS.—Upon completing development of the plan pursuant to paragraph (1), the Director shall—

(A) submit to the congressional intelligence committees, the Subcommittee on Defense of the Committee on Appropriations of the Senate, and the Subcommittee on Defense of the Committee on Appropriations of the House of Representatives a copy of the plan; and

(B) provide such committees and subcommittees a briefing on the plan.

(c) ESTABLISHMENT .—To the extent and in such amounts as specifically provided in advance in appropriations Acts for the purposes detailed in this section, not later than 180 days after the date on which the Director of National Intelligence submits the plan pursuant to subsection (b)(4)(A), the Director of National Intelligence shall establish the Unit within the Office of the Director of National Intelligence.

(d) LIMITATION .—The Unit shall not abrogate or otherwise constrain any element of the intelligence community from conducting authorized activities.

(e) DIRECTOR OF THE INTELLIGENCE COMMUNITY INNOVATION UNIT.—

(1) APPOINTMENT; REPORTING .—The head of the Unit is the Director of the Intelligence Community Innovation Unit, who shall be appointed by the Director of National Intelligence and shall report directly to the Director of National Intelligence.

(2) QUALIFICATIONS.—In selecting an individual for appointment as the Director of the Intelligence Community Innovation Unit, the Director of National Intelligence shall give preference to individuals who the Director of National Intelligence determines have—

(A) significant relevant experience involving commercial emerging technology within the private sector; and

(B) a demonstrated history of fostering the adoption of commercial emerging technologies by the United States Government or the private sector.

(f) STAFF.—

(1) IN GENERAL.— In addition to the Director of the Intelligence Community Innovation Unit, the Unit shall be composed of not more than 50 full- time equivalent positions.

(2) STAFF WITH CERTAIN EXPERTISE .—The Director of National Intelligence shall ensure that there is a sufficient number of staff of the Unit, as determined by the Director, with expertise in—

(A) other transaction authorities and nontraditional and rapid acquisition pathways for emerging technology;

(B) engaging and evaluating small- and medium-sized emerging technology companies;

(C) the mission needs of the intelligence community; and

(D) such other skills or experiences as the Director determines necessary.

(g) AUTHORITY RELATING TO DETAILEES.— Upon request of the Unit, each head of an element of the intelligence community may detail to the Unit any of the personnel of that element to assist in carrying out the duties under subsection (b) on a reimbursable or a nonreimbursable basis.

(h) ENSURING TRANSITION FROM PROTOTYPING TO PRODUCTION .—The Director of the Intelligence Community Innovation Unit shall transition research and prototype projects to products in a production stage upon identifying a demonstrated critical mission need of one or more elements of the intelligence community and a potential mission partner likely to field and further fund upon maturation, including by designating projects as Emerging Technology Transition Projects under the pilot program required by section 6713 of the Intelligence Authorization Act for Fiscal Year 2023 (Public Law 117–263; 50 U.S.C. 3024 note).

(i) ENCOURAGEMENT OF USE BY ELEMENTS.— The Director of National Intelligence shall take such steps as may be necessary to encourage the use of the Unit by the heads of the other elements of the intelligence community.

(j) RULES OF CONSTRUCTION.—

(1) NO PREFERENTIAL TREATMENT FOR PRIVATE SECTOR.— Nothing in this section shall be construed to require any element of the intelligence community to provide preferential treatment for any private sector entity with regard to procurement of technology construed as restricting or preempting any activities of the intelligence community.

(2) NO ADDITIONAL AUTHORITY .—The Unit established pursuant to subsection (c) will be limited to the existing authorities possessed by the Director of National Intelligence.

(k) SUNSET .—The authorities and requirements of this section shall terminate on the date that is 5 years after the date of the establishment of the Unit.

SEC. 103M. [50 U.S.C. 3034d] NATIONAL INTELLIGENCE MANAGEMENT COUNCIL.

(a) ESTABLISHMENT.— There is within the Office of the Director of National Intelligence a National Intelligence Management Council.

(b) COMPOSITION.—

(1) The National Intelligence Management Council shall be composed of senior officials within the intelligence community and substantive experts from the public or private sector, who shall be appointed by, report to, and serve at the pleasure of, the Director of National Intelligence.

(2) The Director shall prescribe appropriate security requirements for personnel appointed from the private sector as a condition of service on the National Intelligence Management Council, or as contractors of the Council or employees of

such contractors, to ensure the protection of intelligence sources and methods while avoiding, wherever possible, unduly intrusive requirements which the Director considers to be unnecessary for this purpose.

(c) DUTIES AND RESPONSIBILITIES.—Members of the National Intelligence Management Council shall work with each other and with other elements of the intelligence community to ensure proper coordination and to minimize duplication of effort, in addition to the following duties and responsibilities:

(1) Provide integrated mission input to support the processes and activities of the intelligence community, including with respect to intelligence planning, programming, budgeting, and evaluation processes.

(2) Identify and pursue opportunities to integrate or coordinate collection and counterintelligence efforts.

(3) In concert with the responsibilities of the National Intelligence Council, ensure the integration and coordination of analytic and collection efforts.

(4) Develop and coordinate intelligence strategies in support of budget planning and programming activities.

(5) Advise the Director of National Intelligence on the development of the National Intelligence Priorities Framework of the Office of the Director of National Intelligence (or any successor mechanism established for the prioritization of programs and activities).

(6) In concert with the responsibilities of the National Intelligence Council, support the role of the Director of National Intelligence as principal advisor to the President on intelligence matters.

(7) Inform the elements of the intelligence community of the activities and decisions related to missions assigned to the National Intelligence Management Council.

(8) Maintain awareness, across various functions and disciplines, of the mission-related activities and budget planning of the intelligence community.

(9) Evaluate, with respect to assigned mission objectives, requirements, and unmet requirements, the implementation of the budget of each element of the intelligence community.

(10) Provide oversight on behalf of, and make recommendations to, the Director of National Intelligence on the extent to which the activities, program recommendations, and budget proposals made by elements of the intelligence community sufficiently address mission objectives, intelligence gaps, and unmet requirements.

(d) MISSION MANAGEMENT OF MEMBERS.—Members of the National Intelligence Management Council, under the direction of the Director of National Intelligence, shall serve as mission managers to ensure integration among the elements of the intelligence community and across intelligence functions, disciplines, and activities for the purpose of achieving unity of effort and effect, including through the following responsibilities:

(1) Planning and programming efforts.

(2) Budget and program execution oversight.

(3) Engagement with elements of the intelligence community and with

policymakers in other agencies.

(4) Workforce competencies and training activities.

(5) Development of capability requirements.

(6) Development of governance fora, policies, and procedures.

(e) STAFF; AVAILABILITY.—

(1) STAFF.— The Director of National Intelligence shall make available to the National Intelligence Management Council such staff as may be necessary to assist the National Intelligence Management Council in carrying out the responsibilities described in this section.

(2) AVAILABILITY.— Under the direction of the Director of National Intelligence, the National Intelligence Management Council shall make reasonable efforts to advise and consult with officers and employees of other departments or agencies, or components thereof, of the United States Government not otherwise associated with the intelligence community.

(f) SUPPORT FROM ELEMENTS OF THE INTELLIGENCE COMMUNITY.— The heads of the elements of the intelligence community shall provide appropriate support to the National Intelligence Management Council, including with respect to intelligence activities, as required by the Director of National Intelligence.

CENTRAL INTELLIGENCE AGENCY

SEC. 104. **[50 U.S.C. 3035]** (a) CENTRAL INTELLIGENCE AGENCY.— There is a Central Intelligence Agency.

(b) FUNCTION.— The function of the Central Intelligence Agency is to assist the Director of the Central Intelligence Agency in carrying out the responsibilities specified in section 104A(c).

DIRECTOR OF THE CENTRAL INTELLIGENCE AGENCY

SEC. 104A. **[50 U.S.C. 3036]** (a) DIRECTOR OF CENTRAL INTELLIGENCE AGENCY.— There is a Director of the Central Intelligence Agency who shall be appointed by the President, by and with the advice and consent of the Senate.

(b) SUPERVISION.— The Director of the Central Intelligence Agency shall report to the Director of National Intelligence regarding the activities of the Central Intelligence Agency.

(c) DUTIES.—The Director of the Central Intelligence Agency shall—

(1) serve as the head of the Central Intelligence Agency; and

(2) carry out the responsibilities specified in subsection (d).

(d) RESPONSIBILITIES.—The Director of the Central Intelligence Agency shall—

(1) collect intelligence through human sources and by other appropriate means, except that the Director of the Central Intelligence Agency shall have no police, subpoena, or law enforcement powers or internal security functions;

(2) correlate and evaluate intelligence related to the national security and provide appropriate dissemination of such intelligence;

(3) provide overall direction for and coordination of the collection of national

intelligence outside the United States through human sources by elements of the intelligence community authorized to undertake such collection and, in coordination with other departments, agencies, or elements of the United States Government which are authorized to undertake such collection, ensure that the most effective use is made of resources and that appropriate account is taken of the risks to the United States and those involved in such collection; and

(4) perform such other functions and duties related to intelligence affecting the national security as the President or the Director of National Intelligence may direct.

(e) TERMINATION OF EMPLOYMENT OF CIA EMPLOYEES.—(1) Notwithstanding the provisions of any other law, the Director of the Central Intelligence Agency may, in the discretion of the Director, terminate the employment of any officer or employee of the Central Intelligence Agency whenever the Director deems the termination of employment of such officer or employee necessary or advisable in the interests of the United States.

(2) Any termination of employment of an officer or employee under paragraph (1) shall not affect the right of the officer or employee to seek or accept employment in any other department, agency, or element of the United States Government if declared eligible for such employment by the Office of Personnel Management.

(f) COORDINATION WITH FOREIGN GOVERNMENTS.— Under the direction of the Director of National Intelligence and in a manner consistent with section 207 of the Foreign Service Act of 1980 (22 U.S.C. 3927), the Director of the Central Intelligence Agency shall coordinate the relationships between elements of the intelligence community and the intelligence or security services of foreign governments or international organizations on all matters involving intelligence related to the national security or involving intelligence acquired through clandestine means.

DEPUTY DIRECTOR OF THE CENTRAL INTELLIGENCE AGENCY

SEC. 104B. [50 U.S.C. 3037] (a) DEPUTY DIRECTOR OF THE CENTRAL INTELLIGENCE AGENCY.— There is a Deputy Director of the Central Intelligence Agency who shall be appointed by the President.

(b) DUTIES.—The Deputy Director of the Central Intelligence Agency shall—

(1) assist the Director of the Central Intelligence Agency in carrying out the duties and responsibilities of the Director of the Central Intelligence Agency; and

(2) during the absence or disability of the Director of the Central Intelligence Agency, or during a vacancy in the position of Director of the Central Intelligence Agency, act for and exercise the powers of the Director of the Central Intelligence Agency.

RESPONSIBILITIES OF THE SECRETARY OF DEFENSE PERTAINING TO THE NATIONAL INTELLIGENCE PROGRAM

SEC. 105. [50 U.S.C. 3038] (a) IN GENERAL.—Consistent with sections 102 and 102A, the Secretary of Defense, in consultation with the Director of National Intelligence, shall—

(1) ensure that the budgets of the elements of the intelligence community within the Department of Defense are adequate to satisfy the overall intelligence needs

of the Department of Defense, including the needs of the Chairman of the Joint Chiefs of Staff and the commanders of the unified and specified commands and, wherever such elements are performing governmentwide functions, the needs of other departments and agencies;

(2) ensure appropriate implementation of the policies and resource decisions of the Director by elements of the Department of Defense within the National Intelligence Program;

(3) ensure that the tactical intelligence activities of the Department of Defense complement and are compatible with intelligence activities under the National Intelligence Program;

(4) ensure that the elements of the intelligence community within the Department of Defense are responsive and timely with respect to satisfying the needs of operational military forces;

(5) eliminate waste and unnecessary duplication among the intelligence activities of the Department of Defense; and

(6) ensure that intelligence activities of the Department of Defense are conducted jointly where appropriate.

(b) Responsibility for the Performance of Specific Functions.—Consistent with sections 102 and 102A of this Act, the Secretary of Defense shall ensure—

(1) through the National Security Agency (except as otherwise directed by the President or the National Security Council), the continued operation of an effective unified organization for the conduct of signals intelligence activities and shall ensure that the product is disseminated in a timely manner to authorized recipients;

(2) through the National Geospatial-Intelligence Agency (except as otherwise directed by the President or the National Security Council), with appropriate representation from the intelligence community, the continued operation of an effective unified organization within the Department of Defense—

(A) for carrying out tasking of imagery collection;

(B) for the coordination of imagery processing and exploitation activities;

(C) for ensuring the dissemination of imagery in a timely manner to authorized recipients; and

(D) notwithstanding any other provision of law, for—

(i) prescribing technical architecture and standards related to imagery intelligence and geospatial information and ensuring compliance with such architecture and standards; and

(ii) developing and fielding systems of common concern related to imagery intelligence and geospatial information;

(3) through the National Reconnaissance Office (except as otherwise directed by the President or the National Security Council), the continued operation of an effective unified organization for the research and development, acquisition, and operation of overhead reconnaissance systems necessary to satisfy the requirements of all elements of the intelligence community;

(4) through the Defense Intelligence Agency (except as otherwise directed by the President or the National Security Council), the continued operation of an

effective unified system within the Department of Defense for the production of timely, objective military and military-related intelligence, based upon all sources available to the intelligence community, and shall ensure the appropriate dissemination of such intelligence to authorized recipients;

(5) through the Defense Intelligence Agency (except as otherwise directed by the President or the National Security Council), effective management of Department of Defense human intelligence and counterintelligence activities, including defense attaches; and

(6) that the military departments maintain sufficient capabilities to collect and produce intelligence to meet—

(A) the requirements of the Director of National Intelligence;

(B) the requirements of the Secretary of Defense or the Chairman of the Joint Chiefs of Staff;

(C) the requirements of the unified and specified combatant commands and of joint operations; and

(D) the specialized requirements of the military departments for intelligence necessary to support tactical commanders, military planners, the research and development process, the acquisition of military equipment, and training and doctrine.

(c) EXPENDITURE OF FUNDS BY THE DEFENSE INTELLIGENCE AGENCY.—(1) Subject to paragraphs (2) and (3), the Director of the Defense Intelligence Agency may expend amounts made available to the Director under the National Intelligence Program for human intelligence and counterintelligence activities for objects of a confidential, extraordinary, or emergency nature, without regard to the provisions of law or regulation relating to the expenditure of Government funds.

(2) The Director of the Defense Intelligence Agency may not expend more than five percent of the amounts made available to the Director under the National Intelligence Program for human intelligence and counterintelligence activities for a fiscal year for objects of a confidential, extraordinary, or emergency nature in accordance with paragraph (1) during such fiscal year unless—

(A) the Director notifies the congressional intelligence committees, the Committee on Armed Services of the Senate, and the Committee on Armed Services of the House of Representatives of the intent to expend the amounts; and

(B) 30 days have elapsed from the date on which the Director notifies the congressional intelligence committees, the Committee on Armed Services of the Senate, and the Committee on Armed Services of the House of Representatives in accordance with subparagraph (A).

(3) For each expenditure referred to in paragraph (1), the Director shall certify that such expenditure was made for an object of a confidential, extraordinary, or emergency nature.

(4) Not later than December 31 of each year, the Director of the Defense Intelligence Agency shall submit to the congressional intelligence committees, the Committee on Armed Services of the Senate, and the Committee on Armed Services of the House of Representatives a report on any expenditures made during the

preceding fiscal year in accordance with paragraph (1).

(d) USE OF ELEMENTS OF DEPARTMENT OF DEFENSE.— The Secretary of Defense, in carrying out the functions described in this section, may use such elements of the Department of Defense as may be appropriate for the execution of those functions, in addition to, or in lieu of, the elements identified in this section.

ASSISTANCE TO UNITED STATES LAW ENFORCEMENT AGENCIES

SEC. 105A. [50 U.S.C. 3039] (a) AUTHORITY TO PROVIDE ASSISTANCE.— Subject to subsection (b), elements of the intelligence community may, upon the request of a United States law enforcement agency, collect information outside the United States about individuals who are not United States persons. Such elements may collect such information notwithstanding that the law enforcement agency intends to use the information collected for purposes of a law enforcement investigation or counterintelligence investigation.

(b) LIMITATION ON ASSISTANCE BY ELEMENTS OF DEPARTMENT OF DEFENSE.—(1) With respect to elements within the Department of Defense, the authority in subsection (a) applies only to the following:

(A) The National Security Agency.

(B) The National Reconnaissance Office.

(C) The National Geospatial-Intelligence Agency.

(D) The Defense Intelligence Agency.

(2) Assistance provided under this section by elements of the Department of Defense may not include the direct participation of a member of the Army, Navy, Air Force, or Marine Corps in an arrest or similar activity.

(3) Assistance may not be provided under this section by an element of the Department of Defense if the provision of such assistance will adversely affect the military preparedness of the United States.

(4) The Secretary of Defense shall prescribe regulations governing the exercise of authority under this section by elements of the Department of Defense, including regulations relating to the protection of sources and methods in the exercise of such authority.

(c) DEFINITIONS.—For purposes of subsection (a):

(1) The term "United States law enforcement agency" means any department or agency of the Federal Government that the Attorney General designates as law enforcement agency for purposes of this section.

(2) The term "United States person" means the following:

(A) A United States citizen.

(B) An alien known by the intelligence agency concerned to be a permanent resident alien.

(C) An unincorporated association substantially composed of United States citizens or permanent resident aliens.

(D) A corporation incorporated in the United States, except for a corporation directed and controlled by a foreign government or governments.

DISCLOSURE OF FOREIGN INTELLIGENCE ACQUIRED IN CRIMINAL INVESTIGATIONS; NOTICE OF CRIMINAL INVESTIGATIONS OF FOREIGN INTELLIGENCE SOURCES

SEC. 105B. [50 U.S.C. 3040] (a) DISCLOSURE OF FOREIGN INTELLIGENCE.—(1) Except as otherwise provided by law and subject to paragraph (2), the Attorney General, or the head of any other department or agency of the Federal Government with law enforcement responsibilities, shall expeditiously disclose to the Director of National Intelligence, pursuant to guidelines developed by the Attorney General in consultation with the Director, foreign intelligence acquired by an element of the Department of Justice or an element of such department or agency, as the case may be, in the course of a criminal investigation.

(2) The Attorney General by regulation and in consultation with the Director may provide for exceptions to the applicability of paragraph (1) for one or more classes of foreign intelligence, or foreign intelligence with respect to one or more targets or matters, if the Attorney General determines that disclosure of such foreign intelligence under that paragraph would jeopardize an ongoing law enforcement investigation or impair other significant law enforcement interests.

(b) PROCEDURES FOR NOTICE OF CRIMINAL INVESTIGATIONS.— Not later than 180 days after the date of enactment of this section, the Attorney General, in consultation with the Director of National Intelligence, shall develop guidelines to ensure that after receipt of a report from an element of the intelligence community of activity of a foreign intelligence source or potential foreign intelligence source that may warrant investigation as criminal activity, the Attorney General provides notice to the Director, within a reasonable period of time, of his intention to commence, or decline to commence, a criminal investigation of such activity.

(c) PROCEDURES.— The Attorney General shall develop procedures for the administration of this section, including the disclosure of foreign intelligence by elements of the Department of Justice, and elements of other departments and agencies of the Federal Government, under subsection (a) and the provision of notice with respect to criminal investigations under subsection (b).

SEC. 105C. [50 U.S.C. 3040a] PROHIBITION ON COLLECTION AND MAINTENANCE OF INFORMATION OF UNITED STATES PERSONS BASED ON FIRST AMENDMENT-PROTECTED ACTIVITIES.

No element of the intelligence community may collect or maintain information concerning a United States person (as defined in section 105A) solely for the purpose of monitoring an activity protected by the first amendment to the Constitution of the United States.

APPOINTMENT OF OFFICIALS RESPONSIBLE FOR INTELLIGENCE-RELATED ACTIVITIES

SEC. 106. [50 U.S.C. 3041] (a) RECOMMENDATION OF DNI IN CERTAIN APPOINTMENTS.—(1) In the event of a vacancy in a position referred to in paragraph (2), the Director of National Intelligence shall recommend to the President an individual for nomination to fill the vacancy.

(2) Paragraph (1) applies to the following positions:

(A) The Principal Deputy Director of National Intelligence.

(B) The Director of the Central Intelligence Agency.

(b) CONCURRENCE OF DNI IN APPOINTMENTS TO POSITIONS IN THE INTELLIGENCE COMMUNITY.—(1) In the event of a vacancy in a position referred to in paragraph (2), the head of the department or agency having jurisdiction over the position shall obtain the concurrence of the Director of National Intelligence before appointing an individual to fill the vacancy or recommending to the President an individual to be nominated to fill the vacancy. If the Director does not concur in the recommendation, the head of the department or agency concerned may not fill the vacancy or make the recommendation to the President (as the case may be). In the case in which the Director does not concur in such a recommendation, the Director and the head of the department or agency concerned may advise the President directly of the intention to withhold concurrence or to make a recommendation, as the case may be.

(2) Paragraph (1) applies to the following positions:

(A) The Director of the National Security Agency.

(B) The Director of the National Reconnaissance Office.

(C) The Director of the National Geospatial-Intelligence Agency.

(D) The Assistant Secretary of State for Intelligence and Research.

(E) The Director of the Office of Intelligence and Counterintelligence of the Department of Energy.

(F) The Assistant Secretary for Intelligence and Analysis of the Department of the Treasury.

(G) The Executive Assistant Director for Intelligence of the Federal Bureau of Investigation or any successor to that position.

(H) The Under Secretary of Homeland Security for Intelligence and Analysis.

(c) CONSULTATION WITH DNI IN CERTAIN POSITIONS.—(1) In the event of a vacancy in a position referred to in paragraph (2), the head of the department or agency having jurisdiction over the position shall consult with the Director of National Intelligence before appointing an individual to fill the vacancy or recommending to the President an individual to be nominated to fill the vacancy.

(2) Paragraph (1) applies to the following positions:

(A) The Director of the Defense Intelligence Agency.

(B) The Assistant Commandant of the Coast Guard for Intelligence.

(C) The Assistant Attorney General designated as the Assistant Attorney General for National Security under section 507A of title 28, United States Code.

SEC. 106A. [50 U.S.C. 3041a] DIRECTOR OF THE NATIONAL RECONNAISSANCE OFFICE.

(a) IN GENERAL.— There is a Director of the National Reconnaissance Office.

(b) APPOINTMENT.— The Director of the National Reconnaissance Office shall be appointed by the President, by and with the advice and consent of the Senate.

(c) FUNCTIONS AND DUTIES.— The Director of the National Reconnaissance Office shall be the head of the National Reconnaissance Office and shall discharge such functions and duties as are provided by this Act or otherwise by law or executive order.

(d) Advisory Board.—

(1) Establishment.— There is established in the National Reconnaissance Office an advisory board (in this section referred to as the "Board").

(2) Duties.—The Board shall—

(A) study matters relating to the mission of the National Reconnaissance Office, including with respect to promoting innovation, competition, and resilience in space, overhead reconnaissance, acquisition, and other matters; and

(B) advise and report directly to the Director with respect to such matters.

(3) Members.—

(A) Number and appointment.—

(i) In general.— The Board shall be composed of up to 8 members appointed by the Director, in consultation with the Director of National Intelligence and the Secretary of Defense, from among individuals with demonstrated academic, government, business, or other expertise relevant to the mission and functions of the National Reconnaissance Office, and who do not present any actual or potential conflict of interest.

(ii) Membership structure.— The Director shall ensure that no more than 2 concurrently serving members of the Board qualify for membership on the Board based predominantly on a single qualification set forth under clause (i).

(iii) Notification.— Not later than 30 days after the date on which the Director appoints a member to the Board, the Director shall notify the congressional intelligence committees and the congressional defense committees (as defined in section 101(a) of title 10, United States Code) of such appointment.

(B) Terms.— Each member shall be appointed for a term of 2 years. Except as provided by subparagraph (C), a member may not serve more than three terms.

(C) Vacancy.— Any member appointed to fill a vacancy occurring before the expiration of the term for which the member's predecessor was appointed shall be appointed only for the remainder of that term. A member may serve after the expiration of that member's term until a successor has taken office.

(D) Chair.— The Board shall have a Chair, who shall be appointed by the Director from among the members.

(E) Travel expenses.— Each member shall receive travel expenses, including per diem in lieu of subsistence, in accordance with applicable provisions under subchapter I of chapter 57 of title 5, United States Code.

(F) Executive secretary.— The Director may appoint an executive secretary, who shall be an employee of the National Reconnaissance Office, to support the Board.

(4) Meetings.— The Board shall meet not less than quarterly, but may meet more frequently at the call of the Director.

(5) Charter.—The Director shall establish a charter for the Board that includes

the following:

(A) Mandatory processes for identifying potential conflicts of interest, including the submission of initial and periodic financial disclosures by Board members.

(B) The vetting of potential conflicts of interest by the designated agency ethics official, except that no individual waiver may be granted for a conflict of interest identified with respect to the Chair of the Board.

(C) The establishment of a process and associated protections for any whistleblower alleging a violation of applicable conflict of interest law, Federal contracting law, or other provision of law.

(6) REPORTS.— Not later than March 31 of each year, the Board shall submit to the Director and to the congressional intelligence committees a report on the activities and significant findings of the Board during the preceding year.

(7) NONAPPLICABILITY OF CERTAIN REQUIREMENTS.— The Federal Advisory Committee Act (5 U.S.C. App.) shall not apply to the Board.

(8) TERMINATION.— The Board shall terminate on August 31, 2027.

[Section 107 was repealed by section 6742(b)(3) of division E of Public Law 116-92.]

ANNUAL NATIONAL SECURITY STRATEGY REPORT

SEC. 108. [50 U.S.C. 3043] (a)(1) The President shall transmit to Congress each year a comprehensive report on the national security strategy of the United States (hereinafter in this section referred to as a national security strategy report").

(2) The national security strategy report for any year shall be transmitted on the date on which the President submits to Congress the budget for the next fiscal year under section 1105 of title 31, United States Code.

(3) Not later than 150 days after the date on which a new President takes office, the President shall transmit to Congress a national security strategy report under this section. That report shall be in addition to the report for that year transmitted at the time specified in paragraph (2).

(b) Each national security strategy report shall set forth the national security strategy of the United States and shall include a comprehensive description and discussion of the following:

(1) The worldwide interests, goals, and objectives of the United States that are vital to the national security of the United States.

(2) The foreign policy, worldwide commitments, and national defense capabilities of the United States necessary to deter aggression and to implement the national security strategy of the United States.

(3) The proposed short-term and long-term uses of the political, economic, military, and other elements of the national power of the United States to protect or promote the interests and achieve the goals and objectives referred to in paragraph (1).

(4) The adequacy of the capabilities of the United States to carry out the national security strategy of the United States, including an evaluation of the balance among the capabilities of all elements of the national power of the United States to support

the implementation of the national security strategy.

(5) Such other information as may be necessary to help inform Congress on matters relating to the national security strategy of the United States.

(c) Each national security strategy report shall be transmitted to Congress in classified form, but may include an unclassified summary.

SEC. 108A. [50 U.S.C. 3043a] NATIONAL INTELLIGENCE STRATEGY.

(a) IN GENERAL.— Beginning in 2017, and once every 4 years thereafter, the Director of National Intelligence shall develop a comprehensive national intelligence strategy to meet national security objectives for the following 4-year period, or a longer period, if appropriate.

(b) REQUIREMENTS.—Each national intelligence strategy required by subsection (a) shall—

(1) delineate a national intelligence strategy consistent with—

(A) the most recent national security strategy report submitted pursuant to section 108;

(B) the strategic plans of other relevant departments and agencies of the United States; and

(C) other relevant national-level plans;

(2) address matters related to national and military intelligence, including counterintelligence;

(3) identify the major national security missions that the intelligence community is currently pursuing and will pursue in the future to meet the anticipated security environment;

(4) describe how the intelligence community will utilize personnel, technology, partnerships, and other capabilities to pursue the major national security missions identified in paragraph (3);

(5) assess current, emerging, and future threats to the intelligence community, including threats from foreign intelligence and security services and insider threats;

(6) outline the organizational roles and missions of the elements of the intelligence community as part of an integrated enterprise to meet customer demands for intelligence products, services, and support;

(7) identify sources of strategic, institutional, programmatic, fiscal, and technological risk; and

(8) analyze factors that may affect the intelligence community's performance in pursuing the major national security missions identified in paragraph (3) during the following 10-year period.

(c) SUBMISSION TO CONGRESS.— The Director of National Intelligence shall submit to the congressional intelligence committees a report on each national intelligence strategy required by subsection (a) not later than 45 days after the date of the completion of such strategy.

SEC. 108B. [50 U.S.C. 3043b] ANNUAL REPORTS ON WORLDWIDE THREATS.

(a) Definition of Appropriate Congressional Committees.—In this section, the term "appropriate congressional committees" means—

(1) the congressional intelligence committees; and

(2) the Committees on Armed Services of the House of Representatives and the Senate.

(b) Annual Reports.— Not later than the first Monday in February 2021, and each year thereafter, the Director of National Intelligence, in coordination with the heads of the elements of the intelligence community, shall submit to the appropriate congressional committees a report containing an assessment of the intelligence community with respect to worldwide threats to the national security of the United States.

(c) Form.— Each report under subsection (b) shall be submitted in unclassified form, but may include a classified annex only for the protection of intelligence sources and methods relating to the matters contained in the report.

(d) Hearings.—

(1) Open hearings.— Upon request by the appropriate congressional committees, the Director (and any other head of an element of the intelligence community determined appropriate by the committees in consultation with the Director) shall testify before such committees in an open setting regarding a report under subsection (b).

(2) Closed hearings.— Any information that may not be disclosed during an open hearing under paragraph (1) in order to protect intelligence sources and methods may instead be discussed in a closed hearing that immediately follows such open hearing.

SEC. 109. [50 U.S.C. 3044] SOFTWARE LICENSING.

(a) Requirement for Inventories of Software Licenses.—The chief information officer of each element of the intelligence community, in consultation with the Chief Information Officer of the Intelligence Community, shall biennially—

(1) conduct an inventory of all existing software licenses of such element, including utilized and unutilized licenses;

(2) assess the actions that could be carried out by such element to achieve the greatest possible economies of scale and associated cost savings in software procurement and usage, including—

(A) increasing the centralization of the management of software licenses;

(B) increasing the regular tracking and maintaining of comprehensive inventories of software licenses using automated discovery and inventory tools and metrics;

(C) analyzing software license data to inform investment decisions; and

(D) providing appropriate personnel with sufficient software licenses management training; and

(3) submit to the Chief Information Officer of the Intelligence Community each inventory required by paragraph (1) and each assessment required by paragraph (2).

(b) INVENTORIES BY THE CHIEF INFORMATION OFFICER OF THE INTELLIGENCE COMMUNITY.—The Chief Information Officer of the Intelligence Community, based on the inventories and assessments required by subsection (a), shall biennially—

(1) compile an inventory of all existing software licenses of the intelligence community, including utilized and unutilized licenses;

(2) assess the actions that could be carried out by the intelligence community to achieve the greatest possible economies of scale and associated cost savings in software procurement and usage, including—

(A) increasing the centralization of the management of software licenses;

(B) increasing the regular tracking and maintaining of comprehensive inventories of software licenses using automated discovery and inventory tools and metrics;

(C) analyzing software license data to inform investment decisions; and

(D) providing appropriate personnel with sufficient software licenses management training; and

(3) based on the assessment required under paragraph (2), make such recommendations with respect to software procurement and usage to the Director of National Intelligence as the Chief Information Officer considers appropriate.

(c) REPORTS TO CONGRESS.— The Chief Information Officer of the Intelligence Community shall submit to the congressional intelligence committees a copy of each inventory compiled under subsection (b)(1).

(d) IMPLEMENTATION OF RECOMMENDATIONS.— Not later than 180 days after the date on which the Director of National Intelligence receives recommendations from the Chief Information Officer of the Intelligence Community in accordance with subsection (b)(3), the Director of National Intelligence shall, to the extent practicable, issue guidelines for the intelligence community on software procurement and usage based on such recommendations.

NATIONAL MISSION OF NATIONAL GEOSPATIAL-INTELLIGENCE AGENCY

SEC. 110. [50 U.S.C. 3045] (a) IN GENERAL.— In addition to the Department of Defense missions set forth in section 442 of title 10, United States Code, the National Geospatial-Intelligence Agency shall support the geospatial intelligence requirements of the Department of State and other departments and agencies of the United States outside the Department of Defense.

(b) REQUIREMENTS AND PRIORITIES.— The Director of National Intelligence shall establish requirements and priorities governing the collection of national intelligence by the National Geospatial-Intelligence Agency under subsection (a).

(c) CORRECTION OF DEFICIENCIES.— The Director of National Intelligence shall develop and implement such programs and policies as the Director and the Secretary of Defense jointly determine necessary to review and correct deficiencies identified in the capabilities of the National Geospatial-Intelligence Agency to accomplish assigned national missions, including support to the all-source analysis and production process. The Director shall consult with the Secretary of Defense on the development and implementation of such programs and policies. The Secretary shall obtain the advice of the Chairman of the Joint Chiefs of Staff regarding the matters on which the Director and the Secretary are to consult under the preceding sentence.

[Section 111 was repealed by section 1075 of Public Law 108–458 (Act of December 17, 2004, 118 Stat. 3694); 50 U.S.C. 3046.]

RESTRICTIONS ON INTELLIGENCE SHARING WITH THE UNITED NATIONS

SEC. 112. [50 U.S.C. 3047] (a) PROVISION OF INTELLIGENCE INFORMATION TO THE UNITED NATIONS.—(1) No United States intelligence information may be provided to the United Nations or any organization affiliated with the United Nations, or to any officials or employees thereof, unless the President certifies to the appropriate committees of Congress that the Director of National Intelligence, in consultation with the Secretary of State and the Secretary of Defense, has established and implemented procedures, and has worked with the United Nations to ensure implementation of procedures, for protecting from unauthorized disclosure United States intelligence sources and methods connected to such information.

(2) Paragraph (1) may be waived upon written certification by the President to the appropriate committees of Congress that providing such information to the United Nations or an organization affiliated with the United Nations, or to any officials or employees thereof, is in the national security interests of the United States.

(b) DELEGATION OF DUTIES.— The President may not delegate or assign the duties of the President under this section.

(c) RELATIONSHIP TO EXISTING LAW.—Nothing in this section shall be construed to—

(1) impair or otherwise affect the authority of the Director of National Intelligence to protect intelligence sources and methods from unauthorized disclosure pursuant to section 102A(i) of this Act; or

(2) supersede or otherwise affect the provisions of title V of this Act.

(d) DEFINITION.— As used in this section, the term "appropriate committees of Congress" means the Committee on Foreign Relations and the Select Committee on Intelligence of the Senate and the Committee on Foreign Relations and the Permanent Select Committee on Intelligence of the House of Representatives.

DETAIL OF INTELLIGENCE COMMUNITY PERSONNEL—INTELLIGENCE COMMUNITY ASSIGNMENT PROGRAM

SEC. 113. [50 U.S.C. 3048] (a) DETAIL.—(1) Notwithstanding any other provision of law, the head of a department with an element in the intelligence community or the head of an intelligence community agency or element may detail any employee within that department, agency, or element to serve in any position in the Intelligence Community Assignment Program on a reimbursable or a nonreimbursable basis.

(2) Nonreimbursable details may be for such periods as are agreed to between the heads of the parent and host agencies, up to a maximum of three years, except that such details may be extended for a period not to exceed one year when the heads of the parent and host agencies determine that such extension is in the public interest.

(b) BENEFITS, ALLOWANCES, TRAVEL, INCENTIVES.—(1) An employee detailed under subsection (a) may be authorized any benefit, allowance, travel, or incentive otherwise provided to enhance staffing by the organization from which the employee is detailed.

(2) The head of an agency of an employee detailed under subsection (a) may pay a lodging allowance for the employee subject to the following conditions:

(A) The allowance shall be the lesser of the cost of the lodging or a maximum amount payable for the lodging as established jointly by the Director of National Intelligence and—

(i) with respect to detailed employees of the Department of Defense, the Secretary of Defense; and

(ii) with respect to detailed employees of other agencies and departments, the head of such agency or department.

(B) The detailed employee maintains a primary residence for the employee's immediate family in the local commuting area of the parent agency duty station from which the employee regularly commuted to such duty station before the detail.

(C) The lodging is within a reasonable proximity of the host agency duty station.

(D) The distance between the detailed employee's parent agency duty station and the host agency duty station is greater than 20 miles.

(E) The distance between the detailed employee's primary residence and the host agency duty station is 10 miles greater than the distance between such primary residence and the employees parent duty station.

(F) The rate of pay applicable to the detailed employee does not exceed the rate of basic pay for grade GS–15 of the General Schedule.

NON-REIMBURSABLE DETAIL OF OTHER PERSONNEL

SEC. 113A. [50 U.S.C. 3049] An officer or employee of the United States or member of the Armed Forces may be detailed to the staff of an element of the intelligence community funded through the National Intelligence Program from another element of the intelligence community or from another element of the United States Government on a non-reimbursable basis, as jointly agreed to by the heads of the receiving and detailing elements, for a period not to exceed three years. This section does not limit any other source of authority for reimbursable or non-reimbursable details. A non-reimbursable detail made under this section shall not be considered an augmentation of the appropriations of the receiving element of the intelligence community.

SEC. 113B. [50 U.S.C. 3049a] SPECIAL PAY AUTHORITY FOR SCIENCE, TECHNOLOGY, ENGINEERING, OR MATHEMATICS POSITIONS AND POSITIONS REQUIRING BANKING OR FINANCIAL SERVICES EXPERTISE.

(a) SPECIAL RATES OF PAY FOR POSITIONS REQUIRING EXPERTISE IN SCIENCE, TECHNOLOGY, ENGINEERING, OR MATHEMATICS OR IN BANKING OR FINANCIAL SERVICES.—

(1) IN GENERAL.—Notwithstanding part III of title 5, United States Code, the head of each element of the intelligence community may, for one or more categories of positions in such element that require expertise in science, technology, engineering, or mathematics or in banking or financial services (including expertise relating

to critical financial infrastructure operations, capital markets, banking compliance programs, or international investments)—

(A) establish higher minimum rates of pay; and

(B) make corresponding increases in all rates of pay of the pay range for each grade or level, subject to subsection (b) or (c), as applicable.

(2) LIMITATION ON NUMBER OF RECIPIENTS.— For each element of the intelligence community, the number of individuals serving in a position in such element who receive a higher rate of pay established or increased under paragraph (1) may not, at any time during a given fiscal year, exceed 50 individuals or 5 percent of the total number of full-time equivalent positions authorized for such element for the preceding fiscal year, whichever is greater.

(3) TREATMENT.— The special rate supplements resulting from the establishment of higher rates under paragraph (1) shall be basic pay for the same or similar purposes as those specified in section 5305(j) of title 5, United States Code.

(b) SPECIAL RATES OF PAY FOR CYBER POSITIONS.—

(1) IN GENERAL.—Notwithstanding subsection (c), the Director of the National Security Agency may establish a special rate of pay—

(A) not to exceed the rate of basic pay payable for level II of the Executive Schedule under section 5313 of title 5, United States Code, if the Director certifies to the Under Secretary of Defense for Intelligence and Security, in consultation with the Under Secretary of Defense for Personnel and Readiness, that the rate of pay is for positions that perform functions that execute the cyber mission of the Agency; or

(B) not to exceed the rate of basic pay payable for the Vice President of the United States under section 104 of title 3, United States Code, if the Director certifies to the Secretary of Defense, by name, individuals that have advanced skills and competencies and that perform critical functions that execute the cyber mission of the Agency.

(2) PAY LIMITATION.—Employees receiving a special rate under paragraph (1) shall be subject to an aggregate pay limitation that parallels the limitation established in section 5307 of title 5, United States Code, except that—

(A) any allowance, differential, bonus, award, or other similar cash payment in addition to basic pay that is authorized under title 10, United States Code, (or any other applicable law in addition to title 5 of such Code, excluding the Fair Labor Standards Act of 1938 (29 U.S.C. 201 et seq.)) shall also be counted as part of aggregate compensation; and

(B) aggregate compensation may not exceed the rate established for the Vice President of the United States under section 104 of title 3, United States Code.

(3) LIMITATION ON NUMBER OF RECIPIENTS.— The number of individuals who receive basic pay established under paragraph (1)(B) may not exceed 100 at any time.

(4) LIMITATION ON USE AS COMPARATIVE REFERENCE.— Notwithstanding any other provision of law, special rates of pay and the limitation established under paragraph (1)(B) may not be used as comparative references for the purpose of fixing the rates of basic pay or maximum pay limitations of qualified positions under section 1599f

of title 10, United States Code, or section 2208 of the Homeland Security Act of 2002 (6 U.S.C. 658).

(c) Maximum Special Rate of Pay.— Except as provided in subsection (b), a minimum rate of pay established for a category of positions under subsection (a) may not exceed the maximum rate of basic pay (excluding any locality-based comparability payment under section 5304 of title 5, United States Code, or similar provision of law) for the position in that category of positions without the authority of subsection (a) by more than 30 percent, and no rate may be established under this section in excess of the rate of basic pay payable for level IV of the Executive Schedule under section 5315 of title 5, United States Code.

(d) Notification of Removal From Special Rate of Pay.—If the head of an element of the intelligence community removes a category of positions from coverage under a rate of pay authorized by subsection (a) or (b) after that rate of pay takes effect—

(1) the head of such element shall provide notice of the loss of coverage of the special rate of pay to each individual in such category; and

(2) the loss of coverage will take effect on the first day of the first pay period after the date of the notice.

(e) Revision of Special Rates of Pay.— Subject to the limitations in this section, rates of pay established under this section by the head of an element of the intelligence community may be revised from time to time by the head of such element and the revisions have the force and effect of statute.

(f) Regulations.— The head of each element of the intelligence community shall promulgate regulations to carry out this section with respect to such element, which shall, to the extent practicable, be comparable to the regulations promulgated to carry out section 5305 of title 5, United States Code.

(g) Reports.—

(1) Requirement for reports.— Not later than 90 days after the date of the enactment of the Damon Paul Nelson and Matthew Young Pollard Intelligence Authorization Act for Fiscal Years 2018 and 2019, the head of each element of the intelligence community shall submit to the congressional intelligence committees a report on any rates of pay established for such element under this section.

(2) Contents.—Each report required by paragraph (1) shall contain for each element of the intelligence community—

(A) a description of any rates of pay established under subsection (a) or (b); and

(B) the number of positions in such element that will be subject to such rates of pay.

SEC. 113C. [50 U.S.C. 3049b] ENABLING INTELLIGENCE COMMUNITY INTEGRATION.

(a) Provision of Goods or Services.— Subject to and in accordance with any guidance and requirements developed by the Director of National Intelligence, the head of an element of the intelligence community may provide goods or services to another element of the intelligence community without reimbursement or transfer of funds for hoteling initiatives for intelligence community employees and affiliates defined in any such guidance and requirements issued by the Director of National Intelligence.

(b) Approval.— Prior to the provision of goods or services pursuant to subsection (a), the head of the element of the intelligence community providing such goods or services and the head of the element of the intelligence community receiving such goods or services shall approve such provision.

(c) Hoteling Defined.— In this section, the term "hoteling" means an alternative work arrangement in which employees of one element of the intelligence community are authorized flexible work arrangements to work part of the time at one or more alternative worksite locations, as appropriately authorized.

ANNUAL REPORT ON HIRING AND RETENTION OF MINORITY EMPLOYEES[5]

Sec. 114. [50 U.S.C. 3050]

(a) The Director of National Intelligence shall, on an annual basis, submit to Congress a report on the employment of covered persons within each element of the intelligence community for the preceding fiscal year and the preceding 5 fiscal years.

(b) Each such report shall include data, disaggregated by category of covered person and by element of the intelligence community, on the following:

(1) Of all individuals employed in the element during the fiscal year involved, the aggregate percentage of such individuals who are covered persons.

(2) Of all individuals employed in the element during the fiscal year involved at the levels referred to in subparagraphs (A) and (B), the percentage of covered persons employed at such levels:

(A) Positions at levels 1 through 15 of the General Schedule.

(B) Positions at levels above GS–15.

(3) Of all individuals hired by the element involved during the fiscal year involved, the percentage of such individuals who are covered persons.

(c) Each such report shall be submitted in unclassified form, but may contain a classified annex.

(d) Nothing in this section shall be construed as providing for the substitution of any similar report required under another provision of law.

(e) In this section the term "covered persons" means—

(1) racial and ethnic minorities;

(2) women; and

(3) individuals with disabilities.

[5] The heading for section 114, as amended by section 329(c)(2)(A) of Public Law 113–126 (as shown above), does not reflect the style as it appears in the enacted law. The enacted law for this element appears in all caps boldface type.

LIMITATION ON ESTABLISHMENT OR OPERATION OF DIPLOMATIC INTELLIGENCE SUPPORT CENTERS

Sec. 115. [50 U.S.C. 3052] (a) In General.—(1) A diplomatic intelligence support center may not be established, operated, or maintained without the prior approval of the Director of National Intelligence.

(2) The Director may only approve the establishment, operation, or maintenance

of a diplomatic intelligence support center if the Director determines that the establishment, operation, or maintenance of such center is required to provide necessary intelligence support in furtherance of the national security interests of the United States.

(b) Prohibition of Use of Appropriations.— Amounts appropriated pursuant to authorizations by law for intelligence and intelligence-related activities may not be obligated or expended for the establishment, operation, or maintenance of a diplomatic intelligence support center that is not approved by the Director of National Intelligence.

(c) Definitions.—In this section:

(1) The term "diplomatic intelligence support center" means an entity to which employees of the various elements of the intelligence community (as defined in section 3(4)) are detailed for the purpose of providing analytical intelligence support that—

(A) consists of intelligence analyses on military or political matters and expertise to conduct limited assessments and dynamic taskings for a chief of mission; and

(B) is not intelligence support traditionally provided to a chief of mission by the Director of National Intelligence.

(2) The term "chief of mission" has the meaning given that term by section 102(3) of the Foreign Service Act of 1980 (22 U.S.C. 3902(3)), and includes ambassadors at large and ministers of diplomatic missions of the United States, or persons appointed to lead United States offices abroad designated by the Secretary of State as diplomatic in nature.

(d) Termination.— This section shall cease to be effective on October 1, 2000.

TRAVEL ON ANY COMMON CARRIER FOR CERTAIN INTELLIGENCE COLLECTION PERSONNEL

Sec. 116. **[50 U.S.C. 3053]** (a) In General.—Notwithstanding any other provision of law, the Director of National Intelligence may authorize travel on any common carrier when such travel, in the discretion of the Director—

(1) is consistent with intelligence community mission requirements, or

(2) is required for cover purposes, operational needs, or other exceptional circumstances necessary for the successful performance of an intelligence community mission.

(b) Authorized Delegation of Duty.— The Director of National Intelligence may only delegate the authority granted by this section to the Principal Deputy Director of National Intelligence, or with respect to employees of the Central Intelligence Agency, to the Director of the Central Intelligence Agency[6], who may delegate such authority to other appropriate officials of the Central Intelligence Agency.

[6] The amendment made by section 1072(a)(5) to strike "to the Deputy Director of Central Intelligence, or with respect to employees of the Central Intelligence Agencythe Director may delegate such authority to the Deputy Director for Operations" and insert "to the Principal Deputy Director of National Intelligence, or with respect to employees of the Central Intelligence Agency, to the Director of the Central Intelligence Agency" was executed to reflect the probable intent of Congress. The comma after "Central Intelligence Agency" in the striken matter does not appear.

POW/MIA ANALYTIC CAPABILITY

SEC. 117. [50 U.S.C. 3054] (a) REQUIREMENT.—(1) The Director of National Intelligence shall, in consultation with the Secretary of Defense, establish and maintain in the intelligence community an analytic capability with responsibility for intelligence in support of the activities of the United States relating to individuals who, after December 31, 1990, are unaccounted for United States personnel.

(2) The analytic capability maintained under paragraph (1) shall be known as the "POW/MIA analytic capability of the intelligence community".

(b) UNACCOUNTED FOR UNITED STATES PERSONNEL.—In this section, the term "unaccounted for United States personnel" means the following:

(1) Any missing person (as that term is defined in section 1513(1) of title 10, United States Code).

(2) Any United States national who was killed while engaged in activities on behalf of the United States and whose remains have not been repatriated to the United States.

ANNUAL REPORT ON FINANCIAL INTELLIGENCE ON TERRORIST ASSETS

SEC. 118. [50 U.S.C. 3055] (a) ANNUAL REPORT.—On an annual basis, the Secretary of the Treasury (acting through the head of the Office of Intelligence Support) shall submit a report to the appropriate congressional committees that fully informs the committees concerning operations against terrorist financial networks. Each such report shall include with respect to the preceding one-year period—

(1) the total number of asset seizures, designations, and other actions against individuals or entities found to have engaged in financial support of terrorism;

(2) the total number of physical searches of offices, residences, or financial records of individuals or entities suspected of having engaged in financial support for terrorist activity; and

(3) whether the financial intelligence information seized in these cases has been shared on a full and timely basis with the all departments, agencies, and other entities of the United States Government involved in intelligence activities participating in the Foreign Terrorist Asset Tracking Center.

(b) IMMEDIATE NOTIFICATION FOR EMERGENCY DESIGNATION.— In the case of a designation of an individual or entity, or the assets of an individual or entity, as having been found to have engaged in terrorist activities, the Secretary of the Treasury shall report such designation within 24 hours of such a designation to the appropriate congressional committees.

(c) SUBMITTAL DATE OF REPORTS TO CONGRESSIONAL INTELLIGENCE COMMITTEES.— In the case of the reports required to be submitted under subsection (a) to the congressional intelligence committees, the submittal dates for such reports shall be as provided in section 507.

(d) APPROPRIATE CONGRESSIONAL COMMITTEES DEFINED.—In this section, the term "appropriate congressional committees" means the following:

(1) The Permanent Select Committee on Intelligence, the Committee on Appropriations, the Committee on Armed Services, and the Committee on Financial

Services of the House of Representatives.

(2) The Select Committee on Intelligence, the Committee on Appropriations, the Committee on Armed Services, and the Committee on Banking, Housing, and Urban Affairs of the Senate.

NATIONAL COUNTERTERRORISM CENTER

SEC. 119. [50 U.S.C. 3056] (a) ESTABLISHMENT OF CENTER.— There is within the Office of the Director of National Intelligence a National Counterterrorism Center.

(b) DIRECTOR OF NATIONAL COUNTERTERRORISM CENTER.—(1) There is a Director of the National Counterterrorism Center, who shall be the head of the National Counterterrorism Center, and who shall be appointed by the President, by and with the advice and consent of the Senate.

(2) The Director of the National Counterterrorism Center may not simultaneously serve in any other capacity in the executive branch.

(c) REPORTING.—(1) The Director of the National Counterterrorism Center shall report to the Director of National Intelligence with respect to matters described in paragraph (2) and the President with respect to matters described in paragraph (3).

(2) The matters described in this paragraph are as follows:

(A) The budget and programs of the National Counterterrorism Center.

(B) The activities of the Directorate of Intelligence of the National Counterterrorism Center under subsection (i).

(C) The conduct of intelligence operations implemented by other elements of the intelligence community; and

(3) The matters described in this paragraph are the planning and progress of joint counterterrorism operations (other than intelligence operations).

(d) PRIMARY MISSIONS.—The primary missions of the National Counterterrorism Center shall be as follows:

(1) To serve as the primary organization in the United States Government for analyzing and integrating all intelligence possessed or acquired by the United States Government pertaining to terrorism and counterterrorism, excepting intelligence pertaining exclusively to domestic terrorists and domestic counterterrorism.

(2) To conduct strategic operational planning for counterterrorism activities, integrating all instruments of national power, including diplomatic, financial, military, intelligence, homeland security, and law enforcement activities within and among agencies.

(3) To assign roles and responsibilities as part of its strategic operational planning duties to lead Departments or agencies, as appropriate, for counterterrorism activities that are consistent with applicable law and that support counterterrorism strategic operational plans, but shall not direct the execution of any resulting operations.

(4) To ensure that agencies, as appropriate, have access to and receive all-source intelligence support needed to execute their counterterrorism plans or perform independent, alternative analysis.

(5) To ensure that such agencies have access to and receive intelligence needed

to accomplish their assigned activities.

(6) To serve as the central and shared knowledge bank on known and suspected terrorists and international terror groups, as well as their goals, strategies, capabilities, and networks of contacts and support.

(e) Domestic Counterterrorism Intelligence.—(1) The Center may, consistent with applicable law, the direction of the President, and the guidelines referred to in section 102A(b), receive intelligence pertaining exclusively to domestic counterterrorism from any Federal, State, or local government or other source necessary to fulfill its responsibilities and retain and disseminate such intelligence.

(2) Any agency authorized to conduct counterterrorism activities may request information from the Center to assist it in its responsibilities, consistent with applicable law and the guidelines referred to in section 102A(b).

(f) Duties and Responsibilities of Director.—(1) The Director of the National Counterterrorism Center shall—

(A) serve as the principal adviser to the Director of National Intelligence on intelligence operations relating to counterterrorism;

(B) provide strategic operational plans for the civilian and military counterterrorism efforts of the United States Government and for the effective integration of counterterrorism intelligence and operations across agency boundaries, both inside and outside the United States;

(C) advise the Director of National Intelligence on the extent to which the counterterrorism program recommendations and budget proposals of the departments, agencies, and elements of the United States Government conform to the priorities established by the President;

(D) disseminate terrorism information, including current terrorism threat analysis, to the President, the Vice President, the Secretaries of State, Defense, and Homeland Security, the Attorney General, the Director of the Central Intelligence Agency, and other officials of the executive branch as appropriate, and to the appropriate committees of Congress;

(E) support the Department of Justice and the Department of Homeland Security, and other appropriate agencies, in fulfillment of their responsibilities to disseminate terrorism information, consistent with applicable law, guidelines referred to in section 102A(b), Executive orders and other Presidential guidance, to State and local government officials, and other entities, and coordinate dissemination of terrorism information to foreign governments as approved by the Director of National Intelligence;

(F) develop a strategy for combining terrorist travel intelligence operations and law enforcement planning and operations into a cohesive effort to intercept terrorists, find terrorist travel facilitators, and constrain terrorist mobility;

(G) have primary responsibility within the United States Government for conducting net assessments of terrorist threats;

(H) consistent with priorities approved by the President, assist the Director of National Intelligence in establishing requirements for the intelligence community for the collection of terrorism information; and

(I) perform such other duties as the Director of National Intelligence may prescribe or are prescribed by law.

(2) Nothing in paragraph (1)(G) shall limit the authority of the departments and agencies of the United States to conduct net assessments.

(g) LIMITATION.— The Director of the National Counterterrorism Center may not direct the execution of counterterrorism operations.

(h) RESOLUTION OF DISPUTES.— The Director of National Intelligence shall resolve disagreements between the National Counterterrorism Center and the head of a department, agency, or element of the United States Government on designations, assignments, plans, or responsibilities under this section. The head of such a department, agency, or element may appeal the resolution of the disagreement by the Director of National Intelligence to the President.

(i) DIRECTORATE OF INTELLIGENCE.— The Director of the National Counterterrorism Center shall establish and maintain within the National Counterterrorism Center a Directorate of Intelligence which shall have primary responsibility within the United States Government for analysis of terrorism and terrorist organizations (except for purely domestic terrorism and domestic terrorist organizations) from all sources of intelligence, whether collected inside or outside the United States.

(j) DIRECTORATE OF STRATEGIC OPERATIONAL PLANNING.—(1) The Director of the National Counterterrorism Center shall establish and maintain within the National Counterterrorism Center a Directorate of Strategic Operational Planning which shall provide strategic operational plans for counterterrorism operations conducted by the United States Government.

(2) Strategic operational planning shall include the mission, objectives to be achieved, tasks to be performed, interagency coordination of operational activities, and the assignment of roles and responsibilities.

(3) The Director of the National Counterterrorism Center shall monitor the implementation of strategic operational plans, and shall obtain information from each element of the intelligence community, and from each other department, agency, or element of the United States Government relevant for monitoring the progress of such entity in implementing such plans.

NATIONAL COUNTERPROLIFERATION AND BIOSECURITY CENTER

SEC. 119A. [50 U.S.C. 3057] (a) ESTABLISHMENT.—(1) The President shall establish a National Counterproliferation and Biosecurity Center, taking into account all appropriate government tools to—

(A) prevent and halt the proliferation of weapons of mass destruction, their delivery systems, and related materials and technologies; and

(B) lead integration and mission management of all intelligence activities pertaining to biosecurity and foreign biological threats.

(2) The head of the National Counterproliferation and Biosecurity Center shall be the Director of the National Counterproliferation and Biosecurity Center, who shall be appointed by the Director of National Intelligence.

(3) The National Counterproliferation and Biosecurity Center shall be located within the Office of the Director of National Intelligence.

(4) The Director of the National Counterproliferation and Biosecurity Center shall serve as the principal coordinator for the intelligence community, and as the principal advisor to the Director of National Intelligence, with respect to counterproliferation, biosecurity, and foreign biological threats.

(b) Missions and Objectives.—

(1) Counterproliferation.—In establishing the National Counterproliferation and Biosecurity Center, the President shall address the following missions and objectives to prevent and halt the proliferation of weapons of mass destruction, their delivery systems, and related materials and technologies:

(A) Establishing a primary organization within the United States Government for integrating all intelligence possessed or acquired by the United States pertaining to proliferation.

(B) Ensuring that appropriate agencies have full access to and receive all-source intelligence support needed to execute their counterproliferation plans or activities, and perform independent, alternative analyses.

(C) Coordinating the establishment of a central repository on known and suspected proliferation activities, including the goals, strategies, capabilities, networks, and any individuals, groups, or entities engaged in proliferation.

(D) Overseeing the dissemination of proliferation information, including proliferation threats and analyses, to the President, to the appropriate departments and agencies, and to the appropriate committees of Congress.

(E) Conducting and coordinating net assessments and warnings about the proliferation of weapons of mass destruction, their delivery systems, and related materials and technologies.

(F) Coordinating counterproliferation plans and activities of the various departments and agencies of the United States Government to prevent and halt the proliferation of weapons of mass destruction, their delivery systems, and related materials and technologies.

(G) Coordinating and advancing strategic operational counterproliferation planning for the United States Government to prevent and halt the proliferation of weapons of mass destruction, their delivery systems, and related materials and technologies.

(2) Biosecurity.—In establishing the National Counterproliferation and Biosecurity Center, the President shall address the following missions and objectives to ensure that the Center serves as the lead for the intelligence community for the integration, mission management, and coordination of intelligence activities pertaining to biosecurity and foreign biological threats, regardless of origin:

(A) Ensuring that the elements of the intelligence community provide timely and effective warnings to the President and the Director of National Intelligence regarding emerging foreign biological threats, including diseases with pandemic potential.

(B) Overseeing and coordinating the collection of intelligence on biosecurity and foreign biological threats in support of the intelligence needs of the Federal departments and agencies responsible for public health, including by conveying collection priorities to elements of the intelligence community.

(C) Overseeing and coordinating the analysis of intelligence on biosecurity and foreign biological threats in support of the intelligence needs of Federal departments and agencies responsible for public health, including by providing analytic priorities to elements of the intelligence community and by coordinating net assessments.

(D) Coordinating intelligence support to the Federal departments and agencies responsible for public health on matters relating to biosecurity and foreign biological threats, including by ensuring that intelligence pertaining to biosecurity and foreign biological threats is disseminated among appropriately cleared personnel of such departments and agencies.

(E) Coordinating with the Federal departments and agencies responsible for public health to encourage information sharing with the intelligence community.

(F) Identifying gaps in the capabilities and authorities of the intelligence community regarding biosecurity and countering foreign biological threats and providing to the Director of National Intelligence recommended solutions for such gaps, including by encouraging research and development of new capabilities[7] to counter foreign biological threats.

[7] Section 6502(2)(B)(v) of division F of Public Law 118–159 provides for an amendment to insert "and authorities" after "capabilities" without referencing the occurrence of the word "capabilities" to carry out such amendment. The amendment was carried out to the first occurrence of such word to reflect the probable intent of Congress.

(G) Enhancing coordination between elements of the intelligence community and private sector entities on information relevant to biosecurity, biotechnology, and foreign biological threats, and coordinating such information with relevant Federal departments and agencies, as applicable.

(c) NATIONAL SECURITY WAIVER.— The President may waive the requirements of this section, and any parts thereof, if the President determines that such requirements do not materially improve the ability of the United States Government to prevent and halt the proliferation of weapons of mass destruction, their delivery systems, and related materials and technologies. Such waiver shall be made in writing to Congress and shall include a description of how the missions and objectives in subsection (b) are being met.

(d) REPORT TO CONGRESS.—(1) Not later than nine months after the implementation of this Act, the President shall submit to Congress, in classified form if necessary, the findings and recommendations of the President's Commission on Weapons of Mass Destruction established by Executive Order in February 2004, together with the views of the President regarding the establishment of a National Counterproliferation and Biosecurity Center.

(2) If the President decides not to exercise the waiver authority granted by subsection (c), the President shall submit to Congress from time to time updates and plans regarding the establishment of a National Counterproliferation and Biosecurity Center.

(e) SENSE OF CONGRESS.— It is the sense of Congress that a central feature of counterproliferation activities, consistent with the President's Proliferation Security

Initiative, should include the physical interdiction, by air, sea, or land, of weapons of mass destruction, their delivery systems, and related materials and technologies, and enhanced law enforcement activities to identify and disrupt proliferation networks, activities, organizations, and persons.

NATIONAL INTELLIGENCE CENTERS

SEC. 119B. [50 U.S.C. 3058] (a) AUTHORITY TO ESTABLISH.— The Director of National Intelligence may establish one or more national intelligence centers to address intelligence priorities, including, but not limited to, regional issues.

(b) RESOURCES OF DIRECTORS OF CENTERS.—(1) The Director of National Intelligence shall ensure that the head of each national intelligence center under subsection (a) has appropriate authority, direction, and control of such center, and of the personnel assigned to such center, to carry out the assigned mission of such center.

(2) The Director of National Intelligence shall ensure that each national intelligence center has appropriate personnel to accomplish effectively the mission of such center.

(c) INFORMATION SHARING.— The Director of National Intelligence shall, to the extent appropriate and practicable, ensure that each national intelligence center under subsection (a) and the other elements of the intelligence community share information in order to facilitate the mission of such center.

(d) MISSION OF CENTERS.—Pursuant to the direction of the Director of National Intelligence, each national intelligence center under subsection (a) may, in the area of intelligence responsibility assigned to such center—

(1) have primary responsibility for providing all-source analysis of intelligence based upon intelligence gathered both domestically and abroad;

(2) have primary responsibility for identifying and proposing to the Director of National Intelligence intelligence collection and analysis and production requirements; and

(3) perform such other duties as the Director of National Intelligence shall specify.

(e) REVIEW AND MODIFICATION OF CENTERS.—The Director of National Intelligence shall determine on a regular basis whether—

(1) the area of intelligence responsibility assigned to each national intelligence center under subsection (a) continues to meet appropriate intelligence priorities; and

(2) the staffing and management of such center remains appropriate for the accomplishment of the mission of such center.

(f) TERMINATION.— The Director of National Intelligence may terminate any national intelligence center under subsection (a).

(g) SEPARATE BUDGET ACCOUNT.— The Director of National Intelligence shall, as appropriate, include in the National Intelligence Program budget a separate line item for each national intelligence center under subsection (a).

SEC. 119C. [50 U.S.C. 3059] FOREIGN MALIGN INFLUENCE CENTER.

(a) ESTABLISHMENT.— There is within the Office of the Director of National Intelligence a Foreign Malign Influence Center (in this section referred to as the "Center").

(b) FUNCTIONS AND COMPOSITION.—The Center shall—

(1) be comprised of analysts from all elements of the intelligence community, including elements with diplomatic and law enforcement functions;

(2) have access to all intelligence and other reporting possessed or acquired by the United States Government pertaining to foreign malign influence;

(3) serve as the primary organization in the United States Government for analyzing and integrating all intelligence possessed or acquired by the United States Government pertaining to foreign malign influence; and

(4) provide to employees and officers of the Federal Government in policy-making positions and Congress comprehensive assessments, and indications and warnings, of foreign malign influence.

(c) DIRECTOR.—

(1) APPOINTMENT.— There is a Director of the Center, who shall be the head of the Center, and who shall be appointed by the Director of National Intelligence.

(2) ROLE.—The Director of the Center shall—

(A) report directly to the Director of National Intelligence;

(B) carry out the functions under subsection (b); and

(C) at the request of the President or the Director of National Intelligence, develop and provide recommendations for potential responses by the United States to foreign malign influence.

(d) ANNUAL REPORTS.—

(1) IN GENERAL.— In addition to the matters submitted pursuant to subsection (b)(4), at the direction of the Director of National Intelligence, but not less than once each year, the Director of the Center shall submit to the congressional intelligence committees, the Committee on Foreign Affairs of the House of Representatives, and the Committee on Foreign Relations of the Senate a report on foreign malign influence.

(2) MATTERS INCLUDED.—Each report under paragraph (1) shall include, with respect to the period covered by the report, a discussion of the following:

(A) The most significant activities of the Center.

(B) Any recommendations the Director determines necessary for legislative or other actions to improve the ability of the Center to carry out its functions, including recommendations regarding the protection of privacy and civil liberties.

(e) DEFINITIONS.—In this section:

(1) COVERED FOREIGN COUNTRY.—The term "covered foreign country" means the following:

(A) The Russian Federation.

(B) The Islamic Republic of Iran.

(C) The Democratic People's Republic of Korea.

(D) The People's Republic of China.

(E) Any other foreign country that the Director of the Center determines appropriate for purposes of this section.

(2) FOREIGN MALIGN INFLUENCE.—The term "foreign malign influence" means any hostile effort undertaken by, at the direction of, or on behalf of or with the substantial support of, the government of a covered foreign country with the objective of influencing, through overt or covert means—

(A) the political, military, economic, or other policies or activities of the United States Government or State or local governments, including any election within the United States; or

(B) the public opinion within the United States.

SEC. 120. [50 U.S.C. 3060] CLIMATE SECURITY ADVISORY COUNCIL.

(a) ESTABLISHMENT.—The Director of National Intelligence shall establish a Climate Security Advisory Council for the purpose of—

(1) assisting intelligence analysts of various elements of the intelligence community with respect to analysis of climate security and its impact on the areas of focus of such analysts;

(2) facilitating coordination between the elements of the intelligence community and elements of the Federal Government that are not elements of the intelligence community in collecting data on, and conducting analysis of, climate change and climate security; and

(3) ensuring that the intelligence community is adequately prioritizing climate change in carrying out its activities.

(b) COMPOSITION OF COUNCIL.—

(1) MEMBERS.—The Council shall be composed of the following individuals appointed by the Director of National Intelligence:

(A) An appropriate official from the National Intelligence Council, who shall chair the Council.

(B) The lead official with respect to climate and environmental security analysis from—

(i) the Central Intelligence Agency;

(ii) the Bureau of Intelligence and Research of the Department of State;

(iii) the National Geospatial-Intelligence Agency;

(iv) the Office of Intelligence and Counterintelligence of the Department of Energy;

(v) the Office of the Under Secretary of Defense for Intelligence and Security; and

(vi) the Defense Intelligence Agency.

(C) Three appropriate officials from elements of the Federal Government that are not elements of the intelligence community that are responsible for—

(i) providing decision makers with a predictive understanding of the climate;

(ii) making observations of our Earth system that can be used by the public, policymakers, and to support strategic decisions; or

(iii) coordinating Federal research and investments in understanding the forces shaping the global environment, both human and natural, and their impacts on society.

(D) Any other officials as the Director of National Intelligence or the chair of the Council may determine appropriate.

(2) RESPONSIBILITIES OF CHAIR.—The chair of the Council shall have responsibility for—

(A) identifying agencies to supply individuals from elements of the Federal Government that are not elements of the intelligence community;

(B) securing the permission of the relevant agency heads for the participation of such individuals on the Council; and

(C) any other duties that the Director of National Intelligence may direct.

(c) DUTIES AND RESPONSIBILITIES OF COUNCIL.—The Council shall carry out the following duties and responsibilities:

(1) To meet at least quarterly to—

(A) exchange appropriate data between elements of the intelligence community and elements of the Federal Government that are not elements of the intelligence community;

(B) discuss processes for the routine exchange of such data and implementation of such processes; and

(C) prepare summaries of the business conducted at each meeting.

(2) To assess and determine best practices with respect to the analysis of climate security, including identifying publicly available information and intelligence acquired through clandestine means that enables such analysis.

(3) To assess and identify best practices with respect to prior efforts of the intelligence community to analyze climate security.

(4) To assess and describe best practices for identifying and disseminating climate intelligence indications and warnings.

(5) To recommend methods of incorporating analysis of climate security and the best practices identified under paragraphs (2) through (4) into existing analytic training programs.

(6) To consult, as appropriate, with other elements of the intelligence community that conduct analysis of climate change or climate security and elements of the Federal Government that are not elements of the intelligence community that conduct analysis of climate change or climate security, for the purpose of sharing information about ongoing efforts and avoiding duplication of existing efforts.

(7) To work with elements of the intelligence community that conduct analysis of climate change or climate security and elements of the Federal Government that are not elements of the intelligence community that conduct analysis of climate change or climate security—

(A) to exchange appropriate data between such elements, establish processes, procedures and practices for the routine exchange of such data, discuss the implementation of such processes; and

(B) to enable and facilitate the sharing of findings and analysis between such elements.

(8) To assess whether the elements of the intelligence community that conduct analysis of climate change or climate security may inform the research direction of academic work and the sponsored work of the United States Government.

(9) At the discretion of the chair of the Council, to convene conferences of analysts and nonintelligence community personnel working on climate change or climate security on subjects that the chair shall direct.

(d) Annual Report.—

(1) Requirement.— Not later than January 31, 2021, and not less frequently than annually thereafter, the chair of the Council shall submit, on behalf of the Council, to the congressional intelligence committees a report describing the activities of the Council as described in subsection (c) during the year preceding the year during which the report is submitted.

(2) Matters included.—Each report under paragraph (1) shall include a description of any obstacles or gaps relating to—

(A) the Council fulfilling its duties and responsibilities under subsection (c); or

(B) the responsiveness of the intelligence community to the climate security needs and priorities of the policymaking elements of the Federal Government.

(e) Sunset.— The Council shall terminate on December 31, 2024.

(f) Definitions.—In this section:

(1) Climate security.—The term “climate security” means the effects of climate change on the following:

(A) The national security of the United States, including national security infrastructure.

(B) Subnational, national, and regional political stability.

(C) The security of allies and partners of the United States.

(D) Ongoing or potential political violence, including unrest, rioting, guerrilla warfare, insurgency, terrorism, rebellion, revolution, civil war, and interstate war.

(2) Climate intelligence indications and warnings.—The term “climate intelligence indications and warnings” means developments relating to climate security with the potential to—

(A) imminently and substantially alter the political stability or degree of human security in a country or region; or

(B) imminently and substantially threaten—

(i) the national security of the United States;

(ii) the military, political, or economic interests of allies and partners of the United States; or

(iii) citizens of the United States abroad.

SEC. 121. [50 U.S.C. 3061] COUNTERINTELLIGENCE AND NATIONAL SECURITY PROTECTIONS FOR INTELLIGENCE COMMUNITY GRANT FUNDING.

(a) DISCLOSURE AS CONDITION FOR RECEIPT OF GRANT.— The head of an element of the intelligence community may not award a grant to a person or entity unless the person or entity has certified to the head of the element that the person or entity has disclosed to the head of the element any material financial or material in-kind support that the person or entity knows, or should have known, derives from the People's Republic of China, the Russian Federation, the Islamic Republic of Iran, the Democratic People's Republic of Korea, or the Republic of Cuba, during the 5-year period ending on the date of the person or entity's application for the grant.

(b) PROCESS FOR REVIEW OF GRANT APPLICANTS PRIOR TO AWARD.—

(1) IN GENERAL.— The head of an element of the intelligence community may not award a grant to a person or entity who submitted a certification under subsection (a) until such certification is received by the head of an element of the intelligence community and submitted to the Director of National Intelligence pursuant to the process set forth in paragraph (2).

(2) PROCESS.—

(A) IN GENERAL.— The Director of National Intelligence, in coordination with such heads of elements of the intelligence community as the Director considers appropriate, shall establish a process to review the awarding of a grant to an applicant who submitted a certification under subsection (a).

(B) ELEMENTS.—The process established under subparagraph (A) shall include the following:

(i) The immediate transmission of a copy of each applicant's certification made under subsection (a) to the Director of National Intelligence.

(ii) The review of the certification and any accompanying disclosures submitted under subsection (a) as soon as practicable.

(iii) Authorization for the heads of the elements of the intelligence community to take such actions as may be necessary, including denial or revocation of a grant, to ensure a grant does not pose an unacceptable risk of—

(I) misappropriation of United States intellectual property, research and development, and innovation efforts; or

(II) other counterintelligence threats.

(c) ANNUAL REPORT REQUIRED.—Not later than 1 year after the date of the enactment of the Intelligence Authorization Act for Fiscal Year 2023 and not less frequently than once each year thereafter, the Director of National Intelligence shall submit to the congressional intelligence committees an annual report identifying the following for the 1-year period covered by the report:

(1) The number of applications for grants received by each element of the intelligence community.

(2) The number of such applications that were reviewed using the process established under subsection (b)(2), disaggregated by element of the intelligence community.

(3) The number of such applications that were denied and the number of grants that were revoked, pursuant to the process established under subsection (b)(2), disaggregated by element of the intelligence community.

SEC. 122. [50 U.S.C. 3062] OFFICE OF ENGAGEMENT.

(a) ESTABLISHMENT .—There is within the Office of the Director of National Intelligence an Office of Engagement (in this section referred to as the "Office").

(b) HEAD; STAFF.—

(1) HEAD.— The Director of National Intelligence shall appoint as head of the Office an individual with requisite experience in matters relating to the duties of the Office, as determined by the Director of National Intelligence. Such head of the Office shall report directly to the Director of National Intelligence.

(2) STAFF.— To assist the head of the Office in fulfilling the duties of the Office, the head shall employ full-time equivalent staff in such number, and with such requisite expertise in matters relating to such duties, as may be determined by the head.

(c) DUTIES.—The duties of the Office shall be as follows:

(1) To ensure coordination across the elements of the intelligence community efforts regarding outreach, relationship development, and associated knowledge and relationship management, with covered entities, consistent with the protection of intelligence sources and methods.

(2) To assist in sharing best practices regarding such efforts among the elements of the intelligence community.

(3) To establish and implement metrics to assess the effectiveness of such efforts.

(d) COVERED ENTITY DEFINED.— In this section, the term "covered entity" means an entity that is not an entity of the United States Government, including private sector companies, institutions of higher education, trade associations, think tanks, laboratories, international organizations, and foreign partners and allies.

TITLE II—THE DEPARTMENT OF DEFENSE

SEC. 201. [50 U.S.C. 3005] DEPARTMENT OF DEFENSE.

Except to the extent inconsistent with the provisions of this Act or other provisions of law, the provisions of title 5, United States Code, shall be applicable to the Department of Defense.

[Sections 202–204 were repealed by section 307 of Public Law 87–651 (Act of September 7, 1962, 76 Stat. 526).]

DEPARTMENT OF THE ARMY

SEC. 205. (a) All laws, orders, regulations, and other actions relating to the Department of War or to any officer or activity whose title is changed under this section shall, insofar as they are not inconsistent with the provisions of this Act, be deemed to relate to the Department of the Army within the Department of Defense or to such officer or activity designated by his or its new title.

(b) **[50 U.S.C. 3004]** the term "Department of the Army" as used in this Act shall be construed to mean the Department of the Army at the seat of government and all field headquarters, forces, reserve components, installations, activities, and functions under the control or supervision of the Department of the Army.

DEPARTMENT OF THE NAVY

SEC. 206. [50 U.S.C. 3004] The term "Department of the Navy" as used in this Act shall be construed to mean the Department of the Navy at the seat of government; the headquarters, United States Marine Corps; the entire operating forces of the United States Navy, including naval aviation, and of the United States Marine Corps, including the reserve components of such forces; all field activities, headquarters, forces, bases, installations, activities and functions under the control or supervision of the Department of the Navy; and the United States Coast Guard when operating as a part of the Navy pursuant to law.

DEPARTMENT OF THE AIR FORCE

SEC. 207. [50 U.S.C. 3004] The term "Department of the Air Force" as used in this Act shall be construed to mean the Department of the Air Force at the seat of government and all field headquarters, forces, reserve components, installations, activities, and functions under the control or supervision of the Department of the Air Force.

TITLE III—MISCELLANEOUS

NATIONAL SECURITY AGENCY VOLUNTARY SEPARATION

SEC. 301. [50 U.S.C. 3071] (a) SHORT TITLE.— This section may be cited as the "National Security Agency Voluntary Separation Act".

(b) DEFINITIONS.—For purposes of this section—

(1) the term "Director" means the Director of the National Security Agency; and

(2) the term "employee" means an employee of the National Security Agency, serving under an appointment without time limitation, who has been currently employed by the National Security Agency for a continuous period of at least 12 months prior to the effective date of the program established under subsection (c), except that such term does not include—

(A) a reemployed annuitant under subchapter III of chapter 83 or chapter 84 of title 5, United States Code, or another retirement system for employees of the Government; or

(B) an employee having a disability on the basis of which such employee is or would be eligible for disability retirement under any of the retirement systems referred to in subparagraph (A).

(c) ESTABLISHMENT OF PROGRAM.— Notwithstanding any other provision of law, the Director, in his sole discretion, may establish a program under which employees may, after October 1, 2000, be eligible for early retirement, offered separation pay to separate from service voluntarily, or both.

(d) EARLY RETIREMENT.—An employee who—

(1) is at least 50 years of age and has completed 20 years of service; or

(2) has at least 25 years of service,

may, pursuant to regulations promulgated under this section, apply and be retired from the National Security Agency and receive benefits in accordance with chapter 83 or 84 of title 5, United States Code, if the employee has not less than 10 years of service with the National Security Agency.

(e) AMOUNT OF SEPARATION PAY AND TREATMENT FOR OTHER PURPOSES.—

(1) AMOUNT.—Separation pay shall be paid in a lump sum and shall be equal to the lesser of—

(A) an amount equal to the amount the employee would be entitled to receive under section 5595(c) of title 5, United States Code, if the employee were entitled to payment under such section; or

(B) $25,000.

(2) TREATMENT.—Separation pay shall not—

(A) be a basis for payment, and shall not be included in the computation, of any other type of Government benefit; and

(B) be taken into account for the purpose of determining the amount of any severance pay to which an individual may be entitled under section 5595 of title 5, United States Code, based on any other separation.

(f) REEMPLOYMENT RESTRICTIONS.— An employee who receives separation pay under such program may not be reemployed by the National Security Agency for the 12-month period beginning on the effective date of the employee's separation. An employee who receives separation pay under this section on the basis of a separation occurring on or after the date of the enactment of the Federal Workforce Restructuring Act of 1994 (Public Law 103–236; 108 Stat. 111) and accepts employment with the Government of the United States within 5 years after the date of the separation on which payment of the separation pay is based shall be required to repay the entire amount of the separation pay to the National Security Agency. If the employment is with an Executive agency (as defined by section 105 of title 5, United States Code), the Director of the Office of Personnel Management may, at the request of the head of the agency, waive the repayment if the individual involved possesses unique abilities and is the only qualified applicant available for the position. If the employment is with an entity in the legislative branch, the head of the entity or the appointing official may waive the repayment if the individual involved possesses unique abilities and is the only qualified applicant available for the position. If the employment is with the judicial branch, the Director of the Administrative Office of the United States Courts may waive the repayment if the individual involved possesses unique abilities and is the only qualified applicant available for the position.

(g) BAR ON CERTAIN EMPLOYMENT.—

(1) BAR.—An employee may not be separated from service under this section unless the employee agrees that the employee will not—

(A) act as agent or attorney for, or otherwise represent, any other person (except the United States) in any formal or informal appearance before, or, with the intent to influence, make any oral or written communication on behalf of any other person (except the United States) to the National Security Agency; or

(B) participate in any manner in the award, modification, or extension of any contract for property or services with the National Security Agency, during the 12-month period beginning on the effective date of the employee's separation from service.

(2) PENALTY.— An employee who violates an agreement under this subsection shall be liable to the United States in the amount of the separation pay paid to the employee pursuant to this section multiplied by the proportion of the 12-month period during which the employee was in violation of the agreement.

(h) LIMITATIONS.—Under this program, early retirement and separation pay may be offered only—

(1) with the prior approval of the Director;

(2) for the period specified by the Director; and

(3) to employees within such occupational groups or geographic locations, or subject to such other similar limitations or conditions, as the Director may require.

(i) REGULATIONS.— Before an employee may be eligible for early retirement, separation pay, or both, under this section, the Director shall prescribe such regulations as may be necessary to carry out this section.

(j) NOTIFICATION OF EXERCISE OF AUTHORITY.— The Director may[8] not make an offer of early retirement, separation pay, or both, pursuant to this section until 15 days after submitting to the congressional intelligence committees a report describing the occupational groups or geographic locations, or other similar limitations or conditions, required by the Director under subsection (h), and including the proposed regulations issued pursuant to subsection (i).

---

[8] Section 941(b)(1) of the Intelligence Authorization Act for Fiscal Year 2003 (P.L. 107–306; 116 Stat. 2431) amended this subsection by striking ```Reporting Require-ments.—' and all that follows through `The Director may' and inserting `Notification of Exercise of Authority.—The Director may'''. There was no hyphen in law within the word ``Requirements''. The amendment has been executed to reflect the probable intent of Congress

---

(k) REMITTANCE OF FUNDS.— In addition to any other payment that is required to be made under subchapter III of chapter 83 or chapter 84 of title 5, United States Code, the National Security Agency shall remit to the Office of Personnel Management for deposit in the Treasury of the United States to the credit of the Civil Service Retirement and Disability Fund, an amount equal to 15 percent of the final basic pay of each employee to whom a voluntary separation payment has been or is to be paid under this section. The remittance required by this subsection shall be in lieu of any remittance required by section 4(a) of the Federal Workforce Restructuring Act of 1994 (5 U.S.C. 8331 note).

AUTHORITY OF FEDERAL BUREAU OF INVESTIGATION TO AWARD PERSONAL SERVICES CONTRACTS

SEC. 302. **[50 U.S.C. 3072]** (a) IN GENERAL.— The Director of the Federal Bureau of Investigation may enter into personal services contracts if the personal services to be provided under such contracts directly support the intelligence or counterintelligence missions of the Federal Bureau of Investigation.

(b) INAPPLICABILITY OF CERTAIN REQUIREMENTS.— Contracts under subsection (a) shall not be subject to the annuity offset requirements of sections 8344 and 8468 of title 5, United States Code, the requirements of section 3109 of title 5, United States Code, or any law or regulation requiring competitive contracting.

(c) CONTRACT TO BE APPROPRIATE MEANS OF SECURING SERVICES.— The Chief Contracting Officer of the Federal Bureau of Investigation shall ensure that each personal services contract entered into by the Director under this section is the appropriate means of securing the services to be provided under such contract.".

ADVISORY COMMITTEES AND PERSONNEL

SEC. 303. [50 U.S.C. 3073] (a) The Director of the Office of Defense Mobilization, the Director of National Intelligence, and the National Security Council, acting through its Executive Secretary, are authorized to appoint such advisory committees and to employ, consistent with other provisions of this Act, such part-time advisory personnel as they may deem necessary in carrying out their respective functions and the functions of agencies under their control. Persons holding other offices or positions under the United States for which they receive compensation, while serving as members of such committees, shall receive no additional compensation for such service. Retired members of the uniformed services employed by the Director of National Intelligence who hold no other office or position under the United States for which they receive compensation, other members of such committees and other part-time advisory personnel so employed may serve without compensation or may receive compensation at a daily rate not to exceed the daily equivalent of the rate of pay in effect for grade GS–18 of the General Schedule established by section 5332 of title 5, United States Code, as determined by the appointing authority.

(b) Service of an individual as a member of any such advisory committee, or in any other part-time capacity for a department or agency hereunder, shall not be considered as service bringing such individual within the provisions of section 203, 205, or 207, of title 18, United States Code, unless the act of such individual, which by such section is made unlawful when performed by an individual referred to in such section, is with respect to any particular matter which directly involves a department or agency which such person is advising or in which such department or agency is directly interested.

SEC. 304. [50 U.S.C. 3073a] REQUIREMENTS FOR CERTAIN EMPLOYMENT ACTIVITIES BY FORMER INTELLIGENCE OFFICERS AND EMPLOYEES.

(a) POST-EMPLOYMENT RESTRICTIONS.—

(1) COVERED POST-SERVICE POSITION.—

(A) PERMANENT RESTRICTION.— Except as provided by paragraph (2)(A), an employee of an element of the intelligence community who occupies a covered intelligence position may not occupy a covered post-service position for a designated prohibited foreign country following the date on which the employee ceases to occupy a covered intelligence position.

(B) TEMPORARY RESTRICTION.— Except as provided by paragraph (2)(A), an employee of an element of the intelligence community who occupies a covered intelligence position may not occupy a covered post-service position during the 30-month period following the date on which the employee ceases to occupy a covered intelligence position.

(2) WAIVER.—

(A) AUTHORITY TO GRANT WAIVERS.—The applicable head of an intelligence community element may waive a restriction in paragraph (1) with respect to an employee or former employee who is subject to that restriction only after—

(i) the employee or former employee submits to the applicable head of the intelligence community element a written application for such waiver in such form and manner as the applicable head of the intelligence community element determines appropriate; and

(ii) the applicable head of the element of the intelligence community determines that granting such waiver will not harm the national security interests of the United States.

(B) Period of waiver.— A waiver issued under subparagraph (A) shall apply for a period not exceeding 5 years. The applicable head of the intelligence community element may renew such a waiver.

(C) Revocation.— The applicable head of the intelligence community element may revoke a waiver issued under subparagraph (A) to an employee or former employee, effective on the date that is 60 days after the date on which the applicable head of the intelligence community element provides the employee or former employee written notice of such revocation.

(D) Tolling.— The 30-month restriction in paragraph (1)(B) shall be tolled for an employee or former employee during the period beginning on the date on which a waiver is issued under subparagraph (A) and ending on the date on which the waiver expires or on the effective date of a revocation under subparagraph (C), as the case may be.

(E) Reporting to congress.—On a quarterly basis, the head of each element of the intelligence community shall submit to the congressional intelligence committees and the congressional defense committees for Department of Defense elements of the intelligence community, a written notification of each waiver or revocation that shall include the following:

(i) With respect to a waiver issued to an employee or former employee—

(I) the covered intelligence position held or formerly held by the employee or former employee; and

(II) a brief description of the covered post-service employment, including the employer and the recipient of the representation, advice, or services.

(ii) With respect to a revocation of a waiver issued to an employee or former employee—

(I) the details of the waiver, including any renewals of such waiver, and the dates of such waiver and renewals; and

(II) the specific reasons why the applicable head of the intelligence community element determined that such revocation is warranted.

(b) Covered Post-service Employment Reporting.—

(1) Requirement.—During the period described in paragraph (2), an employee who ceases to occupy a covered intelligence position shall—

(A) report covered post-service employment to the head of the element of the intelligence community that employed such employee in such covered intelligence position upon accepting such covered post-service employment;

and

(B) annually (or more frequently if the head of such element considers it appropriate) report covered post-service employment to the head of such element.

(2) PERIOD DESCRIBED.— The period described in this paragraph is the period beginning on the date on which an employee ceases to occupy a covered intelligence position.

(3) REGULATIONS.— The head of each element of the intelligence community shall issue regulations requiring, as a condition of employment, each employee of such element occupying a covered intelligence position to sign a written agreement requiring the regular reporting of covered post-service employment to the head of such element pursuant to paragraph (1).

(c) PENALTIES.—

(1) CRIMINAL PENALTIES.— A former employee who knowingly and willfully violates subsection (a) or who knowingly and willfully fails to make a required report under subsection (b) shall be fined under title 18, United States Code, or imprisoned for not more than 5 years, or both. Each report under subsection (b) shall be subject to section 1001 of title 18, United States Code.

(2) SECURITY CLEARANCES.— The head of an element of the intelligence community shall revoke the security clearance of a former employee if the former employee knowingly and willfully fails to make a required report under subsection (b) or knowingly and willfully makes a false report under such subsection.

(d) PROVISION OF INFORMATION.—

(1) TRAINING.— The head of each element of the intelligence community shall regularly provide training on the restrictions under subsection (a) and[9]the reporting requirements under subsection (b) to employees of that element who occupy a covered intelligence position.

[9] Section 7304(1) of Div. G. of P.L. 118-31 provides for an amendment to insert "the restrictions under subsection (a) and" before "the report requirements". However it should have referenced "the reporting requirements" instead. The amendment was carried out due to the probable intent of Congress.

(2) WRITTEN NOTICE ABOUT REPORTING REQUIREMENTS.— The head of each element of the intelligence community shall provide written notice of the reporting requirements under subsection (b) to an employee when the employee occupies a covered intelligence position.

(3) WRITTEN NOTICE ABOUT RESTRICTIONS.—The head of each element of the intelligence community shall provide written notice of the restrictions under subsection (a) to any person who may be subject to such restrictions on or after the date of enactment of the Intelligence Authorization Act for Fiscal Year 2023—

(A) when the head of the element determines that such person may become subject to such covered intelligence position restrictions; and

(B) when the person occupies a covered intelligence position.

(4) WRITTEN ADVISORY OPINIONS.— Upon request from a current employee who occupies a covered intelligence position or a former employee who previously

occupied a covered intelligence position, the applicable head of the element of the intelligence community concerned may provide a written advisory opinion to such current or former employee regarding whether a proposed employment, representation, or provision of advice or services constitutes covered post-service employment as defined in subsection (g).

(e) ANNUAL REPORTS.—

(1) REQUIREMENT.— Not later than March 31 of each year, the Director of National Intelligence shall submit to the congressional intelligence committees a report on covered post-service employment occurring during the year covered by the report.

(2) ELEMENTS.—Each report under paragraph (1) shall include the following:

(A) The number of former employees who occupy a covered post-service position, broken down by—

(i) the name of the employer;

(ii) the foreign government, including by the specific foreign individual, agency, or entity, for whom the covered post-service employment is being performed; and

(iii) the nature of the services provided as part of the covered post-service employment.

(B) A certification by the Director that—

(i) each element of the intelligence community maintains adequate systems and processes for ensuring that former employees are submitting reports required under subsection (b);

(ii) to the knowledge of the heads of the elements of the intelligence community, all former employees who occupy a covered post-service position are in compliance with this section;

(iii) the services provided by former employees who occupy a covered post-service position do not—

(I) pose a current or future threat to the national security of the United States; or

(II) pose a counterintelligence risk; and

(iv) the Director and the heads of such elements are not aware of any credible information or reporting that any former employee who occupies a covered post-service position has engaged in activities that violate Federal law, infringe upon the privacy rights of United States persons, or constitute abuses of human rights.

(3) FORM.— Each report under paragraph (1) shall be submitted in unclassified form, but may include a classified annex.

(f) NOTIFICATION.—In addition to the annual reports under subsection (e), if a head of an element of the intelligence community determines that the services provided by a former employee who occupies a covered post-service position pose a threat or risk described in clause (iii) of paragraph (2)(B) of such subsection, or include activities described in clause (iv) of such paragraph, the head shall notify the congressional intelligence committees of such determination by not later than 7 days after making such determination. The notification shall include the following:

(1) The name of the former employee.

(2) The name of the employer.

(3) The foreign government, including the specific foreign individual, agency, or entity, for whom the covered post-service employment is being performed.

(4) As applicable, a description of—

(A) the risk to national security, the counterintelligence risk, or both; and

(B) the activities that may violate Federal law, infringe upon the privacy rights of United States persons, or constitute abuses of human rights.

(g) DEFINITIONS.—In this section:

(1) COVERED INTELLIGENCE POSITION.— The term "covered intelligence position" means a position within an element of the intelligence community that, based on the level of access of a person occupying such position to information regarding sensitive intelligence sources or methods or other exceptionally sensitive matters, the head of such element determines should be subject to the requirements of this section.

(2) COVERED POST-SERVICE EMPLOYMENT.— The term "covered post-service employment" means direct or indirect employment by, representation of, or any provision of advice or services to the government of a foreign country or any company, entity, or other person whose activities are directly or indirectly supervised, directed, controlled, financed, or subsidized, in whole or in major part, by any government of a foreign country if such employment, representation, or provision of advice or services relates to national security, intelligence, the military, or internal security.

(3) COVERED POST-SERVICE POSITION.— The term "covered post-service position" means a position of employment described in paragraph (2).

(4) DESIGNATED PROHIBITED FOREIGN COUNTRY.—The term "designated prohibited foreign country" means the following:

(A) The People's Republic of China.

(B) The Russian Federation.

(C) The Democratic People's Republic of Korea.

(D) The Islamic Republic of Iran.

(E) The Republic of Cuba.

(F) The Syrian Arab Republic.

(5) EMPLOYEE.— The term "employee", with respect to an employee occupying a covered intelligence position, includes an officer or official of an element of the intelligence community, a contractor of such an element, a detailee to such an element, or a member of the Armed Forces assigned to such an element.

(6) FORMER EMPLOYEE.—The term "former employee" means an individual—

(A) who was an employee occupying a covered intelligence position; and

(B) who is subject to the requirements under subsection (a) or (b).

(7) GOVERNMENT OF A FOREIGN COUNTRY.— The term "government of a foreign country" has the meaning given the term in section 1(e) of the Foreign Agents

Registration Act of 1938 (22 U.S.C. 611(e)).

[Sections 304–306 were repealed by the law enacting title 5, United States Code (Public Law 89–544, September 6, 1966, 80 Stat. 654). Subsequently, section 305(a) of Public Law 113–293 adds after section 303 a new section 304 shown prior to this note (and amended in its entirety by section 308(a)(1) of division X of Public Law 117–103).]

AUTHORIZATION FOR APPROPRIATIONS

SEC. 307. [50 U.S.C. 3074] There are hereby authorized to be appropriated such sums as may be necessary and appropriate to carry out the provisions and purposes of this Act (other than the provisions and purposes of sections 102, 103, 104, 105 and titles V, VI, and VII).

DEFINITIONS

SEC. 308. [50 U.S.C. 3075] (a)[10] As used in sections 2, 101, 102, 103, and 303 of this Act, the term "function" includes functions, powers, and duties.

[10] Section 307 of Public Law 87–651 (Act of September 7, 1962, 76 Stat. 526) repealed section 308(a) *less* its applicability to sections 2, 101–103, and 303.

(b) As used in this Act, the term, "Department of Defense" shall be deemed to include the military departments of the Army, the Navy, and the Air Force, and all agencies created under title II of this Act.

SEPARABILITY

SEC. 309. [50 U.S.C. 3076] If any provision of this Act or the application thereof to any person or circumstances is held invalid, the validity of the remainder of the Act and of the application of such provision to other persons and circumstances shall not be affected thereby.

EFFECTIVE DATE

SEC. 310. [50 U.S.C. 3077] (a) The first sentence of section 202 (a) and sections 1, 2, 307, 308, 309, and 310 shall take effect immediately upon the enactment of this Act.

(b) Except as provided in subsection (a), the provisions of this Act shall take effect on whichever of the following days is the earlier: The day after the day upon which the Secretary of Defense first appointed takes office, or the sixtieth day after the date of the enactment of this Act.

SUCCESSION TO THE PRESIDENCY

SEC. 311. [Section 311 consisted of an amendment to the Act entitled "An Act to provide for the performance of the duties of the office of President in case of the removal, resignation, death, or inability both of the President and Vice President".]

REPEALING AND SAVING PROVISIONS

SEC. 312. [50 U.S.C. 3078] All laws, orders, and regulations inconsistent with the provisions of this title[11] are repealed insofar as they are inconsistent with the powers, duties, and responsibilities enacted hereby: *Provided,* That the powers, duties, and responsibilities of the Secretary of Defense under this title[11] shall be administered in conformance with the policy and requirements for administration of budgetary and fiscal matters in the Government generally, including accounting and financial reporting, and that nothing in this title[11] shall be construed as eliminating or modifying the powers, duties, and responsibilities of any other department, agency, or officer of the Government in connection with such matters, but no such department, agency, or officer shall exercise any such powers, duties, or responsibilities in a manner that will render ineffective the provisions of this title[11].

[11] The references to "this title" originally meant title IV of the National Security Act of 1947, as added by section 11 of the Act of Aug. 10, 1949, Ch. 412, 63 Stat. 585. Title IV of this Act, except for section 411 (subsequently redesignated as section 312 by section 6742(b)(11) of P.L. 116-92; 133 Stat. 2240), was *effectively* repealed by section 307 of Pub. L. 87–651, Sept. 7, 1962, 76 Stat. 526.

SEC. 313. [50 U.S.C. 3079] INSIDER THREAT POLICY COMPLIANCE AND REPORTING.

The head of each element of the intelligence community shall—

(1) implement the policy established in accordance with section 102A(f)(8); and

(2) concurrent with the submission to Congress of budget justification materials in support of the budget of the President for a fiscal year that is submitted to Congress under section 1105(a) of title 31, United States Code, submit to Congress a certification as to whether the element is in compliance with such policy.

[Title IV *less* section 411 was repealed by section 307 of Public Law 87–651 (Act of September 7, 1962, 76 Stat. 526). Such section 411 was redesignated as section 312 by section 6742(b)(11) of Public Law 116–92.]

TITLE V—ACCOUNTABILITY FOR INTELLIGENCE ACTIVITIES

GENERAL CONGRESSIONAL OVERSIGHT PROVISIONS

SEC. 501. [50 U.S.C. 3091] (a)(1) The President shall ensure that the congressional intelligence committees are kept fully and currently informed of the intelligence activities of the United States, including any significant anticipated intelligence activity as required by this title.

(2) Nothing in this title shall be construed as requiring the approval of the congressional intelligence committees as a condition precedent to the initiation of any significant anticipated intelligence activity.

(b) The President shall ensure that any illegal intelligence activity is reported promptly to the congressional intelligence committees, as well as any corrective action that has been taken or is planned in connection with such illegal activity.

(c) The President and the congressional intelligence committees shall each establish such written procedures as may be necessary to carry out the provisions of this title.

(d) The House of Representatives and the Senate shall each establish, by rule or resolution of such House, procedures to protect from unauthorized disclosure all classified information, and all information relating to intelligence sources and methods, that is furnished to the congressional intelligence committees or to Members of

Congress under this title. Such procedures shall be established in consultation with the Director of National Intelligence. In accordance with such procedures, each of the congressional intelligence committees shall promptly call to the attention of its respective House, or to any appropriate committee or committees of its respective House, any matter relating to intelligence activities requiring the attention of such House or such committee or committees.

(e) Nothing in this Act shall be construed as authority to withhold information from the congressional intelligence committees on the grounds that providing the information to the congressional intelligence committees would constitute the unauthorized disclosure of classified information or information relating to intelligence sources and methods.

(f) As used in this section, the term "intelligence activities" includes covert actions as defined in section 503(e), and includes financial intelligence activities.

SEC. 501A. [50 U.S.C. 3091a] CONGRESSIONAL OVERSIGHT OF CONTROLLED ACCESS PROGRAMS.

(a) Periodic Briefings.—

(1) Requirement.— Not less frequently than semiannually or upon request by one of the appropriate congressional committees or a member of congressional leadership, the Director of National Intelligence shall provide to such committees and congressional leadership a briefing on each controlled access program in effect.

(2) Contents.—Each briefing provided under paragraph (1) shall include, at a minimum, the following:

(A) A description of the activity of the controlled access programs during the period covered by the briefing.

(B) Documentation with respect to how the controlled access programs have achieved outcomes consistent with requirements documented by the Director and, as applicable, the Secretary of Defense.

(b) Limitations.—

(1) Establishment.— A head of an element of the intelligence community may not establish a controlled access program, or a compartment or subcompartment therein, until the head notifies the appropriate congressional committees and congressional leadership of such controlled access program, compartment, or subcompartment, as the case may be.

(2) Transfers.—

(A) Limitation.— Except as provided in subparagraph (B), a head of an element of the intelligence community may not transfer a capability from a controlled access program, including from a compartment or subcompartment therein to a compartment or subcompartment of another controlled access program, to a special access program (as defined in section 1152(g) of the National Defense Authorization Act for Fiscal Year 1994 (50 U.S.C. 3348(g))), or to anything else outside the controlled access program, until the head submits to the appropriate congressional committees and congressional leadership notice of the intent of the head to make such transfer.

(B) Exception.—The head of an element of the intelligence community may make a transfer described in subparagraph (A) without prior congressional notification if the head determines that doing so—

(i) is required to mitigate an urgent counterintelligence issue; or

(ii) is necessary to maintain access in the event of an organizational restructuring.

(c) Limitation on Spending.— Funds authorized to be appropriated for the National Intelligence Program may not be obligated or expended for any controlled access program, or a compartment or subcompartment therein, until the head of the element of the intelligence community responsible for the establishment of such program, compartment, or subcompartment, submits the notification required by subsection (b).

(d) Annual Reports.—

(1) Requirement.— On an annual basis, the head of each element of the intelligence community shall submit to the appropriate congressional committees and congressional leadership a report on controlled access programs administered by the head.

(2) Matters included.—Each report submitted under paragraph (1) shall include, with respect to the period covered by the report, the following:

(A) A list of all compartments and subcompartments of controlled access programs active as of the date of the report.

(B) A list of all compartments and subcompartments of controlled access programs terminated during the period covered by the report.

(C) With respect to the report submitted by the Director of National Intelligence, in addition to the matters specified in clauses (A) and (B)—

(i) a certification regarding whether the creation, validation, or substantial modification, including termination, for all existing and proposed controlled access programs, and the compartments and subcompartments within each, are substantiated and justified based on the information required by clause (ii); and

(ii) for each certification—

(I) the rationale for the revalidation, validation, or substantial modification, including termination, of each controlled access program, compartment, and subcompartment;

(II) the identification of a control officer for each controlled access program; and

(III) a statement of protection requirements for each controlled access program.

(e) Definitions.—In this section:

(1) Appropriate congressional committees.—The term "appropriate congressional committees" means—

(A) the congressional intelligence committees;

(B) the Committee on Appropriations of the Senate; and

(C) the Committee on Appropriations of the House of Representatives.

(2) Congressional leadership.—The term "congressional leadership" means—

(A) the majority leader of the Senate;

(B) the minority leader of the Senate;

(C) the Speaker of the House of Representatives; and

(D) the minority leader of the House of Representatives.

(3) CONTROLLED ACCESS PROGRAM.— The term "controlled access program" means a program created or managed pursuant to Intelligence Community Directive 906, or successor directive.

REPORTING OF INTELLIGENCE ACTIVITIES OTHER THAN COVERT ACTIONS

SEC. 502. [50 U.S.C. 3092] (a) IN GENERAL.—To the extent consistent with due regard for the protection from unauthorized disclosure of classified information relating to sensitive intelligence sources and methods or other exceptionally sensitive matters, the Director of National Intelligence and the heads of all departments, agencies, and other entities of the United States Government involved in intelligence activities shall—

(1) keep the congressional intelligence committees fully and currently informed of all intelligence activities, other than a covert action (as defined in section 503(e)), which are the responsibility of, are engaged in by, or are carried out for or on behalf of, any department, agency, or entity of the United States Government, including any significant anticipated intelligence activity and any significant intelligence failure; and

(2) furnish the congressional intelligence committees any information or material concerning intelligence activities (including the legal basis under which the intelligence activity is being or was conducted), other than covert actions, which is within their custody or control, and which is requested by either of the congressional intelligence committees in order to carry out its authorized responsibilities.

(b) FORM AND CONTENTS OF CERTAIN REPORTS.—Any report relating to a significant anticipated intelligence activity or a significant intelligence failure that is submitted to the congressional intelligence committees for purposes of subsection (a)(1) shall be in writing, and shall contain the following:

(1) A concise statement of any facts pertinent to such report.

(2) An explanation of the significance of the intelligence activity or intelligence failure covered by such report.

(c) STANDARDS AND PROCEDURES FOR CERTAIN REPORTS.— The Director of National Intelligence, in consultation with the heads of the departments, agencies, and entities referred to in subsection (a), shall establish standards and procedures applicable to reports covered by subsection (b).

PRESIDENTIAL APPROVAL AND REPORTING OF COVERT ACTIONS

SEC. 503. [50 U.S.C. 3093] (a) The President may not authorize the conduct of a covert action by departments, agencies, or entities of the United States Government unless the President determines such an action is necessary to support identifiable foreign policy objectives of the United States and is important to the national security of the United States, which determination shall be set forth in a finding that shall meet each of the following conditions:

(1) Each finding shall be in writing, unless immediate action by the United States is required and time does not permit the preparation of a written finding, in which case a written record of the President's decision shall be contemporaneously made and shall be reduced to a written finding as soon as possible but in no event more than 48 hours after the decision is made.

(2) Except as permitted by paragraph (1), a finding may not authorize or sanction a covert action, or any aspect of any such action, which already has occurred.

(3) Each finding shall specify each department, agency, or entity of the United States Government authorized to fund or otherwise participate in any significant way in such action. Any employee, contractor, or contract agent of a department, agency, or entity of the United States Government other than the Central Intelligence Agency directed to participate in any way in a covert action shall be subject either to the policies and regulations of the Central Intelligence Agency, or to written policies or regulations adopted by such department, agency, or entity, to govern such participation.

(4) Each finding shall specify whether it is contemplated that any third party which is not an element of, or a contractor or contract agent of, the United States Government, or is not otherwise subject to United States Government policies and regulations, will be used to fund or otherwise participate in any significant way in the covert action concerned, or be used to undertake the covert action concerned on behalf of the United States.

(5) A finding may not authorize any action that would violate the Constitution or any statute of the United States.

(b) To the extent consistent with due regard for the protection from unauthorized disclosure of classified information relating to sensitive intelligence sources and methods or other exceptionally sensitive matters, the Director of National Intelligence and the heads of all departments, agencies, and entities of the United States Government involved in a covert action—

(1) shall keep the congressional intelligence committees fully and currently informed of all covert actions which are the responsibility of, are engaged in by, or are carried out for or on behalf of, any department, agency, or entity of the United States Government, including significant failures; and

(2) shall furnish to the congressional intelligence committees any information or material concerning covert actions (including the legal basis under which the covert action is being or was conducted) which is in the possession, custody, or control of any department, agency, or entity of the United States Government and which is requested by either of the congressional intelligence committees in order to carry out its authorized responsibilities.

(c)(1) The President shall ensure that any finding approved pursuant to subsection (a) shall be reported in writing to the congressional intelligence committees as soon as possible after such approval and before the initiation of the covert action authorized by the finding, except as otherwise provided in paragraph (2) and paragraph (3).

(2) If the President determines that it is essential to limit access to the finding to meet extraordinary circumstances affecting vital interests of the United States,

the finding may be reported to the chairmen and ranking minority members of the congressional intelligence committees, the Speaker and minority leader of the House of Representatives, the majority and minority leaders of the Senate, and such other member or members of the congressional leadership as may be included by the President.

(3) Whenever a finding is not reported pursuant to paragraph (1) or (2) of this subsection, the President shall fully inform the congressional intelligence committees in a timely fashion and shall provide a statement of the reasons for not giving prior notice.

(4) In a case under paragraph (1), (2), or (3), a copy of the finding, signed by the President, shall be provided to the chairman of each congressional intelligence committee.

(5)(A) When access to a finding, or a notification provided under subsection (d)(1), is limited to the Members of Congress specified in paragraph (2), a written statement of the reasons for limiting such access shall also be provided.

(B) Not later than 180 days after a statement of reasons is submitted in accordance with subparagraph (A) or this subparagraph, the President shall ensure that—

(i) all members of the congressional intelligence committees are provided access to the finding or notification; or

(ii) a statement of reasons that it is essential to continue to limit access to such finding or such notification to meet extraordinary circumstances affecting vital interests of the United States is submitted to the Members of Congress specified in paragraph (2).

(d)(1) The President shall ensure that the congressional intelligence committees, or, if applicable, the Members of Congress specified in subsection (c)(2), are notified in writing of any significant change in a previously approved covert action, or any significant undertaking pursuant to a previously approved finding, in the same manner as findings are reported pursuant to subsection (c).

(2) In determining whether an activity constitutes a significant undertaking for purposes of paragraph (1), the President shall consider whether the activity—

(A) involves significant risk of loss of life;

(B) requires an expansion of existing authorities, including authorities relating to research, development, or operations;

(C) results in the expenditure of significant funds or other resources;

(D) requires notification under section 504;

(E) gives rise to a significant risk of disclosing intelligence sources or methods; or

(F) presents a reasonably foreseeable risk of serious damage to the diplomatic relations of the United States if such activity were disclosed without authorization.

(e) As used in this title, the term "covert action" means an activity or activities of the United States Government to influence political, economic, or military conditions abroad, where it is intended that the role of the United States Government will not be apparent or acknowledged publicly, but does not include—

(1) activities the primary purpose of which is to acquire intelligence, traditional counterintelligence activities, traditional activities to improve or maintain the operational security of United States Government programs, or administrative activities;

(2) traditional diplomatic or military activities or routine support to such activities;

(3) traditional law enforcement activities conducted by United States Government law enforcement agencies or routine support to such activities; or

(4) activities to provide routine support to the overt activities (other than activities described in paragraph (1), (2), or (3)) of other United States Government agencies abroad.

(f) No covert action may be conducted which is intended to influence United States political processes, public opinion, policies, or media.

(g)(1) In any case where access to a finding reported under subsection (c) or notification provided under subsection (d)(1) is not made available to all members of a congressional intelligence committee in accordance with subsection (c)(2), the President shall notify all members of such committee that such finding or such notification has been provided only to the members specified in subsection (c)(2).

(2) In any case where access to a finding reported under subsection (c) or notification provided under subsection (d)(1) is not made available to all members of a congressional intelligence committee in accordance with subsection (c)(2), the President shall provide to all members of such committee a general description regarding the finding or notification, as applicable, consistent with the reasons for not yet fully informing all members of such committee.

(3) The President shall maintain—

(A) a record of the members of Congress to whom a finding is reported under subsection (c) or notification is provided under subsection (d)(1) and the date on which each member of Congress receives such finding or notification; and

(B) each written statement provided under subsection (c)(5).

(h) For each type of activity undertaken as part of a covert action, the President shall establish in writing a plan to respond to the unauthorized public disclosure of that type of activity.

FUNDING OF INTELLIGENCE ACTIVITIES

SEC. 504. [50 U.S.C. 3094] (a) Appropriated funds available to an intelligence agency may be obligated or expended for an intelligence or intelligence-related activity only if—

(1) those funds were specifically authorized by Congress for use for such intelligence or intelligence-related activities; or

(2) in the case of funds from the Reserve for Contingencies of the Central Intelligence Agency and consistent with the provisions of section 503 of this Act concerning any significant anticipated intelligence activity, the Director of the Central Intelligence Agency has notified the appropriate congressional committees

of the intent to make such funds available for such activity; or

(3) in the case of funds specifically authorized by the Congress for a different activity—

(A) the activity to be funded is a higher priority intelligence or intelligence-related activity;

(B) the use of such funds for such activity supports an emergent need, improves program effectiveness, or increases efficiency; and

(C) the Director of National Intelligence, the Secretary of Defense, or the Attorney General, as appropriate, has notified the appropriate congressional committees of the intent to make such funds available for such activity;

(4) nothing in this subsection prohibits obligation or expenditure of funds available to an intelligence agency in accordance with sections 1535 and 1536 of title 31, United States Code.

(b) Funds available to an intelligence agency may not be made available for any intelligence or intelligence-related activity for which funds were denied by the Congress.

(c) No funds appropriated for, or otherwise available to, any department, agency, or entity of the United States Government may be expended, or may be directed to be expended, for any covert action, as defined in section 503(e), unless and until a Presidential finding required by subsection (a) of section 503 has been signed or otherwise issued in accordance with that subsection.

(d)(1) Except as otherwise specifically provided by law, funds available to an intelligence agency that are not appropriated funds may be obligated or expended for an intelligence or intelligence-related activity only if those funds are used for activities reported to the appropriate congressional committees pursuant to procedures which identify—

(A) the types of activities for which nonappropriated funds may be expended; and

(B) the circumstances under which an activity must be reported as a significant anticipated intelligence activity before such funds can be expended.

(2) Procedures for purposes of paragraph (1) shall be jointly agreed upon by the congressional intelligence committees and, as appropriate, the Director of National Intelligence or the Secretary of Defense.

(e) As used in this section—

(1) the term "intelligence agency" means any department, agency, or other entity of the United States involved in intelligence or intelligence-related activities;

(2) the term "appropriate congressional committees" means the Permanent Select Committee on Intelligence and the Committee on Appropriations of the House of Representatives and the Select Committee on Intelligence and the Committee on Appropriations of the Senate; and

(3) the term "specifically authorized by the Congress" means that—

(A) the activity and the amount of funds proposed to be used for that activity were identified in a formal budget request to the Congress, but funds shall be deemed to be specifically authorized for that activity only to the extent that the Congress both authorized the funds to be appropriated for that activity and appropriated the funds for that activity; or

(B) although the funds were not formally requested, the Congress both specifically authorized the appropriation of the funds for the activity and appropriated the funds for the activity.

NOTICE TO CONGRESS OF CERTAIN TRANSFERS OF DEFENSE ARTICLES AND DEFENSE SERVICES

SEC. 505. [50 U.S.C. 3095] (a)(1) The transfer of a defense article or defense service, or the anticipated transfer in any fiscal year of any aggregation of defense articles or defense services, exceeding $1,000,000 in value by an intelligence agency to a recipient outside that agency shall be considered a significant anticipated intelligence activity for the purpose of this title.

(2) Paragraph (1) does not apply if—

(A) the transfer is being made to a department, agency, or other entity of the United States (so long as there will not be a subsequent retransfer of the defense articles or defense services outside the United States Government in conjunction with an intelligence or intelligence-related activity); or

(B) the transfer—

(i) is being made pursuant to authorities contained in part II of the Foreign Assistance Act of 1961, the Arms Export Control Act, title 10 of the United States Code (including a law enacted pursuant to section 8677(a) of title 10), or the Federal Property and Administrative Services Act of 1949, and

(ii) is not being made in conjunction with an intelligence or intelligence-related activity.

(3) An intelligence agency may not transfer any defense articles or defense services outside the agency in conjunction with any intelligence or intelligence-related activity for which funds were denied by the Congress.

(b) As used in this section—

(1) the term "intelligence agency" means any department, agency, or other entity of the United States involved in intelligence or intelligence-related activities;

(2) the terms "defense articles" and "defense services" mean the items on the United States Munitions List pursuant to section 38 of the Arms Export Control Act (22 CFR part 121);

(3) the term "transfer" means—

(A) in the case of defense articles, the transfer of possession of those articles; and

(B) in the case of defense services, the provision of those services; and

(4) the term "value" means—

(A) in the case of defense articles, the greater of—

(i) the original acquisition cost to the United States Government, plus the cost of improvements or other modifications made by or on behalf of the Government; or

(ii) the replacement cost; and

(B) in the case of defense services, the full cost to the Government of providing the services.

SPECIFICITY OF NATIONAL INTELLIGENCE PROGRAM BUDGET AMOUNTS FOR COUNTERTERRORISM, COUNTERPROLIFERATION, COUNTERNARCOTICS, AND COUNTERINTELLIGENCE

SEC. 506. [50 U.S.C. 3096] (a) IN GENERAL.—The budget justification materials submitted to Congress in support of the budget of the President for a fiscal year that is submitted to Congress under section 1105(a) of title 31, United States Code, shall set forth separately the aggregate amount requested for that fiscal year for the National Intelligence Program for each of the following:

(1) Counterterrorism.

(2) Counterproliferation.

(3) Counternarcotics.

(4) Counterintelligence.

(b) ELECTION OF CLASSIFIED OR UNCLASSIFIED FORM.— Amounts set forth under subsection (a) may be set forth in unclassified form or classified form, at the election of the Director of National Intelligence.

BUDGET TREATMENT OF COSTS OF ACQUISITION OF MAJOR SYSTEMS BY THE INTELLIGENCE COMMUNITY

SEC. 506A. [50 U.S.C. 3097] (a) INDEPENDENT COST ESTIMATES.—(1) The Director of National Intelligence shall, in consultation with the head of each element of the intelligence community concerned, prepare an independent cost estimate of the full life-cycle cost of development, procurement, and operation of each major system to be acquired by the intelligence community.

(2)(A) Each independent cost estimate for a major system shall, to the maximum extent practicable, specify the amount required to be appropriated and obligated to develop, procure, and operate the major system in each fiscal year of the proposed period of development, procurement, and operation of the major system.

(B) For major system acquisitions requiring a service or capability from another acquisition or program to deliver the end-to-end functionality for the intelligence community end users, independent cost estimates shall include, to the maximum extent practicable, all estimated costs across all pertinent elements of the intelligence community. For collection programs, such cost estimates shall include the cost of new analyst training, new hardware and software for data exploitation and analysis, and any unique or additional costs for data processing, storing, and power, space, and cooling across the life cycle of the program. If such costs for processing, exploitation, dissemination, and storage are scheduled to be executed in other elements of the intelligence community, the independent cost estimate shall identify and annotate such costs for such other elements accordingly.

(3)(A) In the case of a program of the intelligence community that qualifies as a major system, an independent cost estimate shall be prepared before the submission to Congress of the budget of the President for the first fiscal year in which appropriated funds are anticipated to be obligated for the development or procurement of such major system.

(B) In the case of a program of the intelligence community for which an independent cost estimate was not previously required to be prepared under this section, including a program for which development or procurement commenced before the date of the enactment of the Intelligence Authorization Act for Fiscal Year 2004, if the aggregate future costs of development or procurement (or any combination of such activities) of the program will exceed $500,000,000 (in current fiscal year dollars), the program shall qualify as a major system for purposes of this section, and an independent cost estimate for such major system shall be prepared before the submission to Congress of the budget of the President for the first fiscal year thereafter in which appropriated funds are anticipated to be obligated for such major system.

(4) The independent cost estimate for a major system shall be updated upon—

(A) the completion of any preliminary design review associated with the major system;

(B) any significant modification to the anticipated design of the major system; or

(C) any change in circumstances that renders the current independent cost estimate for the major system inaccurate.

(5) Any update of an independent cost estimate for a major system under paragraph (4) shall meet all requirements for independent cost estimates under this section, and shall be treated as the most current independent cost estimate for the major system until further updated under that paragraph.

(b) Preparation of Independent Cost Estimates.—(1) The Director shall establish within the Office of the Director of National Intelligence for Community Management an office which shall be responsible for preparing independent cost estimates, and any updates thereof, under subsection (a), unless a designation is made under paragraph (2).

(2) In the case of the acquisition of a major system for an element of the intelligence community within the Department of Defense, the Director and the Secretary of Defense shall provide that the independent cost estimate, and any updates thereof, under subsection (a) be prepared by an entity jointly designated by the Director and the Secretary in accordance with section 2434(b)(1)(A) of title 10, United States Code.

(c) Utilization in Budgets of President.—(1) If the budget of the President requests appropriations for any fiscal year for the development or procurement of a major system by the intelligence community, the President shall, subject to paragraph (2), request in such budget an amount of appropriations for the development or procurement, as the case may be, of the major system that is equivalent to the amount of appropriations identified in the most current independent cost estimate for the major system for obligation for each fiscal year for which appropriations are requested for the major system in such budget.

(2) If the amount of appropriations requested in the budget of the President for

the development or procurement of a major system is less than the amount of appropriations identified in the most current independent cost estimate for the major system for obligation for each fiscal year for which appropriations are requested for the major system in such budget, the President shall include in the budget justification materials submitted to Congress in support of such budget—

(A) an explanation for the difference between the amount of appropriations requested and the amount of appropriations identified in the most current independent cost estimate;

(B) a description of the importance of the major system to the national security;

(C) an assessment of the consequences for the funding of all programs of the National Intelligence Program in future fiscal years if the most current independent cost estimate for the major system is accurate and additional appropriations are required in future fiscal years to ensure the continued development or procurement of the major system, including the consequences of such funding shortfalls on the major system and all other programs of the National Intelligence Program; and

(D) such other information on the funding of the major system as the President considers appropriate.

(d) Inclusion of Estimates in Budget Justification Materials.— The budget justification materials submitted to Congress in support of the budget of the President shall include the most current independent cost estimate under this section for each major system for which appropriations are requested in such budget for any fiscal year.

(e) Definitions.—In this section:

(1) The term "budget of the President" means the budget of the President for a fiscal year as submitted to Congress under section 1105(a) of title 31, United States Code.

(2)(A) The term "independent cost estimate" means a pragmatic and neutral analysis, assessment, and quantification of all costs and risks associated with the development, acquisition, procurement, operation, and sustainment of a major system across its proposed life cycle, which shall be based on programmatic and technical specifications provided by the office within the element of the intelligence community with primary responsibility for the development, procurement, or operation of the major system.

(B) In accordance with subsection (a)(2)(B), each independent cost estimate shall include all costs required across elements of the intelligence community to develop, acquire, procure, operate, and sustain the system to provide the end-to-end intelligence functionality of the system, including—

(i) for collection programs, the cost of new analyst training, new hardware and software for data exploitation and analysis, and any unique or additional costs for data processing, storing, and power, space, and cooling across the life cycle of the program; and

(ii) costs for processing, exploitation, dissemination, and storage scheduled to be executed in other elements of the intelligence community.

(3) The term "major system" means any significant program of an element

of the intelligence community with projected total development and procurement costs exceeding $500,000,000 (based on fiscal year 2010 constant dollars), which costs shall include all end-to-end program costs, including costs associated with the development and procurement of the program and any other costs associated with the development and procurement of systems required to support or utilize the program.

ANNUAL PERSONNEL LEVEL ASSESSMENTS FOR THE INTELLIGENCE COMMUNITY

SEC. 506B. [50 U.S.C. 3098] (a) REQUIREMENT TO PROVIDE.— The Director of National Intelligence shall, in consultation with the head of each element of the intelligence community, prepare an annual personnel level assessment for such element that assesses the personnel levels for such element for the fiscal year following the fiscal year in which the assessment is submitted.

(b) SCHEDULE.— Each assessment required by subsection (a) shall be submitted to the congressional intelligence committees each year at the time that the President submits to Congress the budget for a fiscal year pursuant to section 1105 of title 31, United States Code.

(c) CONTENTS.—Each assessment required by subsection (a) submitted during a fiscal year shall contain the following information for the element of the intelligence community concerned:

(1) The budget submission for personnel costs for the upcoming fiscal year.

(2) The dollar and percentage increase or decrease of such costs as compared to the personnel costs of the current fiscal year.

(3) The dollar and percentage increase or decrease of such costs as compared to the personnel costs during the prior 5 fiscal years.

(4) The number of full-time equivalent positions that is the basis for which personnel funds are requested for the upcoming fiscal year.

(5) The numerical and percentage increase or decrease of the number referred to in paragraph (4) as compared to the number of full-time equivalent positions of the current fiscal year.

(6) The numerical and percentage increase or decrease of the number referred to in paragraph (4) as compared to the number of full-time equivalent positions during the prior 5 fiscal years.

(7) The best estimate of the number and costs of core contract personnel to be funded by the element for the upcoming fiscal year.

(8) The numerical and percentage increase or decrease of such costs of core contract personnel as compared to the best estimate of the costs of core contract personnel of the current fiscal year.

(9) The numerical and percentage increase or decrease of such number and such costs of core contract personnel as compared to the number and cost of core contract personnel during the prior 5 fiscal years.

(10) A justification for the requested personnel and core contract personnel levels.

(11) The best estimate of the number of intelligence collectors and analysts employed by each element of the intelligence community.

(12) The best estimate of the number of intelligence collectors and analysts contracted by each element of the intelligence community and a description of the functions performed by such contractors.

(13) A statement by the Director of National Intelligence that, based on current and projected funding, the element concerned will have sufficient—

(A) internal infrastructure to support the requested personnel and core contract personnel levels;

(B) training resources to support the requested personnel levels; and

(C) funding to support the administrative and operational activities of the requested personnel levels.

VULNERABILITY ASSESSMENTS OF MAJOR SYSTEMS

SEC. 506C. [50 U.S.C. 3099] (a) INITIAL VULNERABILITY ASSESSMENTS.—(1)(A) Except as provided in subparagraph (B), the Director of National Intelligence shall conduct and submit to the congressional intelligence committees an initial vulnerability assessment for each major system and its significant items of supply—

(i) except as provided in clause (ii), prior to the completion of Milestone B or an equivalent acquisition decision for the major system; or

(ii) prior to the date that is 1 year after the date of the enactment of the Intelligence Authorization Act for Fiscal Year 2010 in the case of a major system for which Milestone B or an equivalent acquisition decision—

(I) was completed prior to such date of enactment; or

(II) is completed on a date during the 180-day period following such date of enactment.

(B) The Director may submit to the congressional intelligence committees an initial vulnerability assessment required by clause (ii) of subparagraph (A) not later than 180 days after the date such assessment is required to be submitted under such clause if the Director notifies the congressional intelligence committees of the extension of the submission date under this subparagraph and provides a justification for such extension.

(C) The initial vulnerability assessment of a major system and its significant items of supply shall include use of an analysis-based approach to—

(i) identify vulnerabilities;

(ii) define exploitation potential;

(iii) examine the system's potential effectiveness;

(iv) determine overall vulnerability; and

(v) make recommendations for risk reduction.

(2) If an initial vulnerability assessment for a major system is not submitted to the congressional intelligence committees as required by paragraph (1), funds appropriated for the acquisition of the major system may not be obligated for a major contract related to the major system. Such prohibition on the obligation of funds for the acquisition of the major system shall cease to apply on the date on which the congressional intelligence committees receive the initial vulnerability assessment.

(b) SUBSEQUENT VULNERABILITY ASSESSMENTS.—(1) The Director of National

Intelligence shall, periodically throughout the procurement of a major system or if the Director determines that a change in circumstances warrants the issuance of a subsequent vulnerability assessment, conduct a subsequent vulnerability assessment of each major system and its significant items of supply within the National Intelligence Program.

(2) Upon the request of a congressional intelligence committee, the Director of National Intelligence may, if appropriate, recertify the previous vulnerability assessment or may conduct a subsequent vulnerability assessment of a particular major system and its significant items of supply within the National Intelligence Program.

(3) Any subsequent vulnerability assessment of a major system and its significant items of supply shall include use of an analysis-based approach and, if applicable, a testing-based approach, to monitor the exploitation potential of such system and reexamine the factors described in clauses (i) through (v) of subsection (a)(1)(C).

(c) MAJOR SYSTEM MANAGEMENT.— The Director of National Intelligence shall give due consideration to the vulnerability assessments prepared for a given major system when developing and determining the National Intelligence Program budget.

(d) CONGRESSIONAL OVERSIGHT.—(1) The Director of National Intelligence shall provide to the congressional intelligence committees a copy of each vulnerability assessment conducted under subsection (a) or (b) not later than 10 days after the date of the completion of such assessment.

(2) The Director of National Intelligence shall provide the congressional intelligence committees with a proposed schedule for subsequent periodic vulnerability assessments of a major system under subsection (b)(1) when providing such committees with the initial vulnerability assessment under subsection (a) of such system as required by paragraph (1).

(e) DEFINITIONS.—In this section:

(1) The term "item of supply" has the meaning given that term in section 4(10) of the Office of Federal Procurement Policy Act (41 U.S.C. 403(10)).

(2) The term "major contract" means each of the 6 largest prime, associate, or Government-furnished equipment contracts under a major system that is in excess of $40,000,000 and that is not a firm, fixed price contract.

(3) The term "major system" has the meaning given that term in section 506A(e).

(4) The term "Milestone B" means a decision to enter into major system development and demonstration pursuant to guidance prescribed by the Director of National Intelligence.

(5) The term "vulnerability assessment" means the process of identifying and quantifying vulnerabilities in a major system and its significant items of supply.

INTELLIGENCE COMMUNITY BUSINESS SYSTEM TRANSFORMATION

SEC. 506D. [50 U.S.C. 3100] (a) LIMITATION ON OBLIGATION OF FUNDS.—(1) Subject to paragraph (3), no funds appropriated to any element of the intelligence community may be obligated for an intelligence community business system transformation that will have a total cost in excess of $3,000,000 unless—

(A) the Director of the Office of Business Transformation of the Office of the Director of National Intelligence makes a certification described in paragraph (2) with respect to such intelligence community business system transformation; and

(B) such certification is approved by the board established under subsection (f).

(2) The certification described in this paragraph for an intelligence community business system transformation is a certification made by the Director of the Office of Business Transformation of the Office of the Director of National Intelligence that the intelligence community business system transformation—

(A) complies with the enterprise architecture under subsection (b) and such other policies and standards that the Director of National Intelligence considers appropriate; or

(B) is necessary—

(i) to achieve a critical national security capability or address a critical requirement; or

(ii) to prevent a significant adverse effect on a project that is needed to achieve an essential capability, taking into consideration any alternative solutions for preventing such adverse effect.

(3) With respect to a fiscal year after fiscal year 2010, the amount referred to in paragraph (1) in the matter preceding subparagraph (A) shall be equal to the sum of—

(A) the amount in effect under such paragraph (1) for the preceding fiscal year (determined after application of this paragraph), plus

(B) such amount multiplied by the annual percentage increase in the consumer price index (all items; U.S. city average) as of September of the previous fiscal year.

(b) Enterprise Architecture for Intelligence Community Business Systems.—(1) The Director of National Intelligence shall, acting through the board established under subsection (f), develop and implement an enterprise architecture to cover all intelligence community business systems, and the functions and activities supported by such business systems. The enterprise architecture shall be sufficiently defined to effectively guide, constrain, and permit implementation of interoperable intelligence community business system solutions, consistent with applicable policies and procedures established by the Director of the Office of Management and Budget.

(2) The enterprise architecture under paragraph (1) shall include the following:

(A) An information infrastructure that will enable the intelligence community to—

(i) comply with all Federal accounting, financial management, and reporting requirements;

(ii) routinely produce timely, accurate, and reliable financial information for management purposes;

(iii) integrate budget, accounting, and program information and systems; and

(iv) provide for the measurement of performance, including the ability to produce timely, relevant, and reliable cost information.

(B) Policies, procedures, data standards, and system interface requirements that apply uniformly throughout the intelligence community.

(c) Responsibilities for Intelligence Community Business System Transformation.— The Director of National Intelligence shall be responsible for the entire life cycle of an intelligence community business system transformation, including review, approval, and oversight of the planning, design, acquisition, deployment, operation, and maintenance of the business system transformation.

(d) Intelligence Community Business System Investment Review.—(1) The Director of the Office of Business Transformation of the Office of the Director of National Intelligence shall establish and implement, not later than 60 days after the enactment of the Intelligence Authorization Act for Fiscal Year 2010, an investment review process for the intelligence community business systems for which the Director of the Office of Business Transformation is responsible.

(2) The investment review process under paragraph (1) shall—

(A) meet the requirements of section 11312 of title 40, United States Code; and

(B) specifically set forth the responsibilities of the Director of the Office of Business Transformation under such review process.

(3) The investment review process under paragraph (1) shall include the following elements:

(A) Review and approval by an investment review board (consisting of appropriate representatives of the intelligence community) of each intelligence community business system as an investment before the obligation of funds for such system.

(B) Periodic review, but not less often than annually, of every intelligence community business system investment.

(C) Thresholds for levels of review to ensure appropriate review of intelligence community business system investments depending on the scope, complexity, and cost of the system involved.

(D) Procedures for making certifications in accordance with the requirements of subsection (a)(2).

[Note: Subsection (e) was repealed by section 310(a)(3) of Public Law 112–277; enacted January 14, 2013.]

(f) Intelligence Community Business System Transformation Governance Board.—(1) The Director of National Intelligence shall establish a board within the intelligence community business system transformation governance structure (in this subsection referred to as the “Board”).

(2) The Board shall—

(A) recommend to the Director policies and procedures necessary to effectively integrate all business activities and any transformation, reform, reorganization, or process improvement initiatives undertaken within the intelligence community;

(B) review and approve any major update of—

(i) the enterprise architecture developed under subsection (b); and

(ii) any plans for an intelligence community business systems modernization;

(C) manage cross-domain integration consistent with such enterprise architecture;

(D) coordinate initiatives for intelligence community business system transformation to maximize benefits and minimize costs for the intelligence community, and periodically report to the Director on the status of efforts to carry out an intelligence community business system transformation;

(E) ensure that funds are obligated for intelligence community business system transformation in a manner consistent with subsection (a); and

(F) carry out such other duties as the Director shall specify.

(g) RELATION TO ANNUAL REGISTRATION REQUIREMENTS.— Nothing in this section shall be construed to alter the requirements of section 8083 of the Department of Defense Appropriations Act, 2005 (Public Law 108–287; 118 Stat. 989), with regard to information technology systems (as defined in subsection (d) of such section).

(h) RELATIONSHIP TO DEFENSE BUSINESS ENTERPRISE ARCHITECTURE.— Nothing in this section shall be construed to exempt funds authorized to be appropriated to the Department of Defense from the requirements of section 2222 of title 10, United States Code, to the extent that such requirements are otherwise applicable.

(i) RELATION TO CLINGER-COHEN ACT.—(1) Executive agency responsibilities in chapter 113 of title 40, United States Code, for any intelligence community business system transformation shall be exercised jointly by—

(A) the Director of National Intelligence and the Chief Information Officer of the Intelligence Community; and

(B) the head of the executive agency that contains the element of the intelligence community involved and the chief information officer of that executive agency.

(2) The Director of National Intelligence and the head of the executive agency referred to in paragraph (1)(B) shall enter into a Memorandum of Understanding to carry out the requirements of this section in a manner that best meets the needs of the intelligence community and the executive agency.

(j) REPORTS.—Not later than March 31 of each of the years 2011 through 2014, the Director of National Intelligence shall submit to the congressional intelligence committees a report on the compliance of the intelligence community with the requirements of this section. Each such report shall—

(1) describe actions taken and proposed for meeting the requirements of subsection (a), including—

(A) specific milestones and actual performance against specified performance measures, and any revision of such milestones and performance measures; and

(B) specific actions on the intelligence community business system transformations submitted for certification under such subsection;

(2) identify the number of intelligence community business system

transformations that received a certification described in subsection (a)(2); and

(3) describe specific improvements in business operations and cost savings resulting from successful intelligence community business systems transformation efforts.

(k) DEFINITIONS.—In this section:

(1) The term "enterprise architecture" has the meaning given that term in section 3601(4) of title 44, United States Code.

(2) The terms "information system" and "information technology" have the meanings given those terms in section 11101 of title 40, United States Code.

(3) The term "intelligence community business system" means an information system, including a national security system, that is operated by, for, or on behalf of an element of the intelligence community, including a financial system, mixed system, financial data feeder system, and the business infrastructure capabilities shared by the systems of the business enterprise architecture, including people, process, and technology, that build upon the core infrastructure used to support business activities, such as acquisition, financial management, logistics, strategic planning and budgeting, installations and environment, and human resource management.

(4) The term "intelligence community business system transformation" means—

(A) the acquisition or development of a new intelligence community business system; or

(B) any significant modification or enhancement of an existing intelligence community business system (other than necessary to maintain current services).

(5) The term "national security system" has the meaning given that term in section 3542 of title 44, United States Code.

(6) The term "Office of Business Transformation of the Office of the Director of National Intelligence" includes any successor office that assumes the functions of the Office of Business Transformation of the Office of the Director of National Intelligence as carried out by the Office of Business Transformation on the date of the enactment of the Intelligence Authorization Act for Fiscal Year 2010.

REPORTS ON THE ACQUISITION OF MAJOR SYSTEMS

SEC. 506E. [50 U.S.C. 3101] (a) DEFINITIONS.—In this section:

(1) The term "cost estimate"—

(A) means an assessment and quantification of all costs and risks associated with the acquisition of a major system based upon reasonably available information at the time the Director establishes the 2010 adjusted total acquisition cost for such system pursuant to subsection (h) or restructures such system pursuant to section 506F(c); and

(B) does not mean an "independent cost estimate".

(2) The term "critical cost growth threshold" means a percentage increase in the total acquisition cost for a major system of at least 25 percent over the total acquisition cost for the major system as shown in the current Baseline Estimate for

the major system.

(3)(A) The term "current Baseline Estimate" means the projected total acquisition cost of a major system that is—

(i) approved by the Director, or a designee of the Director, at Milestone B or an equivalent acquisition decision for the development, procurement, and construction of such system;

(ii) approved by the Director at the time such system is restructured pursuant to section 506F(c); or

(iii) the 2010 adjusted total acquisition cost determined pursuant to subsection (h).

(B) A current Baseline Estimate may be in the form of an independent cost estimate.

(4) Except as otherwise specifically provided, the term "Director" means the Director of National Intelligence.

(5) The term "independent cost estimate" has the meaning given that term in section 506A(e).

(6) The term "major contract" means each of the 6 largest prime, associate, or Government-furnished equipment contracts under a major system that is in excess of $40,000,000 and that is not a firm, fixed price contract.

(7) The term "major system" has the meaning given that term in section 506A(e).

(8) The term "Milestone B" means a decision to enter into major system development and demonstration pursuant to guidance prescribed by the Director.

(9) The term "program manager" means—

(A) the head of the element of the intelligence community that is responsible for the budget, cost, schedule, and performance of a major system; or

(B) in the case of a major system within the Office of the Director of National Intelligence, the deputy who is responsible for the budget, cost, schedule, and performance of the major system.

(10) The term "significant cost growth threshold" means the percentage increase in the total acquisition cost for a major system of at least 15 percent over the total acquisition cost for such system as shown in the current Baseline Estimate for such system.

(11) The term "total acquisition cost" means the amount equal to the total cost for development and procurement of, and system-specific construction for, a major system.

(b) MAJOR SYSTEM COST REPORTS.—(1) The program manager for a major system shall, on a quarterly basis, submit to the Director a major system cost report as described in paragraph (2).

(2) A major system cost report shall include the following information (as of the last day of the quarter for which the report is made):

(A) The total acquisition cost for the major system.

(B) Any cost variance or schedule variance in a major contract for the major system since the contract was entered into.

(C) Any changes from a major system schedule milestones or performances that are known, expected, or anticipated by the program manager.

(D) Any significant changes in the total acquisition cost for development and procurement of any software component of the major system, schedule milestones for such software component of the major system, or expected performance of such software component of the major system that are known, expected, or anticipated by the program manager.

(3) Each major system cost report required by paragraph (1) shall be submitted not more than 30 days after the end of the reporting quarter.

(c) REPORTS FOR BREACH OF SIGNIFICANT OR CRITICAL COST GROWTH THRESHOLDS.— If the program manager of a major system for which a report has previously been submitted under subsection (b) determines at any time during a quarter that there is reasonable cause to believe that the total acquisition cost for the major system has increased by a percentage equal to or greater than the significant cost growth threshold or critical cost growth threshold and if a report indicating an increase of such percentage or more has not previously been submitted to the Director, then the program manager shall immediately submit to the Director a major system cost report containing the information, determined as of the date of the report, required under subsection (b).

(d) NOTIFICATION TO CONGRESS OF COST GROWTH.—(1) Whenever a major system cost report is submitted to the Director, the Director shall determine whether the current acquisition cost for the major system has increased by a percentage equal to or greater than the significant cost growth threshold or the critical cost growth threshold.

(2) If the Director determines that the current total acquisition cost has increased by a percentage equal to or greater than the significant cost growth threshold or critical cost growth threshold, the Director shall submit to Congress a Major System Congressional Report pursuant to subsection (e).

(e) REQUIREMENT FOR MAJOR SYSTEM CONGRESSIONAL REPORT.—(1) Whenever the Director determines under subsection (d) that the total acquisition cost of a major system has increased by a percentage equal to or greater than the significant cost growth threshold for the major system, a Major System Congressional Report shall be submitted to Congress not later than 45 days after the date on which the Director receives the major system cost report for such major system.

(2) If the total acquisition cost of a major system (as determined by the Director under subsection (d)) increases by a percentage equal to or greater than the critical cost growth threshold for the program or subprogram, the Director shall take actions consistent with the requirements of section 506F.

(f) MAJOR SYSTEM CONGRESSIONAL REPORT ELEMENTS.—(1) Except as provided in paragraph (2), each Major System Congressional Report shall include the following:

(A) The name of the major system.

(B) The date of the preparation of the report.

(C) The program phase of the major system as of the date of the preparation of the report.

(D) The estimate of the total acquisition cost for the major system expressed in constant base-year dollars and in current dollars.

(E) The current Baseline Estimate for the major system in constant base-year dollars and in current dollars.

(F) A statement of the reasons for any increase in total acquisition cost for the major system.

(G) The completion status of the major system—

(i) expressed as the percentage that the number of years for which funds have been appropriated for the major system is of the number of years for which it is planned that funds will be appropriated for the major system; and

(ii) expressed as the percentage that the amount of funds that have been appropriated for the major system is of the total amount of funds which it is planned will be appropriated for the major system.

(H) The fiscal year in which the major system was first authorized and in which funds for such system were first appropriated by Congress.

(I) The current change and the total change, in dollars and expressed as a percentage, in the total acquisition cost for the major system, stated both in constant base-year dollars and in current dollars.

(J) The quantity of end items to be acquired under the major system and the current change and total change, if any, in that quantity.

(K) The identities of the officers responsible for management and cost control of the major system.

(L) The action taken and proposed to be taken to control future cost growth of the major system.

(M) Any changes made in the performance or schedule milestones of the major system and the extent to which such changes have contributed to the increase in total acquisition cost for the major system.

(N) The following contract performance assessment information with respect to each major contract under the major system:

(i) The name of the contractor.

(ii) The phase that the contract is in at the time of the preparation of the report.

(iii) The percentage of work under the contract that has been completed.

(iv) Any current change and the total change, in dollars and expressed as a percentage, in the contract cost.

(v) The percentage by which the contract is currently ahead of or behind schedule.

(vi) A narrative providing a summary explanation of the most significant occurrences, including cost and schedule variances under major contracts of the major system, contributing to the changes identified and a discussion of the effect these occurrences will have on the future costs and schedule of the major system.

(O) In any case in which one or more problems with a software component of the major system significantly contributed to the increase in costs of the major system, the action taken and proposed to be taken to solve such problems.

(2) A Major System Congressional Report prepared for a major system for which

the increase in the total acquisition cost is due to termination or cancellation of the entire major system shall include only—

(A) the information described in subparagraphs (A) through (F) of paragraph (1); and

(B) the total percentage change in total acquisition cost for such system.

(g) Prohibition on Obligation of Funds.—If a determination of an increase by a percentage equal to or greater than the significant cost growth threshold is made by the Director under subsection (d) and a Major System Congressional Report containing the information described in subsection (f) is not submitted to Congress under subsection (e)(1), or if a determination of an increase by a percentage equal to or greater than the critical cost growth threshold is made by the Director under subsection (d) and the Major System Congressional Report containing the information described in subsection (f) and section 506F(b)(3) and the certification required by section 506F(b)(2) are not submitted to Congress under subsection (e)(2), funds appropriated for construction, research, development, test, evaluation, and procurement may not be obligated for a major contract under the major system. The prohibition on the obligation of funds for a major system shall cease to apply at the end of the 45-day period that begins on the date—

(1) on which Congress receives the Major System Congressional Report under subsection (e)(1) with respect to that major system, in the case of a determination of an increase by a percentage equal to or greater than the significant cost growth threshold (as determined in subsection (d)); or

(2) on which Congress receives both the Major System Congressional Report under subsection (e)(2) and the certification of the Director under section 506F(b)(2) with respect to that major system, in the case of an increase by a percentage equal to or greater than the critical cost growth threshold (as determined under subsection (d)).

(h) Treatment of Cost Increases Prior to Enactment of Intelligence Authorization Act for Fiscal Year 2010.—(1) Not later than 180 days after the date of the enactment of the Intelligence Authorization Act for Fiscal Year 2010, the Director—

(A) shall, for each major system, determine if the total acquisition cost of such major system increased by a percentage equal to or greater than the significant cost growth threshold or the critical cost growth threshold prior to such date of enactment;

(B) shall establish for each major system for which the total acquisition cost has increased by a percentage equal to or greater than the significant cost growth threshold or the critical cost growth threshold prior to such date of enactment a revised current Baseline Estimate based upon an updated cost estimate;

(C) may, for a major system not described in subparagraph (B), establish a revised current Baseline Estimate based upon an updated cost estimate; and

(D) shall submit to Congress a report describing—

(i) each determination made under subparagraph (A);

(ii) each revised current Baseline Estimate established for a major system under subparagraph (B); and

(iii) each revised current Baseline Estimate established for a major system under subparagraph (C), including the percentage increase of the total acquisition cost of such major system that occurred prior to the date of the enactment of such Act.

(2) The revised current Baseline Estimate established for a major system under subparagraph (B) or (C) of paragraph (1) shall be the 2010 adjusted total acquisition cost for the major system and may include the estimated cost of conducting any vulnerability assessments for such major system required under section 506C.

(i) REQUIREMENTS TO USE BASE YEAR DOLLARS.— Any determination of a percentage increase under this section shall be stated in terms of constant base year dollars.

(j) FORM OF REPORT.— Any report required to be submitted under this section may be submitted in a classified form.

CRITICAL COST GROWTH IN MAJOR SYSTEMS

SEC. 506F. [50 U.S.C. 3102] (a) REASSESSMENT OF MAJOR SYSTEM.—If the Director of National Intelligence determines under section 506E(d) that the total acquisition cost of a major system has increased by a percentage equal to or greater than the critical cost growth threshold for the major system, the Director shall—

(1) determine the root cause or causes of the critical cost growth, in accordance with applicable statutory requirements, policies, procedures, and guidance; and

(2) carry out an assessment of—

(A) the projected cost of completing the major system if current requirements are not modified;

(B) the projected cost of completing the major system based on reasonable modification of such requirements;

(C) the rough order of magnitude of the costs of any reasonable alternative system or capability; and

(D) the need to reduce funding for other systems due to the growth in cost of the major system.

(b) PRESUMPTION OF TERMINATION.—(1) After conducting the reassessment required by subsection (a) with respect to a major system, the Director shall terminate the major system unless the Director submits to Congress a Major System Congressional Report containing a certification in accordance with paragraph (2) and the information described in paragraph (3). The Director shall submit such Major System Congressional Report and certification not later than 90 days after the date the Director receives the relevant major system cost report under subsection (b) or (c) of section 506E.

(2) A certification described by this paragraph with respect to a major system is a written certification that—

(A) the continuation of the major system is essential to the national security;

(B) there are no alternatives to the major system that will provide acceptable capability to meet the intelligence requirement at less cost;

(C) the new estimates of the total acquisition cost have been determined by the Director to be reasonable;

(D) the major system is a higher priority than other systems whose funding must be reduced to accommodate the growth in cost of the major system; and

(E) the management structure for the major system is adequate to manage and control the total acquisition cost.

(3) A Major System Congressional Report accompanying a written certification under paragraph (2) shall include, in addition to the requirements of section 506E(e), the root cause analysis and assessment carried out pursuant to subsection (a), the basis for each determination made in accordance with subparagraphs (A) through (E) of paragraph (2), and a description of all funding changes made as a result of the growth in the cost of the major system, including reductions made in funding for other systems to accommodate such cost growth, together with supporting documentation.

(c) Actions if Major System Not Terminated.—If the Director elects not to terminate a major system pursuant to subsection (b), the Director shall—

(1) restructure the major system in a manner that addresses the root cause or causes of the critical cost growth, as identified pursuant to subsection (a), and ensures that the system has an appropriate management structure as set forth in the certification submitted pursuant to subsection (b)(2)(E);

(2) rescind the most recent Milestone approval for the major system;

(3) require a new Milestone approval for the major system before taking any action to enter a new contract, exercise an option under an existing contract, or otherwise extend the scope of an existing contract under the system, except to the extent determined necessary by the Milestone Decision Authority, on a nondelegable basis, to ensure that the system may be restructured as intended by the Director without unnecessarily wasting resources;

(4) establish a revised current Baseline Estimate for the major system based upon an updated cost estimate; and

(5) conduct regular reviews of the major system.

(d) Actions if Major System Terminated.—If a major system is terminated pursuant to subsection (b), the Director shall submit to Congress a written report setting forth—

(1) an explanation of the reasons for terminating the major system;

(2) the alternatives considered to address any problems in the major system; and

(3) the course the Director plans to pursue to meet any intelligence requirements otherwise intended to be met by the major system.

(e) Form of Report.— Any report or certification required to be submitted under this section may be submitted in a classified form.

(f) Waiver.—(1) The Director may waive the requirements of subsections (d)(2), (e), and (g) of section 506E and subsections (a)(2), (b), (c), and (d) of this section with respect to a major system if the Director determines that at least 90 percent of the amount of the current Baseline Estimate for the major system has been expended.

(2)(A) If the Director grants a waiver under paragraph (1) with respect to a major system, the Director shall submit to the congressional intelligence committees written notice of the waiver that includes—

(i) the information described in section 506E(f); and

(ii) if the current total acquisition cost of the major system has increased by a percentage equal to or greater than the critical cost growth threshold—

(I) a determination of the root cause or causes of the critical cost growth, as described in subsection (a)(1); and

(II) a certification that includes the elements described in subparagraphs (A), (B), and (E) of subsection (b)(2).

(B) The Director shall submit the written notice required by subparagraph (A) not later than 90 days after the date that the Director receives a major system cost report under subsection (b) or (c) of section 506E that indicates that the total acquisition cost for the major system has increased by a percentage equal to or greater than the significant cost growth threshold or critical cost growth threshold.

(g) Definitions.— In this section, the terms "cost estimate", "critical cost growth threshold", "current Baseline Estimate", "major system", and "total acquisition cost" have the meaning given those terms in section 506E(a).

FUTURE BUDGET PROJECTIONS

Sec. 506G. [50 U.S.C. 3103] (a) Future Year Intelligence Plans.—(1) The Director of National Intelligence, with the concurrence of the Director of the Office of Management and Budget, shall provide to the congressional intelligence committees a Future Year Intelligence Plan, as described in paragraph (2), for—

(A) each expenditure center in the National Intelligence Program; and

(B) each major system in the National Intelligence Program.

(2)(A) A Future Year Intelligence Plan submitted under this subsection shall include the year-by-year proposed funding for each center or system referred to in subparagraph (A) or (B) of paragraph (1), for the budget year for which the Plan is submitted and not less than the 4 subsequent fiscal years.

(B) A Future Year Intelligence Plan submitted under subparagraph (B) of paragraph (1) for a major system shall include—

(i) the estimated total life-cycle cost of such major system; and

(ii) major milestones that have significant resource implications for such major system.

(b) Long-term Budget Projections.—(1) The Director of National Intelligence, with the concurrence of the Director of the Office of Management and Budget, shall provide to the congressional intelligence committees a Long-term Budget Projection for each element of the intelligence community funded under the National Intelligence Program acquiring a major system that includes the budget for such element for the 5-year period that begins on the day after the end of the last fiscal year for which year-by-year proposed funding is included in a Future Year Intelligence Plan for such major system in accordance with subsection (a)(2)(A).

(2) A Long-term Budget Projection submitted under paragraph (1) shall include—

(A) projections for the appropriate element of the intelligence community for—

(i) pay and benefits of officers and employees of such element;

(ii) other operating and support costs and minor acquisitions of such element;

(iii) research and technology required by such element;

(iv) current and planned major system acquisitions for such element;

(v) any future major system acquisitions for such element; and

(vi) any additional funding projections that the Director of National Intelligence considers appropriate;

(B) a budget projection based on effective cost and schedule execution of current or planned major system acquisitions and application of Office of Management and Budget inflation estimates to future major system acquisitions;

(C) any additional assumptions and projections that the Director of National Intelligence considers appropriate; and

(D) a description of whether, and to what extent, the total projection for each year exceeds the level that would result from applying the most recent Office of Management and Budget inflation estimate to the budget of that element of the intelligence community.

(c) SUBMISSION TO CONGRESS.— The Director of National Intelligence, with the concurrence of the Director of the Office of Management and Budget, shall submit to the congressional intelligence committees each Future Year Intelligence Plan or Long-term Budget Projection required under subsection (a) or (b) for a fiscal year at the time that the President submits to Congress the budget for such fiscal year pursuant to section 1105 of title 31, United States Code.

(d) MAJOR SYSTEM AFFORDABILITY REPORT.—(1) The Director of National Intelligence, with the concurrence of the Director of the Office of Management and Budget, shall prepare a report on the acquisition of a major system funded under the National Intelligence Program before the time that the President submits to Congress the budget for the first fiscal year in which appropriated funds are anticipated to be obligated for the development or procurement of such major system.

(2) The report on such major system shall include an assessment of whether, and to what extent, such acquisition, if developed, procured, and operated, is projected to cause an increase in the most recent Future Year Intelligence Plan and Long-term Budget Projection submitted under section 506G for an element of the intelligence community.

(3) The Director of National Intelligence shall update the report whenever an independent cost estimate must be updated pursuant to section 506A(a)(4).

(4) The Director of National Intelligence shall submit each report required by this subsection at the time that the President submits to Congress the budget for a fiscal year pursuant to section 1105 of title 31, United States Code.

(e) DEFINITIONS.—In this section:

(1) BUDGET YEAR.— The term "budget year" means the next fiscal year for

which the President is required to submit to Congress a budget pursuant to section 1105 of title 31, United States Code.

(2) INDEPENDENT COST ESTIMATE; MAJOR SYSTEM.— The terms "independent cost estimate" and "major system" have the meaning given those terms in section 506A(e).

REPORTS ON SECURITY CLEARANCES

SEC. 506H. [50 U.S.C. 3104] (a) REPORT ON SECURITY CLEARANCE DETERMINATIONS.—(1) Not later than February 1 of each year, the President shall submit to Congress a report on the security clearance process. Such report shall include, for each security clearance level—

(A) the number of employees of the United States Government who—

(i) held a security clearance at such level as of October 1 of the preceding year; and

(ii) were approved for a security clearance at such level during the preceding fiscal year; and

(B) the number of contractors to the United States Government who—

(i) held a security clearance at such level as of October 1 of the preceding year; and

(ii) were approved for a security clearance at such level during the preceding fiscal year.

(2) For purposes of paragraph (1), the President may consider—

(A) security clearances at the level of confidential and secret as one security clearance level; and

(B) security clearances at the level of top secret or higher as one security clearance level.

(b) INTELLIGENCE COMMUNITY REPORTS.—(1)(A) Not later than March 1 of each year, the Director of National Intelligence shall submit a report to the congressional intelligence committees, the Committee on Homeland Security and Governmental Affairs of the Senate, the Committee on Homeland Security of the House of Representatives, and the Committee on Oversight and Reform of the House of Representatives regarding the security clearances processed by each element of the intelligence community during the preceding fiscal year.

(B) The Director shall submit to the Committee on Armed Services of the Senate and the Committee on Armed Services of the House of Representatives such portions of the report submitted under subparagraph (A) as the Director determines address elements of the intelligence community that are within the Department of Defense.

(C) Each report submitted under this paragraph shall separately identify security clearances processed for Federal employees and contractor employees sponsored by each such element.

(2) Each report submitted under paragraph (1)(A) shall include, for each element of the intelligence community for the fiscal year covered by the report, the following:

(A) The total number of initial security clearance background investigations sponsored for new applicants.

(B) The total number of security clearance periodic reinvestigations sponsored for existing employees.

(C) The total number of initial security clearance background investigations for new applicants that were adjudicated with notice of a determination provided to the prospective applicant, including—

(i) the total number of such adjudications that were adjudicated favorably and granted access to classified information; and

(ii) the total number of such adjudications that were adjudicated unfavorably and resulted in a denial or revocation of a security clearance.

(D) The total number of security clearance periodic background investigations that were adjudicated with notice of a determination provided to the existing employee, including—

(i) the total number of such adjudications that were adjudicated favorably; and

(ii) the total number of such adjudications that were adjudicated unfavorably and resulted in a denial or revocation of a security clearance.

(E) The total number of pending security clearance background investigations, including initial applicant investigations and periodic reinvestigations, that were not adjudicated as of the last day of such year and that remained pending, categorized as follows:

(i) For 180 days or shorter.

(ii) For longer than 180 days, but shorter than 12 months.

(iii) For 12 months or longer, but shorter than 18 months.

(iv) For 18 months or longer, but shorter than 24 months.

(v) For 24 months or longer.

(F) For any security clearance determinations completed or pending during the year preceding the year for which the report is submitted that have taken longer than 12 months to complete—

(i) an explanation of the causes for the delays incurred during the period covered by the report; and

(ii) the number of such delays involving a polygraph requirement.

(G) The percentage of security clearance investigations, including initial and periodic reinvestigations, that resulted in a denial or revocation of a security clearance.

(H) The percentage of security clearance investigations that resulted in incomplete information.

(I) The percentage of security clearance investigations that did not result in enough information to make a decision on potentially adverse information.

(3) The report required under this subsection shall be submitted in unclassified form, but may include a classified annex.

(c) Form.— The reports required under subsections (a)(1) and (b) shall be submitted in unclassified form, but may include a classified annex.

SUMMARY OF INTELLIGENCE RELATING TO TERRORIST RECIDIVISM OF DETAINEES HELD AT UNITED STATES NAVAL STATION, GUANTANAMO BAY, CUBA

SEC. 506I. [50 U.S.C. 3105] (a) IN GENERAL.—The Director of National Intelligence, in consultation with the Director of the Central Intelligence Agency and the Director of the Defense Intelligence Agency, shall make publicly available an unclassified summary of—

(1) intelligence relating to recidivism of detainees currently or formerly held at the Naval Detention Facility at Guantanamo Bay, Cuba, by the Department of Defense; and

(2) an assessment of the likelihood that such detainees will engage in terrorism or communicate with persons in terrorist organizations.

(b) UPDATES.— Not less frequently than annually, the Director of National Intelligence, in consultation with the Director of the Central Intelligence Agency and the Secretary of Defense, shall update and make publicly available an unclassified summary consisting of the information required by subsection (a) and the number of individuals formerly detained at Naval Station, Guantanamo Bay, Cuba, who are confirmed or suspected of returning to terrorist activities after release or transfer from such Naval Station.

SEC. 506J. [50 U.S.C. 3105a] CLASSIFIED INTELLIGENCE BUDGET JUSTIFICATION MATERIALS.

(a) DEFINITIONS .—In this section:

(1) BUDGET .—The term "budget" has the meaning given the term "budget of the President" in section 506A.

(2) CLASSIFIED INTELLIGENCE BUDGET JUSTIFICATION MATERIALS .—The term "classified intelligence budget justification materials" means, with respect to a fiscal year, the materials submitted to Congress by the Director of National Intelligence in support of the budget for that fiscal year that are classified or otherwise protected from public disclosure.

(b) TIMELY SUBMISSION.— Not later than 5 days after the date on which the President submits to Congress the budget for each fiscal year pursuant to section 1105(a) of title 31, United States Code, the Director of National Intelligence shall submit to the congressional intelligence committees the classified intelligence budget justification materials for the element for that budget.

DATES FOR SUBMITTAL OF VARIOUS ANNUAL AND SEMIANNUAL REPORTS TO THE CONGRESSIONAL INTELLIGENCE COMMITTEES

SEC. 507. [50 U.S.C. 3106] (a) ANNUAL REPORTS.—The date for the submittal to the congressional intelligence committees of the following annual reports shall be the date each year provided in subsection (c)(1):

(1) The annual report of the Inspectors General of the intelligence community on proposed resources and activities of their offices required by section 416(h) of title 5, United States Code.

(2) The annual report on certifications for immunity in interdiction of aircraft

engaged in illicit drug trafficking required by section 1012(c)(2) of the National Defense Authorization Act for Fiscal Year 1995 (22 U.S.C. 2291–4(c)(2)).

(3) The annual report on activities under the David L. Boren National Security Education Act of 1991 (title VIII of Public Law 102–183; 50 U.S.C. 1901 et seq.) required by section 806(a) of that Act (50 U.S.C. 1906(a)).

(4) The annual report on hiring and retention of minority employees in the intelligence community required by section 114(a).

(5) The annual report on financial intelligence on terrorist assets required by section 118.

(6) An annual report submitted under section 119C(d)(1).

(b) SEMIANNUAL REPORTS.—The dates for the submittal to the congressional intelligence committees of the following semiannual reports shall be the dates each year provided in subsection (c)(2):

(1) The semiannual reports on decisions not to prosecute certain violations of law under the Classified Information Procedures Act (18 U.S.C. App.) as required by section 13 of that Act.

(2) The semiannual reports on the disclosure of information and consumer reports to the Federal Bureau of Investigation for counterintelligence purposes required by section 624(h)(2) of the Fair Credit Reporting Act (15 U.S.C. 1681u(h)(2)).

(3) The semiannual provision of information on requests for financial information for foreign counterintelligence purposes required by section 1114(a)(5)(C) of the Right to Financial Privacy Act of 1978 (12 U.S.C. 3414(a)(5)(C)).

(c) SUBMITTAL DATES FOR REPORTS.—(1) Except as provided in subsection (d), each annual report listed in subsection (a) shall be submitted not later than February 1.

(2) Except as provided in subsection (d), each semiannual report listed in subsection (b) shall be submitted not later than February 1 and August 1.

(d) POSTPONEMENT OF SUBMITTAL.—(1) Subject to paragraph (3), the date for the submittal of—

(A) an annual report listed in subsection (a) may be postponed until March 1; and

(B) a semiannual report listed in subsection (b) may be postponed until March 1 or September 1, as the case may be,

if the official required to submit such report submits to the congressional intelligence committees a written notification of such postponement.

(2)(A) Notwithstanding any other provision of law and subject to paragraph (3), the date for the submittal to the congressional intelligence committees of any report described in subparagraph (B) may be postponed by not more than 30 days from the date otherwise specified in the provision of law for the submittal of such report if the official required to submit such report submits to the congressional intelligence committees a written notification of such postponement.

(B) A report described in this subparagraph is any report on intelligence or intelligence-related activities of the United States Government that is submitted under a provision of law requiring the submittal of only a single report.

(3)(A) The date for the submittal of a report whose submittal is postponed under paragraph (1) or (2) may be postponed beyond the time provided for the submittal of such report under such paragraph if the official required to submit such report submits to the congressional intelligence committees a written certification that preparation and submittal of such report at such time will impede the work of officers or employees of the intelligence community in a manner that will be detrimental to the national security of the United States.

(B) A certification with respect to a report under subparagraph (A) shall include a proposed submittal date for such report, and such report shall be submitted not later than that date.

CERTIFICATION OF COMPLIANCE WITH OVERSIGHT REQUIREMENTS

SEC. 508. [50 U.S.C. 3107] The head of each element of the intelligence community shall annually submit to the congressional intelligence committees—

(1) a certification that, to the best of the knowledge of the head of such element—

(A) the head of such element is in full compliance with the requirements of this title; and

(B) any information required to be submitted by the head of such element under this Act before the date of the submission of such certification has been properly submitted; or

(2) if the head of such element is unable to submit a certification under paragraph (1), a statement—

(A) of the reasons the head of such element is unable to submit such a certification;

(B) describing any information required to be submitted by the head of such element under this Act before the date of the submission of such statement that has not been properly submitted; and

(C) that the head of such element will submit such information as soon as possible after the submission of such statement.

SEC. 509. [50 U.S.C. 3108] AUDITABILITY OF CERTAIN ELEMENTS OF THE INTELLIGENCE COMMUNITY.

(a) REQUIREMENT FOR ANNUAL AUDITS.— The head of each covered entity shall ensure that there is a full financial audit of such covered entity each year beginning with fiscal year 2014. Such audits may be conducted by an internal or external independent accounting or auditing organization.

(b) REQUIREMENT FOR UNQUALIFIED OPINION.— Beginning as early as practicable, but in no event later than the audit required under subsection (a) for fiscal year 2016, the head of each covered entity shall take all reasonable steps necessary to ensure that each audit required under subsection (a) contains an unqualified opinion on the financial statements of such covered entity for the fiscal year covered by such audit.

(c) REPORTS TO CONGRESS.— The chief financial officer of each covered entity shall provide to the congressional intelligence committees an annual audit report from an accounting or auditing organization on each audit of the covered entity conducted pursuant to subsection (a).

(d) Covered Entity Defined.— In this section, the term "covered entity" means the Office of the Director of National Intelligence, the Central Intelligence Agency, the Defense Intelligence Agency, the National Security Agency, the National Reconnaissance Office, and the National Geospatial-Intelligence Agency.

SEC. 510. [50 U.S.C. 3109] SIGNIFICANT INTERPRETATIONS OF LAW CONCERNING INTELLIGENCE ACTIVITIES.

(a) Notification.— Except as provided in subsection (c) and to the extent consistent with due regard for the protection from unauthorized disclosure of classified information relating to sensitive intelligence sources and methods or other exceptionally sensitive matters, the General Counsel of each element of the intelligence community shall notify the congressional intelligence committees, in writing, of any significant legal interpretation of the United States Constitution or Federal law affecting intelligence activities conducted by such element by not later than 30 days after the date of the commencement of any intelligence activity pursuant to such interpretation.

(b) Content.— Each notification under subsection (a) shall provide a summary of the significant legal interpretation and the intelligence activity or activities conducted pursuant to such interpretation.

(c) Exceptions.—A notification under subsection (a) shall not be required for a significant legal interpretation if—

(1) notice of the significant legal interpretation was previously provided to the congressional intelligence committees under subsection (a); or

(2) the significant legal interpretation was made before the date of the enactment of the Intelligence Authorization Act for Fiscal Year 2014.

(d) Limited Access for Covert Action.— If the President determines that it is essential to limit access to a covert action finding under section 503(c)(2), the President may limit access to information concerning such finding that is subject to notification under this section to those members of Congress who have been granted access to the relevant finding under section 503(c)(2).

SEC. 511. [50 U.S.C. 3110] ANNUAL REPORT ON VIOLATIONS OF LAW OR EXECUTIVE ORDER.

(a) Annual Reports Required.— The Director of National Intelligence shall annually submit to the congressional intelligence committees a report on violations of law or executive order relating to intelligence activities by personnel of an element of the intelligence community that were identified during the previous calendar year.

(b) Elements.—Each report submitted under subsection (a) shall, consistent with the need to preserve ongoing criminal investigations, include a description of, and any action taken in response to, any violation of law or executive order (including Executive Order No. 12333 (50 U.S.C. 3001 note)) relating to intelligence activities committed by personnel of an element of the intelligence community in the course of the employment of such personnel that, during the previous calendar year, was—

(1) determined by the director, head, or general counsel of any element of the intelligence community to have occurred;

(2) referred to the Department of Justice for possible criminal prosecution; or

(3) substantiated by the inspector general of any element of the intelligence community.

SEC. 512. [50 U.S.C. 3111] BRIEFINGS AND NOTIFICATIONS ON COUNTERINTELLIGENCE ACTIVITIES OF THE FEDERAL BUREAU OF INVESTIGATION.

(a) QUARTERLY BRIEFINGS.—In addition to, and without any derogation of, the requirement under section 501 to keep the congressional intelligence committees fully and currently informed of the intelligence and counterintelligence activities of the United States, not less frequently than once each quarter, or more frequently if requested by the congressional intelligence committees, the Director of the Federal Bureau of Investigation shall provide to the congressional intelligence committees a briefing on the counterintelligence activities of the Federal Bureau of Investigation. Such briefings shall include, at a minimum, an overview and update of—

(1) the counterintelligence posture of the Bureau;

(2) counterintelligence investigations; and

(3) any other information relating to the counterintelligence activities of the Bureau that the Director determines necessary.

(b) NOTIFICATIONS.— In addition to the quarterly briefings under subsection (a), the Director of the Federal Bureau of Investigation shall promptly notify the congressional intelligence committees of any counterintelligence investigation carried out by the Bureau with respect to any counterintelligence risk or threat that is related to an election or campaign for Federal office.

(c) GUIDELINES.—

(1) DEVELOPMENT AND CONSULTATION.— The Director shall develop guidelines governing the scope of the briefings provided under subsection (a), the notifications provided under subsection (b), and the information required by section 5304(a)(2) of the Damon Paul Nelson and Matthew Young Pollard Intelligence Authorization Act for Fiscal Years 2018, 2019, and 2020. The Director shall consult the congressional intelligence committees during such development.

(2) SUBMISSION.—The Director shall submit to the congressional intelligence committees—

(A) the guidelines under paragraph (1) upon issuance; and

(B) any updates to such guidelines by not later than 15 days after making such update.

SEC. 513. [50 U.S.C. 3112] ANNUAL REPORTS ON THE DOMESTIC ACTIVITIES OF THE INTELLIGENCE COMMUNITY.

(a) REPORTS.—Not later than January 31 of each year, the Director of National Intelligence shall submit to the congressional intelligence committees a report—

(1) identifying all domestic activities undertaken by each element of the intelligence community during the prior fiscal year; and

(2) for each activity identified under paragraph (1), a statement of the legal authority authorizing such activity to be undertaken.

(b) FORM.— Each report under subsection (a) shall be submitted in unclassified form, but may include a classified annex.

SEC. 514. [50 U.S.C. 3113] UNFUNDED PRIORITIES OF THE INTELLIGENCE COMMUNITY: ANNUAL REPORT.

(a) ANNUAL REPORT.— Not later than 10 days after the date on which the budget of the President for a fiscal year is submitted to Congress pursuant to section 1105 of title 31, United States Code, the head of each element of the intelligence community shall prepare and submit to the Director of National Intelligence, the congressional intelligence committees, the Subcommittee on Defense of the Committee on Appropriations of the Senate, and the Subcommittee on Defense of the Committee on Appropriations of the House of Representatives a report on the unfunded priorities of the programs under the jurisdiction of such head.

(b) ELEMENTS

(1) IN GENERAL .—Each report under subsection (a) shall specify, for each unfunded priority covered by such report, the following:

(A) A summary description of such priority, including the objectives to be achieved if such priority is funded (whether in whole or in part).

(B) Whether such priority will satisfy a covert action or support collection against requirements identified in the National Intelligence Priorities Framework of the Office of the Director of National Intelligence (or any successor mechanism established for the prioritization of programs and activities), including a description of such requirements and the related prioritization level.

(C) The additional amount of funds recommended in connection with the objectives under subparagraph (A).

(D) Budget information with respect to the unfunded priority, including—

(i) the appropriation account;

(ii) the expenditure center; and

(iii) the project and, if applicable, subproject.

(2) PRIORITIZATION OF PRIORITIES.— Each report shall present the unfunded priorities covered by such report in overall order of urgency of priority among unfunded priorities.

(c) UNFUNDED PRIORITY DEFINED.—In this section, the term “unfunded priority”, in the case of a fiscal year, means a program, activity, or mission requirement of an element of the intelligence community that—

(1) is not funded in the budget of the President for the fiscal year as submitted to Congress pursuant to section 1105 of title 31, United States Code;

(2) is necessary to fulfill a covert action or to satisfy an information requirement associated with the collection, analysis, or dissemination of intelligence that has been documented within the National Intelligence Priorities Framework; and

(3) would have been recommended for funding by the head of the element of the intelligence community if—

(A) additional resources had been available for the budget to fund the program, activity, or mission requirement; or

(B) the program, activity, or mission requirement has emerged since the budget was formulated.

SEC. 515. [50 U.S.C. 3114] SUBMISSION OF COVERED DOCUMENTS AND CLASSIFIED ANNEXES.

(a) COVERED DOCUMENT DEFINED.— In this section, the term "covered document" means any executive order, memorandum, or policy directive issued by the President, including national security Presidential memoranda and Presidential policy directives, or such successor memoranda and directives.

(b) REQUIREMENT .—Not later than 7 days after the date on which the President issues or amends a covered document, the President, acting through the Director of National Intelligence, shall submit to the congressional intelligence committees, the Subcommittee on Defense of the Committee on Appropriations of the Senate, and the Subcommittee on Defense of the Committee on Appropriations of the House of Representatives the covered document and any classified annex accompanying that document if such covered document or annex contains a direction to, establishes a requirement for, or includes a restriction on any element of the intelligence community.

SEC. 516. [50 U.S.C. 3115] SUBMISSION OF LEGISLATIVE PROPOSALS.

Not later than 45 days after the date on which the President submits to Congress the budget for each fiscal year pursuant to section 1105(a) of title 31, United States Code, the Director of National Intelligence shall submit to the congressional intelligence committees, the Committee on Appropriations of the Senate, and the Committee on Appropriations of the House of Representatives any legislative provisions that are proposed by the Director to be enacted as part of the annual intelligence authorization bill for that fiscal year.

TITLE VI—PROTECTION OF CERTAIN NATIONAL SECURITY INFORMATION

PROTECTION OF IDENTITIES OF CERTAIN UNITED STATES UNDERCOVER INTELLIGENCE OFFICERS, AGENTS, INFORMANTS, AND SOURCES

SEC. 601. [50 U.S.C. 3121] (a) Whoever, having or having had authorized access to classified information that identifies a covert agent, intentionally discloses any information identifying such covert agent to any individual not authorized to receive classified information, knowing that the information disclosed so identifies such covert agent and that the United States is taking affirmative measures to conceal such covert agent's intelligence relationship to the United States, shall be fined under title 18, United States Code, or imprisoned not more than 15 years, or both.

(b) Whoever, as a result of having authorized access to classified information, learns the identity of a covert agent and intentionally discloses any information identifying such covert agent to any individual not authorized to receive classified information, knowing that the information disclosed so identifies such covert agent and that the United States is taking affirmative measures to conceal such covert agent's intelligence relationship to the United States, shall be fined under title 18, United States Code, or imprisoned not more than 10 years, or both.

(c) Whoever, in the course of a pattern of activities intended to identify and expose covert agents and with reason to believe that such activities would impair or impede the foreign intelligence activities of the United States, discloses any information that identifies an individual as a covert agent to any individual not authorized to receive classified information, knowing that the information disclosed so identifies such individual and that the United States is taking affirmative measures to conceal such individual's classified intelligence relationship to the United States, shall be fined under title 18, United States Code, or imprisoned not more than three years, or both.

(d) A term of imprisonment imposed under this section shall be consecutive to any other sentence of imprisonment.

DEFENSES AND EXCEPTIONS

SEC. 602. [50 U.S.C. 3122] (a) It is a defense to a prosecution under section 601 that before the commission of the offense with which the defendant is charged, the United States had publicly acknowledged or revealed the intelligence relationship to the United States of the individual the disclosure of whose intelligence relationship to the United States is the basis for the prosecution.

(b)(1) Subject to paragraph (2), no person other than a person committing an offense under section 601 shall be subject to prosecution under such section by virtue of section 2 or 4 of title 18, United States Code, or shall be subject to prosecution for conspiracy to commit an offense under such section.

(2) Paragraph (1) shall not apply (A) in the case of a person who acted in the course of a pattern of activities intended to identify and expose covert agents and with reason to believe that such activities would impair or impede the foreign intelligence activities of the United States, or (B) in the case of a person who has authorized access to classified information.

(c) It shall not be an offense under section 601 to transmit information described in such section directly to either congressional intelligence committee.

(d) It shall not be an offense under section 601 for an individual to disclose information that solely identifies himself as a covert agent.

EXTRATERRITORIAL JURISDICTION

SEC. 603. [50 U.S.C. 3124] There is jurisdiction over an offense under section 601 committed outside the United States if the individual committing the offense is a citizen of the United States or an alien lawfully admitted to the United States for permanent residence (as defined in section 101(a)(20) of the Immigration and Nationality Act).

PROVIDING INFORMATION TO CONGRESS

SEC. 604. [50 U.S.C. 3125] Nothing in this title may be construed as authority to withhold information from the Congress or from a committee of either House of Congress.

DEFINITIONS

SEC. 605. [50 U.S.C. 3126] For the purposes of this title:

(1) The term "classified information" means information or material designated and clearly marked or clearly represented, pursuant to the provisions of a statute or Executive order (or a regulation or order issued pursuant to a statute or Executive order), as requiring a specific degree of protection against unauthorized disclosure for reasons of national security.

(2) The term "authorized", when used with respect to access to classified information, means having authority, right, or permission pursuant to the provisions of a statute, Executive order, directive of the head of any department or agency engaged in foreign intelligence or counterintelligence activities, order of any United States court, or provisions of any Rule of the House of Representatives or resolution of the Senate which assigns responsibility within the respective House of Congress for the oversight of intelligence activities.

(3) The term "disclose" means to communicate, provide, impart, transmit, transfer, convey, publish, or otherwise make available.

(4) The term "covert agent" means—

(A) a present or retired officer or employee of an intelligence agency or a present or retired member of the Armed Forces assigned to duty with an intelligence agency whose identity as such an officer, employee, or member is classified information; or

(B) a United States citizen whose intelligence relationship to the United States is classified information, and—

(i) who acts as an agent of, or informant or source of operational assistance to, an intelligence agency, or

(ii) who is at the time of the disclosure acting as an agent of, or informant to, the foreign counterintelligence or foreign counterterrorism components of the Federal Bureau of Investigation; or

(C) an individual, other than a United States citizen, whose past or present intelligence relationship to the United States is classified information and who is a present or former agent of, or a present or former informant or source of operational assistance to, an intelligence agency.

(5) The term "intelligence agency" means the elements of the intelligence community, as that term is defined in section 3(4).[12]

[12] Section 310(a)(4)(B) of Public Law 112–277 provides for an amendment to redesignate section 606 as section 605. Section 506 of such Public Law provides for an amendment to revise paragraph (5) of section 606 in its entirety, which was carried out above to section 605(5) (as so redesignated) to reflect the probable intent of Congress.

(6) The term "informant" means any individual who furnishes information to an intelligence agency in the course of a confidential relationship protecting the identity of such individual from public disclosure.

(7) The terms "officer" and "employee" have the meanings given such terms by section 2104 and 2105, respectively, of title 5, United States Code.

(8) The term "Armed Forces" means the Army, Navy, Air Force, Marine Corps, and Coast Guard.

(9) The term "United States", when used in a geographic sense, means all areas under the territorial sovereignty of the United States and the Trust Territory of the Pacific Islands.

(10) The term "pattern of activities" requires a series of acts with a common purpose or objective.

TITLE VII—PROTECTION OF OPERATIONAL FILES

OPERATIONAL FILES OF THE CENTRAL INTELLIGENCE AGENCY

SEC. 701. [50 U.S.C. 3141] (a) The Director of the Central Intelligence Agency, with the coordination of the Director of National Intelligence, may exempt operational files of the Central Intelligence Agency from the provisions of section 552 of title 5, United States Code (Freedom of Information Act), which require publication or disclosure, or search or review in connection therewith.

(b) In this section, the term "operational files" means—

(1) files of the National Clandestine Service which document the conduct of foreign intelligence or counterintelligence operations or intelligence or security liaison arrangements or information exchanges with foreign governments or their intelligence or security services;

(2) files of the Directorate for Science and Technology which document the means by which foreign intelligence or counterintelligence is collected through scientific and technical systems; and

(3) files of the Office of Personnel Security which document investigations conducted to determine the suitability of potential foreign intelligence or counterintelligence sources;

except that files which are the sole repository of disseminated intelligence are not operational files.

(c) Notwithstanding subsection (a) of this section, exempted operational files shall continue to be subject to search and review for information concerning—

(1) United States citizens or aliens lawfully admitted for permanent residence who have requested information on themselves pursuant to the provisions of section 552 of title 5, United States Code (Freedom of Information Act), or section 552a of title 5, United States Code (Privacy Act of 1974);

(2) any special activity the existence of which is not exempt from disclosure under the provisions of section 552 of title 5, United States Code (Freedom of Information Act); or

(3) the specific subject matter of an investigation by the congressional intelligence committees, the Intelligence Oversight Board, the Department of Justice, the Office of General Counsel of the Central Intelligence Agency, the Office of Inspector General of the Central Intelligence Agency, or the Office of the Director of National Intelligence for any impropriety, or violation of law, Executive order, or Presidential directive, in the conduct of an intelligence activity.

(d)(1) Files that are not exempted under subsection (a) of this section which contain information derived or disseminated from exempted operational files shall be subject to search and review.

(2) The inclusion of information from exempted operational files in files that are not exempted under subsection (a) of this section shall not affect the exemption under subsection (a) of this section of the originating operational files from search, review, publication, or disclosure.

(3) Records from exempted operational files which have been disseminated to

and referenced in files that are not exempted under subsection (a) of this section and which have been returned to exempted operational files for sole retention shall be subject to search and review.

(e) The provisions of subsection (a) of this section shall not be superseded except by a provision of law which is enacted after the date of enactment of subsection (a), and which specifically cites and repeals or modifies its provisions.

(f) Whenever any person who has requested agency records under section 552 of title 5, United States Code (Freedom of Information Act), alleges that the Central Intelligence Agency has improperly withheld records because of failure to comply with any provision of this section, judicial review shall be available under the terms set forth in section 552(a)(4)(B) of title 5, United States Code, except that—

(1) in any case in which information specifically authorized under criteria established by an Executive order to be kept secret in the interest of national defense or foreign relations which is filed with, or produced for, the court by the Central Intelligence Agency, such information shall be examined ex parte, in camera by the court;

(2) the court shall, to the fullest extent practicable, determine issues of fact based on sworn written submissions of the parties;

(3) when a complainant alleges that requested records are improperly withheld because of improper placement solely in exempted operational files, the complainant shall support such allegation with a sworn written submission, based upon personal knowledge or otherwise admissible evidence;

(4)(A) when a complainant alleges that requested records were improperly withheld because of improper exemption of operational files, the Central Intelligence Agency shall meet its burden under section 552(a)(4)(B) of title 5, United States Code, by demonstrating to the court by sworn written submission that exempted operational files likely to contain responsive records currently perform the functions set forth in subsection (b) of this section; and

(B) the court may not order the Central Intelligence Agency to review the content of any exempted operational file or files in order to make the demonstration required under subparagraph (A) of this paragraph, unless the complainant disputes the Central Intelligence Agency's showing with a sworn written submission based on personal knowledge or otherwise admissible evidence;

(5) in proceedings under paragraphs (3) and (4) of this subsection, the parties shall not obtain discovery pursuant to rules 26 through 36 of the Federal Rules of Civil Procedure, except that requests for admission may be made pursuant to rules 26 and 36;

(6) if the court finds under this subsection that the Central Intelligence Agency has improperly withheld requested records because of failure to comply with any provision of this section, the court shall order the Central Intelligence Agency to search and review the appropriate exempted operational file or files for the requested records and make such records, or portions thereof, available in accordance with the provisions of section 552 of title 5, United States Code (Freedom of Information Act), and such order shall be the exclusive remedy for failure to comply with this section; and

(7) if at any time following the filing of a complaint pursuant to this subsection the Central Intelligence Agency agrees to search the appropriate exempted operational file or files for the requested records, the court shall dismiss the claim based upon such complaint.

(g) DECENNIAL REVIEW OF EXEMPTED OPERATIONAL FILES.—(1) Not less than once every ten years, the Director of the Central Intelligence Agency and the Director of National Intelligence shall review the exemptions in force under subsection (a) to determine whether such exemptions may be removed from any category of exempted files or any portion thereof.

(2) The review required by paragraph (1)[13] shall include consideration of the historical value or other public interest in the subject matter of the particular category of files or portions thereof and the potential for declassifying a significant part of the information contained therein.

[13] In section 701(g)(2), the amendment to strike "of subsection (a) of this section" and insert "paragraph (1)" made by section 922(b)(2)(E) of the National Defense Authorization Act for Fiscal Year 2004 (Public Law 108–136; 117 Stat. 1537) was executed by striking "subsection (a) of this section" and inserting "paragraph (1)" in order to reflect the probable intent of Congress.

(3) A complainant who alleges that the Central Intelligence Agency has improperly withheld records because of failure to comply with this subsection may seek judicial review in the district court of the United States of the district in which any of the parties reside, or in the District of Columbia. In such a proceeding, the court's review shall be limited to determining the following:

(A) Whether the Central Intelligence Agency has conducted the review required by paragraph (1) before October 15, 1994, or before the expiration of the 10-year period beginning on the date of the most recent review.

(B) Whether the Central Intelligence Agency, in fact, considered the criteria set forth in paragraph (2) in conducting the required review.

OPERATIONAL FILES OF THE NATIONAL GEOSPATIAL-INTELLIGENCE AGENCY

SEC. 702. [50 U.S.C. 3142] (a) EXEMPTION OF CERTAIN OPERATIONAL FILES FROM SEARCH, REVIEW, PUBLICATION, OR DISCLOSURE.—(1) The Director of the National Geospatial-Intelligence Agency, with the coordination of the Director of National Intelligence, may exempt operational files of the National Geospatial-Intelligence Agency from the provisions of section 552 of title 5, United States Code, which require publication, disclosure, search, or review in connection therewith.

(2)(A) Subject to subparagraph (B), for the purposes of this section, the term "operational files" means files of the National Geospatial-Intelligence Agency (hereafter in this section referred to as "NGA") concerning the activities of NGA that before the establishment of NGA were performed by the National Photographic Interpretation Center of the Central Intelligence Agency (NPIC), that document the means by which foreign intelligence or counterintelligence is collected through scientific and technical systems.

(B) Files which are the sole repository of disseminated intelligence are not operational files.

(3) Notwithstanding paragraph (1), exempted operational files shall continue to be subject to search and review for information concerning—

(A) United States citizens or aliens lawfully admitted for permanent residence who have requested information on themselves pursuant to the provisions of section 552 or 552a of title 5, United States Code;

(B) any special activity the existence of which is not exempt from disclosure under the provisions of section 552 of title 5, United States Code; or

(C) the specific subject matter of an investigation by any of the following for any impropriety, or violation of law, Executive order, or Presidential directive, in the conduct of an intelligence activity:

(i) The congressional intelligence committees.

(ii) The Intelligence Oversight Board.

(iii) The Department of Justice.

(iv) The Office of General Counsel of NGA.

(v) The Office of the Director of NGA.

(vi) The Office of the Inspector General of the National Geospatial-Intelligence Agency.

(4)(A) Files that are not exempted under paragraph (1) which contain information derived or disseminated from exempted operational files shall be subject to search and review.

(B) The inclusion of information from exempted operational files in files that are not exempted under paragraph (1) shall not affect the exemption under paragraph (1) of the originating operational files from search, review, publication, or disclosure.

(C) Records from exempted operational files which have been disseminated to and referenced in files that are not exempted under paragraph (1) and which have been returned to exempted operational files for sole retention shall be subject to search and review.

(5) The provisions of paragraph (1) may not be superseded except by a provision of law which is enacted after the date of the enactment of this section, and which specifically cites and repeals or modifies its provisions.

(6)(A) Except as provided in subparagraph (B), whenever any person who has requested agency records under section 552 of title 5, United States Code, alleges that NGA has withheld records improperly because of failure to comply with any provision of this section, judicial review shall be available under the terms set forth in section 552(a)(4)(B) of title 5, United States Code.

(B) Judicial review shall not be available in the manner provided for under subparagraph (A) as follows:

(i) In any case in which information specifically authorized under criteria established by an Executive order to be kept secret in the interests of national defense or foreign relations is filed with, or produced for, the court by NGA, such information shall be examined ex parte, in camera by the court.

(ii) The court shall, to the fullest extent practicable, determine the issues of fact based on sworn written submissions of the parties.

(iii) When a complainant alleges that requested records are improperly withheld because of improper placement solely in exempted operational files, the complainant shall support such allegation with a sworn written submission based upon personal knowledge or otherwise admissible evidence.

(iv)(I) When a complainant alleges that requested records were improperly withheld because of improper exemption of operational files, NGA shall meet its burden under section 552(a)(4)(B) of title 5, United States Code, by demonstrating to the court by sworn written submission that exempted operational files likely to contain responsive records currently perform the functions set forth in paragraph (2).

(II) The court may not order NGA to review the content of any exempted operational file or files in order to make the demonstration required under subclause (I), unless the complainant disputes NGA's showing with a sworn written submission based on personal knowledge or otherwise admissible evidence.

(v) In proceedings under clauses (iii) and (iv), the parties may not obtain discovery pursuant to rules 26 through 36 of the Federal Rules of Civil Procedure, except that requests for admissions may be made pursuant to rules 26 and 36.

(vi) If the court finds under this paragraph that NGA has improperly withheld requested records because of failure to comply with any provision of this subsection, the court shall order NGA to search and review the appropriate exempted operational file or files for the requested records and make such records, or portions thereof, available in accordance with the provisions of section 552 of title 5, United States Code, and such order shall be the exclusive remedy for failure to comply with this subsection.

(vii) If at any time following the filing of a complaint pursuant to this paragraph NGA agrees to search the appropriate exempted operational file or files for the requested records, the court shall dismiss the claim based upon such complaint.

(viii) Any information filed with, or produced for the court pursuant to clauses (i) and (iv) shall be coordinated with the Director of National Intelligence prior to submission to the court.

(b) Decennial Review of Exempted Operational Files.—(1) Not less than once every 10 years, the Director of the National Geospatial-Intelligence Agency and the Director of National Intelligence shall review the exemptions in force under subsection (a)(1) to determine whether such exemptions may be removed from the category of exempted files or any portion thereof. The Director of National Intelligence must approve any determination to remove such exemptions.

(2) The review required by paragraph (1) shall include consideration of the historical value or other public interest in the subject matter of the particular category of files or portions thereof and the potential for declassifying a significant part of the information contained therein.

(3) A complainant that alleges that NGA has improperly withheld records because of failure to comply with this subsection may seek judicial review in the district

court of the United States of the district in which any of the parties reside, or in the District of Columbia. In such a proceeding, the court's review shall be limited to determining the following:

(A) Whether NGA has conducted the review required by paragraph (1) before the expiration of the 10-year period beginning on the date of the enactment of this section or before the expiration of the 10-year period beginning on the date of the most recent review.

(B) Whether NGA, in fact, considered the criteria set forth in paragraph (2) in conducting the required review.

OPERATIONAL FILES OF THE NATIONAL RECONNAISSANCE OFFICE

SEC. 703. [50 U.S.C. 3143] (a) EXEMPTION OF CERTAIN OPERATIONAL FILES FROM SEARCH, REVIEW, PUBLICATION, OR DISCLOSURE.—(1) The Director of the National Reconnaissance Office, with the coordination of the Director of National Intelligence, may exempt operational files of the National Reconnaissance Office from the provisions of section 552 of title 5, United States Code, which require publication, disclosure, search, or review in connection therewith.

(2)(A) Subject to subparagraph (B), for the purposes of this section, the term "operational files" means files of the National Reconnaissance Office (hereafter in this section referred to as "NRO") that document the means by which foreign intelligence or counterintelligence is collected through scientific and technical systems.

(B) Files which are the sole repository of disseminated intelligence are not operational files.

(3) Notwithstanding paragraph (1), exempted operational files shall continue to be subject to search and review for information concerning—

(A) United States citizens or aliens lawfully admitted for permanent residence who have requested information on themselves pursuant to the provisions of section 552 or 552a of title 5, United States Code;

(B) any special activity the existence of which is not exempt from disclosure under the provisions of section 552 of title 5, United States Code; or

(C) the specific subject matter of an investigation by any of the following for any impropriety, or violation of law, Executive order, or Presidential directive, in the conduct of an intelligence activity:

(i) The Permanent Select Committee on Intelligence of the House of Representatives.

(ii) The Select Committee on Intelligence of the Senate.

(iii) The Intelligence Oversight Board.

(iv) The Department of Justice.

(v) The Office of General Counsel of NRO.

(vi) The Office of the Director of NRO.

(vii) The Office of the Inspector General of the NRO.

(4)(A) Files that are not exempted under paragraph (1) which contain information derived or disseminated from exempted operational files shall be subject to search and review.

(B) The inclusion of information from exempted operational files in files that are not exempted under paragraph (1) shall not affect the exemption under paragraph (1) of the originating operational files from search, review, publication, or disclosure.

(C) The declassification of some of the information contained in exempted operational files shall not affect the status of the operational file as being exempt from search, review, publication, or disclosure.

(D) Records from exempted operational files which have been disseminated to and referenced in files that are not exempted under paragraph (1) and which have been returned to exempted operational files for sole retention shall be subject to search and review.

(5) The provisions of paragraph (1) may not be superseded except by a provision of law which is enacted after the date of the enactment of this section, and which specifically cites and repeals or modifies its provisions.

(6)(A) Except as provided in subparagraph (B), whenever any person who has requested agency records under section 552 of title 5, United States Code, alleges that NRO has withheld records improperly because of failure to comply with any provision of this section, judicial review shall be available under the terms set forth in section 552(a)(4)(B) of title 5, United States Code.

(B) Judicial review shall not be available in the manner provided for under subparagraph (A) as follows:

(i) In any case in which information specifically authorized under criteria established by an Executive order to be kept secret in the interests of national defense or foreign relations is filed with, or produced for, the court by NRO, such information shall be examined ex parte, in camera by the court.

(ii) The court shall, to the fullest extent practicable, determine the issues of fact based on sworn written submissions of the parties.

(iii) When a complainant alleges that requested records are improperly withheld because of improper placement solely in exempted operational files, the complainant shall support such allegation with a sworn written submission based upon personal knowledge or otherwise admissible evidence.

(iv)(I) When a complainant alleges that requested records were improperly withheld because of improper exemption of operational files, NRO shall meet its burden under section 552(a)(4)(B) of title 5, United States Code, by demonstrating to the court by sworn written submission that exempted operational files likely to contain responsive records currently perform the functions set forth in paragraph (2).

(II) The court may not order NRO to review the content of any exempted operational file or files in order to make the demonstration required under subclause (I), unless the complainant disputes NRO's showing with a sworn written submission based on personal knowledge or otherwise admissible evidence.

(v) In proceedings under clauses (iii) and (iv), the parties may not obtain discovery pursuant to rules 26 through 36 of the Federal Rules of Civil Procedure, except that requests for admissions may be made pursuant to rules 26 and 36.

(vi) If the court finds under this paragraph that NRO has improperly withheld requested records because of failure to comply with any provision of this subsection, the court shall order NRO to search and review the appropriate exempted operational file or files for the requested records and make such records, or portions thereof, available in accordance with the provisions of section 552 of title 5, United States Code, and such order shall be the exclusive remedy for failure to comply with this subsection.

(vii) If at any time following the filing of a complaint pursuant to this paragraph NRO agrees to search the appropriate exempted operational file or files for the requested records, the court shall dismiss the claim based upon such complaint.

(viii) Any information filed with, or produced for the court pursuant to clauses (i) and (iv) shall be coordinated with the Director of National Intelligence prior to submission to the court.

(b) Decennial Review of Exempted Operational Files.—(1) Not less than once every 10 years, the Director of the National Reconnaissance Office and the Director of National Intelligence shall review the exemptions in force under subsection (a)(1) to determine whether such exemptions may be removed from the category of exempted files or any portion thereof. The Director of National Intelligence must approve any determination to remove such exemptions.

(2) The review required by paragraph (1) shall include consideration of the historical value or other public interest in the subject matter of the particular category of files or portions thereof and the potential for declassifying a significant part of the information contained therein.

(3) A complainant that alleges that NRO has improperly withheld records because of failure to comply with this subsection may seek judicial review in the district court of the United States of the district in which any of the parties reside, or in the District of Columbia. In such a proceeding, the court's review shall be limited to determining the following:

(A) Whether NRO has conducted the review required by paragraph (1) before the expiration of the 10-year period beginning on the date of the enactment of this section or before the expiration of the 10-year period beginning on the date of the most recent review.

(B) Whether NRO, in fact, considered the criteria set forth in paragraph (2) in conducting the required review.

OPERATIONAL FILES OF THE NATIONAL SECURITY AGENCY

Sec. 704. [50 U.S.C. 3144] (a) Exemption of Certain Operational Files From Search, Review, Publication, or Disclosure.— The Director of the National Security Agency, in coordination with the Director of National Intelligence, may exempt operational files of the National Security Agency from the provisions of section 552 of title 5, United States Code, which require publication, disclosure, search, or review in connection therewith.

(b) Operational Files Defined.—(1) In this section, the term "operational files" means—

(A) files of the Signals Intelligence Directorate of the National Security Agency (and any successor organization of that directorate) that document the means by which foreign intelligence or counterintelligence is collected through technical systems; and

(B) files of the Research Associate Directorate of the National Security Agency (and any successor organization of that directorate) that document the means by which foreign intelligence or counterintelligence is collected through scientific and technical systems.

(2) Files that are the sole repository of disseminated intelligence, and files that have been accessioned into the National Security Agency Archives (or any successor organization) are not operational files.

(c) Search and Review for Information.—Notwithstanding subsection (a), exempted operational files shall continue to be subject to search and review for information concerning any of the following:

(1) United States citizens or aliens lawfully admitted for permanent residence who have requested information on themselves pursuant to the provisions of section 552 or 552a of title 5, United States Code.

(2) Any special activity the existence of which is not exempt from disclosure under the provisions of section 552 of title 5, United States Code.

(3) The specific subject matter of an investigation by any of the following for any impropriety, or violation of law, Executive order, or Presidential directive, in the conduct of an intelligence activity:

(A) The Committee on Armed Services and the Permanent Select Committee on Intelligence of the House of Representatives.

(B) The Committee on Armed Services and the Select Committee on Intelligence of the Senate.

(C) The Intelligence Oversight Board.

(D) The Department of Justice.

(E) The Office of General Counsel of the National Security Agency.

(F) The Office of the Inspector General of the Department of Defense.

(G) The Office of the Director of the National Security Agency.

(H) The Office of the Inspector General of the National Security Agency.

(d) Information Derived or Disseminated from Exempted Operational Files.—(1) Files that are not exempted under subsection (a) that contain information derived or disseminated from exempted operational files shall be subject to search and review.

(2) The inclusion of information from exempted operational files in files that are not exempted under subsection (a) shall not affect the exemption under subsection (a) of the originating operational files from search, review, publication, or disclosure.

(3) The declassification of some of the information contained in exempted operational files shall not affect the status of the operational file as being exempt

from search, review, publication, or disclosure.

(4) Records from exempted operational files that have been disseminated to and referenced in files that are not exempted under subsection (a) and that have been returned to exempted operational files for sole retention shall be subject to search and review.

(e) SUPERCEDURE OF OTHER LAWS.— The provisions of subsection (a) may not be superseded except by a provision of law that is enacted after the date of the enactment of this section and that specifically cites and repeals or modifies such provisions.

(f) ALLEGATION; IMPROPER WITHHOLDING OF RECORDS; JUDICIAL REVIEW.—(1) Except as provided in paragraph (2), whenever any person who has requested agency records under section 552 of title 5, United States Code, alleges that the National Security Agency has withheld records improperly because of failure to comply with any provision of this section, judicial review shall be available under the terms set forth in section 552(a)(4)(B) of title 5, United States Code.

(2) Judicial review shall not be available in the manner provided for under paragraph (1) as follows:

(A) In any case in which information specifically authorized under criteria established by an Executive order to be kept secret in the interests of national defense or foreign relations is filed with, or produced for, the court by the National Security Agency, such information shall be examined ex parte, in camera by the court.

(B) The court shall determine, to the fullest extent practicable, the issues of fact based on sworn written submissions of the parties.

(C) When a complainant alleges that requested records are improperly withheld because of improper placement solely in exempted operational files, the complainant shall support such allegation with a sworn written submission based upon personal knowledge or otherwise admissible evidence.

(D)(i) When a complainant alleges that requested records were improperly withheld because of improper exemption of operational files, the National Security Agency shall meet its burden under section 552(a)(4)(B) of title 5, United States Code, by demonstrating to the court by sworn written submission that exempted operational files likely to contain responsive records currently perform the functions set forth in subsection (b).

(ii) The court may not order the National Security Agency to review the content of any exempted operational file or files in order to make the demonstration required under clause (i), unless the complainant disputes the National Security Agency's showing with a sworn written submission based on personal knowledge or otherwise admissible evidence.

(E) In proceedings under subparagraphs (C) and (D), the parties may not obtain discovery pursuant to rules 26 through 36 of the Federal Rules of Civil Procedure, except that requests for admissions may be made pursuant to rules 26 and 36.

(F) If the court finds under this subsection that the National Security Agency has improperly withheld requested records because of failure to comply with any provision of this subsection, the court shall order the Agency to search and review the appropriate exempted operational file or files for the requested records and make such records, or portions thereof, available in accordance with the provisions of section 552 of title 5, United States Code, and such order shall be the exclusive remedy for failure to comply with this section (other than subsection (g)).

(G) If at any time following the filing of a complaint pursuant to this paragraph the National Security Agency agrees to search the appropriate exempted operational file or files for the requested records, the court shall dismiss the claim based upon such complaint.

(H) Any information filed with, or produced for the court pursuant to subparagraphs (A) and (D) shall be coordinated with the Director of National Intelligence before submission to the court.

(g) DECENNIAL REVIEW OF EXEMPTED OPERATIONAL FILES.—(1) Not less than once every 10 years, the Director of the National Security Agency and the Director of National Intelligence shall review the exemptions in force under subsection (a) to determine whether such exemptions may be removed from a category of exempted files or any portion thereof. The Director of National Intelligence must approve any determination to remove such exemptions.

(2) The review required by paragraph (1) shall include consideration of the historical value or other public interest in the subject matter of a particular category of files or portions thereof and the potential for declassifying a significant part of the information contained therein.

(3) A complainant that alleges that the National Security Agency has improperly withheld records because of failure to comply with this subsection may seek judicial review in the district court of the United States of the district in which any of the parties reside, or in the District of Columbia. In such a proceeding, the court's review shall be limited to determining the following:

(A) Whether the National Security Agency has conducted the review required by paragraph (1) before the expiration of the 10-year period beginning on the date of the enactment of this section or before the expiration of the 10-year period beginning on the date of the most recent review.

(B) Whether the National Security Agency, in fact, considered the criteria set forth in paragraph (2) in conducting the required review.

OPERATIONAL FILES OF THE DEFENSE INTELLIGENCE AGENCY

SEC. 705. [50 U.S.C. 3145] (a) EXEMPTION OF OPERATIONAL FILES.— The Director of the Defense Intelligence Agency, in coordination with the Director of National Intelligence, may exempt operational files of the Defense Intelligence Agency from the provisions of section 552 of title 5, United States Code, which require publication, disclosure, search, or review in connection therewith.

(b) OPERATIONAL FILES DEFINED.—(1) In this section, the term "operational files" means—

(A) files of the Directorate of Human Intelligence of the Defense Intelligence Agency (and any successor organization of that directorate) that document the conduct of foreign intelligence or counterintelligence operations or intelligence or security liaison arrangements or information exchanges with foreign governments or their intelligence or security services; and

(B) files of the Directorate of Technology of the Defense Intelligence Agency (and any successor organization of that directorate) that document the means by which foreign intelligence or counterintelligence is collected through technical systems.

(2) Files that are the sole repository of disseminated intelligence are not operational files.

(c) SEARCH AND REVIEW FOR INFORMATION.—Notwithstanding subsection (a), exempted operational files shall continue to be subject to search and review for information concerning:

(1) United States citizens or aliens lawfully admitted for permanent residence who have requested information on themselves pursuant to the provisions of section 552 or 552a of title 5, United States Code.

(2) Any special activity the existence of which is not exempt from disclosure under the provisions of section 552 of title 5, United States Code.

(3) The specific subject matter of an investigation by any of the following for any impropriety, or violation of law, Executive order, or Presidential directive, in the conduct of an intelligence activity:

(A) The Committee on Armed Services and the Permanent Select Committee on Intelligence of the House of Representatives.

(B) The Committee on Armed Services and the Select Committee on Intelligence of the Senate.

(C) The Intelligence Oversight Board.

(D) The Department of Justice.

(E) The Office of General Counsel of the Department of Defense or of the Defense Intelligence Agency.

(F) The Office of Inspector General of the Department of Defense or of the Defense Intelligence Agency.

(G) The Office of the Director of the Defense Intelligence Agency.

(d) INFORMATION DERIVED OR DISSEMINATED FROM EXEMPTED OPERATIONAL FILES.—(1) Files that are not exempted under subsection (a) that contain information derived or disseminated from exempted operational files shall be subject to search and review.

(2) The inclusion of information from exempted operational files in files that are not exempted under subsection (a) shall not affect the exemption under subsection (a) of the originating operational files from search, review, publication, or disclosure.

(3) The declassification of some of the information contained in an exempted operational file shall not affect the status of the operational file as being exempt from search, review, publication, or disclosure.

(4) Records from exempted operational files that have been disseminated to and referenced in files that are not exempted under subsection (a) and that have been returned to exempted operational files for sole retention shall be subject to search

and review.

(e) Allegation; Improper Withholding of Records; Judicial Review.—(1) Except as provided in paragraph (2), whenever any person who has requested agency records under section 552 of title 5, United States Code, alleges that the Defense Intelligence Agency has withheld records improperly because of failure to comply with any provision of this section, judicial review shall be available under the terms set forth in section 552(a)(4)(B) of title 5, United States Code.

(2) Judicial review shall not be available in the manner provided under paragraph (1) as follows:

(A) In any case in which information specifically authorized under criteria established by an Executive order to be kept secret in the interest of national defense or foreign relations which is filed with, or produced for, the court by the Defense Intelligence Agency, such information shall be examined ex parte, in camera by the court.

(B) The court shall determine, to the fullest extent practicable, issues of fact based on sworn written submissions of the parties.

(C) When a complainant alleges that requested records were improperly withheld because of improper placement solely in exempted operational files, the complainant shall support such allegation with a sworn written submission based upon personal knowledge or otherwise admissible evidence.

(D)(i) When a complainant alleges that requested records were improperly withheld because of improper exemption of operational files, the Defense Intelligence Agency shall meet its burden under section 552(a)(4)(B) of title 5, United States Code, by demonstrating to the court by sworn written submission that exempted operational files likely to contain responsive records currently perform the functions set forth in subsection (b).

(ii) The court may not order the Defense Intelligence Agency to review the content of any exempted operational file or files in order to make the demonstration required under clause (i), unless the complainant disputes the Defense Intelligence Agency's showing with a sworn written submission based on personal knowledge or otherwise admissible evidence.

(E) In proceedings under subparagraphs (C) and (D), the parties shall not obtain discovery pursuant to rules 26 through 36 of the Federal Rules of Civil Procedure, except that requests for admission may be made pursuant to rules 26 and 36.

(F) If the court finds under this subsection that the Defense Intelligence Agency has improperly withheld requested records because of failure to comply with any provision of this subsection, the court shall order the Defense Intelligence Agency to search and review the appropriate exempted operational file or files for the requested records and make such records, or portions thereof, available in accordance with the provisions of section 552 of title 5, United States Code, and such order shall be the exclusive remedy for failure to comply with this section (other than subsection (f)).

(G) If at any time following the filing of a complaint pursuant to this paragraph the Defense Intelligence Agency agrees to search the appropriate exempted operational file or files for the requested records, the court shall dismiss the claim based upon such complaint.

(H) Any information filed with, or produced for the court pursuant to subparagraphs (A) and (D) shall be coordinated with the Director of National Intelligence before submission to the court.

(f) DECENNIAL REVIEW OF EXEMPTED OPERATIONAL FILES.—(1) Not less than once every 10 years, the Director of the Defense Intelligence Agency and the Director of National Intelligence shall review the exemptions in force under subsection (a) to determine whether such exemptions may be removed from a category of exempted files or any portion thereof. The Director of National Intelligence must approve any determinations to remove such exemptions.

(2) The review required by paragraph (1) shall include consideration of the historical value or other public interest in the subject matter of the particular category of files or portions thereof and the potential for declassifying a significant part of the information contained therein.

(3) A complainant that alleges that the Defense Intelligence Agency has improperly withheld records because of failure to comply with this subsection may seek judicial review in the district court of the United States of the district in which any of the parties reside, or in the District of Columbia. In such a proceeding, the court's review shall be limited to determining the following:

(A) Whether the Defense Intelligence Agency has conducted the review required by paragraph (1) before the expiration of the 10-year period beginning on the date of the enactment of this section or before the expiration of the 10-year period beginning on the date of the most recent review.

(B) Whether the Defense Intelligence Agency, in fact, considered the criteria set forth in paragraph (2) in conducting the required review.

(g) TERMINATION.— This section shall cease to be effective on December 31, 2007.

PROTECTION OF CERTAIN FILES OF THE OFFICE OF THE DIRECTOR OF NATIONAL INTELLIGENCE

SEC. 706. [50 U.S.C. 3146] (a) INAPPLICABILITY OF FOIA TO EXEMPTED OPERATIONAL FILES PROVIDED TO ODNI.—(1) Subject to paragraph (2), the provisions of section 552 of title 5, United States Code, that require search, review, publication, or disclosure of a record shall not apply to a record provided to the Office of the Director of National Intelligence by an element of the intelligence community from the exempted operational files of such element.

(2) Paragraph (1) shall not apply with respect to a record of the Office that—

(A) contains information derived or disseminated from an exempted operational file, unless such record is created by the Office for the sole purpose of organizing such exempted operational file for use by the Office;

(B) is disseminated by the Office to a person other than an officer, employee, or contractor of the Office; or

(C) is no longer designated as an exempted operational file in accordance with this title.

(b) EFFECT OF PROVIDING FILES TO ODNI.— Notwithstanding any other provision of this title, an exempted operational file that is provided to the Office by an element of the intelligence community shall not be subject to the provisions of section 552 of title 5, United States Code, that require search, review, publication, or disclosure of a record solely because such element provides such exempted operational file to the Office.

(c) Search and Review for Certain Purposes.—Notwithstanding subsection (a) or (b), an exempted operational file shall continue to be subject to search and review for information concerning any of the following:

(1) United States citizens or aliens lawfully admitted for permanent residence who have requested information on themselves pursuant to the provisions of section 552 or 552a of title 5, United States Code.

(2) Any special activity the existence of which is not exempt from disclosure under the provisions of section 552 of title 5, United States Code.

(3) The specific subject matter of an investigation for any impropriety or violation of law, Executive order, or Presidential directive, in the conduct of an intelligence activity by any of the following:

(A) The Select Committee on Intelligence of the Senate.

(B) The Permanent Select Committee on Intelligence of the House of Representatives.

(C) The Intelligence Oversight Board.

(D) The Department of Justice.

(E) The Office of the Director of National Intelligence.

(F) The Office of the Inspector General of the Intelligence Community.

(d) Decennial Review of Exempted Operational Files.—(1) Not less than once every 10 years, the Director of National Intelligence shall review the exemptions in force under subsection (a) to determine whether such exemptions may be removed from any category of exempted files or any portion thereof.

(2) The review required by paragraph (1) shall include consideration of the historical value or other public interest in the subject matter of the particular category of files or portions thereof and the potential for declassifying a significant part of the information contained therein.

(3) A complainant that alleges that the Director of National Intelligence has improperly withheld records because of failure to comply with this subsection may seek judicial review in the district court of the United States of the district in which any of the parties reside, or in the District of Columbia. In such a proceeding, the court's review shall be limited to determining the following:

(A) Whether the Director has conducted the review required by paragraph (1) before the expiration of the 10-year period beginning on the date of the enactment of the Intelligence Authorization Act for Fiscal Year 2010 or before the expiration of the 10-year period beginning on the date of the most recent review.

(B) Whether the Director of National Intelligence, in fact, considered the criteria set forth in paragraph (2) in conducting the required review.

(e) Supersedure of Other Laws.— The provisions of this section may not be superseded except by a provision of law that is enacted after the date of the enactment of this section and that specifically cites and repeals or modifies such provisions.

(f) ALLEGATION; IMPROPER WITHHOLDING OF RECORDS; JUDICIAL REVIEW.—(1) Except as provided in paragraph (2), whenever any person who has requested agency records under section 552 of title 5, United States Code, alleges that the Office has withheld records improperly because of failure to comply with any provision of this section, judicial review shall be available under the terms set forth in section 552(a)(4)(B) of title 5, United States Code.

(2) Judicial review shall not be available in the manner provided for under paragraph (1) as follows:

(A) In any case in which information specifically authorized under criteria established by an Executive order to be kept secret in the interests of national defense or foreign relations is filed with, or produced for, the court by the Office, such information shall be examined ex parte, in camera by the court.

(B) The court shall determine, to the fullest extent practicable, the issues of fact based on sworn written submissions of the parties.

(C)(i) When a complainant alleges that requested records were improperly withheld because of improper exemption of operational files, the Office may meet the burden of the Office under section 552(a)(4)(B) of title 5, United States Code, by demonstrating to the court by sworn written submission that exempted files likely to contain responsive records are records provided to the Office by an element of the intelligence community from the exempted operational files of such element.

(ii) The court may not order the Office to review the content of any exempted file in order to make the demonstration required under clause (i), unless the complainant disputes the Office's showing with a sworn written submission based on personal knowledge or otherwise admissible evidence.

(D) In proceedings under subparagraph (C), a party may not obtain discovery pursuant to rules 26 through 36 of the Federal Rules of Civil Procedure, except that requests for admissions may be made pursuant to rules 26 and 36 of the Federal Rules of Civil Procedure.

(E) If the court finds under this subsection that the Office has improperly withheld requested records because of failure to comply with any provision of this section, the court shall order the Office to search and review each appropriate exempted file for the requested records and make such records, or portions thereof, available in accordance with the provisions of section 552 of title 5, United States Code (commonly referred to as the Freedom of Information Act), and such order shall be the exclusive remedy for failure to comply with this section.

(F) If at any time following the filing of a complaint pursuant to this paragraph the Office agrees to search each appropriate exempted file for the requested records, the court shall dismiss the claim based upon such complaint.

(g) DEFINITIONS.—In this section:

(1) The term "exempted operational file" means a file of an element of the intelligence community that, in accordance with this title, is exempted from the

provisions of section 552 of title 5, United States Code, that require search, review, publication, or disclosure of such file.

(2) Except as otherwise specifically provided, the term "Office" means the Office of the Director of National Intelligence.

TITLE VIII—ACCESS TO CLASSIFIED INFORMATION

PROCEDURES

SEC. 801. [50 U.S.C 3161] (a) Not later than 180 days after the date of enactment of this title, the President shall, by Executive order or regulation, establish procedures to govern access to classified information which shall be binding upon all departments, agencies, and offices of the executive branch of Government. Such procedures shall, at a minimum—

(1) provide that, except as may be permitted by the President, no employee in the executive branch of Government may be given access to classified information by any department, agency, or office of the executive branch of Government unless, based upon an appropriate background investigation, such access is determined to be clearly consistent with the national security interests of the United States;

(2) establish uniform minimum requirements governing the scope and frequency of background investigations and reinvestigations for all employees in the executive branch of Government who require access to classified information as part of their official responsibilities;

(3) provide that all employees in the executive branch of Government who require access to classified information shall be required as a condition of such access to provide to the employing department or agency written consent which permits access by an authorized investigative agency to relevant financial records, other financial information, consumer reports, travel records, and computers used in the performance of Government duties, as determined by the President, in accordance with section 802 of this title, during the period of access to classified information and for a period of three years thereafter;

(4) provide that all employees in the executive branch of Government who require access to particularly sensitive classified information, as determined by the President, shall be required, as a condition of maintaining access to such information, to submit to the employing department or agency, during the period of such access, relevant information concerning their financial condition and foreign travel, as determined by the President, as may be necessary to ensure appropriate security; and

(5) establish uniform minimum standards to ensure that employees in the executive branch of Government whose access to classified information is being denied or terminated under this title are appropriately advised of the reasons for such denial or termination and are provided an adequate opportunity to respond to all adverse information which forms the basis for such denial or termination before final action by the department or agency concerned.

(b)(1) Subsection (a) shall not be deemed to limit or affect the responsibility and power of an agency head pursuant to other law or Executive order to deny or terminate access to classified information if the national security so requires. Such responsibility and power may be exercised only when the agency head determines that the procedures prescribed by subsection (a) cannot be invoked in a manner that is consistent with the national security.

(2) Upon the exercise of such responsibility, the agency head shall submit a report to the congressional intelligence committees.

REQUESTS BY AUTHORIZED INVESTIGATIVE AGENCIES

SEC. 802. [50 U.S.C. 3162] (a)(1) Any authorized investigative agency may request from any financial agency, financial institution, or holding company, or from any consumer reporting agency, such financial records, other financial information, and consumer reports as may be necessary in order to conduct any authorized law enforcement investigation, counterintelligence inquiry, or security determination. Any authorized investigative agency may also request records maintained by any commercial entity within the United States pertaining to travel by an employee in the executive branch of Government outside the United States.

(2) Requests may be made under this section where—

(A) the records sought pertain to a person who is or was an employee in the executive branch of Government required by the President in an Executive order or regulation, as a condition of access to classified information, to provide consent, during a background investigation and for such time as access to the information is maintained, and for a period of not more than three years thereafter, permitting access to financial records, other financial information, consumer reports, and travel records; and

(B)(i) there are reasonable grounds to believe, based on credible information, that the person is, or may be, disclosing classified information in an unauthorized manner to a foreign power or agent of a foreign power;

(ii) information the employing agency deems credible indicates the person has incurred excessive indebtedness or has acquired a level of affluence which cannot be explained by other information known to the agency; or

(iii) circumstances indicate the person had the capability and opportunity to disclose classified information which is known to have been lost or compromised to a foreign power or an agent of a foreign power.

(3) Each such request—

(A) shall be accompanied by a written certification signed by the department or agency head or deputy department or agency head concerned, or by a senior official designated for this purpose by the department or agency head concerned (whose rank shall be no lower than Assistant Secretary or Assistant Director), and shall certify that—

(i) the person concerned is or was an employee within the meaning of paragraph (2)(A);

(ii) the request is being made pursuant to an authorized inquiry or investigation and is authorized under this section; and

(iii) the records or information to be reviewed are records or information which the employee has previously agreed to make available to the authorized investigative agency for review;

(B) shall contain a copy of the agreement referred to in subparagraph (A)(iii);

(C) shall identify specifically or by category the records or information to be reviewed; and

(D) shall inform the recipient of the request of the prohibition described in subsection (b).

(b) PROHIBITION OF CERTAIN DISCLOSURE.—

(1) PROHIBITION.—

(A) IN GENERAL.— If a certification is issued under subparagraph (B) and notice of the right to judicial review under subsection (c) is provided, no governmental or private entity that receives a request under subsection (a), or officer, employee, or agent thereof, shall disclose to any person that an authorized investigative agency described in subsection (a) has sought or obtained access to information under subsection (a).

(B) CERTIFICATION.—The requirements of subparagraph (A) shall apply if the head of an authorized investigative agency described in subsection (a), or a designee, certifies that the absence of a prohibition of disclosure under this subsection may result in—

(i) a danger to the national security of the United States;

(ii) interference with a criminal, counterterrorism, or counterintelligence investigation;

(iii) interference with diplomatic relations; or

(iv) danger to the life or physical safety of any person.

(2) EXCEPTION.—

(A) IN GENERAL.—A governmental or private entity that receives a request under subsection (a), or officer, employee, or agent thereof, may disclose information otherwise subject to any applicable nondisclosure requirement to—

(i) those persons to whom disclosure is necessary in order to comply with the request;

(ii) an attorney in order to obtain legal advice or assistance regarding the request; or

(iii) other persons as permitted by the head of the authorized investigative agency described in subsection (a) or a designee.

(B) APPLICATION.— A person to whom disclosure is made under subparagraph (A) shall be subject to the nondisclosure requirements applicable to a person to whom a request is issued under subsection (a) in the same manner as the person to whom the request is issued.

(C) NOTICE.— Any recipient that discloses to a person described in subparagraph (A) information otherwise subject to a nondisclosure requirement shall inform the person of the applicable nondisclosure requirement.

(D) IDENTIFICATION OF DISCLOSURE RECIPIENTS.— At the request of the head of an authorized investigative agency described in subsection (a), or a designee, any person making or intending to make a disclosure under clause (i) or (iii) of subparagraph (A) shall identify to the head of the authorized investigative agency or such designee the person to whom such disclosure will be made or to whom such disclosure was made prior to the request.

(c) JUDICIAL REVIEW.—

(1) IN GENERAL.— A request under subsection (a) or a nondisclosure requirement imposed in connection with such request under subsection (b) shall be subject to judicial review under section 3511 of title 18, United States Code.

(2) NOTICE.— A request under subsection (a) shall include notice of the availability of judicial review described in paragraph (1).

(d)(1) Notwithstanding any other provision of law (other than section 6103 of the Internal Revenue Code of 1986), an entity receiving a request for records or information under subsection (a) shall, if the request satisfies the requirements of this section, make available such records or information within 30 days for inspection or copying, as may be appropriate, by the agency requesting such records or information.

(2) Any entity (including any officer, employee, or agent thereof) that discloses records or information for inspection or copying pursuant to this section in good faith reliance upon the certifications made by an agency pursuant to this section shall not be liable for any such disclosure to any person under this title, the constitution of any State, or any law or regulation of any State or any political subdivision of any State.

(e) Any agency requesting records or information under this section may, subject to the availability of appropriations, reimburse a private entity for any cost reasonably incurred by such entity in responding to such request, including the cost of identifying, reproducing, or transporting records or other data.

(f) An agency receiving records or information pursuant to a request under this section may disseminate the records or information obtained pursuant to such request outside the agency only—

(1) to the agency employing the employee who is the subject of the records or information;

(2) to the Department of Justice for law enforcement or counterintelligence purposes; or

(3) with respect to dissemination to an agency of the United States, if such information is clearly relevant to the authorized responsibilities of such agency.

(g) Nothing in this section may be construed to affect the authority of an investigative agency to obtain information pursuant to the Right to Financial Privacy Act (12 U.S.C. 3401 et seq.) or the Fair Credit Reporting Act (15 U.S.C. 1681 et seq.).

SEC. 803. [50 U.S.C. 3162a] SECURITY EXECUTIVE AGENT.

(a) IN GENERAL.— The Director of National Intelligence, or such other officer of the United States as the President may designate, shall serve as the Security Executive Agent for all departments and agencies of the United States.

(b) DUTIES.—The duties of the Security Executive Agent are as follows:

(1) To direct the oversight of investigations, reinvestigations, adjudications,

and, as applicable, polygraphs for eligibility for access to classified information or eligibility to hold a sensitive position made by any Federal agency.

(2) To review the national security background investigation and adjudication programs of Federal agencies to determine whether such programs are being implemented in accordance with this section.

(3) To develop and issue uniform and consistent policies and procedures to ensure the effective, efficient, timely, and secure completion of investigations, polygraphs, and adjudications relating to determinations of eligibility for access to classified information or eligibility to hold a sensitive position.

(4) Unless otherwise designated by law, to serve as the final authority to designate a Federal agency or agencies to conduct investigations of persons who are proposed for access to classified information or for eligibility to hold a sensitive position to ascertain whether such persons satisfy the criteria for obtaining and retaining access to classified information or eligibility to hold a sensitive position, as applicable.

(5) Unless otherwise designated by law, to serve as the final authority to designate a Federal agency or agencies to determine eligibility for access to classified information or eligibility to hold a sensitive position in accordance with Executive Order No. 12968 (50 U.S.C. 3161 note; relating to access to classified information).

(6) To review and approve the policies of the Federal agencies that ensure reciprocal recognition of eligibility for access to classified information or eligibility to hold a sensitive position among Federal agencies, and to act as the final authority to arbitrate and resolve disputes among such agencies involving the reciprocity of investigations and adjudications of eligibility.

(7) To execute all other duties assigned to the Security Executive Agent by law.

(c) AUTHORITIES.—The Security Executive Agent shall—

(1) issue guidelines and instructions to the heads of Federal agencies to ensure appropriate uniformity, centralization, efficiency, effectiveness, timeliness, and security in processes relating to determinations by such agencies of eligibility for access to classified information or eligibility to hold a sensitive position, including such matters as investigations, polygraphs, adjudications, and reciprocity;

(2) have the authority to grant exceptions to, or waivers of, national security investigative requirements, including issuing implementing or clarifying guidance, as necessary;

(3) have the authority to assign, in whole or in part, to the head of any Federal agency (solely or jointly) any of the duties of the Security Executive Agent described in subsection (b) or the authorities described in paragraphs (1) and (2), provided that the exercise of such assigned duties or authorities is subject to the oversight of the Security Executive Agent, including such terms and conditions (including approval by the Security Executive Agent) as the Security Executive Agent determines appropriate;

(4) define and set standards for continuous vetting for continued access to classified information and for eligibility to hold a sensitive position; and

(5) issue guidelines and instructions to the heads of Federal agencies to ensure

that any individual who was appointed by the President to a position in an element of the intelligence community but is no longer employed by the Federal Government shall maintain a security clearance only in accordance with Executive Order 12968 (50 U.S.C. 3161 note; relating to access to classified information), or successor order.

EXCEPTIONS

SEC. 804. [50 U.S.C. 3163] Except as otherwise specifically provided, the provisions of this title shall not apply to the President and Vice President, Members of the Congress, Justices of the Supreme Court, and Federal judges appointed by the President.

DEFINITIONS

SEC. 805. [50 U.S.C. 3164] For purposes of this title—

(1) the term "authorized investigative agency" means an agency authorized by law or regulation to conduct a counterintelligence investigation or investigations of persons who are proposed for access to classified information to ascertain whether such persons satisfy the criteria for obtaining and retaining access to such information;

(2) the term "classified information" means any information that has been determined pursuant to Executive Order No. 12356 of April 2, 1982, or successor orders, or the Atomic Energy Act of 1954, to require protection against unauthorized disclosure and that is so designated;

(3) the term "consumer reporting agency" has the meaning given such term in section 603 of the Consumer Credit Protection Act (15 U.S.C. 1681a);

(4) the term "employee" includes any person who receives a salary or compensation of any kind from the United States Government, is a contractor of the United States Government or an employee thereof, is an unpaid consultant of the United States Government, or otherwise acts for or on behalf of the United States Government, except as otherwise determined by the President;

(5) the terms "financial agency" and "financial institution" have the meanings given to such terms in section 5312(a) of title 31, United States Code, and the term "holding company" has the meaning given to such term in section 1101(6) of the Right to Financial Privacy Act of 1978 (12 U.S.C. 3401);

(6) the terms "foreign power" and "agent of a foreign power" have the same meanings as set forth in subsections (a) and (b) of section 101, respectively, of the Foreign Intelligence Surveillance Act of 1978 (50 U.S.C. 1801);

(7) the term "State" means each of the several States of the United States, the District of Columbia, the Commonwealth of Puerto Rico, the Commonwealth of the Northern Mariana Islands, the United States Virgin Islands, Guam, American Samoa, the Republic of the Marshall Islands, the Federated States of Micronesia, and the Republic of Palau, and any other possession of the United States; and

(8) the term "computer" means any electronic, magnetic, optical, electrochemical, or other high speed data processing device performing logical, arithmetic, or storage functions, and includes any data storage facility or communications facility directly related to or operating in conjunction with such device and any data or other

information stored or contained in such device.

TITLE IX—APPLICATION OF SANCTIONS LAWS TO INTELLIGENCE ACTIVITIES

STAY OF SANCTIONS

SEC. 901. [50 U.S.C. 3171] Notwithstanding any provision of law identified in section 904, the President may stay the imposition of an economic, cultural, diplomatic, or other sanction or related action by the United States Government concerning a foreign country, organization, or person when the President determines and reports to Congress in accordance with section 903 that to proceed without delay would seriously risk the compromise of an ongoing criminal investigation directly related to the activities giving rise to the sanction or an intelligence source or method directly related to the activities giving rise to the sanction. Any such stay shall be effective for a period of time specified by the President, which period may not exceed 120 days, unless such period is extended in accordance with section 902.

EXTENSION OF STAY

SEC. 902. [50 U.S.C. 3172] Whenever the President determines and reports to Congress in accordance with section 903 that a stay of sanctions or related actions pursuant to section 901 has not afforded sufficient time to obviate the risk to an ongoing criminal investigation or to an intelligence source or method that gave rise to the stay, he may extend such stay for a period of time specified by the President, which period may not exceed 120 days. The authority of this section may be used to extend the period of a stay pursuant to section 901 for successive periods of not more than 120 days each.

REPORTS

SEC. 903. [50 U.S.C. 3173] Reports to Congress pursuant to sections 901 and 902 shall be submitted promptly upon determinations under this title. Such reports shall be submitted to the Committee on International Relations of the House of Representatives and the Committee on Foreign Relations of the Senate. With respect to determinations relating to intelligence sources and methods, reports shall also be submitted to the congressional intelligence committees. With respect to determinations relating to ongoing criminal investigations, reports shall also be submitted to the Committees on the Judiciary of the House of Representatives and the Senate.

LAWS SUBJECT TO STAY

SEC. 904. [50 U.S.C. 3174] The President may use the authority of sections 901 and 902 to stay the imposition of an economic, cultural, diplomatic, or other sanction or related action by the United States Government related to the proliferation of weapons of mass destruction, their delivery systems, or advanced conventional weapons otherwise required to be imposed by the Chemical and Biological Weapons Control and Warfare Elimination Act of 1991 (title III of Public Law 102–182); the Nuclear Proliferation Prevention Act of 1994 (title VIII of Public Law 103–236); title XVII of the National Defense Authorization Act for Fiscal Year 1991 (Public Law 101–510) (relating to the nonproliferation of missile technology); the Iran-Iraq Arms Nonproliferation Act of

1992 (title XVI of Public Law 102–484); section 573 of the Foreign Operations, Export Financing Related Programs Appropriations Act, 1994 (Public Law 103–87); section 563 of the Foreign Operations, Export Financing Related Programs Appropriations Act, 1995 (Public Law 103–306); and comparable provisions.[Section 905 was repealed by section 313(a) of Public Law 108–177, December 13, 2003, 117 Stat. 2610; 50 U.S.C. 3175]

TITLE X—EDUCATION IN SUPPORT OF NATIONAL INTELLIGENCE

subtitle A—SCIENCE AND TECHNOLOGY

SCHOLARSHIPS AND WORK-STUDY FOR PURSUIT OF GRADUATE DEGREES IN SCIENCE AND TECHNOLOGY

SEC. 1001. [50 U.S.C. 3191] (a) PROGRAM AUTHORIZED.— The Director of National Intelligence may carry out a program to provide scholarships and work-study for individuals who are pursuing graduate degrees in fields of study in science and technology that are identified by the Director as appropriate to meet the future needs of the intelligence community for qualified scientists and engineers.

(b) ADMINISTRATION.— If the Director of National Intelligence carries out the program under subsection (a), the Director of National Intelligence shall administer the program through the Office of the Director of National Intelligence.

(c) IDENTIFICATION OF FIELDS OF STUDY.— If the Director of National Intelligence carries out the program under subsection (a), the Director shall identify fields of study under subsection (a) in consultation with the other heads of the elements of the intelligence community.

(d) ELIGIBILITY FOR PARTICIPATION.—An individual eligible to participate in the program is any individual who—

(1) either—

(A) is an employee of the intelligence community; or

(B) meets criteria for eligibility for employment in the intelligence community that are established by the Director of National Intelligence;

(2) is accepted in a graduate degree program in a field of study in science or technology identified under subsection (a); and

(3) is eligible for a security clearance at the level of Secret or above.

(e) REGULATIONS.— If the Director of National Intelligence carries out the program under subsection (a), the Director shall prescribe regulations for purposes of the administration of this section.

FRAMEWORK FOR CROSS-DISCIPLINARY EDUCATION AND TRAINING

SEC. 1002. [50 U.S.C. 3192] The Director of National Intelligence shall establish an integrated framework that brings together the educational components of the intelligence community in order to promote a more effective and productive intelligence community through cross-disciplinary education and joint training.

subtitle B—Foreign Languages Program

PROGRAM ON ADVANCEMENT OF FOREIGN LANGUAGES CRITICAL TO THE INTELLIGENCE COMMUNITY

Sec. 1011. [50 U.S.C. 3201] (a) In General.— The Secretary of Defense and the Director of National Intelligence may jointly carry out a program to advance skills in foreign languages that are critical to the capability of the intelligence community to carry out the national security activities of the United States (hereinafter in this subtitle referred to as the "Foreign Languages Program").

(b) Identification of Requisite Actions.— In order to carry out the Foreign Languages Program, the Secretary of Defense and the Director of National Intelligence shall jointly identify actions required to improve the education of personnel in the intelligence community in foreign languages that are critical to the capability of the intelligence community to carry out the national security activities of the United States and to meet the long-term intelligence needs of the United States.

EDUCATION PARTNERSHIPS

Sec. 1012. [50 U.S.C. 3202] (a) In General.— In carrying out the Foreign Languages Program, the head of a covered element of the intelligence community may enter into one or more education partnership agreements with educational institutions in the United States in order to encourage and enhance the study in such educational institutions of foreign languages that are critical to the capability of the intelligence community to carry out the national security activities of the United States.

(b) Assistance Provided Under Educational Partnership Agreements.—Under an educational partnership agreement entered into with an educational institution pursuant to this section, the head of a covered element of the intelligence community may provide the following assistance to the educational institution:

(1) The loan of equipment and instructional materials of the element of the intelligence community to the educational institution for any purpose and duration that the head of the element considers appropriate.

(2) Notwithstanding any other provision of law relating to the transfer of surplus property, the transfer to the educational institution of any computer equipment, or other equipment, that is—

(A) commonly used by educational institutions;

(B) surplus to the needs of the element of the intelligence community; and

(C) determined by the head of the element to be appropriate for support of such agreement.

(3) The provision of dedicated personnel to the educational institution—

(A) to teach courses in foreign languages that are critical to the capability of the intelligence community to carry out the national security activities of the United States; or

(B) to assist in the development for the educational institution of courses and materials on such languages.

(4) The involvement of faculty and students of the educational institution in

research projects of the element of the intelligence community.

(5) Cooperation with the educational institution in developing a program under which students receive academic credit at the educational institution for work on research projects of the element of the intelligence community.

(6) The provision of academic and career advice and assistance to students of the educational institution.

(7) The provision of cash awards and other items that the head of the element of the intelligence community considers appropriate.

VOLUNTARY SERVICES

SEC. 1013. [50 U.S.C. 3203] (a) AUTHORITY TO ACCEPT SERVICES.— Notwithstanding section 1342 of title 31, United States Code, and subject to subsection (b), the Foreign Languages Program under section 1011 shall include authority for the head of a covered element of the intelligence community to accept from any dedicated personnel voluntary services in support of the activities authorized by this subtitle.

(b) REQUIREMENTS AND LIMITATIONS.—(1) In accepting voluntary services from an individual under subsection (a), the head of a covered element of the intelligence community shall—

(A) supervise the individual to the same extent as the head of the element would supervise a compensated employee of that element providing similar services; and

(B) ensure that the individual is licensed, privileged, has appropriate educational or experiential credentials, or is otherwise qualified under applicable law or regulations to provide such services.

(2) In accepting voluntary services from an individual under subsection (a), the head of a covered element of the intelligence community may not—

(A) place the individual in a policymaking position, or other position performing inherently governmental functions; or

(B) compensate the individual for the provision of such services.

(c) AUTHORITY TO RECRUIT AND TRAIN INDIVIDUALS PROVIDING SERVICES.— The head of a covered element of the intelligence community may recruit and train individuals to provide voluntary services under subsection (a).

(d) STATUS OF INDIVIDUALS PROVIDING SERVICES.—(1) Subject to paragraph (2), while providing voluntary services under subsection (a) or receiving training under subsection (c), an individual shall be considered to be an employee of the Federal Government only for purposes of the following provisions of law:

(A) Section 552a of title 5, United States Code (relating to maintenance of records on individuals).

(B) Chapter 11 of title 18, United States Code (relating to conflicts of interest).

(2)(A) With respect to voluntary services under paragraph (1) provided by an individual that are within the scope of the services accepted under that paragraph, the individual shall be deemed to be a volunteer of a governmental entity or nonprofit institution for purposes of the Volunteer Protection Act of 1997 (42 U.S.C. 14501 et seq.).

(B) In the case of any claim against such an individual with respect to the provision of such services, section 4(d) of such Act (42 U.S.C. 14503(d)) shall not apply.

(3) Acceptance of voluntary services under this section shall have no bearing on the issuance or renewal of a security clearance.

(e) REIMBURSEMENT OF INCIDENTAL EXPENSES.—(1) The head of a covered element of the intelligence community may reimburse an individual for incidental expenses incurred by the individual in providing voluntary services under subsection (a). The head of a covered element of the intelligence community shall determine which expenses are eligible for reimbursement under this subsection.

(2) Reimbursement under paragraph (1) may be made from appropriated or nonappropriated funds.

(f) AUTHORITY TO INSTALL EQUIPMENT.—(1) The head of a covered element of the intelligence community may install telephone lines and any necessary telecommunication equipment in the private residences of individuals who provide voluntary services under subsection (a).

(2) The head of a covered element of the intelligence community may pay the charges incurred for the use of equipment installed under paragraph (1) for authorized purposes.

(3) Notwithstanding section 1348 of title 31, United States Code, the head of a covered element of the intelligence community may use appropriated funds or nonappropriated funds of the element in carrying out this subsection.

REGULATIONS

SEC. 1014. [50 U.S.C. 3204] (a) IN GENERAL.— The Secretary of Defense and the Director of National Intelligence shall jointly prescribe regulations to carry out the Foreign Languages Program.

(b) ELEMENTS OF THE INTELLIGENCE COMMUNITY.—The head of each covered element of the intelligence community shall prescribe regulations to carry out sections 1012 and 1013 with respect to that element including the following:

(1) Procedures to be utilized for the acceptance of voluntary services under section 1013.

(2) Procedures and requirements relating to the installation of equipment under section 1013(f).

DEFINITIONS

SEC. 1015. [50 U.S.C. 3205] In this subtitle:

(1) The term "covered element of the intelligence community" means an agency, office, bureau, or element referred to in subparagraphs (B) through (L) of section 3(4).

(2) The term "educational institution" means—

(A) a local educational agency (as that term is defined in section 8101 of the Elementary and Secondary Education Act of 1965);

(B) an institution of higher education (as defined in section 102 of the Higher Education Act of 1965 (20 U.S.C. 1002) other than institutions referred to in subsection (a)(1)(C) of such section); or

(C) any other nonprofit institution that provides instruction of foreign languages in languages that are critical to the capability of the intelligence community to carry out national security activities of the United States.

(3) The term "dedicated personnel" means employees of the intelligence community and private citizens (including former civilian employees of the Federal Government who have been voluntarily separated, and members of the United States Armed Forces who have been honorably discharged, honorably separated, or generally discharged under honorable circumstances and rehired on a voluntary basis specifically to perform the activities authorized under this subtitle).

subtitle C—Additional Education Provisions

ASSIGNMENT OF INTELLIGENCE COMMUNITY PERSONNEL AS LANGUAGE STUDENTS

Sec. 1021. [50 U.S.C. 3221] (a) In General.— The Director of National Intelligence, acting through the heads of the elements of the intelligence community, may assign employees of such elements in analyst positions requiring foreign language expertise as students at accredited professional, technical, or other institutions of higher education for training at the graduate or undergraduate level in foreign languages required for the conduct of duties and responsibilities of such positions.

(b) Authority for Reimbursement of Costs of Tuition and Training.—(1) The Director of National Intelligence may reimburse an employee assigned under subsection (a) for the total cost of the training described in that subsection, including costs of educational and supplementary reading materials.

(2) The authority under paragraph (1) shall apply to employees who are assigned on a full-time or part-time basis.

(3) Reimbursement under paragraph (1) may be made from appropriated or nonappropriated funds.

(c) Relationship to Compensation as an Analyst.— Reimbursement under this section to an employee who is an analyst is in addition to any benefits, allowances, travel expenses, or other compensation the employee is entitled to by reason of serving in such an analyst position.

SEC. 1022. [U.S.C. ????] PROGRAM ON RECRUITMENT AND TRAINING.

(a) Program.—

(1) Requirement.—The Director of National Intelligence, in consultation with the heads of the elements of the intelligence community, shall carry out a program to ensure that selected individuals are provided funds for academic training (including with respect to both undergraduate and postgraduate education), or to reimburse for academic training previously obtained—

(A) in capabilities, missions, or skillsets, especially in the fields of science, technology, math, and engineering, to address workforce requirements in which the intelligence community is deficient or likely to be deficient in the future; or

(B) for such individuals who have backgrounds or experiences that the Director has identified as—

(i) contributing to capabilities, missions, or skillsets in which the intelligence community is deficient or likely to be deficient in future; and

(ii) being underrepresented in the intelligence community or likely to be underrepresented in the future.

(2) COMMITMENT.— An individual selected for participation in the program shall commit to employment with an element of the intelligence community for a period that the Director determines is commensurate with the amount of funding provided to the individual under the program and under such terms and conditions as the Director considers appropriate.

(3) DESIGNATION.— The program shall be known as the Pat Roberts Intelligence Scholars Program.

(4) OUTREACH.—The Director, in consultation with the heads of the elements of the intelligence community, shall maintain a publicly available internet website on the program that describes—

(A) the intent of the program;

(B) the conditions and requirements for selection and participation;

(C) application instructions;

(D) the areas covered by the program pursuant to the review conducted under subsection (b)(2); and

(E) any other details the Director determines appropriate.

(b) ELEMENTS.—In carrying out the program under subsection (a), the Director shall—

(1) establish such requirements relating to the academic training of participants as the Director considers appropriate to ensure that participants are prepared for employment as intelligence professionals; and

(2) on an annual basis, review the areas that will contribute to the capabilities, missions, and skillsets in which the intelligence community is deficient or is likely to be deficient in the future.

(c) USE OF FUNDS.—Funds made available for the program under subsection (a) shall be used—

(1) to provide a monthly stipend for each month that a participant is pursuing a course of study;

(2) to pay the partial or full tuition of a participant for the completion of such course of study;

(3) to reimburse a participant for tuition paid by the participant before becoming an employee of an element of the intelligence community, including with respect to providing payments for student loans used for such tuition;

(4) to pay for books and materials that the participant requires or required to complete such course of study;

(5) to pay the expenses of the participant for travel requested by an element of the intelligence community in relation to such program; or

(6) for such other purposes the Director considers reasonably appropriate to carry out such program.

EDUCATIONAL SCHOLARSHIP PROGRAM

SEC. 1023. [50 U.S.C. 3223] The head of a department or agency containing an element of the intelligence community may establish an undergraduate or graduate training program with respect to civilian employees and prospective civilian employees of such element similar in purpose, conditions, content, and administration to the program that the Secretary of Defense is authorized to establish under section 16 of the National Security Agency Act of 1959 (50 U.S.C. 402 note).

INTELLIGENCE OFFICER TRAINING PROGRAM

SEC. 1024. [50 U.S.C. 3224] (a) PROGRAMS.—(1) The Director of National Intelligence may carry out grant programs in accordance with subsections (b) and (c) to enhance the recruitment and retention of an ethnically and culturally diverse intelligence community workforce with capabilities critical to the national security interests of the United States.

(2) In carrying out paragraph (1), the Director shall identify the skills necessary to meet current or emergent needs of the intelligence community and the educational disciplines that will provide individuals with such skills.

(b) INSTITUTIONAL GRANT PROGRAM.—(1) The Director may provide grants to institutions of higher education to support the establishment or continued development of programs of study in educational disciplines identified under subsection (a)(2).

(2) A grant provided under paragraph (1) may, with respect to the educational disciplines identified under subsection (a)(2), be used for the following purposes:

(A) Curriculum or program development.

(B) Faculty development.

(C) Laboratory equipment or improvements.

(D) Faculty research.

(c) GRANT PROGRAM FOR CERTAIN MINORITY-SERVING COLLEGES AND UNIVERSITIES.—(1) The Director may provide grants to historically black colleges and universities, Predominantly Black Institutions, Hispanic-serving institutions, and Asian American and Native American Pacific Islander-serving institutions to provide programs of study in educational disciplines identified under subsection (a)(2) or described in paragraph (2).

(2) A grant provided under paragraph (1) may be used to provide programs of study in the following educational disciplines:

(A) Intermediate and advanced foreign languages deemed in the immediate interest of the intelligence community, including Farsi, Pashto, Middle Eastern, African, and South Asian dialects.

(B) Study abroad programs and cultural immersion programs.

(d) APPLICATION.— An institution of higher education seeking a grant under this section shall submit an application describing the proposed use of the grant at such time and in such manner as the Director may require.

(e) REPORTS.—An institution of higher education that receives a grant under this section shall submit to the Director regular reports regarding the use of such grant, including—

(1) a description of the benefits to students who participate in the course of study funded by such grant;

(2) a description of the results and accomplishments related to such course of study; and

(3) any other information that the Director may require.

(f) REGULATIONS.— The Director shall prescribe such regulations as may be necessary to carry out this section.

(g) DEFINITIONS.—In this section:

(1) The term "Director" means the Director of National Intelligence.

(2) HISTORICALLY BLACK COLLEGE AND UNIVERSITY.— The term "historically black college and university" has the meaning given the term "part B institution" in section 322 of the Higher Education Act of 1965 (20 U.S.C. 1061).

(3) The term "institution of higher education" has the meaning given the term in section 101 of the Higher Education Act of 1965 (20 U.S.C. 1001).

(4) PREDOMINANTLY BLACK INSTITUTION.— The term "Predominantly Black Institution" has the meaning given the term in section 318 of the Higher education Act of 1965 (20 U.S.C. 1059e).

(5) HISPANIC-SERVING INSTITUTION.— The term "Hispanic-serving institution" has the meaning given that term in section 502(a)(5) of the Higher Education Act of 1965 (20 U.S.C. 1101a(a)(5)).

(6) ASIAN AMERICAN AND NATIVE AMERICAN PACIFIC ISLANDER-SERVING INSTITUTION.— The term "Asian American and Native American Pacific Islander-serving institution" has the meaning given that term in section 320(b)(2) of the Higher Education Act of 1965 (20 U.S.C. 1059g(b)(2)).

(7) STUDY ABROAD PROGRAM.—The term "study abroad program" means a program of study that—

(A) takes place outside the geographical boundaries of the United States;

(B) focuses on areas of the world that are critical to the national security interests of the United States and are generally underrepresented in study abroad programs at institutions of higher education, including Africa, Asia, Central and Eastern Europe, Eurasia, Latin America, and the Middle East; and

(C) is a credit or noncredit program.

SEC. 1025. [50 U.SC. 3224a] AUTHORIZATION OF SUPPORT BY DIRECTOR OF NATIONAL INTELLIGENCE FOR CERTAIN WORKFORCE ACTIVITIES.

(a) AUTHORIZATION.— The Director may, with or without reimbursement, obligate or expend amounts authorized to be appropriated or otherwise made available for the Office of the Director of National Intelligence for covered workforce activities for the purpose of supporting a covered workforce activity of an element of the intelligence community.

(b) NOTIFICATION.— Not later than 30 days after the date on which the Director exercises the authority in subsection (a), the Director shall submit to the congressional intelligence committees and the Committees on Appropriations of the House of Representatives and the Senate written notification of such exercise.

(c) Covered Workforce Activity Defined.—In this section, the term "covered workforce activity" means an activity relating to—

(1) recruitment or retention of the intelligence community workforce; or

(2) diversity, equality, inclusion, or accessibility, with respect to such workforce.

Subtitle D—National Intelligence University

SEC. 1031. [50 U.SC. 3227] TRANSFER DATE.

In this subtitle, the term "transfer date" means the date on which the National Intelligence University is transferred from the Defense Intelligence Agency to the Director of National Intelligence under section 5324(a) of the National Defense Authorization Act for Fiscal Year 2020 (Public Law 116–92).

SEC. 1032. [50 U.SC. 3227a] DEGREE-GRANTING AUTHORITY.

(a) In General.— Beginning on the transfer date, under regulations prescribed by the Director of National Intelligence, the President of the National Intelligence University may, upon the recommendation of the faculty of the University, confer appropriate degrees upon graduates who meet the degree requirements.

(b) Limitation.—A degree may not be conferred under this section unless—

(1) the Secretary of Education has recommended approval of the degree in accordance with the Federal Policy Governing Granting of Academic Degrees by Federal Agencies; and

(2) the University is accredited by the appropriate academic accrediting agency or organization to award the degree, as determined by the Secretary of Education.

SEC. 1033. [50 U.SC. 3227b] REPORTING.

(a) In General.— Not less frequently than once each year, the Director of National Intelligence shall submit to the congressional intelligence committees a plan for employing professors, instructors, and lecturers at the National Intelligence University.

(b) Elements.—Each plan submitted under subsection (a) shall include the following:

(1) The total number of proposed personnel to be employed at the National Intelligence University.

(2) The total annual compensation to be provided the personnel described in paragraph (1).

(3) Such other matters as the Director considers appropriate.

(c) Form of Submittal.— Each plan submitted by the Director to the congressional intelligence committees under subsection (a) shall be submitted as part of another annual submission from the Director to the congressional intelligence committees.

SEC. 1034. [50 U.SC. 3227c] CONTINUED APPLICABILITY OF THE FEDERAL ADVISORY COMMITTEE ACT TO THE BOARD OF VISITORS.

The Federal Advisory Committee Act (5 U.S.C. App.) shall continue to apply to the Board of Visitors of the National Intelligence University on and after the transfer date.

§ 1035. [50 U.SC. 3227d] NATIONAL INTELLIGENCE UNIVERSITY ACCEPTANCE OF GRANTS[14]

(a) AUTHORITY.— The Director of National Intelligence may authorize the President of the National Intelligence University to accept qualifying research grants.

(b) QUALIFYING GRANTS.— A qualifying research grant under this section is a grant that is awarded on a competitive basis by an entity referred to in subsection (c) for a research project with a scientific, literary, or educational purpose.

(c) ENTITIES FROM WHICH GRANTS MAY BE ACCEPTED.— A qualifying research grant may be accepted under this section only from a Federal agency or from a corporation, fund, foundation, educational institution, or similar entity that is organized and operated primarily for scientific, literary, or educational purposes.

(d) ADMINISTRATION OF GRANT FUNDS.—

(1) ESTABLISHMENT OF ACCOUNT.— The Director shall establish an account for administering funds received as qualifying research grants under this section.

(2) USE OF FUNDS.— The President of the University shall use the funds in the account established pursuant to paragraph (1) in accordance with applicable provisions of the regulations and the terms and conditions of the grants received.

(e) RELATED EXPENSES.— Subject to such limitations as may be provided in appropriations Acts, appropriations available for the National Intelligence University may be used to pay expenses incurred by the University in applying for, and otherwise pursuing, the award of qualifying research grants.

(f) REGULATIONS.— The Director of National Intelligence shall prescribe regulations for the administration of this section.

14 The style of the section heading for section 1035, as added by section 6305(a) of division F of Public Law 118–159, does not conform with the style of section headings of the Act.

TITLE XI—ADDITIONAL MISCELLANEOUS PROVISIONS

APPLICABILITY TO UNITED STATES INTELLIGENCE ACTIVITIES OF FEDERAL LAWS IMPLEMENTING INTERNATIONAL TREATIES AND AGREEMENTS

SEC. 1101. [50 U.S.C. 3231] (a) IN GENERAL.— No Federal law enacted on or after the date of the enactment of the Intelligence Authorization Act for Fiscal Year 2001 that implements a treaty or other international agreement shall be construed as making unlawful an otherwise lawful and authorized intelligence activity of the United States Government or its employees, or any other person to the extent such other person is carrying out such activity on behalf of, and at the direction of, the United States, unless such Federal law specifically addresses such intelligence activity.

(b) AUTHORIZED INTELLIGENCE ACTIVITIES.— An intelligence activity shall be treated as authorized for purposes of subsection (a) if the intelligence activity is authorized by an appropriate official of the United States Government, acting within the scope of the official duties of that official and in compliance with Federal law and any applicable Presidential directive.

COUNTERINTELLIGENCE INITIATIVES

SEC. 1102. [50 U.S. C. 3232] (a) INSPECTION PROCESS.— In order to protect intelligence sources and methods from unauthorized disclosure, the Director of National Intelligence shall establish and implement an inspection process for all agencies and departments of the United States that handle classified information relating to the national security of the United States intended to assure that those agencies and departments maintain effective operational security practices and programs directed against counterintelligence activities.

(b) ANNUAL REVIEW OF DISSEMINATION LISTS.— The Director of National Intelligence shall establish and implement a process for all elements of the intelligence community to review, on an annual basis, individuals included on distribution lists for access to classified information. Such process shall ensure that only individuals who have a particularized "need to know" (as determined by the Director) are continued on such distribution lists.

(c) COMPLETION OF FINANCIAL DISCLOSURE STATEMENTS REQUIRED FOR ACCESS TO CERTAIN CLASSIFIED INFORMATION.— The Director of National Intelligence shall establish and implement a process by which each head of an element of the intelligence community directs that all employees of that element, in order to be granted access to classified information referred to in subsection (a) of section 1.3 of Executive Order No. 12968 (August 2, 1995; 60 Fed. Reg. 40245; 50 U.S.C. 435 note), submit financial disclosure forms as required under subsection (b) of such section.

(d) ARRANGEMENTS TO HANDLE SENSITIVE INFORMATION.— The Director of National Intelligence shall establish, for all elements of the intelligence community, programs and procedures by which sensitive classified information relating to human intelligence is safeguarded against unauthorized disclosure by employees of those elements.

SEC. 1102A. [U.S.C. 3232a] MEASURES TO MITIGATE COUNTERINTELLIGENCE THREATS FROM PROLIFERATION AND USE OF FOREIGN COMMERCIAL SPYWARE

(a) DEFINITIONS.—In this section:

(1) APPROPRIATE CONGRESSIONAL COMMITTEES .—The term "appropriate congressional committees" means—

(A) the Select Committee on Intelligence, the Committee on Foreign Relations, the Committee on Armed Services, the Committee on Banking, Housing, and Urban Affairs, the Committee on the Judiciary, the Committee on Appropriations, and the Committee on Homeland Security and Governmental Affairs of the Senate; and

(B) the Permanent Select Committee on Intelligence, the Committee on Foreign Affairs, the Committee on Armed Services, the Committee on Financial Services, the Committee on the Judiciary, the Committee on Appropriations, the Committee on Homeland Security, and the Committee on Oversight and Reform of the House of Representatives.

(2) COVERED ENTITY .—The term "covered entity" means any foreign company that either directly or indirectly develops, maintains, owns, operates, brokers, markets, sells, leases, licenses, or otherwise makes available spyware.

(3) FOREIGN COMMERCIAL SPYWARE .—The term "foreign commercial spyware" means spyware that is developed (solely or in partnership with a foreign company), maintained, sold, leased, licensed, marketed, sourced (in whole or in part), or

otherwise provided, either directly or indirectly, by a foreign company.

(4) Foreign company .—The term "foreign company" means a company that is incorporated or domiciled outside of the United States, including any subsidiaries or affiliates wherever such subsidiaries or affiliates are domiciled or incorporated.

(5) Spyware.—The term "spyware" means a tool or set of tools that operate as an end-to-end system of software to provide an unauthorized user remote access to information stored on or transiting through an electronic device connected to the Internet and not owned or operated by the unauthorized user, including end-to-end systems that—

(A) allow an unauthorized user to remotely infect electronic devices with malicious software, including without any action required by the user of the device;

(B) can record telecommunications or other audio captured on a device not owned by the unauthorized user;

(C) undertake geolocation, collect cell site location information, or otherwise track the location of a device or person using the internal sensors of an electronic device not owned by the unauthorized user;

(D) allow an unauthorized user access to and the ability to retrieve information on the electronic device, including text messages, files, e-mails, transcripts of chats, contacts, photos, and browsing history; or

(E) any additional criteria described in publicly available documents published by the Director of National Intelligence, such as whether the end-to-end system is used outside the context of a codified lawful intercept system.

(b) Annual assessments of counterintelligence threats.—

(1) Requirement.— Not later than 90 days after the enactment of the Intelligence Authorization Act for Fiscal Year 2023, and annually thereafter, the Director of National Intelligence, in coordination with the Director of the Central Intelligence Agency, the Director of the National Security Agency, and the Director of the Federal Bureau of Investigation, shall submit to the appropriate congressional committees a report with an accompanying classified annex containing an assessment of the counterintelligence threats and other risks to the national security of the United States posed by the proliferation of foreign commercial spyware. The assessment shall incorporate all credible data, including open-source information.

(2) Elements .—Each report under paragraph (1) shall include the following, if known:

(A) A list of the most significant covered entities.

(B) A description of the foreign commercial spyware marketed by the covered entities identified under subparagraph (A) and an assessment by the intelligence community of the foreign commercial spyware.

(C) An assessment of the counterintelligence risk to the intelligence community or personnel of the intelligence community posed by foreign commercial spyware.

(D) For each covered entity identified in subparagraph (A), details of any subsidiaries, resellers, or other agents acting on behalf of the covered entity.

(E) Details of where each covered entity identified under subparagraphs (A) and (D) is domiciled.

(F) A description of how each covered entity identified under subparagraphs (A) and (D) is financed, where the covered entity acquired its capital, and the organizations and individuals having substantial investments or other equities in the covered entity.

(G) An assessment by the intelligence community of any relationship between each covered entity identified in subparagraphs (A) and (D) and any foreign government, including any export controls and processes to which the covered entity is subject.

(H) A list of the foreign customers of each covered entity identified in subparagraphs (A) and (D), including the understanding by the intelligence community of the organizations and end-users within any foreign government.

(I) With respect to each foreign customer identified under subparagraph (H), an assessment by the intelligence community regarding how the foreign customer is using the spyware, including whether the foreign customer has targeted personnel of the intelligence community.

(J) With respect to the first report required under paragraph (1), a mitigation plan to reduce the exposure of personnel of the intelligence community to foreign commercial spyware.

(K) With respect to each report following the first report required under paragraph (1), details of steps taken by the intelligence community since the previous report to implement measures to reduce the exposure of personnel of the intelligence community to foreign commercial spyware.

(3) Classified annex .—In submitting the report under paragraph (1), the Director shall also include an accompanying but separate classified annex, providing a watchlist of companies selling, leasing, or otherwise providing foreign commercial spyware that the Director determines are engaged in activities that pose a counterintelligence risk to personnel of the intelligence community.

(4) Form.— Each report under paragraph (1) shall be submitted in classified form.

(5) Dissemination.— The Director of National Intelligence shall separately distribute each report under paragraph (1) and each annex under paragraph (3) to the President, the heads of all elements of the intelligence community, the Secretary of State, the Attorney General, the Secretary of Commerce, the Secretary of Homeland Security, the National Cyber Director, and the heads of any other departments or agencies the Director of National Intelligence determines appropriate.

(c) Authority to prohibit purchase or use by intelligence community.—

(1) Foreign commercial spyware.—

(A) In general .—The Director of National Intelligence may prohibit any element of the intelligence community from procuring, leasing, or otherwise acquiring on the commercial market, or extending or renewing a contract to procure, lease, or otherwise acquire, foreign commercial spyware.

(B) Considerations.—In determining whether and how to exercise the authority under subparagraph (A), the Director of National Intelligence shall consider—

(i) the assessment of the intelligence community of the counterintelligence threats or other risks to the United States posed by foreign commercial spyware;

(ii) the assessment of the intelligence community of whether the foreign commercial spyware has been used to target United States Government personnel;

(iii) whether the original owner or developer retains any of the physical property or intellectual property associated with the foreign commercial spyware;

(iv) whether the original owner or developer has verifiably destroyed all copies of the data collected by or associated with the foreign commercial spyware;

(v) whether the personnel of the original owner or developer retain any access to data collected by or associated with the foreign commercial spyware;

(vi) whether the use of the foreign commercial spyware requires the user to connect to an information system of the original owner or developer or information system of a foreign government; and

(vii) whether the foreign commercial spyware poses a counterintelligence risk to the United States or any other threat to the national security of the United States.

(2) COMPANY THAT HAS ACQUIRED FOREIGN COMMERCIAL SPYWARE.—

(A) AUTHORITY .—The Director of National Intelligence may prohibit any element of the intelligence community from entering into any contract or other agreement for any purpose with a company that has acquired, in whole or in part, any foreign commercial spyware.

(B) CONSIDERATIONS.—In considering whether and how to exercise the authority under subparagraph (A), the Director of National Intelligence shall consider—

(i) whether the original owner or developer of the foreign commercial spyware retains any of the physical property or intellectual property associated with the spyware;

(ii) whether the original owner or developer of the foreign commercial spyware has verifiably destroyed all data, and any copies thereof, collected by or associated with the spyware;

(iii) whether the personnel of the original owner or developer of the foreign commercial spyware retain any access to data collected by or associated with the foreign commercial spyware;

(iv) whether the use of the foreign commercial spyware requires the user to connect to an information system of the original owner or developer or information system of a foreign government; and

(v) whether the foreign commercial spyware poses a counterintelligence risk to the United States or any other threat to the national security of the United States.

(3) NOTIFICATIONS OF PROHIBITION.—Not later than 30 days after the date on

which the Director of National Intelligence exercises the authority to issue a prohibition under subsection (c), the Director of National Intelligence shall notify the congressional intelligence committees of such exercise of authority. Such notice shall include—

(A) a description of the circumstances under which the prohibition was issued;

(B) an identification of the company or product covered by the prohibition;

(C) any information that contributed to the decision of the Director of National Intelligence to exercise the authority, including any information relating to counterintelligence or other risks to the national security of the United States posed by the company or product, as assessed by the intelligence community; and

(D) an identification of each element of the intelligence community to which the prohibition has been applied.

(4) WAIVER AUTHORITY.—

(A) IN GENERAL .—The head of an element of the intelligence community may request from the Director of National Intelligence the waiver of a prohibition made under paragraph (1) or (2).

(B) DIRECTOR OF NATIONAL INTELLIGENCE DETERMINATION .—The Director of National Intelligence, upon receiving the waiver request in subparagraph (A), may issue a waiver for a period not to exceed one year in response to the request from the head of an element of the intelligence community if such waiver is in the national security interest of the United States.

(C) NOTICE .—Not later than 30 days after approving a waiver request pursuant to subparagraph (B), the Director of National Intelligence shall submit to the congressional intelligence committees, the Subcommittee on Defense of the Committee on Appropriations of the Senate, and the Subcommittee on Defense of the Committee on Appropriations of the House of Representatives a written notification. The notification shall include—

(i) an identification of the head of the element of the intelligence community that requested the waiver;

(ii) the details of the waiver request, including the national security interests of the United States;

(iii) the rationale and basis for the determination that the waiver is in the national security interests of the United States;

(iv) the considerations that informed the ultimate determination of the Director of National Intelligence to issue the waiver; and

(v) and any other considerations contributing to the determination, made by the Director of National Intelligence.

(D) WAIVER TERMINATION The Director of National Intelligence may revoke a previously granted waiver at any time. Upon revocation of a waiver, the Director of National Intelligence shall submit a written notification to the congressional intelligence committees, the Subcommittee on Defense of the Committee on Appropriations of the Senate, and the Subcommittee on Defense of the Committee on Appropriations of the House of Representatives not later than 30 days after making a revocation determination.

(5) TERMINATION OF PROHIBITION.— The Director of National Intelligence may terminate a prohibition made under paragraph (1) or (2) at any time. Upon termination of a prohibition, the Director of National Intelligence shall submit a notification of the termination to the congressional intelligence committees, the Subcommittee on Defense of the Committee on Appropriations of the Senate, and the Subcommittee on Defense of the Committee on Appropriations of the House of Representatives not later than 30 days after terminating a prohibition, detailing the basis for the termination, including any United States national security interests that may be affected by such termination.

MISUSE OF THE OFFICE OF THE DIRECTOR OF NATIONAL INTELLIGENCE NAME, INITIALS, OR SEAL

SEC. 1103. [50 U.S.C. 3233] (a) PROHIBITED ACTS.— No person may, except with the written permission of the Director of National Intelligence, or a designee of the Director, knowingly use the words "Office of the Director of National Intelligence", the initials "ODNI", the seal of the Office of the Director of National Intelligence, or any colorable imitation of such words, initials, or seal in connection with any merchandise, impersonation, solicitation, or commercial activity in a manner reasonably calculated to convey the impression that such use is approved, endorsed, or authorized by the Director of National Intelligence.

(b) INJUNCTION.— Whenever it appears to the Attorney General that any person is engaged or is about to engage in an act or practice which constitutes or will constitute conduct prohibited by subsection (a), the Attorney General may initiate a civil proceeding in a district court of the United States to enjoin such act or practice. Such court shall proceed as soon as practicable to the hearing and determination of such action and may, at any time before final determination, enter such restraining orders or prohibitions, or take such other action as is warranted, to prevent injury to the United States or to any person or class of persons for whose protection the action is brought.

SEC. 1104. [50 U.S.C. 3234] PROHIBITED PERSONNEL PRACTICES IN THE INTELLIGENCE COMMUNITY.

(a) DEFINITIONS.—In this section:

(1) AGENCY.— The term "agency" means an executive department or independent establishment, as defined under sections 101 and 104 of title 5, United States Code, that contains an intelligence community element, except the Federal Bureau of Investigation.

(2) COVERED INTELLIGENCE COMMUNITY ELEMENT.—The term "covered intelligence community element"—

(A) means—

(i) the Central Intelligence Agency, the Defense Intelligence Agency, the National Geospatial-Intelligence Agency, the National Security Agency, the Office of the Director of National Intelligence, and the National Reconnaissance Office; and

(ii) any executive agency or unit thereof determined by the President under section 2302(a)(2)(C)(ii) of title 5, United States Code, to have as its principal function the conduct of foreign intelligence or counterintelligence activities; and

(B) does not include the Federal Bureau of Investigation.

(3) PERSONNEL ACTION.—The term "personnel action" means, with respect to an employee in a position in a covered intelligence community element (other than a position excepted from the competitive service due to its confidential, policy-determining, policymaking, or policy-advocating character) or a contractor employee—

(A) an appointment;

(B) a promotion;

(C) a disciplinary or corrective action;

(D) a detail, transfer, or reassignment;

(E) a demotion, suspension, or termination;

(F) a reinstatement or restoration;

(G) a performance evaluation;

(H) a decision concerning pay, benefits, or awards;

(I) a decision concerning education or training if such education or training may reasonably be expected to lead to an appointment, promotion, or performance evaluation; or

(J) any other significant change in duties, responsibilities, or working conditions.

(4) CONTRACTOR EMPLOYEE.— The term "contractor employee" means an employee of a contractor, subcontractor, grantee, subgrantee, or personal services contractor, of a covered intelligence community element.

(b) AGENCY EMPLOYEES.—Any employee of a covered intelligence community element or an agency who has authority to take, direct others to take, recommend, or approve any personnel action, shall not, with respect to such authority, take or fail to take, or threaten to take or fail to take, a personnel action with respect to any employee of a covered intelligence community element as a reprisal for—

(1) any lawful disclosure of information by the employee to the Director of National Intelligence (or an employee designated by the Director of National Intelligence for such purpose), the Inspector General of the Intelligence Community, a supervisor in the employee's direct chain of command, or a supervisor of the employing agency with responsibility for the subject matter of the disclosure, up to and including the head of the employing agency (or an employee designated by the head of that agency for such purpose), the appropriate inspector general of the employing agency or covered intelligence community element, a congressional intelligence committee, or a member of a congressional intelligence committee, which the employee reasonably believes evidences—

(A) a violation of any Federal law, rule, or regulation; or

(B) mismanagement, a gross waste of funds, an abuse of authority, or a substantial and specific danger to public health or safety;

(2) any lawful disclosure that complies with—

(A) subsections (b)(1), (e), and (h) of section 416 of title 5, United States

Code;

(B) subparagraphs (A), (D), and (H) of section 17(d)(5) of the Central Intelligence Agency Act of 1949 (50 U.S.C. 3517(d)(5)); or

(C) subparagraphs (A), (D), and (I) of section 103H(k)(5); or

(3) if the actions do not result in the employee unlawfully disclosing information specifically required by Executive order to be kept classified in the interest of national defense or the conduct of foreign affairs, any lawful disclosure in conjunction with—

(A) the exercise of any appeal, complaint, or grievance right granted by any law, rule, or regulation;

(B) testimony for or otherwise lawfully assisting any individual in the exercise of any right referred to in subparagraph (A); or

(C) cooperation with or disclosing information to the Inspector General of an agency, in accordance with applicable provisions of law in connection with an audit, inspection, or investigation conducted by the Inspector General.

(c) CONTRACTOR EMPLOYEES.—(1) Any employee of an agency or of a contractor, subcontractor, grantee, subgrantee, or personal services contractor, of a covered intelligence community element who has authority to take, direct others to take, recommend, or approve any personnel action, shall not, with respect to such authority, take or fail to take, or threaten to take or fail to take, a personnel action with respect to any contractor employee as a reprisal for—

(A) any lawful disclosure of information by the contractor employee to the Director of National Intelligence (or an employee designated by the Director of National Intelligence for such purpose), the Inspector General of the Intelligence Community, a supervisor in the contractor employee's direct chain of command, or a supervisor of the employing or contracting agency or employing contractor with responsibility for the subject matter of the disclosure, up to and including the head of the employing or contracting agency (or an employee designated by the head of that agency for that purpose) or employing contractor, the appropriate inspector general of the employing or contracting agency or covered intelligence community element, a congressional intelligence committee, or a member of a congressional intelligence committee, which the contractor employee reasonably believes evidences—

(i) a violation of any Federal law, rule, or regulation (including with respect to evidence of another employee or contractor employee accessing or sharing classified information without authorization); or

(ii) mismanagement, a gross waste of funds, an abuse of authority, or a substantial and specific danger to public health or safety;

(B) any lawful disclosure that complies with—

(i) subsections (b)(1), (e), and (h) of section 416 of title 5, United States Code;

(ii) subparagraphs (A), (D), and (H) of section 17(d)(5) of the Central Intelligence Agency Act of 1949 (50 U.S.C. 3517(d)(5)); or

(iii) subparagraphs (A), (D), and (I) of section 103H(k)(5); or

(C) if the actions do not result in the contractor employee unlawfully disclosing information specifically required by Executive order to be kept classified in the interest of national defense or the conduct of foreign affairs, any lawful disclosure in conjunction with—

(i) the exercise of any appeal, complaint, or grievance right granted by any law, rule, or regulation;

(ii) testimony for or otherwise lawfully assisting any individual in the exercise of any right referred to in clause (i); or

(iii) cooperation with or disclosing information to the Inspector General of an agency, in accordance with applicable provisions of law in connection with an audit, inspection, or investigation conducted by the Inspector General.

(2) A personnel action under paragraph (1) is prohibited even if the action is undertaken at the request of an agency official, unless the request takes the form of a nondiscretionary directive and is within the authority of the agency official making the request.

(d) RULE OF CONSTRUCTION.—Consistent with the protection of intelligence sources and methods, nothing in subsection (b) or (c) shall be construed to authorize—

(1) the withholding of information from Congress; or

(2) the taking of any personnel action against an employee who lawfully discloses information to Congress.

(e) DISCLOSURES.—A disclosure shall not be excluded from this section because—

(1) the disclosure was made to an individual, including a supervisor, who participated in an activity that the employee reasonably believed to be covered under subsection (b)(1)(B) or the contractor employee reasonably believed to be covered under subsection (c)(1)(A)(ii);

(2) the disclosure revealed information that had been previously disclosed;

(3) the disclosure was not made in writing;

(4) the disclosure was made while the employee was off duty;

(5) of the amount of time which has passed since the occurrence of the events described in the disclosure; or

(6) the disclosure was made during the normal course of duties of an employee or contractor employee.

(f) ENFORCEMENT.— The President shall provide for the enforcement of this section consistent, to the fullest extent possible, with the policies and procedures used to adjudicate alleged violations of section 2302(b)(8) of title 5, United States Code.

(g) EXISTING RIGHTS PRESERVED.—Nothing in this section shall be construed to—

(1) preempt or preclude any employee, contractor employee, or applicant for employment, at the Federal Bureau of Investigation from exercising rights provided under any other law, rule, or regulation, including section 2303 of title 5, United States Code; or

(2) repeal section 2303 of title 5, United States Code.

SEC. 1105. [50 U.S.C. 3235] SEMIANNUAL REPORTS ON INVESTIGATIONS OF UNAUTHORIZED DISCLOSURES OF CLASSIFIED INFORMATION.

(a) DEFINITIONS.—In this section:

(1) COVERED OFFICIAL.—The term "covered official" means—

(A) the heads of each element of the intelligence community; and

(B) the inspectors general with oversight responsibility for an element of the intelligence community.

(2) INVESTIGATION.— The term "investigation" means any inquiry, whether formal or informal, into the existence of an unauthorized public disclosure of classified information.

(3) UNAUTHORIZED DISCLOSURE OF CLASSIFIED INFORMATION.— The term "unauthorized disclosure of classified information" means any unauthorized disclosure of classified information to any recipient.

(4) UNAUTHORIZED PUBLIC DISCLOSURE OF CLASSIFIED INFORMATION.— The term "unauthorized public disclosure of classified information" means the unauthorized disclosure of classified information to a journalist or media organization.

(b) INTELLIGENCE COMMUNITY REPORTING.—

(1) IN GENERAL.— Not less frequently than once every 6 months, each covered official shall submit to the congressional intelligence committees a report on investigations of unauthorized public disclosures of classified information.

(2) ELEMENTS.—Each report submitted under paragraph (1) shall include, with respect to the preceding 6-month period, the following:

(A) The number of investigations opened by the covered official regarding an unauthorized public disclosure of classified information.

(B) The number of investigations completed by the covered official regarding an unauthorized public disclosure of classified information.

(C) Of the number of such completed investigations identified under subparagraph (B), the number referred to the Attorney General for criminal investigation.

(c) DEPARTMENT OF JUSTICE REPORTING.—

(1) IN GENERAL.— Not less frequently than once every 6 months, the Assistant Attorney General for National Security of the Department of Justice, in consultation with the Director of the Federal Bureau of Investigation, shall submit to the congressional intelligence committees, the Committee on the Judiciary of the Senate, and the Committee on the Judiciary of the House of Representatives a report on the status of each referral made to the Department of Justice from any element of the intelligence community regarding an unauthorized disclosure of classified information made during the most recent 365-day period or any referral that has not yet been closed, regardless of the date the referral was made.

(2) CONTENTS.—Each report submitted under paragraph (1) shall include, for each referral covered by the report, at a minimum, the following:

(A) The date the referral was received.

(B) A statement indicating whether the alleged unauthorized disclosure described in the referral was substantiated by the Department of Justice.

(C) A statement indicating the highest level of classification of the information that was revealed in the unauthorized disclosure.

(D) A statement indicating whether an open criminal investigation related to the referral is active.

(E) A statement indicating whether any criminal charges have been filed related to the referral.

(F) A statement indicating whether the Department of Justice has been able to attribute the unauthorized disclosure to a particular entity or individual.

(d) Form of Reports.— Each report submitted under this section shall be submitted in unclassified form, but may have a classified annex.

SEC. 1105A. [50 U.S.C. 3235a] NOTICE AND DAMAGE ASSESSMENT WITH RESPECT TO SIGNIFICANT UNAUTHORIZED DISCLOSURE OR COMPROMISE OF CLASSIFIED NATIONAL INTELLIGENCE.

(a) Notification and Damage Assessment Requirements.—

(1) Requirements .—If the Director of National Intelligence becomes aware of an actual or potential significant unauthorized disclosure or compromise of classified national intelligence—

(A) as soon as practicable, but not later than 7 days after the date on which the Director becomes so aware, the Director shall notify the congressional intelligence committees of such actual or potential disclosure or compromise; and

(B) in the case of an actual disclosure or compromise, not later than 7 days after the date on which the Director becomes so aware, the Director or the head of any element of the intelligence community from which the significant unauthorized disclosure or compromise originated shall initiate a damage assessment consistent with the procedures set forth in Intelligence Community Directive 732 (relating to the conduct of damage assessments), or successor directive, with respect to such disclosure or compromise.

(2) Contents of notification .—A notification submitted to the congressional intelligence committees under paragraph (1)(A) with respect to an actual or potential significant unauthorized disclosure or compromise of classified national intelligence shall include—

(A) a summary of the facts and circumstances of such disclosure or compromise;

(B) a summary of the contents of the national intelligence revealed or potentially revealed, as the case may be, by such disclosure or compromise;

(C) an initial appraisal of the level of actual or potential damage, as the case may be, to the national security of the United States as a result of such disclosure or compromise; and

(D) in the case of an actual disclosure or compromise, which elements of the intelligence community will be involved in the damage assessment conducted with respect to such disclosure or compromise pursuant to paragraph (1)(B).

(b) Damage Assessment Reporting Requirements.—

(1) Recurring reporting requirement .—Not later than 30 days after the date of the initiation of a damage assessment pursuant to subsection (a)(1)(B), and every 90 days thereafter until the completion of the damage assessment or upon the request of the congressional intelligence committees, the Director of National Intelligence

shall—

(A) submit to the congressional intelligence committees copies of any documents or materials disclosed as a result of the significant unauthorized disclosure or compromise of the classified national intelligence that is the subject of the damage assessment; and

(B) provide to the congressional intelligence committees a briefing on such documents and materials and a status of the damage assessment.

(2) FINAL DAMAGE ASSESSMENT .—As soon as practicable after completing a damage assessment pursuant to subsection (a)(1)(B), the Director of National Intelligence shall submit the final damage assessment to the congressional intelligence committees.

(c) NOTIFICATION OF REFERRAL TO DEPARTMENT OF JUSTICE .—If a referral is made to the Department of Justice from any element of the intelligence community regarding a significant unauthorized disclosure or compromise of classified national intelligence under this section, the Director of National Intelligence shall notify the congressional intelligence committees of the referral on the date such referral is made.

SEC. 1106. [50 U.S.C. 3236] INSPECTOR GENERAL EXTERNAL REVIEW PANEL.

(a) REQUEST FOR REVIEW.— An individual with a claim described in subsection (b) may submit to the Inspector General of the Intelligence Community a request for a review of such claim by an external review panel convened under subsection (c).

(b) CLAIMS AND INDIVIDUALS DESCRIBED.—A claim described in this subsection is any—

(1) claim by an individual—

(A) that the individual has been subjected to a personnel action that is prohibited under section 1104; and

(B) who has exhausted the applicable review process for the claim pursuant to enforcement of such section; or

(2) claim by an individual—

(A) that he or she has been subjected to a reprisal prohibited by paragraph (1) of section 3001(j) of the Intelligence Reform and Terrorism Prevention Act of 2004 (50 U.S.C. 3341(j)); and

(B) who received a decision on an appeal regarding that claim under paragraph (4) of such section.

(c) EXTERNAL REVIEW PANEL CONVENED.—

(1) DISCRETION TO CONVENE.— Upon receipt of a request under subsection (a) regarding a claim, the Inspector General of the Intelligence Community may, at the discretion of the Inspector General, convene an external review panel under this subsection to review the claim.

(2) MEMBERSHIP.—

(A) COMPOSITION.—An external review panel convened under this subsection shall be composed of three members as follows:

(i) The Inspector General of the Intelligence Community.

(ii) Except as provided in subparagraph (B), two members selected by the

Inspector General as the Inspector General considers appropriate on a case-by-case basis from among inspectors general of the following:

(I) The Department of Defense.

(II) The Department of Energy.

(III) The Department of Homeland Security.

(IV) The Department of Justice.

(V) The Department of State.

(VI) The Department of the Treasury.

(VII) The Central Intelligence Agency.

(VIII) The Defense Intelligence Agency.

(IX) The National Geospatial-Intelligence Agency.

(X) The National Reconnaissance Office.

(XI) The National Security Agency.

(B) LIMITATION.— An inspector general of an agency may not be selected to sit on the panel under subparagraph (A)(ii) to review any matter relating to a decision made by such agency.

(C) CHAIRPERSON.—

(i) IN GENERAL.— Except as provided in clause (ii), the chairperson of any panel convened under this subsection shall be the Inspector General of the Intelligence Community.

(ii) CONFLICTS OF INTEREST.—If the Inspector General of the Intelligence Community finds cause to recuse himself or herself from a panel convened under this subsection, the Inspector General of the Intelligence Community shall—

(I) select a chairperson from inspectors general of the elements listed under subparagraph (A)(ii) whom the Inspector General of the Intelligence Community considers appropriate; and

(II) notify the congressional intelligence committees of such selection.

(3) PERIOD OF REVIEW.— Each external review panel convened under this subsection to review a claim shall complete review of the claim no later than 270 days after the date on which the Inspector General convenes the external review panel.

(d) REMEDIES.—

(1) PANEL RECOMMENDATIONS.—If an external review panel convened under subsection (c) determines, pursuant to a review of a claim submitted by an individual under subsection (a), that the individual was the subject of a personnel action prohibited under section 1104 or was subjected to a reprisal prohibited by section 3001(j)(1) of the Intelligence Reform and Terrorism Prevention Act of 2004 (50 U.S.C. 3341(j)(1)), the panel may recommend that the agency head take corrective action—

(A) in the case of an employee or former employee—

(i) to return the employee or former employee, as nearly as practicable and reasonable, to the position such employee or former employee would have held had the reprisal not occurred; or

(ii) reconsider the employee's or former employee's eligibility for access to classified information consistent with national security; or

(B) in any other case, such other action as the external review panel considers appropriate.

(2) AGENCY ACTION.—

(A) IN GENERAL.—Not later than 90 days after the date on which the head of an agency receives a recommendation from an external review panel under paragraph (1), the head shall—

(i) give full consideration to such recommendation; and

(ii) inform the panel and the Director of National Intelligence of what action the head has taken with respect to the recommendation.

(B) FAILURE TO INFORM.— The Director shall notify the President of any failures to comply with subparagraph (A)(ii).

(e) ANNUAL REPORTS.—

(1) IN GENERAL.— Not less frequently than once each year, the Inspector General of the Intelligence Community shall submit to the congressional intelligence committees and the Director of National Intelligence a report on the activities under this section during the previous year.

(2) CONTENTS.—Subject to such limitations as the Inspector General of the Intelligence Community considers necessary to protect the privacy of an individual who has made a claim described in subsection (b), each report submitted under paragraph (1) shall include, for the period covered by the report, the following:

(A) The determinations and recommendations made by the external review panels convened under this section.

(B) The responses of the heads of agencies that received recommendations from the external review panels.

SEC. 1107. [50 U.S.C. 3237] ANNUAL REPORTS ON INFLUENCE OPERATIONS AND CAMPAIGNS IN THE UNITED STATES BY THE CHINESE COMMUNIST PARTY.

(a) REQUIREMENT.— On an annual basis, consistent with the protection of intelligence sources and methods, the Director of the National Counterintelligence and Security Center shall submit to the congressional intelligence committees, the Committee on Foreign Affairs of the House of Representatives, and the Committee on Foreign Relations of the Senate a report on the influence operations and campaigns in the United States conducted by the Chinese Communist Party.

(b) CONTENTS.—Each report under subsection (a) shall include the following:

(1) A description of the organization of the United Front Work Department of the People's Republic of China, or the successors of the United Front Work Department, and the links between the United Front Work Department and the Central Committee of the Chinese Communist Party.

(2) An assessment of the degree to which organizations that are associated with or receive funding from the United Front Work Department, particularly such

entities operating in the United States, are formally tasked by the Chinese Communist Party or the Government of China.

(3) A description of the efforts by the United Front Work Department and subsidiary organizations of the United Front Work Department to target, coerce, and influence foreign populations, particularly those of ethnic Chinese descent.

(4) An assessment of attempts by the Chinese Embassy, consulates, and organizations affiliated with the Chinese Communist Party (including, at a minimum, the United Front Work Department) to influence the United States-based Chinese Student Scholar Associations.

(5) A description of the evolution of the role of the United Front Work Department under the leadership of the President of China.

(6) An assessment of the activities of the United Front Work Department designed to influence the opinions of elected leaders of the United States, or candidates for elections in the United States, with respect to issues of importance to the Chinese Communist Party.

(7) A listing of all known organizations affiliated with the United Front Work Department that are operating in the United States as of the date of the report.

(8) An identification of influence activities and operations employed by the Chinese Communist Party against the United States science and technology sectors, specifically employees of the United States Government, researchers, scientists, and students in the science and technology sector in the United States.

(9) A listing of all known Chinese talent recruitment programs operating in the United States as of the date of the report.

(10) With respect to reports submitted after the first report, an assessment of the change in goals, tactics, techniques, and procedures of the influence operations and campaigns conducted by the Chinese Communist Party.

(c) COORDINATION.— In carrying out subsection (a), the Director shall coordinate with the Director of the Federal Bureau of Investigation, the Director of the Central Intelligence Agency, the Director of the National Security Agency, and any other relevant head of an element of the intelligence community.

(d) FORM.— Each report submitted under subsection (a) shall be submitted in unclassified form, but may include a classified annex.

SEC. 1108. [50 U.S.C. 3238] ANNUAL REPORTS ON INFLUENCE OPERATIONS AND CAMPAIGNS IN THE UNITED STATES BY THE RUSSIAN FEDERATION.

(a) REQUIREMENT.— On an annual basis, the Director of the National Counterintelligence and Security Center shall submit to the congressional intelligence committees a report on the influence operations and campaigns in the United States conducted by the Russian Federation.

(b) CONTENTS.—Each report under subsection (a) shall include the following:

(1) A description and listing of the Russian organizations and persons involved in influence operations and campaigns operating in the United States as of the date of the report.

(2) An assessment of organizations that are associated with or receive funding from organizations and persons identified in paragraph (1), particularly such entities

operating in the United States.

(3) A description of the efforts by the organizations and persons identified in paragraph (1) to target, coerce, and influence populations within the United States.

(4) An assessment of the activities of the organizations and persons identified in paragraph (1) designed to influence the opinions of elected leaders of the United States or candidates for election in the United States.

(5) With respect to reports submitted after the first report, an assessment of the change in goals, tactics, techniques, and procedures of the influence operations and campaigns conducted by the organizations and persons identified in paragraph (1).

(c) COORDINATION.— In carrying out subsection (a), the Director shall coordinate with the Director of the Federal Bureau of Investigation, the Director of the Central Intelligence Agency, the Director of the National Security Agency, and any other relevant head of an element of the intelligence community.

(d) FORM.— Each report submitted under subsection (a) shall be submitted in unclassified form, but may include a classified annex.

SEC. 1109. [50 U.S.C. 3239] REQUIREMENT TO BUY CERTAIN SATELLITE COMPONENT FROM AMERICAN SOURCES.

(a) DEFINITIONS.—In this section:

(1) COVERED ELEMENT OF THE INTELLIGENCE COMMUNITY.— The term "covered element of the intelligence community" means an element of the intelligence community that is not an element of the Department of Defense.

(2) NATIONAL SECURITY SATELLITE.— The term "national security satellite" means a satellite weighing over 400 pounds whose principle purpose is to support the national security or intelligence needs of the United States Government.

(3) UNITED STATES.— The term "United States" means the several States, the District of Columbia, and the territories and possessions of the United States.

(b) REQUIREMENT.— Beginning January 1, 2021, except as provided in subsection (c), a covered element of the intelligence community may not award a contract for a national security satellite if the satellite uses a star tracker that is not produced in the United States, including with respect to both the software and the hardware of the star tracker.

(c) EXCEPTION.—The head of a covered element of the intelligence community may waive the requirement under subsection (b) if, on a case-by-case basis, the head certifies in writing to the congressional intelligence committees that—

(1) there is no available star tracker produced in the United States that meets the mission and design requirements of the national security satellite for which the star tracker will be used;

(2) the cost of a star tracker produced in the United States is unreasonable, based on a market survey; or

(3) such waiver is necessary for the national security interests of the United States based on an urgent and compelling need.

SEC. 1110. [50 U.S.C. 3240] REPORT ON BEST PRACTICES TO PROTECT PRIVACY , CIVIL LIBERTIES, AND CIVIL RIGHTS OF CHINESE AMERICANS.

(a) SENSE OF CONGRESS.—It is the sense of Congress that—

(1) the People's Republic of China appears to be specifically targeting the Chinese-American community for intelligence purposes;

(2) such targeting carries a substantial risk that the loyalty of such Americans may be generally questioned and lead to unacceptable stereotyping, targeting, and racial profiling;

(3) the United States Government has a duty to warn and protect all Americans including those of Chinese descent from these intelligence efforts by the People's Republic of China;

(4) the broad stereotyping, targeting, and racial profiling of Americans of Chinese descent is contrary to the values of the United States and reinforces the flawed narrative perpetuated by the People's Republic of China that ethnically Chinese individuals worldwide have a duty to support the People's Republic of China; and

(5) the United States efforts to combat the People's Republic of China's intelligence activities should actively safeguard and promote the constitutional rights of all Chinese Americans.

(b) REPORT.—On an annual basis, the Director of National Intelligence, acting through the Office of Civil Liberties, Privacy, and Transparency, in coordination with the civil liberties and privacy officers of the elements of the intelligence community, shall submit a report to the congressional intelligence committees containing—

(1) a review of how the policies, procedures, and practices of the intelligence community that govern the intelligence activities and operations targeting the People's Republic of China affect policies, procedures, and practices relating to the privacy , civil liberties, and civil rights of Americans of Chinese descent who may be targets of espionage and influence operations by China; and

(2) recommendations to ensure that the privacy , civil liberties, and civil rights of Americans of Chinese descent are sufficiently protected.

(c) FORM.— The report under subsection (b) shall be submitted in unclassified form, but may include a classified annex.

SEC. 1111. [50 U.S.C. 3241] BIENNIAL REPORTS ON FOREIGN BIOLOGICAL THREATS.

(a) REPORTS.— On a biennial basis until the date that is 10 years after the date of the enactment of the Intelligence Authorization Act for Fiscal Year 2022, the Director of National Intelligence shall submit to the congressional intelligence committees a comprehensive report on the activities, prioritization, and responsibilities of the intelligence community with respect to foreign biological threats emanating from the territory of, or sponsored by, a covered country.

(b) MATTERS INCLUDED.—Each report under subsection (a) shall include, with respect to foreign biological threats emanating from the territory of, or sponsored by, a covered country, the following:

(1) A detailed description of all activities relating to such threats undertaken by each element of the intelligence community, and an assessment of any gaps in such activities.

(2) A detailed description of all duties and responsibilities relating to such

threats explicitly authorized or otherwise assigned, exclusively or jointly, to each element of the intelligence community, and an assessment of any identified gaps in such duties or responsibilities.

(3) A description of the coordination among the relevant elements of the intelligence community with respect to the activities specified in paragraph (1) and the duties and responsibilities specified in paragraph (2).

(4) An inventory of the strategies, plans, policies, and interagency agreements of the intelligence community relating to the collection, monitoring, analysis, mitigation, and attribution of such threats, and an assessment of any identified gaps therein.

(5) A description of the coordination and interactions among the relevant elements of the intelligence community and non-intelligence community partners.

(6) An assessment of foreign malign influence efforts relating to such threats, including any foreign academics engaged in such efforts, and a description of how the intelligence community contributes to efforts by non-intelligence community partners to counter such foreign malign influence.

(c) FORM.— Each report submitted under subsection (a) may be submitted in classified form, but if so submitted shall include an unclassified executive summary.

(d) DEFINITIONS.—In this section:

(1) COVERED COUNTRY.—The term "covered country" means—

(A) China;

(B) Iran;

(C) North Korea;

(D) Russia; and

(E) any other foreign country—

(i) from which the Director of National Intelligence determines a biological threat emanates; or

(ii) that the Director determines has a known history of, or has been assessed as having conditions present for, infectious disease outbreaks or epidemics.

(2) FOREIGN BIOLOGICAL THREAT.— The term "foreign biological threat" means biological warfare, bioterrorism, naturally occurring infectious diseases, or accidental exposures to biological materials, without regard to whether the threat originates from a state actor, a non-state actor, natural conditions, or an undetermined source.

(3) FOREIGN MALIGN INFLUENCE.— The term "foreign malign influence" has the meaning given such term in section 119C(e) of this Act.

(4) NON-INTELLIGENCE COMMUNITY PARTNER.— The term "non-intelligence community partner" means a Federal department or agency that is not an element of the intelligence community.

SEC. 1112. [50 U.S.C. 3242] ANNUAL REPORTS ON CERTAIN CYBER VULNERABILITIES PROCURED BY INTELLIGENCE COMMUNITY AND FOREIGN COMMERCIAL PROVIDERS OF CYBER VULNERABILITIES.

(a) Annual Reports.— On an annual basis through 2026, the Director of the Central Intelligence Agency and the Director of the National Security Agency, in coordination with the Director of National Intelligence, shall jointly submit to the congressional intelligence committees a report containing information on foreign commercial providers and the cyber vulnerabilities procured by the intelligence community through foreign commercial providers.

(b) Elements.—Each report under subsection (a) shall include, with respect to the period covered by the report, the following:

(1) A description of each cyber vulnerability procured through a foreign commercial provider, including—

(A) a description of the vulnerability;

(B) the date of the procurement;

(C) whether the procurement consisted of only that vulnerability or included other vulnerabilities;

(D) the cost of the procurement;

(E) the identity of the commercial provider and, if the commercial provider was not the original supplier of the vulnerability, a description of the original supplier;

(F) the country of origin of the vulnerability; and

(G) an assessment of the ability of the intelligence community to use the vulnerability, including whether such use will be operational or for research and development, and the approximate timeline for such use.

(2) An assessment of foreign commercial providers that—

(A) pose a significant threat to the national security of the United States; or

(B) have provided cyber vulnerabilities to any foreign government that—

(i) has used the cyber vulnerabilities to target United States persons, the United States Government, journalists, or dissidents; or

(ii) has an established pattern or practice of violating human rights or suppressing dissent.

(3) An assessment of whether the intelligence community has conducted business with the foreign commercial providers identified under paragraph (2) during the 5-year period preceding the date of the report.

(c) Form.— Each report under subsection (a) may be submitted in classified form.

(d) Definitions.—In this section:

(1) Commercial provider.— The term "commercial provider" means any person that sells, or acts as a broker, for a cyber vulnerability.

(2) Cyber vulnerability.— The term "cyber vulnerability" means any tool, exploit, vulnerability, or code that is intended to compromise a device, network, or system, including such a tool, exploit, vulnerability, or code procured by the intelligence community for purposes of research and development.

SEC. 1113. [50 U.S.C. 3243] PERIODIC REPORTS ON TECHNOLOGY STRATEGY OF INTELLIGENCE COMMUNITY.

(a) Reports.— On a basis that is not less frequent than once every 4 years, the

Director of National Intelligence, in coordination with the Director of the Office of Science and Technology Policy, the Secretary of Commerce, and the heads of such other agencies as the Director considers appropriate, shall submit to the congressional intelligence committees a comprehensive report on the technology strategy of the intelligence community, which shall be designed to support the maintenance of the leadership of the United States in critical and emerging technologies essential to the national security of the United States.

(b) ELEMENTS.—Each report submitted under subsection (a) shall include the following:

(1) An assessment of technologies critical to the national security of the United States, particularly those technologies with respect to which foreign countries that are adversarial to the United States have or are poised to match or surpass the technology leadership of the United States.

(2) A review of current technology policies of the intelligence community, including long-term goals.

(3) An identification of sectors and supply chains the Director determines to be of the greatest strategic importance to national security.

(4) An identification of opportunities to protect the leadership of the United States, and the allies and partners of the United States, in critical technologies, including through targeted export controls, investment screening, and counterintelligence activities.

(5) An identification of research and development areas the Director determines critical to the national security of the United States, including areas in which the private sector does not focus.

(6) Recommendations for growing talent in key critical and emerging technologies and enhancing the ability of the intelligence community to recruit and retain individuals with critical skills relating to such technologies.

(7) An identification of opportunities to improve the leadership of the United States in critical technologies, including opportunities to develop international partnerships to reinforce domestic policy actions, develop new markets, engage in collaborative research, and maintain an international environment that reflects the values of the United States and protects the interests of the United States.

(8) A technology annex to establish an approach for the identification, prioritization, development, and fielding of emerging technologies critical to the mission of the intelligence community.

(9) Such other information as the Director determines may be necessary to inform Congress on matters relating to the technology strategy of the intelligence community and related implications for the national security of the United States.

(c) FORM OF ANNEX.— Each annex submitted under subsection (b)(8) may be submitted in classified form.

SEC. 1114. [50 U.S.C. 3244] ANNUAL REPORT ON REPORTING REQUIREMENTS.

(a) ANNUAL REPORT REQUIRED.— Not later than March 1 of each fiscal year, the Director of National Intelligence shall submit to the congressional intelligence committees, the Committee on Appropriations of the Senate, and the Committee on

Appropriations of the House of Representatives a report detailing all congressionally mandated reporting requirements applicable to the Office of the Director of National Intelligence for the upcoming fiscal year.

(b) CONTENTS.—Each report submitted pursuant to subsection (a) shall include, for the fiscal year covered by the report and for each congressionally mandated reporting requirement detailed in the report:

(1) A description of the reporting requirement.

(2) A citation to the provision of law (or other source of congressional directive) imposing the reporting requirement.

(3) Whether the reporting requirement is recurring, conditional, or subject to a termination provision.

(4) Whether the Director recommends repealing or modifying the requirement.

(c) FORM.— Each report submitted pursuant to subsection (a) may be submitted in classified form.

NATIONAL SECURITY AGENCY ACT OF 1959

PUBLIC LAW 86–36

AS AMENDED THROUGH P.L. 118–159

NATIONAL SECURITY AGENCY ACT OF 1959

PUBLIC LAW 86–36

AS AMENDED THROUGH P.L. 118–159

NATIONAL SECURITY ACT OF 1947

[Chapter 343; 61 Stat. 496; approved July 26, 1947]

[As Amended Through P.L. 118–159, Enacted December 23, 2024]

AN ACT To promote the national security by providing for a Secretary of Defense; for a National Military Establishment; for a Department of the Army, a Department of the Navy, and a Department of the Air Force; and for the coordination of the activities of the National Military Establishment with other departments and agencies of the Government concerned with the national security.

Be it enacted by the Senate and House of Representatives of the United States of America in Congress assembled,

SHORT TITLE

That [50 U.S.C. 3001] this Act may be cited as the "National Security Act of 1947".

TABLE OF CONTENTS

[1] The toc item of section 108B does not match the section heading. The toc item reads “world-wide” while the section heading reads “worldwide”. See amendments made by section 617 of division W of Public Law 116-260.

ACTIVITIES

* * * * * * *

DECLARATION OF POLICY

SEC. 2. [50 U.S.C. 3002] In enacting this legislation, it is the intent of Congress to provide a comprehensive program for the future security of the United States; to provide for the establishment of integrated policies and procedures for the departments, agencies, and functions of the Government relating to the national security; to provide a Department of Defense, including the three military Departments of the Army, the Navy (including naval aviation and the United States Marine Corps), and the Air Force under the direction, authority, and control of the Secretary of Defense; to provide that each military department shall be separately organized under its own Secretary and shall function under the direction, authority, and control of the Secretary of Defense; to provide for their unified direction under civilian control of the Secretary of Defense but not to merge these departments or services; to provide for the establishment of unified or specified combatant commands, and a clear and direct line of command to such commands; to eliminate unnecessary duplication in the Department of Defense, and particularly in the field of research and engineering by vesting its overall direction and control in the Secretary of Defense; to provide more effective, efficient, and economical administration in the Department of Defense; to provide for the unified strategic direction of the combatant forces, for their operation under unified command, and for their integration into an efficient team of land, naval, and air forces but not to establish a single Chief of Staff over the armed forces nor an overall armed forces general staff.

DEFINITIONS

SEC. 3. [50 U.S.C. 3003] As used in this Act:

(1) The term "intelligence" includes foreign intelligence and counterintelligence.

(2) The term "foreign intelligence" means information relating to the capabilities, intentions, or activities of foreign governments or elements thereof, foreign organizations, or foreign persons, or international terrorist activities.

(3) The term "counterintelligence" means information gathered, and activities conducted, to protect against espionage, other intelligence activities, sabotage, or assassinations conducted by or on behalf of foreign governments or elements thereof, foreign organizations, or foreign persons, or international terrorist activities.

(4) The term "intelligence community" includes the following:

(A) The Office of the Director of National Intelligence.

(B) The Central Intelligence Agency.

(C) The National Security Agency.

(D) The Defense Intelligence Agency.

(E) The National Geospatial-Intelligence Agency.

(F) The National Reconnaissance Office.

(G) Other offices within the Department of Defense for the collection of specialized national intelligence through reconnaissance programs.

(H) The intelligence elements of the Army, the Navy, the Air Force, the Marine Corps, the Space Force, the Coast Guard, the Federal Bureau of Investigation, the Drug Enforcement Administration, and the Department of Energy.

(I) The Bureau of Intelligence and Research of the Department of State.

(J) The Office of Intelligence and Analysis of the Department of the Treasury.

(K) The Office of Intelligence and Analysis of the Department of Homeland Security.

(L) Such other elements of any department or agency as may be designated by the President, or designated jointly by the Director of National Intelligence and the head of the department or agency concerned, as an element of the intelligence community.

(5) The terms "national intelligence" and "intelligence related to national security" refer to all intelligence, regardless of the source from which derived and including information gathered within or outside the United States, that—

(A) pertains, as determined consistent with any guidance issued by the President, to more than one United States Government agency; and

(B) that involves—

(i) threats to the United States, its people, property, or interests;

(ii) the development, proliferation, or use of weapons of mass destruction; or

(iii) any other matter bearing on United States national or homeland security.

(6) The term "National Intelligence Program" refers to all programs, projects, and activities of the intelligence community, as well as any other programs of the intelligence community designated jointly by the Director of National Intelligence and the head of a United States department or agency or by the President. Such term does not include programs, projects, or activities of the military departments to acquire intelligence solely for the planning and conduct of tactical military operations by United States Armed Forces.

(7) The term "congressional intelligence committees" means—

(A) the Select Committee on Intelligence of the Senate; and

(B) the Permanent Select Committee on Intelligence of the House of Representatives.

TITLE I—COORDINATION FOR NATIONAL SECURITY

SEC. 101. [50 U.S.C. 3021] NATIONAL SECURITY COUNCIL.

(a) National Security Council.— There is a council known as the National Security Council (in this section referred to as the "Council").

(b) Functions.—Consistent with the direction of the President, the functions of the Council shall be to—

(1) advise the President with respect to the integration of domestic, foreign, and military policies relating to the national security so as to enable the Armed Forces and the other departments and agencies of the United States Government to cooperate more effectively in matters involving the national security;

(2) assess and appraise the objectives, commitments, and risks of the United States in relation to the actual and potential military power of the United States, and make recommendations thereon to the President;

(3) make recommendations to the President concerning policies on matters of common interest to the departments and agencies of the United States Government concerned with the national security; and

(4) coordinate, without assuming operational authority, the United States Government response to malign foreign influence operations and campaigns.

(c) Membership.—

(1) In general.— The Council consists of the President, the Vice President, the Secretary of State, the Secretary of Defense, the Secretary of Energy, the Secretary of the Treasury, the Director of the Office of Pandemic Preparedness and Response Policy and such other officers of the United States Government as the President may designate.

(2) Attendance and participation in meetings.— The President may designate such other officers of the United States Government as the President considers appropriate, including the Director of National Intelligence, the Director of National Drug Control Policy, the Chairman of the Joint Chiefs of Staff, and the

National Cyber Director, to attend and participate in meetings of the Council.

(d) PRESIDING OFFICERS.— At meetings of the Council, the President shall preside or, in the absence of the President, a member of the Council designated by the President shall preside.

(e) STAFF.—

(1) IN GENERAL.— The Council shall have a staff headed by a civilian executive secretary appointed by the President.

(2) STAFF.— Consistent with the direction of the President and subject to paragraph (3), the executive secretary may, subject to the civil service laws and chapter 51 and subchapter III of chapter 53 of title 5, United States Code, appoint and fix the compensation of such personnel as may be necessary to perform such duties as may be prescribed by the President in connection with performance of the functions of the Council.

(3)[2] NUMBER OF PROFESSIONAL STAFF.— The professional staff for which this subsection provides shall not exceed 200 persons, including persons employed by, assigned to, detailed to, under contract to serve on, or otherwise serving or affiliated with the staff. The limitation in this paragraph does not apply to personnel serving substantially in support or administrative positions.

---

[2] Section 1085(b) of division A of Public Law 114-328 states "The limitation on the number of professional staff of the National Security Council specified in subsection (e)(3) of section 101 of the National Security Act of 1947, as amended by subsection (a) of this section, shall take effect on the date that is 18 months after the date of the enactment of this Act.".

(f) SPECIAL ADVISOR TO THE PRESIDENT ON INTERNATIONAL RELIGIOUS FREEDOM.— It is the sense of Congress that there should be within the staff of the Council a Special Adviser to the President on International Religious Freedom, whose position should be comparable to that of a director within the Executive Office of the President. The Special Adviser should serve as a resource for executive branch officials, compiling and maintaining information on the facts and circumstances of violations of religious freedom (as defined in section 3 of the International Religious Freedom Act of 1998 (22 U.S.C. 6402)), and making policy recommendations. The Special Adviser should serve as liaison with the Ambassador at Large for International Religious Freedom, the United States Commission on International Religious Freedom, Congress and, as advisable, religious nongovernmental organizations.

(g) COORDINATOR FOR COMBATING MALIGN FOREIGN INFLUENCE OPERATIONS AND CAMPAIGNS.—

(1) IN GENERAL.— The President shall designate an employee of the National Security Council to be responsible for the coordination of the interagency process for combating malign foreign influence operations and campaigns.

(2) CONGRESSIONAL BRIEFING.—

(A) IN GENERAL.— Not less frequently than twice each year, the employee designated under this subsection, or the employee's designee, shall provide to the congressional committees specified in subparagraph (B) a briefing on the responsibilities and activities of the employee designated under this subsection.

(B) COMMITTEES SPECIFIED.—The congressional committees specified in this subparagraph are the following:

(i) The Committees on Armed Services, Foreign Affairs, and Oversight and Government Reform, and the Permanent Select Committee on Intelligence of the House of Representatives.

(ii) The Committees on Armed Services, Foreign Relations, and Homeland Security and Governmental Affairs, and the Select Committee on Intelligence of the Senate.

(h) DEFINITION OF MALIGN FOREIGN INFLUENCE OPERATIONS AND CAMPAIGNS.— In this section, the term "malign foreign influence operations and campaigns" means the coordinated, direct or indirect application of national diplomatic, informational, military, economic, business, corruption, educational, and other capabilities by hostile foreign powers to affect attitudes, behaviors, decisions, or outcomes within the United States.

JOINT INTELLIGENCE COMMUNITY COUNCIL

SEC. 101A. [50 U.S.C. 3022] (a) JOINT INTELLIGENCE COMMUNITY COUNCIL.— There is a Joint Intelligence Community Council.

(b) MEMBERSHIP.—The Joint Intelligence Community Council shall consist of the following:

(1) The Director of National Intelligence, who shall chair the Council.

(2) The Secretary of State.

(3) The Secretary of the Treasury.

(4) The Secretary of Defense.

(5) The Attorney General.

(6) The Secretary of Energy.

(7) The Secretary of Homeland Security.

(8) Such other officers of the United States Government as the President may designate from time to time.

(c) FUNCTIONS.—The Joint Intelligence Community Council shall assist the Director of National Intelligence in developing and implementing a joint, unified national intelligence effort to protect national security by—

(1) advising the Director on establishing requirements, developing budgets, financial management, and monitoring and evaluating the performance of the intelligence community, and on such other matters as the Director may request; and

(2) ensuring the timely execution of programs, policies, and directives established or developed by the Director.

(d) MEETINGS.— The Director of National Intelligence shall convene meetings of the Joint Intelligence Community Council as the Director considers appropriate.

(e) ADVICE AND OPINIONS OF MEMBERS OTHER THAN CHAIRMAN.—(1) A member of the Joint Intelligence Community Council (other than the Chairman) may submit to the Chairman advice or an opinion in disagreement with, or advice or an opinion in addition to, the advice presented by the Director of National Intelligence to the President or the National Security Council, in the role of the Chairman as Chairman of the Joint Intelligence Community Council. If a member submits such advice or opinion, the Chairman shall present the advice or opinion of such member at the same time the Chairman presents the advice of the Chairman to the President or the National Security Council, as the case may be.

(2) The Chairman shall establish procedures to ensure that the presentation of the advice of the Chairman to the President or the National Security Council is not unduly delayed by reason of the submission of the individual advice or opinion of another member of the Council.

(f) Recommendations to Congress.— Any member of the Joint Intelligence Community Council may make such recommendations to Congress relating to the intelligence community as such member considers appropriate.

DIRECTOR OF NATIONAL INTELLIGENCE

Sec. 102. [50 U.S.C. 3023] (a) Director of National Intelligence.—(1) There is a Director of National Intelligence who shall be appointed by the President, by and with the advice and consent of the Senate. Any individual nominated for appointment as Director of National Intelligence shall have extensive national security expertise.

(2) The Director of National Intelligence shall not be located within the Executive Office of the President.

(b) Principal Responsibility.—Subject to the authority, direction, and control of the President, the Director of National Intelligence shall—

(1) serve as head of the intelligence community;

(2) act as the principal adviser to the President, to the National Security Council, and the Homeland Security Council for intelligence matters related to the national security; and

(3) consistent with section 1018 of the National Security Intelligence Reform Act of 2004, oversee and direct the implementation of the National Intelligence Program.

(c) Prohibition on Dual Service.— The individual serving in the position of Director of National Intelligence shall not, while so serving, also serve as the Director of the Central Intelligence Agency or as the head of any other element of the intelligence community.

RESPONSIBILITIES AND AUTHORITIES OF THE DIRECTOR OF NATIONAL INTELLIGENCE

Sec. 102A. [50 U.S.C. 3024] (a) Provision of Intelligence.—(1) The Director of National Intelligence shall be responsible for ensuring that national intelligence is provided—

(A) to the President;

(B) to the heads of departments and agencies of the executive branch;

(C) to the Chairman of the Joint Chiefs of Staff and senior military commanders;

(D) to the Senate and House of Representatives and the committees thereof; and

(E) to such other persons as the Director of National Intelligence determines to be appropriate.

(2) Such national intelligence should be timely, objective, independent of political considerations, and based upon all sources available to the intelligence community and other appropriate entities.

(b) Access to Intelligence.— Unless otherwise directed by the President, the Director of National Intelligence shall have access to all national intelligence and intelligence related to the national security which is collected by any Federal department, agency, or other entity, except as otherwise provided by law or, as appropriate, under guidelines agreed upon by the Attorney General and the Director of National Intelligence.

(c) Budget Authorities.—(1) With respect to budget requests and appropriations for the National Intelligence Program, the Director of National Intelligence shall—

(A) based on intelligence priorities set by the President, provide to the heads of departments containing agencies or organizations within the intelligence community, and to the heads of such agencies and organizations, guidance for developing the National Intelligence Program budget pertaining to such agencies and organizations;

(B) based on budget proposals provided to the Director of National Intelligence by the heads of agencies and organizations within the intelligence community and the heads of their respective departments and, as appropriate, after obtaining the advice of the Joint Intelligence Community Council, develop and determine an annual consolidated National Intelligence Program budget; and

(C) present such consolidated National Intelligence Program budget, together with any comments from the heads of departments containing agencies or organizations within the intelligence community, to the President for approval.

(2) In addition to the information provided under paragraph (1)(B), the heads of agencies and organizations within the intelligence community shall provide the Director of National Intelligence such other information as the Director shall request for the purpose of determining the annual consolidated National Intelligence Program budget under that paragraph.

(3)(A) The Director of National Intelligence shall participate in the development by the Secretary of Defense of the annual budget for the Military Intelligence Program or any successor program or programs.

(B) The Director of National Intelligence shall provide guidance for the development of the annual budget for each element of the intelligence community that is not within the National Intelligence Program.

(4) The Director of National Intelligence shall ensure the effective execution of the annual budget for intelligence and intelligence-related activities.

(5)(A) The Director of National Intelligence shall be responsible for managing appropriations for the National Intelligence Program by directing the allotment or allocation of such appropriations through the heads of the departments containing agencies or organizations within the intelligence community and the Director of the Central Intelligence Agency, with prior notice (including the provision of appropriate supporting information) to the head of the department containing an agency or organization receiving any such allocation or allotment or the Director of the Central Intelligence Agency.

(B) Notwithstanding any other provision of law, pursuant to relevant appropriations Acts for the National Intelligence Program, the Director of the Office of Management and Budget shall exercise the authority of the Director of the Office of Management and Budget to apportion funds, at the exclusive direction of the Director of National Intelligence, for allocation to the elements of the intelligence community through the relevant host executive departments and the Central Intelligence Agency. Department comptrollers or appropriate budget execution officers shall allot, allocate, reprogram, or transfer funds appropriated for the National Intelligence Program in an expeditious manner.

(C) The Director of National Intelligence shall monitor the implementation and execution of the National Intelligence Program by the heads of the elements of the intelligence community that manage programs and activities that are part of the National Intelligence Program, which shall include audits and evaluations.

(D) Consistent with subparagraph (C), the Director of National Intelligence shall ensure that the programs and activities that are part of the National Intelligence Program, including those of the Federal Bureau of Investigation, are structured and executed in a manner than enables budget traceability.

(6) Apportionment and allotment of funds under this subsection shall be subject to chapter 13 and section 1517 of title 31, United States Code, and the Congressional Budget and Impoundment Control Act of 1974 (2 U.S.C. 621 et seq.).

(7)(A) The Director of National Intelligence shall provide a semi-annual report, beginning April 1, 2005, and ending April 1, 2007, to the President and the Congress regarding implementation of this section.

(B) The Director of National Intelligence shall report to the President and the Congress not later than 15 days after learning of any instance in which a departmental comptroller acts in a manner inconsistent with the law (including permanent statutes, authorization Acts, and appropriations Acts), or the direction of the Director of National Intelligence, in carrying out the National Intelligence Program.

(d) Role of Director of National Intelligence in Transfer and Reprogramming of Funds.—(1)(A) No funds made available under the National Intelligence Program may be transferred or reprogrammed without the prior approval of the Director of National Intelligence, except in accordance with procedures prescribed by the Director of National Intelligence.

(B) The Secretary of Defense shall consult with the Director of National Intelligence before transferring or reprogramming funds made available under the Military Intelligence Program or any successor program or programs.

(2) Subject to the succeeding provisions of this subsection, the Director of National Intelligence may transfer or reprogram funds appropriated for a program within the National Intelligence Program—

(A) to another such program;

(B) to other departments or agencies of the United States Government for the development and fielding of systems of common concern related to the collection, processing, analysis, exploitation, and dissemination of intelligence information; or

(C) to a program funded by appropriations not within the National Intelligence Program to address critical gaps in intelligence information sharing or access capabilities.

(3) The Director of National Intelligence may only transfer or reprogram funds referred to in paragraph (1)(A)—

(A) with the approval of the Director of the Office of Management and Budget; and

(B) after consultation with the heads of departments containing agencies or organizations within the intelligence community to the extent such agencies or organizations are affected, and, in the case of the Central Intelligence Agency, after consultation with the Director of the Central Intelligence Agency.

(4) The amounts available for transfer or reprogramming in the National Intelligence Program in any given fiscal year, and the terms and conditions governing such transfers and reprogrammings, are subject to the provisions of annual appropriations Acts and this subsection.

(5)(A) A transfer or reprogramming of funds may be made under this subsection only if—

(i) the funds are being transferred to an activity that is a higher priority intelligence activity;

(ii) the transfer or reprogramming supports an emergent need, improves program effectiveness, or increases efficiency;

(iii) the transfer or reprogramming does not involve a transfer or reprogramming of funds to a Reserve for Contingencies of the Director of National Intelligence or the Reserve for Contingencies of the Central Intelligence Agency;

(iv) the transfer or reprogramming results in a cumulative transfer or reprogramming of funds out of any department or agency, as appropriate, funded in the National Intelligence Program in a single fiscal year—

(I) that is less than $150,000,000, and

(II) that is less than 5 percent of amounts available to a department or agency under the National Intelligence Program; and

(v) the transfer or reprogramming does not terminate an acquisition program.

(B) A transfer or reprogramming may be made without regard to a limitation set forth in clause (iv) or (v) of subparagraph (A) if the transfer has the concurrence of the head of the department involved or the Director of the Central Intelligence Agency (in the case of the Central Intelligence Agency). The authority to provide such concurrence may only be delegated by the head of the department involved or the Director of the Central Intelligence Agency (in the case of the Central Intelligence Agency) to the deputy of such officer.

(6) Funds transferred or reprogrammed under this subsection shall remain available for the same period as the appropriations account to which transferred or reprogrammed.

(7) Any transfer or reprogramming of funds under this subsection shall be carried out in accordance with existing procedures applicable to reprogramming notifications for the appropriate congressional committees. Any proposed transfer or reprogramming for which notice is given to the appropriate congressional committees shall be accompanied by a report explaining the nature of the proposed transfer or reprogramming and how it satisfies the requirements of this subsection. In addition, the congressional intelligence committees shall be promptly notified of any transfer or reprogramming of funds made pursuant to this subsection in any case in which the transfer or reprogramming would not have otherwise required reprogramming notification under procedures in effect as of the date of the enactment of this subsection.

(e) TRANSFER OF PERSONNEL.—(1)(A) In addition to any other authorities available under law for such purposes, in the first twelve months after establishment of a new national intelligence center, the Director of National Intelligence, with the approval of the Director of the Office of Management and Budget and in consultation with the congressional committees of jurisdiction referred to in subparagraph (B), may transfer not more than 100 personnel authorized for elements of the intelligence community to such center.

(B) The Director of National Intelligence shall promptly provide notice of any transfer of personnel made pursuant to this paragraph to—

(i) the congressional intelligence committees;

(ii) the Committees on Appropriations of the Senate and the House of Representatives;

(iii) in the case of the transfer of personnel to or from the Department of Defense, the Committees on Armed Services of the Senate and the House of Representatives; and

(iv) in the case of the transfer of personnel to or from the Department of Justice, to the Committees on the Judiciary of the Senate and the House of Representatives.

(C) The Director shall include in any notice under subparagraph (B) an explanation of the nature of the transfer and how it satisfies the requirements of this subsection.

(2)(A) The Director of National Intelligence, with the approval of the Director of the Office of Management and Budget and in accordance with procedures to be developed by the Director of National Intelligence and the heads of the departments and agencies concerned, may transfer personnel authorized for an element of the intelligence community to another such element for a period of not more than 2 years.

(B) A transfer of personnel may be made under this paragraph only if—

(i) the personnel are being transferred to an activity that is a higher priority intelligence activity; and

(ii) the transfer supports an emergent need, improves program effectiveness, or increases efficiency.

(C) The Director of National Intelligence shall promptly provide notice of any transfer of personnel made pursuant to this paragraph to—

(i) the congressional intelligence committees;

(ii) in the case of the transfer of personnel to or from the Department of Defense, the Committees on Armed Services of the Senate and the House of Representatives; and

(iii) in the case of the transfer of personnel to or from the Department of Justice, to the Committees on the Judiciary of the Senate and the House of Representatives.

(D) The Director shall include in any notice under subparagraph (C) an explanation of the nature of the transfer and how it satisfies the requirements of this paragraph.

(3)(A) In addition to the number of full-time equivalent positions authorized for the Office of the Director of National Intelligence for a fiscal year, there is authorized for such Office for each fiscal year an additional 100 full-time equivalent positions that may be used only for the purposes described in subparagraph (B).

(B) Except as provided in subparagraph (C), the Director of National Intelligence may use a full-time equivalent position authorized under subparagraph (A) only for the purpose of providing a temporary transfer of personnel made in accordance with paragraph (2) to an element of the intelligence community to enable such element to increase the total number of personnel authorized for such element, on a temporary basis—

(i) during a period in which a permanent employee of such element is absent to participate in critical language training; or

(ii) to accept a permanent employee of another element of the intelligence community to provide language-capable services.

(C) Paragraph (2)(B) shall not apply with respect to a transfer of personnel made under subparagraph (B).

(D) For each of the fiscal years 2010, 2011, and 2012, the Director of National Intelligence shall submit to the congressional intelligence committees an annual report on the use of authorities under this paragraph. Each such report shall include a description of—

(i) the number of transfers of personnel made by the Director pursuant to subparagraph (B), disaggregated by each element of the intelligence community;

(ii) the critical language needs that were fulfilled or partially fulfilled through the use of such transfers; and

(iii) the cost to carry out subparagraph (B).

(4) It is the sense of Congress that—

(A) the nature of the national security threats facing the United States will continue to challenge the intelligence community to respond rapidly and flexibly to bring analytic resources to bear against emerging and unforeseen requirements;

(B) both the Office of the Director of National Intelligence and any analytic centers determined to be necessary should be fully and properly supported with appropriate levels of personnel resources and that the President's yearly budget requests adequately support those needs; and

(C) the President should utilize all legal and administrative discretion to ensure that the Director of National Intelligence and all other elements of the intelligence community have the necessary resources and procedures to respond promptly and effectively to emerging and unforeseen national security challenges.

(f) TASKING AND OTHER AUTHORITIES.—(1)(A) The Director of National Intelligence shall—

(i) establish objectives, priorities, and guidance for the intelligence community to ensure timely and effective collection, processing, analysis, and dissemination (including access by users to collected data consistent with applicable law and, as appropriate, the guidelines referred to in subsection (b) and analytic products generated by or within the intelligence community) of national intelligence;

(ii) determine requirements and priorities for, and manage and direct the tasking of, collection, analysis, production, and dissemination of national intelligence by elements of the intelligence community, including—

(I) approving requirements (including those requirements responding to needs provided by consumers) for collection and analysis; and

(II) resolving conflicts in collection requirements and in the tasking of national collection assets of the elements of the intelligence community; and

(iii) provide advisory tasking to intelligence elements of those agencies and departments not within the National Intelligence Program.

(B) The authority of the Director of National Intelligence under subparagraph (A) shall not apply—

(i) insofar as the President so directs;

(ii) with respect to clause (ii) of subparagraph (A), insofar as the Secretary of Defense exercises tasking authority under plans or arrangements agreed upon by the Secretary of Defense and the Director of National Intelligence; or

(iii) to the direct dissemination of information to State government and local government officials and private sector entities pursuant to sections 201 and 892 of the Homeland Security Act of 2002 (6 U.S.C. 121, 482).

(2) The Director of National Intelligence shall oversee the National Counterterrorism Center, the National Counterproliferation Center, and the National Counterintelligence and Security Center and may establish such other national intelligence centers as the Director determines necessary.

(3)(A) The Director of National Intelligence shall prescribe, in consultation with the heads of other agencies or elements of the intelligence community, and the heads of their respective departments, binding personnel policies and programs applicable to the intelligence community that—

(i) require and facilitate assignments and details of personnel to national intelligence centers, and between elements of the intelligence community over the course of the careers of such personnel;

(ii) set standards for education, training, and career development of personnel of the intelligence community;

(iii) encourage and facilitate the recruitment and retention by the intelligence community of highly qualified individuals for the effective conduct of intelligence activities;

(iv) ensure that the personnel of the intelligence community are sufficiently diverse for purposes of the collection and analysis of intelligence through the recruitment and training of women, minorities, and individuals with diverse ethnic, cultural, and linguistic backgrounds;

(v) require service in more than one element of the intelligence community as a condition of promotion to such positions within the intelligence community as the Director shall specify, and take requisite steps to ensure compliance among elements of the intelligence community; and

(vi) ensure the effective management of intelligence community personnel who are responsible for intelligence community-wide matters.

(B) Policies prescribed under subparagraph (A) shall not be inconsistent with the personnel policies otherwise applicable to members of the uniformed services.

(4) The Director of National Intelligence shall ensure compliance with the Constitution and laws of the United States by the Central Intelligence Agency and shall ensure such compliance by other elements of the intelligence community through the host executive departments that manage the programs and activities that are part of the National Intelligence Program.

(5) The Director of National Intelligence shall ensure the elimination of waste and unnecessary duplication within the intelligence community.

(6) The Director of National Intelligence shall establish requirements and priorities for foreign intelligence information to be collected under the Foreign Intelligence Surveillance Act of 1978 (50 U.S.C. 1801 et seq.), and provide assistance to the Attorney General to ensure that information derived from electronic surveillance or physical searches under that Act is disseminated so it may be used efficiently and effectively for national intelligence purposes, except that the Director

shall have no authority to direct or undertake electronic surveillance or physical search operations pursuant to that Act unless authorized by statute or Executive order.

(7)(A) The Director of National Intelligence shall, if the Director determines it is necessary, or may, if requested by a congressional intelligence committee, conduct an accountability review of an element of the intelligence community or the personnel of such element in relation to a failure or deficiency within the intelligence community.

(B) The Director of National Intelligence, in consultation with the Attorney General, shall establish guidelines and procedures for conducting an accountability review under subparagraph (A).

(C)(i) The Director of National Intelligence shall provide the findings of an accountability review conducted under subparagraph (A) and the Director's recommendations for corrective or punitive action, if any, to the head of the applicable element of the intelligence community. Such recommendations may include a recommendation for dismissal of personnel.

(ii) If the head of such element does not implement a recommendation made by the Director under clause (i), the head of such element shall submit to the congressional intelligence committees a notice of the determination not to implement the recommendation, including the reasons for the determination.

(D) The requirements of this paragraph shall not be construed to limit any authority of the Director of National Intelligence under subsection (m) or with respect to supervision of the Central Intelligence Agency.

(8) The Director of National Intelligence shall—

(A) conduct assessments and audits of the compliance of each element of the intelligence community with minimum insider threat policy;

(B) receive information from each element of the intelligence community regarding the collection, sharing, and use by such element of audit and monitoring data for insider threat detection across all classified and unclassified information technology systems within such element;

(C) provide guidance and oversight to Federal departments and agencies to fully implement automated records checks, consistent with personnel vetting reforms and the Trusted Workforce 2.0 initiative, or successor initiative, and ensure that information collected pursuant to such records checks is appropriately shared in support of intelligence community-wide insider threat initiatives;

(D) carry out evaluations of the effectiveness of counterintelligence, security, and insider threat program activities of each element of the intelligence community, including with respect to the lowest organizational unit of each such element, that include an identification of any gaps, shortfalls, or resource needs of each such element;

(E) identify gaps, shortfalls, resources needs, and recommendations for adjustments in allocations and additional resources and other remedies to strengthen counterintelligence, security, and insider threat detection programs;

(F) pursuant to final damage assessments facilitated by the National Counterintelligence and Security Center that have been undertaken as a result of an unauthorized disclosure, determine whether the heads of the elements of the intelligence community implement recommended mitigation, and notify the congressional intelligence committees of such determinations and notify the Committee on Armed Services of the Senate and the Committee on Armed Services of the House of Representatives in cases involving elements of the intelligence community within the Department of Defense; and

(G) study the data collected during the course of background investigations and adjudications for security clearances granted to individuals who subsequently commit unauthorized disclosures, and issue findings regarding the quality of such data as a predictor for insider threat activity, delineated by the severity of the unauthorized disclosure.

(9) The Director of National Intelligence shall ensure there is established a policy for minimum insider threat standards for the intelligence community and ensure compliance by the elements of the intelligence community with that policy.

(10) The Director of National Intelligence shall perform such other intelligence-related functions as the President may direct, and upon receiving any such direction, the Director shall notify the congressional intelligence committees immediately in writing with a description of such other intelligence-related functions directed by the President.

(11) Nothing in this title shall be construed as affecting the role of the Department of Justice or the Attorney General under the Foreign Intelligence Surveillance Act of 1978.

(g) Intelligence Information Sharing.—(1) The Director of National Intelligence shall have principal authority to ensure maximum availability of and access to intelligence information within the intelligence community consistent with national security requirements. The Director of National Intelligence shall—

(A) establish uniform security standards and procedures;

(B) establish common information technology standards, protocols, and interfaces;

(C) ensure development of information technology systems that include multi-level security and intelligence integration capabilities;

(D) establish policies and procedures to resolve conflicts between the need to share intelligence information and the need to protect intelligence sources and methods;

(E) develop an enterprise architecture for the intelligence community and ensure that elements of the intelligence community comply with such architecture;

(F) have procurement approval authority over all enterprise architecture-related information technology items funded in the National Intelligence Program; and

(G) in accordance with Executive Order No. 13526 (75 Fed. Reg. 707; relating to classified national security information) (or any subsequent corresponding executive order), and part 2001 of title 32, Code of Federal Regulations (or any subsequent corresponding regulation), establish—

(i) guidance to standardize, in appropriate cases, the formats for classified and unclassified intelligence products created by elements of the intelligence community for purposes of promoting the sharing of intelligence products; and

(ii) policies and procedures requiring the increased use, in appropriate cases, and including portion markings, of the classification of portions of information within one intelligence product.

(2) The President shall ensure that the Director of National Intelligence has all necessary support and authorities to fully and effectively implement paragraph (1).

(3) Except as otherwise directed by the President or with the specific written agreement of the head of the department or agency in question, a Federal agency or official shall not be considered to have met any obligation to provide any information, report, assessment, or other material (including unevaluated intelligence information) to that department or agency solely by virtue of having provided that information, report, assessment, or other material to the Director of National Intelligence or the National Counterterrorism Center.

(4) The Director of National Intelligence shall, in a timely manner, report to Congress any statute, regulation, policy, or practice that the Director believes impedes the ability of the Director to fully and effectively ensure maximum availability of access to intelligence information within the intelligence community consistent with the protection of the national security of the United States.

(h) Analysis.—To ensure the most accurate analysis of intelligence is derived from all sources to support national security needs, the Director of National Intelligence shall—

(1) implement policies and procedures—

(A) to require sound analytic methods and tradecraft, independent of political considerations, throughout the elements of the intelligence community;

(B) to ensure that analysis is based upon all sources available; and

(C) to ensure that the elements of the intelligence community regularly conduct competitive analysis of analytic products, whether such products are produced by or disseminated to such elements;

(2) ensure that resource allocation for intelligence analysis is appropriately proportional to resource allocation for intelligence collection systems and operations in order to maximize analysis of all collected data;

(3) ensure that substantial differences in analytic judgment are fully considered, brought to the attention of policymakers, and documented in analytic products; and

(4) ensure that sufficient relationships are established between intelligence collectors and analysts to facilitate greater understanding of the needs of analysts.

(i) Protection of Intelligence Sources and Methods.—(1) The Director of

National Intelligence shall protect, and shall establish and enforce policies to protect, intelligence sources and methods from unauthorized disclosure.

(2) Consistent with paragraph (1), in order to maximize the dissemination of intelligence, the Director of National Intelligence shall establish and implement requirements for the intelligence community for the following purposes:

(A) Classification of information under applicable law, Executive orders, or other Presidential directives.

(B) Access to and dissemination of intelligence, both in final form and in the form when initially gathered.

(C) Preparation of intelligence products in such a way that source information is removed to allow for dissemination at the lowest level of classification possible or in unclassified form to the extent practicable.

(3) The Director may only delegate a duty or authority given the Director under this subsection to the Principal Deputy Director of National Intelligence.

(4)(A) Each head of an element of the intelligence community shall ensure that any congressionally mandated report submitted to Congress by the head, other than such a report submitted solely to the congressional intelligence committees, shall be consistent with the protection of intelligence sources and methods in accordance with the policies established by the Director under paragraph (1), regardless of whether the provision of law mandating the report explicitly requires such protection.

(B) Nothing in this paragraph shall be construed to alter any congressional leadership's or congressional committee's jurisdiction or access to information from any element of the intelligence community under the rules of either chamber of Congress.

(j) Uniform Procedures for Classified Information.—The Director of National Intelligence, subject to the direction of the President, shall—

(1) establish uniform standards and procedures for the grant of access to sensitive compartmented information to any officer or employee of any agency or department of the United States and to employees of contractors of those agencies or departments;

(2) ensure the consistent implementation of those standards and procedures throughout such agencies and departments;

(3) ensure that security clearances granted by individual elements of the intelligence community are recognized by all elements of the intelligence community, and under contracts entered into by those agencies;

(4) ensure that the process for investigation and adjudication of an application for access to sensitive compartmented information is performed in the most expeditious manner possible consistent with applicable standards for national security;

(5) ensure that the background of each employee or officer of an element of the intelligence community, each contractor to an element of the intelligence community, and each individual employee of such a contractor who has been

determined to be eligible for access to classified information is monitored on a continual basis under standards developed by the Director, including with respect to the frequency of evaluation, during the period of eligibility of such employee or officer of an element of the intelligence community, such contractor, or such individual employee to such a contractor to determine whether such employee or officer of an element of the intelligence community, such contractor, and such individual employee of such a contractor continues to meet the requirements for eligibility for access to classified information; and

(6) develop procedures to require information sharing between elements of the intelligence community concerning potentially derogatory security information regarding an employee or officer of an element of the intelligence community, a contractor to an element of the intelligence community, or an individual employee of such a contractor that may impact the eligibility of such employee or officer of an element of the intelligence community, such contractor, or such individual employee of such a contractor for a security clearance.

(k) Coordination With Foreign Governments.— Under the direction of the President and in a manner consistent with section 207 of the Foreign Service Act of 1980 (22 U.S.C. 3927), the Director of National Intelligence shall oversee the coordination of the relationships between elements of the intelligence community and the intelligence or security services of foreign governments or international organizations on all matters involving intelligence related to the national security or involving intelligence acquired through clandestine means.

(l) Enhanced Personnel Management.—(1)(A) The Director of National Intelligence shall, under regulations prescribed by the Director, provide incentives for personnel of elements of the intelligence community to serve—

(i) on the staff of the Director of National Intelligence;

(ii) on the staff of the national intelligence centers;

(iii) on the staff of the National Counterterrorism Center; and

(iv) in other positions in support of the intelligence community management functions of the Director.

(B) Incentives under subparagraph (A) may include financial incentives, bonuses, and such other awards and incentives as the Director considers appropriate.

(2)(A) Notwithstanding any other provision of law, the personnel of an element of the intelligence community who are assigned or detailed under paragraph (1)(A) to service under the Director of National Intelligence shall be promoted at rates equivalent to or better than personnel of such element who are not so assigned or detailed.

(B) The Director may prescribe regulations to carry out this paragraph.

(3)(A) The Director of National Intelligence shall prescribe mechanisms to facilitate the rotation of personnel of the intelligence community through various elements of the intelligence community in the course of their careers in order to facilitate the widest possible understanding by such personnel of the variety of intelligence requirements, methods, users, and capabilities.

(B) The mechanisms prescribed under subparagraph (A) may include the following:

(i) The establishment of special occupational categories involving service, over the course of a career, in more than one element of the intelligence community.

(ii) The provision of rewards for service in positions undertaking analysis and planning of operations involving two or more elements of the intelligence community.

(iii) The establishment of requirements for education, training, service, and evaluation for service involving more than one element of the intelligence community.

(C) It is the sense of Congress that the mechanisms prescribed under this subsection should, to the extent practical, seek to duplicate for civilian personnel within the intelligence community the joint officer management policies established by chapter 38 of title 10, United States Code, and the other amendments made by title IV of the Goldwater-Nichols Department of Defense Reorganization Act of 1986 (Public Law 99–433).

(D) The mechanisms prescribed under subparagraph (A) and any other policies of the Director—

(i) may not require an employee of an office of inspector general for an element of the intelligence community, including the Office of the Inspector General of the Intelligence Community, to rotate to a position in an office or organization of such an element over which such office of inspector general exercises jurisdiction; and

(ii) shall be implemented in a manner that exempts employees of an office of inspector general from a rotation that may impact the independence of such office.

(4)(A) Except as provided in subparagraph (B) and subparagraph (D), this subsection shall not apply with respect to personnel of the elements of the intelligence community who are members of the uniformed services.

(B) Mechanisms that establish requirements for education and training pursuant to paragraph (3)(B)(iii) may apply with respect to members of the uniformed services who are assigned to an element of the intelligence community funded through the National Intelligence Program, but such mechanisms shall not be inconsistent with personnel policies and education and training requirements otherwise applicable to members of the uniformed services.

(C) The personnel policies and programs developed and implemented under this subsection with respect to law enforcement officers (as that term is defined in section 5541(3) of title 5, United States Code) shall not affect the ability of law enforcement entities to conduct operations or, through the applicable chain of command, to control the activities of such law enforcement officers.

(D) Assignment to the Office of the Director of National Intelligence of commissioned officers of the Armed Forces shall be considered a joint-duty assignment for purposes of the joint officer management policies prescribed by chapter 38 of title 10, United States Code, and other provisions of that title.

(m) Additional Authority With Respect to Personnel.—(1) In addition to the authorities under subsection (f)(3), the Director of National Intelligence may exercise with respect to the personnel of the Office of the Director of National Intelligence any authority of the Director of the Central Intelligence Agency with respect to the personnel of the Central Intelligence Agency under the Central Intelligence Agency Act of 1949 (50 U.S.C. 403a et seq.), and other applicable provisions of law, as of the date of the enactment of this subsection to the same extent, and subject to the same conditions and limitations, that the Director of the Central Intelligence Agency may exercise such authority with respect to personnel of the Central Intelligence Agency, including with respect to the notification requirement under section 8(c) of such Act (50 U.S.C. 3510(c)).

(2) Employees and applicants for employment of the Office of the Director of National Intelligence shall have the same rights and protections under the Office of the Director of National Intelligence as employees of the Central Intelligence Agency have under the Central Intelligence Agency Act of 1949, and other applicable provisions of law, as of the date of the enactment of this subsection.

(n) Acquisition and Other Authorities.—(1) In carrying out the responsibilities and authorities under this section, the Director of National Intelligence may exercise the acquisition and appropriations authorities referred to in the Central Intelligence Agency Act of 1949 (50 U.S.C. 403a et seq.) other than the authorities referred to in section 8(b) of that Act (50 U.S.C. 403j(b)).

(2) For the purpose of the exercise of any authority referred to in paragraph (1), a reference to the head of an agency shall be deemed to be a reference to the Director of National Intelligence or the Principal Deputy Director of National Intelligence.

(3)(A) Any determination or decision to be made under an authority referred to in paragraph (1) by the head of an agency may be made with respect to individual purchases and contracts or with respect to classes of purchases or contracts, and shall be final.

(B) Except as provided in subparagraph (C), the Director of National Intelligence or the Principal Deputy Director of National Intelligence may, in such official's discretion, delegate to any officer or other official of the Office of the Director of National Intelligence any authority to make a determination or decision as the head of the agency under an authority referred to in paragraph (1).

(C) The limitations and conditions set forth in section 3(d) of the Central Intelligence Agency Act of 1949 (50 U.S.C. 403c(d)) shall apply to the exercise by the Director of National Intelligence of an authority referred to in paragraph (1).

(D) Each determination or decision required by an authority referred to in the second sentence of section 3(d) of the Central Intelligence Agency Act of 1949 shall be based upon written findings made by the official making such determination or decision, which findings shall be final and shall be available within the Office of the Director of National Intelligence for a period of at least six years following the date of such determination or decision.

(4)(A) In addition to the authority referred to in paragraph (1), the Director of National Intelligence may authorize the head of an element of the intelligence community to exercise an acquisition authority referred to in section 3 or 8(a) of the Central Intelligence Agency Act of 1949 (50 U.S.C. 403c and 403j(a)) for an acquisition by such element that is more than 50 percent funded under the National Intelligence Program.

(B) The head of an element of the intelligence community may not exercise an authority referred to in subparagraph (A) until—

(i) the head of such element (without delegation) submits to the Director of National Intelligence a written request that includes—

(I) a description of such authority requested to be exercised;

(II) an explanation of the need for such authority, including an explanation of the reasons that other authorities are insufficient; and

(III) a certification that the mission of such element would be—

(aa) impaired if such authority is not exercised; or

(bb) significantly and measurably enhanced if such authority is exercised; and

(ii) the Director of National Intelligence issues a written authorization that includes—

(I) a description of the authority referred to in subparagraph (A) that is authorized to be exercised; and

(II) a justification to support the exercise of such authority.

(C) A request and authorization to exercise an authority referred to in subparagraph (A) may be made with respect to an individual acquisition or with respect to a specific class of acquisitions described in the request and authorization referred to in subparagraph (B).

(D)(i) A request from a head of an element of the intelligence community located within one of the departments described in clause (ii) to exercise an authority referred to in subparagraph (A) shall be submitted to the Director of National Intelligence in accordance with any procedures established by the head of such department.

(ii) The departments described in this clause are the Department of Defense, the Department of Energy, the Department of Homeland Security, the Department of Justice, the Department of State, and the Department of the Treasury.

(E)(i) The head of an element of the intelligence community may not be authorized to utilize an authority referred to in subparagraph (A) for a class of acquisitions for a period of more than 3 years, except that the Director of National Intelligence (without delegation) may authorize the use of such an authority for not more than 6 years.

(ii) Each authorization to utilize an authority referred to in subparagraph (A) may be extended in accordance with the requirements of subparagraph (B) for successive periods of not more than 3 years, except that the Director of National Intelligence (without delegation) may authorize an extension period of not more than 6 years.

(F) Subject to clauses (i) and (ii) of subparagraph (E), the Director of National Intelligence may only delegate the authority of the Director under subparagraphs (A) through (E) to the Principal Deputy Director of National Intelligence or a Deputy Director of National Intelligence.

(G) The Director of National Intelligence shall submit—

(i) to the congressional intelligence committees a notification of an authorization to exercise an authority referred to in subparagraph (A) or an extension of such authorization that includes the written authorization referred to in subparagraph (B)(ii); and

(ii) to the Director of the Office of Management and Budget a notification of an authorization to exercise an authority referred to in subparagraph (A) for an acquisition or class of acquisitions that will exceed $50,000,000 annually.

(H) Requests and authorizations to exercise an authority referred to in subparagraph (A) shall remain available within the Office of the Director of National Intelligence for a period of at least 6 years following the date of such request or authorization.

(I) Nothing in this paragraph may be construed to alter or otherwise limit the authority of the Central Intelligence Agency to independently exercise an authority under section 3 or 8(a) of the Central Intelligence Agency Act of 1949 (50 U.S.C. 403c and 403j(a)).

(5) Any authority provided to the Director of National Intelligence or the head of an element of the intelligence community pursuant to this subsection to make an expenditure referred to in subsection (a) of section 8 of the Central Intelligence Agency Act of 1949 (50 U.S.C. 3510) is subject to the notification requirement under subsection (c) of such section. If the Director of National Intelligence is required to make a notification for a specific expenditure pursuant to both this paragraph and paragraph (4)(G), the Director may make a single notification.

(6) Other transaction authority.—

(A) In general.— In addition to other acquisition authorities, the Director of National Intelligence may exercise the acquisition authorities referred to in sections 4021 and 4022 of title 10, United States Code, subject to the provisions of this paragraph.

(B) Delegation.—(i) The Director shall delegate the authorities provided by subparagraph (A) to the heads of elements of the intelligence community.

(ii) The heads of elements of the intelligence community shall, to the maximum extent practicable, delegate the authority delegated under clause (i) to the official of the respective element of the intelligence community responsible for decisions with respect to basic, applied, or advanced research activities or the adoption of such activities within such element.

(C) INTELLIGENCE COMMUNITY AUTHORITY.—(i) For purposes of this paragraph, the limitation in section 4022(a)(1) of title 10, United States Code, shall not apply to elements of the intelligence community.

(ii) Subject to section 4022(a)(2) of such title, the Director may enter into transactions and agreements (other than contracts, cooperative agreements, and grants) of amounts not to exceed $75,000,000 under this paragraph to carry out basic, applied, and advanced research projects and prototype projects in support of intelligence activities.

(iii) For purposes of this paragraph, the limitations specified in section 4022(a)(2) of such title shall apply to the intelligence community in lieu of the Department of Defense, and the Director shall—

(I) identify appropriate officials who can make the determinations required in subparagraph (B)(i) of such section for the intelligence community; and

(II) brief the congressional intelligence committees, the Subcommittee on Defense of the Committee on Appropriations of the Senate, and the Subcommittee on Defense of the Committee on Appropriations of the House of Representatives in lieu of the congressional defense committees, as specified in subparagraph (B)(ii) of such section.

(iv) For purposes of this paragraph, the limitation in section 4022(a)(3) of such title shall not apply to elements of the intelligence community.

(v) In carrying out this paragraph, section 4022(d)(1) of such title shall be applied by substituting "Director of National Intelligence" for "Secretary of Defense".

(vi) For purposes of this paragraph, the limitations in section 4022(d)(2) of such title shall not apply to elements of the intelligence community.

(vii) In addition to the follow-on production contract criteria in section 4022(f)(2) of such title, the following additional criteria shall apply:

(I) The authorizing official of the relevant element of the intelligence community determines that Government users of the proposed production product or production service have been consulted.

(II) In the case of a proposed production product that is software, there are mechanisms in place for Government users to provide ongoing feedback to participants to the follow-on production contract.

(III) In the case of a proposed production product that is software, there are mechanisms in place to promote the interoperability and accessibility with and between Government and commercial software providers, including by the promotion of open application programming interfaces and requirement of appropriate software documentation.

(IV) The award follows a documented market analysis as mandated by the Federal Acquisition Regulations surveying available and comparable products.

(V) In the case of a proposed production product that is software, the follow-on production contract includes a requirement that, for the duration of such contract (or such other period of time as may be agreed to as a term of such contract)—

(aa) the participants provide the most up-to-date version of the product that is available in the commercial marketplace and is consistent with security requirements;

(bb) there are mechanisms in place for the participants to provide timely updates to the production product; and

(cc) the authority specified in section 4022(f)(5) of such title shall be exercised by the Director in lieu of the Secretary of Defense.

(D) IMPLEMENTATION POLICY.—The Director, in consultation with the heads of the elements of the intelligence community, shall—

(i) not later than 180 days after the date of the enactment of the Intelligence Authorization Act for Fiscal Year 2023, establish and implement an intelligence community-wide policy prescribing the use and limitations of the authority under this paragraph, particularly with respect to the application of subparagraphs (B) and (C);

(ii) periodically review and update the policy established under clause (i); and

(iii) submit to the congressional intelligence committees, the Committee on Appropriations of the Senate, and the Committee on Appropriations of the House of Representatives the policy when established under clause (i) or updated under clause (ii).

(E) ANNUAL REPORT.—

(i) IN GENERAL.— Not less frequently than annually, the Director shall submit to the congressional intelligence committees, the Committee on Appropriations of the Senate, and the Committee on Appropriations of the House of Representatives a report detailing the use by the intelligence community of the authority provided by this paragraph.

(ii) ELEMENTS.—

(I) REQUIRED ELEMENTS.—Each report required by clause (i) shall detail the following:

(aa) The number of transactions.

(bb) The participants to such transactions.

(cc) The purpose of the transaction.

(dd) The amount of each transaction.

(ee) Concerns with the efficiency of the policy.

(ff) Any recommendations for how to improve the process.

(II) OTHER ELEMENTS.— Each report required by clause (i) may describe such transactions which have been awarded follow-on production contracts either pursuant to the authority provided by this paragraph or another acquisition authority available to the intelligence community.

(o) CONSIDERATION OF VIEWS OF ELEMENTS OF INTELLIGENCE COMMUNITY.— In carrying out the duties and responsibilities under this section, the Director of National Intelligence shall take into account the views of a head of a department containing an element of the intelligence community and of the Director of the Central Intelligence Agency.

(p) CERTAIN RESPONSIBILITIES OF DIRECTOR OF NATIONAL INTELLIGENCE RELATING TO NATIONAL INTELLIGENCE PROGRAM.—(1) Subject to the direction of the President, the Director of National Intelligence shall, after consultation with the Secretary of Defense, ensure that the National Intelligence Program budgets for the elements of the intelligence community that are within the Department of Defense are adequate to satisfy the national intelligence needs of the Department of Defense, including the needs of the Chairman of the Joint Chiefs of Staff and the commanders of the unified and specified commands, and wherever such elements are performing Government-wide functions, the needs of other Federal departments and agencies.

(2) Consistent with subsection (c)(5)(C), the Director of National Intelligence shall, after consultation with the Director of the Federal Bureau of Investigation, ensure that the programs and activities of the Federal Bureau of Investigation that are part of the National Intelligence Program are executed in a manner that conforms with the requirements of the national intelligence strategy under section 108A of this Act and the National Intelligence Priorities Framework of the Office of the Director of National Intelligence (or any successor mechanism established for the prioritization of such programs and activities).

(3) Not later than March 1 of each year, the President, acting through the Director of National Intelligence, shall submit to the congressional intelligence committees, the Subcommittee on Defense of the Committee on Appropriations of the Senate, and the Subcommittee on Defense of the Committee on Appropriations of the House of Representatives a copy of the most recently updated National Intelligence Priorities Framework of the Office of the Director of National Intelligence (or any such successor mechanism).

(q) ACQUISITIONS OF MAJOR SYSTEMS.—(1) For each intelligence program within the National Intelligence Program for the acquisition of a major system, the Director of National Intelligence shall—

(A) require the development and implementation of a program management plan that includes cost, schedule, security risks, and performance goals and program milestone criteria, except that with respect to Department of Defense programs the Director shall consult with the Secretary of Defense;

(B) serve as exclusive milestone decision authority, except that with respect to Department of Defense programs the Director shall serve as milestone decision authority jointly with the Secretary of Defense or the designee of the Secretary; and

(C) periodically—

(i) review and assess the progress made toward the achievement of the goals and milestones established in such plan; and

(ii) submit to Congress a report on the results of such review and assessment.

(2) If the Director of National Intelligence and the Secretary of Defense are unable to reach an agreement on a milestone decision under paragraph (1)(B), the President shall resolve the conflict.

(3) Nothing in this subsection may be construed to limit the authority of the Director of National Intelligence to delegate to any other official any authority to perform the responsibilities of the Director under this subsection.

(4) In this subsection:

(A) The term "intelligence program", with respect to the acquisition of a major system, means a program that—

(i) is carried out to acquire such major system for an element of the intelligence community; and

(ii) is funded in whole out of amounts available for the National Intelligence Program.

(B) The term "major system" has the meaning given such term in section 4(9) of the Federal Property and Administrative Services Act of 1949 (41 U.S.C. 403(9)).

(r) Performance of Common Services.— The Director of National Intelligence shall, in consultation with the heads of departments and agencies of the United States Government containing elements within the intelligence community and with the Director of the Central Intelligence Agency, coordinate the performance by the elements of the intelligence community within the National Intelligence Program of such services as are of common concern to the intelligence community, which services the Director of National Intelligence determines can be more efficiently accomplished in a consolidated manner.

(s) Pay Authority for Critical Positions.—(1) Notwithstanding any pay limitation established under any other provision of law applicable to employees in elements of the intelligence community, the Director of National Intelligence may, in coordination with the Director of the Office of Personnel Management and the Director of the Office of Management and Budget, grant authority to the head of a department or agency to fix the rate of basic pay for one or more positions within the intelligence community at a rate in excess of any applicable limitation, subject to the provisions of this subsection. The exercise of authority so granted is at the discretion of the head of the department or agency employing the individual in a position covered by such authority, subject to the provisions of this subsection and any conditions established by the Director of National Intelligence when granting such authority.

(2) Authority under this subsection may be granted or exercised only—

(A) with respect to a position that requires an extremely high level of expertise and is critical to successful accomplishment of an important mission;

and

(B) to the extent necessary to recruit or retain an individual exceptionally well qualified for the position.

(3) The head of a department or agency may not fix a rate of basic pay under this subsection at a rate greater than the rate payable for level II of the Executive Schedule under section 5313 of title 5, United States Code, except upon written approval of the Director of National Intelligence or as otherwise authorized by law.

(4) The head of a department or agency may not fix a rate of basic pay under this subsection at a rate greater than the rate payable for level I of the Executive Schedule under section 5312 of title 5, United States Code, except upon written approval of the President in response to a request by the Director of National Intelligence or as otherwise authorized by law.

(5) Any grant of authority under this subsection for a position shall terminate at the discretion of the Director of National Intelligence.

(6)(A) The Director of National Intelligence shall notify the congressional intelligence committees not later than 30 days after the date on which the Director grants authority to the head of a department or agency under this subsection.

(B) The head of a department or agency to which the Director of National Intelligence grants authority under this subsection shall notify the congressional intelligence committees and the Director of the exercise of such authority not later than 30 days after the date on which such head exercises such authority.

(t) Award of Rank to Members of the Senior National Intelligence Service.—(1) The President, based on the recommendation of the Director of National Intelligence, may award a rank to a member of the Senior National Intelligence Service or other intelligence community senior civilian officer not already covered by such a rank award program in the same manner in which a career appointee of an agency may be awarded a rank under section 4507 of title 5, United States Code.

(2) The President may establish procedures to award a rank under paragraph (1) to a member of the Senior National Intelligence Service or a senior civilian officer of the intelligence community whose identity as such a member or officer is classified information (as defined in section 606(1)).

(u) Conflict of Interest Regulations.— The Director of National Intelligence, in consultation with the Director of the Office of Government Ethics, shall issue regulations prohibiting an officer or employee of an element of the intelligence community from engaging in outside employment if such employment creates a conflict of interest or appearance thereof.

(v) Authority To Establish Positions in Excepted Service.—(1) The Director of National Intelligence, with the concurrence of the head of the covered department concerned and in consultation with the Director of the Office of Personnel Management, may—

(A) convert competitive service positions, and the incumbents of such positions, within an element of the intelligence community in such department, to excepted service positions as the Director of National Intelligence determines necessary to carry out the intelligence functions of such element; and

(B) establish new positions in the excepted service within an element of the intelligence community in such department, if the Director of National Intelligence determines such positions are necessary to carry out the intelligence functions of such element.

(2) An incumbent occupying a position on the date of the enactment of the Intelligence Authorization Act for Fiscal Year 2012 selected to be converted to the excepted service under this section shall have the right to refuse such conversion. Once such individual no longer occupies the position, the position may be converted to the excepted service.

(3) A covered department may appoint an individual to a position converted or established pursuant to this subsection without regard to the civil-service laws, including parts II and III of title 5, United States Code.

(4) In this subsection, the term "covered department" means the Department of Energy, the Department of Homeland Security, the Department of State, or the Department of the Treasury.

(w) Nuclear Proliferation Assessment Statements Intelligence Community Addendum.— The Director of National Intelligence, in consultation with the heads of the appropriate elements of the intelligence community and the Secretary of State, shall provide to the President, the congressional intelligence committees, the Committee on Foreign Affairs of the House of Representatives, and the Committee on Foreign Relations of the Senate an addendum to each Nuclear Proliferation Assessment Statement accompanying a civilian nuclear cooperation agreement, containing a comprehensive analysis of the country's export control system with respect to nuclear-related matters, including interactions with other countries of proliferation concern and the actual or suspected nuclear, dual-use, or missile-related transfers to such countries.

(x) Requirements for Intelligence Community Contractors.—The Director of National Intelligence, in consultation with the heads of the elements of the intelligence community, shall—

(1) ensure that—

(A) any contractor to an element of the intelligence community with access to a classified network or classified information develops and operates a security plan that is consistent with standards established by the Director of National Intelligence for intelligence community networks; and

(B) each contract awarded by an element of the intelligence community includes provisions requiring the contractor comply with such plan and such standards;

(2) conduct periodic assessments of each security plan required under paragraph (1)(A) to ensure such security plan complies with the requirements of such paragraph; and

(3) ensure that the insider threat detection capabilities and insider threat policies of the intelligence community, including the policy under subsection (f)(8), apply to facilities of contractors with access to a classified network.

(y) Fundraising.—(1) The Director of National Intelligence may engage in fundraising in an official capacity for the benefit of nonprofit organizations that—

(A) provide support to surviving family members of a deceased employee of an element of the intelligence community; or

(B) otherwise provide support for the welfare, education, or recreation of employees of an element of the intelligence community, former employees of an element of the intelligence community, or family members of such employees.

(2) In this subsection, the term "fundraising" means the raising of funds through the active participation in the promotion, production, or presentation of an event designed to raise funds and does not include the direct solicitation of money by any other means.

(3) Not later than 7 days after the date the Director engages in fundraising authorized by this subsection or at the time the decision is made to participate in such fundraising, the Director shall notify the congressional intelligence committees of such fundraising.

(4) The Director, in consultation with the Director of the Office of Government Ethics, shall issue regulations to carry out the authority provided in this subsection. Such regulations shall ensure that such authority is exercised in a manner that is consistent with all relevant ethical constraints and principles, including the avoidance of any prohibited conflict of interest or appearance of impropriety.

(z) Analyses and Impact Statements Regarding Proposed Investment Into the United States.—(1) Not later than 20 days after the completion of a review or an investigation of any proposed investment into the United States for which the Director has prepared analytic materials, the Director shall submit to the Select Committee on Intelligence of the Senate and the Permanent Select Committee on Intelligence of the House of Representative copies of such analytic materials, including any supplements or amendments to such analysis made by the Director.

(2) Not later than 60 days after the completion of consideration by the United States Government of any investment described in paragraph (1), the Director shall determine whether such investment will have an operational impact on the intelligence community, and, if so, shall submit a report on such impact to the Select Committee on Intelligence of the Senate and the Permanent Select Committee on Intelligence of the House of Representatives. Each such report shall—

(A) describe the operational impact of the investment on the intelligence community, including with respect to counterintelligence; and

(B) describe any actions that have been or will be taken to mitigate such impact.

(3) Definitions.—In this subsection:

(A) The term "a review or an investigation of any proposed investment into the United States for which the Director has prepared analytic materials" includes a review, investigation, assessment, or analysis conducted by the Director pursuant to section 7 or 10(g) of Executive Order 13913 (85 Fed. Reg. 19643; relating to Establishing the Committee for the Assessment of Foreign Participation in the United States Telecommunications Services Sector), or successor order.

(B) The term "investment" includes any activity reviewed, investigated, assessed, or analyzed by the Director pursuant to section 7 or 10(g) of Executive Order 13913, or successor order.

OFFICE OF THE DIRECTOR OF NATIONAL INTELLIGENCE

SEC. 103. [50 U.S.C. 3025] (a) OFFICE OF DIRECTOR OF NATIONAL INTELLIGENCE.— There is an Office of the Director of National Intelligence.

(b) FUNCTION.— The function of the Office of the Director of National Intelligence is to assist the Director of National Intelligence in carrying out the duties and responsibilities of the Director under this Act and other applicable provisions of law, and to carry out such other duties as may be prescribed by the President or by law.

(c) COMPOSITION.—The Office of the Director of National Intelligence is composed of the following:

(1) The Director of National Intelligence.

(2) The Principal Deputy Director of National Intelligence.

(3) Any Deputy Director of National Intelligence appointed under section 103A.

(4) The National Intelligence Council.

(5) The National Intelligence Management Council.

(6) The General Counsel.

(7) The Civil Liberties Protection Officer.

(8) The Director of Science and Technology.

(9) The Director of the National Counterintelligence and Security Center.

(10) The Chief Information Officer of the Intelligence Community.

(11) The Inspector General of the Intelligence Community.

(12) The Director of the National Counterterrorism Center.

(13) The Director of the National Counter Proliferation Center.

(14) The Chief Financial Officer of the Intelligence Community.

(15) Such other offices and officials as may be established by law or the Director may establish or designate in the Office, including national intelligence centers.

(d) STAFF.—(1) To assist the Director of National Intelligence in fulfilling the duties and responsibilities of the Director, the Director shall employ and utilize in the Office of the Director of National Intelligence a professional staff having an expertise in matters relating to such duties and responsibilities, and may establish permanent positions and appropriate rates of pay with respect to that staff.

(2) The staff of the Office of the Director of National Intelligence under paragraph (1) shall include the staff of the Office of the Deputy Director of Central Intelligence for Community Management that is transferred to the Office of the Director of National Intelligence under section 1091 of the National Security Intelligence Reform Act of 2004.

(e) TEMPORARY FILLING OF VACANCIES.—With respect to filling temporarily a vacancy in an office within the Office of the Director of National Intelligence (other than that of the Director of National Intelligence), section 3345(a)(3) of title 5, United States Code, may be applied—

(1) in the matter preceding subparagraph (A), by substituting "an element of the intelligence community, as that term is defined in section 3(4) of the National Security Act of 1947 (50 U.S.C. 401a(4))," for "such Executive agency"; and

(2) in subparagraph (A), by substituting "the intelligence community" for "such agency".

(f) LOCATION OF THE OFFICE OF THE DIRECTOR OF NATIONAL INTELLIGENCE.— The headquarters of the Office of the Director of National Intelligence may be located in the Washington metropolitan region, as that term is defined in section 8301 of title 40, United States Code.

DEPUTY DIRECTORS OF NATIONAL INTELLIGENCE

SEC. 103A. [50 U.S.C. 3026] (a) PRINCIPAL DEPUTY DIRECTOR OF NATIONAL INTELLIGENCE.—(1) There is a Principal Deputy Director of National Intelligence who shall be appointed by the President, by and with the advice and consent of the Senate.

(2) In the event of a vacancy in the position of Principal Deputy Director of National Intelligence, the Director of National Intelligence shall recommend to the President an individual for appointment as Principal Deputy Director of National Intelligence.

(3) Any individual nominated for appointment as Principal Deputy Director of National Intelligence shall have extensive national security experience and management expertise.

(4) The individual serving as Principal Deputy Director of National Intelligence shall not, while so serving, serve in any capacity in any other element of the intelligence community.

(5) The Principal Deputy Director of National Intelligence shall assist the Director of National Intelligence in carrying out the duties and responsibilities of the Director.

(6) The Principal Deputy Director of National Intelligence shall act for, and exercise the powers of, the Director of National Intelligence during the absence or disability of the Director of National Intelligence or during a vacancy in the position of Director of National Intelligence.

(b) DEPUTY DIRECTORS OF NATIONAL INTELLIGENCE.—(1) There may be not more than four Deputy Directors of National Intelligence who shall be appointed by the Director of National Intelligence.

(2) Each Deputy Director of National Intelligence appointed under this subsection shall have such duties, responsibilities, and authorities as the Director of National Intelligence may assign or are specified by law.

(c) MILITARY STATUS OF DIRECTOR OF NATIONAL INTELLIGENCE AND PRINCIPAL DEPUTY DIRECTOR OF NATIONAL INTELLIGENCE.—(1) Not more than one of the individuals serving in the positions specified in paragraph (2) may be a commissioned officer of the Armed Forces in active status.

(2) The positions referred to in this paragraph are the following:

(A) The Director of National Intelligence.

(B) The Principal Deputy Director of National Intelligence.

(3) It is the sense of Congress that, under ordinary circumstances, it is desirable that one of the individuals serving in the positions specified in paragraph (2)—

(A) be a commissioned officer of the Armed Forces, in active status; or

(B) have, by training or experience, an appreciation of military intelligence activities and requirements.

(4) A commissioned officer of the Armed Forces, while serving in a position specified in paragraph (2)—

(A) shall not be subject to supervision or control by the Secretary of Defense or by any officer or employee of the Department of Defense;

(B) shall not exercise, by reason of the officer's status as a commissioned officer, any supervision or control with respect to any of the military or civilian personnel of the Department of Defense except as otherwise authorized by law; and

(C) shall not be counted against the numbers and percentages of commissioned officers of the rank and grade of such officer authorized for the military department of that officer.

(5) Except as provided in subparagraph (A) or (B) of paragraph (4), the appointment of an officer of the Armed Forces to a position specified in paragraph (2) shall not affect the status, position, rank, or grade of such officer in the Armed Forces, or any emolument, perquisite, right, privilege, or benefit incident to or arising out of such status, position, rank, or grade.

(6) A commissioned officer of the Armed Forces on active duty who is appointed to a position specified in paragraph (2), while serving in such position and while remaining on active duty, shall continue to receive military pay and allowances and shall not receive the pay prescribed for such position. Funds from which such pay and allowances are paid shall be reimbursed from funds available to the Director of National Intelligence.

NATIONAL INTELLIGENCE COUNCIL

SEC. 103B. [50 U.S.C. 3027] (a) NATIONAL INTELLIGENCE COUNCIL.— There is a National Intelligence Council.

(b) COMPOSITION.—(1) The National Intelligence Council shall be composed of senior analysts within the intelligence community and substantive experts from the public and private sector, who shall be appointed by, report to, and serve at the pleasure of, the Director of National Intelligence.

(2) The Director shall prescribe appropriate security requirements for personnel appointed from the private sector as a condition of service on the Council, or as

contractors of the Council or employees of such contractors, to ensure the protection of intelligence sources and methods while avoiding, wherever possible, unduly intrusive requirements which the Director considers to be unnecessary for this purpose.

(c) Duties and Responsibilities.—(1) The National Intelligence Council shall—

(A) produce national intelligence estimates for the United States Government, including alternative views held by elements of the intelligence community and other information as specified in paragraph (2);

(B) evaluate community-wide collection and production of intelligence by the intelligence community and the requirements and resources of such collection and production; and

(C) otherwise assist the Director of National Intelligence in carrying out the responsibilities of the Director under section 102A.

(2) The Director of National Intelligence shall ensure that the Council satisfies the needs of policymakers and other consumers of intelligence.

(d) Service as Senior Intelligence Advisers.— Within their respective areas of expertise and under the direction of the Director of National Intelligence, the members of the National Intelligence Council shall constitute the senior intelligence advisers of the intelligence community for purposes of representing the views of the intelligence community within the United States Government.

(e) Authority To Contract.— Subject to the direction and control of the Director of National Intelligence, the National Intelligence Council may carry out its responsibilities under this section by contract, including contracts for substantive experts necessary to assist the Council with particular assessments under this section.

(f) Staff.— The Director of National Intelligence shall make available to the National Intelligence Council such staff as may be necessary to permit the Council to carry out its responsibilities under this section.

(g) Availability of Council and Staff.—(1) The Director of National Intelligence shall take appropriate measures to ensure that the National Intelligence Council and its staff satisfy the needs of policymaking officials and other consumers of intelligence.

(2) The Council shall be readily accessible to policymaking officials and other appropriate individuals not otherwise associated with the intelligence community.

(h) Support.— The heads of the elements of the intelligence community shall, as appropriate, furnish such support to the National Intelligence Council, including the preparation of intelligence analyses, as may be required by the Director of National Intelligence.

(i) National Intelligence Council Product.— For purposes of this section, the term "National Intelligence Council product" includes a National Intelligence Estimate and any other intelligence community assessment that sets forth the judgment of the intelligence community as a whole on a matter covered by such product.

GENERAL COUNSEL

Sec. 103C. [50 U.S.C. 3028] (a) General Counsel.— There is a General Counsel of the

Office of the Director of National Intelligence who shall be appointed by the President, by and with the advice and consent of the Senate.

(b) Prohibition on Dual Service as General Counsel of Another Agency.— The individual serving in the position of General Counsel may not, while so serving, also serve as the General Counsel of any other department, agency, or element of the United States Government.

(c) Scope of Position.— The General Counsel is the chief legal officer of the Office of the Director of National Intelligence.

(d) Functions.— The General Counsel shall perform such functions as the Director of National Intelligence may prescribe.

CIVIL LIBERTIES PROTECTION OFFICER

Sec. 103D. [50 U.S.C. 3029] (a) Civil Liberties Protection Officer.—(1) Within the Office of the Director of National Intelligence, there is a Civil Liberties Protection Officer who shall be appointed by the Director of National Intelligence.

(2) The Civil Liberties Protection Officer shall report directly to the Director of National Intelligence.

(b) Duties.—The Civil Liberties Protection Officer shall—

(1) ensure that the protection of civil liberties and privacy is appropriately incorporated in the policies and procedures developed for and implemented by the Office of the Director of National Intelligence and the elements of the intelligence community within the National Intelligence Program;

(2) oversee compliance by the Office and the Director of National Intelligence with requirements under the Constitution and all laws, regulations, Executive orders, and implementing guidelines relating to civil liberties and privacy;

(3) review and assess complaints and other information indicating possible abuses of civil liberties and privacy in the administration of the programs and operations of the Office and the Director of National Intelligence and, as appropriate, investigate any such complaint or information;

(4) ensure that the use of technologies sustain, and do not erode, privacy protections relating to the use, collection, and disclosure of personal information;

(5) ensure that personal information contained in a system of records subject to section 552a of title 5, United States Code (popularly referred to as the "Privacy Act"), is handled in full compliance with fair information practices as set out in that section;

(6) conduct privacy impact assessments when appropriate or as required by law; and

(7) perform such other duties as may be prescribed by the Director of National Intelligence or specified by law.

(c) Use of Agency Inspectors General.— When appropriate, the Civil Liberties Protection Officer may refer complaints to the Office of Inspector General having responsibility for the affected element of the department or agency of the intelligence community to conduct an investigation under paragraph (3) of subsection (b).

DIRECTOR OF SCIENCE AND TECHNOLOGY

SEC. 103E. [50 U.S.C. 3030] (a) DIRECTOR OF SCIENCE AND TECHNOLOGY.— There is a Director of Science and Technology within the Office of the Director of National Intelligence who shall be appointed by the Director of National Intelligence.

(b) REQUIREMENT RELATING TO APPOINTMENT.— An individual appointed as Director of Science and Technology shall have a professional background and experience appropriate for the duties of the Director of Science and Technology. In making such appointment, the Director of National Intelligence may give preference to an individual with experience outside of the United States Government.

(c) DUTIES.—The Director of Science and Technology shall—

(1) act as the chief representative of the Director of National Intelligence for science and technology;

(2) chair the Director of National Intelligence Science and Technology Committee under subsection (d);

(3) assist the Director in formulating a long-term strategy for scientific advances in the field of intelligence;

(4) assist the Director on the science and technology elements of the budget of the Office of the Director of National Intelligence; and

(5) perform other such duties as may be prescribed by the Director of National Intelligence or specified by law.

(d) DIRECTOR OF NATIONAL INTELLIGENCE SCIENCE AND TECHNOLOGY COMMITTEE.—(1) There is within the Office of the Director of Science and Technology a Director of National Intelligence Science and Technology Committee.

(2) The Committee shall be composed of the principal science officers of the National Intelligence Program.

(3) The Committee shall—

(A) coordinate advances in research and development related to intelligence; and

(B) perform such other functions as the Director of Science and Technology shall prescribe.

DIRECTOR OF THE NATIONAL COUNTERINTELLIGENCE AND SECURITY CENTER

SEC. 103F. [50 U.S.C. 3031] (a) DIRECTOR OF THE NATIONAL COUNTERINTELLIGENCE AND SECURITY CENTER.— The Director of the National Counterintelligence and Security Center appointed under section 902 of the Counterintelligence Enhancement Act of 2002 (50 U.S.C. 3382) is a component of the Office of the Director of National Intelligence.

(b) DUTIES.— The Director of the National Counterintelligence and Security Center shall perform the duties provided in the Counterintelligence Enhancement Act of 2002 and such other duties as may be prescribed by the Director of National Intelligence or specified by law.

CHIEF INFORMATION OFFICER

SEC. 103G. [50 U.S.C. 3032] (a) CHIEF INFORMATION OFFICER.— To assist the Director of National Intelligence in carrying out the responsibilities of the Director under this Act and other applicable provisions of law, there shall be within the Office of the Director of National Intelligence a Chief Information Officer of the Intelligence Community who shall be appointed by the Director. The Chief Information Officer shall report directly to the Director of National Intelligence.

(b) DUTIES AND RESPONSIBILITIES.—Subject to the direction of the Director of National Intelligence, the Chief Information Officer of the Intelligence Community shall—

(1) manage activities relating to the information technology infrastructure and enterprise architecture requirements of the intelligence community;

(2) have procurement approval authority over all information technology items related to the enterprise architectures of all intelligence community components;

(3) direct and manage all information technology-related procurement for the intelligence community; and

(4) ensure that all expenditures for information technology and research and development activities are consistent with the intelligence community enterprise architecture and the strategy of the Director for such architecture.

(c) PROHIBITION ON SIMULTANEOUS SERVICE AS OTHER CHIEF INFORMATION OFFICER.— An individual serving in the position of Chief Information Officer of the Intelligence Community may not, while so serving, serve as the chief information officer of any other department or agency, or component thereof, of the United States Government.

(d) PROHIBITION ON SIMULTANEOUS SERVICE AS CHIEF DATA OFFICER AND CHIEF INFORMATION OFFICER.— An individual serving in the position of Chief Information Officer of the Intelligence Community or chief information officer of any other element of the intelligence community shall not concurrently serve as the Intelligence Community Chief Data Officer under section 103K and as the chief data officer of any other element of the intelligence community.

INSPECTOR GENERAL OF THE INTELLIGENCE COMMUNITY

SEC. 103H. [50 U.S.C. 3033] (a) OFFICE OF INSPECTOR GENERAL OF THE INTELLIGENCE COMMUNITY.— There is within the Office of the Director of National Intelligence an Office of the Inspector General of the Intelligence Community.

(b) PURPOSE.—The purpose of the Office of the Inspector General of the Intelligence Community is—

(1) to create an objective and effective office, appropriately accountable to Congress, to initiate and conduct independent investigations, inspections, audits, and reviews on programs and activities within the responsibility and authority of the Director of National Intelligence;

(2) to provide leadership and coordination and recommend policies for activities designed—

(A) to promote economy, efficiency, and effectiveness in the administration and implementation of such programs and activities; and

(B) to prevent and detect fraud and abuse in such programs and activities;

(3) to provide a means for keeping the Director of National Intelligence fully and currently informed about—

(A) problems and deficiencies relating to the administration of programs and activities within the responsibility and authority of the Director of National Intelligence; and

(B) the necessity for, and the progress of, corrective actions; and

(4) in the manner prescribed by this section, to ensure that the congressional intelligence committees are kept similarly informed of—

(A) significant problems and deficiencies relating to programs and activities within the responsibility and authority of the Director of National Intelligence; and

(B) the necessity for, and the progress of, corrective actions.

(c) INSPECTOR GENERAL OF THE INTELLIGENCE COMMUNITY[3].—(1) There is an Inspector General of the Intelligence Community, who shall be the head of the Office of the Inspector General of the Intelligence Community, who shall be appointed by the President, by and with the advice and consent of the Senate.

[3] Sections 5202(a)(3)(A)(i) and 5203(b) of division E of P.L. 117-263 provide for amendments to this subsection of the "National Security Act", but such amendments should have been made to the "National Security Act of 1947". Such amendments have been executed to show the probable intent of Congress.

(2) The nomination of an individual for appointment as Inspector General shall be made—

(A) without regard to political affiliation;

(B) on the basis of integrity, compliance with security standards of the intelligence community, and prior experience in the field of intelligence or national security; and

(C) on the basis of demonstrated ability in accounting, financial analysis, law, management analysis, public administration, or investigations.

(3) The Inspector General shall report directly to and be under the general supervision of the Director of National Intelligence.

(4)(A) The Inspector General may be removed from office only by the President. The President shall communicate in writing to the congressional intelligence committees the substantive rationale, including detailed and case-specific reasons, for the removal not later than 30 days prior to the effective date of such removal. Nothing in this paragraph shall be construed to prohibit a personnel action otherwise authorized by law, other than transfer or removal.

(B) If there is an open or completed inquiry into the Inspector General that relates to the removal or transfer of the Inspector General under subparagraph (A), the written communication required under that subparagraph shall—

(i) identify each entity that is conducting, or that conducted, the inquiry; and

(ii) in the case of a completed inquiry, contain the findings made during the inquiry.

(5)(A) Subject to the other provisions of this paragraph, only the President may place the Inspector General on nonduty status.

(B) If the President places the Inspector General on nonduty status, the President shall communicate in writing the substantive rationale, including detailed and case-specific reasons, for the change in status to the congressional intelligence committees not later than 15 days before the date on which the change in status takes effect, except that the President may submit that communication not later than the date on which the change in status takes effect if—

(i) the President has made a determination that the continued presence of the Inspector General in the workplace poses a threat described in any of clauses (i) through (iv) of section 6329b(b)(2)(A) of title 5, United States Code; and

(ii) in the communication, the President includes a report on the determination described in clause (i), which shall include—

(I) a specification of which clause of section 6329b(b)(2)(A) of title 5, United States Code, the President has determined applies under clause (i);

(II) the substantive rationale, including detailed and case-specific reasons, for the determination made under clause (i);

(III) an identification of each entity that is conducting, or that conducted, any inquiry upon which the determination under clause (i) was made; and

(IV) in the case of an inquiry described in subclause (III) that is completed, the findings made during that inquiry.

(C) The President may not place the Inspector General on nonduty status during the 30-day period preceding the date on which the Inspector General is removed or transferred under paragraph (4)(A) unless the President—

(i) has made a determination that the continued presence of the Inspector General in the workplace poses a threat described in any of clauses (i) through (iv) of section 6329b(b)(2)(A) of title 5, United States Code; and

(ii) not later than the date on which the change in status takes effect, submits to the congressional intelligence committees a written communication that contains the information required under subparagraph (B), including the report required under clause (ii) of that subparagraph.

(6)(A) In this subsection, the term "first assistant to the position of Inspector General" has the meaning given in section 3 of the Inspector General Act of 1978 (5 U.S.C. App.).

(B) If the Inspector General dies, resigns, or is otherwise unable to perform the functions and duties of the position—

(i) section 3345(a) of title 5, United States Code, and section 103(e) of the National Security Act of 1947 (50 U.S.C. 3025(e)) shall not apply;

(ii) subject to subparagraph (D), the first assistant to the position of Inspector General shall perform the functions and duties of the Inspector General temporarily in an acting capacity subject to the time limitations of section 3346 of title 5, United States Code; and

(iii) notwithstanding clause (ii), and subject to subparagraphs (D) and (E), the President (and only the President) may direct an officer or employee of any Office of an Inspector General to perform the functions and duties of the Inspector General temporarily in an acting capacity subject to the time limitations of section 3346 of title 5, United States Code, only if—

(I) during the 365-day period preceding the date of death, resignation, or beginning of inability to serve of the Inspector General, the officer or employee served in a position in an Office of an Inspector General for not less than 90 days, except that—

(aa) the requirement under this subclause shall not apply if the officer is an Inspector General; and

(bb) for the purposes of this clause, performing the functions and duties of an Inspector General temporarily in an acting capacity does not qualify as service in a position in an Office of an Inspector General;

(II) the rate of pay for the position of the officer or employee described in subclause (I) is equal to or greater than the minimum rate of pay payable for a position at GS–15 of the General Schedule;

(III) the officer or employee has demonstrated ability in accounting, auditing, financial analysis, law, management analysis, public administration, or investigations; and

(IV) not later than 30 days before the date on which the direction takes effect, the President communicates in writing to the congressional intelligence committees the substantive rationale, including the detailed and case-specific reasons, for such direction, including the reason for the direction that someone other than the individual who is performing the functions and duties of the Inspector General temporarily in an acting capacity (as of the date on which the President issues that direction) perform those functions and duties temporarily in an acting capacity.

(C) Notwithstanding section 3345(a) of title 5, United States Code, section 103(e) of the National Security Act of 1947 (50 U.S.C. 3025(e)), and clauses (ii) and (iii) of subparagraph (B), and subject to subparagraph (D), during any period in which the Inspector General is on nonduty status—

(i) the first assistant to the position of Inspector General shall perform the functions and duties of the position temporarily in an acting capacity subject to the time limitations of section 3346 of title 5, United States Code; and

(ii) if the first assistant described in clause (i) dies, resigns, or becomes otherwise unable to perform those functions and duties, the President (and only the President) may direct an officer or employee in the Office of Inspector General to perform those functions and duties temporarily in an acting capacity, subject to the time limitations of section 3346 of title 5, United States Code, if—

(I) that direction satisfies the requirements under subclauses (II), (III), and (IV) of subparagraph (B)(iii); and

(II) that officer or employee served in a position in that Office of Inspector General for not fewer than 90 of the 365 days preceding the date on which the President makes that direction.

(D) An individual may perform the functions and duties of the Inspector General temporarily and in an acting capacity under clause (ii) or (iii) of subparagraph (B), or under subparagraph (C), with respect to only 1 Inspector General position at any given time.

(E) If the President makes a direction under subparagraph (B)(iii), during the 30-day period preceding the date on which the direction of the President takes effect, the functions and duties of the position of the Inspector General shall be performed by—

(i) the first assistant to the position of Inspector General; or

(ii) the individual performing those functions and duties temporarily in an acting capacity, as of the date on which the President issues that direction, if that individual is an individual other than the first assistant to the position of Inspector General.

(d) Assistant Inspectors General.—Subject to the policies of the Director of National Intelligence, the Inspector General of the Intelligence Community shall—

(1) appoint an Assistant Inspector General for Audit who shall have the responsibility for supervising the performance of auditing activities relating to programs and activities within the responsibility and authority of the Director;

(2) appoint an Assistant Inspector General for Investigations who shall have the responsibility for supervising the performance of investigative activities relating to such programs and activities; and

(3) appoint other Assistant Inspectors General that, in the judgment of the Inspector General, are necessary to carry out the duties of the Inspector General.

(e) Duties and Responsibilities.—It shall be the duty and responsibility of the Inspector General of the Intelligence Community—

(1) to provide policy direction for, and to plan, conduct, supervise, and coordinate independently, the investigations, inspections, audits, and reviews relating to programs and activities within the responsibility and authority of the Director of National Intelligence;

(2) to keep the Director of National Intelligence fully and currently informed concerning violations of law and regulations, fraud, and other serious problems, abuses, and deficiencies relating to the programs and activities within the responsibility and authority of the Director, to recommend corrective action concerning such problems, and to report on the progress made in implementing such corrective action;

(3) to take due regard for the protection of intelligence sources and methods in the preparation of all reports issued by the Inspector General, and, to the extent consistent with the purpose and objective of such reports, take such measures as may be appropriate to minimize the disclosure of intelligence sources and methods described in such reports; and

(4) in the execution of the duties and responsibilities under this section, to comply with generally accepted government auditing.

(f) LIMITATIONS ON ACTIVITIES.—(1) The Director of National Intelligence may prohibit the Inspector General of the Intelligence Community from initiating, carrying out, or completing any investigation, inspection, audit, or review if the Director determines that such prohibition is necessary to protect vital national security interests of the United States.

(2) Not later than seven days after the date on which the Director exercises the authority under paragraph (1), the Director shall submit to the congressional intelligence committees an appropriately classified statement of the reasons for the exercise of such authority.

(3) The Director shall advise the Inspector General at the time a statement under paragraph (2) is submitted, and, to the extent consistent with the protection of intelligence sources and methods, provide the Inspector General with a copy of such statement.

(4) The Inspector General may submit to the congressional intelligence committees any comments on the statement of which the Inspector General has notice under paragraph (3) that the Inspector General considers appropriate.

(g) AUTHORITIES.—(1) The Inspector General of the Intelligence Community shall have direct and prompt access to the Director of National Intelligence when necessary for any purpose pertaining to the performance of the duties of the Inspector General.

(2)(A) The Inspector General shall, subject to the limitations in subsection (f), make such investigations and reports relating to the administration of the programs and activities within the authorities and responsibilities of the Director as are, in the judgment of the Inspector General, necessary or desirable.

(B) The Inspector General shall have access to any employee, or any employee of a contractor, of any element of the intelligence community needed for the performance of the duties of the Inspector General.

(C) The Inspector General shall have direct access to all records, reports, audits, reviews, documents, papers, recommendations, or other materials that relate to the programs and activities with respect to which the Inspector General has responsibilities under this section.

(D) The level of classification or compartmentation of information shall not, in and of itself, provide a sufficient rationale for denying the Inspector General access to any materials under subparagraph (C).

(E) The Director, or on the recommendation of the Director, another appropriate official of the intelligence community, shall take appropriate administrative actions against an employee, or an employee of a contractor, of an element of the intelligence community that fails to cooperate with the Inspector General. Such administrative action may include loss of employment or the termination of an existing contractual relationship.

(3)(A) The Inspector General is authorized to receive and investigate, pursuant to subsection (h), complaints or information from any person concerning the existence of an activity within the authorities and responsibilities of the Director of National Intelligence constituting a violation of laws, rules, or regulations, or mismanagement, gross waste of funds, abuse of authority, or a substantial and specific danger to the public health and safety. Once such complaint or information has been received from an employee of the intelligence community—

(i) the Inspector General shall not disclose the identity of the employee without the consent of the employee, unless the Inspector General determines that such disclosure is unavoidable during the course of the investigation or the disclosure is made to an official of the Department of Justice responsible for determining whether a prosecution should be undertaken, and this provision shall qualify as a withholding statute pursuant to subsection (b)(3) of section 552 of title 5, United States Code (commonly known as the "Freedom of Information Act"); and

(ii) no action constituting a reprisal, or threat of reprisal, for making such complaint or disclosing such information to the Inspector General may be taken by any employee in a position to take such actions, unless the complaint was made or the information was disclosed with the knowledge that it was false or with willful disregard for its truth or falsity.

(B)(i) An individual may disclose classified information to the Inspector General in accordance with the applicable security standards and procedures established under section 102A or 803 of this Act, chapter 12 of the Atomic Energy Act of 1954 (42 U.S.C. 2161 et seq.), Executive Order 13526 (50 U.S.C. 3161 note; relating to Classified National Security Information), or any applicable provision of law.

(ii) A disclosure under clause (i) of classified information made by an individual without appropriate clearance or authority to access such classified information at the time of the disclosure, but that is otherwise made in accordance with applicable security standards and procedures, shall be treated as an authorized disclosure that does not violate a covered provision.

(iii) Nothing in clause (ii) may be construed to limit or modify the obligation of an individual to appropriately store, handle, or disseminate classified information in accordance with applicable security guidance and procedures, including with respect to the removal or retention of classified information.

(iv) In this subparagraph, the term "covered provision" means—

(I) any otherwise applicable nondisclosure agreement;

(II) any otherwise applicable regulation or order issued under the authority of chapter 18 of the Atomic Energy Act of 1954 (42 U.S.C. 2271 et seq.) or Executive Order 13526;

(III) section 798 of title 18, United States Code; or

(IV) any other provision of law with respect to the unauthorized disclosure of national security information.

(4) The Inspector General shall have the authority to administer to or take from any person an oath, affirmation, or affidavit, whenever necessary in the performance of the duties of the Inspector General, which oath, affirmation, or affidavit when administered or taken by or before an employee of the Office of the Inspector General of the Intelligence Community designated by the Inspector General shall have the same force and effect as if administered or taken by, or before, an officer having a seal.

(5)(A) Except as provided in subparagraph (B), the Inspector General is authorized to require by subpoena the production of all information, documents, reports, answers, records, accounts, papers, and other data in any medium (including electronically stored information, as well as any tangible thing) and documentary evidence necessary in the performance of the duties and responsibilities of the Inspector General.

(B) In the case of departments, agencies, and other elements of the United States Government, the Inspector General shall obtain information, documents, reports, answers, records, accounts, papers, and other data and evidence for the purpose specified in subparagraph (A) using procedures other than by subpoenas.

(C) The Inspector General may not issue a subpoena for, or on behalf of, any component of the Office of the Director of National Intelligence or any element of the intelligence community, including the Office of the Director of National Intelligence.

(D) In the case of contumacy or refusal to obey a subpoena issued under this paragraph, the subpoena shall be enforceable by order of any appropriate district court of the United States.

(6) The Inspector General may obtain services as authorized by section 3109 of title 5, United States Code, at rates for individuals not to exceed the daily equivalent of the maximum annual rate of basic pay payable for grade GS–15 of the General Schedule under section 5332 of title 5, United States Code.

(7) The Inspector General may, to the extent and in such amounts as may be provided in appropriations, enter into contracts and other arrangements for audits, studies, analyses, and other services with public agencies and with private persons, and to make such payments as may be necessary to carry out the provisions of this section.

(h) Coordination Among Inspectors General.—(1)(A) In the event of a matter within the jurisdiction of the Inspector General of the Intelligence Community that may be subject to an investigation, inspection, audit, or review by both the Inspector General of the Intelligence Community and an inspector general with oversight responsibility for an element of the intelligence community, the Inspector General of the Intelligence Community and such other inspector general shall expeditiously resolve the question of which inspector general shall conduct such investigation, inspection, audit, or review to avoid unnecessary duplication of the activities of the inspectors general.

(B) In attempting to resolve a question under subparagraph (A), the inspectors general concerned may request the assistance of the Intelligence Community Inspectors General Forum established under paragraph (2). In the event of a dispute between an inspector general within a department or agency of the United States Government and the Inspector General of the Intelligence Community that has not been resolved with the assistance of such Forum, the inspectors general shall submit the question to the Director of National Intelligence and the head of the affected department or agency for resolution.

(2)(A) There is established the Intelligence Community Inspectors General Forum, which shall consist of all statutory or administrative inspectors general with oversight responsibility for an element of the intelligence community.

(B) The Inspector General of the Intelligence Community shall serve as the Chair of the Forum established under subparagraph (A). The Forum shall have no administrative authority over any inspector general, but shall serve as a mechanism for informing its members of the work of individual members of the Forum that may be of common interest and discussing questions about jurisdiction or access to employees, employees of contract personnel, records, audits, reviews, documents, recommendations, or other materials that may involve or be of assistance to more than one of its members.

(3) The inspector general conducting an investigation, inspection, audit, or review covered by paragraph (1) shall submit the results of such investigation, inspection, audit, or review to any other inspector general, including the Inspector General of the Intelligence Community, with jurisdiction to conduct such investigation, inspection, audit, or review who did not conduct such investigation, inspection, audit, or review.

(i) Counsel to the Inspector General.—(1) The Inspector General of the Intelligence Community shall—

(A) appoint a Counsel to the Inspector General who shall report to the Inspector General; or

(B) obtain the services of a counsel appointed by and directly reporting to another inspector general or the Council of the Inspectors General on Integrity and Efficiency on a reimbursable basis.

(2) The counsel appointed or obtained under paragraph (1) shall perform such functions as the Inspector General may prescribe.

(j) Staff and Other Support.—(1) The Director of National Intelligence shall provide the Inspector General of the Intelligence Community with appropriate and adequate office space at central and field office locations, together with such equipment, office supplies, maintenance services, and communications facilities and services as may be necessary for the operation of such offices.

(2)(A) Subject to applicable law and the policies of the Director of National Intelligence, the Inspector General shall select, appoint, and employ such officers and employees as may be necessary to carry out the functions, powers, and duties of the Inspector General. The Inspector General shall ensure that any officer or employee so selected, appointed, or employed has security clearances appropriate for the assigned duties of such officer or employee.

(B) In making selections under subparagraph (A), the Inspector General shall ensure that such officers and employees have the requisite training and experience to enable the Inspector General to carry out the duties of the Inspector General effectively.

(C) In meeting the requirements of this paragraph, the Inspector General shall create within the Office of the Inspector General of the Intelligence Community a career cadre of sufficient size to provide appropriate continuity and objectivity needed for the effective performance of the duties of the Inspector General.

(3) Consistent with budgetary and personnel resources allocated by the Director of National Intelligence, the Inspector General has final approval of—

(A) the selection of internal and external candidates for employment with the Office of the Inspector General; and

(B) all other personnel decisions concerning personnel permanently assigned to the Office of the Inspector General, including selection and appointment to the Senior Intelligence Service, but excluding all security-based determinations that are not within the authority of a head of a component of the Office of the Director of National Intelligence.

(4)(A) Subject to the concurrence of the Director of National Intelligence, the Inspector General may request such information or assistance as may be necessary for carrying out the duties and responsibilities of the Inspector General from any Federal, State (as defined in section 805), or local governmental agency or unit thereof.

(B) Upon request of the Inspector General for information or assistance from a department, agency, or element of the Federal Government under subparagraph (A), the head of the department, agency, or element concerned shall, insofar as is practicable and not in contravention of any existing statutory restriction or regulation of the department, agency, or element, furnish to the Inspector General, such information or assistance.

(C) The Inspector General of the Intelligence Community may, upon reasonable notice to the head of any element of the intelligence community and in coordination with that element's inspector general pursuant to subsection (h), conduct, as authorized by this section, an investigation, inspection, audit, or review of such element and may enter into any place occupied by such element for purposes of the performance of the duties of the Inspector General.

(k) Reports.—(1)(A) The Inspector General of the Intelligence Community shall, not later than October 31 and April 30 of each year, prepare and submit to the Director of National Intelligence a classified, and, as appropriate, unclassified semiannual report summarizing the activities of the Office of the Inspector General of the Intelligence Community during the immediately preceding 6-month period ending September 30 and March 31, respectively. The Inspector General of the Intelligence Community shall provide any portion of the report involving a component of a department of the United States Government to the head of that department simultaneously with submission of the report to the Director of National Intelligence.

(B) Each report under this paragraph shall include, at a minimum, the following:

(i) A list of the title or subject of each investigation, inspection, audit, or review conducted during the period covered by such report.

(ii) A description of significant problems, abuses, and deficiencies relating to the administration of programs and activities of the intelligence community within the responsibility and authority of the Director of National Intelligence, and in the relationships between elements of the intelligence community, identified by the Inspector General during the period covered by such report.

(iii) A description of the recommendations for corrective action made by the Inspector General during the period covered by such report with respect to significant problems, abuses, or deficiencies identified in clause (ii).

(iv) A statement of whether or not corrective action has been completed on each significant recommendation described in previous semiannual reports, and, in a case where corrective action has been completed, a description of such corrective action.

(v) A certification of whether or not the Inspector General has had full and direct access to all information relevant to the performance of the functions of the Inspector General.

(vi) A description of the exercise of the subpoena authority under subsection (g)(5) by the Inspector General during the period covered by such report.

(vii) Such recommendations as the Inspector General considers appropriate for legislation to promote economy, efficiency, and effectiveness in the administration and implementation of programs and activities within the responsibility and authority of the Director of National Intelligence, and to detect and eliminate fraud and abuse in such programs and activities.

(C) Not later than 30 days after the date of receipt of a report under subparagraph (A), the Director shall transmit the report to the congressional intelligence committees together with any comments the Director considers appropriate. The Director shall transmit to the committees of the Senate and of the House of Representatives with jurisdiction over a department of the United States Government any portion of the report involving a component of such department simultaneously with submission of the report to the congressional intelligence committees.

(2)(A) The Inspector General shall report immediately to the Director whenever the Inspector General becomes aware of particularly serious or flagrant problems, abuses, or deficiencies relating to programs and activities within the responsibility and authority of the Director of National Intelligence.

(B) The Director shall transmit to the congressional intelligence committees each report under subparagraph (A) within 7 calendar days of receipt of such report, together with such comments as the Director considers appropriate. The Director shall transmit to the committees of the Senate and of the House of Representatives with jurisdiction over a department of the United States Government any portion of each report under subparagraph (A) that involves a problem, abuse, or deficiency related to a component of such department simultaneously with transmission of the report to the congressional intelligence committees.

(3)(A) In the event that—

(i) the Inspector General is unable to resolve any differences with the Director affecting the execution of the duties or responsibilities of the Inspector General;

(ii) an investigation, inspection, audit, or review carried out by the Inspector General focuses on any current or former intelligence community official who—

(I) holds or held a position in an element of the intelligence community that is subject to appointment by the President, whether or not by and with the advice and consent of the Senate, including such a position held on an acting basis;

(II) holds or held a position in an element of the intelligence community, including a position held on an acting basis, that is appointed by the Director of National Intelligence; or

(III) holds or held a position as head of an element of the intelligence community or a position covered by subsection (b) or (c) of section 106;

(iii) a matter requires a report by the Inspector General to the Department of Justice on possible criminal conduct by a current or former official described in clause (ii);

(iv) the Inspector General receives notice from the Department of Justice declining or approving prosecution of possible criminal conduct of any current or former official described in clause (ii); or

(v) the Inspector General, after exhausting all possible alternatives, is unable to obtain significant documentary information in the course of an investigation, inspection, audit, or review,

the Inspector General shall immediately notify, and submit a report to, the congressional intelligence committees on such matter.

(B) The Inspector General shall submit to the committees of the Senate and of the House of Representatives with jurisdiction over a department of the United States Government any portion of each report under subparagraph (A) that involves an investigation, inspection, audit, or review carried out by the Inspector General focused on any current or former official of a component of such department simultaneously with submission of the report to the congressional intelligence committees.

(4) The Director shall submit to the congressional intelligence committees any report or findings and recommendations of an investigation, inspection, audit, or review conducted by the office which has been requested by the Chairman or Vice Chairman or ranking minority member of either committee.

(5)(A)(i) An employee of an element of the intelligence community, an employee assigned or detailed to an element of the intelligence community, or an employee of a contractor to the intelligence community who intends to report to Congress a complaint or information with respect to an urgent concern may report such complaint or information in writing to the Inspector General.

(ii) The Inspector General shall—

(I) provide reasonable support necessary to ensure that an employee can report a complaint or information under this subparagraph in writing; and

(II) if such submission is not feasible, create a written record of the employee's verbal complaint or information and treat such written record as a written submission.

(B)(i) In accordance with clause (ii), the Inspector General shall determine whether a complaint or information reported under subparagraph (A) appears credible. Upon making such a determination, the Inspector General shall transmit to the Director a notice of that determination, together with the complaint or information.

(ii) The Inspector General shall make the determination under clause (i) with respect to a complaint or information under subparagraph (A) by not later than the end of the 14-calendar-day period beginning on the date on which the employee who reported the complaint or information confirms to the Inspector General the intent of the employee to report to Congress that complaint or information.

(C) Upon receipt of a transmittal from the Inspector General under subparagraph (B), the Director shall, within 7 calendar days of such receipt, forward such transmittal to the congressional intelligence committees, together with any comments the Director considers appropriate.

(D)(i) If the Inspector General does not find credible under subparagraph (B) a complaint or information submitted under subparagraph (A), or does not transmit the complaint or information to the Director in accurate form under subparagraph (B), the employee (subject to clause (ii)) may submit the complaint or information to Congress by contacting either or both of the congressional intelligence committees directly.

(ii) An employee may contact the congressional intelligence committees directly as described in clause (i) only if the employee—

(I) before making such a contact, furnishes to the Director, through the Inspector General, a statement of the employee's complaint or information and notice of the employee's intent to contact the congressional intelligence committees directly; and

(II) obtains and follows from the Director, through the Inspector

General, direction on how to contact the congressional intelligence committees in accordance with appropriate security practices.

(iii) A member or employee of one of the congressional intelligence committees who receives a complaint or information under this subparagraph does so in that member or employee's official capacity as a member or employee of such committee.

(E) The Inspector General shall notify an employee who reports a complaint or information to the Inspector General under this paragraph of each action taken under this paragraph with respect to the complaint or information. Such notice shall be provided not later than 3 days after any such action is taken.

(F) An action taken by the Director or the Inspector General under this paragraph shall not be subject to judicial review.

(G)(i) In this paragraph, the term "urgent concern" means any of the following:

(I) A serious or flagrant problem, abuse, violation of law or Executive order, or deficiency relating to the funding, administration, or operation of an intelligence activity of the Federal Government that is—

(aa)[4] a matter of national security; and

(bb) not a difference of opinion concerning public policy matters.

[4] The margins of items (aa) and (bb) are so in law. See amendment made by section 6609(a) of division F of Public Law 117–263 (136 Stat. 3559).

(II) A false statement to Congress, or a willful withholding from Congress, on an issue of material fact relating to the funding, administration, or operation of an intelligence activity.

(III) An action, including a personnel action described in section 2302(a)(2)(A) of title 5, United States Code, constituting reprisal or threat of reprisal prohibited under subsection (g)(3)(B) of this section in response to an employee's reporting an urgent concern in accordance with this paragraph.

(ii) Within the executive branch, the Inspector General shall have sole authority to determine whether any complaint or information reported to the Inspector General is a matter of urgent concern under this paragraph.

(H) Nothing in this section shall be construed to limit the protections afforded to an employee under section 17(d) of the Central Intelligence Agency Act of 1949 (50 U.S.C. 403q(d)) or section 416 of title 5, United States Code.

(I) An individual who has submitted a complaint or information to the Inspector General under this section may notify any member of either of the congressional intelligence committees, or a staff member of either of such committees, of the fact that such individual has made a submission to the Inspector General, and of the date on which such submission was made.

(J) In this paragraph, the term "employee" includes a former employee, if the complaint or information reported under subparagraph (A) arises from or relates to the period during which the former employee was an employee.

(6) In accordance with section 535 of title 28, United States Code, the Inspector General shall expeditiously report to the Attorney General any information, allegation, or complaint received by the Inspector General relating to violations of Federal criminal law that involve a program or operation of an element of the intelligence community, or in the relationships between the elements of the intelligence community, consistent with such guidelines as may be issued by the Attorney General pursuant to subsection (b)(2) of such section. A copy of each such report shall be furnished to the Director.

(l) Construction of Duties Regarding Elements of Intelligence Community.— Except as resolved pursuant to subsection (h), the performance by the Inspector General of the Intelligence Community of any duty, responsibility, or function regarding an element of the intelligence community shall not be construed to modify or affect the duties and responsibilities of any other inspector general having duties and responsibilities relating to such element.

(m) Separate Budget Account.— The Director of National Intelligence shall, in accordance with procedures issued by the Director in consultation with the congressional intelligence committees, include in the National Intelligence Program budget a separate account for the Office of the Inspector General of the Intelligence Community.

(n) Budget.—(1) For each fiscal year, the Inspector General of the Intelligence Community shall transmit a budget estimate and request to the Director of National Intelligence that specifies for such fiscal year—

(A) the aggregate amount requested for the operations of the Inspector General;

(B) the amount requested for all training requirements of the Inspector General, including a certification from the Inspector General that the amount requested is sufficient to fund all training requirements for the Office of the Inspector General; and

(C) thc amount requested to support the Council of the Inspectors General on Integrity and Efficiency, including a justification for such amount.

(2) In transmitting a proposed budget to the President for a fiscal year, the Director of National Intelligence shall include for such fiscal year—

(A) the aggregate amount requested for the Inspector General of the Intelligence Community;

(B) the amount requested for Inspector General training;

(C) the amount requested to support the Council of the Inspectors General on Integrity and Efficiency; and

(D) the comments of the Inspector General, if any, with respect to such proposed budget.

(3) The Director of National Intelligence shall submit to the congressional intelligence committees, the Committee on Appropriations of the Senate, and the

Committee on Appropriations of the House of Representatives for each fiscal year—

(A) a separate statement of the budget estimate transmitted pursuant to paragraph (1);

(B) the amount requested by the Director for the Inspector General pursuant to paragraph (2)(A);

(C) the amount requested by the Director for the training of personnel of the Office of the Inspector General pursuant to paragraph (2)(B);

(D) the amount requested by the Director for support for the Council of the Inspectors General on Integrity and Efficiency pursuant to paragraph (2)(C); and

(E) the comments of the Inspector General under paragraph (2)(D), if any, on the amounts requested pursuant to paragraph (2), including whether such amounts would substantially inhibit the Inspector General from performing the duties of the Office of the Inspector General.

(o) INFORMATION ON WEBSITE.—(1) The Director of National Intelligence shall establish and maintain on the homepage of the publicly accessible website of the Office of the Director of National Intelligence information relating to the Office of the Inspector General of the Intelligence Community including methods to contact the Inspector General.

(2) The information referred to in paragraph (1) shall be obvious and facilitate accessibility to the information related to the Office of the Inspector General of the Intelligence Community.

CHIEF FINANCIAL OFFICER OF THE INTELLIGENCE COMMUNITY

SEC. 103I. [50 U.S.C. 3034] (a) CHIEF FINANCIAL OFFICER OF THE INTELLIGENCE COMMUNITY.— To assist the Director of National Intelligence in carrying out the responsibilities of the Director under this Act and other applicable provisions of law, there is within the Office of the Director of National Intelligence a Chief Financial Officer of the Intelligence Community who shall be appointed by the Director. The Chief Financial Officer shall report directly to the Director of National Intelligence.

(b) DUTIES AND RESPONSIBILITIES.—Subject to the direction of the Director of National Intelligence, the Chief Financial Officer of the Intelligence Community shall—

(1) serve as the principal advisor to the Director of National Intelligence and the Principal Deputy Director of National Intelligence on the management and allocation of intelligence community budgetary resources;

(2) participate in overseeing a comprehensive and integrated strategic process for resource management within the intelligence community;

(3) ensure that the strategic plan of the Director of National Intelligence—

(A) is based on budgetary constraints as specified in the Future Year Intelligence Plans and Long-term Budget Projections required under section 506G; and

(B) contains specific goals and objectives to support a performance-based budget;

(4) prior to the obligation or expenditure of funds for the acquisition of any major system pursuant to a Milestone A or Milestone B decision, receive verification from appropriate authorities that the national requirements for meeting the strategic plan of the Director have been established, and that such requirements are prioritized based on budgetary constraints as specified in the Future Year Intelligence Plans and the Long-term Budget Projections for such major system required under section 506G;

(5) ensure that the collection architectures of the Director are based on budgetary constraints as specified in the Future Year Intelligence Plans and the Long-term Budget Projections required under section 506G;

(6) coordinate or approve representations made to Congress by the intelligence community regarding National Intelligence Program budgetary resources;

(7) participate in key mission requirements, acquisitions, or architectural boards formed within or by the Office of the Director of National Intelligence; and

(8) perform such other duties as may be prescribed by the Director of National Intelligence.

(c) Other Law.— The Chief Financial Officer of the Intelligence Community shall serve as the Chief Financial Officer of the intelligence community and, to the extent applicable, shall have the duties, responsibilities, and authorities specified in chapter 9 of title 31, United States Code.

(d) Prohibition on Simultaneous Service as Other Chief Financial Officer.— An individual serving in the position of Chief Financial Officer of the Intelligence Community may not, while so serving, serve as the chief financial officer of any other department or agency, or component thereof, of the United States Government.

(e) Definitions.—In this section:

(1) The term “major system” has the meaning given that term in section 506A(e).

(2) The term “Milestone A” has the meaning given that term in section 506G(f).

(3) The term “Milestone B” has the meaning given that term in section 506C(e).

SEC. 103J. [50 U.S.C. 3034a] FUNCTIONAL MANAGERS FOR THE INTELLIGENCE COMMUNITY.

(a) Functional Managers Authorized.— The Director of National Intelligence may establish within the intelligence community one or more positions of manager of an intelligence function. Any position so established may be known as the “Functional Manager” of the intelligence function concerned.

(b) Personnel.— The Director shall designate individuals to serve as manager of intelligence functions established under subsection (a) from among officers and employees of elements of the intelligence community.

(c) Duties.—Each manager of an intelligence function established under subsection

(a) shall have the duties as follows:

(1) To act as principal advisor to the Director on the intelligence function.

(2) To carry out such other responsibilities with respect to the intelligence function as the Director may specify for purposes of this section.

SEC. 103K. [U.S.C. 3034b] INTELLIGENCE COMMUNITY CHIEF DATA OFFICER.

(a) INTELLIGENCE COMMUNITY CHIEF DATA OFFICER .—There is an Intelligence Community Chief Data Officer within the Office of the Director of National Intelligence who shall be appointed by the Director of National Intelligence.

(b) REQUIREMENT RELATING TO APPOINTMENT.— An individual appointed as the Intelligence Community Chief Data Officer shall have a professional background and experience appropriate for the duties of the Intelligence Community Chief Data Officer. In making such appointment, the Director of National Intelligence may give preference to an individual with experience outside of the United States Government.

(c) DUTIES.—The Intelligence Community Chief Data Officer shall—

(1) act as the chief representative of the Director of National Intelligence for data issues within the intelligence community;

(2) coordinate, to the extent practicable and advisable, with the Chief Data Officer of the Department of Defense to ensure consistent data policies, standards, and procedures between the intelligence community and the Department of Defense;

(3) assist the Director of National Intelligence regarding data elements of the budget of the Office of the Director of National Intelligence; and

(4) perform other such duties relating to data as may be prescribed by the Director of National Intelligence or specified in law.

SEC. 103L. [U.S.C. 3034c] INTELLIGENCE COMMUNITY INNOVATION UNIT.

(a) DEFINITIONS .—In this section:

(1) EMERGING TECHNOLOGY .—the term “emerging technology” has the meaning given that term in section 6701 of the Intelligence Authorization Act for Fiscal Year 2023 (Public Law 117–263; 50 U.S.C. 3024 note).

(2) UNIT .—The term “Unit” means the Intelligence Community Innovation Unit.

(b) PLAN FOR IMPLEMENTATION OF INTELLIGENCE COMMUNITY INNOVATION UNIT.—

(1) PLAN REQUIRED .—Not later than 180 days after the date of the enactment of the Intelligence Authorization Act for Fiscal Year 2024, the Director of National Intelligence shall develop a plan for how to implement the Intelligence Community Innovation Unit within the intelligence community.

(2) MATTERS COVERED.—The plan developed pursuant to paragraph (1) shall cover how the Unit will—

(A) benefit heads of the elements of the intelligence community in identifying commercial emerging technologies and associated capabilities to address critical mission needs of elements of the intelligence community;

(B) provide to the heads of the elements of the intelligence community seeking to field commercial emerging technologies technical expertise with respect to such technologies.

(C) facilitate the transition of potential prototypes and solutions to critical mission needs of the intelligence community from research and prototype projects to production; and

(D) serve as a liaison between the intelligence community and the private sector, in which capacity such liaison shall focus on small- and medium-sized companies and other organizations that do not have significant experience engaging with the intelligence community.

(3) Requirements.—The plan developed pursuant to paragraph (1) shall—

(A) plan for not more than 50 full-time equivalent personnel; and

(B) include an assessment as to how the establishment of the Unit would benefit the identification and evaluation of commercial emerging technologies for prototyping and potential adoption by the intelligence community to fulfill critical mission needs.

(4) Submission to Congress.—Upon completing development of the plan pursuant to paragraph (1), the Director shall—

(A) submit to the congressional intelligence committees, the Subcommittee on Defense of the Committee on Appropriations of the Senate, and the Subcommittee on Defense of the Committee on Appropriations of the House of Representatives a copy of the plan; and

(B) provide such committees and subcommittees a briefing on the plan.

(c) Establishment .—To the extent and in such amounts as specifically provided in advance in appropriations Acts for the purposes detailed in this section, not later than 180 days after the date on which the Director of National Intelligence submits the plan pursuant to subsection (b)(4)(A), the Director of National Intelligence shall establish the Unit within the Office of the Director of National Intelligence.

(d) Limitation .—The Unit shall not abrogate or otherwise constrain any element of the intelligence community from conducting authorized activities.

(e) Director of the Intelligence Community Innovation Unit.—

(1) Appointment; reporting .—The head of the Unit is the Director of the Intelligence Community Innovation Unit, who shall be appointed by the Director of National Intelligence and shall report directly to the Director of National Intelligence.

(2) Qualifications.—In selecting an individual for appointment as the Director of the Intelligence Community Innovation Unit, the Director of National Intelligence shall give preference to individuals who the Director of National Intelligence determines have—

(A) significant relevant experience involving commercial emerging technology within the private sector; and

(B) a demonstrated history of fostering the adoption of commercial emerging technologies by the United States Government or the private sector.

(f) STAFF.—

(1) IN GENERAL.— In addition to the Director of the Intelligence Community Innovation Unit, the Unit shall be composed of not more than 50 full- time equivalent positions.

(2) STAFF WITH CERTAIN EXPERTISE .—The Director of National Intelligence shall ensure that there is a sufficient number of staff of the Unit, as determined by the Director, with expertise in—

(A) other transaction authorities and nontraditional and rapid acquisition pathways for emerging technology;

(B) engaging and evaluating small- and medium-sized emerging technology companies;

(C) the mission needs of the intelligence community; and

(D) such other skills or experiences as the Director determines necessary.

(g) AUTHORITY RELATING TO DETAILEES.— Upon request of the Unit, each head of an element of the intelligence community may detail to the Unit any of the personnel of that element to assist in carrying out the duties under subsection (b) on a reimbursable or a nonreimbursable basis.

(h) ENSURING TRANSITION FROM PROTOTYPING TO PRODUCTION .—The Director of the Intelligence Community Innovation Unit shall transition research and prototype projects to products in a production stage upon identifying a demonstrated critical mission need of one or more elements of the intelligence community and a potential mission partner likely to field and further fund upon maturation, including by designating projects as Emerging Technology Transition Projects under the pilot program required by section 6713 of the Intelligence Authorization Act for Fiscal Year 2023 (Public Law 117–263; 50 U.S.C. 3024 note).

(i) ENCOURAGEMENT OF USE BY ELEMENTS.— The Director of National Intelligence shall take such steps as may be necessary to encourage the use of the Unit by the heads of the other elements of the intelligence community.

(j) RULES OF CONSTRUCTION.—

(1) NO PREFERENTIAL TREATMENT FOR PRIVATE SECTOR.— Nothing in this section shall be construed to require any element of the intelligence community to provide preferential treatment for any private sector entity with regard to procurement of technology construed as restricting or preempting any activities of the intelligence community.

(2) NO ADDITIONAL AUTHORITY .—The Unit established pursuant to subsection (c) will be limited to the existing authorities possessed by the Director of National Intelligence.

(k) SUNSET .—The authorities and requirements of this section shall terminate on the date that is 5 years after the date of the establishment of the Unit.

SEC. 103M. [50 U.S.C. 3034d] NATIONAL INTELLIGENCE MANAGEMENT COUNCIL.

(a) ESTABLISHMENT.— There is within the Office of the Director of National Intelligence a National Intelligence Management Council.

(b) COMPOSITION.—

(1) The National Intelligence Management Council shall be composed of senior officials within the intelligence community and substantive experts from the public or private sector, who shall be appointed by, report to, and serve at the pleasure of, the Director of National Intelligence.

(2) The Director shall prescribe appropriate security requirements for personnel appointed from the private sector as a condition of service on the National Intelligence Management Council, or as contractors of the Council or employees of such contractors, to ensure the protection of intelligence sources and methods while avoiding, wherever possible, unduly intrusive requirements which the Director considers to be unnecessary for this purpose.

(c) DUTIES AND RESPONSIBILITIES.—Members of the National Intelligence Management Council shall work with each other and with other elements of the intelligence community to ensure proper coordination and to minimize duplication of effort, in addition to the following duties and responsibilities:

(1) Provide integrated mission input to support the processes and activities of the intelligence community, including with respect to intelligence planning, programming, budgeting, and evaluation processes.

(2) Identify and pursue opportunities to integrate or coordinate collection and counterintelligence efforts.

(3) In concert with the responsibilities of the National Intelligence Council, ensure the integration and coordination of analytic and collection efforts.

(4) Develop and coordinate intelligence strategies in support of budget planning and programming activities.

(5) Advise the Director of National Intelligence on the development of the National Intelligence Priorities Framework of the Office of the Director of National Intelligence (or any successor mechanism established for the prioritization of programs and activities).

(6) In concert with the responsibilities of the National Intelligence Council, support the role of the Director of National Intelligence as principal advisor to the President on intelligence matters.

(7) Inform the elements of the intelligence community of the activities and decisions related to missions assigned to the National Intelligence Management Council.

(8) Maintain awareness, across various functions and disciplines, of the mission-related activities and budget planning of the intelligence community.

(9) Evaluate, with respect to assigned mission objectives, requirements, and unmet requirements, the implementation of the budget of each element of the intelligence community.

(10) Provide oversight on behalf of, and make recommendations to, the Director

of National Intelligence on the extent to which the activities, program recommendations, and budget proposals made by elements of the intelligence community sufficiently address mission objectives, intelligence gaps, and unmet requirements.

(d) MISSION MANAGEMENT OF MEMBERS.—Members of the National Intelligence Management Council, under the direction of the Director of National Intelligence, shall serve as mission managers to ensure integration among the elements of the intelligence community and across intelligence functions, disciplines, and activities for the purpose of achieving unity of effort and effect, including through the following responsibilities:

(1) Planning and programming efforts.

(2) Budget and program execution oversight.

(3) Engagement with elements of the intelligence community and with policymakers in other agencies.

(4) Workforce competencies and training activities.

(5) Development of capability requirements.

(6) Development of governance fora, policies, and procedures.

(e) STAFF; AVAILABILITY.—

(1) STAFF.— The Director of National Intelligence shall make available to the National Intelligence Management Council such staff as may be necessary to assist the National Intelligence Management Council in carrying out the responsibilities described in this section.

(2) AVAILABILITY.— Under the direction of the Director of National Intelligence, the National Intelligence Management Council shall make reasonable efforts to advise and consult with officers and employees of other departments or agencies, or components thereof, of the United States Government not otherwise associated with the intelligence community.

(f) SUPPORT FROM ELEMENTS OF THE INTELLIGENCE COMMUNITY.— The heads of the elements of the intelligence community shall provide appropriate support to the National Intelligence Management Council, including with respect to intelligence activities, as required by the Director of National Intelligence.

CENTRAL INTELLIGENCE AGENCY

SEC. 104. [50 U.S.C. 3035] (a) CENTRAL INTELLIGENCE AGENCY.— There is a Central Intelligence Agency.

(b) FUNCTION.— The function of the Central Intelligence Agency is to assist the Director of the Central Intelligence Agency in carrying out the responsibilities specified in section 104A(c).

DIRECTOR OF THE CENTRAL INTELLIGENCE AGENCY

SEC. 104A. [50 U.S.C. 3036] (a) DIRECTOR OF CENTRAL INTELLIGENCE AGENCY.— There is a Director of the Central Intelligence Agency who shall be appointed by the President, by and with the advice and consent of the Senate.

(b) SUPERVISION.— The Director of the Central Intelligence Agency shall report to the Director of National Intelligence regarding the activities of the Central Intelligence Agency.

(c) Duties.—The Director of the Central Intelligence Agency shall—

(1) serve as the head of the Central Intelligence Agency; and

(2) carry out the responsibilities specified in subsection (d).

(d) Responsibilities.—The Director of the Central Intelligence Agency shall—

(1) collect intelligence through human sources and by other appropriate means, except that the Director of the Central Intelligence Agency shall have no police, subpoena, or law enforcement powers or internal security functions;

(2) correlate and evaluate intelligence related to the national security and provide appropriate dissemination of such intelligence;

(3) provide overall direction for and coordination of the collection of national intelligence outside the United States through human sources by elements of the intelligence community authorized to undertake such collection and, in coordination with other departments, agencies, or elements of the United States Government which are authorized to undertake such collection, ensure that the most effective use is made of resources and that appropriate account is taken of the risks to the United States and those involved in such collection; and

(4) perform such other functions and duties related to intelligence affecting the national security as the President or the Director of National Intelligence may direct.

(e) Termination of Employment of CIA Employees.—(1) Notwithstanding the provisions of any other law, the Director of the Central Intelligence Agency may, in the discretion of the Director, terminate the employment of any officer or employee of the Central Intelligence Agency whenever the Director deems the termination of employment of such officer or employee necessary or advisable in the interests of the United States.

(2) Any termination of employment of an officer or employee under paragraph (1) shall not affect the right of the officer or employee to seek or accept employment in any other department, agency, or element of the United States Government if declared eligible for such employment by the Office of Personnel Management.

(f) Coordination With Foreign Governments.— Under the direction of the Director of National Intelligence and in a manner consistent with section 207 of the Foreign Service Act of 1980 (22 U.S.C. 3927), the Director of the Central Intelligence Agency shall coordinate the relationships between elements of the intelligence community and the intelligence or security services of foreign governments or international organizations on all matters involving intelligence related to the national security or involving intelligence acquired through clandestine means.

DEPUTY DIRECTOR OF THE CENTRAL INTELLIGENCE AGENCY

Sec. 104B. **[50 U.S.C. 3037]** (a) Deputy Director of the Central Intelligence Agency.— There is a Deputy Director of the Central Intelligence Agency who shall be appointed by the President.

(b) DUTIES.—The Deputy Director of the Central Intelligence Agency shall—

(1) assist the Director of the Central Intelligence Agency in carrying out the duties and responsibilities of the Director of the Central Intelligence Agency; and

(2) during the absence or disability of the Director of the Central Intelligence Agency, or during a vacancy in the position of Director of the Central Intelligence Agency, act for and exercise the powers of the Director of the Central Intelligence Agency.

RESPONSIBILITIES OF THE SECRETARY OF DEFENSE PERTAINING TO THE NATIONAL INTELLIGENCE PROGRAM

SEC. 105. [50 U.S.C. 3038] (a) IN GENERAL.—Consistent with sections 102 and 102A, the Secretary of Defense, in consultation with the Director of National Intelligence, shall—

(1) ensure that the budgets of the elements of the intelligence community within the Department of Defense are adequate to satisfy the overall intelligence needs of the Department of Defense, including the needs of the Chairman of the Joint Chiefs of Staff and the commanders of the unified and specified commands and, wherever such elements are performing governmentwide functions, the needs of other departments and agencies;

(2) ensure appropriate implementation of the policies and resource decisions of the Director by elements of the Department of Defense within the National Intelligence Program;

(3) ensure that the tactical intelligence activities of the Department of Defense complement and are compatible with intelligence activities under the National Intelligence Program;

(4) ensure that the elements of the intelligence community within the Department of Defense are responsive and timely with respect to satisfying the needs of operational military forces;

(5) eliminate waste and unnecessary duplication among the intelligence activities of the Department of Defense; and

(6) ensure that intelligence activities of the Department of Defense are conducted jointly where appropriate.

(b) RESPONSIBILITY FOR THE PERFORMANCE OF SPECIFIC FUNCTIONS.—Consistent with sections 102 and 102A of this Act, the Secretary of Defense shall ensure—

(1) through the National Security Agency (except as otherwise directed by the President or the National Security Council), the continued operation of an effective unified organization for the conduct of signals intelligence activities and shall ensure that the product is disseminated in a timely manner to authorized recipients;

(2) through the National Geospatial-Intelligence Agency (except as otherwise directed by the President or the National Security Council),. with appropriate representation from the intelligence community, the continued operation of an effective unified organization within the Department of Defense—

(A) for carrying out tasking of imagery collection;

(B) for the coordination of imagery processing and exploitation activities;

(C) for ensuring the dissemination of imagery in a timely manner to authorized recipients; and

(D) notwithstanding any other provision of law, for—

(i) prescribing technical architecture and standards related to imagery intelligence and geospatial information and ensuring compliance with such architecture and standards; and

(ii) developing and fielding systems of common concern related to imagery intelligence and geospatial information;

(3) through the National Reconnaissance Office (except as otherwise directed by the President or the National Security Council), the continued operation of an effective unified organization for the research and development, acquisition, and operation of overhead reconnaissance systems necessary to satisfy the requirements of all elements of the intelligence community;

(4) through the Defense Intelligence Agency (except as otherwise directed by the President or the National Security Council), the continued operation of an effective unified system within the Department of Defense for the production of timely, objective military and military-related intelligence, based upon all sources available to the intelligence community, and shall ensure the appropriate dissemination of such intelligence to authorized recipients;

(5) through the Defense Intelligence Agency (except as otherwise directed by the President or the National Security Council), effective management of Department of Defense human intelligence and counterintelligence activities, including defense attaches; and

(6) that the military departments maintain sufficient capabilities to collect and produce intelligence to meet—

(A) the requirements of the Director of National Intelligence;

(B) the requirements of the Secretary of Defense or the Chairman of the Joint Chiefs of Staff;

(C) the requirements of the unified and specified combatant commands and of joint operations; and

(D) the specialized requirements of the military departments for intelligence necessary to support tactical commanders, military planners, the research and development process, the acquisition of military equipment, and training and doctrine.

(c) Expenditure of Funds by the Defense Intelligence Agency.—(1) Subject to paragraphs (2) and (3), the Director of the Defense Intelligence Agency may expend amounts made available to the Director under the National Intelligence Program for human intelligence and counterintelligence activities for objects of a confidential, extraordinary, or emergency nature, without regard to the provisions of law or regulation relating to the expenditure of Government funds.

(2) The Director of the Defense Intelligence Agency may not expend more than

five percent of the amounts made available to the Director under the National Intelligence Program for human intelligence and counterintelligence activities for a fiscal year for objects of a confidential, extraordinary, or emergency nature in accordance with paragraph (1) during such fiscal year unless—

(A) the Director notifies the congressional intelligence committees, the Committee on Armed Services of the Senate, and the Committee on Armed Services of the House of Representatives of the intent to expend the amounts; and

(B) 30 days have elapsed from the date on which the Director notifies the congressional intelligence committees, the Committee on Armed Services of the Senate, and the Committee on Armed Services of the House of Representatives in accordance with subparagraph (A).

(3) For each expenditure referred to in paragraph (1), the Director shall certify that such expenditure was made for an object of a confidential, extraordinary, or emergency nature.

(4) Not later than December 31 of each year, the Director of the Defense Intelligence Agency shall submit to the congressional intelligence committees, the Committee on Armed Services of the Senate, and the Committee on Armed Services of the House of Representatives a report on any expenditures made during the preceding fiscal year in accordance with paragraph (1).

(d) USE OF ELEMENTS OF DEPARTMENT OF DEFENSE.— The Secretary of Defense, in carrying out the functions described in this section, may use such elements of the Department of Defense as may be appropriate for the execution of those functions, in addition to, or in lieu of, the elements identified in this section.

ASSISTANCE TO UNITED STATES LAW ENFORCEMENT AGENCIES

SEC. 105A. [50 U.S.C. 3039] (a) AUTHORITY TO PROVIDE ASSISTANCE.— Subject to subsection (b), elements of the intelligence community may, upon the request of a United States law enforcement agency, collect information outside the United States about individuals who are not United States persons. Such elements may collect such information notwithstanding that the law enforcement agency intends to use the information collected for purposes of a law enforcement investigation or counterintelligence investigation.

(b) LIMITATION ON ASSISTANCE BY ELEMENTS OF DEPARTMENT OF DEFENSE.—(1) With respect to elements within the Department of Defense, the authority in subsection (a) applies only to the following:

(A) The National Security Agency.

(B) The National Reconnaissance Office.

(C) The National Geospatial-Intelligence Agency.

(D) The Defense Intelligence Agency.

(2) Assistance provided under this section by elements of the Department of Defense may not include the direct participation of a member of the Army, Navy, Air Force, or Marine Corps in an arrest or similar activity.

(3) Assistance may not be provided under this section by an element of the Department of Defense if the provision of such assistance will adversely affect the military preparedness of the United States.

(4) The Secretary of Defense shall prescribe regulations governing the exercise of authority under this section by elements of the Department of Defense, including regulations relating to the protection of sources and methods in the exercise of such authority.

(c) Definitions.—For purposes of subsection (a):

(1) The term "United States law enforcement agency" means any department or agency of the Federal Government that the Attorney General designates as law enforcement agency for purposes of this section.

(2) The term "United States person" means the following:

(A) A United States citizen.

(B) An alien known by the intelligence agency concerned to be a permanent resident alien.

(C) An unincorporated association substantially composed of United States citizens or permanent resident aliens.

(D) A corporation incorporated in the United States, except for a corporation directed and controlled by a foreign government or governments.

DISCLOSURE OF FOREIGN INTELLIGENCE ACQUIRED IN CRIMINAL INVESTIGATIONS; NOTICE OF CRIMINAL INVESTIGATIONS OF FOREIGN INTELLIGENCE SOURCES

Sec. 105B. [50 U.S.C. 3040] (a) Disclosure of Foreign Intelligence.—(1) Except as otherwise provided by law and subject to paragraph (2), the Attorney General, or the head of any other department or agency of the Federal Government with law enforcement responsibilities, shall expeditiously disclose to the Director of National Intelligence, pursuant to guidelines developed by the Attorney General in consultation with the Director, foreign intelligence acquired by an element of the Department of Justice or an element of such department or agency, as the case may be, in the course of a criminal investigation.

(2) The Attorney General by regulation and in consultation with the Director may provide for exceptions to the applicability of paragraph (1) for one or more classes of foreign intelligence, or foreign intelligence with respect to one or more targets or matters, if the Attorney General determines that disclosure of such foreign intelligence under that paragraph would jeopardize an ongoing law enforcement investigation or impair other significant law enforcement interests.

(b) Procedures for Notice of Criminal Investigations.— Not later than 180 days after the date of enactment of this section, the Attorney General, in consultation with the Director of National Intelligence, shall develop guidelines to ensure that after receipt of a report from an element of the intelligence community of activity of a foreign intelligence source or potential foreign intelligence source that may warrant investigation as criminal activity, the Attorney General provides notice to the Director, within a reasonable period of time, of his intention to commence, or decline to commence, a criminal investigation of such activity.

(c) PROCEDURES.— The Attorney General shall develop procedures for the administration of this section, including the disclosure of foreign intelligence by elements of the Department of Justice, and elements of other departments and agencies of the Federal Government, under subsection (a) and the provision of notice with respect to criminal investigations under subsection (b).

SEC. 105C. [50 U.S.C. 3040a] PROHIBITION ON COLLECTION AND MAINTENANCE OF INFORMATION OF UNITED STATES PERSONS BASED ON FIRST AMENDMENT-PROTECTED ACTIVITIES.

No element of the intelligence community may collect or maintain information concerning a United States person (as defined in section 105A) solely for the purpose of monitoring an activity protected by the first amendment to the Constitution of the United States.

APPOINTMENT OF OFFICIALS RESPONSIBLE FOR INTELLIGENCE-RELATED ACTIVITIES

SEC. 106. [50 U.S.C. 3041] (a) RECOMMENDATION OF DNI IN CERTAIN APPOINTMENTS.—(1) In the event of a vacancy in a position referred to in paragraph (2), the Director of National Intelligence shall recommend to the President an individual for nomination to fill the vacancy.

(2) Paragraph (1) applies to the following positions:

(A) The Principal Deputy Director of National Intelligence.

(B) The Director of the Central Intelligence Agency.

(b) CONCURRENCE OF DNI IN APPOINTMENTS TO POSITIONS IN THE INTELLIGENCE COMMUNITY.—(1) In the event of a vacancy in a position referred to in paragraph (2), the head of the department or agency having jurisdiction over the position shall obtain the concurrence of the Director of National Intelligence before appointing an individual to fill the vacancy or recommending to the President an individual to be nominated to fill the vacancy. If the Director does not concur in the recommendation, the head of the department or agency concerned may not fill the vacancy or make the recommendation to the President (as the case may be). In the case in which the Director does not concur in such a recommendation, the Director and the head of the department or agency concerned may advise the President directly of the intention to withhold concurrence or to make a recommendation, as the case may be.

(2) Paragraph (1) applies to the following positions:

(A) The Director of the National Security Agency.

(B) The Director of the National Reconnaissance Office.

(C) The Director of the National Geospatial-Intelligence Agency.

(D) The Assistant Secretary of State for Intelligence and Research.

(E) The Director of the Office of Intelligence and Counterintelligence of the Department of Energy.

(F) The Assistant Secretary for Intelligence and Analysis of the Department of the Treasury.

(G) The Executive Assistant Director for Intelligence of the Federal Bureau of Investigation or any successor to that position.

(H) The Under Secretary of Homeland Security for Intelligence and Analysis.

(c) Consultation With DNI in Certain Positions.—(1) In the event of a vacancy in a position referred to in paragraph (2), the head of the department or agency having jurisdiction over the position shall consult with the Director of National Intelligence before appointing an individual to fill the vacancy or recommending to the President an individual to be nominated to fill the vacancy.

(2) Paragraph (1) applies to the following positions:

(A) The Director of the Defense Intelligence Agency.

(B) The Assistant Commandant of the Coast Guard for Intelligence.

(C) The Assistant Attorney General designated as the Assistant Attorney General for National Security under section 507A of title 28, United States Code.

SEC. 106A. [50 U.S.C. 3041a] DIRECTOR OF THE NATIONAL RECONNAISSANCE OFFICE.

(a) In General.— There is a Director of the National Reconnaissance Office.

(b) Appointment.— The Director of the National Reconnaissance Office shall be appointed by the President, by and with the advice and consent of the Senate.

(c) Functions and Duties.— The Director of the National Reconnaissance Office shall be the head of the National Reconnaissance Office and shall discharge such functions and duties as are provided by this Act or otherwise by law or executive order.

(d) Advisory Board.—

(1) Establishment.— There is established in the National Reconnaissance Office an advisory board (in this section referred to as the "Board").

(2) Duties.—The Board shall—

(A) study matters relating to the mission of the National Reconnaissance Office, including with respect to promoting innovation, competition, and resilience in space, overhead reconnaissance, acquisition, and other matters; and

(B) advise and report directly to the Director with respect to such matters.

(3) Members.—

(A) Number and appointment.—

(i) In general.— The Board shall be composed of up to 8 members appointed by the Director, in consultation with the Director of National Intelligence and the Secretary of Defense, from among individuals with demonstrated academic, government, business, or other expertise relevant to the mission and functions of the National Reconnaissance Office, and who do not present any actual or potential conflict of interest.

(ii) Membership structure.— The Director shall ensure that no more than 2 concurrently serving members of the Board qualify for membership on the Board based predominantly on a single qualification set forth under clause (i).

(iii) NOTIFICATION.— Not later than 30 days after the date on which the Director appoints a member to the Board, the Director shall notify the congressional intelligence committees and the congressional defense committees (as defined in section 101(a) of title 10, United States Code) of such appointment.

(B) TERMS.— Each member shall be appointed for a term of 2 years. Except as provided by subparagraph (C), a member may not serve more than three terms.

(C) VACANCY.— Any member appointed to fill a vacancy occurring before the expiration of the term for which the member's predecessor was appointed shall be appointed only for the remainder of that term. A member may serve after the expiration of that member's term until a successor has taken office.

(D) CHAIR.— The Board shall have a Chair, who shall be appointed by the Director from among the members.

(E) TRAVEL EXPENSES.— Each member shall receive travel expenses, including per diem in lieu of subsistence, in accordance with applicable provisions under subchapter I of chapter 57 of title 5, United States Code.

(F) EXECUTIVE SECRETARY.— The Director may appoint an executive secretary, who shall be an employee of the National Reconnaissance Office, to support the Board.

(4) MEETINGS.— The Board shall meet not less than quarterly, but may meet more frequently at the call of the Director.

(5) CHARTER.—The Director shall establish a charter for the Board that includes the following:

(A) Mandatory processes for identifying potential conflicts of interest, including the submission of initial and periodic financial disclosures by Board members.

(B) The vetting of potential conflicts of interest by the designated agency ethics official, except that no individual waiver may be granted for a conflict of interest identified with respect to the Chair of the Board.

(C) The establishment of a process and associated protections for any whistleblower alleging a violation of applicable conflict of interest law, Federal contracting law, or other provision of law.

(6) REPORTS.— Not later than March 31 of each year, the Board shall submit to the Director and to the congressional intelligence committees a report on the activities and significant findings of the Board during the preceding year.

(7) NONAPPLICABILITY OF CERTAIN REQUIREMENTS.— The Federal Advisory Committee Act (5 U.S.C. App.) shall not apply to the Board.

(8) TERMINATION.— The Board shall terminate on August 31, 2027.

[Section 107 was repealed by section 6742(b)(3) of division E of Public Law 116-92.]

ANNUAL NATIONAL SECURITY STRATEGY REPORT

SEC. 108. [50 U.S.C. 3043] (a)(1) The President shall transmit to Congress each year a comprehensive report on the national security strategy of the United States (hereinafter in this section referred to as a national security strategy report").

(2) The national security strategy report for any year shall be transmitted on the date on which the President submits to Congress the budget for the next fiscal year under section 1105 of title 31, United States Code.

(3) Not later than 150 days after the date on which a new President takes office, the President shall transmit to Congress a national security strategy report under this section. That report shall be in addition to the report for that year transmitted at the time specified in paragraph (2).

(b) Each national security strategy report shall set forth the national security strategy of the United States and shall include a comprehensive description and discussion of the following:

(1) The worldwide interests, goals, and objectives of the United States that are vital to the national security of the United States.

(2) The foreign policy, worldwide commitments, and national defense capabilities of the United States necessary to deter aggression and to implement the national security strategy of the United States.

(3) The proposed short-term and long-term uses of the political, economic, military, and other elements of the national power of the United States to protect or promote the interests and achieve the goals and objectives referred to in paragraph (1).

(4) The adequacy of the capabilities of the United States to carry out the national security strategy of the United States, including an evaluation of the balance among the capabilities of all elements of the national power of the United States to support the implementation of the national security strategy.

(5) Such other information as may be necessary to help inform Congress on matters relating to the national security strategy of the United States.

(c) Each national security strategy report shall be transmitted to Congress in classified form, but may include an unclassified summary.

SEC. 108A. [50 U.S.C. 3043a] NATIONAL INTELLIGENCE STRATEGY.

(a) IN GENERAL.— Beginning in 2017, and once every 4 years thereafter, the Director of National Intelligence shall develop a comprehensive national intelligence strategy to meet national security objectives for the following 4-year period, or a longer period, if appropriate.

(b) REQUIREMENTS.—Each national intelligence strategy required by subsection (a) shall—

(1) delineate a national intelligence strategy consistent with—

(A) the most recent national security strategy report submitted pursuant to section 108;

(B) the strategic plans of other relevant departments and agencies of the United States; and

(C) other relevant national-level plans;

(2) address matters related to national and military intelligence, including counterintelligence;

(3) identify the major national security missions that the intelligence community is currently pursuing and will pursue in the future to meet the anticipated security environment;

(4) describe how the intelligence community will utilize personnel, technology, partnerships, and other capabilities to pursue the major national security missions identified in paragraph (3);

(5) assess current, emerging, and future threats to the intelligence community, including threats from foreign intelligence and security services and insider threats;

(6) outline the organizational roles and missions of the elements of the intelligence community as part of an integrated enterprise to meet customer demands for intelligence products, services, and support;

(7) identify sources of strategic, institutional, programmatic, fiscal, and technological risk; and

(8) analyze factors that may affect the intelligence community's performance in pursuing the major national security missions identified in paragraph (3) during the following 10-year period.

(c) SUBMISSION TO CONGRESS.— The Director of National Intelligence shall submit to the congressional intelligence committees a report on each national intelligence strategy required by subsection (a) not later than 45 days after the date of the completion of such strategy.

SEC. 108B. [50 U.S.C. 3043b] ANNUAL REPORTS ON WORLDWIDE THREATS.

(a) DEFINITION OF APPROPRIATE CONGRESSIONAL COMMITTEES.—In this section, the term "appropriate congressional committees" means—

(1) the congressional intelligence committees; and

(2) the Committees on Armed Services of the House of Representatives and the Senate.

(b) ANNUAL REPORTS.— Not later than the first Monday in February 2021, and each year thereafter, the Director of National Intelligence, in coordination with the heads of the elements of the intelligence community, shall submit to the appropriate congressional committees a report containing an assessment of the intelligence community with respect to worldwide threats to the national security of the United States.

(c) FORM.— Each report under subsection (b) shall be submitted in unclassified form, but may include a classified annex only for the protection of intelligence sources and methods relating to the matters contained in the report.

(d) HEARINGS.—

(1) OPEN HEARINGS.— Upon request by the appropriate congressional committees, the Director (and any other head of an element of the intelligence community determined appropriate by the committees in consultation with the Director) shall testify before such committees in an open setting regarding a report under subsection (b).

(2) CLOSED HEARINGS.— Any information that may not be disclosed during an open hearing under paragraph (1) in order to protect intelligence sources and methods may instead be discussed in a closed hearing that immediately follows such open hearing.

SEC. 109. [50 U.S.C. 3044] SOFTWARE LICENSING.

(a) REQUIREMENT FOR INVENTORIES OF SOFTWARE LICENSES.—The chief information officer of each element of the intelligence community, in consultation with the Chief Information Officer of the Intelligence Community, shall biennially—

(1) conduct an inventory of all existing software licenses of such element, including utilized and unutilized licenses;

(2) assess the actions that could be carried out by such element to achieve the greatest possible economies of scale and associated cost savings in software procurement and usage, including—

(A) increasing the centralization of the management of software licenses;

(B) increasing the regular tracking and maintaining of comprehensive inventories of software licenses using automated discovery and inventory tools and metrics;

(C) analyzing software license data to inform investment decisions; and

(D) providing appropriate personnel with sufficient software licenses management training; and

(3) submit to the Chief Information Officer of the Intelligence Community each inventory required by paragraph (1) and each assessment required by paragraph (2).

(b) INVENTORIES BY THE CHIEF INFORMATION OFFICER OF THE INTELLIGENCE COMMUNITY.—The Chief Information Officer of the Intelligence Community, based on the inventories and assessments required by subsection (a), shall biennially—

(1) compile an inventory of all existing software licenses of the intelligence community, including utilized and unutilized licenses;

(2) assess the actions that could be carried out by the intelligence community to achieve the greatest possible economies of scale and associated cost savings in software procurement and usage, including—

(A) increasing the centralization of the management of software licenses;

(B) increasing the regular tracking and maintaining of comprehensive inventories of software licenses using automated discovery and inventory tools and metrics;

(C) analyzing software license data to inform investment decisions; and

(D) providing appropriate personnel with sufficient software licenses management training; and

(3) based on the assessment required under paragraph (2), make such recommendations with respect to software procurement and usage to the Director of National Intelligence as the Chief Information Officer considers appropriate.

(c) Reports to Congress.— The Chief Information Officer of the Intelligence Community shall submit to the congressional intelligence committees a copy of each inventory compiled under subsection (b)(1).

(d) Implementation of Recommendations.— Not later than 180 days after the date on which the Director of National Intelligence receives recommendations from the Chief Information Officer of the Intelligence Community in accordance with subsection (b)(3), the Director of National Intelligence shall, to the extent practicable, issue guidelines for the intelligence community on software procurement and usage based on such recommendations.

NATIONAL MISSION OF NATIONAL GEOSPATIAL-INTELLIGENCE AGENCY

Sec. 110. [50 U.S.C. 3045] (a) In General.— In addition to the Department of Defense missions set forth in section 442 of title 10, United States Code, the National Geospatial-Intelligence Agency shall support the geospatial intelligence requirements of the Department of State and other departments and agencies of the United States outside the Department of Defense.

(b) Requirements and Priorities.— The Director of National Intelligence shall establish requirements and priorities governing the collection of national intelligence by the National Geospatial-Intelligence Agency under subsection (a).

(c) Correction of Deficiencies.— The Director of National Intelligence shall develop and implement such programs and policies as the Director and the Secretary of Defense jointly determine necessary to review and correct deficiencies identified in the capabilities of the National Geospatial-Intelligence Agency to accomplish assigned national missions, including support to the all-source analysis and production process. The Director shall consult with the Secretary of Defense on the development and implementation of such programs and policies. The Secretary shall obtain the advice of the Chairman of the Joint Chiefs of Staff regarding the matters on which the Director and the Secretary are to consult under the preceding sentence.

[Section 111 was repealed by section 1075 of Public Law 108–458 (Act of December 17, 2004, 118 Stat. 3694); 50 U.S.C. 3046.]

RESTRICTIONS ON INTELLIGENCE SHARING WITH THE UNITED NATIONS

Sec. 112. [50 U.S.C. 3047] (a) Provision of Intelligence Information to the United Nations.—(1) No United States intelligence information may be provided to the United Nations or any organization affiliated with the United Nations, or to any officials or employees thereof, unless the President certifies to the appropriate committees of Congress that the Director of National Intelligence, in consultation with the Secretary of State and the Secretary of Defense, has established and implemented procedures, and has worked with the United Nations to ensure implementation of procedures, for protecting from unauthorized disclosure United States intelligence sources and methods connected to such information.

(2) Paragraph (1) may be waived upon written certification by the President to the appropriate committees of Congress that providing such information to the United Nations or an organization affiliated with the United Nations, or to any officials or employees thereof, is in the national security interests of the United States.

(b) DELEGATION OF DUTIES.— The President may not delegate or assign the duties of the President under this section.

(c) RELATIONSHIP TO EXISTING LAW.—Nothing in this section shall be construed to—

(1) impair or otherwise affect the authority of the Director of National Intelligence to protect intelligence sources and methods from unauthorized disclosure pursuant to section 102A(i) of this Act; or

(2) supersede or otherwise affect the provisions of title V of this Act.

(d) DEFINITION.— As used in this section, the term "appropriate committees of Congress" means the Committee on Foreign Relations and the Select Committee on Intelligence of the Senate and the Committee on Foreign Relations and the Permanent Select Committee on Intelligence of the House of Representatives.

DETAIL OF INTELLIGENCE COMMUNITY PERSONNEL—INTELLIGENCE COMMUNITY ASSIGNMENT PROGRAM

SEC. 113. [50 U.S.C. 3048] (a) DETAIL.—(1) Notwithstanding any other provision of law, the head of a department with an element in the intelligence community or the head of an intelligence community agency or element may detail any employee within that department, agency, or element to serve in any position in the Intelligence Community Assignment Program on a reimbursable or a nonreimbursable basis.

(2) Nonreimbursable details may be for such periods as are agreed to between the heads of the parent and host agencies, up to a maximum of three years, except that such details may be extended for a period not to exceed one year when the heads of the parent and host agencies determine that such extension is in the public interest.

(b) BENEFITS, ALLOWANCES, TRAVEL, INCENTIVES.—(1) An employee detailed under subsection (a) may be authorized any benefit, allowance, travel, or incentive otherwise provided to enhance staffing by the organization from which the employee is detailed.

(2) The head of an agency of an employee detailed under subsection (a) may pay a lodging allowance for the employee subject to the following conditions:

(A) The allowance shall be the lesser of the cost of the lodging or a maximum amount payable for the lodging as established jointly by the Director of National Intelligence and—

(i) with respect to detailed employees of the Department of Defense, the Secretary of Defense; and

(ii) with respect to detailed employees of other agencies and departments, the head of such agency or department.

(B) The detailed employee maintains a primary residence for the employee's immediate family in the local commuting area of the parent agency duty station from which the employee regularly commuted to such duty station before the detail.

(C) The lodging is within a reasonable proximity of the host agency duty station.

(D) The distance between the detailed employee's parent agency duty station and the host agency duty station is greater than 20 miles.

(E) The distance between the detailed employee's primary residence and the host agency duty station is 10 miles greater than the distance between such primary residence and the employees parent duty station.

(F) The rate of pay applicable to the detailed employee does not exceed the rate of basic pay for grade GS–15 of the General Schedule.

NON-REIMBURSABLE DETAIL OF OTHER PERSONNEL

SEC. 113A. [50 U.S.C. 3049] An officer or employee of the United States or member of the Armed Forces may be detailed to the staff of an element of the intelligence community funded through the National Intelligence Program from another element of the intelligence community or from another element of the United States Government on a non-reimbursable basis, as jointly agreed to by the heads of the receiving and detailing elements, for a period not to exceed three years. This section does not limit any other source of authority for reimbursable or non-reimbursable details. A non-reimbursable detail made under this section shall not be considered an augmentation of the appropriations of the receiving element of the intelligence community.

SEC. 113B. [50 U.S.C. 3049a] SPECIAL PAY AUTHORITY FOR SCIENCE, TECHNOLOGY, ENGINEERING, OR MATHEMATICS POSITIONS AND POSITIONS REQUIRING BANKING OR FINANCIAL SERVICES EXPERTISE.

(a) SPECIAL RATES OF PAY FOR POSITIONS REQUIRING EXPERTISE IN SCIENCE, TECHNOLOGY, ENGINEERING, OR MATHEMATICS OR IN BANKING OR FINANCIAL SERVICES.—

(1) IN GENERAL.—Notwithstanding part III of title 5, United States Code, the head of each element of the intelligence community may, for one or more categories of positions in such element that require expertise in science, technology, engineering, or mathematics or in banking or financial services (including expertise relating to critical financial infrastructure operations, capital markets, banking compliance programs, or international investments)—

(A) establish higher minimum rates of pay; and

(B) make corresponding increases in all rates of pay of the pay range for each grade or level, subject to subsection (b) or (c), as applicable.

(2) LIMITATION ON NUMBER OF RECIPIENTS.— For each element of the intelligence community, the number of individuals serving in a position in such element who receive a higher rate of pay established or increased under paragraph (1) may not, at any time during a given fiscal year, exceed 50 individuals or 5 percent of the total number of full-time equivalent positions authorized for such element for the

preceding fiscal year, whichever is greater.

(3) TREATMENT.— The special rate supplements resulting from the establishment of higher rates under paragraph (1) shall be basic pay for the same or similar purposes as those specified in section 5305(j) of title 5, United States Code.

(b) SPECIAL RATES OF PAY FOR CYBER POSITIONS.—

(1) IN GENERAL.—Notwithstanding subsection (c), the Director of the National Security Agency may establish a special rate of pay—

(A) not to exceed the rate of basic pay payable for level II of the Executive Schedule under section 5313 of title 5, United States Code, if the Director certifies to the Under Secretary of Defense for Intelligence and Security, in consultation with the Under Secretary of Defense for Personnel and Readiness, that the rate of pay is for positions that perform functions that execute the cyber mission of the Agency; or

(B) not to exceed the rate of basic pay payable for the Vice President of the United States under section 104 of title 3, United States Code, if the Director certifies to the Secretary of Defense, by name, individuals that have advanced skills and competencies and that perform critical functions that execute the cyber mission of the Agency.

(2) PAY LIMITATION.—Employees receiving a special rate under paragraph (1) shall be subject to an aggregate pay limitation that parallels the limitation established in section 5307 of title 5, United States Code, except that—

(A) any allowance, differential, bonus, award, or other similar cash payment in addition to basic pay that is authorized under title 10, United States Code, (or any other applicable law in addition to title 5 of such Code, excluding the Fair Labor Standards Act of 1938 (29 U.S.C. 201 et seq.)) shall also be counted as part of aggregate compensation; and

(B) aggregate compensation may not exceed the rate established for the Vice President of the United States under section 104 of title 3, United States Code.

(3) LIMITATION ON NUMBER OF RECIPIENTS.— The number of individuals who receive basic pay established under paragraph (1)(B) may not exceed 100 at any time.

(4) LIMITATION ON USE AS COMPARATIVE REFERENCE.— Notwithstanding any other provision of law, special rates of pay and the limitation established under paragraph (1)(B) may not be used as comparative references for the purpose of fixing the rates of basic pay or maximum pay limitations of qualified positions under section 1599f of title 10, United States Code, or section 2208 of the Homeland Security Act of 2002 (6 U.S.C. 658).

(c) MAXIMUM SPECIAL RATE OF PAY.— Except as provided in subsection (b), a minimum rate of pay established for a category of positions under subsection (a) may not exceed the maximum rate of basic pay (excluding any locality-based comparability payment under section 5304 of title 5, United States Code, or similar provision of law) for the position in that category of positions without the authority of subsection (a) by more than 30 percent, and no rate may be established under this section in excess of the rate of basic pay payable for level IV of the Executive Schedule under section 5315 of title 5, United States Code.

(d) NOTIFICATION OF REMOVAL FROM SPECIAL RATE OF PAY.—If the head of an element of the intelligence community removes a category of positions from coverage under a rate of pay authorized by subsection (a) or (b) after that rate of pay takes effect—

(1) the head of such element shall provide notice of the loss of coverage of the special rate of pay to each individual in such category; and

(2) the loss of coverage will take effect on the first day of the first pay period after the date of the notice.

(e) REVISION OF SPECIAL RATES OF PAY.— Subject to the limitations in this section, rates of pay established under this section by the head of an element of the intelligence community may be revised from time to time by the head of such element and the revisions have the force and effect of statute.

(f) REGULATIONS.— The head of each element of the intelligence community shall promulgate regulations to carry out this section with respect to such element, which shall, to the extent practicable, be comparable to the regulations promulgated to carry out section 5305 of title 5, United States Code.

(g) REPORTS.—

(1) REQUIREMENT FOR REPORTS.— Not later than 90 days after the date of the enactment of the Damon Paul Nelson and Matthew Young Pollard Intelligence Authorization Act for Fiscal Years 2018 and 2019, the head of each element of the intelligence community shall submit to the congressional intelligence committees a report on any rates of pay established for such element under this section.

(2) CONTENTS.—Each report required by paragraph (1) shall contain for each element of the intelligence community—

(A) a description of any rates of pay established under subsection (a) or (b); and

(B) the number of positions in such element that will be subject to such rates of pay.

SEC. 113C. [50 U.S.C. 3049b] ENABLING INTELLIGENCE COMMUNITY INTEGRATION.

(a) PROVISION OF GOODS OR SERVICES.— Subject to and in accordance with any guidance and requirements developed by the Director of National Intelligence, the head of an element of the intelligence community may provide goods or services to another element of the intelligence community without reimbursement or transfer of funds for hoteling initiatives for intelligence community employees and affiliates defined in any such guidance and requirements issued by the Director of National Intelligence.

(b) APPROVAL.— Prior to the provision of goods or services pursuant to subsection (a), the head of the element of the intelligence community providing such goods or services and the head of the element of the intelligence community receiving such goods or services shall approve such provision.

(c) HOTELING DEFINED.— In this section, the term "hoteling" means an alternative work arrangement in which employees of one element of the intelligence community are authorized flexible work arrangements to work part of the time at one or more alternative worksite locations, as appropriately authorized.

ANNUAL REPORT ON HIRING AND RETENTION OF MINORITY EMPLOYEES[5]

SEC. 114. [50 U.S.C. 3050]

(a) The Director of National Intelligence shall, on an annual basis, submit to Congress a report on the employment of covered persons within each element of the intelligence community for the preceding fiscal year and the preceding 5 fiscal years.

(b) Each such report shall include data, disaggregated by category of covered person and by element of the intelligence community, on the following:

(1) Of all individuals employed in the element during the fiscal year involved, the aggregate percentage of such individuals who are covered persons.

(2) Of all individuals employed in the element during the fiscal year involved at the levels referred to in subparagraphs (A) and (B), the percentage of covered persons employed at such levels:

(A) Positions at levels 1 through 15 of the General Schedule.

(B) Positions at levels above GS–15.

(3) Of all individuals hired by the element involved during the fiscal year involved, the percentage of such individuals who are covered persons.

(c) Each such report shall be submitted in unclassified form, but may contain a classified annex.

(d) Nothing in this section shall be construed as providing for the substitution of any similar report required under another provision of law.

(e) In this section the term "covered persons" means—

(1) racial and ethnic minorities;

(2) women; and

(3) individuals with disabilities.

[5] The heading for section 114, as amended by section 329(c)(2)(A) of Public Law 113–126 (as shown above), does not reflect the style as it appears in the enacted law. The enacted law for this element appears in all caps boldface type.

LIMITATION ON ESTABLISHMENT OR OPERATION OF DIPLOMATIC INTELLIGENCE SUPPORT CENTERS

SEC. 115. [50 U.S.C. 3052] (a) IN GENERAL.—(1) A diplomatic intelligence support center may not be established, operated, or maintained without the prior approval of the Director of National Intelligence.

(2) The Director may only approve the establishment, operation, or maintenance of a diplomatic intelligence support center if the Director determines that the establishment, operation, or maintenance of such center is required to provide necessary intelligence support in furtherance of the national security interests of the United States.

(b) PROHIBITION OF USE OF APPROPRIATIONS.— Amounts appropriated pursuant to authorizations by law for intelligence and intelligence-related activities may not be obligated or expended for the establishment, operation, or maintenance of a diplomatic intelligence support center that is not approved by the Director of National Intelligence.

(c) DEFINITIONS.—In this section:

(1) The term "diplomatic intelligence support center" means an entity to which employees of the various elements of the intelligence community (as defined in section 3(4)) are detailed for the purpose of providing analytical intelligence support that—

(A) consists of intelligence analyses on military or political matters and expertise to conduct limited assessments and dynamic taskings for a chief of mission; and

(B) is not intelligence support traditionally provided to a chief of mission by the Director of National Intelligence.

(2) The term "chief of mission" has the meaning given that term by section 102(3) of the Foreign Service Act of 1980 (22 U.S.C. 3902(3)), and includes ambassadors at large and ministers of diplomatic missions of the United States, or persons appointed to lead United States offices abroad designated by the Secretary of State as diplomatic in nature.

(d) TERMINATION.— This section shall cease to be effective on October 1, 2000.

TRAVEL ON ANY COMMON CARRIER FOR CERTAIN INTELLIGENCE COLLECTION PERSONNEL

SEC. 116. [50 U.S.C. 3053] (a) IN GENERAL.—Notwithstanding any other provision of law, the Director of National Intelligence may authorize travel on any common carrier when such travel, in the discretion of the Director—

(1) is consistent with intelligence community mission requirements, or

(2) is required for cover purposes, operational needs, or other exceptional circumstances necessary for the successful performance of an intelligence community mission.

(b) AUTHORIZED DELEGATION OF DUTY.— The Director of National Intelligence may only delegate the authority granted by this section to the Principal Deputy Director of National Intelligence, or with respect to employees of the Central Intelligence Agency, to the Director of the Central Intelligence Agency[6], who may delegate such authority to other appropriate officials of the Central Intelligence Agency.

[6] The amendment made by section 1072(a)(5) to strike "to the Deputy Director of Central Intelligence, or with respect to employees of the Central Intelligence Agencythe Director may delegate such authority to the Deputy Director for Operations" and insert "to the Principal Deputy Director of National Intelligence, or with respect to employees of the Central Intelligence Agency, to the Director of the Central Intelligence Agency" was executed to reflect the probable intent of Congress. The comma after "Central Intelligence Agency" in the striken matter does not appear.

POW/MIA ANALYTIC CAPABILITY

SEC. 117. [50 U.S.C. 3054] (a) REQUIREMENT.—(1) The Director of National Intelligence shall, in consultation with the Secretary of Defense, establish and maintain in the intelligence community an analytic capability with responsibility for intelligence in support of the activities of the United States relating to individuals who, after December

31, 1990, are unaccounted for United States personnel.

(2) The analytic capability maintained under paragraph (1) shall be known as the "POW/MIA analytic capability of the intelligence community".

(b) UNACCOUNTED FOR UNITED STATES PERSONNEL.—In this section, the term "unaccounted for United States personnel" means the following:

(1) Any missing person (as that term is defined in section 1513(1) of title 10, United States Code).

(2) Any United States national who was killed while engaged in activities on behalf of the United States and whose remains have not been repatriated to the United States.

ANNUAL REPORT ON FINANCIAL INTELLIGENCE ON TERRORIST ASSETS

SEC. 118. [50 U.S.C. 3055] (a) ANNUAL REPORT.—On an annual basis, the Secretary of the Treasury (acting through the head of the Office of Intelligence Support) shall submit a report to the appropriate congressional committees that fully informs the committees concerning operations against terrorist financial networks. Each such report shall include with respect to the preceding one-year period—

(1) the total number of asset seizures, designations, and other actions against individuals or entities found to have engaged in financial support of terrorism;

(2) the total number of physical searches of offices, residences, or financial records of individuals or entities suspected of having engaged in financial support for terrorist activity; and

(3) whether the financial intelligence information seized in these cases has been shared on a full and timely basis with the all departments, agencies, and other entities of the United States Government involved in intelligence activities participating in the Foreign Terrorist Asset Tracking Center.

(b) IMMEDIATE NOTIFICATION FOR EMERGENCY DESIGNATION.— In the case of a designation of an individual or entity, or the assets of an individual or entity, as having been found to have engaged in terrorist activities, the Secretary of the Treasury shall report such designation within 24 hours of such a designation to the appropriate congressional committees.

(c) SUBMITTAL DATE OF REPORTS TO CONGRESSIONAL INTELLIGENCE COMMITTEES.— In the case of the reports required to be submitted under subsection (a) to the congressional intelligence committees, the submittal dates for such reports shall be as provided in section 507.

(d) APPROPRIATE CONGRESSIONAL COMMITTEES DEFINED.—In this section, the term "appropriate congressional committees" means the following:

(1) The Permanent Select Committee on Intelligence, the Committee on Appropriations, the Committee on Armed Services, and the Committee on Financial Services of the House of Representatives.

(2) The Select Committee on Intelligence, the Committee on Appropriations, the Committee on Armed Services, and the Committee on Banking, Housing, and Urban Affairs of the Senate.

NATIONAL COUNTERTERRORISM CENTER

SEC. 119. [50 U.S.C. 3056] (a) ESTABLISHMENT OF CENTER.— There is within the Office of the Director of National Intelligence a National Counterterrorism Center.

(b) DIRECTOR OF NATIONAL COUNTERTERRORISM CENTER.—(1) There is a Director of the National Counterterrorism Center, who shall be the head of the National Counterterrorism Center, and who shall be appointed by the President, by and with the advice and consent of the Senate.

(2) The Director of the National Counterterrorism Center may not simultaneously serve in any other capacity in the executive branch.

(c) REPORTING.—(1) The Director of the National Counterterrorism Center shall report to the Director of National Intelligence with respect to matters described in paragraph (2) and the President with respect to matters described in paragraph (3).

(2) The matters described in this paragraph are as follows:

(A) The budget and programs of the National Counterterrorism Center.

(B) The activities of the Directorate of Intelligence of the National Counterterrorism Center under subsection (i).

(C) The conduct of intelligence operations implemented by other elements of the intelligence community; and

(3) The matters described in this paragraph are the planning and progress of joint counterterrorism operations (other than intelligence operations).

(d) PRIMARY MISSIONS.—The primary missions of the National Counterterrorism Center shall be as follows:

(1) To serve as the primary organization in the United States Government for analyzing and integrating all intelligence possessed or acquired by the United States Government pertaining to terrorism and counterterrorism, excepting intelligence pertaining exclusively to domestic terrorists and domestic counterterrorism.

(2) To conduct strategic operational planning for counterterrorism activities, integrating all instruments of national power, including diplomatic, financial, military, intelligence, homeland security, and law enforcement activities within and among agencies.

(3) To assign roles and responsibilities as part of its strategic operational planning duties to lead Departments or agencies, as appropriate, for counterterrorism activities that are consistent with applicable law and that support counterterrorism strategic operational plans, but shall not direct the execution of any resulting operations.

(4) To ensure that agencies, as appropriate, have access to and receive all-source intelligence support needed to execute their counterterrorism plans or perform independent, alternative analysis.

(5) To ensure that such agencies have access to and receive intelligence needed to accomplish their assigned activities.

(6) To serve as the central and shared knowledge bank on known and suspected terrorists and international terror groups, as well as their goals, strategies,

capabilities, and networks of contacts and support.

(e) DOMESTIC COUNTERTERRORISM INTELLIGENCE.—(1) The Center may, consistent with applicable law, the direction of the President, and the guidelines referred to in section 102A(b), receive intelligence pertaining exclusively to domestic counterterrorism from any Federal, State, or local government or other source necessary to fulfill its responsibilities and retain and disseminate such intelligence.

(2) Any agency authorized to conduct counterterrorism activities may request information from the Center to assist it in its responsibilities, consistent with applicable law and the guidelines referred to in section 102A(b).

(f) DUTIES AND RESPONSIBILITIES OF DIRECTOR.—(1) The Director of the National Counterterrorism Center shall—

(A) serve as the principal adviser to the Director of National Intelligence on intelligence operations relating to counterterrorism;

(B) provide strategic operational plans for the civilian and military counterterrorism efforts of the United States Government and for the effective integration of counterterrorism intelligence and operations across agency boundaries, both inside and outside the United States;

(C) advise the Director of National Intelligence on the extent to which the counterterrorism program recommendations and budget proposals of the departments, agencies, and elements of the United States Government conform to the priorities established by the President;

(D) disseminate terrorism information, including current terrorism threat analysis, to the President, the Vice President, the Secretaries of State, Defense, and Homeland Security, the Attorney General, the Director of the Central Intelligence Agency, and other officials of the executive branch as appropriate, and to the appropriate committees of Congress;

(E) support the Department of Justice and the Department of Homeland Security, and other appropriate agencies, in fulfillment of their responsibilities to disseminate terrorism information, consistent with applicable law, guidelines referred to in section 102A(b), Executive orders and other Presidential guidance, to State and local government officials, and other entities, and coordinate dissemination of terrorism information to foreign governments as approved by the Director of National Intelligence;

(F) develop a strategy for combining terrorist travel intelligence operations and law enforcement planning and operations into a cohesive effort to intercept terrorists, find terrorist travel facilitators, and constrain terrorist mobility;

(G) have primary responsibility within the United States Government for conducting net assessments of terrorist threats;

(H) consistent with priorities approved by the President, assist the Director of National Intelligence in establishing requirements for the intelligence community for the collection of terrorism information; and

(I) perform such other duties as the Director of National Intelligence may prescribe or are prescribed by law.

(2) Nothing in paragraph (1)(G) shall limit the authority of the departments and agencies of the United States to conduct net assessments.

(g) Limitation.— The Director of the National Counterterrorism Center may not direct the execution of counterterrorism operations.

(h) Resolution of Disputes.— The Director of National Intelligence shall resolve disagreements between the National Counterterrorism Center and the head of a department, agency, or element of the United States Government on designations, assignments, plans, or responsibilities under this section. The head of such a department, agency, or element may appeal the resolution of the disagreement by the Director of National Intelligence to the President.

(i) Directorate of Intelligence.— The Director of the National Counterterrorism Center shall establish and maintain within the National Counterterrorism Center a Directorate of Intelligence which shall have primary responsibility within the United States Government for analysis of terrorism and terrorist organizations (except for purely domestic terrorism and domestic terrorist organizations) from all sources of intelligence, whether collected inside or outside the United States.

(j) Directorate of Strategic Operational Planning.—(1) The Director of the National Counterterrorism Center shall establish and maintain within the National Counterterrorism Center a Directorate of Strategic Operational Planning which shall provide strategic operational plans for counterterrorism operations conducted by the United States Government.

(2) Strategic operational planning shall include the mission, objectives to be achieved, tasks to be performed, interagency coordination of operational activities, and the assignment of roles and responsibilities.

(3) The Director of the National Counterterrorism Center shall monitor the implementation of strategic operational plans, and shall obtain information from each element of the intelligence community, and from each other department, agency, or element of the United States Government relevant for monitoring the progress of such entity in implementing such plans.

NATIONAL COUNTERPROLIFERATION AND BIOSECURITY CENTER

Sec. 119A. [50 U.S.C. 3057] (a) Establishment.—(1) The President shall establish a National Counterproliferation and Biosecurity Center, taking into account all appropriate government tools to—

(A) prevent and halt the proliferation of weapons of mass destruction, their delivery systems, and related materials and technologies; and

(B) lead integration and mission management of all intelligence activities pertaining to biosecurity and foreign biological threats.

(2) The head of the National Counterproliferation and Biosecurity Center shall be the Director of the National Counterproliferation and Biosecurity Center, who shall be appointed by the Director of National Intelligence.

(3) The National Counterproliferation and Biosecurity Center shall be located within the Office of the Director of National Intelligence.

(4) The Director of the National Counterproliferation and Biosecurity Center shall serve as the principal coordinator for the intelligence community, and as the principal advisor to the Director of National Intelligence, with respect to counterproliferation, biosecurity, and foreign biological threats.

(b) Missions and Objectives.—

(1) Counterproliferation.—In establishing the National Counterproliferation and Biosecurity Center, the President shall address the following missions and objectives to prevent and halt the proliferation of weapons of mass destruction, their delivery systems, and related materials and technologies:

(A) Establishing a primary organization within the United States Government for integrating all intelligence possessed or acquired by the United States pertaining to proliferation.

(B) Ensuring that appropriate agencies have full access to and receive all-source intelligence support needed to execute their counterproliferation plans or activities, and perform independent, alternative analyses.

(C) Coordinating the establishment of a central repository on known and suspected proliferation activities, including the goals, strategies, capabilities, networks, and any individuals, groups, or entities engaged in proliferation.

(D) Overseeing the dissemination of proliferation information, including proliferation threats and analyses, to the President, to the appropriate departments and agencies, and to the appropriate committees of Congress.

(E) Conducting and coordinating net assessments and warnings about the proliferation of weapons of mass destruction, their delivery systems, and related materials and technologies.

(F) Coordinating counterproliferation plans and activities of the various departments and agencies of the United States Government to prevent and halt the proliferation of weapons of mass destruction, their delivery systems, and related materials and technologies.

(G) Coordinating and advancing strategic operational counterproliferation planning for the United States Government to prevent and halt the proliferation of weapons of mass destruction, their delivery systems, and related materials and technologies.

(2) Biosecurity.—In establishing the National Counterproliferation and Biosecurity Center, the President shall address the following missions and objectives to ensure that the Center serves as the lead for the intelligence community for the integration, mission management, and coordination of intelligence activities pertaining to biosecurity and foreign biological threats, regardless of origin:

(A) Ensuring that the elements of the intelligence community provide timely and effective warnings to the President and the Director of National Intelligence regarding emerging foreign biological threats, including diseases with pandemic potential.

(B) Overseeing and coordinating the collection of intelligence on biosecurity and foreign biological threats in support of the intelligence needs of the Federal departments and agencies responsible for public health, including by conveying collection priorities to elements of the intelligence community.

(C) Overseeing and coordinating the analysis of intelligence on biosecurity and foreign biological threats in support of the intelligence needs of Federal departments and agencies responsible for public health, including by providing analytic priorities to elements of the intelligence community and by coordinating net assessments.

(D) Coordinating intelligence support to the Federal departments and agencies responsible for public health on matters relating to biosecurity and foreign biological threats, including by ensuring that intelligence pertaining to biosecurity and foreign biological threats is disseminated among appropriately cleared personnel of such departments and agencies.

(E) Coordinating with the Federal departments and agencies responsible for public health to encourage information sharing with the intelligence community.

(F) Identifying gaps in the capabilities and authorities of the intelligence community regarding biosecurity and countering foreign biological threats and providing to the Director of National Intelligence recommended solutions for such gaps, including by encouraging research and development of new capabilities[7] to counter foreign biological threats.

[7] Section 6502(2)(B)(v) of division F of Public Law 118–159 provides for an amendment to insert "and authorities" after "capabilities" without referencing the occurrence of the word "capabilities" to carry out such amendment. The amendment was carried out to the first occurrence of such word to reflect the probable intent of Congress.

(G) Enhancing coordination between elements of the intelligence community and private sector entities on information relevant to biosecurity, biotechnology, and foreign biological threats, and coordinating such information with relevant Federal departments and agencies, as applicable.

(c) NATIONAL SECURITY WAIVER.— The President may waive the requirements of this section, and any parts thereof, if the President determines that such requirements do not materially improve the ability of the United States Government to prevent and halt the proliferation of weapons of mass destruction, their delivery systems, and related materials and technologies. Such waiver shall be made in writing to Congress and shall include a description of how the missions and objectives in subsection (b) are being met.

(d) REPORT TO CONGRESS.—(1) Not later than nine months after the implementation of this Act, the President shall submit to Congress, in classified form if necessary, the findings and recommendations of the President's Commission on Weapons of Mass Destruction established by Executive Order in February 2004, together with the views of the President regarding the establishment of a National Counterproliferation and Biosecurity Center.

(2) If the President decides not to exercise the waiver authority granted by subsection (c), the President shall submit to Congress from time to time updates and plans regarding the establishment of a National Counterproliferation and Biosecurity

Center.

(e) Sense of Congress.— It is the sense of Congress that a central feature of counterproliferation activities, consistent with the President's Proliferation Security Initiative, should include the physical interdiction, by air, sea, or land, of weapons of mass destruction, their delivery systems, and related materials and technologies, and enhanced law enforcement activities to identify and disrupt proliferation networks, activities, organizations, and persons.

NATIONAL INTELLIGENCE CENTERS

Sec. 119B. [50 U.S.C. 3058] (a) Authority To Establish.— The Director of National Intelligence may establish one or more national intelligence centers to address intelligence priorities, including, but not limited to, regional issues.

(b) Resources of Directors of Centers.—(1) The Director of National Intelligence shall ensure that the head of each national intelligence center under subsection (a) has appropriate authority, direction, and control of such center, and of the personnel assigned to such center, to carry out the assigned mission of such center.

(2) The Director of National Intelligence shall ensure that each national intelligence center has appropriate personnel to accomplish effectively the mission of such center.

(c) Information Sharing.— The Director of National Intelligence shall, to the extent appropriate and practicable, ensure that each national intelligence center under subsection (a) and the other elements of the intelligence community share information in order to facilitate the mission of such center.

(d) Mission of Centers.—Pursuant to the direction of the Director of National Intelligence, each national intelligence center under subsection (a) may, in the area of intelligence responsibility assigned to such center—

(1) have primary responsibility for providing all-source analysis of intelligence based upon intelligence gathered both domestically and abroad;

(2) have primary responsibility for identifying and proposing to the Director of National Intelligence intelligence collection and analysis and production requirements; and

(3) perform such other duties as the Director of National Intelligence shall specify.

(e) Review and Modification of Centers.—The Director of National Intelligence shall determine on a regular basis whether—

(1) the area of intelligence responsibility assigned to each national intelligence center under subsection (a) continues to meet appropriate intelligence priorities; and

(2) the staffing and management of such center remains appropriate for the accomplishment of the mission of such center.

(f) Termination.— The Director of National Intelligence may terminate any national intelligence center under subsection (a).

(g) Separate Budget Account.— The Director of National Intelligence shall, as appropriate, include in the National Intelligence Program budget a separate line item for each national intelligence center under subsection (a).

SEC. 119C. [50 U.S.C. 3059] FOREIGN MALIGN INFLUENCE CENTER.

(a) ESTABLISHMENT.— There is within the Office of the Director of National Intelligence a Foreign Malign Influence Center (in this section referred to as the "Center").

(b) FUNCTIONS AND COMPOSITION.—The Center shall—

(1) be comprised of analysts from all elements of the intelligence community, including elements with diplomatic and law enforcement functions;

(2) have access to all intelligence and other reporting possessed or acquired by the United States Government pertaining to foreign malign influence;

(3) serve as the primary organization in the United States Government for analyzing and integrating all intelligence possessed or acquired by the United States Government pertaining to foreign malign influence; and

(4) provide to employees and officers of the Federal Government in policy-making positions and Congress comprehensive assessments, and indications and warnings, of foreign malign influence.

(c) DIRECTOR.—

(1) APPOINTMENT.— There is a Director of the Center, who shall be the head of the Center, and who shall be appointed by the Director of National Intelligence.

(2) ROLE.—The Director of the Center shall—

(A) report directly to the Director of National Intelligence;

(B) carry out the functions under subsection (b); and

(C) at the request of the President or the Director of National Intelligence, develop and provide recommendations for potential responses by the United States to foreign malign influence.

(d) ANNUAL REPORTS.—

(1) IN GENERAL.— In addition to the matters submitted pursuant to subsection (b)(4), at the direction of the Director of National Intelligence, but not less than once each year, the Director of the Center shall submit to the congressional intelligence committees, the Committee on Foreign Affairs of the House of Representatives, and the Committee on Foreign Relations of the Senate a report on foreign malign influence.

(2) MATTERS INCLUDED.—Each report under paragraph (1) shall include, with respect to the period covered by the report, a discussion of the following:

(A) The most significant activities of the Center.

(B) Any recommendations the Director determines necessary for legislative or other actions to improve the ability of the Center to carry out its functions, including recommendations regarding the protection of privacy and civil liberties.

(e) DEFINITIONS.—In this section:

(1) COVERED FOREIGN COUNTRY.—The term "covered foreign country" means the following:

(A) The Russian Federation.

(B) The Islamic Republic of Iran.

(C) The Democratic People's Republic of Korea.

(D) The People's Republic of China.

(E) Any other foreign country that the Director of the Center determines appropriate for purposes of this section.

(2) FOREIGN MALIGN INFLUENCE.—The term "foreign malign influence" means any hostile effort undertaken by, at the direction of, or on behalf of or with the substantial support of, the government of a covered foreign country with the objective of influencing, through overt or covert means—

(A) the political, military, economic, or other policies or activities of the United States Government or State or local governments, including any election within the United States; or

(B) the public opinion within the United States.

SEC. 120. [50 U.S.C. 3060] CLIMATE SECURITY ADVISORY COUNCIL.

(a) ESTABLISHMENT.—The Director of National Intelligence shall establish a Climate Security Advisory Council for the purpose of—

(1) assisting intelligence analysts of various elements of the intelligence community with respect to analysis of climate security and its impact on the areas of focus of such analysts;

(2) facilitating coordination between the elements of the intelligence community and elements of the Federal Government that are not elements of the intelligence community in collecting data on, and conducting analysis of, climate change and climate security; and

(3) ensuring that the intelligence community is adequately prioritizing climate change in carrying out its activities.

(b) COMPOSITION OF COUNCIL.—

(1) MEMBERS.—The Council shall be composed of the following individuals appointed by the Director of National Intelligence:

(A) An appropriate official from the National Intelligence Council, who shall chair the Council.

(B) The lead official with respect to climate and environmental security analysis from—

(i) the Central Intelligence Agency;

(ii) the Bureau of Intelligence and Research of the Department of State;

(iii) the National Geospatial-Intelligence Agency;

(iv) the Office of Intelligence and Counterintelligence of the Department of Energy;

(v) the Office of the Under Secretary of Defense for Intelligence and Security; and

(vi) the Defense Intelligence Agency.

(C) Three appropriate officials from elements of the Federal Government that are not elements of the intelligence community that are responsible for—

(i) providing decision makers with a predictive understanding of the climate;

(ii) making observations of our Earth system that can be used by the public, policymakers, and to support strategic decisions; or

(iii) coordinating Federal research and investments in understanding the forces shaping the global environment, both human and natural, and their impacts on society.

(D) Any other officials as the Director of National Intelligence or the chair of the Council may determine appropriate.

(2) Responsibilities of chair.—The chair of the Council shall have responsibility for—

(A) identifying agencies to supply individuals from elements of the Federal Government that are not elements of the intelligence community;

(B) securing the permission of the relevant agency heads for the participation of such individuals on the Council; and

(C) any other duties that the Director of National Intelligence may direct.

(c) Duties and Responsibilities of Council.—The Council shall carry out the following duties and responsibilities:

(1) To meet at least quarterly to—

(A) exchange appropriate data between elements of the intelligence community and elements of the Federal Government that are not elements of the intelligence community;

(B) discuss processes for the routine exchange of such data and implementation of such processes; and

(C) prepare summaries of the business conducted at each meeting.

(2) To assess and determine best practices with respect to the analysis of climate security, including identifying publicly available information and intelligence acquired through clandestine means that enables such analysis.

(3) To assess and identify best practices with respect to prior efforts of the intelligence community to analyze climate security.

(4) To assess and describe best practices for identifying and disseminating climate intelligence indications and warnings.

(5) To recommend methods of incorporating analysis of climate security and

the best practices identified under paragraphs (2) through (4) into existing analytic training programs.

(6) To consult, as appropriate, with other elements of the intelligence community that conduct analysis of climate change or climate security and elements of the Federal Government that are not elements of the intelligence community that conduct analysis of climate change or climate security, for the purpose of sharing information about ongoing efforts and avoiding duplication of existing efforts.

(7) To work with elements of the intelligence community that conduct analysis of climate change or climate security and elements of the Federal Government that are not elements of the intelligence community that conduct analysis of climate change or climate security—

(A) to exchange appropriate data between such elements, establish processes, procedures and practices for the routine exchange of such data, discuss the implementation of such processes; and

(B) to enable and facilitate the sharing of findings and analysis between such elements.

(8) To assess whether the elements of the intelligence community that conduct analysis of climate change or climate security may inform the research direction of academic work and the sponsored work of the United States Government.

(9) At the discretion of the chair of the Council, to convene conferences of analysts and nonintelligence community personnel working on climate change or climate security on subjects that the chair shall direct.

(d) Annual Report.—

(1) Requirement.— Not later than January 31, 2021, and not less frequently than annually thereafter, the chair of the Council shall submit, on behalf of the Council, to the congressional intelligence committees a report describing the activities of the Council as described in subsection (c) during the year preceding the year during which the report is submitted.

(2) Matters included.—Each report under paragraph (1) shall include a description of any obstacles or gaps relating to—

(A) the Council fulfilling its duties and responsibilities under subsection (c); or

(B) the responsiveness of the intelligence community to the climate security needs and priorities of the policymaking elements of the Federal Government.

(e) Sunset.— The Council shall terminate on December 31, 2024.

(f) Definitions.—In this section:

(1) Climate security.—The term "climate security" means the effects of climate change on the following:

(A) The national security of the United States, including national security infrastructure.

(B) Subnational, national, and regional political stability.

(C) The security of allies and partners of the United States.

(D) Ongoing or potential political violence, including unrest, rioting, guerrilla warfare, insurgency, terrorism, rebellion, revolution, civil war, and interstate war.

(2) CLIMATE INTELLIGENCE INDICATIONS AND WARNINGS.—The term "climate intelligence indications and warnings" means developments relating to climate security with the potential to—

(A) imminently and substantially alter the political stability or degree of human security in a country or region; or

(B) imminently and substantially threaten—

(i) the national security of the United States;

(ii) the military, political, or economic interests of allies and partners of the United States; or

(iii) citizens of the United States abroad.

SEC. 121. [50 U.S.C. 3061] COUNTERINTELLIGENCE AND NATIONAL SECURITY PROTECTIONS FOR INTELLIGENCE COMMUNITY GRANT FUNDING.

(a) DISCLOSURE AS CONDITION FOR RECEIPT OF GRANT.— The head of an element of the intelligence community may not award a grant to a person or entity unless the person or entity has certified to the head of the element that the person or entity has disclosed to the head of the element any material financial or material in-kind support that the person or entity knows, or should have known, derives from the People's Republic of China, the Russian Federation, the Islamic Republic of Iran, the Democratic People's Republic of Korea, or the Republic of Cuba, during the 5-year period ending on the date of the person or entity's application for the grant.

(b) PROCESS FOR REVIEW OF GRANT APPLICANTS PRIOR TO AWARD.—

(1) IN GENERAL.— The head of an element of the intelligence community may not award a grant to a person or entity who submitted a certification under subsection (a) until such certification is received by the head of an element of the intelligence community and submitted to the Director of National Intelligence pursuant to the process set forth in paragraph (2).

(2) PROCESS.—

(A) IN GENERAL.— The Director of National Intelligence, in coordination with such heads of elements of the intelligence community as the Director considers appropriate, shall establish a process to review the awarding of a grant to an applicant who submitted a certification under subsection (a).

(B) ELEMENTS.—The process established under subparagraph (A) shall include the following:

(i) The immediate transmission of a copy of each applicant's certification made under subsection (a) to the Director of National Intelligence.

(ii) The review of the certification and any accompanying disclosures submitted under subsection (a) as soon as practicable.

(iii) Authorization for the heads of the elements of the intelligence community to take such actions as may be necessary, including denial or revocation of a grant, to ensure a grant does not pose an unacceptable risk of—

(I) misappropriation of United States intellectual property, research and development, and innovation efforts; or

(II) other counterintelligence threats.

(c) Annual Report Required.—Not later than 1 year after the date of the enactment of the Intelligence Authorization Act for Fiscal Year 2023 and not less frequently than once each year thereafter, the Director of National Intelligence shall submit to the congressional intelligence committees an annual report identifying the following for the 1-year period covered by the report:

(1) The number of applications for grants received by each element of the intelligence community.

(2) The number of such applications that were reviewed using the process established under subsection (b)(2), disaggregated by element of the intelligence community.

(3) The number of such applications that were denied and the number of grants that were revoked, pursuant to the process established under subsection (b)(2), disaggregated by element of the intelligence community.

SEC. 122. [50 U.S.C. 3062] Office of Engagement.

(a) Establishment .—There is within the Office of the Director of National Intelligence an Office of Engagement (in this section referred to as the "Office").

(b) Head; staff.—

(1) Head.— The Director of National Intelligence shall appoint as head of the Office an individual with requisite experience in matters relating to the duties of the Office, as determined by the Director of National Intelligence. Such head of the Office shall report directly to the Director of National Intelligence.

(2) Staff.— To assist the head of the Office in fulfilling the duties of the Office, the head shall employ full-time equivalent staff in such number, and with such requisite expertise in matters relating to such duties, as may be determined by the head.

(c) Duties.—The duties of the Office shall be as follows:

(1) To ensure coordination across the elements of the intelligence community efforts regarding outreach, relationship development, and associated knowledge and relationship management, with covered entities, consistent with the protection of intelligence sources and methods.

(2) To assist in sharing best practices regarding such efforts among the elements of the intelligence community.

(3) To establish and implement metrics to assess the effectiveness of such efforts.

(d) Covered entity defined.— In this section, the term "covered entity" means an entity that is not an entity of the United States Government, including private sector companies, institutions of higher education, trade associations, think tanks, laboratories, international organizations, and foreign partners and allies.

TITLE II—THE DEPARTMENT OF DEFENSE

SEC. 201. [50 U.S.C. 3005] DEPARTMENT OF DEFENSE.

Except to the extent inconsistent with the provisions of this Act or other provisions of law, the provisions of title 5, United States Code, shall be applicable to the Department of Defense.

[Sections 202–204 were repealed by section 307 of Public Law 87–651 (Act of September 7, 1962, 76 Stat. 526).]

DEPARTMENT OF THE ARMY

SEC. 205. (a) All laws, orders, regulations, and other actions relating to the Department of War or to any officer or activity whose title is changed under this section shall, insofar as they are not inconsistent with the provisions of this Act, be deemed to relate to the Department of the Army within the Department of Defense or to such officer or activity designated by his or its new title.

(b) [50 U.S.C. 3004] the term "Department of the Army" as used in this Act shall be construed to mean the Department of the Army at the seat of government and all field headquarters, forces, reserve components, installations, activities, and functions under the control or supervision of the Department of the Army.

DEPARTMENT OF THE NAVY

SEC. 206. [50 U.S.C. 3004] The term "Department of the Navy" as used in this Act shall be construed to mean the Department of the Navy at the seat of government; the headquarters, United States Marine Corps; the entire operating forces of the United States Navy, including naval aviation, and of the United States Marine Corps, including the reserve components of such forces; all field activities, headquarters, forces, bases, installations, activities and functions under the control or supervision of the Department of the Navy; and the United States Coast Guard when operating as a part of the Navy pursuant to law.

DEPARTMENT OF THE AIR FORCE

SEC. 207. [50 U.S.C. 3004] The term "Department of the Air Force" as used in this Act shall be construed to mean the Department of the Air Force at the seat of government and all field headquarters, forces, reserve components, installations, activities, and functions under the control or supervision of the Department of the Air Force.

TITLE III—MISCELLANEOUS

NATIONAL SECURITY AGENCY VOLUNTARY SEPARATION

SEC. 301. [50 U.S.C. 3071] (a) SHORT TITLE.— This section may be cited as the "National Security Agency Voluntary Separation Act".

(b) DEFINITIONS.—For purposes of this section—

(1) the term "Director" means the Director of the National Security Agency; and

(2) the term "employee" means an employee of the National Security Agency, serving under an appointment without time limitation, who has been currently employed by the National Security Agency for a continuous period of at least 12 months prior to the effective date of the program established under subsection (c), except that such term does not include—

(A) a reemployed annuitant under subchapter III of chapter 83 or chapter 84 of title 5, United States Code, or another retirement system for employees of the Government; or

(B) an employee having a disability on the basis of which such employee is or would be eligible for disability retirement under any of the retirement systems referred to in subparagraph (A).

(c) ESTABLISHMENT OF PROGRAM.— Notwithstanding any other provision of law, the Director, in his sole discretion, may establish a program under which employees may, after October 1, 2000, be eligible for early retirement, offered separation pay to separate from service voluntarily, or both.

(d) EARLY RETIREMENT.—An employee who—

(1) is at least 50 years of age and has completed 20 years of service; or

(2) has at least 25 years of service,

may, pursuant to regulations promulgated under this section, apply and be retired from the National Security Agency and receive benefits in accordance with chapter 83 or 84 of title 5, United States Code, if the employee has not less than 10 years of service with the National Security Agency.

(e) AMOUNT OF SEPARATION PAY AND TREATMENT FOR OTHER PURPOSES.—

(1) AMOUNT.—Separation pay shall be paid in a lump sum and shall be equal to the lesser of—

(A) an amount equal to the amount the employee would be entitled to receive under section 5595(c) of title 5, United States Code, if the employee were entitled to payment under such section; or

(B) $25,000.

(2) TREATMENT.—Separation pay shall not—

(A) be a basis for payment, and shall not be included in the computation, of any other type of Government benefit; and

(B) be taken into account for the purpose of determining the amount of any severance pay to which an individual may be entitled under section 5595 of title 5, United States Code, based on any other separation.

(f) REEMPLOYMENT RESTRICTIONS.— An employee who receives separation pay under such program may not be reemployed by the National Security Agency for the 12-month period beginning on the effective date of the employee's separation. An employee who receives separation pay under this section on the basis of a separation occurring on or after the date of the enactment of the Federal Workforce Restructuring Act of 1994 (Public Law 103–236; 108 Stat. 111) and accepts employment with the Government of the United States within 5 years after the date of the separation on which payment of the separation pay is based shall be required to repay the entire amount of the separation pay to the National Security Agency. If the employment is with an Executive agency (as defined by section 105 of title 5, United States Code), the Director of the Office of Personnel Management may, at the request of the head of the agency, waive the repayment if the individual involved possesses unique abilities and is the only qualified applicant available for the position. If the employment is with an entity in the legislative branch, the head of the entity or the appointing official may waive the repayment if the individual involved possesses unique abilities and is the only qualified applicant available for the position. If the employment is with the judicial branch, the Director of the Administrative Office of the United States Courts may waive the repayment if the individual involved possesses unique abilities and is the only qualified applicant available for the position.

(g) Bar on Certain Employment.—

(1) Bar.—An employee may not be separated from service under this section unless the employee agrees that the employee will not—

(A) act as agent or attorney for, or otherwise represent, any other person (except the United States) in any formal or informal appearance before, or, with the intent to influence, make any oral or written communication on behalf of any other person (except the United States) to the National Security Agency; or

(B) participate in any manner in the award, modification, or extension of any contract for property or services with the National Security Agency,

during the 12-month period beginning on the effective date of the employee's separation from service.

(2) Penalty.— An employee who violates an agreement under this subsection shall be liable to the United States in the amount of the separation pay paid to the employee pursuant to this section multiplied by the proportion of the 12-month period during which the employee was in violation of the agreement.

(h) Limitations.—Under this program, early retirement and separation pay may be offered only—

(1) with the prior approval of the Director;

(2) for the period specified by the Director; and

(3) to employees within such occupational groups or geographic locations, or subject to such other similar limitations or conditions, as the Director may require.

(i) Regulations.— Before an employee may be eligible for early retirement, separation pay, or both, under this section, the Director shall prescribe such regulations as may be necessary to carry out this section.

(j) Notification of Exercise of Authority.— The Director may[8] not make an offer of early retirement, separation pay, or both, pursuant to this section until 15 days after submitting to the congressional intelligence committees a report describing the occupational groups or geographic locations, or other similar limitations or conditions, required by the Director under subsection (h), and including the proposed regulations issued pursuant to subsection (i).

[8] Section 941(b)(1) of the Intelligence Authorization Act for Fiscal Year 2003 (P.L. 107–306; 116 Stat. 2431) amended this subsection by striking ```Reporting Require-ments.—' and all that follows through `The Director may' and inserting `Notification of Exercise of Authority.—The Director may'''. There was no hyphen in law within the word ``Requirements''. The amendment has been executed to reflect the probable intent of Congress

(k) Remittance of Funds.— In addition to any other payment that is required to be made under subchapter III of chapter 83 or chapter 84 of title 5, United States Code, the National Security Agency shall remit to the Office of Personnel Management for deposit in the Treasury of the United States to the credit of the Civil Service Retirement and Disability Fund, an amount equal to 15 percent of the final basic pay of each employee to whom a voluntary separation payment has been or is to be paid under this section. The remittance required by this subsection shall be in lieu of any remittance required by section 4(a) of the Federal Workforce Restructuring Act of 1994 (5 U.S.C. 8331 note).

AUTHORITY OF FEDERAL BUREAU OF INVESTIGATION TO AWARD PERSONAL SERVICES CONTRACTS

Sec. 302. [50 U.S.C. 3072] (a) In General.— The Director of the Federal Bureau of Investigation may enter into personal services contracts if the personal services to be provided under such contracts directly support the intelligence or counterintelligence missions of the Federal Bureau of Investigation.

(b) Inapplicability of Certain Requirements.— Contracts under subsection (a) shall not be subject to the annuity offset requirements of sections 8344 and 8468 of title 5, United States Code, the requirements of section 3109 of title 5, United States Code, or any law or regulation requiring competitive contracting.

(c) Contract To Be Appropriate Means of Securing Services.— The Chief Contracting Officer of the Federal Bureau of Investigation shall ensure that each personal services contract entered into by the Director under this section is the appropriate means of securing the services to be provided under such contract.''.

ADVISORY COMMITTEES AND PERSONNEL

Sec. 303. [50 U.S.C. 3073] (a) The Director of the Office of Defense Mobilization, the Director of National Intelligence, and the National Security Council, acting through its Executive Secretary, are authorized to appoint such advisory committees and to employ, consistent with other provisions of this Act, such part-time advisory personnel as they may deem necessary in carrying out their respective functions and the functions of agencies under their control. Persons holding other offices or positions under the United States for which they receive compensation, while serving as members of such committees, shall receive no additional compensation for such service. Retired members of the uniformed services employed by the Director of National Intelligence who hold no other office or position under the United States for which they receive compensation, other members of such committees and other part-time advisory personnel so employed may serve without compensation or may receive compensation at a daily rate not to exceed the daily equivalent of the rate of pay in effect for grade GS–18 of the General Schedule established by section 5332 of title 5, United States Code, as determined by the appointing authority.

(b) Service of an individual as a member of any such advisory committee, or in any other part-time capacity for a department or agency hereunder, shall not be considered as service bringing such individual within the provisions of section 203, 205, or 207, of title 18, United States Code, unless the act of such individual, which by such section is made unlawful when performed by an individual referred to in such section, is with respect to any particular matter which directly involves a department or agency which such person is advising or in which such department or agency is directly interested.

SEC. 304. [50 U.S.C. 3073a] REQUIREMENTS FOR CERTAIN EMPLOYMENT ACTIVITIES BY FORMER INTELLIGENCE OFFICERS AND EMPLOYEES.

(a) Post-employment Restrictions.—

(1) Covered post-service position.—

(A) Permanent restriction.— Except as provided by paragraph (2)(A), an employee of an element of the intelligence community who occupies a covered intelligence position may not occupy a covered post-service position for a designated prohibited foreign country following the date on which the employee ceases to occupy a covered intelligence position.

(B) Temporary restriction.— Except as provided by paragraph (2)(A), an employee of an element of the intelligence community who occupies a covered intelligence position may not occupy a covered post-service position during the 30-month period following the date on which the employee ceases to occupy a covered intelligence position.

(2) Waiver.—

(A) Authority to grant waivers.—The applicable head of an intelligence community element may waive a restriction in paragraph (1) with respect to an employee or former employee who is subject to that restriction only after—

(i) the employee or former employee submits to the applicable head of the intelligence community element a written application for such waiver in such form and manner as the applicable head of the intelligence community element determines appropriate; and

(ii) the applicable head of the element of the intelligence community determines that granting such waiver will not harm the national security interests of the United States.

(B) Period of waiver.— A waiver issued under subparagraph (A) shall apply for a period not exceeding 5 years. The applicable head of the intelligence community element may renew such a waiver.

(C) Revocation.— The applicable head of the intelligence community element may revoke a waiver issued under subparagraph (A) to an employee or former employee, effective on the date that is 60 days after the date on which the applicable head of the intelligence community element provides the employee or former employee written notice of such revocation.

(D) Tolling.— The 30-month restriction in paragraph (1)(B) shall be tolled for an employee or former employee during the period beginning on the date on which a waiver is issued under subparagraph (A) and ending on the date on which the waiver expires or on the effective date of a revocation under subparagraph (C), as the case may be.

(E) REPORTING TO CONGRESS.—On a quarterly basis, the head of each element of the intelligence community shall submit to the congressional intelligence committees and the congressional defense committees for Department of Defense elements of the intelligence community, a written notification of each waiver or revocation that shall include the following:

(i) With respect to a waiver issued to an employee or former employee—

(I) the covered intelligence position held or formerly held by the employee or former employee; and

(II) a brief description of the covered post-service employment, including the employer and the recipient of the representation, advice, or services.

(ii) With respect to a revocation of a waiver issued to an employee or former employee—

(I) the details of the waiver, including any renewals of such waiver, and the dates of such waiver and renewals; and

(II) the specific reasons why the applicable head of the intelligence community element determined that such revocation is warranted.

(b) COVERED POST-SERVICE EMPLOYMENT REPORTING.—

(1) REQUIREMENT.—During the period described in paragraph (2), an employee who ceases to occupy a covered intelligence position shall—

(A) report covered post-service employment to the head of the element of the intelligence community that employed such employee in such covered intelligence position upon accepting such covered post-service employment; and

(B) annually (or more frequently if the head of such element considers it appropriate) report covered post-service employment to the head of such element.

(2) PERIOD DESCRIBED.— The period described in this paragraph is the period beginning on the date on which an employee ceases to occupy a covered intelligence position.

(3) REGULATIONS.— The head of each element of the intelligence community shall issue regulations requiring, as a condition of employment, each employee of such element occupying a covered intelligence position to sign a written agreement requiring the regular reporting of covered post-service employment to the head of such element pursuant to paragraph (1).

(c) PENALTIES.—

(1) CRIMINAL PENALTIES.— A former employee who knowingly and willfully violates subsection (a) or who knowingly and willfully fails to make a required

report under subsection (b) shall be fined under title 18, United States Code, or imprisoned for not more than 5 years, or both. Each report under subsection (b) shall be subject to section 1001 of title 18, United States Code.

(2) SECURITY CLEARANCES.— The head of an element of the intelligence community shall revoke the security clearance of a former employee if the former employee knowingly and willfully fails to make a required report under subsection (b) or knowingly and willfully makes a false report under such subsection.

(d) PROVISION OF INFORMATION.—

(1) TRAINING.— The head of each element of the intelligence community shall regularly provide training on the restrictions under subsection (a) and[9] the reporting requirements under subsection (b) to employees of that element who occupy a covered intelligence position.

[9] Section 7304(1) of Div. G. of P.L. 118-31 provides for an amendment to insert "the restrictions under subsection (a) and" before "the report requirements". However it should have referenced "the reporting requirements" instead. The amendment was carried out due to the probable intent of Congress.

(2) WRITTEN NOTICE ABOUT REPORTING REQUIREMENTS.— The head of each element of the intelligence community shall provide written notice of the reporting requirements under subsection (b) to an employee when the employee occupies a covered intelligence position.

(3) WRITTEN NOTICE ABOUT RESTRICTIONS.—The head of each element of the intelligence community shall provide written notice of the restrictions under subsection (a) to any person who may be subject to such restrictions on or after the date of enactment of the Intelligence Authorization Act for Fiscal Year 2023—

(A) when the head of the element determines that such person may become subject to such covered intelligence position restrictions; and

(B) when the person occupies a covered intelligence position.

(4) WRITTEN ADVISORY OPINIONS.— Upon request from a current employee who occupies a covered intelligence position or a former employee who previously occupied a covered intelligence position, the applicable head of the element of the intelligence community concerned may provide a written advisory opinion to such current or former employee regarding whether a proposed employment, representation, or provision of advice or services constitutes covered post-service employment as defined in subsection (g).

(e) ANNUAL REPORTS.—

(1) REQUIREMENT.— Not later than March 31 of each year, the Director of National Intelligence shall submit to the congressional intelligence committees a report on covered post-service employment occurring during the year covered by the report.

(2) ELEMENTS.—Each report under paragraph (1) shall include the following:

(A) The number of former employees who occupy a covered post-service position, broken down by—

(i) the name of the employer;

(ii) the foreign government, including by the specific foreign individual, agency, or entity, for whom the covered post-service employment is being performed; and

(iii) the nature of the services provided as part of the covered post-service employment.

(B) A certification by the Director that—

(i) each element of the intelligence community maintains adequate systems and processes for ensuring that former employees are submitting reports required under subsection (b);

(ii) to the knowledge of the heads of the elements of the intelligence community, all former employees who occupy a covered post-service position are in compliance with this section;

(iii) the services provided by former employees who occupy a covered post-service position do not—

(I) pose a current or future threat to the national security of the United States; or

(II) pose a counterintelligence risk; and

(iv) the Director and the heads of such elements are not aware of any credible information or reporting that any former employee who occupies a covered post-service position has engaged in activities that violate Federal law, infringe upon the privacy rights of United States persons, or constitute abuses of human rights.

(3) Form.— Each report under paragraph (1) shall be submitted in unclassified form, but may include a classified annex.

(f) Notification.—In addition to the annual reports under subsection (e), if a head of an element of the intelligence community determines that the services provided by a former employee who occupies a covered post-service position pose a threat or risk described in clause (iii) of paragraph (2)(B) of such subsection, or include activities described in clause (iv) of such paragraph, the head shall notify the congressional intelligence committees of such determination by not later than 7 days after making such determination. The notification shall include the following:

(1) The name of the former employee.

(2) The name of the employer.

(3) The foreign government, including the specific foreign individual, agency, or entity, for whom the covered post-service employment is being performed.

(4) As applicable, a description of—

(A) the risk to national security, the counterintelligence risk, or both; and

(B) the activities that may violate Federal law, infringe upon the privacy rights of United States persons, or constitute abuses of human rights.

(g) Definitions.—In this section:

(1) COVERED INTELLIGENCE POSITION.— The term "covered intelligence position" means a position within an element of the intelligence community that, based on the level of access of a person occupying such position to information regarding sensitive intelligence sources or methods or other exceptionally sensitive matters, the head of such element determines should be subject to the requirements of this section.

(2) COVERED POST-SERVICE EMPLOYMENT.— The term "covered post-service employment" means direct or indirect employment by, representation of, or any provision of advice or services to the government of a foreign country or any company, entity, or other person whose activities are directly or indirectly supervised, directed, controlled, financed, or subsidized, in whole or in major part, by any government of a foreign country if such employment, representation, or provision of advice or services relates to national security, intelligence, the military, or internal security.

(3) COVERED POST-SERVICE POSITION.— The term "covered post-service position" means a position of employment described in paragraph (2).

(4) DESIGNATED PROHIBITED FOREIGN COUNTRY.—The term "designated prohibited foreign country" means the following:

(A) The People's Republic of China.

(B) The Russian Federation.

(C) The Democratic People's Republic of Korea.

(D) The Islamic Republic of Iran.

(E) The Republic of Cuba.

(F) The Syrian Arab Republic.

(5) EMPLOYEE.— The term "employee", with respect to an employee occupying a covered intelligence position, includes an officer or official of an element of the intelligence community, a contractor of such an element, a detailee to such an element, or a member of the Armed Forces assigned to such an element.

(6) FORMER EMPLOYEE.—The term "former employee" means an individual—

(A) who was an employee occupying a covered intelligence position; and

(B) who is subject to the requirements under subsection (a) or (b).

(7) GOVERNMENT OF A FOREIGN COUNTRY.— The term "government of a foreign country" has the meaning given the term in section 1(e) of the Foreign Agents Registration Act of 1938 (22 U.S.C. 611(e)).

[Sections 304–306 were repealed by the law enacting title 5, United States Code (Public Law 89–544, September 6, 1966, 80 Stat. 654). Subsequently, section 305(a) of Public Law 113–293 adds after section 303 a new section 304 shown prior to this note (and amended in its entirety by section 308(a)(1) of division X of Public Law 117–103).]

AUTHORIZATION FOR APPROPRIATIONS

SEC. 307. [50 U.S.C. 3074] There are hereby authorized to be appropriated such sums as may be necessary and appropriate to carry out the provisions and purposes of this Act (other than the provisions and purposes of sections 102, 103, 104, 105 and titles V, VI, and VII).

DEFINITIONS

SEC. 308. [50 U.S.C. 3075] (a)[10] As used in sections 2, 101, 102, 103, and 303 of this Act, the term "function" includes functions, powers, and duties.

[10] Section 307 of Public Law 87–651 (Act of September 7, 1962, 76 Stat. 526) repealed section 308(a) *less* its applicability to sections 2, 101–103, and 303.

(b) As used in this Act, the term, "Department of Defense" shall be deemed to include the military departments of the Army, the Navy, and the Air Force, and all agencies created under title II of this Act.

SEPARABILITY

SEC. 309. [50 U.S.C. 3076] If any provision of this Act or the application thereof to any person or circumstances is held invalid, the validity of the remainder of the Act and of the application of such provision to other persons and circumstances shall not be affected thereby.

EFFECTIVE DATE

SEC. 310. [50 U.S.C. 3077] (a) The first sentence of section 202 (a) and sections 1, 2, 307, 308, 309, and 310 shall take effect immediately upon the enactment of this Act.

(b) Except as provided in subsection (a), the provisions of this Act shall take effect on whichever of the following days is the earlier: The day after the day upon which the Secretary of Defense first appointed takes office, or the sixtieth day after the date of the enactment of this Act.

SUCCESSION TO THE PRESIDENCY

SEC. 311. [Section 311 consisted of an amendment to the Act entitled "An Act to provide for the performance of the duties of the office of President in case of the removal, resignation, death, or inability both of the President and Vice President".]

REPEALING AND SAVING PROVISIONS

SEC. 312. [50 U.S.C. 3078] All laws, orders, and regulations inconsistent with the provisions of this title[11] are repealed insofar as they are inconsistent with the powers, duties, and responsibilities enacted hereby: *Provided,* That the powers, duties, and responsibilities of the Secretary of Defense under this title[11] shall be administered in conformance with the policy and requirements for administration of budgetary and fiscal matters in the Government generally, including accounting and financial reporting, and that nothing in this title[11] shall be construed as eliminating or modifying the powers, duties, and responsibilities of any other department, agency, or officer of the Government in connection with such matters, but no such department, agency, or officer shall exercise any such powers, duties, or responsibilities in a manner that will render ineffective the provisions of this title[11].

[11] The references to “this title” originally meant title IV of the National Security Act of 1947, as added by section 11 of the Act of Aug. 10, 1949, Ch. 412, 63 Stat. 585. Title IV of this Act, except for section 411 (subsequently redesignated as section 312 by section 6742(b)(11) of P.L. 116-92; 133 Stat. 2240), was *effectively* repealed by section 307 of Pub. L. 87–651, Sept. 7, 1962, 76 Stat. 526.

SEC. 313. [50 U.S.C. 3079] INSIDER THREAT POLICY COMPLIANCE AND REPORTING.

The head of each element of the intelligence community shall—

(1) implement the policy established in accordance with section 102A(f)(8); and

(2) concurrent with the submission to Congress of budget justification materials in support of the budget of the President for a fiscal year that is submitted to Congress under section 1105(a) of title 31, United States Code, submit to Congress a certification as to whether the element is in compliance with such policy.

[Title IV *less* section 411 was repealed by section 307 of Public Law 87–651 (Act of September 7, 1962, 76 Stat. 526). Such section 411 was redesignated as section 312 by section 6742(b)(11) of Public Law 116–92.]

TITLE V—ACCOUNTABILITY FOR INTELLIGENCE ACTIVITIES

GENERAL CONGRESSIONAL OVERSIGHT PROVISIONS

SEC. 501. [50 U.S.C. 3091] (a)(1) The President shall ensure that the congressional intelligence committees are kept fully and currently informed of the intelligence activities of the United States, including any significant anticipated intelligence activity as required by this title.

(2) Nothing in this title shall be construed as requiring the approval of the congressional intelligence committees as a condition precedent to the initiation of any significant anticipated intelligence activity.

(b) The President shall ensure that any illegal intelligence activity is reported promptly to the congressional intelligence committees, as well as any corrective action that has been taken or is planned in connection with such illegal activity.

(c) The President and the congressional intelligence committees shall each establish such written procedures as may be necessary to carry out the provisions of this title.

(d) The House of Representatives and the Senate shall each establish, by rule or resolution of such House, procedures to protect from unauthorized disclosure all classified information, and all information relating to intelligence sources and methods, that is furnished to the congressional intelligence committees or to Members of Congress under this title. Such procedures shall be established in consultation with the Director of National Intelligence. In accordance with such procedures, each of the congressional intelligence committees shall promptly call to the attention of its respective House, or to any appropriate committee or committees of its respective House, any matter relating to intelligence activities requiring the attention of such House or such committee or committees.

(e) Nothing in this Act shall be construed as authority to withhold information from the congressional intelligence committees on the grounds that providing the information to the congressional intelligence committees would constitute the unauthorized disclosure of classified information or information relating to intelligence sources and methods.

(f) As used in this section, the term "intelligence activities" includes covert actions as defined in section 503(e), and includes financial intelligence activities.

SEC. 501A. [50 U.S.C. 3091a] CONGRESSIONAL OVERSIGHT OF CONTROLLED ACCESS PROGRAMS.

(a) PERIODIC BRIEFINGS.—

(1) REQUIREMENT.— Not less frequently than semiannually or upon request by one of the appropriate congressional committees or a member of congressional leadership, the Director of National Intelligence shall provide to such committees and congressional leadership a briefing on each controlled access program in effect.

(2) CONTENTS.—Each briefing provided under paragraph (1) shall include, at a minimum, the following:

(A) A description of the activity of the controlled access programs during the period covered by the briefing.

(B) Documentation with respect to how the controlled access programs have achieved outcomes consistent with requirements documented by the Director and, as applicable, the Secretary of Defense.

(b) LIMITATIONS.—

(1) ESTABLISHMENT.— A head of an element of the intelligence community may not establish a controlled access program, or a compartment or subcompartment therein, until the head notifies the appropriate congressional committees and congressional leadership of such controlled access program, compartment, or subcompartment, as the case may be.

(2) TRANSFERS.—

(A) LIMITATION.— Except as provided in subparagraph (B), a head of an element of the intelligence community may not transfer a capability from a controlled access program, including from a compartment or subcompartment therein to a compartment or subcompartment of another controlled access program, to a special access program (as defined in section 1152(g) of the National Defense Authorization Act for Fiscal Year 1994 (50 U.S.C. 3348(g))), or to anything else outside the controlled access program, until the head submits to the appropriate congressional committees and congressional leadership notice of the intent of the head to make such transfer.

(B) EXCEPTION.—The head of an element of the intelligence community may make a transfer described in subparagraph (A) without prior congressional notification if the head determines that doing so—

(i) is required to mitigate an urgent counterintelligence issue; or

(ii) is necessary to maintain access in the event of an organizational restructuring.

(c) LIMITATION ON SPENDING.— Funds authorized to be appropriated for the National Intelligence Program may not be obligated or expended for any controlled access program, or a compartment or subcompartment therein, until the head of the element of the intelligence community responsible for the establishment of such program, compartment, or subcompartment, submits the notification required by subsection (b).

(d) ANNUAL REPORTS.—

(1) REQUIREMENT.— On an annual basis, the head of each element of the intelligence community shall submit to the appropriate congressional committees and congressional leadership a report on controlled access programs administered by the head.

(2) MATTERS INCLUDED.—Each report submitted under paragraph (1) shall include, with respect to the period covered by the report, the following:

(A) A list of all compartments and subcompartments of controlled access programs active as of the date of the report.

(B) A list of all compartments and subcompartments of controlled access programs terminated during the period covered by the report.

(C) With respect to the report submitted by the Director of National Intelligence, in addition to the matters specified in clauses (A) and (B)—

(i) a certification regarding whether the creation, validation, or substantial modification, including termination, for all existing and proposed controlled access programs, and the compartments and subcompartments within each, are substantiated and justified based on the information required by clause (ii); and

(ii) for each certification—

(I) the rationale for the revalidation, validation, or substantial modification, including termination, of each controlled access program, compartment, and subcompartment;

(II) the identification of a control officer for each controlled access program; and

(III) a statement of protection requirements for each controlled access program.

(e) DEFINITIONS.—In this section:

(1) APPROPRIATE CONGRESSIONAL COMMITTEES.—The term “appropriate congressional committees” means—

(A) the congressional intelligence committees;

(B) the Committee on Appropriations of the Senate; and

(C) the Committee on Appropriations of the House of Representatives.

(2) CONGRESSIONAL LEADERSHIP.—The term “congressional leadership” means—

(A) the majority leader of the Senate;

(B) the minority leader of the Senate;

(C) the Speaker of the House of Representatives; and

(D) the minority leader of the House of Representatives.

(3) CONTROLLED ACCESS PROGRAM.— The term "controlled access program" means a program created or managed pursuant to Intelligence Community Directive 906, or successor directive.

REPORTING OF INTELLIGENCE ACTIVITIES OTHER THAN COVERT ACTIONS

SEC. 502. [50 U.S.C. 3092] (a) IN GENERAL.—To the extent consistent with due regard for the protection from unauthorized disclosure of classified information relating to sensitive intelligence sources and methods or other exceptionally sensitive matters, the Director of National Intelligence and the heads of all departments, agencies, and other entities of the United States Government involved in intelligence activities shall—

(1) keep the congressional intelligence committees fully and currently informed of all intelligence activities, other than a covert action (as defined in section 503(e)), which are the responsibility of, are engaged in by, or are carried out for or on behalf of, any department, agency, or entity of the United States Government, including any significant anticipated intelligence activity and any significant intelligence failure; and

(2) furnish the congressional intelligence committees any information or material concerning intelligence activities (including the legal basis under which the intelligence activity is being or was conducted), other than covert actions, which is within their custody or control, and which is requested by either of the congressional intelligence committees in order to carry out its authorized responsibilities.

(b) FORM AND CONTENTS OF CERTAIN REPORTS.—Any report relating to a significant anticipated intelligence activity or a significant intelligence failure that is submitted to the congressional intelligence committees for purposes of subsection (a)(1) shall be in writing, and shall contain the following:

(1) A concise statement of any facts pertinent to such report.

(2) An explanation of the significance of the intelligence activity or intelligence failure covered by such report.

(c) STANDARDS AND PROCEDURES FOR CERTAIN REPORTS.— The Director of National Intelligence, in consultation with the heads of the departments, agencies, and entities referred to in subsection (a), shall establish standards and procedures applicable to reports covered by subsection (b).

PRESIDENTIAL APPROVAL AND REPORTING OF COVERT ACTIONS

SEC. 503. [50 U.S.C. 3093] (a) The President may not authorize the conduct of a covert action by departments, agencies, or entities of the United States Government unless the President determines such an action is necessary to support identifiable foreign policy objectives of the United States and is important to the national security of the United States, which determination shall be set forth in a finding that shall meet each of the following conditions:

(1) Each finding shall be in writing, unless immediate action by the United States is required and time does not permit the preparation of a written finding, in

which case a written record of the President's decision shall be contemporaneously made and shall be reduced to a written finding as soon as possible but in no event more than 48 hours after the decision is made.

(2) Except as permitted by paragraph (1), a finding may not authorize or sanction a covert action, or any aspect of any such action, which already has occurred.

(3) Each finding shall specify each department, agency, or entity of the United States Government authorized to fund or otherwise participate in any significant way in such action. Any employee, contractor, or contract agent of a department, agency, or entity of the United States Government other than the Central Intelligence Agency directed to participate in any way in a covert action shall be subject either to the policies and regulations of the Central Intelligence Agency, or to written policies or regulations adopted by such department, agency, or entity, to govern such participation.

(4) Each finding shall specify whether it is contemplated that any third party which is not an element of, or a contractor or contract agent of, the United States Government, or is not otherwise subject to United States Government policies and regulations, will be used to fund or otherwise participate in any significant way in the covert action concerned, or be used to undertake the covert action concerned on behalf of the United States.

(5) A finding may not authorize any action that would violate the Constitution or any statute of the United States.

(b) To the extent consistent with due regard for the protection from unauthorized disclosure of classified information relating to sensitive intelligence sources and methods or other exceptionally sensitive matters, the Director of National Intelligence and the heads of all departments, agencies, and entities of the United States Government involved in a covert action—

(1) shall keep the congressional intelligence committees fully and currently informed of all covert actions which are the responsibility of, are engaged in by, or are carried out for or on behalf of, any department, agency, or entity of the United States Government, including significant failures; and

(2) shall furnish to the congressional intelligence committees any information or material concerning covert actions (including the legal basis under which the covert action is being or was conducted) which is in the possession, custody, or control of any department, agency, or entity of the United States Government and which is requested by either of the congressional intelligence committees in order to carry out its authorized responsibilities.

(c)(1) The President shall ensure that any finding approved pursuant to subsection (a) shall be reported in writing to the congressional intelligence committees as soon as possible after such approval and before the initiation of the covert action authorized by the finding, except as otherwise provided in paragraph (2) and paragraph (3).

(2) If the President determines that it is essential to limit access to the finding to meet extraordinary circumstances affecting vital interests of the United States, the finding may be reported to the chairmen and ranking minority members of the

congressional intelligence committees, the Speaker and minority leader of the House of Representatives, the majority and minority leaders of the Senate, and such other member or members of the congressional leadership as may be included by the President.

(3) Whenever a finding is not reported pursuant to paragraph (1) or (2) of this subsection, the President shall fully inform the congressional intelligence committees in a timely fashion and shall provide a statement of the reasons for not giving prior notice.

(4) In a case under paragraph (1), (2), or (3), a copy of the finding, signed by the President, shall be provided to the chairman of each congressional intelligence committee.

(5)(A) When access to a finding, or a notification provided under subsection (d)(1), is limited to the Members of Congress specified in paragraph (2), a written statement of the reasons for limiting such access shall also be provided.

(B) Not later than 180 days after a statement of reasons is submitted in accordance with subparagraph (A) or this subparagraph, the President shall ensure that—

(i) all members of the congressional intelligence committees are provided access to the finding or notification; or

(ii) a statement of reasons that it is essential to continue to limit access to such finding or such notification to meet extraordinary circumstances affecting vital interests of the United States is submitted to the Members of Congress specified in paragraph (2).

(d)(1) The President shall ensure that the congressional intelligence committees, or, if applicable, the Members of Congress specified in subsection (c)(2), are notified in writing of any significant change in a previously approved covert action, or any significant undertaking pursuant to a previously approved finding, in the same manner as findings are reported pursuant to subsection (c).

(2) In determining whether an activity constitutes a significant undertaking for purposes of paragraph (1), the President shall consider whether the activity—

(A) involves significant risk of loss of life;

(B) requires an expansion of existing authorities, including authorities relating to research, development, or operations;

(C) results in the expenditure of significant funds or other resources;

(D) requires notification under section 504;

(E) gives rise to a significant risk of disclosing intelligence sources or methods; or

(F) presents a reasonably foreseeable risk of serious damage to the diplomatic relations of the United States if such activity were disclosed without authorization.

(e) As used in this title, the term "covert action" means an activity or activities of the United States Government to influence political, economic, or military conditions abroad, where it is intended that the role of the United States Government will not be apparent or acknowledged publicly, but does not include—

(1) activities the primary purpose of which is to acquire intelligence, traditional counterintelligence activities, traditional activities to improve or maintain the operational security of United States Government programs, or administrative activities;

(2) traditional diplomatic or military activities or routine support to such activities;

(3) traditional law enforcement activities conducted by United States Government law enforcement agencies or routine support to such activities; or

(4) activities to provide routine support to the overt activities (other than activities described in paragraph (1), (2), or (3)) of other United States Government agencies abroad.

(f) No covert action may be conducted which is intended to influence United States political processes, public opinion, policies, or media.

(g)(1) In any case where access to a finding reported under subsection (c) or notification provided under subsection (d)(1) is not made available to all members of a congressional intelligence committee in accordance with subsection (c)(2), the President shall notify all members of such committee that such finding or such notification has been provided only to the members specified in subsection (c)(2).

(2) In any case where access to a finding reported under subsection (c) or notification provided under subsection (d)(1) is not made available to all members of a congressional intelligence committee in accordance with subsection (c)(2), the President shall provide to all members of such committee a general description regarding the finding or notification, as applicable, consistent with the reasons for not yet fully informing all members of such committee.

(3) The President shall maintain—

(A) a record of the members of Congress to whom a finding is reported under subsection (c) or notification is provided under subsection (d)(1) and the date on which each member of Congress receives such finding or notification; and

(B) each written statement provided under subsection (c)(5).

(h) For each type of activity undertaken as part of a covert action, the President shall establish in writing a plan to respond to the unauthorized public disclosure of that type of activity.

FUNDING OF INTELLIGENCE ACTIVITIES

SEC. 504. [50 U.S.C. 3094] (a) Appropriated funds available to an intelligence agency may be obligated or expended for an intelligence or intelligence-related activity only if—

(1) those funds were specifically authorized by Congress for use for such intelligence or intelligence-related activities; or

(2) in the case of funds from the Reserve for Contingencies of the Central Intelligence Agency and consistent with the provisions of section 503 of this Act

concerning any significant anticipated intelligence activity, the Director of the Central Intelligence Agency has notified the appropriate congressional committees of the intent to make such funds available for such activity; or

(3) in the case of funds specifically authorized by the Congress for a different activity—

(A) the activity to be funded is a higher priority intelligence or intelligence-related activity;

(B) the use of such funds for such activity supports an emergent need, improves program effectiveness, or increases efficiency; and

(C) the Director of National Intelligence, the Secretary of Defense, or the Attorney General, as appropriate, has notified the appropriate congressional committees of the intent to make such funds available for such activity;

(4) nothing in this subsection prohibits obligation or expenditure of funds available to an intelligence agency in accordance with sections 1535 and 1536 of title 31, United States Code.

(b) Funds available to an intelligence agency may not be made available for any intelligence or intelligence-related activity for which funds were denied by the Congress.

(c) No funds appropriated for, or otherwise available to, any department, agency, or entity of the United States Government may be expended, or may be directed to be expended, for any covert action, as defined in section 503(e), unless and until a Presidential finding required by subsection (a) of section 503 has been signed or otherwise issued in accordance with that subsection.

(d)(1) Except as otherwise specifically provided by law, funds available to an intelligence agency that are not appropriated funds may be obligated or expended for an intelligence or intelligence-related activity only if those funds are used for activities reported to the appropriate congressional committees pursuant to procedures which identify—

(A) the types of activities for which nonappropriated funds may be expended; and

(B) the circumstances under which an activity must be reported as a significant anticipated intelligence activity before such funds can be expended.

(2) Procedures for purposes of paragraph (1) shall be jointly agreed upon by the congressional intelligence committees and, as appropriate, the Director of National Intelligence or the Secretary of Defense.

(e) As used in this section—

(1) the term "intelligence agency" means any department, agency, or other entity of the United States involved in intelligence or intelligence-related activities;

(2) the term "appropriate congressional committees" means the Permanent Select Committee on Intelligence and the Committee on Appropriations of the House of Representatives and the Select Committee on Intelligence and the Committee on Appropriations of the Senate; and

(3) the term "specifically authorized by the Congress" means that—

(A) the activity and the amount of funds proposed to be used for that activity were identified in a formal budget request to the Congress, but funds shall be deemed to be specifically authorized for that activity only to the extent that the Congress both authorized the funds to be appropriated for that activity and appropriated the funds for that activity; or

(B) although the funds were not formally requested, the Congress both specifically authorized the appropriation of the funds for the activity and appropriated the funds for the activity.

NOTICE TO CONGRESS OF CERTAIN TRANSFERS OF DEFENSE ARTICLES AND DEFENSE SERVICES

SEC. 505. [50 U.S.C. 3095] (a)(1) The transfer of a defense article or defense service, or the anticipated transfer in any fiscal year of any aggregation of defense articles or defense services, exceeding $1,000,000 in value by an intelligence agency to a recipient outside that agency shall be considered a significant anticipated intelligence activity for the purpose of this title.

(2) Paragraph (1) does not apply if—

(A) the transfer is being made to a department, agency, or other entity of the United States (so long as there will not be a subsequent retransfer of the defense articles or defense services outside the United States Government in conjunction with an intelligence or intelligence-related activity); or

(B) the transfer—

(i) is being made pursuant to authorities contained in part II of the Foreign Assistance Act of 1961, the Arms Export Control Act, title 10 of the United States Code (including a law enacted pursuant to section 8677(a) of title 10), or the Federal Property and Administrative Services Act of 1949, and

(ii) is not being made in conjunction with an intelligence or intelligence-related activity.

(3) An intelligence agency may not transfer any defense articles or defense services outside the agency in conjunction with any intelligence or intelligence-related activity for which funds were denied by the Congress.

(b) As used in this section—

(1) the term "intelligence agency" means any department, agency, or other entity of the United States involved in intelligence or intelligence-related activities;

(2) the terms "defense articles" and "defense services" mean the items on the United States Munitions List pursuant to section 38 of the Arms Export Control Act (22 CFR part 121);

(3) the term "transfer" means—

(A) in the case of defense articles, the transfer of possession of those articles; and

(B) in the case of defense services, the provision of those services; and

(4) the term "value" means—

(A) in the case of defense articles, the greater of—

(i) the original acquisition cost to the United States Government, plus the cost of improvements or other modifications made by or on behalf of the Government; or

(ii) the replacement cost; and

(B) in the case of defense services, the full cost to the Government of providing the services.

SPECIFICITY OF NATIONAL INTELLIGENCE PROGRAM BUDGET AMOUNTS FOR COUNTERTERRORISM, COUNTERPROLIFERATION, COUNTERNARCOTICS, AND COUNTERINTELLIGENCE

SEC. 506. [50 U.S.C. 3096] (a) IN GENERAL.—The budget justification materials submitted to Congress in support of the budget of the President for a fiscal year that is submitted to Congress under section 1105(a) of title 31, United States Code, shall set forth separately the aggregate amount requested for that fiscal year for the National Intelligence Program for each of the following:

(1) Counterterrorism.

(2) Counterproliferation.

(3) Counternarcotics.

(4) Counterintelligence.

(b) ELECTION OF CLASSIFIED OR UNCLASSIFIED FORM.— Amounts set forth under subsection (a) may be set forth in unclassified form or classified form, at the election of the Director of National Intelligence.

BUDGET TREATMENT OF COSTS OF ACQUISITION OF MAJOR SYSTEMS BY THE INTELLIGENCE COMMUNITY

SEC. 506A. [50 U.S.C. 3097] (a) INDEPENDENT COST ESTIMATES.—(1) The Director of National Intelligence shall, in consultation with the head of each element of the intelligence community concerned, prepare an independent cost estimate of the full life-cycle cost of development, procurement, and operation of each major system to be acquired by the intelligence community.

(2)(A) Each independent cost estimate for a major system shall, to the maximum extent practicable, specify the amount required to be appropriated and obligated to develop, procure, and operate the major system in each fiscal year of the proposed period of development, procurement, and operation of the major system.

(B) For major system acquisitions requiring a service or capability from another acquisition or program to deliver the end-to-end functionality for the intelligence community end users, independent cost estimates shall include, to the maximum extent practicable, all estimated costs across all pertinent elements of the intelligence community. For collection programs, such cost estimates shall include the cost of new analyst training, new hardware and software for data exploitation and analysis, and any unique or additional costs for data processing, storing, and power, space, and cooling across the life cycle of the program. If such costs for processing, exploitation, dissemination, and storage are scheduled to be executed in other elements of the intelligence community, the independent cost estimate shall identify and annotate such costs for such other elements accordingly.

(3)(A) In the case of a program of the intelligence community that qualifies as a major system, an independent cost estimate shall be prepared before the submission to Congress of the budget of the President for the first fiscal year in which appropriated funds are anticipated to be obligated for the development or procurement of such major system.

(B) In the case of a program of the intelligence community for which an independent cost estimate was not previously required to be prepared under this section, including a program for which development or procurement commenced before the date of the enactment of the Intelligence Authorization Act for Fiscal Year 2004, if the aggregate future costs of development or procurement (or any combination of such activities) of the program will exceed $500,000,000 (in current fiscal year dollars), the program shall qualify as a major system for purposes of this section, and an independent cost estimate for such major system shall be prepared before the submission to Congress of the budget of the President for the first fiscal year thereafter in which appropriated funds are anticipated to be obligated for such major system.

(4) The independent cost estimate for a major system shall be updated upon—

(A) the completion of any preliminary design review associated with the major system;

(B) any significant modification to the anticipated design of the major system; or

(C) any change in circumstances that renders the current independent cost estimate for the major system inaccurate.

(5) Any update of an independent cost estimate for a major system under paragraph (4) shall meet all requirements for independent cost estimates under this section, and shall be treated as the most current independent cost estimate for the major system until further updated under that paragraph.

(b) Preparation of Independent Cost Estimates.—(1) The Director shall establish within the Office of the Director of National Intelligence for Community Management an office which shall be responsible for preparing independent cost estimates, and any updates thereof, under subsection (a), unless a designation is made under paragraph (2).

(2) In the case of the acquisition of a major system for an element of the intelligence community within the Department of Defense, the Director and the Secretary of Defense shall provide that the independent cost estimate, and any updates thereof, under subsection (a) be prepared by an entity jointly designated by the Director and the Secretary in accordance with section 2434(b)(1)(A) of title 10, United States Code.

(c) UTILIZATION IN BUDGETS OF PRESIDENT.—(1) If the budget of the President requests appropriations for any fiscal year for the development or procurement of a major system by the intelligence community, the President shall, subject to paragraph (2), request in such budget an amount of appropriations for the development or procurement, as the case may be, of the major system that is equivalent to the amount of appropriations identified in the most current independent cost estimate for the major system for obligation for each fiscal year for which appropriations are requested for the major system in such budget.

(2) If the amount of appropriations requested in the budget of the President for the development or procurement of a major system is less than the amount of appropriations identified in the most current independent cost estimate for the major system for obligation for each fiscal year for which appropriations are requested for the major system in such budget, the President shall include in the budget justification materials submitted to Congress in support of such budget—

(A) an explanation for the difference between the amount of appropriations requested and the amount of appropriations identified in the most current independent cost estimate;

(B) a description of the importance of the major system to the national security;

(C) an assessment of the consequences for the funding of all programs of the National Intelligence Program in future fiscal years if the most current independent cost estimate for the major system is accurate and additional appropriations are required in future fiscal years to ensure the continued development or procurement of the major system, including the consequences of such funding shortfalls on the major system and all other programs of the National Intelligence Program; and

(D) such other information on the funding of the major system as the President considers appropriate.

(d) INCLUSION OF ESTIMATES IN BUDGET JUSTIFICATION MATERIALS.— The budget justification materials submitted to Congress in support of the budget of the President shall include the most current independent cost estimate under this section for each major system for which appropriations are requested in such budget for any fiscal year.

(e) DEFINITIONS.—In this section:

(1) The term "budget of the President" means the budget of the President for a fiscal year as submitted to Congress under section 1105(a) of title 31, United States Code.

(2)(A) The term "independent cost estimate" means a pragmatic and neutral analysis, assessment, and quantification of all costs and risks associated with the development, acquisition, procurement, operation, and sustainment of a major system across its proposed life cycle, which shall be based on programmatic and technical specifications provided by the office within the element of the intelligence community with primary responsibility for the development, procurement, or operation of the major system.

(B) In accordance with subsection (a)(2)(B), each independent cost estimate shall include all costs required across elements of the intelligence community to develop, acquire, procure, operate, and sustain the system to provide the end-to-end intelligence functionality of the system, including—

(i) for collection programs, the cost of new analyst training, new hardware and software for data exploitation and analysis, and any unique or additional costs for data processing, storing, and power, space, and cooling across the life cycle of the program; and

(ii) costs for processing, exploitation, dissemination, and storage scheduled to be executed in other elements of the intelligence community.

(3) The term "major system" means any significant program of an element of the intelligence community with projected total development and procurement costs exceeding $500,000,000 (based on fiscal year 2010 constant dollars), which costs shall include all end-to-end program costs, including costs associated with the development and procurement of the program and any other costs associated with the development and procurement of systems required to support or utilize the program.

ANNUAL PERSONNEL LEVEL ASSESSMENTS FOR THE INTELLIGENCE COMMUNITY

SEC. 506B. [50 U.S.C. 3098] (a) REQUIREMENT TO PROVIDE.— The Director of National Intelligence shall, in consultation with the head of each element of the intelligence community, prepare an annual personnel level assessment for such element that assesses the personnel levels for such element for the fiscal year following the fiscal year in which the assessment is submitted.

(b) SCHEDULE.— Each assessment required by subsection (a) shall be submitted to the congressional intelligence committees each year at the time that the President submits to Congress the budget for a fiscal year pursuant to section 1105 of title 31, United States Code.

(c) CONTENTS.—Each assessment required by subsection (a) submitted during a fiscal year shall contain the following information for the element of the intelligence community concerned:

(1) The budget submission for personnel costs for the upcoming fiscal year.

(2) The dollar and percentage increase or decrease of such costs as compared to the personnel costs of the current fiscal year.

(3) The dollar and percentage increase or decrease of such costs as compared to the personnel costs during the prior 5 fiscal years.

(4) The number of full-time equivalent positions that is the basis for which personnel funds are requested for the upcoming fiscal year.

(5) The numerical and percentage increase or decrease of the number referred to in paragraph (4) as compared to the number of full-time equivalent positions of the current fiscal year.

(6) The numerical and percentage increase or decrease of the number referred to in paragraph (4) as compared to the number of full-time equivalent positions during the prior 5 fiscal years.

(7) The best estimate of the number and costs of core contract personnel to be funded by the element for the upcoming fiscal year.

(8) The numerical and percentage increase or decrease of such costs of core contract personnel as compared to the best estimate of the costs of core contract personnel of the current fiscal year.

(9) The numerical and percentage increase or decrease of such number and such costs of core contract personnel as compared to the number and cost of core contract personnel during the prior 5 fiscal years.

(10) A justification for the requested personnel and core contract personnel levels.

(11) The best estimate of the number of intelligence collectors and analysts employed by each element of the intelligence community.

(12) The best estimate of the number of intelligence collectors and analysts contracted by each element of the intelligence community and a description of the functions performed by such contractors.

(13) A statement by the Director of National Intelligence that, based on current and projected funding, the element concerned will have sufficient—

(A) internal infrastructure to support the requested personnel and core contract personnel levels;

(B) training resources to support the requested personnel levels; and

(C) funding to support the administrative and operational activities of the requested personnel levels.

VULNERABILITY ASSESSMENTS OF MAJOR SYSTEMS

SEC. 506C. [50 U.S.C. 3099] (a) INITIAL VULNERABILITY ASSESSMENTS.—(1)(A) Except as provided in subparagraph (B), the Director of National Intelligence shall conduct and submit to the congressional intelligence committees an initial vulnerability assessment for each major system and its significant items of supply—

(i) except as provided in clause (ii), prior to the completion of Milestone B or an equivalent acquisition decision for the major system; or

(ii) prior to the date that is 1 year after the date of the enactment of the Intelligence Authorization Act for Fiscal Year 2010 in the case of a major system for which Milestone B or an equivalent acquisition decision—

(I) was completed prior to such date of enactment; or

(II) is completed on a date during the 180-day period following such date of enactment.

(B) The Director may submit to the congressional intelligence committees an initial vulnerability assessment required by clause (ii) of subparagraph (A) not later than 180 days after the date such assessment is required to be submitted under such clause if the Director notifies the congressional intelligence committees of the extension of the submission date under this subparagraph and provides a justification for such extension.

(C) The initial vulnerability assessment of a major system and its significant items of supply shall include use of an analysis-based approach to—

(i) identify vulnerabilities;

(ii) define exploitation potential;

(iii) examine the system's potential effectiveness;

(iv) determine overall vulnerability; and

(v) make recommendations for risk reduction.

(2) If an initial vulnerability assessment for a major system is not submitted to the congressional intelligence committees as required by paragraph (1), funds appropriated for the acquisition of the major system may not be obligated for a major contract related to the major system. Such prohibition on the obligation of funds for the acquisition of the major system shall cease to apply on the date on which the congressional intelligence committees receive the initial vulnerability assessment.

(b) SUBSEQUENT VULNERABILITY ASSESSMENTS.—(1) The Director of National Intelligence shall, periodically throughout the procurement of a major system or if the Director determines that a change in circumstances warrants the issuance of a subsequent vulnerability assessment, conduct a subsequent vulnerability assessment of each major system and its significant items of supply within the National Intelligence Program.

(2) Upon the request of a congressional intelligence committee, the Director of National Intelligence may, if appropriate, recertify the previous vulnerability assessment or may conduct a subsequent vulnerability assessment of a particular major system and its significant items of supply within the National Intelligence Program.

(3) Any subsequent vulnerability assessment of a major system and its significant items of supply shall include use of an analysis-based approach and, if applicable, a testing-based approach, to monitor the exploitation potential of such system and reexamine the factors described in clauses (i) through (v) of subsection (a)(1)(C).

(c) MAJOR SYSTEM MANAGEMENT.— The Director of National Intelligence shall give due consideration to the vulnerability assessments prepared for a given major system when developing and determining the National Intelligence Program budget.

(d) CONGRESSIONAL OVERSIGHT.—(1) The Director of National Intelligence shall provide to the congressional intelligence committees a copy of each vulnerability assessment conducted under subsection (a) or (b) not later than 10 days after the date of the completion of such assessment.

(2) The Director of National Intelligence shall provide the congressional intelligence committees with a proposed schedule for subsequent periodic vulnerability assessments of a major system under subsection (b)(1) when providing such committees with the initial vulnerability assessment under subsection (a) of such system as required by paragraph (1).

(e) DEFINITIONS.—In this section:

(1) The term “item of supply” has the meaning given that term in section 4(10)

of the Office of Federal Procurement Policy Act (41 U.S.C. 403(10)).

(2) The term "major contract" means each of the 6 largest prime, associate, or Government-furnished equipment contracts under a major system that is in excess of $40,000,000 and that is not a firm, fixed price contract.

(3) The term "major system" has the meaning given that term in section 506A(e).

(4) The term "Milestone B" means a decision to enter into major system development and demonstration pursuant to guidance prescribed by the Director of National Intelligence.

(5) The term "vulnerability assessment" means the process of identifying and quantifying vulnerabilities in a major system and its significant items of supply.

INTELLIGENCE COMMUNITY BUSINESS SYSTEM TRANSFORMATION

SEC. 506D. [50 U.S.C. 3100] (a) LIMITATION ON OBLIGATION OF FUNDS.—(1) Subject to paragraph (3), no funds appropriated to any element of the intelligence community may be obligated for an intelligence community business system transformation that will have a total cost in excess of $3,000,000 unless—

(A) the Director of the Office of Business Transformation of the Office of the Director of National Intelligence makes a certification described in paragraph (2) with respect to such intelligence community business system transformation; and

(B) such certification is approved by the board established under subsection (f).

(2) The certification described in this paragraph for an intelligence community business system transformation is a certification made by the Director of the Office of Business Transformation of the Office of the Director of National Intelligence that the intelligence community business system transformation—

(A) complies with the enterprise architecture under subsection (b) and such other policies and standards that the Director of National Intelligence considers appropriate; or

(B) is necessary—

(i) to achieve a critical national security capability or address a critical requirement; or

(ii) to prevent a significant adverse effect on a project that is needed to achieve an essential capability, taking into consideration any alternative solutions for preventing such adverse effect.

(3) With respect to a fiscal year after fiscal year 2010, the amount referred to in paragraph (1) in the matter preceding subparagraph (A) shall be equal to the sum of—

(A) the amount in effect under such paragraph (1) for the preceding fiscal year (determined after application of this paragraph), plus

(B) such amount multiplied by the annual percentage increase in the consumer price index (all items; U.S. city average) as of September of the previous fiscal year.

(b) ENTERPRISE ARCHITECTURE FOR INTELLIGENCE COMMUNITY BUSINESS SYSTEMS.—(1) The Director of National Intelligence shall, acting through the board established under subsection (f), develop and implement an enterprise architecture to cover all intelligence community business systems, and the functions and activities supported by such business systems. The enterprise architecture shall be sufficiently defined to effectively guide, constrain, and permit implementation of interoperable intelligence community business system solutions, consistent with applicable policies and procedures established by the Director of the Office of Management and Budget.

(2) The enterprise architecture under paragraph (1) shall include the following:

(A) An information infrastructure that will enable the intelligence community to—

(i) comply with all Federal accounting, financial management, and reporting requirements;

(ii) routinely produce timely, accurate, and reliable financial information for management purposes;

(iii) integrate budget, accounting, and program information and systems; and

(iv) provide for the measurement of performance, including the ability to produce timely, relevant, and reliable cost information.

(B) Policies, procedures, data standards, and system interface requirements that apply uniformly throughout the intelligence community.

(c) RESPONSIBILITIES FOR INTELLIGENCE COMMUNITY BUSINESS SYSTEM TRANSFORMATION.— The Director of National Intelligence shall be responsible for the entire life cycle of an intelligence community business system transformation, including review, approval, and oversight of the planning, design, acquisition, deployment, operation, and maintenance of the business system transformation.

(d) INTELLIGENCE COMMUNITY BUSINESS SYSTEM INVESTMENT REVIEW.—(1) The Director of the Office of Business Transformation of the Office of the Director of National Intelligence shall establish and implement, not later than 60 days after the enactment of the Intelligence Authorization Act for Fiscal Year 2010, an investment review process for the intelligence community business systems for which the Director of the Office of Business Transformation is responsible.

(2) The investment review process under paragraph (1) shall—

(A) meet the requirements of section 11312 of title 40, United States Code; and

(B) specifically set forth the responsibilities of the Director of the Office of Business Transformation under such review process.

(3) The investment review process under paragraph (1) shall include the following elements:

(A) Review and approval by an investment review board (consisting of appropriate representatives of the intelligence community) of each intelligence community business system as an investment before the obligation of funds for such system.

(B) Periodic review, but not less often than annually, of every intelligence community business system investment.

(C) Thresholds for levels of review to ensure appropriate review of intelligence community business system investments depending on the scope, complexity, and cost of the system involved.

(D) Procedures for making certifications in accordance with the requirements of subsection (a)(2).

[Note: Subsection (e) was repealed by section 310(a)(3) of Public Law 112–277; enacted January 14, 2013.]

(f) INTELLIGENCE COMMUNITY BUSINESS SYSTEM TRANSFORMATION GOVERNANCE BOARD.—(1) The Director of National Intelligence shall establish a board within the intelligence community business system transformation governance structure (in this subsection referred to as the "Board").

(2) The Board shall—

(A) recommend to the Director policies and procedures necessary to effectively integrate all business activities and any transformation, reform, reorganization, or process improvement initiatives undertaken within the intelligence community;

(B) review and approve any major update of—

(i) the enterprise architecture developed under subsection (b); and

(ii) any plans for an intelligence community business systems modernization;

(C) manage cross-domain integration consistent with such enterprise architecture;

(D) coordinate initiatives for intelligence community business system transformation to maximize benefits and minimize costs for the intelligence community, and periodically report to the Director on the status of efforts to carry out an intelligence community business system transformation;

(E) ensure that funds are obligated for intelligence community business system transformation in a manner consistent with subsection (a); and

(F) carry out such other duties as the Director shall specify.

(g) RELATION TO ANNUAL REGISTRATION REQUIREMENTS.— Nothing in this section shall be construed to alter the requirements of section 8083 of the Department of Defense Appropriations Act, 2005 (Public Law 108–287; 118 Stat. 989), with regard to information technology systems (as defined in subsection (d) of such section).

(h) RELATIONSHIP TO DEFENSE BUSINESS ENTERPRISE ARCHITECTURE.— Nothing in this section shall be construed to exempt funds authorized to be appropriated to the Department of Defense from the requirements of section 2222 of title 10, United States Code, to the extent that such requirements are otherwise applicable.

(i) RELATION TO CLINGER-COHEN ACT.—(1) Executive agency responsibilities in chapter 113 of title 40, United States Code, for any intelligence community business system transformation shall be exercised jointly by—

(A) the Director of National Intelligence and the Chief Information Officer of the Intelligence Community; and

(B) the head of the executive agency that contains the element of the intelligence community involved and the chief information officer of that executive agency.

(2) The Director of National Intelligence and the head of the executive agency referred to in paragraph (1)(B) shall enter into a Memorandum of Understanding to carry out the requirements of this section in a manner that best meets the needs of the intelligence community and the executive agency.

(j) Reports.—Not later than March 31 of each of the years 2011 through 2014, the Director of National Intelligence shall submit to the congressional intelligence committees a report on the compliance of the intelligence community with the requirements of this section. Each such report shall—

(1) describe actions taken and proposed for meeting the requirements of subsection (a), including—

(A) specific milestones and actual performance against specified performance measures, and any revision of such milestones and performance measures; and

(B) specific actions on the intelligence community business system transformations submitted for certification under such subsection;

(2) identify the number of intelligence community business system transformations that received a certification described in subsection (a)(2); and

(3) describe specific improvements in business operations and cost savings resulting from successful intelligence community business systems transformation efforts.

(k) Definitions.—In this section:

(1) The term "enterprise architecture" has the meaning given that term in section 3601(4) of title 44, United States Code.

(2) The terms "information system" and "information technology" have the meanings given those terms in section 11101 of title 40, United States Code.

(3) The term "intelligence community business system" means an information system, including a national security system, that is operated by, for, or on behalf of an element of the intelligence community, including a financial system, mixed system, financial data feeder system, and the business infrastructure capabilities shared by the systems of the business enterprise architecture, including people, process, and technology, that build upon the core infrastructure used to support business activities, such as acquisition, financial management, logistics, strategic planning and budgeting, installations and environment, and human resource management.

(4) The term "intelligence community business system transformation" means—

(A) the acquisition or development of a new intelligence community business system; or

(B) any significant modification or enhancement of an existing intelligence community business system (other than necessary to maintain current services).

(5) The term "national security system" has the meaning given that term in section 3542 of title 44, United States Code.

(6) The term "Office of Business Transformation of the Office of the Director of National Intelligence" includes any successor office that assumes the functions of the Office of Business Transformation of the Office of the Director of National Intelligence as carried out by the Office of Business Transformation on the date of the enactment of the Intelligence Authorization Act for Fiscal Year 2010.

REPORTS ON THE ACQUISITION OF MAJOR SYSTEMS

SEC. 506E. [50 U.S.C. 3101] (a) DEFINITIONS.—In this section:

(1) The term "cost estimate"—

(A) means an assessment and quantification of all costs and risks associated with the acquisition of a major system based upon reasonably available information at the time the Director establishes the 2010 adjusted total acquisition cost for such system pursuant to subsection (h) or restructures such system pursuant to section 506F(c); and

(B) does not mean an "independent cost estimate".

(2) The term "critical cost growth threshold" means a percentage increase in the total acquisition cost for a major system of at least 25 percent over the total acquisition cost for the major system as shown in the current Baseline Estimate for the major system.

(3)(A) The term "current Baseline Estimate" means the projected total acquisition cost of a major system that is—

(i) approved by the Director, or a designee of the Director, at Milestone B or an equivalent acquisition decision for the development, procurement, and construction of such system;

(ii) approved by the Director at the time such system is restructured pursuant to section 506F(c); or

(iii) the 2010 adjusted total acquisition cost determined pursuant to subsection (h).

(B) A current Baseline Estimate may be in the form of an independent cost estimate.

(4) Except as otherwise specifically provided, the term "Director" means the Director of National Intelligence.

(5) The term "independent cost estimate" has the meaning given that term in section 506A(e).

(6) The term "major contract" means each of the 6 largest prime, associate, or Government-furnished equipment contracts under a major system that is in excess

of $40,000,000 and that is not a firm, fixed price contract.

(7) The term "major system" has the meaning given that term in section 506A(e).

(8) The term "Milestone B" means a decision to enter into major system development and demonstration pursuant to guidance prescribed by the Director.

(9) The term "program manager" means—

(A) the head of the element of the intelligence community that is responsible for the budget, cost, schedule, and performance of a major system; or

(B) in the case of a major system within the Office of the Director of National Intelligence, the deputy who is responsible for the budget, cost, schedule, and performance of the major system.

(10) The term "significant cost growth threshold" means the percentage increase in the total acquisition cost for a major system of at least 15 percent over the total acquisition cost for such system as shown in the current Baseline Estimate for such system.

(11) The term "total acquisition cost" means the amount equal to the total cost for development and procurement of, and system-specific construction for, a major system.

(b) Major System Cost Reports.—(1) The program manager for a major system shall, on a quarterly basis, submit to the Director a major system cost report as described in paragraph (2).

(2) A major system cost report shall include the following information (as of the last day of the quarter for which the report is made):

(A) The total acquisition cost for the major system.

(B) Any cost variance or schedule variance in a major contract for the major system since the contract was entered into.

(C) Any changes from a major system schedule milestones or performances that are known, expected, or anticipated by the program manager.

(D) Any significant changes in the total acquisition cost for development and procurement of any software component of the major system, schedule milestones for such software component of the major system, or expected performance of such software component of the major system that are known, expected, or anticipated by the program manager.

(3) Each major system cost report required by paragraph (1) shall be submitted not more than 30 days after the end of the reporting quarter.

(c) Reports for Breach of Significant or Critical Cost Growth Thresholds.— If the program manager of a major system for which a report has previously been submitted under subsection (b) determines at any time during a quarter that there is reasonable cause to believe that the total acquisition cost for the major system has increased by a percentage equal to or greater than the significant cost growth threshold or critical cost growth threshold and if a report indicating an increase of such percentage or more has not previously been submitted to the Director, then the program manager shall immediately submit to the Director a major system cost report containing the information, determined as of the date of the report, required under subsection (b).

(d) NOTIFICATION TO CONGRESS OF COST GROWTH.—(1) Whenever a major system cost report is submitted to the Director, the Director shall determine whether the current acquisition cost for the major system has increased by a percentage equal to or greater than the significant cost growth threshold or the critical cost growth threshold.

(2) If the Director determines that the current total acquisition cost has increased by a percentage equal to or greater than the significant cost growth threshold or critical cost growth threshold, the Director shall submit to Congress a Major System Congressional Report pursuant to subsection (e).

(e) REQUIREMENT FOR MAJOR SYSTEM CONGRESSIONAL REPORT.—(1) Whenever the Director determines under subsection (d) that the total acquisition cost of a major system has increased by a percentage equal to or greater than the significant cost growth threshold for the major system, a Major System Congressional Report shall be submitted to Congress not later than 45 days after the date on which the Director receives the major system cost report for such major system.

(2) If the total acquisition cost of a major system (as determined by the Director under subsection (d)) increases by a percentage equal to or greater than the critical cost growth threshold for the program or subprogram, the Director shall take actions consistent with the requirements of section 506F.

(f) MAJOR SYSTEM CONGRESSIONAL REPORT ELEMENTS.—(1) Except as provided in paragraph (2), each Major System Congressional Report shall include the following:

(A) The name of the major system.

(B) The date of the preparation of the report.

(C) The program phase of the major system as of the date of the preparation of the report.

(D) The estimate of the total acquisition cost for the major system expressed in constant base-year dollars and in current dollars.

(E) The current Baseline Estimate for the major system in constant base-year dollars and in current dollars.

(F) A statement of the reasons for any increase in total acquisition cost for the major system.

(G) The completion status of the major system—

(i) expressed as the percentage that the number of years for which funds have been appropriated for the major system is of the number of years for which it is planned that funds will be appropriated for the major system; and

(ii) expressed as the percentage that the amount of funds that have been appropriated for the major system is of the total amount of funds which it is planned will be appropriated for the major system.

(H) The fiscal year in which the major system was first authorized and in which funds for such system were first appropriated by Congress.

(I) The current change and the total change, in dollars and expressed as a percentage, in the total acquisition cost for the major system, stated both in constant base-year dollars and in current dollars.

(J) The quantity of end items to be acquired under the major system and the current change and total change, if any, in that quantity.

(K) The identities of the officers responsible for management and cost control of the major system.

(L) The action taken and proposed to be taken to control future cost growth of the major system.

(M) Any changes made in the performance or schedule milestones of the major system and the extent to which such changes have contributed to the increase in total acquisition cost for the major system.

(N) The following contract performance assessment information with respect to each major contract under the major system:

(i) The name of the contractor.

(ii) The phase that the contract is in at the time of the preparation of the report.

(iii) The percentage of work under the contract that has been completed.

(iv) Any current change and the total change, in dollars and expressed as a percentage, in the contract cost.

(v) The percentage by which the contract is currently ahead of or behind schedule.

(vi) A narrative providing a summary explanation of the most significant occurrences, including cost and schedule variances under major contracts of the major system, contributing to the changes identified and a discussion of the effect these occurrences will have on the future costs and schedule of the major system.

(O) In any case in which one or more problems with a software component of the major system significantly contributed to the increase in costs of the major system, the action taken and proposed to be taken to solve such problems.

(2) A Major System Congressional Report prepared for a major system for which the increase in the total acquisition cost is due to termination or cancellation of the entire major system shall include only—

(A) the information described in subparagraphs (A) through (F) of paragraph (1); and

(B) the total percentage change in total acquisition cost for such system.

(g) Prohibition on Obligation of Funds.—If a determination of an increase by a percentage equal to or greater than the significant cost growth threshold is made by the Director under subsection (d) and a Major System Congressional Report containing the information described in subsection (f) is not submitted to Congress under subsection (e)(1), or if a determination of an increase by a percentage equal to or greater than the critical cost growth threshold is made by the Director under subsection (d) and the Major System Congressional Report containing the information described in subsection

(f) and section 506F(b)(3) and the certification required by section 506F(b)(2) are not submitted to Congress under subsection (e)(2), funds appropriated for construction, research, development, test, evaluation, and procurement may not be obligated for a major contract under the major system. The prohibition on the obligation of funds for a major system shall cease to apply at the end of the 45-day period that begins on the date—

(1) on which Congress receives the Major System Congressional Report under subsection (e)(1) with respect to that major system, in the case of a determination of an increase by a percentage equal to or greater than the significant cost growth threshold (as determined in subsection (d)); or

(2) on which Congress receives both the Major System Congressional Report under subsection (e)(2) and the certification of the Director under section 506F(b)(2) with respect to that major system, in the case of an increase by a percentage equal to or greater than the critical cost growth threshold (as determined under subsection (d)).

(h) Treatment of Cost Increases Prior to Enactment of Intelligence Authorization Act for Fiscal Year 2010.—(1) Not later than 180 days after the date of the enactment of the Intelligence Authorization Act for Fiscal Year 2010, the Director—

(A) shall, for each major system, determine if the total acquisition cost of such major system increased by a percentage equal to or greater than the significant cost growth threshold or the critical cost growth threshold prior to such date of enactment;

(B) shall establish for each major system for which the total acquisition cost has increased by a percentage equal to or greater than the significant cost growth threshold or the critical cost growth threshold prior to such date of enactment a revised current Baseline Estimate based upon an updated cost estimate;

(C) may, for a major system not described in subparagraph (B), establish a revised current Baseline Estimate based upon an updated cost estimate; and

(D) shall submit to Congress a report describing—

(i) each determination made under subparagraph (A);

(ii) each revised current Baseline Estimate established for a major system under subparagraph (B); and

(iii) each revised current Baseline Estimate established for a major system under subparagraph (C), including the percentage increase of the total acquisition cost of such major system that occurred prior to the date of the enactment of such Act.

(2) The revised current Baseline Estimate established for a major system under subparagraph (B) or (C) of paragraph (1) shall be the 2010 adjusted total acquisition cost for the major system and may include the estimated cost of conducting any vulnerability assessments for such major system required under section 506C.

(i) Requirements To Use Base Year Dollars.— Any determination of a percentage increase under this section shall be stated in terms of constant base year dollars.

(j) FORM OF REPORT.— Any report required to be submitted under this section may be submitted in a classified form.

CRITICAL COST GROWTH IN MAJOR SYSTEMS

SEC. 506F. [50 U.S.C. 3102] (a) REASSESSMENT OF MAJOR SYSTEM.—If the Director of National Intelligence determines under section 506E(d) that the total acquisition cost of a major system has increased by a percentage equal to or greater than the critical cost growth threshold for the major system, the Director shall—

(1) determine the root cause or causes of the critical cost growth, in accordance with applicable statutory requirements, policies, procedures, and guidance; and

(2) carry out an assessment of—

(A) the projected cost of completing the major system if current requirements are not modified;

(B) the projected cost of completing the major system based on reasonable modification of such requirements;

(C) the rough order of magnitude of the costs of any reasonable alternative system or capability; and

(D) the need to reduce funding for other systems due to the growth in cost of the major system.

(b) PRESUMPTION OF TERMINATION.—(1) After conducting the reassessment required by subsection (a) with respect to a major system, the Director shall terminate the major system unless the Director submits to Congress a Major System Congressional Report containing a certification in accordance with paragraph (2) and the information described in paragraph (3). The Director shall submit such Major System Congressional Report and certification not later than 90 days after the date the Director receives the relevant major system cost report under subsection (b) or (c) of section 506E.

(2) A certification described by this paragraph with respect to a major system is a written certification that—

(A) the continuation of the major system is essential to the national security;

(B) there are no alternatives to the major system that will provide acceptable capability to meet the intelligence requirement at less cost;

(C) the new estimates of the total acquisition cost have been determined by the Director to be reasonable;

(D) the major system is a higher priority than other systems whose funding must be reduced to accommodate the growth in cost of the major system; and

(E) the management structure for the major system is adequate to manage and control the total acquisition cost.

(3) A Major System Congressional Report accompanying a written certification under paragraph (2) shall include, in addition to the requirements of section 506E(e), the root cause analysis and assessment carried out pursuant to subsection (a), the

basis for each determination made in accordance with subparagraphs (A) through (E) of paragraph (2), and a description of all funding changes made as a result of the growth in the cost of the major system, including reductions made in funding for other systems to accommodate such cost growth, together with supporting documentation.

(c) Actions if Major System Not Terminated.—If the Director elects not to terminate a major system pursuant to subsection (b), the Director shall—

(1) restructure the major system in a manner that addresses the root cause or causes of the critical cost growth, as identified pursuant to subsection (a), and ensures that the system has an appropriate management structure as set forth in the certification submitted pursuant to subsection (b)(2)(E);

(2) rescind the most recent Milestone approval for the major system;

(3) require a new Milestone approval for the major system before taking any action to enter a new contract, exercise an option under an existing contract, or otherwise extend the scope of an existing contract under the system, except to the extent determined necessary by the Milestone Decision Authority, on a nondelegable basis, to ensure that the system may be restructured as intended by the Director without unnecessarily wasting resources;

(4) establish a revised current Baseline Estimate for the major system based upon an updated cost estimate; and

(5) conduct regular reviews of the major system.

(d) Actions if Major System Terminated.—If a major system is terminated pursuant to subsection (b), the Director shall submit to Congress a written report setting forth—

(1) an explanation of the reasons for terminating the major system;

(2) the alternatives considered to address any problems in the major system; and

(3) the course the Director plans to pursue to meet any intelligence requirements otherwise intended to be met by the major system.

(e) Form of Report.— Any report or certification required to be submitted under this section may be submitted in a classified form.

(f) Waiver.—(1) The Director may waive the requirements of subsections (d)(2), (e), and (g) of section 506E and subsections (a)(2), (b), (c), and (d) of this section with respect to a major system if the Director determines that at least 90 percent of the amount of the current Baseline Estimate for the major system has been expended.

(2)(A) If the Director grants a waiver under paragraph (1) with respect to a major system, the Director shall submit to the congressional intelligence committees written notice of the waiver that includes—

(i) the information described in section 506E(f); and

(ii) if the current total acquisition cost of the major system has increased by a percentage equal to or greater than the critical cost growth threshold—

(I) a determination of the root cause or causes of the critical cost growth, as described in subsection (a)(1); and

(II) a certification that includes the elements described in subparagraphs (A), (B), and (E) of subsection (b)(2).

(B) The Director shall submit the written notice required by subparagraph (A) not later than 90 days after the date that the Director receives a major system cost report under subsection (b) or (c) of section 506E that indicates that the total acquisition cost for the major system has increased by a percentage equal to or greater than the significant cost growth threshold or critical cost growth threshold.

(g) DEFINITIONS.— In this section, the terms "cost estimate", "critical cost growth threshold", "current Baseline Estimate", "major system", and "total acquisition cost" have the meaning given those terms in section 506E(a).

FUTURE BUDGET PROJECTIONS

SEC. 506G. [50 U.S.C. 3103] (a) FUTURE YEAR INTELLIGENCE PLANS.—(1) The Director of National Intelligence, with the concurrence of the Director of the Office of Management and Budget, shall provide to the congressional intelligence committees a Future Year Intelligence Plan, as described in paragraph (2), for—

(A) each expenditure center in the National Intelligence Program; and

(B) each major system in the National Intelligence Program.

(2)(A) A Future Year Intelligence Plan submitted under this subsection shall include the year-by-year proposed funding for each center or system referred to in subparagraph (A) or (B) of paragraph (1), for the budget year for which the Plan is submitted and not less than the 4 subsequent fiscal years.

(B) A Future Year Intelligence Plan submitted under subparagraph (B) of paragraph (1) for a major system shall include—

(i) the estimated total life-cycle cost of such major system; and

(ii) major milestones that have significant resource implications for such major system.

(b) LONG-TERM BUDGET PROJECTIONS.—(1) The Director of National Intelligence, with the concurrence of the Director of the Office of Management and Budget, shall provide to the congressional intelligence committees a Long-term Budget Projection for each element of the intelligence community funded under the National Intelligence Program acquiring a major system that includes the budget for such element for the 5-year period that begins on the day after the end of the last fiscal year for which year-by-year proposed funding is included in a Future Year Intelligence Plan for such major system in accordance with subsection (a)(2)(A).

(2) A Long-term Budget Projection submitted under paragraph (1) shall include—

(A) projections for the appropriate element of the intelligence community for—

(i) pay and benefits of officers and employees of such element;

(ii) other operating and support costs and minor acquisitions of such element;

(iii) research and technology required by such element;

(iv) current and planned major system acquisitions for such element;

(v) any future major system acquisitions for such element; and

(vi) any additional funding projections that the Director of National Intelligence considers appropriate;

(B) a budget projection based on effective cost and schedule execution of current or planned major system acquisitions and application of Office of Management and Budget inflation estimates to future major system acquisitions;

(C) any additional assumptions and projections that the Director of National Intelligence considers appropriate; and

(D) a description of whether, and to what extent, the total projection for each year exceeds the level that would result from applying the most recent Office of Management and Budget inflation estimate to the budget of that element of the intelligence community.

(c) SUBMISSION TO CONGRESS.— The Director of National Intelligence, with the concurrence of the Director of the Office of Management and Budget, shall submit to the congressional intelligence committees each Future Year Intelligence Plan or Long-term Budget Projection required under subsection (a) or (b) for a fiscal year at the time that the President submits to Congress the budget for such fiscal year pursuant to section 1105 of title 31, United States Code.

(d) MAJOR SYSTEM AFFORDABILITY REPORT.—(1) The Director of National Intelligence, with the concurrence of the Director of the Office of Management and Budget, shall prepare a report on the acquisition of a major system funded under the National Intelligence Program before the time that the President submits to Congress the budget for the first fiscal year in which appropriated funds are anticipated to be obligated for the development or procurement of such major system.

(2) The report on such major system shall include an assessment of whether, and to what extent, such acquisition, if developed, procured, and operated, is projected to cause an increase in the most recent Future Year Intelligence Plan and Long-term Budget Projection submitted under section 506G for an element of the intelligence community.

(3) The Director of National Intelligence shall update the report whenever an independent cost estimate must be updated pursuant to section 506A(a)(4).

(4) The Director of National Intelligence shall submit each report required by this subsection at the time that the President submits to Congress the budget for a fiscal year pursuant to section 1105 of title 31, United States Code.

(e) DEFINITIONS.—In this section:

(1) BUDGET YEAR.— The term "budget year" means the next fiscal year for which the President is required to submit to Congress a budget pursuant to section 1105 of title 31, United States Code.

(2) INDEPENDENT COST ESTIMATE; MAJOR SYSTEM.— The terms "independent cost estimate" and "major system" have the meaning given those terms in section 506A(e).

REPORTS ON SECURITY CLEARANCES

SEC. 506H. [50 U.S.C. 3104] (a) REPORT ON SECURITY CLEARANCE DETERMINATIONS.—(1) Not later than February 1 of each year, the President shall submit to Congress a report on the security clearance process. Such report shall include, for each security clearance level—

(A) the number of employees of the United States Government who—

(i) held a security clearance at such level as of October 1 of the preceding year; and

(ii) were approved for a security clearance at such level during the preceding fiscal year; and

(B) the number of contractors to the United States Government who—

(i) held a security clearance at such level as of October 1 of the preceding year; and

(ii) were approved for a security clearance at such level during the preceding fiscal year.

(2) For purposes of paragraph (1), the President may consider—

(A) security clearances at the level of confidential and secret as one security clearance level; and

(B) security clearances at the level of top secret or higher as one security clearance level.

(b) INTELLIGENCE COMMUNITY REPORTS.—(1)(A) Not later than March 1 of each year, the Director of National Intelligence shall submit a report to the congressional intelligence committees, the Committee on Homeland Security and Governmental Affairs of the Senate, the Committee on Homeland Security of the House of Representatives, and the Committee on Oversight and Reform of the House of Representatives regarding the security clearances processed by each element of the intelligence community during the preceding fiscal year.

(B) The Director shall submit to the Committee on Armed Services of the Senate and the Committee on Armed Services of the House of Representatives such portions of the report submitted under subparagraph (A) as the Director determines address elements of the intelligence community that are within the Department of Defense.

(C) Each report submitted under this paragraph shall separately identify security clearances processed for Federal employees and contractor employees sponsored by each such element.

(2) Each report submitted under paragraph (1)(A) shall include, for each element of the intelligence community for the fiscal year covered by the report, the following:

(A) The total number of initial security clearance background investigations sponsored for new applicants.

(B) The total number of security clearance periodic reinvestigations sponsored for existing employees.

(C) The total number of initial security clearance background investigations for new applicants that were adjudicated with notice of a determination provided to the prospective applicant, including—

(i) the total number of such adjudications that were adjudicated favorably and granted access to classified information; and

(ii) the total number of such adjudications that were adjudicated unfavorably and resulted in a denial or revocation of a security clearance.

(D) The total number of security clearance periodic background investigations that were adjudicated with notice of a determination provided to the existing employee, including—

(i) the total number of such adjudications that were adjudicated favorably; and

(ii) the total number of such adjudications that were adjudicated unfavorably and resulted in a denial or revocation of a security clearance.

(E) The total number of pending security clearance background investigations, including initial applicant investigations and periodic reinvestigations, that were not adjudicated as of the last day of such year and that remained pending, categorized as follows:

(i) For 180 days or shorter.

(ii) For longer than 180 days, but shorter than 12 months.

(iii) For 12 months or longer, but shorter than 18 months.

(iv) For 18 months or longer, but shorter than 24 months.

(v) For 24 months or longer.

(F) For any security clearance determinations completed or pending during the year preceding the year for which the report is submitted that have taken longer than 12 months to complete—

(i) an explanation of the causes for the delays incurred during the period covered by the report; and

(ii) the number of such delays involving a polygraph requirement.

(G) The percentage of security clearance investigations, including initial and periodic reinvestigations, that resulted in a denial or revocation of a security clearance.

(H) The percentage of security clearance investigations that resulted in incomplete information.

(I) The percentage of security clearance investigations that did not result in enough information to make a decision on potentially adverse information.

(3) The report required under this subsection shall be submitted in unclassified form, but may include a classified annex.

(c) FORM.— The reports required under subsections (a)(1) and (b) shall be submitted in unclassified form, but may include a classified annex.

SUMMARY OF INTELLIGENCE RELATING TO TERRORIST RECIDIVISM OF DETAINEES HELD AT UNITED STATES NAVAL STATION, GUANTANAMO BAY, CUBA

SEC. 506I. [50 U.S.C. 3105] (a) IN GENERAL.—The Director of National Intelligence, in consultation with the Director of the Central Intelligence Agency and the Director of the Defense Intelligence Agency, shall make publicly available an unclassified summary of—

(1) intelligence relating to recidivism of detainees currently or formerly held at the Naval Detention Facility at Guantanamo Bay, Cuba, by the Department of Defense; and

(2) an assessment of the likelihood that such detainees will engage in terrorism or communicate with persons in terrorist organizations.

(b) UPDATES.— Not less frequently than annually, the Director of National Intelligence, in consultation with the Director of the Central Intelligence Agency and the Secretary of Defense, shall update and make publicly available an unclassified summary consisting of the information required by subsection (a) and the number of individuals formerly detained at Naval Station, Guantanamo Bay, Cuba, who are confirmed or suspected of returning to terrorist activities after release or transfer from such Naval Station.

SEC. 506J. [50 U.S.C. 3105a] CLASSIFIED INTELLIGENCE BUDGET JUSTIFICATION MATERIALS.

(a) DEFINITIONS .—In this section:

(1) BUDGET .—The term “budget” has the meaning given the term “budget of the President” in section 506A.

(2) CLASSIFIED INTELLIGENCE BUDGET JUSTIFICATION MATERIALS .—The term “classified intelligence budget justification materials” means, with respect to a fiscal year, the materials submitted to Congress by the Director of National Intelligence in support of the budget for that fiscal year that are classified or otherwise protected from public disclosure.

(b) TIMELY SUBMISSION.— Not later than 5 days after the date on which the President submits to Congress the budget for each fiscal year pursuant to section 1105(a) of title 31, United States Code, the Director of National Intelligence shall submit to the congressional intelligence committees the classified intelligence budget justification materials for the element for that budget.

DATES FOR SUBMITTAL OF VARIOUS ANNUAL AND SEMIANNUAL REPORTS TO THE CONGRESSIONAL INTELLIGENCE COMMITTEES

SEC. 507. [50 U.S.C. 3106] (a) ANNUAL REPORTS.—The date for the submittal to the congressional intelligence committees of the following annual reports shall be the date each year provided in subsection (c)(1):

(1) The annual report of the Inspectors General of the intelligence community on proposed resources and activities of their offices required by section 416(h) of title 5, United States Code.

(2) The annual report on certifications for immunity in interdiction of aircraft engaged in illicit drug trafficking required by section 1012(c)(2) of the National Defense Authorization Act for Fiscal Year 1995 (22 U.S.C. 2291–4(c)(2)).

(3) The annual report on activities under the David L. Boren National Security Education Act of 1991 (title VIII of Public Law 102–183; 50 U.S.C. 1901 et seq.) required by section 806(a) of that Act (50 U.S.C. 1906(a)).

(4) The annual report on hiring and retention of minority employees in the intelligence community required by section 114(a).

(5) The annual report on financial intelligence on terrorist assets required by section 118.

(6) An annual report submitted under section 119C(d)(1).

(b) SEMIANNUAL REPORTS.—The dates for the submittal to the congressional intelligence committees of the following semiannual reports shall be the dates each year provided in subsection (c)(2):

(1) The semiannual reports on decisions not to prosecute certain violations of law under the Classified Information Procedures Act (18 U.S.C. App.) as required by section 13 of that Act.

(2) The semiannual reports on the disclosure of information and consumer reports to the Federal Bureau of Investigation for counterintelligence purposes required by section 624(h)(2) of the Fair Credit Reporting Act (15 U.S.C. 1681u(h)(2)).

(3) The semiannual provision of information on requests for financial information for foreign counterintelligence purposes required by section 1114(a)(5)(C) of the Right to Financial Privacy Act of 1978 (12 U.S.C. 3414(a)(5)(C)).

(c) SUBMITTAL DATES FOR REPORTS.—(1) Except as provided in subsection (d), each annual report listed in subsection (a) shall be submitted not later than February 1.

(2) Except as provided in subsection (d), each semiannual report listed in subsection (b) shall be submitted not later than February 1 and August 1.

(d) POSTPONEMENT OF SUBMITTAL.—(1) Subject to paragraph (3), the date for the submittal of—

(A) an annual report listed in subsection (a) may be postponed until March 1; and

(B) a semiannual report listed in subsection (b) may be postponed until March 1 or September 1, as the case may be,

if the official required to submit such report submits to the congressional intelligence committees a written notification of such postponement.

(2)(A) Notwithstanding any other provision of law and subject to paragraph (3), the date for the submittal to the congressional intelligence committees of any report described in subparagraph (B) may be postponed by not more than 30 days from the date otherwise specified in the provision of law for the submittal of such report if the official required to submit such report submits to the congressional intelligence committees a written notification of such postponement.

(B) A report described in this subparagraph is any report on intelligence or intelligence-related activities of the United States Government that is submitted under a provision of law requiring the submittal of only a single report.

(3)(A) The date for the submittal of a report whose submittal is postponed under paragraph (1) or (2) may be postponed beyond the time provided for the submittal of such report under such paragraph if the official required to submit such report submits to the congressional intelligence committees a written certification that preparation and submittal of such report at such time will impede the work of officers or employees of the intelligence community in a manner that will be detrimental to the national security of the United States.

(B) A certification with respect to a report under subparagraph (A) shall include a proposed submittal date for such report, and such report shall be submitted not later than that date.

CERTIFICATION OF COMPLIANCE WITH OVERSIGHT REQUIREMENTS

SEC. 508. [50 U.S.C. 3107] The head of each element of the intelligence community shall annually submit to the congressional intelligence committees—

(1) a certification that, to the best of the knowledge of the head of such element—

(A) the head of such element is in full compliance with the requirements of this title; and

(B) any information required to be submitted by the head of such element under this Act before the date of the submission of such certification has been properly submitted; or

(2) if the head of such element is unable to submit a certification under paragraph (1), a statement—

(A) of the reasons the head of such element is unable to submit such a certification;

(B) describing any information required to be submitted by the head of such element under this Act before the date of the submission of such statement that has not been properly submitted; and

(C) that the head of such element will submit such information as soon as possible after the submission of such statement.

SEC. 509. [50 U.S.C. 3108] AUDITABILITY OF CERTAIN ELEMENTS OF THE INTELLIGENCE COMMUNITY.

(a) REQUIREMENT FOR ANNUAL AUDITS.— The head of each covered entity shall ensure that there is a full financial audit of such covered entity each year beginning with fiscal year 2014. Such audits may be conducted by an internal or external independent accounting or auditing organization.

(b) Requirement for Unqualified Opinion.— Beginning as early as practicable, but in no event later than the audit required under subsection (a) for fiscal year 2016, the head of each covered entity shall take all reasonable steps necessary to ensure that each audit required under subsection (a) contains an unqualified opinion on the financial statements of such covered entity for the fiscal year covered by such audit.

(c) Reports to Congress.— The chief financial officer of each covered entity shall provide to the congressional intelligence committees an annual audit report from an accounting or auditing organization on each audit of the covered entity conducted pursuant to subsection (a).

(d) Covered Entity Defined.— In this section, the term "covered entity" means the Office of the Director of National Intelligence, the Central Intelligence Agency, the Defense Intelligence Agency, the National Security Agency, the National Reconnaissance Office, and the National Geospatial-Intelligence Agency.

SEC. 510. [50 U.S.C. 3109] SIGNIFICANT INTERPRETATIONS OF LAW CONCERNING INTELLIGENCE ACTIVITIES.

(a) Notification.— Except as provided in subsection (c) and to the extent consistent with due regard for the protection from unauthorized disclosure of classified information relating to sensitive intelligence sources and methods or other exceptionally sensitive matters, the General Counsel of each element of the intelligence community shall notify the congressional intelligence committees, in writing, of any significant legal interpretation of the United States Constitution or Federal law affecting intelligence activities conducted by such element by not later than 30 days after the date of the commencement of any intelligence activity pursuant to such interpretation.

(b) Content.— Each notification under subsection (a) shall provide a summary of the significant legal interpretation and the intelligence activity or activities conducted pursuant to such interpretation.

(c) Exceptions.—A notification under subsection (a) shall not be required for a significant legal interpretation if—

(1) notice of the significant legal interpretation was previously provided to the congressional intelligence committees under subsection (a); or

(2) the significant legal interpretation was made before the date of the enactment of the Intelligence Authorization Act for Fiscal Year 2014.

(d) Limited Access for Covert Action.— If the President determines that it is essential to limit access to a covert action finding under section 503(c)(2), the President may limit access to information concerning such finding that is subject to notification under this section to those members of Congress who have been granted access to the relevant finding under section 503(c)(2).

SEC. 511. [50 U.S.C. 3110] ANNUAL REPORT ON VIOLATIONS OF LAW OR EXECUTIVE ORDER.

(a) Annual Reports Required.— The Director of National Intelligence shall annually submit to the congressional intelligence committees a report on violations of law or executive order relating to intelligence activities by personnel of an element of the intelligence community that were identified during the previous calendar year.

(b) ELEMENTS.—Each report submitted under subsection (a) shall, consistent with the need to preserve ongoing criminal investigations, include a description of, and any action taken in response to, any violation of law or executive order (including Executive Order No. 12333 (50 U.S.C. 3001 note)) relating to intelligence activities committed by personnel of an element of the intelligence community in the course of the employment of such personnel that, during the previous calendar year, was—

(1) determined by the director, head, or general counsel of any element of the intelligence community to have occurred;

(2) referred to the Department of Justice for possible criminal prosecution; or

(3) substantiated by the inspector general of any element of the intelligence community.

SEC. 512. [50 U.S.C. 3111] BRIEFINGS AND NOTIFICATIONS ON COUNTERINTELLIGENCE ACTIVITIES OF THE FEDERAL BUREAU OF INVESTIGATION.

(a) QUARTERLY BRIEFINGS.—In addition to, and without any derogation of, the requirement under section 501 to keep the congressional intelligence committees fully and currently informed of the intelligence and counterintelligence activities of the United States, not less frequently than once each quarter, or more frequently if requested by the congressional intelligence committees, the Director of the Federal Bureau of Investigation shall provide to the congressional intelligence committees a briefing on the counterintelligence activities of the Federal Bureau of Investigation. Such briefings shall include, at a minimum, an overview and update of—

(1) the counterintelligence posture of the Bureau;

(2) counterintelligence investigations; and

(3) any other information relating to the counterintelligence activities of the Bureau that the Director determines necessary.

(b) NOTIFICATIONS.— In addition to the quarterly briefings under subsection (a), the Director of the Federal Bureau of Investigation shall promptly notify the congressional intelligence committees of any counterintelligence investigation carried out by the Bureau with respect to any counterintelligence risk or threat that is related to an election or campaign for Federal office.

(c) GUIDELINES.—

(1) DEVELOPMENT AND CONSULTATION.— The Director shall develop guidelines governing the scope of the briefings provided under subsection (a), the notifications provided under subsection (b), and the information required by section 5304(a)(2) of the Damon Paul Nelson and Matthew Young Pollard Intelligence Authorization Act for Fiscal Years 2018, 2019, and 2020. The Director shall consult the congressional intelligence committees during such development.

(2) SUBMISSION.—The Director shall submit to the congressional intelligence committees—

(A) the guidelines under paragraph (1) upon issuance; and

(B) any updates to such guidelines by not later than 15 days after making such update.

SEC. 513. [50 U.S.C. 3112] ANNUAL REPORTS ON THE DOMESTIC ACTIVITIES OF THE INTELLIGENCE COMMUNITY.

(a) REPORTS.—Not later than January 31 of each year, the Director of National Intelligence shall submit to the congressional intelligence committees a report—

(1) identifying all domestic activities undertaken by each element of the intelligence community during the prior fiscal year; and

(2) for each activity identified under paragraph (1), a statement of the legal authority authorizing such activity to be undertaken.

(b) FORM.— Each report under subsection (a) shall be submitted in unclassified form, but may include a classified annex.

SEC. 514. [50 U.S.C. 3113] UNFUNDED PRIORITIES OF THE INTELLIGENCE COMMUNITY: ANNUAL REPORT.

(a) ANNUAL REPORT.— Not later than 10 days after the date on which the budget of the President for a fiscal year is submitted to Congress pursuant to section 1105 of title 31, United States Code, the head of each element of the intelligence community shall prepare and submit to the Director of National Intelligence, the congressional intelligence committees, the Subcommittee on Defense of the Committee on Appropriations of the Senate, and the Subcommittee on Defense of the Committee on Appropriations of the House of Representatives a report on the unfunded priorities of the programs under the jurisdiction of such head.

(b) ELEMENTS

(1) IN GENERAL .—Each report under subsection (a) shall specify, for each unfunded priority covered by such report, the following:

(A) A summary description of such priority, including the objectives to be achieved if such priority is funded (whether in whole or in part).

(B) Whether such priority will satisfy a covert action or support collection against requirements identified in the National Intelligence Priorities Framework of the Office of the Director of National Intelligence (or any successor mechanism established for the prioritization of programs and activities), including a description of such requirements and the related prioritization level.

(C) The additional amount of funds recommended in connection with the objectives under subparagraph (A).

(D) Budget information with respect to the unfunded priority, including—

(i) the appropriation account;

(ii) the expenditure center; and

(iii) the project and, if applicable, subproject.

(2) PRIORITIZATION OF PRIORITIES.— Each report shall present the unfunded priorities covered by such report in overall order of urgency of priority among unfunded priorities.

(c) UNFUNDED PRIORITY DEFINED.—In this section, the term “unfunded priority”, in the case of a fiscal year, means a program, activity, or mission requirement of an element of the intelligence community that—

(1) is not funded in the budget of the President for the fiscal year as submitted to Congress pursuant to section 1105 of title 31, United States Code;

(2) is necessary to fulfill a covert action or to satisfy an information requirement associated with the collection, analysis, or dissemination of intelligence that has been documented within the National Intelligence Priorities Framework; and

(3) would have been recommended for funding by the head of the element of the intelligence community if—

(A) additional resources had been available for the budget to fund the program, activity, or mission requirement; or

(B) the program, activity, or mission requirement has emerged since the budget was formulated.

SEC. 515. [50 U.S.C. 3114] SUBMISSION OF COVERED DOCUMENTS AND CLASSIFIED ANNEXES.

(a) COVERED DOCUMENT DEFINED.— In this section, the term "covered document" means any executive order, memorandum, or policy directive issued by the President, including national security Presidential memoranda and Presidential policy directives, or such successor memoranda and directives.

(b) REQUIREMENT .—Not later than 7 days after the date on which the President issues or amends a covered document, the President, acting through the Director of National Intelligence, shall submit to the congressional intelligence committees, the Subcommittee on Defense of the Committee on Appropriations of the Senate, and the Subcommittee on Defense of the Committee on Appropriations of the House of Representatives the covered document and any classified annex accompanying that document if such covered document or annex contains a direction to, establishes a requirement for, or includes a restriction on any element of the intelligence community.

SEC. 516. [50 U.S.C. 3115] SUBMISSION OF LEGISLATIVE PROPOSALS.

Not later than 45 days after the date on which the President submits to Congress the budget for each fiscal year pursuant to section 1105(a) of title 31, United States Code, the Director of National Intelligence shall submit to the congressional intelligence committees, the Committee on Appropriations of the Senate, and the Committee on Appropriations of the House of Representatives any legislative provisions that are proposed by the Director to be enacted as part of the annual intelligence authorization bill for that fiscal year.

TITLE VI—PROTECTION OF CERTAIN NATIONAL SECURITY INFORMATION

PROTECTION OF IDENTITIES OF CERTAIN UNITED STATES UNDERCOVER INTELLIGENCE OFFICERS, AGENTS, INFORMANTS, AND SOURCES

SEC. 601. [50 U.S.C. 3121] (a) Whoever, having or having had authorized access to classified information that identifies a covert agent, intentionally discloses any information identifying such covert agent to any individual not authorized to receive classified information, knowing that the information disclosed so identifies such covert agent and that the United States is taking affirmative measures to conceal such covert agent's intelligence relationship to the United States, shall be fined under title 18, United States Code, or imprisoned not more than 15 years, or both.

(b) Whoever, as a result of having authorized access to classified information, learns the identity of a covert agent and intentionally discloses any information identifying such covert agent to any individual not authorized to receive classified information, knowing that the information disclosed so identifies such covert agent and that the United States is taking affirmative measures to conceal such covert agent's intelligence relationship to the United States, shall be fined under title 18, United States Code, or imprisoned not more than 10 years, or both.

(c) Whoever, in the course of a pattern of activities intended to identify and expose covert agents and with reason to believe that such activities would impair or impede the foreign intelligence activities of the United States, discloses any information that identifies an individual as a covert agent to any individual not authorized to receive classified information, knowing that the information disclosed so identifies such individual and that the United States is taking affirmative measures to conceal such individual's classified intelligence relationship to the United States, shall be fined under title 18, United States Code, or imprisoned not more than three years, or both.

(d) A term of imprisonment imposed under this section shall be consecutive to any other sentence of imprisonment.

DEFENSES AND EXCEPTIONS

SEC. 602. **[50 U.S.C. 3122]** (a) It is a defense to a prosecution under section 601 that before the commission of the offense with which the defendant is charged, the United States had publicly acknowledged or revealed the intelligence relationship to the United States of the individual the disclosure of whose intelligence relationship to the United States is the basis for the prosecution.

(b)(1) Subject to paragraph (2), no person other than a person committing an offense under section 601 shall be subject to prosecution under such section by virtue of section 2 or 4 of title 18, United States Code, or shall be subject to prosecution for conspiracy to commit an offense under such section.

(2) Paragraph (1) shall not apply (A) in the case of a person who acted in the course of a pattern of activities intended to identify and expose covert agents and with reason to believe that such activities would impair or impede the foreign intelligence activities of the United States, or (B) in the case of a person who has authorized access to classified information.

(c) It shall not be an offense under section 601 to transmit information described in such section directly to either congressional intelligence committee.

(d) It shall not be an offense under section 601 for an individual to disclose information that solely identifies himself as a covert agent.

EXTRATERRITORIAL JURISDICTION

SEC. 603. **[50 U.S.C. 3124]** There is jurisdiction over an offense under section 601 committed outside the United States if the individual committing the offense is a citizen of the United States or an alien lawfully admitted to the United States for permanent residence (as defined in section 101(a)(20) of the Immigration and Nationality Act).

PROVIDING INFORMATION TO CONGRESS

SEC. 604. [50 U.S.C. 3125] Nothing in this title may be construed as authority to withhold information from the Congress or from a committee of either House of Congress.

DEFINITIONS

SEC. 605. [50 U.S.C. 3126] For the purposes of this title:

(1) The term "classified information" means information or material designated and clearly marked or clearly represented, pursuant to the provisions of a statute or Executive order (or a regulation or order issued pursuant to a statute or Executive order), as requiring a specific degree of protection against unauthorized disclosure for reasons of national security.

(2) The term "authorized", when used with respect to access to classified information, means having authority, right, or permission pursuant to the provisions of a statute, Executive order, directive of the head of any department or agency engaged in foreign intelligence or counterintelligence activities, order of any United States court, or provisions of any Rule of the House of Representatives or resolution of the Senate which assigns responsibility within the respective House of Congress for the oversight of intelligence activities.

(3) The term "disclose" means to communicate, provide, impart, transmit, transfer, convey, publish, or otherwise make available.

(4) The term "covert agent" means—

(A) a present or retired officer or employee of an intelligence agency or a present or retired member of the Armed Forces assigned to duty with an intelligence agency whose identity as such an officer, employee, or member is classified information; or

(B) a United States citizen whose intelligence relationship to the United States is classified information, and—

(i) who acts as an agent of, or informant or source of operational assistance to, an intelligence agency, or

(ii) who is at the time of the disclosure acting as an agent of, or informant to, the foreign counterintelligence or foreign counterterrorism components of the Federal Bureau of Investigation; or

(C) an individual, other than a United States citizen, whose past or present intelligence relationship to the United States is classified information and who is a present or former agent of, or a present or former informant or source of operational assistance to, an intelligence agency.

(5) The term "intelligence agency" means the elements of the intelligence community, as that term is defined in section 3(4).[12]

[12] Section 310(a)(4)(B) of Public Law 112–277 provides for an amendment to redesignate section 606 as section 605. Section 506 of such Public Law provides for an amendment to revise paragraph (5) of section 606 in its entirety, which was carried out above to section 605(5) (as so redesignated) to

reflect the probable intent of Congress.

(6) The term "informant" means any individual who furnishes information to an intelligence agency in the course of a confidential relationship protecting the identity of such individual from public disclosure.

(7) The terms "officer" and "employee" have the meanings given such terms by section 2104 and 2105, respectively, of title 5, United States Code.

(8) The term "Armed Forces" means the Army, Navy, Air Force, Marine Corps, and Coast Guard.

(9) The term "United States", when used in a geographic sense, means all areas under the territorial sovereignty of the United States and the Trust Territory of the Pacific Islands.

(10) The term "pattern of activities" requires a series of acts with a common purpose or objective.

TITLE VII—PROTECTION OF OPERATIONAL FILES

OPERATIONAL FILES OF THE CENTRAL INTELLIGENCE AGENCY

SEC. 701. [50 U.S.C. 3141] (a) The Director of the Central Intelligence Agency, with the coordination of the Director of National Intelligence, may exempt operational files of the Central Intelligence Agency from the provisions of section 552 of title 5, United States Code (Freedom of Information Act), which require publication or disclosure, or search or review in connection therewith.

(b) In this section, the term "operational files" means—

(1) files of the National Clandestine Service which document the conduct of foreign intelligence or counterintelligence operations or intelligence or security liaison arrangements or information exchanges with foreign governments or their intelligence or security services;

(2) files of the Directorate for Science and Technology which document the means by which foreign intelligence or counterintelligence is collected through scientific and technical systems; and

(3) files of the Office of Personnel Security which document investigations conducted to determine the suitability of potential foreign intelligence or counterintelligence sources;

except that files which are the sole repository of disseminated intelligence are not operational files.

(c) Notwithstanding subsection (a) of this section, exempted operational files shall continue to be subject to search and review for information concerning—

(1) United States citizens or aliens lawfully admitted for permanent residence who have requested information on themselves pursuant to the provisions of section 552 of title 5, United States Code (Freedom of Information Act), or section 552a of title 5, United States Code (Privacy Act of 1974);

(2) any special activity the existence of which is not exempt from disclosure

under the provisions of section 552 of title 5, United States Code (Freedom of Information Act); or

(3) the specific subject matter of an investigation by the congressional intelligence committees, the Intelligence Oversight Board, the Department of Justice, the Office of General Counsel of the Central Intelligence Agency, the Office of Inspector General of the Central Intelligence Agency, or the Office of the Director of National Intelligence for any impropriety, or violation of law, Executive order, or Presidential directive, in the conduct of an intelligence activity.

(d)(1) Files that are not exempted under subsection (a) of this section which contain information derived or disseminated from exempted operational files shall be subject to search and review.

(2) The inclusion of information from exempted operational files in files that are not exempted under subsection (a) of this section shall not affect the exemption under subsection (a) of this section of the originating operational files from search, review, publication, or disclosure.

(3) Records from exempted operational files which have been disseminated to and referenced in files that are not exempted under subsection (a) of this section and which have been returned to exempted operational files for sole retention shall be subject to search and review.

(e) The provisions of subsection (a) of this section shall not be superseded except by a provision of law which is enacted after the date of enactment of subsection (a), and which specifically cites and repeals or modifies its provisions.

(f) Whenever any person who has requested agency records under section 552 of title 5, United States Code (Freedom of Information Act), alleges that the Central Intelligence Agency has improperly withheld records because of failure to comply with any provision of this section, judicial review shall be available under the terms set forth in section 552(a)(4)(B) of title 5, United States Code, except that—

(1) in any case in which information specifically authorized under criteria established by an Executive order to be kept secret in the interest of national defense or foreign relations which is filed with, or produced for, the court by the Central Intelligence Agency, such information shall be examined ex parte, in camera by the court;

(2) the court shall, to the fullest extent practicable, determine issues of fact based on sworn written submissions of the parties;

(3) when a complainant alleges that requested records are improperly withheld because of improper placement solely in exempted operational files, the complainant shall support such allegation with a sworn written submission, based upon personal knowledge or otherwise admissible evidence;

(4)(A) when a complainant alleges that requested records were improperly withheld because of improper exemption of operational files, the Central Intelligence Agency shall meet its burden under section 552(a)(4)(B) of title 5, United States Code, by demonstrating to the court by sworn written submission that exempted operational files likely to contain responsive records currently perform the functions set forth in subsection (b) of this section; and

(B) the court may not order the Central Intelligence Agency to review the content of any exempted operational file or files in order to make the demonstration required under subparagraph (A) of this paragraph, unless the complainant disputes the Central Intelligence Agency's showing with a sworn written submission based on personal knowledge or otherwise admissible evidence;

(5) in proceedings under paragraphs (3) and (4) of this subsection, the parties shall not obtain discovery pursuant to rules 26 through 36 of the Federal Rules of Civil Procedure, except that requests for admission may be made pursuant to rules 26 and 36;

(6) if the court finds under this subsection that the Central Intelligence Agency has improperly withheld requested records because of failure to comply with any provision of this section, the court shall order the Central Intelligence Agency to search and review the appropriate exempted operational file or files for the requested records and make such records, or portions thereof, available in accordance with the provisions of section 552 of title 5, United States Code (Freedom of Information Act), and such order shall be the exclusive remedy for failure to comply with this section; and

(7) if at any time following the filing of a complaint pursuant to this subsection the Central Intelligence Agency agrees to search the appropriate exempted operational file or files for the requested records, the court shall dismiss the claim based upon such complaint.

(g) DECENNIAL REVIEW OF EXEMPTED OPERATIONAL FILES.—(1) Not less than once every ten years, the Director of the Central Intelligence Agency and the Director of National Intelligence shall review the exemptions in force under subsection (a) to determine whether such exemptions may be removed from any category of exempted files or any portion thereof.

(2) The review required by paragraph (1)[13] shall include consideration of the historical value or other public interest in the subject matter of the particular category of files or portions thereof and the potential for declassifying a significant part of the information contained therein.

[13] In section 701(g)(2), the amendment to strike "of subsection (a) of this section" and insert "paragraph (1)" made by section 922(b)(2)(E) of the National Defense Authorization Act for Fiscal Year 2004 (Public Law 108–136; 117 Stat. 1537) was executed by striking "subsection (a) of this section" and inserting "paragraph (1)" in order to reflect the probable intent of Congress.

(3) A complainant who alleges that the Central Intelligence Agency has improperly withheld records because of failure to comply with this subsection may seek judicial review in the district court of the United States of the district in which any of the parties reside, or in the District of Columbia. In such a proceeding, the court's review shall be limited to determining the following:

(A) Whether the Central Intelligence Agency has conducted the review required by paragraph (1) before October 15, 1994, or before the expiration of the 10-year period beginning on the date of the most recent review.

(B) Whether the Central Intelligence Agency, in fact, considered the criteria set forth in paragraph (2) in conducting the required review.

OPERATIONAL FILES OF THE NATIONAL GEOSPATIAL-INTELLIGENCE AGENCY

SEC. 702. [50 U.S.C. 3142] (a) EXEMPTION OF CERTAIN OPERATIONAL FILES FROM SEARCH, REVIEW, PUBLICATION, OR DISCLOSURE.—(1) The Director of the National Geospatial-Intelligence Agency, with the coordination of the Director of National Intelligence, may exempt operational files of the National Geospatial-Intelligence Agency from the provisions of section 552 of title 5, United States Code, which require publication, disclosure, search, or review in connection therewith.

(2)(A) Subject to subparagraph (B), for the purposes of this section, the term "operational files" means files of the National Geospatial-Intelligence Agency (hereafter in this section referred to as "NGA") concerning the activities of NGA that before the establishment of NGA were performed by the National Photographic Interpretation Center of the Central Intelligence Agency (NPIC), that document the means by which foreign intelligence or counterintelligence is collected through scientific and technical systems.

(B) Files which are the sole repository of disseminated intelligence are not operational files.

(3) Notwithstanding paragraph (1), exempted operational files shall continue to be subject to search and review for information concerning—

(A) United States citizens or aliens lawfully admitted for permanent residence who have requested information on themselves pursuant to the provisions of section 552 or 552a of title 5, United States Code;

(B) any special activity the existence of which is not exempt from disclosure under the provisions of section 552 of title 5, United States Code; or

(C) the specific subject matter of an investigation by any of the following for any impropriety, or violation of law, Executive order, or Presidential directive, in the conduct of an intelligence activity:

(i) The congressional intelligence committees.

(ii) The Intelligence Oversight Board.

(iii) The Department of Justice.

(iv) The Office of General Counsel of NGA.

(v) The Office of the Director of NGA.

(vi) The Office of the Inspector General of the National Geospatial-Intelligence Agency.

(4)(A) Files that are not exempted under paragraph (1) which contain information derived or disseminated from exempted operational files shall be subject to search and review.

(B) The inclusion of information from exempted operational files in files that are not exempted under paragraph (1) shall not affect the exemption under paragraph (1) of the originating operational files from search, review, publication, or disclosure.

(C) Records from exempted operational files which have been disseminated to and referenced in files that are not exempted under paragraph (1) and which have been returned to exempted operational files for sole retention shall be subject to search and review.

(5) The provisions of paragraph (1) may not be superseded except by a provision of law which is enacted after the date of the enactment of this section, and which specifically cites and repeals or modifies its provisions.

(6)(A) Except as provided in subparagraph (B), whenever any person who has requested agency records under section 552 of title 5, United States Code, alleges that NGA has withheld records improperly because of failure to comply with any provision of this section, judicial review shall be available under the terms set forth in section 552(a)(4)(B) of title 5, United States Code.

(B) Judicial review shall not be available in the manner provided for under subparagraph (A) as follows:

(i) In any case in which information specifically authorized under criteria established by an Executive order to be kept secret in the interests of national defense or foreign relations is filed with, or produced for, the court by NGA, such information shall be examined ex parte, in camera by the court.

(ii) The court shall, to the fullest extent practicable, determine the issues of fact based on sworn written submissions of the parties.

(iii) When a complainant alleges that requested records are improperly withheld because of improper placement solely in exempted operational files, the complainant shall support such allegation with a sworn written submission based upon personal knowledge or otherwise admissible evidence.

(iv)(I) When a complainant alleges that requested records were improperly withheld because of improper exemption of operational files, NGA shall meet its burden under section 552(a)(4)(B) of title 5, United States Code, by demonstrating to the court by sworn written submission that exempted operational files likely to contain responsive records currently perform the functions set forth in paragraph (2).

(II) The court may not order NGA to review the content of any exempted operational file or files in order to make the demonstration required under subclause (I), unless the complainant disputes NGA's showing with a sworn written submission based on personal knowledge or otherwise admissible evidence.

(v) In proceedings under clauses (iii) and (iv), the parties may not obtain discovery pursuant to rules 26 through 36 of the Federal Rules of Civil Procedure, except that requests for admissions may be made pursuant to rules 26 and 36.

(vi) If the court finds under this paragraph that NGA has improperly withheld requested records because of failure to comply with any provision of this subsection, the court shall order NGA to search and review the appropriate exempted operational file or files for the requested records and make such records, or portions thereof, available in accordance with the provisions of section 552 of title 5, United States Code, and such order shall be the exclusive remedy for failure to comply with this subsection.

(vii) If at any time following the filing of a complaint pursuant to this paragraph NGA agrees to search the appropriate exempted operational file or files for the requested records, the court shall dismiss the claim based upon such complaint.

(viii) Any information filed with, or produced for the court pursuant to clauses (i) and (iv) shall be coordinated with the Director of National Intelligence prior to submission to the court.

(b) DECENNIAL REVIEW OF EXEMPTED OPERATIONAL FILES.—(1) Not less than once every 10 years, the Director of the National Geospatial-Intelligence Agency and the Director of National Intelligence shall review the exemptions in force under subsection (a)(1) to determine whether such exemptions may be removed from the category of exempted files or any portion thereof. The Director of National Intelligence must approve any determination to remove such exemptions.

(2) The review required by paragraph (1) shall include consideration of the historical value or other public interest in the subject matter of the particular category of files or portions thereof and the potential for declassifying a significant part of the information contained therein.

(3) A complainant that alleges that NGA has improperly withheld records because of failure to comply with this subsection may seek judicial review in the district court of the United States of the district in which any of the parties reside, or in the District of Columbia. In such a proceeding, the court's review shall be limited to determining the following:

(A) Whether NGA has conducted the review required by paragraph (1) before the expiration of the 10-year period beginning on the date of the enactment of this section or before the expiration of the 10-year period beginning on the date of the most recent review.

(B) Whether NGA, in fact, considered the criteria set forth in paragraph (2) in conducting the required review.

OPERATIONAL FILES OF THE NATIONAL RECONNAISSANCE OFFICE

SEC. 703. **[50 U.S.C. 3143]** (a) EXEMPTION OF CERTAIN OPERATIONAL FILES FROM SEARCH, REVIEW, PUBLICATION, OR DISCLOSURE.—(1) The Director of the National Reconnaissance Office, with the coordination of the Director of National Intelligence, may exempt operational files of the National Reconnaissance Office from the provisions of section 552 of title 5, United States Code, which require publication, disclosure, search, or review in connection therewith.

(2)(A) Subject to subparagraph (B), for the purposes of this section, the term "operational files" means files of the National Reconnaissance Office (hereafter in this section referred to as "NRO") that document the means by which foreign intelligence or counterintelligence is collected through scientific and technical systems.

(B) Files which are the sole repository of disseminated intelligence are not operational files.

(3) Notwithstanding paragraph (1), exempted operational files shall continue to be subject to search and review for information concerning—

(A) United States citizens or aliens lawfully admitted for permanent residence who have requested information on themselves pursuant to the provisions of section 552 or 552a of title 5, United States Code;

(B) any special activity the existence of which is not exempt from disclosure under the provisions of section 552 of title 5, United States Code; or

(C) the specific subject matter of an investigation by any of the following for any impropriety, or violation of law, Executive order, or Presidential directive, in the conduct of an intelligence activity:

(i) The Permanent Select Committee on Intelligence of the House of Representatives.

(ii) The Select Committee on Intelligence of the Senate.

(iii) The Intelligence Oversight Board.

(iv) The Department of Justice.

(v) The Office of General Counsel of NRO.

(vi) The Office of the Director of NRO.

(vii) The Office of the Inspector General of the NRO.

(4)(A) Files that are not exempted under paragraph (1) which contain information derived or disseminated from exempted operational files shall be subject to search and review.

(B) The inclusion of information from exempted operational files in files that are not exempted under paragraph (1) shall not affect the exemption under paragraph (1) of the originating operational files from search, review, publication, or disclosure.

(C) The declassification of some of the information contained in exempted operational files shall not affect the status of the operational file as being exempt from search, review, publication, or disclosure.

(D) Records from exempted operational files which have been disseminated to and referenced in files that are not exempted under paragraph (1) and which have been returned to exempted operational files for sole retention shall be subject to search and review.

(5) The provisions of paragraph (1) may not be superseded except by a provision of law which is enacted after the date of the enactment of this section, and which specifically cites and repeals or modifies its provisions.

(6)(A) Except as provided in subparagraph (B), whenever any person who has requested agency records under section 552 of title 5, United States Code, alleges that NRO has withheld records improperly because of failure to comply with any provision of this section, judicial review shall be available under the terms set forth in section 552(a)(4)(B) of title 5, United States Code.

(B) Judicial review shall not be available in the manner provided for under subparagraph (A) as follows:

(i) In any case in which information specifically authorized under criteria established by an Executive order to be kept secret in the interests of national defense or foreign relations is filed with, or produced for, the court by NRO, such information shall be examined ex parte, in camera by the court.

(ii) The court shall, to the fullest extent practicable, determine the issues of fact based on sworn written submissions of the parties.

(iii) When a complainant alleges that requested records are improperly withheld because of improper placement solely in exempted operational files, the complainant shall support such allegation with a sworn written submission based upon personal knowledge or otherwise admissible evidence.

(iv)(I) When a complainant alleges that requested records were improperly withheld because of improper exemption of operational files, NRO shall meet its burden under section 552(a)(4)(B) of title 5, United States Code, by demonstrating to the court by sworn written submission that exempted operational files likely to contain responsive records currently perform the functions set forth in paragraph (2).

(II) The court may not order NRO to review the content of any exempted operational file or files in order to make the demonstration required under subclause (I), unless the complainant disputes NRO's showing with a sworn written submission based on personal knowledge or otherwise admissible evidence.

(v) In proceedings under clauses (iii) and (iv), the parties may not obtain discovery pursuant to rules 26 through 36 of the Federal Rules of Civil Procedure, except that requests for admissions may be made pursuant to rules 26 and 36.

(vi) If the court finds under this paragraph that NRO has improperly withheld requested records because of failure to comply with any provision of this subsection, the court shall order NRO to search and review the appropriate exempted operational file or files for the requested records and make such records, or portions thereof, available in accordance with the provisions of section 552 of title 5, United States Code, and such order shall be the exclusive remedy for failure to comply with this subsection.

(vii) If at any time following the filing of a complaint pursuant to this paragraph NRO agrees to search the appropriate exempted operational file or files for the requested records, the court shall dismiss the claim based upon such complaint.

(viii) Any information filed with, or produced for the court pursuant to clauses (i) and (iv) shall be coordinated with the Director of National Intelligence prior to submission to the court.

(b) DECENNIAL REVIEW OF EXEMPTED OPERATIONAL FILES.—(1) Not less than once every 10 years, the Director of the National Reconnaissance Office and the Director of National Intelligence shall review the exemptions in force under subsection (a)(1) to determine whether such exemptions may be removed from the category of exempted files or any portion thereof. The Director of National Intelligence must approve any determination to remove such exemptions.

(2) The review required by paragraph (1) shall include consideration of the historical value or other public interest in the subject matter of the particular category of files or portions thereof and the potential for declassifying a significant part of the information contained therein.

(3) A complainant that alleges that NRO has improperly withheld records because of failure to comply with this subsection may seek judicial review in the district court of the United States of the district in which any of the parties reside, or in the District of Columbia. In such a proceeding, the court's review shall be limited to determining the following:

(A) Whether NRO has conducted the review required by paragraph (1) before the expiration of the 10-year period beginning on the date of the enactment of this section or before the expiration of the 10-year period beginning on the date of the most recent review.

(B) Whether NRO, in fact, considered the criteria set forth in paragraph (2) in conducting the required review.

OPERATIONAL FILES OF THE NATIONAL SECURITY AGENCY

SEC. 704. [50 U.S.C. 3144] (a) EXEMPTION OF CERTAIN OPERATIONAL FILES FROM SEARCH, REVIEW, PUBLICATION, OR DISCLOSURE.— The Director of the National Security Agency, in coordination with the Director of National Intelligence, may exempt operational files of the National Security Agency from the provisions of section 552 of title 5, United States Code, which require publication, disclosure, search, or review in connection therewith.

(b) OPERATIONAL FILES DEFINED.—(1) In this section, the term "operational files" means—

(A) files of the Signals Intelligence Directorate of the National Security Agency (and any successor organization of that directorate) that document the means by which foreign intelligence or counterintelligence is collected through technical systems; and

(B) files of the Research Associate Directorate of the National Security Agency (and any successor organization of that directorate) that document the means by which foreign intelligence or counterintelligence is collected through scientific and technical systems.

(2) Files that are the sole repository of disseminated intelligence, and files that have been accessioned into the National Security Agency Archives (or any successor organization) are not operational files.

(c) SEARCH AND REVIEW FOR INFORMATION.—Notwithstanding subsection (a), exempted operational files shall continue to be subject to search and review for information concerning any of the following:

(1) United States citizens or aliens lawfully admitted for permanent residence who have requested information on themselves pursuant to the provisions of section 552 or 552a of title 5, United States Code.

(2) Any special activity the existence of which is not exempt from disclosure under the provisions of section 552 of title 5, United States Code.

(3) The specific subject matter of an investigation by any of the following for any impropriety, or violation of law, Executive order, or Presidential directive, in the conduct of an intelligence activity:

(A) The Committee on Armed Services and the Permanent Select Committee on Intelligence of the House of Representatives.

(B) The Committee on Armed Services and the Select Committee on Intelligence of the Senate.

(C) The Intelligence Oversight Board.

(D) The Department of Justice.

(E) The Office of General Counsel of the National Security Agency.

(F) The Office of the Inspector General of the Department of Defense.

(G) The Office of the Director of the National Security Agency.

(H) The Office of the Inspector General of the National Security Agency.

(d) Information Derived or Disseminated from Exempted Operational Files.—(1) Files that are not exempted under subsection (a) that contain information derived or disseminated from exempted operational files shall be subject to search and review.

(2) The inclusion of information from exempted operational files in files that are not exempted under subsection (a) shall not affect the exemption under subsection (a) of the originating operational files from search, review, publication, or disclosure.

(3) The declassification of some of the information contained in exempted operational files shall not affect the status of the operational file as being exempt from search, review, publication, or disclosure.

(4) Records from exempted operational files that have been disseminated to and referenced in files that are not exempted under subsection (a) and that have been returned to exempted operational files for sole retention shall be subject to search and review.

(e) Supercedure of Other Laws.— The provisions of subsection (a) may not be superseded except by a provision of law that is enacted after the date of the enactment of this section and that specifically cites and repeals or modifies such provisions.

(f) Allegation; Improper Withholding of Records; Judicial Review.—(1) Except as provided in paragraph (2), whenever any person who has requested agency records under section 552 of title 5, United States Code, alleges that the National Security Agency has withheld records improperly because of failure to comply with any provision of this section, judicial review shall be available under the terms set forth in section 552(a)(4)(B) of title 5, United States Code.

(2) Judicial review shall not be available in the manner provided for under paragraph (1) as follows:

(A) In any case in which information specifically authorized under criteria established by an Executive order to be kept secret in the interests of national defense or foreign relations is filed with, or produced for, the court by the National Security Agency, such information shall be examined ex parte, in camera by the court.

(B) The court shall determine, to the fullest extent practicable, the issues of fact based on sworn written submissions of the parties.

(C) When a complainant alleges that requested records are improperly withheld because of improper placement solely in exempted operational files, the complainant shall support such allegation with a sworn written submission based upon personal knowledge or otherwise admissible evidence.

(D)(i) When a complainant alleges that requested records were improperly withheld because of improper exemption of operational files, the National Security Agency shall meet its burden under section 552(a)(4)(B) of title 5, United States Code, by demonstrating to the court by sworn written submission that exempted operational files likely to contain responsive records currently perform the functions set forth in subsection (b).

(ii) The court may not order the National Security Agency to review the content of any exempted operational file or files in order to make the demonstration required under clause (i), unless the complainant disputes the National Security Agency's showing with a sworn written submission based on personal knowledge or otherwise admissible evidence.

(E) In proceedings under subparagraphs (C) and (D), the parties may not obtain discovery pursuant to rules 26 through 36 of the Federal Rules of Civil Procedure, except that requests for admissions may be made pursuant to rules 26 and 36.

(F) If the court finds under this subsection that the National Security Agency has improperly withheld requested records because of failure to comply with any provision of this subsection, the court shall order the Agency to search and review the appropriate exempted operational file or files for the requested records and make such records, or portions thereof, available in accordance with the provisions of section 552 of title 5, United States Code, and such order shall be the exclusive remedy for failure to comply with this section (other than subsection (g)).

(G) If at any time following the filing of a complaint pursuant to this paragraph the National Security Agency agrees to search the appropriate exempted operational file or files for the requested records, the court shall dismiss the claim based upon such complaint.

(H) Any information filed with, or produced for the court pursuant to subparagraphs (A) and (D) shall be coordinated with the Director of National

Intelligence before submission to the court.

(g) Decennial Review of Exempted Operational Files.—(1) Not less than once every 10 years, the Director of the National Security Agency and the Director of National Intelligence shall review the exemptions in force under subsection (a) to determine whether such exemptions may be removed from a category of exempted files or any portion thereof. The Director of National Intelligence must approve any determination to remove such exemptions.

(2) The review required by paragraph (1) shall include consideration of the historical value or other public interest in the subject matter of a particular category of files or portions thereof and the potential for declassifying a significant part of the information contained therein.

(3) A complainant that alleges that the National Security Agency has improperly withheld records because of failure to comply with this subsection may seek judicial review in the district court of the United States of the district in which any of the parties reside, or in the District of Columbia. In such a proceeding, the court's review shall be limited to determining the following:

(A) Whether the National Security Agency has conducted the review required by paragraph (1) before the expiration of the 10-year period beginning on the date of the enactment of this section or before the expiration of the 10-year period beginning on the date of the most recent review.

(B) Whether the National Security Agency, in fact, considered the criteria set forth in paragraph (2) in conducting the required review.

OPERATIONAL FILES OF THE DEFENSE INTELLIGENCE AGENCY

Sec. 705. [50 U.S.C. 3145] (a) Exemption of Operational Files.— The Director of the Defense Intelligence Agency, in coordination with the Director of National Intelligence, may exempt operational files of the Defense Intelligence Agency from the provisions of section 552 of title 5, United States Code, which require publication, disclosure, search, or review in connection therewith.

(b) Operational Files Defined.—(1) In this section, the term “operational files” means—

(A) files of the Directorate of Human Intelligence of the Defense Intelligence Agency (and any successor organization of that directorate) that document the conduct of foreign intelligence or counterintelligence operations or intelligence or security liaison arrangements or information exchanges with foreign governments or their intelligence or security services; and

(B) files of the Directorate of Technology of the Defense Intelligence Agency (and any successor organization of that directorate) that document the means by which foreign intelligence or counterintelligence is collected through technical systems.

(2) Files that are the sole repository of disseminated intelligence are not operational files.

(c) Search and Review for Information.—Notwithstanding subsection (a), exempted operational files shall continue to be subject to search and review for information concerning:

(1) United States citizens or aliens lawfully admitted for permanent residence who have requested information on themselves pursuant to the provisions of section 552 or 552a of title 5, United States Code.

(2) Any special activity the existence of which is not exempt from disclosure under the provisions of section 552 of title 5, United States Code.

(3) The specific subject matter of an investigation by any of the following for any impropriety, or violation of law, Executive order, or Presidential directive, in the conduct of an intelligence activity:

(A) The Committee on Armed Services and the Permanent Select Committee on Intelligence of the House of Representatives.

(B) The Committee on Armed Services and the Select Committee on Intelligence of the Senate.

(C) The Intelligence Oversight Board.

(D) The Department of Justice.

(E) The Office of General Counsel of the Department of Defense or of the Defense Intelligence Agency.

(F) The Office of Inspector General of the Department of Defense or of the Defense Intelligence Agency.

(G) The Office of the Director of the Defense Intelligence Agency.

(d) INFORMATION DERIVED OR DISSEMINATED FROM EXEMPTED OPERATIONAL FILES.—(1) Files that are not exempted under subsection (a) that contain information derived or disseminated from exempted operational files shall be subject to search and review.

(2) The inclusion of information from exempted operational files in files that are not exempted under subsection (a) shall not affect the exemption under subsection (a) of the originating operational files from search, review, publication, or disclosure.

(3) The declassification of some of the information contained in an exempted operational file shall not affect the status of the operational file as being exempt from search, review, publication, or disclosure.

(4) Records from exempted operational files that have been disseminated to and referenced in files that are not exempted under subsection (a) and that have been returned to exempted operational files for sole retention shall be subject to search and review.

(e) ALLEGATION; IMPROPER WITHHOLDING OF RECORDS; JUDICIAL REVIEW.—(1) Except as provided in paragraph (2), whenever any person who has requested agency records under section 552 of title 5, United States Code, alleges that the Defense Intelligence Agency has withheld records improperly because of failure to comply with any provision of this section, judicial review shall be available under the terms set forth in section 552(a)(4)(B) of title 5, United States Code.

(2) Judicial review shall not be available in the manner provided under paragraph

(1) as follows:

(A) In any case in which information specifically authorized under criteria established by an Executive order to be kept secret in the interest of national defense or foreign relations which is filed with, or produced for, the court by the Defense Intelligence Agency, such information shall be examined ex parte, in camera by the court.

(B) The court shall determine, to the fullest extent practicable, issues of fact based on sworn written submissions of the parties.

(C) When a complainant alleges that requested records were improperly withheld because of improper placement solely in exempted operational files, the complainant shall support such allegation with a sworn written submission based upon personal knowledge or otherwise admissible evidence.

(D)(i) When a complainant alleges that requested records were improperly withheld because of improper exemption of operational files, the Defense Intelligence Agency shall meet its burden under section 552(a)(4)(B) of title 5, United States Code, by demonstrating to the court by sworn written submission that exempted operational files likely to contain responsive records currently perform the functions set forth in subsection (b).

(ii) The court may not order the Defense Intelligence Agency to review the content of any exempted operational file or files in order to make the demonstration required under clause (i), unless the complainant disputes the Defense Intelligence Agency's showing with a sworn written submission based on personal knowledge or otherwise admissible evidence.

(E) In proceedings under subparagraphs (C) and (D), the parties shall not obtain discovery pursuant to rules 26 through 36 of the Federal Rules of Civil Procedure, except that requests for admission may be made pursuant to rules 26 and 36.

(F) If the court finds under this subsection that the Defense Intelligence Agency has improperly withheld requested records because of failure to comply with any provision of this subsection, the court shall order the Defense Intelligence Agency to search and review the appropriate exempted operational file or files for the requested records and make such records, or portions thereof, available in accordance with the provisions of section 552 of title 5, United States Code, and such order shall be the exclusive remedy for failure to comply with this section (other than subsection (f)).

(G) If at any time following the filing of a complaint pursuant to this paragraph the Defense Intelligence Agency agrees to search the appropriate exempted operational file or files for the requested records, the court shall dismiss the claim based upon such complaint.

(H) Any information filed with, or produced for the court pursuant to subparagraphs (A) and (D) shall be coordinated with the Director of National Intelligence before submission to the court.

(f) Decennial Review of Exempted Operational Files.—(1) Not less than once every 10 years, the Director of the Defense Intelligence Agency and the Director of

National Intelligence shall review the exemptions in force under subsection (a) to determine whether such exemptions may be removed from a category of exempted files or any portion thereof. The Director of National Intelligence must approve any determinations to remove such exemptions.

(2) The review required by paragraph (1) shall include consideration of the historical value or other public interest in the subject matter of the particular category of files or portions thereof and the potential for declassifying a significant part of the information contained therein.

(3) A complainant that alleges that the Defense Intelligence Agency has improperly withheld records because of failure to comply with this subsection may seek judicial review in the district court of the United States of the district in which any of the parties reside, or in the District of Columbia. In such a proceeding, the court's review shall be limited to determining the following:

(A) Whether the Defense Intelligence Agency has conducted the review required by paragraph (1) before the expiration of the 10-year period beginning on the date of the enactment of this section or before the expiration of the 10-year period beginning on the date of the most recent review.

(B) Whether the Defense Intelligence Agency, in fact, considered the criteria set forth in paragraph (2) in conducting the required review.

(g) TERMINATION.— This section shall cease to be effective on December 31, 2007.

PROTECTION OF CERTAIN FILES OF THE OFFICE OF THE DIRECTOR OF NATIONAL INTELLIGENCE

SEC. 706. **[50 U.S.C. 3146]** (a) INAPPLICABILITY OF FOIA TO EXEMPTED OPERATIONAL FILES PROVIDED TO ODNI.—(1) Subject to paragraph (2), the provisions of section 552 of title 5, United States Code, that require search, review, publication, or disclosure of a record shall not apply to a record provided to the Office of the Director of National Intelligence by an element of the intelligence community from the exempted operational files of such element.

(2) Paragraph (1) shall not apply with respect to a record of the Office that—

(A) contains information derived or disseminated from an exempted operational file, unless such record is created by the Office for the sole purpose of organizing such exempted operational file for use by the Office;

(B) is disseminated by the Office to a person other than an officer, employee, or contractor of the Office; or

(C) is no longer designated as an exempted operational file in accordance with this title.

(b) EFFECT OF PROVIDING FILES TO ODNI.— Notwithstanding any other provision of this title, an exempted operational file that is provided to the Office by an element of the intelligence community shall not be subject to the provisions of section 552 of title 5, United States Code, that require search, review, publication, or disclosure of a record solely because such element provides such exempted operational file to the Office.

(c) SEARCH AND REVIEW FOR CERTAIN PURPOSES.—Notwithstanding subsection (a) or (b), an exempted operational file shall continue to be subject to search and review for information concerning any of the following:

(1) United States citizens or aliens lawfully admitted for permanent residence who have requested information on themselves pursuant to the provisions of section 552 or 552a of title 5, United States Code.

(2) Any special activity the existence of which is not exempt from disclosure under the provisions of section 552 of title 5, United States Code.

(3) The specific subject matter of an investigation for any impropriety or violation of law, Executive order, or Presidential directive, in the conduct of an intelligence activity by any of the following:

(A) The Select Committee on Intelligence of the Senate.

(B) The Permanent Select Committee on Intelligence of the House of Representatives.

(C) The Intelligence Oversight Board.

(D) The Department of Justice.

(E) The Office of the Director of National Intelligence.

(F) The Office of the Inspector General of the Intelligence Community.

(d) DECENNIAL REVIEW OF EXEMPTED OPERATIONAL FILES.—(1) Not less than once every 10 years, the Director of National Intelligence shall review the exemptions in force under subsection (a) to determine whether such exemptions may be removed from any category of exempted files or any portion thereof.

(2) The review required by paragraph (1) shall include consideration of the historical value or other public interest in the subject matter of the particular category of files or portions thereof and the potential for declassifying a significant part of the information contained therein.

(3) A complainant that alleges that the Director of National Intelligence has improperly withheld records because of failure to comply with this subsection may seek judicial review in the district court of the United States of the district in which any of the parties reside, or in the District of Columbia. In such a proceeding, the court's review shall be limited to determining the following:

(A) Whether the Director has conducted the review required by paragraph (1) before the expiration of the 10-year period beginning on the date of the enactment of the Intelligence Authorization Act for Fiscal Year 2010 or before the expiration of the 10-year period beginning on the date of the most recent review.

(B) Whether the Director of National Intelligence, in fact, considered the criteria set forth in paragraph (2) in conducting the required review.

(e) SUPERSEDURE OF OTHER LAWS.— The provisions of this section may not be superseded except by a provision of law that is enacted after the date of the enactment of this section and that specifically cites and repeals or modifies such provisions.

(f) ALLEGATION; IMPROPER WITHHOLDING OF RECORDS; JUDICIAL REVIEW.—(1) Except as provided in paragraph (2), whenever any person who has requested agency records under section 552 of title 5, United States Code, alleges that the Office has withheld records improperly because of failure to comply with any provision of this section, judicial review shall be available under the terms set forth in section 552(a)(4)(B) of title 5, United States Code.

(2) Judicial review shall not be available in the manner provided for under paragraph (1) as follows:

(A) In any case in which information specifically authorized under criteria established by an Executive order to be kept secret in the interests of national defense or foreign relations is filed with, or produced for, the court by the Office, such information shall be examined ex parte, in camera by the court.

(B) The court shall determine, to the fullest extent practicable, the issues of fact based on sworn written submissions of the parties.

(C)(i) When a complainant alleges that requested records were improperly withheld because of improper exemption of operational files, the Office may meet the burden of the Office under section 552(a)(4)(B) of title 5, United States Code, by demonstrating to the court by sworn written submission that exempted files likely to contain responsive records are records provided to the Office by an element of the intelligence community from the exempted operational files of such element.

(ii) The court may not order the Office to review the content of any exempted file in order to make the demonstration required under clause (i), unless the complainant disputes the Office's showing with a sworn written submission based on personal knowledge or otherwise admissible evidence.

(D) In proceedings under subparagraph (C), a party may not obtain discovery pursuant to rules 26 through 36 of the Federal Rules of Civil Procedure, except that requests for admissions may be made pursuant to rules 26 and 36 of the Federal Rules of Civil Procedure.

(E) If the court finds under this subsection that the Office has improperly withheld requested records because of failure to comply with any provision of this section, the court shall order the Office to search and review each appropriate exempted file for the requested records and make such records, or portions thereof, available in accordance with the provisions of section 552 of title 5, United States Code (commonly referred to as the Freedom of Information Act), and such order shall be the exclusive remedy for failure to comply with this section.

(F) If at any time following the filing of a complaint pursuant to this paragraph the Office agrees to search each appropriate exempted file for the requested records, the court shall dismiss the claim based upon such complaint.

(g) DEFINITIONS.—In this section:

(1) The term “exempted operational file” means a file of an element of the intelligence community that, in accordance with this title, is exempted from the provisions of section 552 of title 5, United States Code, that require search, review, publication, or disclosure of such file.

(2) Except as otherwise specifically provided, the term "Office" means the Office of the Director of National Intelligence.

TITLE VIII—ACCESS TO CLASSIFIED INFORMATION

PROCEDURES

SEC. 801. [50 U.S.C 3161] (a) Not later than 180 days after the date of enactment of this title, the President shall, by Executive order or regulation, establish procedures to govern access to classified information which shall be binding upon all departments, agencies, and offices of the executive branch of Government. Such procedures shall, at a minimum—

(1) provide that, except as may be permitted by the President, no employee in the executive branch of Government may be given access to classified information by any department, agency, or office of the executive branch of Government unless, based upon an appropriate background investigation, such access is determined to be clearly consistent with the national security interests of the United States;

(2) establish uniform minimum requirements governing the scope and frequency of background investigations and reinvestigations for all employees in the executive branch of Government who require access to classified information as part of their official responsibilities;

(3) provide that all employees in the executive branch of Government who require access to classified information shall be required as a condition of such access to provide to the employing department or agency written consent which permits access by an authorized investigative agency to relevant financial records, other financial information, consumer reports, travel records, and computers used in the performance of Government duties, as determined by the President, in accordance with section 802 of this title, during the period of access to classified information and for a period of three years thereafter;

(4) provide that all employees in the executive branch of Government who require access to particularly sensitive classified information, as determined by the President, shall be required, as a condition of maintaining access to such information, to submit to the employing department or agency, during the period of such access, relevant information concerning their financial condition and foreign travel, as determined by the President, as may be necessary to ensure appropriate security; and

(5) establish uniform minimum standards to ensure that employees in the executive branch of Government whose access to classified information is being denied or terminated under this title are appropriately advised of the reasons for such denial or termination and are provided an adequate opportunity to respond to all adverse information which forms the basis for such denial or termination before final action by the department or agency concerned.

(b)(1) Subsection (a) shall not be deemed to limit or affect the responsibility and power of an agency head pursuant to other law or Executive order to deny or terminate access to classified information if the national security so requires. Such responsibility and power may be exercised only when the agency head determines that the procedures prescribed by subsection (a) cannot be invoked in a manner that is consistent with the national security.

(2) Upon the exercise of such responsibility, the agency head shall submit a report to the congressional intelligence committees.

REQUESTS BY AUTHORIZED INVESTIGATIVE AGENCIES

SEC. 802. [50 U.S.C. 3162] (a)(1) Any authorized investigative agency may request from any financial agency, financial institution, or holding company, or from any consumer reporting agency, such financial records, other financial information, and consumer reports as may be necessary in order to conduct any authorized law enforcement investigation, counterintelligence inquiry, or security determination. Any authorized investigative agency may also request records maintained by any commercial entity within the United States pertaining to travel by an employee in the executive branch of Government outside the United States.

(2) Requests may be made under this section where—

(A) the records sought pertain to a person who is or was an employee in the executive branch of Government required by the President in an Executive order or regulation, as a condition of access to classified information, to provide consent, during a background investigation and for such time as access to the information is maintained, and for a period of not more than three years thereafter, permitting access to financial records, other financial information, consumer reports, and travel records; and

(B)(i) there are reasonable grounds to believe, based on credible information, that the person is, or may be, disclosing classified information in an unauthorized manner to a foreign power or agent of a foreign power;

(ii) information the employing agency deems credible indicates the person has incurred excessive indebtedness or has acquired a level of affluence which cannot be explained by other information known to the agency; or

(iii) circumstances indicate the person had the capability and opportunity to disclose classified information which is known to have been lost or compromised to a foreign power or an agent of a foreign power.

(3) Each such request—

(A) shall be accompanied by a written certification signed by the department or agency head or deputy department or agency head concerned, or by a senior official designated for this purpose by the department or agency head concerned (whose rank shall be no lower than Assistant Secretary or Assistant Director), and shall certify that—

(i) the person concerned is or was an employee within the meaning of paragraph (2)(A);

(ii) the request is being made pursuant to an authorized inquiry or investigation and is authorized under this section; and

(iii) the records or information to be reviewed are records or information which the employee has previously agreed to make available to the authorized investigative agency for review;

(B) shall contain a copy of the agreement referred to in subparagraph (A)(iii);

(C) shall identify specifically or by category the records or information to be reviewed; and

(D) shall inform the recipient of the request of the prohibition described in subsection (b).

(b) PROHIBITION OF CERTAIN DISCLOSURE.—

(1) PROHIBITION.—

(A) IN GENERAL.— If a certification is issued under subparagraph (B) and notice of the right to judicial review under subsection (c) is provided, no governmental or private entity that receives a request under subsection (a), or officer, employee, or agent thereof, shall disclose to any person that an authorized investigative agency described in subsection (a) has sought or obtained access to information under subsection (a).

(B) CERTIFICATION.—The requirements of subparagraph (A) shall apply if the head of an authorized investigative agency described in subsection (a), or a designee, certifies that the absence of a prohibition of disclosure under this subsection may result in—

(i) a danger to the national security of the United States;

(ii) interference with a criminal, counterterrorism, or counterintelligence investigation;

(iii) interference with diplomatic relations; or

(iv) danger to the life or physical safety of any person.

(2) EXCEPTION.—

(A) IN GENERAL.—A governmental or private entity that receives a request under subsection (a), or officer, employee, or agent thereof, may disclose information otherwise subject to any applicable nondisclosure requirement to—

(i) those persons to whom disclosure is necessary in order to comply with the request;

(ii) an attorney in order to obtain legal advice or assistance regarding the request; or

(iii) other persons as permitted by the head of the authorized investigative agency described in subsection (a) or a designee.

(B) APPLICATION.— A person to whom disclosure is made under subparagraph (A) shall be subject to the nondisclosure requirements applicable to a person to whom a request is issued under subsection (a) in the same manner as the person to whom the request is issued.

(C) NOTICE.— Any recipient that discloses to a person described in subparagraph (A) information otherwise subject to a nondisclosure requirement shall inform the person of the applicable nondisclosure requirement.

(D) IDENTIFICATION OF DISCLOSURE RECIPIENTS.— At the request of the head of an authorized investigative agency described in subsection (a), or a designee, any person making or intending to make a disclosure under clause (i) or (iii) of subparagraph (A) shall identify to the head of the authorized investigative agency or such designee the person to whom such disclosure will be made or to whom such disclosure was made prior to the request.

(c) JUDICIAL REVIEW.—

(1) IN GENERAL.— A request under subsection (a) or a nondisclosure requirement imposed in connection with such request under subsection (b) shall be subject to judicial review under section 3511 of title 18, United States Code.

(2) NOTICE.— A request under subsection (a) shall include notice of the availability of judicial review described in paragraph (1).

(d)(1) Notwithstanding any other provision of law (other than section 6103 of the Internal Revenue Code of 1986), an entity receiving a request for records or information under subsection (a) shall, if the request satisfies the requirements of this section, make available such records or information within 30 days for inspection or copying, as may be appropriate, by the agency requesting such records or information.

(2) Any entity (including any officer, employee, or agent thereof) that discloses records or information for inspection or copying pursuant to this section in good faith reliance upon the certifications made by an agency pursuant to this section shall not be liable for any such disclosure to any person under this title, the constitution of any State, or any law or regulation of any State or any political subdivision of any State.

(e) Any agency requesting records or information under this section may, subject to the availability of appropriations, reimburse a private entity for any cost reasonably incurred by such entity in responding to such request, including the cost of identifying, reproducing, or transporting records or other data.

(f) An agency receiving records or information pursuant to a request under this section may disseminate the records or information obtained pursuant to such request outside the agency only—

(1) to the agency employing the employee who is the subject of the records or information;

(2) to the Department of Justice for law enforcement or counterintelligence purposes; or

(3) with respect to dissemination to an agency of the United States, if such information is clearly relevant to the authorized responsibilities of such agency.

(g) Nothing in this section may be construed to affect the authority of an investigative agency to obtain information pursuant to the Right to Financial Privacy Act (12 U.S.C. 3401 et seq.) or the Fair Credit Reporting Act (15 U.S.C. 1681 et seq.).

SEC. 803. [50 U.S.C. 3162a] SECURITY EXECUTIVE AGENT.

(a) IN GENERAL.— The Director of National Intelligence, or such other officer of the United States as the President may designate, shall serve as the Security Executive Agent for all departments and agencies of the United States.

(b) Duties.—The duties of the Security Executive Agent are as follows:

(1) To direct the oversight of investigations, reinvestigations, adjudications, and, as applicable, polygraphs for eligibility for access to classified information or eligibility to hold a sensitive position made by any Federal agency.

(2) To review the national security background investigation and adjudication programs of Federal agencies to determine whether such programs are being implemented in accordance with this section.

(3) To develop and issue uniform and consistent policies and procedures to ensure the effective, efficient, timely, and secure completion of investigations, polygraphs, and adjudications relating to determinations of eligibility for access to classified information or eligibility to hold a sensitive position.

(4) Unless otherwise designated by law, to serve as the final authority to designate a Federal agency or agencies to conduct investigations of persons who are proposed for access to classified information or for eligibility to hold a sensitive position to ascertain whether such persons satisfy the criteria for obtaining and retaining access to classified information or eligibility to hold a sensitive position, as applicable.

(5) Unless otherwise designated by law, to serve as the final authority to designate a Federal agency or agencies to determine eligibility for access to classified information or eligibility to hold a sensitive position in accordance with Executive Order No. 12968 (50 U.S.C. 3161 note; relating to access to classified information).

(6) To review and approve the policies of the Federal agencies that ensure reciprocal recognition of eligibility for access to classified information or eligibility to hold a sensitive position among Federal agencies, and to act as the final authority to arbitrate and resolve disputes among such agencies involving the reciprocity of investigations and adjudications of eligibility.

(7) To execute all other duties assigned to the Security Executive Agent by law.

(c) Authorities.—The Security Executive Agent shall—

(1) issue guidelines and instructions to the heads of Federal agencies to ensure appropriate uniformity, centralization, efficiency, effectiveness, timeliness, and security in processes relating to determinations by such agencies of eligibility for access to classified information or eligibility to hold a sensitive position, including such matters as investigations, polygraphs, adjudications, and reciprocity;

(2) have the authority to grant exceptions to, or waivers of, national security investigative requirements, including issuing implementing or clarifying guidance, as necessary;

(3) have the authority to assign, in whole or in part, to the head of any Federal agency (solely or jointly) any of the duties of the Security Executive Agent described in subsection (b) or the authorities described in paragraphs (1) and (2), provided that the exercise of such assigned duties or authorities is subject to the

oversight of the Security Executive Agent, including such terms and conditions (including approval by the Security Executive Agent) as the Security Executive Agent determines appropriate;

(4) define and set standards for continuous vetting for continued access to classified information and for eligibility to hold a sensitive position; and

(5) issue guidelines and instructions to the heads of Federal agencies to ensure that any individual who was appointed by the President to a position in an element of the intelligence community but is no longer employed by the Federal Government shall maintain a security clearance only in accordance with Executive Order 12968 (50 U.S.C. 3161 note; relating to access to classified information), or successor order.

EXCEPTIONS

SEC. 804. [50 U.S.C. 3163] Except as otherwise specifically provided, the provisions of this title shall not apply to the President and Vice President, Members of the Congress, Justices of the Supreme Court, and Federal judges appointed by the President.

DEFINITIONS

SEC. 805. [50 U.S.C. 3164] For purposes of this title—

(1) the term "authorized investigative agency" means an agency authorized by law or regulation to conduct a counterintelligence investigation or investigations of persons who are proposed for access to classified information to ascertain whether such persons satisfy the criteria for obtaining and retaining access to such information;

(2) the term "classified information" means any information that has been determined pursuant to Executive Order No. 12356 of April 2, 1982, or successor orders, or the Atomic Energy Act of 1954, to require protection against unauthorized disclosure and that is so designated;

(3) the term "consumer reporting agency" has the meaning given such term in section 603 of the Consumer Credit Protection Act (15 U.S.C. 1681a);

(4) the term "employee" includes any person who receives a salary or compensation of any kind from the United States Government, is a contractor of the United States Government or an employee thereof, is an unpaid consultant of the United States Government, or otherwise acts for or on behalf of the United States Government, except as otherwise determined by the President;

(5) the terms "financial agency" and "financial institution" have the meanings given to such terms in section 5312(a) of title 31, United States Code, and the term "holding company" has the meaning given to such term in section 1101(6) of the Right to Financial Privacy Act of 1978 (12 U.S.C. 3401);

(6) the terms "foreign power" and "agent of a foreign power" have the same meanings as set forth in subsections (a) and (b) of section 101, respectively, of the Foreign Intelligence Surveillance Act of 1978 (50 U.S.C. 1801);

(7) the term "State" means each of the several States of the United States, the

District of Columbia, the Commonwealth of Puerto Rico, the Commonwealth of the Northern Mariana Islands, the United States Virgin Islands, Guam, American Samoa, the Republic of the Marshall Islands, the Federated States of Micronesia, and the Republic of Palau, and any other possession of the United States; and

(8) the term "computer" means any electronic, magnetic, optical, electrochemical, or other high speed data processing device performing logical, arithmetic, or storage functions, and includes any data storage facility or communications facility directly related to or operating in conjunction with such device and any data or other information stored or contained in such device.

TITLE IX—APPLICATION OF SANCTIONS LAWS TO INTELLIGENCE ACTIVITIES

STAY OF SANCTIONS

SEC. 901. [50 U.S.C. 3171] Notwithstanding any provision of law identified in section 904, the President may stay the imposition of an economic, cultural, diplomatic, or other sanction or related action by the United States Government concerning a foreign country, organization, or person when the President determines and reports to Congress in accordance with section 903 that to proceed without delay would seriously risk the compromise of an ongoing criminal investigation directly related to the activities giving rise to the sanction or an intelligence source or method directly related to the activities giving rise to the sanction. Any such stay shall be effective for a period of time specified by the President, which period may not exceed 120 days, unless such period is extended in accordance with section 902.

EXTENSION OF STAY

SEC. 902. [50 U.S.C. 3172] Whenever the President determines and reports to Congress in accordance with section 903 that a stay of sanctions or related actions pursuant to section 901 has not afforded sufficient time to obviate the risk to an ongoing criminal investigation or to an intelligence source or method that gave rise to the stay, he may extend such stay for a period of time specified by the President, which period may not exceed 120 days. The authority of this section may be used to extend the period of a stay pursuant to section 901 for successive periods of not more than 120 days each.

REPORTS

SEC. 903. [50 U.S.C. 3173] Reports to Congress pursuant to sections 901 and 902 shall be submitted promptly upon determinations under this title. Such reports shall be submitted to the Committee on International Relations of the House of Representatives and the Committee on Foreign Relations of the Senate. With respect to determinations relating to intelligence sources and methods, reports shall also be submitted to the congressional intelligence committees. With respect to determinations relating to ongoing criminal investigations, reports shall also be submitted to the Committees on the Judiciary of the House of Representatives and the Senate.

LAWS SUBJECT TO STAY

SEC. 904. [50 U.S.C. 3174] The President may use the authority of sections 901 and 902 to stay the imposition of an economic, cultural, diplomatic, or other sanction or related action by the United States Government related to the proliferation of weapons of mass destruction, their delivery systems, or advanced conventional weapons otherwise required to be imposed by the Chemical and Biological Weapons Control and Warfare Elimination Act of 1991 (title III of Public Law 102–182); the Nuclear Proliferation Prevention Act of 1994 (title VIII of Public Law 103–236); title XVII of the National Defense Authorization Act for Fiscal Year 1991 (Public Law 101–510) (relating to the nonproliferation of missile technology); the Iran-Iraq Arms Nonproliferation Act of 1992 (title XVI of Public Law 102–484); section 573 of the Foreign Operations, Export Financing Related Programs Appropriations Act, 1994 (Public Law 103–87); section 563 of the Foreign Operations, Export Financing Related Programs Appropriations Act, 1995 (Public Law 103–306); and comparable provisions.[Section 905 was repealed by section 313(a) of Public Law 108–177, December 13, 2003, 117 Stat. 2610; 50 U.S.C. 3175]

TITLE X—EDUCATION IN SUPPORT OF NATIONAL INTELLIGENCE

subtitle A—SCIENCE AND TECHNOLOGY

SCHOLARSHIPS AND WORK-STUDY FOR PURSUIT OF GRADUATE DEGREES IN SCIENCE AND TECHNOLOGY

SEC. 1001. [50 U.S.C. 3191] (a) PROGRAM AUTHORIZED.— The Director of National Intelligence may carry out a program to provide scholarships and work-study for individuals who are pursuing graduate degrees in fields of study in science and technology that are identified by the Director as appropriate to meet the future needs of the intelligence community for qualified scientists and engineers.

(b) ADMINISTRATION.— If the Director of National Intelligence carries out the program under subsection (a), the Director of National Intelligence shall administer the program through the Office of the Director of National Intelligence.

(c) IDENTIFICATION OF FIELDS OF STUDY.— If the Director of National Intelligence carries out the program under subsection (a), the Director shall identify fields of study under subsection (a) in consultation with the other heads of the elements of the intelligence community.

(d) ELIGIBILITY FOR PARTICIPATION.—An individual eligible to participate in the program is any individual who—

(1) either—

(A) is an employee of the intelligence community; or

(B) meets criteria for eligibility for employment in the intelligence community that are established by the Director of National Intelligence;

(2) is accepted in a graduate degree program in a field of study in science or technology identified under subsection (a); and

(3) is eligible for a security clearance at the level of Secret or above.

(e) Regulations.— If the Director of National Intelligence carries out the program under subsection (a), the Director shall prescribe regulations for purposes of the administration of this section.

FRAMEWORK FOR CROSS-DISCIPLINARY EDUCATION AND TRAINING

Sec. 1002. [50 U.S.C. 3192] The Director of National Intelligence shall establish an integrated framework that brings together the educational components of the intelligence community in order to promote a more effective and productive intelligence community through cross-disciplinary education and joint training.

subtitle B—Foreign Languages Program

PROGRAM ON ADVANCEMENT OF FOREIGN LANGUAGES CRITICAL TO THE INTELLIGENCE COMMUNITY

Sec. 1011. [50 U.S.C. 3201] (a) In General.— The Secretary of Defense and the Director of National Intelligence may jointly carry out a program to advance skills in foreign languages that are critical to the capability of the intelligence community to carry out the national security activities of the United States (hereinafter in this subtitle referred to as the "Foreign Languages Program").

(b) Identification of Requisite Actions.— In order to carry out the Foreign Languages Program, the Secretary of Defense and the Director of National Intelligence shall jointly identify actions required to improve the education of personnel in the intelligence community in foreign languages that are critical to the capability of the intelligence community to carry out the national security activities of the United States and to meet the long-term intelligence needs of the United States.

EDUCATION PARTNERSHIPS

Sec. 1012. [50 U.S.C. 3202] (a) In General.— In carrying out the Foreign Languages Program, the head of a covered element of the intelligence community may enter into one or more education partnership agreements with educational institutions in the United States in order to encourage and enhance the study in such educational institutions of foreign languages that are critical to the capability of the intelligence community to carry out the national security activities of the United States.

(b) Assistance Provided Under Educational Partnership Agreements.—Under an educational partnership agreement entered into with an educational institution pursuant to this section, the head of a covered element of the intelligence community may provide the following assistance to the educational institution:

(1) The loan of equipment and instructional materials of the element of the intelligence community to the educational institution for any purpose and duration that the head of the element considers appropriate.

(2) Notwithstanding any other provision of law relating to the transfer of surplus property, the transfer to the educational institution of any computer equipment, or other equipment, that is—

(A) commonly used by educational institutions;

(B) surplus to the needs of the element of the intelligence community; and

(C) determined by the head of the element to be appropriate for support of such agreement.

(3) The provision of dedicated personnel to the educational institution—

(A) to teach courses in foreign languages that are critical to the capability of the intelligence community to carry out the national security activities of the United States; or

(B) to assist in the development for the educational institution of courses and materials on such languages.

(4) The involvement of faculty and students of the educational institution in research projects of the element of the intelligence community.

(5) Cooperation with the educational institution in developing a program under which students receive academic credit at the educational institution for work on research projects of the element of the intelligence community.

(6) The provision of academic and career advice and assistance to students of the educational institution.

(7) The provision of cash awards and other items that the head of the element of the intelligence community considers appropriate.

VOLUNTARY SERVICES

SEC. 1013. [50 U.S.C. 3203] (a) AUTHORITY TO ACCEPT SERVICES.— Notwithstanding section 1342 of title 31, United States Code, and subject to subsection (b), the Foreign Languages Program under section 1011 shall include authority for the head of a covered element of the intelligence community to accept from any dedicated personnel voluntary services in support of the activities authorized by this subtitle.

(b) REQUIREMENTS AND LIMITATIONS.—(1) In accepting voluntary services from an individual under subsection (a), the head of a covered element of the intelligence community shall—

(A) supervise the individual to the same extent as the head of the element would supervise a compensated employee of that element providing similar services; and

(B) ensure that the individual is licensed, privileged, has appropriate educational or experiential credentials, or is otherwise qualified under applicable law or regulations to provide such services.

(2) In accepting voluntary services from an individual under subsection (a), the head of a covered element of the intelligence community may not—

(A) place the individual in a policymaking position, or other position performing inherently governmental functions; or

(B) compensate the individual for the provision of such services.

(c) AUTHORITY TO RECRUIT AND TRAIN INDIVIDUALS PROVIDING SERVICES.— The head of a covered element of the intelligence community may recruit and train individuals to provide voluntary services under subsection (a).

(d) STATUS OF INDIVIDUALS PROVIDING SERVICES.—(1) Subject to paragraph (2), while providing voluntary services under subsection (a) or receiving training under subsection (c), an individual shall be considered to be an employee of the Federal Government only for purposes of the following provisions of law:

(A) Section 552a of title 5, United States Code (relating to maintenance of records on individuals).

(B) Chapter 11 of title 18, United States Code (relating to conflicts of interest).

(2)(A) With respect to voluntary services under paragraph (1) provided by an individual that are within the scope of the services accepted under that paragraph, the individual shall be deemed to be a volunteer of a governmental entity or nonprofit institution for purposes of the Volunteer Protection Act of 1997 (42 U.S.C. 14501 et seq.).

(B) In the case of any claim against such an individual with respect to the provision of such services, section 4(d) of such Act (42 U.S.C. 14503(d)) shall not apply.

(3) Acceptance of voluntary services under this section shall have no bearing on the issuance or renewal of a security clearance.

(e) Reimbursement of Incidental Expenses.—(1) The head of a covered element of the intelligence community may reimburse an individual for incidental expenses incurred by the individual in providing voluntary services under subsection (a). The head of a covered element of the intelligence community shall determine which expenses are eligible for reimbursement under this subsection.

(2) Reimbursement under paragraph (1) may be made from appropriated or nonappropriated funds.

(f) Authority To Install Equipment.—(1) The head of a covered element of the intelligence community may install telephone lines and any necessary telecommunication equipment in the private residences of individuals who provide voluntary services under subsection (a).

(2) The head of a covered element of the intelligence community may pay the charges incurred for the use of equipment installed under paragraph (1) for authorized purposes.

(3) Notwithstanding section 1348 of title 31, United States Code, the head of a covered element of the intelligence community may use appropriated funds or nonappropriated funds of the element in carrying out this subsection.

REGULATIONS

Sec. 1014. [50 U.S.C. 3204] (a) In General.— The Secretary of Defense and the Director of National Intelligence shall jointly prescribe regulations to carry out the Foreign Languages Program.

(b) Elements of the Intelligence Community.—The head of each covered element of the intelligence community shall prescribe regulations to carry out sections 1012 and 1013 with respect to that element including the following:

(1) Procedures to be utilized for the acceptance of voluntary services under section 1013.

(2) Procedures and requirements relating to the installation of equipment under section 1013(f).

DEFINITIONS

SEC. 1015. [50 U.S.C. 3205] In this subtitle:

(1) The term "covered element of the intelligence community" means an agency, office, bureau, or element referred to in subparagraphs (B) through (L) of section 3(4).

(2) The term "educational institution" means—

(A) a local educational agency (as that term is defined in section 8101 of the Elementary and Secondary Education Act of 1965);

(B) an institution of higher education (as defined in section 102 of the Higher Education Act of 1965 (20 U.S.C. 1002) other than institutions referred to in subsection (a)(1)(C) of such section); or

(C) any other nonprofit institution that provides instruction of foreign languages in languages that are critical to the capability of the intelligence community to carry out national security activities of the United States.

(3) The term "dedicated personnel" means employees of the intelligence community and private citizens (including former civilian employees of the Federal Government who have been voluntarily separated, and members of the United States Armed Forces who have been honorably discharged, honorably separated, or generally discharged under honorable circumstances and rehired on a voluntary basis specifically to perform the activities authorized under this subtitle).

subtitle C—ADDITIONAL EDUCATION PROVISIONS

ASSIGNMENT OF INTELLIGENCE COMMUNITY PERSONNEL AS LANGUAGE STUDENTS

SEC. 1021. [50 U.S.C. 3221] (a) IN GENERAL.— The Director of National Intelligence, acting through the heads of the elements of the intelligence community, may assign employees of such elements in analyst positions requiring foreign language expertise as students at accredited professional, technical, or other institutions of higher education for training at the graduate or undergraduate level in foreign languages required for the conduct of duties and responsibilities of such positions.

(b) AUTHORITY FOR REIMBURSEMENT OF COSTS OF TUITION AND TRAINING.—(1) The Director of National Intelligence may reimburse an employee assigned under subsection (a) for the total cost of the training described in that subsection, including costs of educational and supplementary reading materials.

(2) The authority under paragraph (1) shall apply to employees who are assigned on a full-time or part-time basis.

(3) Reimbursement under paragraph (1) may be made from appropriated or nonappropriated funds.

(c) RELATIONSHIP TO COMPENSATION AS AN ANALYST.— Reimbursement under this section to an employee who is an analyst is in addition to any benefits, allowances, travel expenses, or other compensation the employee is entitled to by reason of serving in such an analyst position.

SEC. 1022. [U.S.C. ????] PROGRAM ON RECRUITMENT AND TRAINING.

(a) PROGRAM.—

(1) REQUIREMENT.—The Director of National Intelligence, in consultation with the heads of the elements of the intelligence community, shall carry out a program to ensure that selected individuals are provided funds for academic training (including with respect to both undergraduate and postgraduate education), or to reimburse for academic training previously obtained—

(A) in capabilities, missions, or skillsets, especially in the fields of science, technology, math, and engineering, to address workforce requirements in which the intelligence community is deficient or likely to be deficient in the future; or

(B) for such individuals who have backgrounds or experiences that the Director has identified as—

(i) contributing to capabilities, missions, or skillsets in which the intelligence community is deficient or likely to be deficient in future; and

(ii) being underrepresented in the intelligence community or likely to be underrepresented in the future.

(2) COMMITMENT.— An individual selected for participation in the program shall commit to employment with an element of the intelligence community for a period that the Director determines is commensurate with the amount of funding provided to the individual under the program and under such terms and conditions as the Director considers appropriate.

(3) DESIGNATION.— The program shall be known as the Pat Roberts Intelligence Scholars Program.

(4) OUTREACH.—The Director, in consultation with the heads of the elements of the intelligence community, shall maintain a publicly available internet website on the program that describes—

(A) the intent of the program;

(B) the conditions and requirements for selection and participation;

(C) application instructions;

(D) the areas covered by the program pursuant to the review conducted under subsection (b)(2); and

(E) any other details the Director determines appropriate.

(b) ELEMENTS.—In carrying out the program under subsection (a), the Director shall—

(1) establish such requirements relating to the academic training of participants as the Director considers appropriate to ensure that participants are prepared for employment as intelligence professionals; and

(2) on an annual basis, review the areas that will contribute to the capabilities, missions, and skillsets in which the intelligence community is deficient or is likely

to be deficient in the future.

(c) USE OF FUNDS.—Funds made available for the program under subsection (a) shall be used—

(1) to provide a monthly stipend for each month that a participant is pursuing a course of study;

(2) to pay the partial or full tuition of a participant for the completion of such course of study;

(3) to reimburse a participant for tuition paid by the participant before becoming an employee of an element of the intelligence community, including with respect to providing payments for student loans used for such tuition;

(4) to pay for books and materials that the participant requires or required to complete such course of study;

(5) to pay the expenses of the participant for travel requested by an element of the intelligence community in relation to such program; or

(6) for such other purposes the Director considers reasonably appropriate to carry out such program.

EDUCATIONAL SCHOLARSHIP PROGRAM

SEC. 1023. [50 U.S.C. 3223] The head of a department or agency containing an element of the intelligence community may establish an undergraduate or graduate training program with respect to civilian employees and prospective civilian employees of such element similar in purpose, conditions, content, and administration to the program that the Secretary of Defense is authorized to establish under section 16 of the National Security Agency Act of 1959 (50 U.S.C. 402 note).

INTELLIGENCE OFFICER TRAINING PROGRAM

SEC. 1024. [50 U.S.C. 3224] (a) PROGRAMS.—(1) The Director of National Intelligence may carry out grant programs in accordance with subsections (b) and (c) to enhance the recruitment and retention of an ethnically and culturally diverse intelligence community workforce with capabilities critical to the national security interests of the United States.

(2) In carrying out paragraph (1), the Director shall identify the skills necessary to meet current or emergent needs of the intelligence community and the educational disciplines that will provide individuals with such skills.

(b) INSTITUTIONAL GRANT PROGRAM.—(1) The Director may provide grants to institutions of higher education to support the establishment or continued development of programs of study in educational disciplines identified under subsection (a)(2).

(2) A grant provided under paragraph (1) may, with respect to the educational disciplines identified under subsection (a)(2), be used for the following purposes:

(A) Curriculum or program development.

(B) Faculty development.

(C) Laboratory equipment or improvements.

(D) Faculty research.

(c) GRANT PROGRAM FOR CERTAIN MINORITY-SERVING COLLEGES AND UNIVERSITIES.—(1) The Director may provide grants to historically black colleges and universities, Predominantly Black Institutions, Hispanic-serving institutions, and Asian American and Native American Pacific Islander-serving institutions to provide programs of study in educational disciplines identified under subsection (a)(2) or described in paragraph (2).

(2) A grant provided under paragraph (1) may be used to provide programs of study in the following educational disciplines:

(A) Intermediate and advanced foreign languages deemed in the immediate interest of the intelligence community, including Farsi, Pashto, Middle Eastern, African, and South Asian dialects.

(B) Study abroad programs and cultural immersion programs.

(d) APPLICATION.— An institution of higher education seeking a grant under this section shall submit an application describing the proposed use of the grant at such time and in such manner as the Director may require.

(e) REPORTS.—An institution of higher education that receives a grant under this section shall submit to the Director regular reports regarding the use of such grant, including—

(1) a description of the benefits to students who participate in the course of study funded by such grant;

(2) a description of the results and accomplishments related to such course of study; and

(3) any other information that the Director may require.

(f) REGULATIONS.— The Director shall prescribe such regulations as may be necessary to carry out this section.

(g) DEFINITIONS.—In this section:

(1) The term "Director" means the Director of National Intelligence.

(2) HISTORICALLY BLACK COLLEGE AND UNIVERSITY.— The term "historically black college and university" has the meaning given the term "part B institution" in section 322 of the Higher Education Act of 1965 (20 U.S.C. 1061).

(3) The term "institution of higher education" has the meaning given the term in section 101 of the Higher Education Act of 1965 (20 U.S.C. 1001).

(4) PREDOMINANTLY BLACK INSTITUTION.— The term "Predominantly Black Institution" has the meaning given the term in section 318 of the Higher education Act of 1965 (20 U.S.C. 1059e).

(5) HISPANIC-SERVING INSTITUTION.— The term "Hispanic-serving institution" has the meaning given that term in section 502(a)(5) of the Higher Education Act of 1965 (20 U.S.C. 1101a(a)(5)).

(6) ASIAN AMERICAN AND NATIVE AMERICAN PACIFIC ISLANDER-SERVING INSTITUTION.— The term "Asian American and Native American Pacific Islander-serving institution" has the meaning given that term in section 320(b)(2) of the

Higher Education Act of 1965 (20 U.S.C. 1059g(b)(2)).

(7) STUDY ABROAD PROGRAM.—The term "study abroad program" means a program of study that—

(A) takes place outside the geographical boundaries of the United States;

(B) focuses on areas of the world that are critical to the national security interests of the United States and are generally underrepresented in study abroad programs at institutions of higher education, including Africa, Asia, Central and Eastern Europe, Eurasia, Latin America, and the Middle East; and

(C) is a credit or noncredit program.

SEC. 1025. [50 U.SC. 3224a] AUTHORIZATION OF SUPPORT BY DIRECTOR OF NATIONAL INTELLIGENCE FOR CERTAIN WORKFORCE ACTIVITIES.

(a) AUTHORIZATION.— The Director may, with or without reimbursement, obligate or expend amounts authorized to be appropriated or otherwise made available for the Office of the Director of National Intelligence for covered workforce activities for the purpose of supporting a covered workforce activity of an element of the intelligence community.

(b) NOTIFICATION.— Not later than 30 days after the date on which the Director exercises the authority in subsection (a), the Director shall submit to the congressional intelligence committees and the Committees on Appropriations of the House of Representatives and the Senate written notification of such exercise.

(c) COVERED WORKFORCE ACTIVITY DEFINED.—In this section, the term "covered workforce activity" means an activity relating to—

(1) recruitment or retention of the intelligence community workforce; or

(2) diversity, equality, inclusion, or accessibility, with respect to such workforce.

Subtitle D—NATIONAL INTELLIGENCE UNIVERSITY

SEC. 1031. [50 U.SC. 3227] TRANSFER DATE.

In this subtitle, the term "transfer date" means the date on which the National Intelligence University is transferred from the Defense Intelligence Agency to the Director of National Intelligence under section 5324(a) of the National Defense Authorization Act for Fiscal Year 2020 (Public Law 116–92).

SEC. 1032. [50 U.SC. 3227a] DEGREE-GRANTING AUTHORITY.

(a) IN GENERAL.— Beginning on the transfer date, under regulations prescribed by the Director of National Intelligence, the President of the National Intelligence University may, upon the recommendation of the faculty of the University, confer appropriate degrees upon graduates who meet the degree requirements.

(b) LIMITATION.—A degree may not be conferred under this section unless—

(1) the Secretary of Education has recommended approval of the degree in accordance with the Federal Policy Governing Granting of Academic Degrees by Federal Agencies; and

(2) the University is accredited by the appropriate academic accrediting agency or organization to award the degree, as determined by the Secretary of Education.

SEC. 1033. [50 U.SC. 3227b] REPORTING.

(a) In General.— Not less frequently than once each year, the Director of National Intelligence shall submit to the congressional intelligence committees a plan for employing professors, instructors, and lecturers at the National Intelligence University.

(b) Elements.—Each plan submitted under subsection (a) shall include the following:

(1) The total number of proposed personnel to be employed at the National Intelligence University.

(2) The total annual compensation to be provided the personnel described in paragraph (1).

(3) Such other matters as the Director considers appropriate.

(c) Form of Submittal.— Each plan submitted by the Director to the congressional intelligence committees under subsection (a) shall be submitted as part of another annual submission from the Director to the congressional intelligence committees.

SEC. 1034. [50 U.SC. 3227c] CONTINUED APPLICABILITY OF THE FEDERAL ADVISORY COMMITTEE ACT TO THE BOARD OF VISITORS.

The Federal Advisory Committee Act (5 U.S.C. App.) shall continue to apply to the Board of Visitors of the National Intelligence University on and after the transfer date.

§ 1035. [50 U.SC. 3227d] National Intelligence University acceptance of grants[14]

(a) Authority.— The Director of National Intelligence may authorize the President of the National Intelligence University to accept qualifying research grants.

(b) Qualifying Grants.— A qualifying research grant under this section is a grant that is awarded on a competitive basis by an entity referred to in subsection (c) for a research project with a scientific, literary, or educational purpose.

(c) Entities From Which Grants May Be Accepted.— A qualifying research grant may be accepted under this section only from a Federal agency or from a corporation, fund, foundation, educational institution, or similar entity that is organized and operated primarily for scientific, literary, or educational purposes.

(d) Administration of Grant Funds.—

(1) Establishment of account.— The Director shall establish an account for administering funds received as qualifying research grants under this section.

(2) Use of funds.— The President of the University shall use the funds in the account established pursuant to paragraph (1) in accordance with applicable provisions of the regulations and the terms and conditions of the grants received.

(e) Related Expenses.— Subject to such limitations as may be provided in appropriations Acts, appropriations available for the National Intelligence University may be used to pay expenses incurred by the University in applying for, and otherwise pursuing, the award of qualifying research grants.

(f) Regulations.— The Director of National Intelligence shall prescribe regulations for the administration of this section.

[14] The style of the section heading for section 1035, as added by section 6305(a) of division F of Public Law 118–159, does not conform with the style of section headings of the Act.

TITLE XI—ADDITIONAL MISCELLANEOUS PROVISIONS

APPLICABILITY TO UNITED STATES INTELLIGENCE ACTIVITIES OF FEDERAL LAWS IMPLEMENTING INTERNATIONAL TREATIES AND AGREEMENTS

SEC. 1101. [50 U.S.C. 3231] (a) IN GENERAL.— No Federal law enacted on or after the date of the enactment of the Intelligence Authorization Act for Fiscal Year 2001 that implements a treaty or other international agreement shall be construed as making unlawful an otherwise lawful and authorized intelligence activity of the United States Government or its employees, or any other person to the extent such other person is carrying out such activity on behalf of, and at the direction of, the United States, unless such Federal law specifically addresses such intelligence activity.

(b) AUTHORIZED INTELLIGENCE ACTIVITIES.— An intelligence activity shall be treated as authorized for purposes of subsection (a) if the intelligence activity is authorized by an appropriate official of the United States Government, acting within the scope of the official duties of that official and in compliance with Federal law and any applicable Presidential directive.

COUNTERINTELLIGENCE INITIATIVES

SEC. 1102. [50 U.S. C. 3232] (a) INSPECTION PROCESS.— In order to protect intelligence sources and methods from unauthorized disclosure, the Director of National Intelligence shall establish and implement an inspection process for all agencies and departments of the United States that handle classified information relating to the national security of the United States intended to assure that those agencies and departments maintain effective operational security practices and programs directed against counterintelligence activities.

(b) ANNUAL REVIEW OF DISSEMINATION LISTS.— The Director of National Intelligence shall establish and implement a process for all elements of the intelligence community to review, on an annual basis, individuals included on distribution lists for access to classified information. Such process shall ensure that only individuals who have a particularized “need to know” (as determined by the Director) are continued on such distribution lists.

(c) COMPLETION OF FINANCIAL DISCLOSURE STATEMENTS REQUIRED FOR ACCESS TO CERTAIN CLASSIFIED INFORMATION.— The Director of National Intelligence shall establish and implement a process by which each head of an element of the intelligence community directs that all employees of that element, in order to be granted access to classified information referred to in subsection (a) of section 1.3 of Executive Order No. 12968 (August 2, 1995; 60 Fed. Reg. 40245; 50 U.S.C. 435 note), submit financial disclosure forms as required under subsection (b) of such section.

(d) ARRANGEMENTS TO HANDLE SENSITIVE INFORMATION.— The Director of National

Intelligence shall establish, for all elements of the intelligence community, programs and procedures by which sensitive classified information relating to human intelligence is safeguarded against unauthorized disclosure by employees of those elements.

SEC. 1102A. [U.S.C. 3232a] MEASURES TO MITIGATE COUNTERINTELLIGENCE THREATS FROM PROLIFERATION AND USE OF FOREIGN COMMERCIAL SPYWARE

(a) DEFINITIONS.—In this section:

(1) APPROPRIATE CONGRESSIONAL COMMITTEES .—The term "appropriate congressional committees" means—

(A) the Select Committee on Intelligence, the Committee on Foreign Relations, the Committee on Armed Services, the Committee on Banking, Housing, and Urban Affairs, the Committee on the Judiciary, the Committee on Appropriations, and the Committee on Homeland Security and Governmental Affairs of the Senate; and

(B) the Permanent Select Committee on Intelligence, the Committee on Foreign Affairs, the Committee on Armed Services, the Committee on Financial Services, the Committee on the Judiciary, the Committee on Appropriations, the Committee on Homeland Security, and the Committee on Oversight and Reform of the House of Representatives.

(2) COVERED ENTITY .—The term "covered entity" means any foreign company that either directly or indirectly develops, maintains, owns, operates, brokers, markets, sells, leases, licenses, or otherwise makes available spyware.

(3) FOREIGN COMMERCIAL SPYWARE .—The term "foreign commercial spyware" means spyware that is developed (solely or in partnership with a foreign company), maintained, sold, leased, licensed, marketed, sourced (in whole or in part), or otherwise provided, either directly or indirectly, by a foreign company.

(4) FOREIGN COMPANY .—The term "foreign company" means a company that is incorporated or domiciled outside of the United States, including any subsidiaries or affiliates wherever such subsidiaries or affiliates are domiciled or incorporated.

(5) SPYWARE.—The term "spyware" means a tool or set of tools that operate as an end-to-end system of software to provide an unauthorized user remote access to information stored on or transiting through an electronic device connected to the Internet and not owned or operated by the unauthorized user, including end-to-end systems that—

(A) allow an unauthorized user to remotely infect electronic devices with malicious software, including without any action required by the user of the device;

(B) can record telecommunications or other audio captured on a device not owned by the unauthorized user;

(C) undertake geolocation, collect cell site location information, or otherwise track the location of a device or person using the internal sensors of an electronic device not owned by the unauthorized user;

(D) allow an unauthorized user access to and the ability to retrieve information on the electronic device, including text messages, files, e-mails, transcripts of chats, contacts, photos, and browsing history; or

(E) any additional criteria described in publicly available documents published by the Director of National Intelligence, such as whether the end-to-end system is used outside the context of a codified lawful intercept system.

(b) ANNUAL ASSESSMENTS OF COUNTERINTELLIGENCE THREATS.—

(1) REQUIREMENT.— Not later than 90 days after the enactment of the Intelligence Authorization Act for Fiscal Year 2023, and annually thereafter, the Director of National Intelligence, in coordination with the Director of the Central Intelligence Agency, the Director of the National Security Agency, and the Director of the Federal Bureau of Investigation, shall submit to the appropriate congressional committees a report with an accompanying classified annex containing an assessment of the counterintelligence threats and other risks to the national security of the United States posed by the proliferation of foreign commercial spyware. The assessment shall incorporate all credible data, including open-source information.

(2) ELEMENTS .—Each report under paragraph (1) shall include the following, if known:

(A) A list of the most significant covered entities.

(B) A description of the foreign commercial spyware marketed by the covered entities identified under subparagraph (A) and an assessment by the intelligence community of the foreign commercial spyware.

(C) An assessment of the counterintelligence risk to the intelligence community or personnel of the intelligence community posed by foreign commercial spyware.

(D) For each covered entity identified in subparagraph (A), details of any subsidiaries, resellers, or other agents acting on behalf of the covered entity.

(E) Details of where each covered entity identified under subparagraphs (A) and (D) is domiciled.

(F) A description of how each covered entity identified under subparagraphs (A) and (D) is financed, where the covered entity acquired its capital, and the organizations and individuals having substantial investments or other equities in the covered entity.

(G) An assessment by the intelligence community of any relationship between each covered entity identified in subparagraphs (A) and (D) and any foreign government, including any export controls and processes to which the covered entity is subject.

(H) A list of the foreign customers of each covered entity identified in subparagraphs (A) and (D), including the understanding by the intelligence community of the organizations and end-users within any foreign government.

(I) With respect to each foreign customer identified under subparagraph (H), an assessment by the intelligence community regarding how the foreign customer is using the spyware, including whether the foreign customer has targeted personnel of the intelligence community.

(J) With respect to the first report required under paragraph (1), a mitigation plan to reduce the exposure of personnel of the intelligence community to foreign commercial spyware.

(K) With respect to each report following the first report required under paragraph (1), details of steps taken by the intelligence community since the previous report to implement measures to reduce the exposure of personnel of the intelligence community to foreign commercial spyware.

(3) CLASSIFIED ANNEX .—In submitting the report under paragraph (1), the Director shall also include an accompanying but separate classified annex, providing a watchlist of companies selling, leasing, or otherwise providing foreign commercial spyware that the Director determines are engaged in activities that pose a counterintelligence risk to personnel of the intelligence community.

(4) FORM.— Each report under paragraph (1) shall be submitted in classified form.

(5) DISSEMINATION.— The Director of National Intelligence shall separately distribute each report under paragraph (1) and each annex under paragraph (3) to the President, the heads of all elements of the intelligence community, the Secretary of State, the Attorney General, the Secretary of Commerce, the Secretary of Homeland Security, the National Cyber Director, and the heads of any other departments or agencies the Director of National Intelligence determines appropriate.

(c) AUTHORITY TO PROHIBIT PURCHASE OR USE BY INTELLIGENCE COMMUNITY.—

(1) FOREIGN COMMERCIAL SPYWARE.—

(A) IN GENERAL .—The Director of National Intelligence may prohibit any element of the intelligence community from procuring, leasing, or otherwise acquiring on the commercial market, or extending or renewing a contract to procure, lease, or otherwise acquire, foreign commercial spyware.

(B) CONSIDERATIONS.—In determining whether and how to exercise the authority under subparagraph (A), the Director of National Intelligence shall consider—

(i) the assessment of the intelligence community of the counterintelligence threats or other risks to the United States posed by foreign commercial spyware;

(ii) the assessment of the intelligence community of whether the foreign commercial spyware has been used to target United States Government personnel;

(iii) whether the original owner or developer retains any of the physical property or intellectual property associated with the foreign commercial spyware;

(iv) whether the original owner or developer has verifiably destroyed all copies of the data collected by or associated with the foreign commercial spyware;

(v) whether the personnel of the original owner or developer retain any access to data collected by or associated with the foreign commercial spyware;

(vi) whether the use of the foreign commercial spyware requires the user to connect to an information system of the original owner or developer or information system of a foreign government; and

(vii) whether the foreign commercial spyware poses a counterintelligence risk to the United States or any other threat to the national security of the United States.

(2) COMPANY THAT HAS ACQUIRED FOREIGN COMMERCIAL SPYWARE.—

(A) AUTHORITY .—The Director of National Intelligence may prohibit any element of the intelligence community from entering into any contract or other agreement for any purpose with a company that has acquired, in whole or in part, any foreign commercial spyware.

(B) CONSIDERATIONS.—In considering whether and how to exercise the authority under subparagraph (A), the Director of National Intelligence shall consider—

(i) whether the original owner or developer of the foreign commercial spyware retains any of the physical property or intellectual property associated with the spyware;

(ii) whether the original owner or developer of the foreign commercial spyware has verifiably destroyed all data, and any copies thereof, collected by or associated with the spyware;

(iii) whether the personnel of the original owner or developer of the foreign commercial spyware retain any access to data collected by or associated with the foreign commercial spyware;

(iv) whether the use of the foreign commercial spyware requires the user to connect to an information system of the original owner or developer or information system of a foreign government; and

(v) whether the foreign commercial spyware poses a counterintelligence risk to the United States or any other threat to the national security of the United States.

(3) NOTIFICATIONS OF PROHIBITION.—Not later than 30 days after the date on which the Director of National Intelligence exercises the authority to issue a prohibition under subsection (c), the Director of National Intelligence shall notify the congressional intelligence committees of such exercise of authority. Such notice shall include—

(A) a description of the circumstances under which the prohibition was issued;

(B) an identification of the company or product covered by the prohibition;

(C) any information that contributed to the decision of the Director of National Intelligence to exercise the authority, including any information relating to counterintelligence or other risks to the national security of the United States posed by the company or product, as assessed by the intelligence community; and

(D) an identification of each element of the intelligence community to which the prohibition has been applied.

(4) WAIVER AUTHORITY.—

(A) IN GENERAL .—The head of an element of the intelligence community may request from the Director of National Intelligence the waiver of a prohibition made under paragraph (1) or (2).

(B) DIRECTOR OF NATIONAL INTELLIGENCE DETERMINATION .—The Director of National Intelligence, upon receiving the waiver request in subparagraph (A), may issue a waiver for a period not to exceed one year in response to the request from the head of an element of the intelligence community if such waiver is in the national security interest of the United States.

(C) NOTICE .—Not later than 30 days after approving a waiver request pursuant to subparagraph (B), the Director of National Intelligence shall submit to the congressional intelligence committees, the Subcommittee on Defense of the Committee on Appropriations of the Senate, and the Subcommittee on Defense of the Committee on Appropriations of the House of Representatives a written notification. The notification shall include—

(i) an identification of the head of the element of the intelligence community that requested the waiver;

(ii) the details of the waiver request, including the national security interests of the United States;

(iii) the rationale and basis for the determination that the waiver is in the national security interests of the United States;

(iv) the considerations that informed the ultimate determination of the Director of National Intelligence to issue the waiver; and

(v) and any other considerations contributing to the determination, made by the Director of National Intelligence.

(D) WAIVER TERMINATION The Director of National Intelligence may revoke a previously granted waiver at any time. Upon revocation of a waiver, the Director of National Intelligence shall submit a written notification to the congressional intelligence committees, the Subcommittee on Defense of the Committee on Appropriations of the Senate, and the Subcommittee on Defense of the Committee on Appropriations of the House of Representatives not later than 30 days after making a revocation determination.

(5) TERMINATION OF PROHIBITION.— The Director of National Intelligence may terminate a prohibition made under paragraph (1) or (2) at any time. Upon termination of a prohibition, the Director of National Intelligence shall submit a notification of the termination to the congressional intelligence committees, the Subcommittee on Defense of the Committee on Appropriations of the Senate, and the Subcommittee on Defense of the Committee on Appropriations of the House of Representatives not later than 30 days after terminating a prohibition, detailing the basis for the termination, including any United States national security interests that

may be affected by such termination.

MISUSE OF THE OFFICE OF THE DIRECTOR OF NATIONAL INTELLIGENCE NAME, INITIALS, OR SEAL

SEC. 1103. [50 U.S.C. 3233] (a) PROHIBITED ACTS.— No person may, except with the written permission of the Director of National Intelligence, or a designee of the Director, knowingly use the words "Office of the Director of National Intelligence", the initials "ODNI", the seal of the Office of the Director of National Intelligence, or any colorable imitation of such words, initials, or seal in connection with any merchandise, impersonation, solicitation, or commercial activity in a manner reasonably calculated to convey the impression that such use is approved, endorsed, or authorized by the Director of National Intelligence.

(b) INJUNCTION.— Whenever it appears to the Attorney General that any person is engaged or is about to engage in an act or practice which constitutes or will constitute conduct prohibited by subsection (a), the Attorney General may initiate a civil proceeding in a district court of the United States to enjoin such act or practice. Such court shall proceed as soon as practicable to the hearing and determination of such action and may, at any time before final determination, enter such restraining orders or prohibitions, or take such other action as is warranted, to prevent injury to the United States or to any person or class of persons for whose protection the action is brought.

SEC. 1104. [50 U.S.C. 3234] PROHIBITED PERSONNEL PRACTICES IN THE INTELLIGENCE COMMUNITY.

(a) DEFINITIONS.—In this section:

(1) AGENCY.— The term "agency" means an executive department or independent establishment, as defined under sections 101 and 104 of title 5, United States Code, that contains an intelligence community element, except the Federal Bureau of Investigation.

(2) COVERED INTELLIGENCE COMMUNITY ELEMENT.—The term "covered intelligence community element"—

(A) means—

(i) the Central Intelligence Agency, the Defense Intelligence Agency, the National Geospatial-Intelligence Agency, the National Security Agency, the Office of the Director of National Intelligence, and the National Reconnaissance Office; and

(ii) any executive agency or unit thereof determined by the President under section 2302(a)(2)(C)(ii) of title 5, United States Code, to have as its principal function the conduct of foreign intelligence or counterintelligence activities; and

(B) does not include the Federal Bureau of Investigation.

(3) PERSONNEL ACTION.—The term "personnel action" means, with respect to an employee in a position in a covered intelligence community element (other than a position excepted from the competitive service due to its confidential, policy-determining, policymaking, or policy-advocating character) or a contractor

employee—

(A) an appointment;

(B) a promotion;

(C) a disciplinary or corrective action;

(D) a detail, transfer, or reassignment;

(E) a demotion, suspension, or termination;

(F) a reinstatement or restoration;

(G) a performance evaluation;

(H) a decision concerning pay, benefits, or awards;

(I) a decision concerning education or training if such education or training may reasonably be expected to lead to an appointment, promotion, or performance evaluation; or

(J) any other significant change in duties, responsibilities, or working conditions.

(4) CONTRACTOR EMPLOYEE.— The term "contractor employee" means an employee of a contractor, subcontractor, grantee, subgrantee, or personal services contractor, of a covered intelligence community element.

(b) AGENCY EMPLOYEES.—Any employee of a covered intelligence community element or an agency who has authority to take, direct others to take, recommend, or approve any personnel action, shall not, with respect to such authority, take or fail to take, or threaten to take or fail to take, a personnel action with respect to any employee of a covered intelligence community element as a reprisal for—

(1) any lawful disclosure of information by the employee to the Director of National Intelligence (or an employee designated by the Director of National Intelligence for such purpose), the Inspector General of the Intelligence Community, a supervisor in the employee's direct chain of command, or a supervisor of the employing agency with responsibility for the subject matter of the disclosure, up to and including the head of the employing agency (or an employee designated by the head of that agency for such purpose), the appropriate inspector general of the employing agency or covered intelligence community element, a congressional intelligence committee, or a member of a congressional intelligence committee, which the employee reasonably believes evidences—

(A) a violation of any Federal law, rule, or regulation; or

(B) mismanagement, a gross waste of funds, an abuse of authority, or a substantial and specific danger to public health or safety;

(2) any lawful disclosure that complies with—

(A) subsections (b)(1), (e), and (h) of section 416 of title 5, United States Code;

(B) subparagraphs (A), (D), and (H) of section 17(d)(5) of the Central Intelligence Agency Act of 1949 (50 U.S.C. 3517(d)(5)); or

(C) subparagraphs (A), (D), and (I) of section 103H(k)(5); or

(3) if the actions do not result in the employee unlawfully disclosing information specifically required by Executive order to be kept classified in the interest of national defense or the conduct of foreign affairs, any lawful disclosure in conjunction with—

(A) the exercise of any appeal, complaint, or grievance right granted by any law, rule, or regulation;

(B) testimony for or otherwise lawfully assisting any individual in the exercise of any right referred to in subparagraph (A); or

(C) cooperation with or disclosing information to the Inspector General of an agency, in accordance with applicable provisions of law in connection with an audit, inspection, or investigation conducted by the Inspector General.

(c) CONTRACTOR EMPLOYEES.—(1) Any employee of an agency or of a contractor, subcontractor, grantee, subgrantee, or personal services contractor, of a covered intelligence community element who has authority to take, direct others to take, recommend, or approve any personnel action, shall not, with respect to such authority, take or fail to take, or threaten to take or fail to take, a personnel action with respect to any contractor employee as a reprisal for—

(A) any lawful disclosure of information by the contractor employee to the Director of National Intelligence (or an employee designated by the Director of National Intelligence for such purpose), the Inspector General of the Intelligence Community, a supervisor in the contractor employee's direct chain of command, or a supervisor of the employing or contracting agency or employing contractor with responsibility for the subject matter of the disclosure, up to and including the head of the employing or contracting agency (or an employee designated by the head of that agency for that purpose) or employing contractor, the appropriate inspector general of the employing or contracting agency or covered intelligence community element, a congressional intelligence committee, or a member of a congressional intelligence committee, which the contractor employee reasonably believes evidences—

(i) a violation of any Federal law, rule, or regulation (including with respect to evidence of another employee or contractor employee accessing or sharing classified information without authorization); or

(ii) mismanagement, a gross waste of funds, an abuse of authority, or a substantial and specific danger to public health or safety;

(B) any lawful disclosure that complies with—

(i) subsections (b)(1), (e), and (h) of section 416 of title 5, United States Code;

(ii) subparagraphs (A), (D), and (H) of section 17(d)(5) of the Central Intelligence Agency Act of 1949 (50 U.S.C. 3517(d)(5)); or

(iii) subparagraphs (A), (D), and (I) of section 103H(k)(5); or

(C) if the actions do not result in the contractor employee unlawfully disclosing information specifically required by Executive order to be kept classified in the interest of national defense or the conduct of foreign affairs, any lawful disclosure in conjunction with—

(i) the exercise of any appeal, complaint, or grievance right granted by any law, rule, or regulation;

(ii) testimony for or otherwise lawfully assisting any individual in the exercise of any right referred to in clause (i); or

(iii) cooperation with or disclosing information to the Inspector General of an agency, in accordance with applicable provisions of law in connection with an audit, inspection, or investigation conducted by the Inspector General.

(2) A personnel action under paragraph (1) is prohibited even if the action is undertaken at the request of an agency official, unless the request takes the form of a nondiscretionary directive and is within the authority of the agency official making the request.

(d) RULE OF CONSTRUCTION.—Consistent with the protection of intelligence sources and methods, nothing in subsection (b) or (c) shall be construed to authorize—

(1) the withholding of information from Congress; or

(2) the taking of any personnel action against an employee who lawfully discloses information to Congress.

(e) DISCLOSURES.—A disclosure shall not be excluded from this section because—

(1) the disclosure was made to an individual, including a supervisor, who participated in an activity that the employee reasonably believed to be covered under subsection (b)(1)(B) or the contractor employee reasonably believed to be covered under subsection (c)(1)(A)(ii);

(2) the disclosure revealed information that had been previously disclosed;

(3) the disclosure was not made in writing;

(4) the disclosure was made while the employee was off duty;

(5) of the amount of time which has passed since the occurrence of the events described in the disclosure; or

(6) the disclosure was made during the normal course of duties of an employee or contractor employee.

(f) ENFORCEMENT.— The President shall provide for the enforcement of this section consistent, to the fullest extent possible, with the policies and procedures used to adjudicate alleged violations of section 2302(b)(8) of title 5, United States Code.

(g) EXISTING RIGHTS PRESERVED.—Nothing in this section shall be construed to—

(1) preempt or preclude any employee, contractor employee, or applicant for employment, at the Federal Bureau of Investigation from exercising rights provided under any other law, rule, or regulation, including section 2303 of title 5, United States Code; or

(2) repeal section 2303 of title 5, United States Code.

SEC. 1105. [50 U.S.C. 3235] SEMIANNUAL REPORTS ON INVESTIGATIONS OF UNAUTHORIZED DISCLOSURES OF CLASSIFIED INFORMATION.

(a) DEFINITIONS.—In this section:

(1) COVERED OFFICIAL.—The term "covered official" means—

(A) the heads of each element of the intelligence community; and

(B) the inspectors general with oversight responsibility for an element of the intelligence community.

(2) INVESTIGATION.— The term "investigation" means any inquiry, whether formal or informal, into the existence of an unauthorized public disclosure of classified information.

(3) UNAUTHORIZED DISCLOSURE OF CLASSIFIED INFORMATION.— The term "unauthorized disclosure of classified information" means any unauthorized disclosure of classified information to any recipient.

(4) UNAUTHORIZED PUBLIC DISCLOSURE OF CLASSIFIED INFORMATION.— The term "unauthorized public disclosure of classified information" means the unauthorized disclosure of classified information to a journalist or media organization.

(b) INTELLIGENCE COMMUNITY REPORTING.—

(1) IN GENERAL.— Not less frequently than once every 6 months, each covered official shall submit to the congressional intelligence committees a report on investigations of unauthorized public disclosures of classified information.

(2) ELEMENTS.—Each report submitted under paragraph (1) shall include, with respect to the preceding 6-month period, the following:

(A) The number of investigations opened by the covered official regarding an unauthorized public disclosure of classified information.

(B) The number of investigations completed by the covered official regarding an unauthorized public disclosure of classified information.

(C) Of the number of such completed investigations identified under subparagraph (B), the number referred to the Attorney General for criminal investigation.

(c) DEPARTMENT OF JUSTICE REPORTING.—

(1) IN GENERAL.— Not less frequently than once every 6 months, the Assistant Attorney General for National Security of the Department of Justice, in consultation with the Director of the Federal Bureau of Investigation, shall submit to the congressional intelligence committees, the Committee on the Judiciary of the Senate, and the Committee on the Judiciary of the House of Representatives a report on the status of each referral made to the Department of Justice from any element of the intelligence community regarding an unauthorized disclosure of classified information made during the most recent 365-day period or any referral that has not yet been closed, regardless of the date the referral was made.

(2) CONTENTS.—Each report submitted under paragraph (1) shall include, for each referral covered by the report, at a minimum, the following:

(A) The date the referral was received.

(B) A statement indicating whether the alleged unauthorized disclosure described in the referral was substantiated by the Department of Justice.

(C) A statement indicating the highest level of classification of the information that was revealed in the unauthorized disclosure.

(D) A statement indicating whether an open criminal investigation related to the referral is active.

(E) A statement indicating whether any criminal charges have been filed related to the referral.

(F) A statement indicating whether the Department of Justice has been able to attribute the unauthorized disclosure to a particular entity or individual.

(d) Form of Reports.— Each report submitted under this section shall be submitted in unclassified form, but may have a classified annex.

SEC. 1105A. [50 U.S.C. 3235a] NOTICE AND DAMAGE ASSESSMENT WITH RESPECT TO SIGNIFICANT UNAUTHORIZED DISCLOSURE OR COMPROMISE OF CLASSIFIED NATIONAL INTELLIGENCE.

(a) Notification and Damage Assessment Requirements.—

(1) Requirements .—If the Director of National Intelligence becomes aware of an actual or potential significant unauthorized disclosure or compromise of classified national intelligence—

(A) as soon as practicable, but not later than 7 days after the date on which the Director becomes so aware, the Director shall notify the congressional intelligence committees of such actual or potential disclosure or compromise; and

(B) in the case of an actual disclosure or compromise, not later than 7 days after the date on which the Director becomes so aware, the Director or the head of any element of the intelligence community from which the significant unauthorized disclosure or compromise originated shall initiate a damage assessment consistent with the procedures set forth in Intelligence Community Directive 732 (relating to the conduct of damage assessments), or successor directive, with respect to such disclosure or compromise.

(2) Contents of notification .—A notification submitted to the congressional intelligence committees under paragraph (1)(A) with respect to an actual or potential significant unauthorized disclosure or compromise of classified national intelligence shall include—

(A) a summary of the facts and circumstances of such disclosure or compromise;

(B) a summary of the contents of the national intelligence revealed or potentially revealed, as the case may be, by such disclosure or compromise;

(C) an initial appraisal of the level of actual or potential damage, as the case may be, to the national security of the United States as a result of such disclosure or compromise; and

(D) in the case of an actual disclosure or compromise, which elements of the intelligence community will be involved in the damage assessment conducted with respect to such disclosure or compromise pursuant to paragraph (1)(B).

(b) DAMAGE ASSESSMENT REPORTING REQUIREMENTS.—

(1) RECURRING REPORTING REQUIREMENT .—Not later than 30 days after the date of the initiation of a damage assessment pursuant to subsection (a)(1)(B), and every 90 days thereafter until the completion of the damage assessment or upon the request of the congressional intelligence committees, the Director of National Intelligence shall—

(A) submit to the congressional intelligence committees copies of any documents or materials disclosed as a result of the significant unauthorized disclosure or compromise of the classified national intelligence that is the subject of the damage assessment; and

(B) provide to the congressional intelligence committees a briefing on such documents and materials and a status of the damage assessment.

(2) FINAL DAMAGE ASSESSMENT .—As soon as practicable after completing a damage assessment pursuant to subsection (a)(1)(B), the Director of National Intelligence shall submit the final damage assessment to the congressional intelligence committees.

(c) NOTIFICATION OF REFERRAL TO DEPARTMENT OF JUSTICE .—If a referral is made to the Department of Justice from any element of the intelligence community regarding a significant unauthorized disclosure or compromise of classified national intelligence under this section, the Director of National Intelligence shall notify the congressional intelligence committees of the referral on the date such referral is made.

SEC. 1106. [50 U.S.C. 3236] INSPECTOR GENERAL EXTERNAL REVIEW PANEL.

(a) REQUEST FOR REVIEW.— An individual with a claim described in subsection (b) may submit to the Inspector General of the Intelligence Community a request for a review of such claim by an external review panel convened under subsection (c).

(b) CLAIMS AND INDIVIDUALS DESCRIBED.—A claim described in this subsection is any—

(1) claim by an individual—

(A) that the individual has been subjected to a personnel action that is prohibited under section 1104; and

(B) who has exhausted the applicable review process for the claim pursuant to enforcement of such section; or

(2) claim by an individual—

(A) that he or she has been subjected to a reprisal prohibited by paragraph (1) of section 3001(j) of the Intelligence Reform and Terrorism Prevention Act of 2004 (50 U.S.C. 3341(j)); and

(B) who received a decision on an appeal regarding that claim under paragraph (4) of such section.

(c) EXTERNAL REVIEW PANEL CONVENED.—

(1) DISCRETION TO CONVENE.— Upon receipt of a request under subsection (a) regarding a claim, the Inspector General of the Intelligence Community may, at the

discretion of the Inspector General, convene an external review panel under this subsection to review the claim.

(2) MEMBERSHIP.—

(A) COMPOSITION.—An external review panel convened under this subsection shall be composed of three members as follows:

(i) The Inspector General of the Intelligence Community.

(ii) Except as provided in subparagraph (B), two members selected by the Inspector General as the Inspector General considers appropriate on a case-by-case basis from among inspectors general of the following:

(I) The Department of Defense.

(II) The Department of Energy.

(III) The Department of Homeland Security.

(IV) The Department of Justice.

(V) The Department of State.

(VI) The Department of the Treasury.

(VII) The Central Intelligence Agency.

(VIII) The Defense Intelligence Agency.

(IX) The National Geospatial-Intelligence Agency.

(X) The National Reconnaissance Office.

(XI) The National Security Agency.

(B) LIMITATION.— An inspector general of an agency may not be selected to sit on the panel under subparagraph (A)(ii) to review any matter relating to a decision made by such agency.

(C) CHAIRPERSON.—

(i) IN GENERAL.— Except as provided in clause (ii), the chairperson of any panel convened under this subsection shall be the Inspector General of the Intelligence Community.

(ii) CONFLICTS OF INTEREST.—If the Inspector General of the Intelligence Community finds cause to recuse himself or herself from a panel convened under this subsection, the Inspector General of the Intelligence Community shall—

(I) select a chairperson from inspectors general of the elements listed under subparagraph (A)(ii) whom the Inspector General of the Intelligence Community considers appropriate; and

(II) notify the congressional intelligence committees of such selection.

(3) PERIOD OF REVIEW.— Each external review panel convened under this subsection to review a claim shall complete review of the claim no later than 270 days after the date on which the Inspector General convenes the external review

panel.

(d) REMEDIES.—

(1) PANEL RECOMMENDATIONS.—If an external review panel convened under subsection (c) determines, pursuant to a review of a claim submitted by an individual under subsection (a), that the individual was the subject of a personnel action prohibited under section 1104 or was subjected to a reprisal prohibited by section 3001(j)(1) of the Intelligence Reform and Terrorism Prevention Act of 2004 (50 U.S.C. 3341(j)(1)), the panel may recommend that the agency head take corrective action—

(A) in the case of an employee or former employee—

(i) to return the employee or former employee, as nearly as practicable and reasonable, to the position such employee or former employee would have held had the reprisal not occurred; or

(ii) reconsider the employee's or former employee's eligibility for access to classified information consistent with national security; or

(B) in any other case, such other action as the external review panel considers appropriate.

(2) AGENCY ACTION.—

(A) IN GENERAL.—Not later than 90 days after the date on which the head of an agency receives a recommendation from an external review panel under paragraph (1), the head shall—

(i) give full consideration to such recommendation; and

(ii) inform the panel and the Director of National Intelligence of what action the head has taken with respect to the recommendation.

(B) FAILURE TO INFORM.— The Director shall notify the President of any failures to comply with subparagraph (A)(ii).

(e) ANNUAL REPORTS.—

(1) IN GENERAL.— Not less frequently than once each year, the Inspector General of the Intelligence Community shall submit to the congressional intelligence committees and the Director of National Intelligence a report on the activities under this section during the previous year.

(2) CONTENTS.—Subject to such limitations as the Inspector General of the Intelligence Community considers necessary to protect the privacy of an individual who has made a claim described in subsection (b), each report submitted under paragraph (1) shall include, for the period covered by the report, the following:

(A) The determinations and recommendations made by the external review panels convened under this section.

(B) The responses of the heads of agencies that received recommendations from the external review panels.

SEC. 1107. [50 U.S.C. 3237] ANNUAL REPORTS ON INFLUENCE OPERATIONS AND CAMPAIGNS IN THE UNITED STATES BY THE CHINESE COMMUNIST PARTY.

(a) REQUIREMENT.— On an annual basis, consistent with the protection of intelligence sources and methods, the Director of the National Counterintelligence and Security Center shall submit to the congressional intelligence committees, the Committee on Foreign Affairs of the House of Representatives, and the Committee on Foreign Relations of the Senate a report on the influence operations and campaigns in the United States conducted by the Chinese Communist Party.

(b) CONTENTS.—Each report under subsection (a) shall include the following:

(1) A description of the organization of the United Front Work Department of the People's Republic of China, or the successors of the United Front Work Department, and the links between the United Front Work Department and the Central Committee of the Chinese Communist Party.

(2) An assessment of the degree to which organizations that are associated with or receive funding from the United Front Work Department, particularly such entities operating in the United States, are formally tasked by the Chinese Communist Party or the Government of China.

(3) A description of the efforts by the United Front Work Department and subsidiary organizations of the United Front Work Department to target, coerce, and influence foreign populations, particularly those of ethnic Chinese descent.

(4) An assessment of attempts by the Chinese Embassy, consulates, and organizations affiliated with the Chinese Communist Party (including, at a minimum, the United Front Work Department) to influence the United States-based Chinese Student Scholar Associations.

(5) A description of the evolution of the role of the United Front Work Department under the leadership of the President of China.

(6) An assessment of the activities of the United Front Work Department designed to influence the opinions of elected leaders of the United States, or candidates for elections in the United States, with respect to issues of importance to the Chinese Communist Party.

(7) A listing of all known organizations affiliated with the United Front Work Department that are operating in the United States as of the date of the report.

(8) An identification of influence activities and operations employed by the Chinese Communist Party against the United States science and technology sectors, specifically employees of the United States Government, researchers, scientists, and students in the science and technology sector in the United States.

(9) A listing of all known Chinese talent recruitment programs operating in the United States as of the date of the report.

(10) With respect to reports submitted after the first report, an assessment of the change in goals, tactics, techniques, and procedures of the influence operations and campaigns conducted by the Chinese Communist Party.

(c) COORDINATION.— In carrying out subsection (a), the Director shall coordinate with the Director of the Federal Bureau of Investigation, the Director of the Central Intelligence Agency, the Director of the National Security Agency, and any other relevant head of an element of the intelligence community.

(d) FORM.— Each report submitted under subsection (a) shall be submitted in unclassified form, but may include a classified annex.

SEC. 1108. [50 U.S.C. 3238] ANNUAL REPORTS ON INFLUENCE OPERATIONS AND CAMPAIGNS IN THE UNITED STATES BY THE RUSSIAN FEDERATION.

(a) REQUIREMENT.— On an annual basis, the Director of the National Counterintelligence and Security Center shall submit to the congressional intelligence committees a report on the influence operations and campaigns in the United States conducted by the Russian Federation.

(b) CONTENTS.—Each report under subsection (a) shall include the following:

(1) A description and listing of the Russian organizations and persons involved in influence operations and campaigns operating in the United States as of the date of the report.

(2) An assessment of organizations that are associated with or receive funding from organizations and persons identified in paragraph (1), particularly such entities operating in the United States.

(3) A description of the efforts by the organizations and persons identified in paragraph (1) to target, coerce, and influence populations within the United States.

(4) An assessment of the activities of the organizations and persons identified in paragraph (1) designed to influence the opinions of elected leaders of the United States or candidates for election in the United States.

(5) With respect to reports submitted after the first report, an assessment of the change in goals, tactics, techniques, and procedures of the influence operations and campaigns conducted by the organizations and persons identified in paragraph (1).

(c) COORDINATION.— In carrying out subsection (a), the Director shall coordinate with the Director of the Federal Bureau of Investigation, the Director of the Central Intelligence Agency, the Director of the National Security Agency, and any other relevant head of an element of the intelligence community.

(d) FORM.— Each report submitted under subsection (a) shall be submitted in unclassified form, but may include a classified annex.

SEC. 1109. [50 U.S.C. 3239] REQUIREMENT TO BUY CERTAIN SATELLITE COMPONENT FROM AMERICAN SOURCES.

(a) DEFINITIONS.—In this section:

(1) COVERED ELEMENT OF THE INTELLIGENCE COMMUNITY.— The term “covered element of the intelligence community” means an element of the intelligence community that is not an element of the Department of Defense.

(2) NATIONAL SECURITY SATELLITE.— The term “national security satellite” means a satellite weighing over 400 pounds whose principle purpose is to support the national security or intelligence needs of the United States Government.

(3) UNITED STATES.— The term “United States” means the several States, the District of Columbia, and the territories and possessions of the United States.

(b) REQUIREMENT.— Beginning January 1, 2021, except as provided in subsection (c), a covered element of the intelligence community may not award a contract for a national security satellite if the satellite uses a star tracker that is not produced in the United States, including with respect to both the software and the hardware of the star tracker.

(c) EXCEPTION.—The head of a covered element of the intelligence community may waive the requirement under subsection (b) if, on a case-by-case basis, the head certifies in writing to the congressional intelligence committees that—

(1) there is no available star tracker produced in the United States that meets the mission and design requirements of the national security satellite for which the star tracker will be used;

(2) the cost of a star tracker produced in the United States is unreasonable, based on a market survey; or

(3) such waiver is necessary for the national security interests of the United States based on an urgent and compelling need.

SEC. 1110. [50 U.S.C. 3240] REPORT ON BEST PRACTICES TO PROTECT PRIVACY , CIVIL LIBERTIES, AND CIVIL RIGHTS OF CHINESE AMERICANS.

(a) SENSE OF CONGRESS.—It is the sense of Congress that—

(1) the People's Republic of China appears to be specifically targeting the Chinese-American community for intelligence purposes;

(2) such targeting carries a substantial risk that the loyalty of such Americans may be generally questioned and lead to unacceptable stereotyping, targeting, and racial profiling;

(3) the United States Government has a duty to warn and protect all Americans including those of Chinese descent from these intelligence efforts by the People's Republic of China;

(4) the broad stereotyping, targeting, and racial profiling of Americans of Chinese descent is contrary to the values of the United States and reinforces the flawed narrative perpetuated by the People's Republic of China that ethnically Chinese individuals worldwide have a duty to support the People's Republic of China; and

(5) the United States efforts to combat the People's Republic of China's intelligence activities should actively safeguard and promote the constitutional rights of all Chinese Americans.

(b) REPORT.—On an annual basis, the Director of National Intelligence, acting through the Office of Civil Liberties, Privacy, and Transparency, in coordination with the civil liberties and privacy officers of the elements of the intelligence community, shall submit a report to the congressional intelligence committees containing—

(1) a review of how the policies, procedures, and practices of the intelligence community that govern the intelligence activities and operations targeting the People's Republic of China affect policies, procedures, and practices relating to the privacy , civil liberties, and civil rights of Americans of Chinese descent who may be targets of espionage and influence operations by China; and

(2) recommendations to ensure that the privacy , civil liberties, and civil rights of Americans of Chinese descent are sufficiently protected.

(c) FORM.— The report under subsection (b) shall be submitted in unclassified form, but may include a classified annex.

SEC. 1111. [50 U.S.C. 3241] BIENNIAL REPORTS ON FOREIGN BIOLOGICAL THREATS.

(a) REPORTS.— On a biennial basis until the date that is 10 years after the date of the enactment of the Intelligence Authorization Act for Fiscal Year 2022, the Director of National Intelligence shall submit to the congressional intelligence committees a comprehensive report on the activities, prioritization, and responsibilities of the intelligence community with respect to foreign biological threats emanating from the territory of, or sponsored by, a covered country.

(b) MATTERS INCLUDED.—Each report under subsection (a) shall include, with respect to foreign biological threats emanating from the territory of, or sponsored by, a covered country, the following:

(1) A detailed description of all activities relating to such threats undertaken by each element of the intelligence community, and an assessment of any gaps in such activities.

(2) A detailed description of all duties and responsibilities relating to such threats explicitly authorized or otherwise assigned, exclusively or jointly, to each element of the intelligence community, and an assessment of any identified gaps in such duties or responsibilities.

(3) A description of the coordination among the relevant elements of the intelligence community with respect to the activities specified in paragraph (1) and the duties and responsibilities specified in paragraph (2).

(4) An inventory of the strategies, plans, policies, and interagency agreements of the intelligence community relating to the collection, monitoring, analysis, mitigation, and attribution of such threats, and an assessment of any identified gaps therein.

(5) A description of the coordination and interactions among the relevant elements of the intelligence community and non-intelligence community partners.

(6) An assessment of foreign malign influence efforts relating to such threats, including any foreign academics engaged in such efforts, and a description of how the intelligence community contributes to efforts by non-intelligence community partners to counter such foreign malign influence.

(c) FORM.— Each report submitted under subsection (a) may be submitted in classified form, but if so submitted shall include an unclassified executive summary.

(d) DEFINITIONS.—In this section:

(1) COVERED COUNTRY.—The term "covered country" means—

(A) China;

(B) Iran;

(C) North Korea;

(D) Russia; and

(E) any other foreign country—

(i) from which the Director of National Intelligence determines a biological threat emanates; or

(ii) that the Director determines has a known history of, or has been assessed as having conditions present for, infectious disease outbreaks or epidemics.

(2) FOREIGN BIOLOGICAL THREAT.— The term "foreign biological threat" means biological warfare, bioterrorism, naturally occurring infectious diseases, or accidental exposures to biological materials, without regard to whether the threat originates from a state actor, a non-state actor, natural conditions, or an undetermined source.

(3) FOREIGN MALIGN INFLUENCE.— The term "foreign malign influence" has the meaning given such term in section 119C(e) of this Act.

(4) NON-INTELLIGENCE COMMUNITY PARTNER.— The term "non-intelligence community partner" means a Federal department or agency that is not an element of the intelligence community.

SEC. 1112. [50 U.S.C. 3242] ANNUAL REPORTS ON CERTAIN CYBER VULNERABILITIES PROCURED BY INTELLIGENCE COMMUNITY AND FOREIGN COMMERCIAL PROVIDERS OF CYBER VULNERABILITIES.

(a) ANNUAL REPORTS.— On an annual basis through 2026, the Director of the Central Intelligence Agency and the Director of the National Security Agency, in coordination with the Director of National Intelligence, shall jointly submit to the congressional intelligence committees a report containing information on foreign commercial providers and the cyber vulnerabilities procured by the intelligence community through foreign commercial providers.

(b) ELEMENTS.—Each report under subsection (a) shall include, with respect to the period covered by the report, the following:

(1) A description of each cyber vulnerability procured through a foreign commercial provider, including—

(A) a description of the vulnerability;

(B) the date of the procurement;

(C) whether the procurement consisted of only that vulnerability or included other vulnerabilities;

(D) the cost of the procurement;

(E) the identity of the commercial provider and, if the commercial provider was not the original supplier of the vulnerability, a description of the original supplier;

(F) the country of origin of the vulnerability; and

(G) an assessment of the ability of the intelligence community to use the vulnerability, including whether such use will be operational or for research and development, and the approximate timeline for such use.

(2) An assessment of foreign commercial providers that—

(A) pose a significant threat to the national security of the United States; or

(B) have provided cyber vulnerabilities to any foreign government that—

(i) has used the cyber vulnerabilities to target United States persons, the United States Government, journalists, or dissidents; or

(ii) has an established pattern or practice of violating human rights or suppressing dissent.

(3) An assessment of whether the intelligence community has conducted business with the foreign commercial providers identified under paragraph (2) during the 5-year period preceding the date of the report.

(c) FORM.— Each report under subsection (a) may be submitted in classified form.

(d) DEFINITIONS.—In this section:

(1) COMMERCIAL PROVIDER.— The term "commercial provider" means any person that sells, or acts as a broker, for a cyber vulnerability.

(2) CYBER VULNERABILITY.— The term "cyber vulnerability" means any tool, exploit, vulnerability, or code that is intended to compromise a device, network, or system, including such a tool, exploit, vulnerability, or code procured by the intelligence community for purposes of research and development.

SEC. 1113. [50 U.S.C. 3243] PERIODIC REPORTS ON TECHNOLOGY STRATEGY OF INTELLIGENCE COMMUNITY.

(a) REPORTS.— On a basis that is not less frequent than once every 4 years, the Director of National Intelligence, in coordination with the Director of the Office of Science and Technology Policy, the Secretary of Commerce, and the heads of such other agencies as the Director considers appropriate, shall submit to the congressional intelligence committees a comprehensive report on the technology strategy of the intelligence community, which shall be designed to support the maintenance of the leadership of the United States in critical and emerging technologies essential to the national security of the United States.

(b) ELEMENTS.—Each report submitted under subsection (a) shall include the following:

(1) An assessment of technologies critical to the national security of the United States, particularly those technologies with respect to which foreign countries that are adversarial to the United States have or are poised to match or surpass the technology leadership of the United States.

(2) A review of current technology policies of the intelligence community, including long-term goals.

(3) An identification of sectors and supply chains the Director determines to be of the greatest strategic importance to national security.

(4) An identification of opportunities to protect the leadership of the United States, and the allies and partners of the United States, in critical technologies,

including through targeted export controls, investment screening, and counterintelligence activities.

(5) An identification of research and development areas the Director determines critical to the national security of the United States, including areas in which the private sector does not focus.

(6) Recommendations for growing talent in key critical and emerging technologies and enhancing the ability of the intelligence community to recruit and retain individuals with critical skills relating to such technologies.

(7) An identification of opportunities to improve the leadership of the United States in critical technologies, including opportunities to develop international partnerships to reinforce domestic policy actions, develop new markets, engage in collaborative research, and maintain an international environment that reflects the values of the United States and protects the interests of the United States.

(8) A technology annex to establish an approach for the identification, prioritization, development, and fielding of emerging technologies critical to the mission of the intelligence community.

(9) Such other information as the Director determines may be necessary to inform Congress on matters relating to the technology strategy of the intelligence community and related implications for the national security of the United States.

(c) FORM OF ANNEX.— Each annex submitted under subsection (b)(8) may be submitted in classified form.

SEC. 1114. [50 U.S.C. 3244] ANNUAL REPORT ON REPORTING REQUIREMENTS.

(a) ANNUAL REPORT REQUIRED.— Not later than March 1 of each fiscal year, the Director of National Intelligence shall submit to the congressional intelligence committees, the Committee on Appropriations of the Senate, and the Committee on Appropriations of the House of Representatives a report detailing all congressionally mandated reporting requirements applicable to the Office of the Director of National Intelligence for the upcoming fiscal year.

(b) CONTENTS.—Each report submitted pursuant to subsection (a) shall include, for the fiscal year covered by the report and for each congressionally mandated reporting requirement detailed in the report:

(1) A description of the reporting requirement.

(2) A citation to the provision of law (or other source of congressional directive) imposing the reporting requirement.

(3) Whether the reporting requirement is recurring, conditional, or subject to a termination provision.

(4) Whether the Director recommends repealing or modifying the requirement.

(c) FORM.— Each report submitted pursuant to subsection (a) may be submitted in classified form.

INTELLIGENCE REFORM AND TERRORISM PREVENTION ACT OF 2004

TITLE I IS CITED AS THE NATIONAL SECURITY INTELLIGENCE REFORM ACT OF 2004

PUBLIC LAW 108–458
AS AMENDED THROUGH P.L. 118–158

INTELLIGENCE REFORM AND TERRORISM PREVENTION ACT OF 2004

National Security Intelligence Reform Act of 2004 (Title I)

[(Public Law 108–458; December 17, 2004)]

[As Amended Through P.L. 118–159, Enacted December 23, 2024]

AN ACT To reform the intelligence community and the intelligence and intelligence-related activities of the United States Government, and for other purposes.

Be it enacted by the Senate and House of Representatives of the United States of America in Congress assembled,

SECTION 1. SHORT TITLE; TABLE OF CONTENTS.

(a) **[50 U.S.C. 3001 note]** SHORT TITLE.— This Act may be cited as the "Intelligence Reform and Terrorism Prevention Act of 2004".

(b) TABLE OF CONTENTS.— The table of contents for this Act is as follows:

* * * * * * *

TITLE I—REFORM OF THE INTELLIGENCE COMMUNITY

SEC. 1001. [50 U.S.C. 3001 note] SHORT TITLE.

This title may be cited as the "National Security Intelligence Reform Act of 2004".

SEC. 1011. REORGANIZATION AND IMPROVEMENT OF MANAGEMENT OF INTELLIGENCE COMMUNITY.

(a)

* * *

(b) **[50 U.S.C. 3506a note]** SENSE OF CONGRESS.—It is the sense of Congress that—

(1) the human intelligence officers of the intelligence community have performed admirably and honorably in the face of great personal dangers;

(2) during an extended period of unprecedented investment and improvements in technical collection means, the human intelligence capabilities of the United States have not received the necessary and commensurate priorities;

(3) human intelligence is becoming an increasingly important capability to provide information on the asymmetric threats to the national security of the United States;

(4) the continued development and improvement of a robust and empowered and flexible human intelligence work force is critical to identifying, understanding, and countering the plans and intentions of the adversaries of the United States; and

(5) an increased emphasis on, and resources applied to, enhancing the depth and breadth of human intelligence capabilities of the United States intelligence community must be among the top priorities of the Director of National Intelligence.

(c) **[50 U.S.C. 3506a]** TRANSFORMATION OF CENTRAL INTELLIGENCE AGENCY.—The Director of the Central Intelligence Agency shall, in accordance with standards developed by the Director in consultation with the Director of National Intelligence—

(1) enhance the analytic, human intelligence, and other capabilities of the Central Intelligence Agency;

(2) develop and maintain an effective language program within the Agency;

(3) emphasize the hiring of personnel of diverse backgrounds for purposes of improving the capabilities of the Agency;

(4) establish and maintain effective relationships between human intelligence and signals intelligence within the Agency at the operational level; and

(5) achieve a more effective balance within the Agency with respect to unilateral operations and liaison operations.

(d) REPORT.—(1) Not later than 180 days after the date of the enactment of this Act, the Director of the Central Intelligence Agency shall submit to the Director of National Intelligence and the congressional intelligence committees a report setting forth the following:

(A) A strategy for improving the conduct of analysis (including strategic analysis) by the Central Intelligence Agency, and the progress of the Agency in implementing that strategy.

(B) A strategy for improving the human intelligence and other capabilities of the Agency, and the progress of the Agency in implementing that strategy.

(2)(A) The information in the report under paragraph (1) on the strategy referred to in paragraph (1)(B) shall—

(i) identify the number and types of personnel required to implement that strategy;

(ii) include a plan for the recruitment, training, equipping, and deployment of such personnel; and

(iii) set forth an estimate of the costs of such activities.

(B) If as of the date of the report under paragraph (1), a proper balance does not exist between unilateral operations and liaison operations, such report shall set forth the steps to be taken to achieve such balance.

* * * * * * *

SEC. 1013. [50 U.S.C. 3024 note] JOINT PROCEDURES FOR OPERATIONAL COORDINATION BETWEEN DEPARTMENT OF DEFENSE AND CENTRAL INTELLIGENCE AGENCY.

(a) Development of Procedures.—The Director of National Intelligence, in consultation with the Secretary of Defense and the Director of the Central Intelligence Agency, shall develop joint procedures to be used by the Department of Defense and the Central Intelligence Agency to improve the coordination and deconfliction of operations that involve elements of both the Armed Forces and the Central Intelligence Agency consistent with national security and the protection of human intelligence sources and methods. Those procedures shall, at a minimum, provide the following:

(1) Methods by which the Director of the Central Intelligence Agency and the Secretary of Defense can improve communication and coordination in the planning, execution, and sustainment of operations, including, as a minimum—

(A) information exchange between senior officials of the Central Intelligence Agency and senior officers and officials of the Department of Defense when planning for such an operation commences by either organization; and

(B) exchange of information between the Secretary and the Director of the Central Intelligence Agency to ensure that senior operational officials in both the Department of Defense and the Central Intelligence Agency have knowledge of the existence of the ongoing operations of the other.

(2) When appropriate, in cases where the Department of Defense and the Central Intelligence Agency are conducting separate missions in the same geographical area, a mutual agreement on the tactical and strategic objectives for the region and a clear delineation of operational responsibilities to prevent conflict and duplication of effort.

(b) Implementation Report.— Not later than 180 days after the date of the enactment of the Act, the Director of National Intelligence shall submit to the congressional defense committees (as defined in section 101 of title 10, United States Code) and the congressional intelligence committees (as defined in section 3(7) of the National Security Act of 1947 (50 U.S.C. 401a(7))) a report describing the procedures established pursuant to subsection (a) and the status of the implementation of those procedures.

* * * * * * *

SEC. 1016. [6 U.S.C. 485] INFORMATION SHARING.

(a) Definitions.—In this section:

(1) Homeland security information.— The term “homeland security information” has the meaning given that term in section 892(f) of the Homeland Security Act of 2002 (6 U.S.C. 482(f)).

(2) Information sharing council.— The term “Information Sharing Council” means the Information Systems Council established by Executive Order 13356, or any successor body designated by the President, and referred to under subsection (g).

(3) Information sharing environment.— The terms "information sharing environment" and "ISE" mean an approach that facilitates the sharing of terrorism and homeland security information, which may include any method determined necessary and appropriate for carrying out this section.

(4) Program manager.— The term "program manager" means the program manager designated under subsection (f).

(5) Terrorism information.—The term "terrorism information"—

(A) means all information, whether collected, produced, or distributed by intelligence, law enforcement, military, homeland security, or other activities relating to—

(i) the existence, organization, capabilities, plans, intentions, vulnerabilities, means of finance or material support, or activities of foreign or international terrorist groups or individuals, or of domestic groups or individuals involved in transnational terrorism;

(ii) threats posed by such groups or individuals to the United States, United States persons, or United States interests, or to those of other nations;

(iii) communications of or by such groups or individuals; or

(iv) groups or individuals reasonably believed to be assisting or associated with such groups or individuals; and

(B) includes weapons of mass destruction information.

(6) Weapons of mass destruction information.— The term "weapons of mass destruction information" means information that could reasonably be expected to assist in the development, proliferation, or use of a weapon of mass destruction (including a chemical, biological, radiological, or nuclear weapon) that could be used by a terrorist or a terrorist organization against the United States, including information about the location of any stockpile of nuclear materials that could be exploited for use in such a weapon that could be used by a terrorist or a terrorist organization against the United States.

(b) Information Sharing Environment.—

(1) Establishment.—The President shall—

(A) create an information sharing environment for the sharing of terrorism information in a manner consistent with national security and with applicable legal standards relating to privacy and civil liberties;

(B) designate the organizational and management structures that will be used to operate and manage the ISE; and

(C) determine and enforce the policies, directives, and rules that will govern the content and usage of the ISE.

(2) Attributes.—The President shall, through the structures described in subparagraphs (B) and (C) of paragraph (1), ensure that the ISE provides and facilitates the means for sharing terrorism information among all appropriate Federal, State, local, and tribal entities, and the private sector through the use of policy guidelines and technologies. The President shall, to the greatest extent practicable, ensure that the ISE provides the functional equivalent of, or otherwise supports, a decentralized, distributed, and coordinated environment that—

(A) connects existing systems, where appropriate, provides no single points of failure, and allows users to share information among agencies, between levels of government, and, as appropriate, with the private sector;

(B) ensures direct and continuous online electronic access to information;

(C) facilitates the availability of information in a form and manner that facilitates its use in analysis, investigations and operations;

(D) builds upon existing systems capabilities currently in use across the Government;

(E) employs an information access management approach that controls access to data rather than just systems and networks, without sacrificing security;

(F) facilitates the sharing of information at and across all levels of security;

(G) provides directory services, or the functional equivalent, for locating people and information;

(H) incorporates protections for individuals' privacy and civil liberties;

(I) incorporates strong mechanisms to enhance accountability and facilitate oversight, including audits, authentication, and access controls;

(J) integrates the information within the scope of the information sharing environment, including any such information in legacy technologies;

(K) integrates technologies, including all legacy technologies, through Internet-based services, consistent with appropriate security protocols and safeguards, to enable connectivity among required users at the Federal, State, and local levels;

(L) allows the full range of analytic and operational activities without the need to centralize information within the scope of the information sharing environment;

(M) permits analysts to collaborate both independently and in a group (commonly known as "collective and noncollective collaboration"), and across multiple levels of national security information and controlled unclassified information;

(N) provides a resolution process that enables changes by authorized officials regarding rules and policies for the access, use, and retention of information within the scope of the information sharing environment; and

(O) incorporates continuous, real-time, and immutable audit capabilities, to the maximum extent practicable.

(3) Delegation.—

(A) In general.— Subject to subparagraph (B), the President may delegate responsibility for carrying out this subsection.

(B) Limitation.— The President may not delegate responsibility for carrying out this subsection to the Director of National Intelligence.

(c) Preliminary Report.—Not later than 180 days after the date of the enactment of this Act, the program manager shall, in consultation with the Information Sharing Council—

(1) submit to the President and Congress a description of the technological,

legal, and policy issues presented by the creation of the ISE, and the way in which these issues will be addressed;

(2) establish an initial capability to provide electronic directory services, or the functional equivalent, to assist in locating in the Federal Government intelligence and terrorism information and people with relevant knowledge about intelligence and terrorism information; and

(3) conduct a review of relevant current Federal agency capabilities, databases, and systems for sharing information.

(d) GUIDELINES AND REQUIREMENTS.—As soon as possible, but in no event later than 270 days after the date of the enactment of this Act, the President shall—

(1) leverage all ongoing efforts consistent with establishing the ISE and issue guidelines for acquiring, accessing, sharing, and using information, including guidelines to ensure that information is provided in its most shareable form, such as by using tearlines to separate out data from the sources and methods by which the data are obtained;

(2) in consultation with the Privacy and Civil Liberties Oversight Board established under section 1061, issue guidelines that—

(A) protect privacy and civil liberties in the development and use of the ISE; and

(B) shall be made public, unless nondisclosure is clearly necessary to protect national security; and

(3) require the heads of Federal departments and agencies to promote a culture of information sharing by—

(A) reducing disincentives to information sharing, including over-classification of information and unnecessary requirements for originator approval, consistent with applicable laws and regulations; and

(B) providing affirmative incentives for information sharing.

(e) IMPLEMENTATION PLAN REPORT.—Not later than one year after the date of the enactment of this Act, the President shall, with the assistance of the program manager, submit to Congress a report containing an implementation plan for the ISE. The report shall include the following:

(1) A description of the functions, capabilities, resources, and conceptual design of the ISE, including standards.

(2) A description of the impact on enterprise architectures of participating agencies.

(3) A budget estimate that identifies the incremental costs associated with designing, testing, integrating, deploying, and operating the ISE.

(4) A project plan for designing, testing, integrating, deploying, and operating the ISE.

(5) The policies and directives referred to in subsection (b)(1)(C), as well as the metrics and enforcement mechanisms that will be utilized.

(6) Objective, systemwide performance measures to enable the assessment of progress toward achieving the full implementation of the ISE.

(7) A description of the training requirements needed to ensure that the ISE will

be adequately implemented and properly utilized.

(8) A description of the means by which privacy and civil liberties will be protected in the design and operation of the ISE.

(9) The recommendations of the program manager, in consultation with the Information Sharing Council, regarding whether, and under what conditions, the ISE should be expanded to include other intelligence information.

(10) A delineation of the roles of the Federal departments and agencies that will participate in the ISE, including an identification of the agencies that will deliver the infrastructure needed to operate and manage the ISE (as distinct from individual department or agency components that are part of the ISE), with such delineation of roles to be consistent with—

(A) the authority of the Director of National Intelligence under this title, and the amendments made by this title, to set standards for information sharing throughout the intelligence community; and

(B) the authority of the Secretary of Homeland Security and the Attorney General, and the role of the Department of Homeland Security and the Department of Justice, in coordinating with State, local, and tribal officials and the private sector.

(11) The recommendations of the program manager, in consultation with the Information Sharing Council, for a future management structure for the ISE, including whether the position of program manager should continue to remain in existence.

(f) PROGRAM MANAGER.—

(1) DESIGNATION.— Not later than 120 days after the date of the enactment of this Act, with notification to Congress, the President shall designate an individual as the program manager responsible for information sharing across the Federal Government. Beginning on the date of the enactment of the Damon Paul Nelson and Matthew Young Pollard Intelligence Authorization Act for Fiscal Years 2018, 2019 and 2020, each individual designated as the program manager shall be appointed by the Director of National Intelligence. The program manager, in consultation with the head of any affected department or agency, shall have and exercise governmentwide authority over the sharing of information within the scope of the information sharing environment, including homeland security information, terrorism information, and weapons of mass destruction information, by all Federal departments, agencies, and components, irrespective of the Federal department, agency, or component in which the program manager may be administratively located, except as otherwise expressly provided by law.

(2) DUTIES AND RESPONSIBILITIES.—

(A) IN GENERAL.—The program manager shall, in consultation with the Information Sharing Council—

(i) plan for and oversee the implementation of, and manage, the ISE;

(ii) assist in the development of policies, as appropriate, to foster the development and proper operation of the ISE;

(iii) consistent with the direction and policies issued by the President, the Director of National Intelligence, and the Director of the Office of

Management and Budget, issue governmentwide procedures, guidelines, instructions, and functional standards, as appropriate, for the management, development, and proper operation of the ISE;

(iv) identify and resolve information sharing disputes between Federal departments, agencies, and components; and

(v) assist, monitor, and assess the implementation of the ISE by Federal departments and agencies to ensure adequate progress, technological consistency and policy compliance; and regularly report the findings to Congress.

(B) CONTENT OF POLICIES, PROCEDURES, GUIDELINES, RULES, AND STANDARDS.—The policies, procedures, guidelines, rules, and standards under subparagraph (A)(ii) shall—

(i) take into account the varying missions and security requirements of agencies participating in the ISE;

(ii) address development, implementation, and oversight of technical standards and requirements;

(iii) take into account ongoing and planned efforts that support development, implementation and management of the ISE;

(iv) address and facilitate information sharing between and among departments and agencies of the intelligence community, the Department of Defense, the homeland security community and the law enforcement community;

(v) address and facilitate information sharing between Federal departments and agencies and State, tribal, and local governments;

(vi) address and facilitate, as appropriate, information sharing between Federal departments and agencies and the private sector;

(vii) address and facilitate, as appropriate, information sharing between Federal departments and agencies with foreign partners and allies; and

(viii) ensure the protection of privacy and civil liberties.

(g) INFORMATION SHARING COUNCIL.—

(1) ESTABLISHMENT.— There is established an Information Sharing Council that shall assist the President and the program manager in their duties under this section. The Information Sharing Council shall serve until removed from service or replaced by the President (at the sole discretion of the President) with a successor body.

(2) SPECIFIC DUTIES.—In assisting the President and the program manager in their duties under this section, the Information Sharing Council shall—

(A) advise the President and the program manager in developing policies, procedures, guidelines, roles, and standards necessary to establish, implement, and maintain the ISE;

(B) work to ensure coordination among the Federal departments and agencies participating in the ISE in the establishment, implementation, and maintenance of the ISE;

(C) identify and, as appropriate, recommend the consolidation and elimination of current programs, systems, and processes used by Federal departments and agencies to share information, and recommend, as appropriate, the redirection of existing resources to support the ISE;

(D) identify gaps, if any, between existing technologies, programs and systems used by Federal departments and agencies to share information and the parameters of the proposed information sharing environment;

(E) recommend solutions to address any gaps identified under subparagraph (D);

(F) recommend means by which the ISE can be extended to allow interchange of information between Federal departments and agencies and appropriate authorities of State and local governments;

(G) assist the program manager in identifying and resolving information sharing disputes between Federal departments, agencies, and components;

(H) identify appropriate personnel for assignment to the program manager to support staffing needs identified by the program manager; and

(I) recommend whether or not, and by which means, the ISE should be expanded so as to allow future expansion encompassing other relevant categories of information.

(3) CONSULTATION.— In performing its duties, the Information Sharing Council shall consider input from persons and entities outside the Federal Government having significant experience and expertise in policy, technical matters, and operational matters relating to the ISE.

(4) INAPPLICABILITY OF CHAPTER 10 OF TITLE 5, UNITED STATES CODE.— The Information Sharing Council (including any subsidiary group of the Information Sharing Council) shall not be subject to the requirements of chapter 10 of title 5, United States Code.

(5) DETAILEES.— Upon a request by the Director of National Intelligence, the departments and agencies represented on the Information Sharing Council shall detail to the program manager, on a reimbursable basis, appropriate personnel identified under paragraph (2)(H).

(h) AGENCY RESPONSIBILITIES.—The head of each department or agency that possesses or uses intelligence or terrorism information, operates a system in the ISE, or otherwise participates (or expects to participate) in the ISE shall—

(1) ensure full department or agency compliance with information sharing policies, procedures, guidelines, rules, and standards established under subsections (b) and (f);

(2) ensure the provision of adequate resources for systems and activities supporting operation of and participation in the ISE;

(3) ensure full department or agency cooperation in the development of the ISE to implement governmentwide information sharing; and

(4) submit, at the request of the President or the program manager, any reports on the implementation of the requirements of the ISE within such department or agency.

(i) REPORT ON THE INFORMATION SHARING ENVIRONMENT.—

(1) IN GENERAL.—Not later than 180 days after the date of enactment of the

Implementing Recommendations of the 9/11 Commission Act of 2007, the President shall report to the Committee on Homeland Security and Governmental Affairs of the Senate, the Select Committee on Intelligence of the Senate, the Committee on Homeland Security of the House of Representatives, and the Permanent Select Committee on Intelligence of the House of Representatives on the feasibility of—

(A) eliminating the use of any marking or process (including "Originator Control") intended to, or having the effect of, restricting the sharing of information within the scope of the information sharing environment, including homeland security information, terrorism information, and weapons of mass destruction information, between and among participants in the information sharing environment, unless the President has—

(i) specifically exempted categories of information from such elimination; and

(ii) reported that exemption to the committees of Congress described in the matter preceding this subparagraph; and

(B) continuing to use Federal agency standards in effect on such date of enactment for the collection, sharing, and access to information within the scope of the information sharing environment, including homeland security information, terrorism information, and weapons of mass destruction information, relating to citizens and lawful permanent residents;

(C) replacing the standards described in subparagraph (B) with a standard that would allow mission-based or threat-based permission to access or share information within the scope of the information sharing environment, including homeland security information, terrorism information, and weapons of mass destruction information, for a particular purpose that the Federal Government, through an appropriate process established in consultation with the Privacy and Civil Liberties Oversight Board established under section 1061, has determined to be lawfully permissible for a particular agency, component, or employee (commonly known as an "authorized use" standard); and

(D) the use of anonymized data by Federal departments, agencies, or components collecting, possessing, disseminating, or handling information within the scope of the information sharing environment, including homeland security information, terrorism information, and weapons of mass destruction information, in any cases in which—

(i) the use of such information is reasonably expected to produce results materially equivalent to the use of information that is transferred or stored in a non-anonymized form; and

(ii) such use is consistent with any mission of that department, agency, or component (including any mission under a Federal statute or directive of the President) that involves the storage, retention, sharing, or exchange of personally identifiable information.

(2) Definition.— In this subsection, the term "anonymized data" means data in which the individual to whom the data pertains is not identifiable with reasonable efforts, including information that has been encrypted or hidden through the use of other technology.

(j) Additional Positions.—The program manager is authorized to hire not more than 40 full-time employees to assist the program manager in—

(1) activities associated with the implementation of the information sharing environment, including—

(A) implementing the requirements under subsection (b)(2); and

(B) any additional implementation initiatives to enhance and expedite the creation of the information sharing environment; and

(2) identifying and resolving information sharing disputes between Federal departments, agencies, and components under subsection (f)(2)(A)(iv).

(k) Authorization of Appropriations.— There is authorized to be appropriated to carry out this section $30,000,000 for each of fiscal years 2008 and 2009.

SEC. 1017. [50 U.S.C. 3024 note] ALTERNATIVE ANALYSIS OF INTELLIGENCE BY THE INTELLIGENCE COMMUNITY.

(a) In General.— Not later than 180 days after the effective date of this Act, the Director of National Intelligence shall establish a process and assign an individual or entity the responsibility for ensuring that, as appropriate, elements of the intelligence community conduct alternative analysis (commonly referred to as "red-team analysis") of the information and conclusions in intelligence products.

(b) Report.— Not later than 270 days after the effective date of this Act, the Director of National Intelligence shall provide a report to the Select Committee on Intelligence of the Senate and the Permanent Select Committee of the House of Representatives on the implementation of subsection (a).

SEC. 1018. [50 U.S.C. 3023 note] PRESIDENTIAL GUIDELINES ON IMPLEMENTATION AND PRESERVATION OF AUTHORITIES.

The President shall issue guidelines to ensure the effective implementation and execution within the executive branch of the authorities granted to the Director of National Intelligence by this title and the amendments made by this title, in a manner that respects and does not abrogate the statutory responsibilities of the heads of the departments of the United States Government concerning such departments, including, but not limited to:

(1) the authority of the Director of the Office of Management and Budget; and

(2) the authority of the principal officers of the executive departments as heads of their respective departments, including, but not limited to, under—

(A) section 199 of the Revised Statutes (22 U.S.C. 2651);

(B) title II of the Department of Energy Organization Act (42 U.S.C. 7131 et seq.);

(C) the State Department Basic Authorities Act of 1956;

(D) section 102(a) of the Homeland Security Act of 2002 (6 U.S.C. 112(a)); and

(E) sections 301 of title 5, 113(b) and 162(b) of title 10, 503 of title 28, and 301(b) of title 31, United States Code.

SEC. 1019. [50 U.S.C. 3364] ASSIGNMENT OF RESPONSIBILITIES RELATING TO ANALYTIC

INTEGRITY.

(a) Assignment of Responsibilities.— For purposes of carrying out section 102A(h) of the National Security Act of 1947 (as added by section 1011(a)), the Director of National Intelligence shall, not later than 180 days after the date of the enactment of this Act, assign an individual or entity to be responsible for ensuring that finished intelligence products produced by any element or elements of the intelligence community are timely, objective, independent of political considerations, based upon all sources of available intelligence, and employ the standards of proper analytic tradecraft.

(b) Responsibilities.—(1) The individual or entity assigned responsibility under subsection (a)—

(A) may be responsible for general oversight and management of analysis and production, but may not be directly responsible for, or involved in, the specific production of any finished intelligence product;

(B) shall perform, on a regular basis, detailed reviews of finished intelligence product or other analytic products by an element or elements of the intelligence community covering a particular topic or subject matter;

(C) shall be responsible for identifying on an annual basis functional or topical areas of analysis for specific review under subparagraph (B); and

(D) upon completion of any review under subparagraph (B), may draft lessons learned, identify best practices, or make recommendations for improvement to the analytic tradecraft employed in the production of the reviewed product or products.

(2) Each review under paragraph (1)(B) should—

(A) include whether the product or products concerned were based on all sources of available intelligence, properly describe the quality and reliability of underlying sources, properly caveat and express uncertainties or confidence in analytic judgments, properly distinguish between underlying intelligence and the assumptions and judgments of analysts, and incorporate, where appropriate, alternative analyses; and

(B) ensure that the analytic methodologies, tradecraft, and practices used by the element or elements concerned in the production of the product or products concerned meet the standards set forth in subsection (a).

(3) Information drafted under paragraph (1)(D) should, as appropriate, be included in analysis teaching modules and case studies for use throughout the intelligence community.

(c) Annual Briefings.— Not later than February 1 each year, the Director of National Intelligence shall provide to the congressional intelligence committees, the heads of the relevant elements of the intelligence community, and the heads of analytic training departments a briefing with a description, and the associated findings, of each review under subsection (b)(1)(B) during such year.

(d) Congressional Intelligence Committees Defined.—In this section, the term "congressional intelligence committees" means—

(1) the Select Committee on Intelligence of the Senate; and

(2) the Permanent Select Committee on Intelligence of the House of Representatives.

SEC. 1020. [50 U.S.C. 3364 note] SAFEGUARD OF OBJECTIVITY IN INTELLIGENCE ANALYSIS.

(a) In General.— Not later than 180 days after the effective date of this Act, the Director of National Intelligence shall identify an individual within the Office of the Director of National Intelligence who shall be available to analysts within the Office of the Director of National Intelligence to counsel, conduct arbitration, offer recommendations, and, as appropriate, initiate inquiries into real or perceived problems of analytic tradecraft or politicization, biased reporting, or lack of objectivity in intelligence analysis.

(b) Report.— Not later than 270 days after the effective date of this Act, the Director of National Intelligence shall provide a report to the Select Committee on Intelligence of the Senate and the Permanent Select Committee on Intelligence of the House of Representatives on the implementation of subsection (a).

* * * * * * *

Subtitle D—Improvement of Education for the Intelligence Community

SEC. 1041. [50 U.S.C. 3322] ADDITIONAL EDUCATION AND TRAINING REQUIREMENTS.

(a) Findings.—Congress makes the following findings:

(1) Foreign language education is essential for the development of a highly-skilled workforce for the intelligence community.

(2) Since September 11, 2001, the need for language proficiency levels to meet required national security functions has been raised, and the ability to comprehend and articulate technical and scientific information in foreign languages has become critical.

(b) Linguistic Requirements.—(1) The Director of National Intelligence shall—

(A) identify the linguistic requirements for the Office of the Director of National Intelligence;

(B) identify specific requirements for the range of linguistic skills necessary for the intelligence community, including proficiency in scientific and technical vocabularies of critical foreign languages; and

(C) develop a comprehensive plan for the Office to meet such requirements through the education, recruitment, and training of linguists.

(2) In carrying out activities under paragraph (1), the Director shall take into account education grant programs of the Department of Defense and the Department of Education that are in

(c) Professional Intelligence Training.—The Director of National Intelligence shall require the head of each element and component within the Office of the Director of National Intelligence who has responsibility for professional intelligence training to periodically review and revise the curriculum for the professional intelligence training of the senior and intermediate level personnel of such element or component in order to—

(1) strengthen the focus of such curriculum on the integration of intelligence

collection and analysis throughout the Office; and

(2) prepare such personnel for duty with other departments, agencies, and elements of the intelligence community.

* * * * * * *

Subtitle E—Additional Improvements of Intelligence Activities

SEC. 1051. SERVICE AND NATIONAL LABORATORIES AND THE INTELLIGENCE COMMUNITY.

The Director of National Intelligence, in cooperation with the Secretary of Defense and the Secretary of Energy, should seek to ensure that each service laboratory of the Department of Defense and each national laboratory of the Department of Energy may, acting through the relevant Secretary and in a manner consistent with the missions and commitments of the laboratory—

(1) assist the Director of National Intelligence in all aspects of technical intelligence, including research, applied sciences, analysis, technology evaluation and assessment, and any other aspect that the relevant Secretary considers appropriate; and

(2) make available to the intelligence community, on a community-wide basis—

(A) the analysis and production services of the service and national laboratories, in a manner that maximizes the capacity and services of such laboratories; and

(B) the facilities and human resources of the service and national laboratories, in a manner that improves the technological capabilities of the intelligence community.

SEC. 1052. OPEN-SOURCE INTELLIGENCE.

(a) Sense of Congress.—It is the sense of Congress that—

(1) the Director of National Intelligence should establish an intelligence center for the purpose of coordinating the collection, analysis, production, and dissemination of open-source intelligence to elements of the intelligence community;

(2) open-source intelligence is a valuable source that must be integrated into the intelligence cycle to ensure that United States policymakers are fully and completely informed; and

(3) the intelligence center should ensure that each element of the intelligence community uses open-source intelligence consistent with the mission of such element.

(b) [50 U.S.C. 3367] Requirement for Efficient Use by Intelligence Community of Open-source Intelligence.— The Director of National Intelligence shall ensure that the intelligence community makes efficient and effective use of open-source information and analysis.

(c) Report.— Not later than June 30, 2005, the Director of National Intelligence shall submit to the congressional intelligence committees a report containing the decision of the Director as to whether an open-source intelligence center will be established. If the Director decides not to establish an open-source intelligence center, such report shall also contain a description of how the intelligence community will use open-source intelligence and effectively integrate open-source intelligence into the national intelligence cycle.

(d) CONGRESSIONAL INTELLIGENCE COMMITTEES DEFINED.—In this section, the term "congressional intelligence committees" means—

(1) the Select Committee on Intelligence of the Senate; and

(2) the Permanent Select Committee on Intelligence of the House of Representatives.

SEC. 1053. [50 U.S.C. 3321] NATIONAL INTELLIGENCE RESERVE CORPS.

(a) ESTABLISHMENT.— The Director of National Intelligence may provide for the establishment and training of a National Intelligence Reserve Corps (in this section referred to as "National Intelligence Reserve Corps") for the temporary reemployment on a voluntary basis of former employees of elements of the intelligence community during periods of emergency, as determined by the Director.

(b) ELIGIBLE INDIVIDUALS.— An individual may participate in the National Intelligence Reserve Corps only if the individual previously served as a full time employee of an element of the intelligence community.

(c) TERMS OF PARTICIPATION.— The Director of National Intelligence shall prescribe the terms and conditions under which eligible individuals may participate in the National Intelligence Reserve Corps.

(d) EXPENSES.— The Director of National Intelligence may provide members of the National Intelligence Reserve Corps transportation and per diem in lieu of subsistence for purposes of participating in any training that relates to service as a member of the Reserve Corps.

(e) TREATMENT OF ANNUITANTS.—(1) If an annuitant receiving an annuity from the Civil Service Retirement and Disability Fund becomes temporarily reemployed pursuant to this section, such annuity shall not be discontinued thereby.

(2) An annuitant so reemployed shall not be considered an employee for the purposes of chapter 83 or 84 of title 5, United States Code.

(f) TREATMENT UNDER OFFICE OF DIRECTOR OF NATIONAL INTELLIGENCE PERSONNEL CEILING.— A member of the National Intelligence Reserve Corps who is reemployed on a temporary basis pursuant to this section shall not count against any personnel ceiling applicable to the Office of the Director of National Intelligence.

Subtitle F—PRIVACY AND CIVIL LIBERTIES

SEC. 1061. [42 U.S.C. 2000ee] PRIVACY AND CIVIL LIBERTIES OVERSIGHT BOARD.

(a) IN GENERAL.— There is established as an independent agency within the executive branch a Privacy and Civil Liberties Oversight Board (referred to in this section as the "Board").

(b) FINDINGS.—Consistent with the report of the National Commission on Terrorist Attacks Upon the United States, Congress makes the following findings:

(1) In conducting the war on terrorism, the Government may need additional powers and may need to enhance the use of its existing powers.

(2) This shift of power and authority to the Government calls for an enhanced system of checks and balances to protect the precious liberties that are vital to our way of life and to ensure that the Government uses its powers for the purposes for which the powers were given.

(3) The National Commission on Terrorist Attacks Upon the United States correctly concluded that "The choice between security and liberty is a false choice, as nothing is more likely to endanger America's liberties than the success of a terrorist attack at home. Our history has shown us that insecurity threatens liberty. Yet, if our liberties are curtailed, we lose the values that we are struggling to defend.".

(c) PURPOSE.—The Board shall—

(1) analyze and review actions the executive branch takes to protect the Nation from terrorism, ensuring that the need for such actions is balanced with the need to protect privacy and civil liberties; and

(2) ensure that liberty concerns are appropriately considered in the development and implementation of laws, regulations, and policies related to efforts to protect the Nation against terrorism.

(d) FUNCTIONS.—

(1) ADVICE AND COUNSEL ON POLICY DEVELOPMENT AND IMPLEMENTATION.—The Board shall—

(A) review proposed legislation, regulations, and policies related to efforts to protect the Nation from terrorism, including the development and adoption of information sharing guidelines under subsections (d) and (f) of section 1016;

(B) review the implementation of new and existing legislation, regulations, and policies related to efforts to protect the Nation from terrorism, including the implementation of information sharing guidelines under subsections (d) and (f) of section 1016;

(C) advise the President and the departments, agencies, and elements of the executive branch to ensure that privacy and civil liberties are appropriately considered in the development and implementation of such legislation, regulations, policies, and guidelines; and

(D) in providing advice on proposals to retain or enhance a particular governmental power, consider whether the department, agency, or element of the executive branch has established—

(i) that the need for the power is balanced with the need to protect privacy and civil liberties;

(ii) that there is adequate supervision of the use by the executive branch of the power to ensure protection of privacy and civil liberties; and

(iii) that there are adequate guidelines and oversight to properly confine its use.

(2) OVERSIGHT.—The Board shall continually review—

(A) the regulations, policies, and procedures, and the implementation of the regulations, policies, and procedures, of the departments, agencies, and elements of the executive branch relating to efforts to protect the Nation from terrorism to ensure that privacy and civil liberties are protected;

(B) the information sharing practices of the departments, agencies, and elements of the executive branch relating to efforts to protect the Nation from terrorism to determine whether they appropriately protect privacy and civil liberties and adhere to the information sharing guidelines issued or developed under subsections (d) and (f) of section 1016 and to other governing laws, regulations, and policies regarding privacy and civil liberties; and

(C) other actions by the executive branch relating to efforts to protect the Nation from terrorism to determine whether such actions—

(i) appropriately protect privacy and civil liberties; and

(ii) are consistent with governing laws, regulations, and policies regarding privacy and civil liberties.

(3) RELATIONSHIP WITH PRIVACY AND CIVIL LIBERTIES OFFICERS.—The Board shall—

(A) receive and review reports and other information from privacy officers and civil liberties officers under section 1062;

(B) when appropriate, make recommendations to such privacy officers and civil liberties officers regarding their activities; and

(C) when appropriate, coordinate the activities of such privacy officers and civil liberties officers on relevant interagency matters.

(4) TESTIMONY.— The members of the Board shall appear and testify before Congress upon request.

(e) REPORTS.—

(1) IN GENERAL.—The Board shall—

(A) receive and review reports from privacy officers and civil liberties officers under section 1062; and

(B) periodically submit, not less than semiannually, reports—

(i)(I) to the appropriate committees of Congress, including the Committee on the Judiciary of the Senate, the Committee on the Judiciary of the House of Representatives, the Committee on Homeland Security and Governmental Affairs of the Senate, the Committee on Homeland Security of the House of Representatives, the Committee on Oversight and Government Reform of the House of Representatives, the Select Committee on Intelligence of the Senate, and the Permanent Select Committee on Intelligence of the House of Representatives; and

(II) to the President; and

(ii) which shall be in unclassified form to the greatest extent possible, with a classified annex where necessary.

(2) CONTENTS.—Not less than 2 reports submitted each year under paragraph (1)(B) shall include—

(A) a description of the major activities of the Board during the preceding period;

(B) information on the findings, conclusions, and recommendations of the Board resulting from its advice and oversight functions under subsection (d);

(C) the minority views on any findings, conclusions, and recommendations of the Board resulting from its advice and oversight functions under subsection (d);

(D) each proposal reviewed by the Board under subsection (d)(1) that—

(i) the Board advised against implementation; and

(ii) notwithstanding such advice, actions were taken to implement; and

(E) for the preceding period, any requests submitted under subsection (g)(1)(D) for the issuance of subpoenas that were modified or denied by the Attorney General.

(f) Informing the Public.—The Board—

(1) shall make its reports, including its reports to Congress, available to the public to the greatest extent that is consistent with the protection of classified information and applicable law; and

(2) shall hold public hearings and otherwise inform the public of its activities, as appropriate and in a manner consistent with the protection of classified information and applicable law, but may, notwithstanding section 552b of title 5, United States Code, meet or otherwise communicate in any number to confer or deliberate in a manner that is closed to the public.

(g) Access to Information.—

(1) Authorization.—If determined by the Board to be necessary to carry out its responsibilities under this section, the Board is authorized to—

(A) have access from any department, agency, or element of the executive branch, or any Federal officer or employee of any such department, agency, or element, to all relevant records, reports, audits, reviews, documents, papers, recommendations, or other relevant material, including classified information consistent with applicable law;

(B) interview, take statements from, or take public testimony from personnel of any department, agency, or element of the executive branch, or any Federal officer or employee of any such department, agency, or element;

(C) request information or assistance from any State, tribal, or local government; and

(D) at the direction of a majority of the members of the Board, submit a written request to the Attorney General of the United States that the Attorney General require, by subpoena, persons (other than departments, agencies, and elements of the executive branch) to produce any relevant information, documents, reports, answers, records, accounts, papers, and other documentary or testimonial evidence.

(2) Review of subpoena request.—

(A) In general.—Not later than 30 days after the date of receipt of a request by the Board under paragraph (1)(D), the Attorney General shall—

(i) issue the subpoena as requested; or

(ii) provide the Board, in writing, with an explanation of the grounds on which the subpoena request has been modified or denied.

(B) NOTIFICATION.— If a subpoena request is modified or denied under subparagraph (A)(ii), the Attorney General shall, not later than 30 days after the date of that modification or denial, notify the Committee on the Judiciary of the Senate and the Committee on the Judiciary of the House of Representatives.

(3) ENFORCEMENT OF SUBPOENA.— In the case of contumacy or failure to obey a subpoena issued pursuant to paragraph (1)(D), the United States district court for the judicial district in which the subpoenaed person resides, is served, or may be found may issue an order requiring such person to produce the evidence required by such subpoena.

(4) AGENCY COOPERATION.— Whenever information or assistance requested under subparagraph (A) or (B) of paragraph (1) is, in the judgment of the Board, unreasonably refused or not provided, the Board shall report the circumstances to the head of the department, agency, or element concerned without delay. The head of the department, agency, or element concerned shall ensure that the Board is given access to the information, assistance, material, or personnel the Board determines to be necessary to carry out its functions.

(5) ACCESS.— Nothing in this section shall be construed to authorize the Board, or any agent thereof, to gain access to information regarding an activity covered by section 503(a) of the National Security Act of 1947 (50 U.S.C. 3093(a)).

(h) MEMBERSHIP.—

(1) MEMBERS.— The Board shall be composed of a full-time chairman and 4 additional members, who shall be appointed by the President, by and with the advice and consent of the Senate.

(2) QUALIFICATIONS.— Members of the Board shall be selected solely on the basis of their professional qualifications, achievements, public stature, expertise in civil liberties and privacy, and relevant experience, and without regard to political affiliation, but in no event shall more than 3 members of the Board be members of the same political party. The President shall, before appointing an individual who is not a member of the same political party as the President, consult with the leadership of that party, if any, in the Senate and House of Representatives.

(3) INCOMPATIBLE OFFICE.— An individual appointed to the Board may not, while serving on the Board, be an elected official, officer, or employee of the Federal Government, other than in the capacity as a member of the Board.

(4) TERM.—

(A) COMMENCEMENT.— Each member of the Board shall serve a term of 6 years, commencing on the date of the appointment of the member to the Board.

(B) REAPPOINTMENT.— A member may be reappointed to one or more additional terms.

(C) VACANCY.— A vacancy on the Board shall be filled in the manner in which the original appointment was made.

(D) EXTENSION.—Upon the expiration of the term of office of a member, the member may continue to serve for up to one year after the date of expiration, at the election of the member—

(i) during the period preceding the reappointment of the member pursuant to subparagraph (B); or

(ii) until the member's successor has been appointed and qualified.

(5) QUORUM AND MEETINGS.— The Board shall meet upon the call of the chairman or a majority of its members. Three members of the Board shall constitute a quorum.

(i) COMPENSATION AND TRAVEL EXPENSES.—

(1) COMPENSATION.—

(A) CHAIRMAN.— The chairman of the Board shall be compensated at the rate of pay payable for a position at level III of the Executive Schedule under section 5314 of title 5, United States Code.

(B) MEMBERS.— Each member of the Board shall be compensated at a rate of pay payable for a position at level IV of the Executive Schedule under section 5315 of title 5, United States Code, for each day during which that member is engaged in the actual performance of the duties of the Board.

(2) TRAVEL EXPENSES.— Members of the Board shall be allowed travel expenses, including per diem in lieu of subsistence, at rates authorized for persons employed intermittently by the Government under section 5703(b) of title 5, United States Code, while away from their homes or regular places of business in the performance of services for the Board.

(j) STAFF.—

(1) APPOINTMENT AND COMPENSATION.— The chairman of the Board, in accordance with rules agreed upon by the Board, shall appoint and fix the compensation of a full-time executive director and such other personnel as may be necessary to enable the Board to carry out its functions, without regard to the provisions of title 5, United States Code, governing appointments in the competitive service, and without regard to the provisions of chapter 51 and subchapter III of chapter 53 of such title relating to classification and General Schedule pay rates, except that no rate of pay fixed under this subsection may exceed the equivalent of that payable for a position at level V of the Executive Schedule under section 5316 of title 5, United States Code.

(2) APPOINTMENT IN ABSENCE OF CHAIRMAN.— If the position of chairman of the Board is vacant, during the period of the vacancy, the Board, at the direction of the unanimous vote of the serving members of the Board, may exercise the authority of the chairman under paragraph (1).

(3) DETAILEES.— Any Federal employee may be detailed to the Board without reimbursement from the Board, and such detailee shall retain the rights, status, and privileges of the detailee's regular employment without interruption.

(4) CONSULTANT SERVICES.— The Board may procure the temporary or intermittent services of experts and consultants in accordance with section 3109 of title 5, United States Code, at rates that do not exceed the daily rate paid a person occupying a position at level IV of the Executive Schedule under section 5315 of such title.

(k) SECURITY CLEARANCES.—

(1) IN GENERAL.— The appropriate departments, agencies, and elements of the executive branch shall cooperate with the Board to expeditiously provide the Board members and staff with appropriate security clearances to the extent possible under existing procedures and requirements.

(2) RULES AND PROCEDURES.— After consultation with the Secretary of Defense, the Attorney General, and the Director of National Intelligence, the Board shall adopt rules and procedures of the Board for physical, communications, computer, document, personnel, and other security relating to carrying out the functions of the Board.

(l) TREATMENT AS AGENCY, NOT AS ADVISORY COMMITTEE.—The Board—

(1) is an agency (as defined in section 551(1) of title 5, United States Code); and

(2) is not an advisory committee (as defined in section 1001(2) of title 5, United States Code).

(m) AUTHORIZATION OF APPROPRIATIONS.—There are authorized to be appropriated to carry out this section amounts as follows:

(1) For fiscal year 2008, $5,000,000.

(2) For fiscal year 2009, $6,650,000.

(3) For fiscal year 2010, $8,300,000.

(4) For fiscal year 2011, $10,000,000.

(5) For fiscal year 2012 and each subsequent fiscal year, such sums as may be necessary.

SEC. 1062. [42 U.S.C. 2000ee–1] PRIVACY AND CIVIL LIBERTIES OFFICERS.

(a) DESIGNATION AND FUNCTIONS.—The Attorney General, the Secretary of Defense, the Secretary of State, the Secretary of the Treasury, the Secretary of Health and Human Services, the Secretary of Homeland Security, the Director of National Intelligence, the Director of the Central Intelligence Agency, the Director of the National Security Agency, the Director of the Federal Bureau of Investigation, and the head of any other department, agency, or element of the executive branch designated by the Privacy and Civil Liberties Oversight Board under section 1061 to be appropriate for coverage under this section shall designate not less than 1 senior officer to serve as the principal advisor to—

(1) assist the head of such department, agency, or element and other officials of such department, agency, or element in appropriately considering privacy and civil liberties concerns when such officials are proposing, developing, or implementing laws, regulations, policies, procedures, or guidelines related to efforts to protect the Nation against terrorism;

(2) periodically investigate and review department, agency, or element actions, policies, procedures, guidelines, and related laws and their implementation to ensure that such department, agency, or element is adequately considering privacy and civil liberties in its actions;

(3) ensure that such department, agency, or element has adequate procedures to receive, investigate, respond to, and redress complaints from individuals who allege such department, agency, or element has violated their privacy or civil liberties;

and

(4) in providing advice on proposals to retain or enhance a particular governmental power the officer shall consider whether such department, agency, or element has established—

(A) that the need for the power is balanced with the need to protect privacy and civil liberties;

(B) that there is adequate supervision of the use by such department, agency, or element of the power to ensure protection of privacy and civil liberties; and

(C) that there are adequate guidelines and oversight to properly confine its use.

(b) Exception to Designation Authority.—

(1) Privacy officers.— In any department, agency, or element referred to in subsection (a) or designated by the Privacy and Civil Liberties Oversight Board, which has a statutorily created privacy officer, such officer shall perform the functions specified in subsection (a) with respect to privacy.

(2) Civil liberties officers.— In any department, agency, or element referred to in subsection (a) or designated by the Board, which has a statutorily created civil liberties officer, such officer shall perform the functions specified in subsection (a) with respect to civil liberties.

(c) Supervision and Coordination.—Each privacy officer or civil liberties officer described in subsection (a) or (b) shall—

(1) report directly to the head of the department, agency, or element concerned; and

(2) coordinate their activities with the Inspector General of such department, agency, or element to avoid duplication of effort.

(d) Agency Cooperation.—The head of each department, agency, or element shall ensure that each privacy officer and civil liberties officer—

(1) has the information, material, and resources necessary to fulfill the functions of such officer;

(2) is advised of proposed policy changes;

(3) is consulted by decision makers; and

(4) is given access to material and personnel the officer determines to be necessary to carry out the functions of such officer.

(e) Reprisal for Making Complaint.— No action constituting a reprisal, or threat of reprisal, for making a complaint or for disclosing information to a privacy officer or civil liberties officer described in subsection (a) or (b), or to the Privacy and Civil Liberties Oversight Board, that indicates a possible violation of privacy protections or civil liberties in the administration of the programs and operations of the Federal Government relating to efforts to protect the Nation from terrorism shall be taken by any Federal employee in a position to take such action, unless the complaint was made or the information was disclosed with the knowledge that it was false or with willful disregard for its truth or falsity.

(f) Periodic Reports.—

(1) In general.—The privacy officers and civil liberties officers of each

department, agency, or element referred to or described in subsection (a) or (b) shall periodically, but not less than annually, submit a report on the activities of such officers—

(A)(i) to the appropriate committees of Congress, including the Committee on the Judiciary of the Senate, the Committee on the Judiciary of the House of Representatives, the Committee on Homeland Security and Governmental Affairs of the Senate, the Committee on Oversight and Government Reform of the House of Representatives, the Select Committee on Intelligence of the Senate, and the Permanent Select Committee on Intelligence of the House of Representatives;

(ii) to the head of such department, agency, or element; and

(iii) to the Privacy and Civil Liberties Oversight Board; and

(B) which shall be in unclassified form to the greatest extent possible, with a classified annex where necessary.

(2) CONTENTS.—Each report submitted under paragraph (1) shall include information on the discharge of each of the functions of the officer concerned, including—

(A) information on the number and types of reviews undertaken;

(B) the type of advice provided and the response given to such advice;

(C) the number and nature of the complaints received by the department, agency, or element concerned for alleged violations; and

(D) a summary of the disposition of such complaints, the reviews and inquiries conducted, and the impact of the activities of such officer.

(g) INFORMING THE PUBLIC.—Each privacy officer and civil liberties officer shall—

(1) make the reports of such officer, including reports to Congress, available to the public to the greatest extent that is consistent with the protection of classified information and applicable law; and

(2) otherwise inform the public of the activities of such officer, as appropriate and in a manner consistent with the protection of classified information and applicable law.

(h) SAVINGS CLAUSE.— Nothing in this section shall be construed to limit or otherwise supplant any other authorities or responsibilities provided by law to privacy officers or civil liberties officers.

Subtitle G—CONFORMING AND OTHER AMENDMENTS

* * * * * * *

SEC. 1081. [50 U.S.C. 3001 note] GENERAL REFERENCES.

(a) DIRECTOR OF CENTRAL INTELLIGENCE AS HEAD OF INTELLIGENCE COMMUNITY.— Any reference to the Director of Central Intelligence or the Director of the Central Intelligence Agency in the Director's capacity as the head of the intelligence community in any law, regulation, document, paper, or other record of the United States shall be deemed to be a reference to the Director of National Intelligence.

(b) DIRECTOR OF CENTRAL INTELLIGENCE AS HEAD OF CIA.— Any reference to the Director of Central Intelligence or the Director of the Central Intelligence Agency in the Director's capacity as the head of the Central Intelligence Agency in any law, regulation, document, paper, or other record of the United States shall be deemed to be a reference to the Director of the Central Intelligence Agency.

(c) COMMUNITY MANAGEMENT STAFF.— Any reference to the Community Management Staff in any law, regulation, document, paper, or other record of the United States shall be deemed to be a reference to the staff of the Office of the Director of National Intelligence.

Subtitle H—TRANSFER, TERMINATION, TRANSITION, AND OTHER PROVISIONS

SEC. 1091. [50 U.S.C. 3001 note] TRANSFER OF COMMUNITY MANAGEMENT STAFF.

(a) TRANSFER.— There shall be transferred to the Office of the Director of National Intelligence such staff of the Community Management Staff as of the date of the enactment of this Act as the Director of National Intelligence determines to be appropriate, including all functions and activities discharged by the Community Management Staff as of that date.

(b) ADMINISTRATION.— The Director of National Intelligence shall administer the Community Management Staff after the date of the enactment of this Act as a component of the Office of the Director of National Intelligence under section 103 of the National Security Act of 1947, as amended by section 1011(a) of this Act.

SEC. 1092. [50 U.S.C. 3001 note] TRANSFER OF TERRORIST THREAT INTEGRATION CENTER.

(a) TRANSFER.— There shall be transferred to the National Counterterrorism Center the Terrorist Threat Integration Center (TTIC) or its successor entity, including all functions and activities discharged by the Terrorist Threat Integration Center or its successor entity as of the date of the enactment of this Act.

(b) ADMINISTRATION.— The Director of the National Counterterrorism Center shall administer the Terrorist Threat Integration Center after the date of the enactment of this Act as a component of the Directorate of Intelligence of the National Counterterrorism Center under section 119(i) of the National Security Act of 1947, as added by section 1021(a) of this Act.

SEC. 1093. [50 U.S.C. 3001 note] TERMINATION OF POSITIONS OF ASSISTANT DIRECTORS OF CENTRAL INTELLIGENCE.

(a) TERMINATION.— The positions referred to in subsection (b) are hereby abolished.

(b) COVERED POSITIONS.—The positions referred to in this subsection are as follows:

(1) The Assistant Director of Central Intelligence for Collection.

(2) The Assistant Director of Central Intelligence for Analysis and Production.

(3) The Assistant Director of Central Intelligence for Administration.

SEC. 1094. [50 U.S.C. 3001 note] IMPLEMENTATION PLAN.

The President shall transmit to Congress a plan for the implementation of this title and the amendments made by this title. The plan shall address, at a minimum, the following:

(1) The transfer of personnel, assets, and obligations to the Director of National Intelligence pursuant to this title.

(2) Any consolidation, reorganization, or streamlining of activities transferred to the Director of National Intelligence pursuant to this title.

(3) The establishment of offices within the Office of the Director of National Intelligence to implement the duties and responsibilities of the Director of National Intelligence as described in this title.

(4) Specification of any proposed disposition of property, facilities, contracts, records, and other assets and obligations to be transferred to the Director of National Intelligence.

(5) Recommendations for additional legislative or administrative action as the President considers appropriate.

SEC. 1095. [50 U.S.C. 3001 note] DIRECTOR OF NATIONAL INTELLIGENCE REPORT ON IMPLEMENTATION OF INTELLIGENCE COMMUNITY REFORM.

(a) REPORT.— Not later than one year after the effective date of this Act, the Director of National Intelligence shall submit to the congressional intelligence committees a report on the progress made in the implementation of this title, including the amendments made by this title. The report shall include a comprehensive description of the progress made, and may include such recommendations for additional legislative or administrative action as the Director considers appropriate.

(b) CONGRESSIONAL INTELLIGENCE COMMITTEES DEFINED.—In this section, the term "congressional intelligence committees" means—

(1) the Select Committee on Intelligence of the Senate; and

(2) the Permanent Select Committee on Intelligence of the House of Representatives.

SEC. 1096. [50 U.S.C. 3001 note] TRANSITIONAL AUTHORITIES.

(a) IN GENERAL.—(1) Upon the request of the Director of National Intelligence, the head of any executive agency may, on a reimbursable basis, provide services or detail personnel to the Director of National Intelligence. Any records of the Office of the Director of National Intelligence that are maintained by the agency as a service for the Office of the Director of National Intelligence under section 1535 of title 31, United States Code, (popularly known as the "Economy Act") may be treated as the records of the agency when dispositioned as required by law, and any disclosure of such records between the two agencies shall not be subject to any otherwise applicable legal consent requirements or disclosure accounting requirements.

(2) The records of the Office of the Director of National Intelligence may not be dispositioned pursuant to paragraph (1) without the authorization of the Director of National Intelligence.

(b) TRANSFER OF PERSONNEL.—In addition to any other authorities available under law for such purposes, in the fiscal years 2005 and 2006, the Director of National Intelligence—

(1) is authorized within the Office of the Director of National Intelligence the total of 500 new personnel positions; and

(2) with the approval of the Director of the Office of Management and Budget, may detail not more than 150 personnel funded within the National Intelligence Program to the Office of the Director of National Intelligence for a period of not more than 2 years.

SEC. 1097. [50 U.S.C. 3001 note] EFFECTIVE DATES.

(a) In General.— Except as otherwise expressly provided in this Act, this title and the amendments made by this title shall take effect not later than six months after the date of the enactment of this Act.

(b) Specific Effective Dates.—(1)(A) Not later than 60 days after the date of the appointment of the first Director of National Intelligence, the Director of National Intelligence shall first appoint individuals to positions within the Office of the Director of National Intelligence.

(B) Subparagraph (A) shall not apply with respect to the Principal Deputy Director of National Intelligence.

(2) Not later than 180 days after the effective date of this Act, the President shall transmit to Congress the implementation plan required by section 1094.

(3) Not later than one year after the date of the enactment of this Act, the Director of National Intelligence shall prescribe regulations, policies, procedures, standards, and guidelines required under section 102A of the National Security Act of 1947, as amended by section 1011(a) of this Act.

Subtitle I—Other Matters

SEC. 1101. STUDY OF PROMOTION AND PROFESSIONAL MILITARY EDUCATION SCHOOL SELECTION RATES FOR MILITARY INTELLIGENCE OFFICERS.

(a) Study.— The Secretary of Defense shall conduct a study of the promotion selection rates, and the selection rates for attendance at professional military education schools, of intelligence officers of the Armed Forces, particularly in comparison to the rates for other officers of the same Armed Force who are in the same grade and competitive category.

(b) Report.— The Secretary shall submit to the Committees on Armed Services of the Senate and House of Representatives a report providing the Secretary's findings resulting from the study under subsection (a) and the Secretary's recommendations (if any) for such changes in law as the Secretary considers needed to ensure that intelligence officers, as a group, are selected for promotion, and for attendance at professional military education schools, at rates not less than the rates for all line (or the equivalent) officers of the same Armed Force (both in the zone and below the zone) in the same grade. The report shall be submitted not later than April 1, 2005.

* * * * * * *

SEC. 1103. [50 U.S.C. 3001 note] SEVERABILITY.

If any provision of this Act, or an amendment made by this Act, or the application of such provision to any person or circumstance is held invalid, the remainder of this Act, or the application of such provision to persons or circumstances other those to which such provision is held invalid shall not be affected thereby.

TITLE II—FEDERAL BUREAU OF INVESTIGATION

SEC. 2001. [28 U.S.C. 532 note] IMPROVEMENT OF INTELLIGENCE CAPABILITIES OF THE FEDERAL BUREAU OF INVESTIGATION.

(a) FINDINGS.—Congress makes the following findings:

(1) The National Commission on Terrorist Attacks Upon the United States in its final report stated that, under Director Robert Mueller, the Federal Bureau of Investigation has made significant progress in improving its intelligence capabilities.

(2) In the report, the members of the Commission also urged that the Federal Bureau of Investigation fully institutionalize the shift of the Bureau to a preventive counterterrorism posture.

(b) IMPROVEMENT OF INTELLIGENCE CAPABILITIES.— The Director of the Federal Bureau of Investigation shall continue efforts to improve the intelligence capabilities of the Federal Bureau of Investigation and to develop and maintain within the Bureau a national intelligence workforce.

(c) NATIONAL INTELLIGENCE WORKFORCE.—(1) In developing and maintaining a national intelligence workforce under subsection (b), the Director of the Federal Bureau of Investigation shall develop and maintain a specialized and integrated national intelligence workforce consisting of agents, analysts, linguists, and surveillance specialists who are recruited, trained, and rewarded in a manner which ensures the existence within the Federal Bureau of Investigation of an institutional culture with substantial expertise in, and commitment to, the intelligence mission of the Bureau.

(2) Each agent employed by the Bureau after the date of the enactment of this Act shall receive basic training in both criminal justice matters and national intelligence matters.

(3) Each agent employed by the Bureau after the date of the enactment of this Act shall, to the maximum extent practicable, be given the opportunity to undergo, during such agent's early service with the Bureau, meaningful assignments in criminal justice matters and in national intelligence matters.

(4) The Director shall—

(A) establish career positions in national intelligence matters for agents, analysts, and related personnel of the Bureau; and

(B) in furtherance of the requirement under subparagraph (A) and to the maximum extent practicable, afford agents, analysts, and related personnel of the Bureau the opportunity to work in the career specialty selected by such agents, analysts, and related personnel over their entire career with the Bureau.

(5) The Director shall carry out a program to enhance the capacity of the Bureau to recruit and retain individuals with backgrounds in intelligence, international relations, language, technology, and other skills relevant to the intelligence mission

of the Bureau.

(6) The Director shall, to the maximum extent practicable, afford the analysts of the Bureau training and career opportunities commensurate with the training and career opportunities afforded analysts in other elements of the intelligence community.

(7) Commencing as soon as practicable after the date of the enactment of this Act, each direct supervisor of a Field Intelligence Group, and each Bureau Operational Manager at the Section Chief and Assistant Special Agent in Charge (ASAC) level and above, shall be a certified intelligence officer.

(8) The Director shall, to the maximum extent practicable, ensure that the successful discharge of advanced training courses, and of one or more assignments to another element of the intelligence community, is a precondition to advancement to higher level intelligence assignments within the Bureau.

(d) Field Office Matters.—(1) In improving the intelligence capabilities of the Federal Bureau of Investigation under subsection (b), the Director of the Federal Bureau of Investigation shall ensure that each Field Intelligence Group reports directly to a field office senior manager responsible for intelligence matters.

(2) The Director shall provide for such expansion of the secure facilities in the field offices of the Bureau as is necessary to ensure the discharge by the field offices of the intelligence mission of the Bureau.

(3) The Director shall require that each Field Intelligence Group manager ensures the integration of analysts, agents, linguists, and surveillance personnel in the field.

(e) Discharge of Improvements.—(1) The Director of the Federal Bureau of Investigation shall carry out subsections (b) through (d) through the head of the Directorate of Intelligence of the Federal Bureau of Investigation.

(2) The Director of the Federal Bureau of Investigation shall carry out subsections (b) through (d) under the joint guidance of the Attorney General and the Director of National Intelligence in a manner consistent with applicable law.

(f) Budget Matters.—The Director of the Federal Bureau of Investigation shall establish a budget structure of the Federal Bureau of Investigation to reflect the four principal missions of the Bureau as follows:

(1) Intelligence.

(2) Counterterrorism and counterintelligence.

(3) Criminal Enterprises/Federal Crimes.

(4) Criminal justice services.

(g) Reports.—(1) Not later than 180 days after the date of the enactment of this Act, the Director of the Federal Bureau of Investigation shall submit to Congress a report on the progress made as of the date of such report in carrying out the requirements of this section.

(2) The Director shall include in each annual program review of the Federal Bureau of Investigation that is submitted to Congress a report on the progress made by each field office of the Bureau during the period covered by such review in addressing Bureau and national program priorities.

(3) Not later than 180 days after the date of the enactment of this Act, and every 12 months thereafter, the Director shall submit to Congress a report on the progress of the Bureau in implementing information-sharing principles.

SEC. 2002. [28 U.S.C. 532 note] DIRECTORATE OF INTELLIGENCE OF THE FEDERAL BUREAU OF INVESTIGATION.

(a) DIRECTORATE OF INTELLIGENCE OF FEDERAL BUREAU OF INVESTIGATION.— The element of the Federal Bureau of Investigation known as of the date of the enactment of this Act as the Office of Intelligence is hereby redesignated as the Directorate of Intelligence of the Federal Bureau of Investigation.

(b) HEAD OF DIRECTORATE.— The head of the Directorate of Intelligence shall be the Executive Assistant Director for Intelligence of the Federal Bureau of Investigation.

(c) RESPONSIBILITIES.—The Directorate of Intelligence shall be responsible for the following:

(1) Supervision of all national intelligence programs, projects, and activities of the Bureau.

(2) The discharge by the Bureau of the requirements in section 105B of the National Security Act of 1947 (50 U.S.C. 403–5b).

(3) The oversight of Bureau field intelligence operations.

(4) Coordinating human source development and management by the Bureau.

(5) Coordinating collection by the Bureau against nationally-determined intelligence requirements.

(6) Strategic analysis.

(7) Intelligence program and budget management.

(8) The intelligence workforce.

(9) Any other responsibilities specified by the Director of the Federal Bureau of Investigation or specified by law.

(d) STAFF.— The Directorate of Intelligence shall consist of such staff as the Director of the Federal Bureau of Investigation considers appropriate for the activities of the Directorate.

SEC. 2003. [28 U.S.C. 532 note] FEDERAL BUREAU OF INVESTIGATION INTELLIGENCE CAREER SERVICE.

(a) ESTABLISHMENT OF FEDERAL BUREAU OF INVESTIGATION INTELLIGENCE CAREER SERVICE.—The Director of the Federal Bureau of Investigation may—

(1) in consultation with the Director of the Office of Personnel Management—

(A) establish positions for intelligence analysts, and prescribe standards and procedures for establishing and classifying such positions, without regard to chapter 51 of title 5, United States Code; and

(B) fix the rate of basic pay for such positions, without regard to subchapter III of chapter 53 of title 5, United States Code, if the rate of pay is not greater than the rate of basic pay payable for level IV of the Executive Schedule;

(2) appoint individuals to such positions; and

(3) establish a performance management system for such individuals with at

least one level of performance above a retention standard.

(b) Reporting Requirement.— Not less than 60 days before the date of the implementation of authorities authorized under this section, the Director of the Federal Bureau of Investigation shall submit an operating plan describing the Director's intended use of the authorities under this section to the appropriate committees of Congress.

(c) Annual Report.— Not later than December 31, 2005, and annually thereafter for 4 years, the Director of the Federal Bureau of Investigation shall submit an annual report of the use of the permanent authorities provided under this section during the preceding fiscal year to the appropriate committees of Congress.

(d) Appropriate Committees of Congress Defined.—In this section, the term "appropriate committees of Congress means"—

(1) the Committees on Appropriations, Homeland Security and Governmental Affairs, and the Judiciary and the Select Committee on Intelligence of the Senate; and

(2) the Committees on Appropriations, Government Reform, and the Judiciary and the Permanent Select Committee on Intelligence of the House of Representatives.

* * * * * * *

SEC. 2006. [28 U.S.C. 509 note] FEDERAL BUREAU OF INVESTIGATION USE OF TRANSLATORS.

Not later than 30 days after the date of the enactment of this Act, and annually thereafter, the Attorney General of the United States shall submit to the Committee on the Judiciary of the Senate and the Committee on the Judiciary of the House of Representatives a report that contains, with respect to each preceding 12-month period—

(1) the number of translators employed, or contracted for, by the Federal Bureau of Investigation or other components of the Department of Justice;

(2) any legal or practical impediments to using translators employed by Federal, State, or local agencies on a full-time, part-time, or shared basis;

(3) the needs of the Federal Bureau of Investigation for specific translation services in certain languages, and recommendations for meeting those needs;

(4) the status of any automated statistical reporting system, including implementation and future viability;

(5) the storage capabilities of the digital collection system or systems utilized;

(6) a description of the establishment and compliance with audio retention policies that satisfy the investigative and intelligence goals of the Federal Bureau of Investigation; and

(7) a description of the implementation of quality control procedures and mechanisms for monitoring compliance with quality control procedures.

TITLE III—SECURITY CLEARANCES

SEC. 3001. [50 U.S.C. 3341] SECURITY CLEARANCES.

(a) DEFINITIONS.—In this section:

(1) The term "agency" means—

(A) an executive agency (as that term is defined in section 105 of title 5, United States Code);

(B) a military department (as that term is defined in section 102 of title 5, United States Code); or

(C) an element of the intelligence community.

(2) The term "authorized investigative agency" means an agency designated by the head of the agency selected pursuant to subsection (b) to conduct a counterintelligence investigation or investigation of persons who are proposed for access to classified information to ascertain whether such persons satisfy the criteria for obtaining and retaining access to such information.

(3) The term "authorized adjudicative agency" means an agency authorized by law, regulation, or direction of the Director of National Intelligence to determine eligibility for access to classified information in accordance with Executive Order 12968.

(4) The term "highly sensitive program" means—

(A) a government program designated as a Special Access Program (as that term is defined in section 4.1(h) of Executive Order 12958 or any successor Executive order); or

(B) a government program that applies restrictions required for—

(i) restricted data (as that term is defined in section 11 y. of the Atomic Energy Act of 1954 (42 U.S.C. 2014(y))); or

(ii) other information commonly referred to as "sensitive compartmented information".

(5) The term "current investigation file" means, with respect to a security clearance, a file on an investigation or adjudication that has been conducted during—

(A) the 5-year period beginning on the date the security clearance was granted, in the case of a Top Secret Clearance, or the date access was granted to a highly sensitive program;

(B) the 10-year period beginning on the date the security clearance was granted in the case of a Secret Clearance; and

(C) the 15-year period beginning on the date the security clearance was granted in the case of a Confidential Clearance.

(6) The term "personnel security investigation" means any investigation required for the purpose of determining the eligibility of any military, civilian, or government contractor personnel to access classified information.

(7) The term "periodic reinvestigations" means investigations conducted for the purpose of updating a previously completed background investigation—

(A) every 5 years in the case of a top secret clearance or access to a highly sensitive program;

(B) every 10 years in the case of a secret clearance; or

(C) every 15 years in the case of a Confidential Clearance.

(8) The term "appropriate committees of Congress" means—

(A) the Permanent Select Committee on Intelligence and the Committees on Armed Services, Homeland Security, Government Reform, and the Judiciary of the House of Representatives; and

(B) the Select Committee on Intelligence and the Committees on Armed Services, Homeland Security and Governmental Affairs, and the Judiciary of the Senate.

(9) ACCESS DETERMINATION.—The term "access determination" means the determination regarding whether an employee—

(A) is eligible for access to classified information in accordance with Executive Order 12968 (60 Fed. Reg. 40245; relating to access to classified information), or any successor thereto, and Executive Order 10865 (25 Fed. Reg. 1583; relating to safeguarding classified information within industry), or any successor thereto; and

(B) possesses a need to know under such an Order.

(b) SELECTION OF ENTITY.—Except as otherwise provided, not later than 90 days after the date of the enactment of this Act, the President shall select a single department, agency, or element of the executive branch to be responsible for—

(1) directing day-to-day oversight of investigations and adjudications for personnel security clearances, including for highly sensitive programs, throughout the United States Government;

(2) developing and implementing uniform and consistent policies and procedures to ensure the effective, efficient, and timely completion of security clearances and determinations for access to highly sensitive programs, including the standardization of security questionnaires, financial disclosure requirements for security clearance applicants, and polygraph policies and procedures;

(3) serving as the final authority to designate an authorized investigative agency or authorized adjudicative agency;

(4) ensuring reciprocal recognition of access to classified information among the agencies of the United States Government, including acting as the final authority to arbitrate and resolve disputes involving the reciprocity of security clearances and access to highly sensitive programs pursuant to subsection (d);

(5) ensuring, to the maximum extent practicable, that sufficient resources are available in each agency to achieve clearance and investigative program goals;

(6) reviewing and coordinating the development of tools and techniques for enhancing the conduct of investigations and granting of clearances; and

(7) not later than 180 days after the date of the enactment of the Intelligence Authorization Act for Fiscal Year 2014, and consistent with subsection (j)—

(A) developing policies and procedures that permit, to the extent practicable, individuals alleging reprisal for having made a protected disclosure (provided the individual does not disclose classified information or other information contrary to law) to appeal any action affecting an employee's access to classified information and to retain their government employment status while such challenge is pending; and

(B) developing and implementing uniform and consistent policies and procedures to ensure proper protections during the process for denying, suspending, or revoking a security clearance or access to classified information following a protected disclosure, including the ability to appeal such a denial, suspension, or revocation, except that there shall be no appeal of an agency's suspension of a security clearance or access determination for purposes of conducting an investigation, if that suspension lasts no longer than 1 year or the head of the agency or a designee of the head of the agency certifies that a longer suspension is needed before a final decision on denial or revocation to prevent imminent harm to the national security.

(c) PERFORMANCE OF SECURITY CLEARANCE INVESTIGATIONS.—(1) Notwithstanding any other provision of law, not later than 180 days after the date of the enactment of this Act, the President shall, in consultation with the head of the entity selected pursuant to subsection (b), select a single agency of the executive branch to conduct, to the maximum extent practicable, security clearance investigations of employees and contractor personnel of the United States Government who require access to classified information and to provide and maintain all security clearances of such employees and contractor personnel. The head of the entity selected pursuant to subsection (b) may designate other agencies to conduct such investigations if the head of the entity selected pursuant to subsection (b) considers it appropriate for national security and efficiency purposes.

(2) The agency selected under paragraph (1) shall—

(A) take all necessary actions to carry out the requirements of this section, including entering into a memorandum of understanding with any agency carrying out responsibilities relating to security clearances or security clearance investigations before the date of the enactment of this Act;

(B) as soon as practicable, integrate reporting of security clearance applications, security clearance investigations, and determinations of eligibility for security clearances, with the database required by subsection (e); and

(C) ensure that security clearance investigations are conducted in accordance with uniform standards and requirements established under subsection (b), including uniform security questionnaires and financial disclosure requirements.

(d) RECIPROCITY OF SECURITY CLEARANCE AND ACCESS DETERMINATIONS.—(1) All security clearance background investigations and determinations completed by an authorized investigative agency or authorized adjudicative agency shall be accepted by all agencies.

(2) All security clearance background investigations initiated by an authorized investigative agency shall be transferable to any other authorized investigative agency.

(3)(A) An authorized investigative agency or authorized adjudicative agency may not establish additional investigative or adjudicative requirements (other than requirements for the conduct of a polygraph examination) that exceed requirements specified in Executive Orders establishing security requirements for access to classified information without the approval of the head of the entity selected pursuant to subsection (b).

(B) Notwithstanding subparagraph (A), the head of the entity selected pursuant to subsection (b) may establish such additional requirements as the head of such entity considers necessary for national security purposes.

(4) An authorized investigative agency or authorized adjudicative agency may not conduct an investigation for purposes of determining whether to grant a security clearance to an individual where a current investigation or clearance of equal level already exists or has been granted by another authorized adjudicative agency.

(5) The head of the entity selected pursuant to subsection (b) may disallow the reciprocal recognition of an individual security clearance by an agency under this section on a case-by-case basis if the head of the entity selected pursuant to subsection (b) determines that such action is necessary for national security purposes.

(6) The head of the entity selected pursuant to subsection (b) shall establish a review procedure by which agencies can seek review of actions required under this section.

(e) Database on Security Clearances.—(1) Not later than 12 months after the date of the enactment of this Act, the Director of the Office of Personnel Management shall, in cooperation with the heads of the entities selected pursuant to subsections (b) and (c), establish and commence operating and maintaining an integrated, secure, database into which appropriate data relevant to the granting, denial, or revocation of a security clearance or access pertaining to military, civilian, or government contractor personnel shall be entered from all authorized investigative and adjudicative agencies.

(2) The database under this subsection shall function to integrate information from existing Federal clearance tracking systems from other authorized investigative and adjudicative agencies into a single consolidated database.

(3) Each authorized investigative or adjudicative agency shall check the database under this subsection to determine whether an individual the agency has identified as requiring a security clearance has already been granted or denied a security clearance, or has had a security clearance revoked, by any other authorized investigative or adjudicative agency.

(4) The head of the entity selected pursuant to subsection (b) shall evaluate the extent to which an agency is submitting information to, and requesting information from, the database under this subsection as part of a determination of whether to certify the agency as an authorized investigative agency or authorized adjudicative agency.

(5) The head of the entity selected pursuant to subsection (b) may authorize an agency to withhold information about certain individuals from the database under this subsection if the head of the entity considers it necessary for national security purposes.

(f) Evaluation of Use of Available Technology in Clearance Investigations and Adjudications.—(1) The head of the entity selected pursuant to subsection (b) shall evaluate the use of available information technology and databases to expedite investigative and adjudicative processes for all and to verify standard information submitted as part of an application for a security clearance.

(2) The evaluation shall assess the application of the technologies described in paragraph (1) for—

(A) granting interim clearances to applicants at the secret, top secret, and special access program levels before the completion of the appropriate full investigation;

(B) expediting investigations and adjudications of security clearances, including verification of information submitted by the applicant;

(C) ongoing verification of suitability of personnel with security clearances in effect for continued access to classified information;

(D) use of such technologies to augment periodic reinvestigations;

(E) assessing the impact of the use of such technologies on the rights of applicants to verify, correct, or challenge information obtained through such technologies; and

(F) such other purposes as the head of the entity selected pursuant to subsection (b) considers appropriate.

(3) An individual subject to verification utilizing the technology described in paragraph (1) shall be notified of such verification, shall provide consent to such use, and shall have access to data being verified in order to correct errors or challenge information the individual believes is incorrect.

(4) Not later than one year after the date of the enactment of this Act, the head of the entity selected pursuant to subsection (b) shall submit to the President and the appropriate committees of Congress a report on the results of the evaluation, including recommendations on the use of technologies described in paragraph (1).

(i) AUTHORIZATION OF APPROPRIATIONS.— There is authorized to be appropriated such sums as may be necessary for fiscal year 2005 and each fiscal year thereafter for the implementation, maintenance, and operation of the database required by subsection (e).

(j) RETALIATORY REVOCATION OF SECURITY CLEARANCES AND ACCESS DETERMINATIONS.—

(1) IN GENERAL.—Agency personnel with authority to take, direct others to take, recommend, or approve personnel security clearance or access determinations shall not take or fail to take, or threaten to take or fail to take, any action with respect to any employee's security clearance or access determination in retaliation for—

(A) any lawful disclosure of information to the Director of National Intelligence (or an employee designated by the Director of National Intelligence for such purpose) or a supervisor in the employee's direct chain of command, or a supervisor of the employing agency with responsibility for the subject matter of the disclosure, up to and including the head of the employing agency (or employee designated by the head of that agency for such purpose) by an employee that the employee reasonably believes evidences—

(i) a violation of any Federal law, rule, or regulation; or

(ii) mismanagement, a gross waste of funds, an abuse of authority, or a substantial and specific danger to public health or safety;

(B) any lawful disclosure to the Inspector General of an agency or another employee designated by the head of the agency to receive such disclosures, of information which the employee reasonably believes evidences—

(i) a violation of any Federal law, rule, or regulation; or

(ii) mismanagement, a gross waste of funds, an abuse of authority, or a substantial and specific danger to public health or safety;

(C) any lawful disclosure that complies with—

(i) subsections (a)(1), (d), and (h) of section 8H of the Inspector General Act of 1978 (5 U.S.C. App.);

(ii) subparagraphs (A), (D), and (H) of section 17(d)(5) of the Central Intelligence Agency Act of 1949 (50 U.S.C. 3517(d)(5)); or

(iii) subparagraphs (A), (D), and (I) of section 103H(k)(5) of the National Security Act of 1947 (50 U.S.C. 3033(k)(5)); and

(D) if the actions do not result in the employee or applicant unlawfully disclosing information specifically required by Executive order to be kept classified in the interest of national defense or the conduct of foreign affairs, any lawful disclosure in conjunction with—

(i) the exercise of any appeal, complaint, or grievance right granted by any law, rule, or regulation;

(ii) testimony for or otherwise lawfully assisting any individual in the exercise of any right referred to in clause (i); or

(iii) cooperation with or disclosing information to the Inspector General of an agency, in accordance with applicable provisions of law in connection with an audit, inspection, or investigation conducted by the Inspector General.

(2) Rule of construction.— Consistent with the protection of sources and methods, nothing in paragraph (1) shall be construed to authorize the withholding of information from Congress or the taking of any personnel action or clearance action against an employee who lawfully discloses information to Congress.

(3) Disclosures.—A disclosure shall not be excluded from paragraph (1) because—

(A) the disclosure was made to a person, including a supervisor, who participated in an activity that the employee reasonably believed to be covered by paragraph (1)(A)(ii);

(B) the disclosure revealed information that had been previously disclosed;

(C) the disclosure was not made in writing;

(D) the disclosure was made while the employee was off duty;

(E) of the amount of time which has passed since the occurrence of the events described in the disclosure; or

(F) the disclosure was made during the normal course of duties of an employee.

(4) Agency adjudication.—

(A) Remedial procedure.— An employee or former employee who believes that he or she has been subjected to a reprisal prohibited by paragraph (1) may, within 90 days (except as provided by subparagraph (D)) after the issuance of notice of such decision, appeal that decision within the agency of that employee or former employee through proceedings authorized by subsection (b)(7), except that there shall be no appeal of an agency's suspension of a security clearance or access determination for purposes of conducting an investigation, if that suspension lasts not longer than 1 year (or a longer period in accordance with a certification made under subsection (b)(7)).

(B) CORRECTIVE ACTION.— If, in the course of proceedings authorized under subparagraph (A), it is determined that the adverse security clearance or access determination violated paragraph (1), the agency shall take specific corrective action to return the employee or former employee, as nearly as practicable and reasonable, to the position such employee or former employee would have held had the violation not occurred. Such corrective action may include back pay and related benefits, travel expenses, and compensatory damages not to exceed $300,000.

(C) CONTRIBUTING FACTOR.— In determining whether the adverse security clearance or access determination violated paragraph (1), the agency shall find that paragraph (1) was violated if a disclosure described in paragraph (1) was a contributing factor in the adverse security clearance or access determination taken against the individual, unless the agency demonstrates by a preponderance of the evidence that it would have taken the same action in the absence of such disclosure, giving the utmost deference to the agency's assessment of the particular threat to the national security interests of the United States in the instant matter.

(D) TOLLING.—The time requirement established by subparagraph (A) for an employee or former employee to appeal the decision of an agency may be tolled if the employee or former employee presents substantial credible evidence showing why the employee or former employee did not timely initiate the appeal and why the enforcement of the time requirement would be unfair, such as evidence showing that the employee or former employee—

(i) did not receive notice of the decision; or

(ii) could not timely initiate the appeal because of factors beyond the control of the employee or former employee.

(5) APPELLATE REVIEW OF SECURITY CLEARANCE ACCESS DETERMINATIONS BY DIRECTOR OF NATIONAL INTELLIGENCE.—

(A) APPEAL.— Within 60 days after receiving notice of an adverse final agency determination under a proceeding under paragraph (4), an employee or former employee may appeal that determination in accordance with the procedures established under subparagraph (B).

(B) POLICIES AND PROCEDURES.— The Director of National Intelligence, in consultation with the Attorney General and the Secretary of Defense, shall develop and implement policies and procedures for adjudicating the appeals authorized by subparagraph (A).

(C) CONGRESSIONAL NOTIFICATION.— Consistent with the protection of sources and methods, at the time the Director of National Intelligence issues an order regarding an appeal pursuant to the policies and procedures established by this paragraph, the Director of National Intelligence shall notify the congressional intelligence committees.

(6) JUDICIAL REVIEW.—Nothing in this section shall be construed to permit or

require judicial review of any—

(A) agency action under this section; or

(B) action of the appellate review procedures established under paragraph (5).

(7) PRIVATE CAUSE OF ACTION.— Nothing in this section shall be construed to permit, authorize, or require a private cause of action to challenge the merits of a security clearance determination.

(8) ENFORCEMENT.— Except as otherwise provided in this subsection, the President shall provide for the enforcement of this section consistent, to the fullest extent possible, with the policies and procedures used to adjudicate alleged violations of section 2302(b)(8) of title 5, United States Code.

(9) INCLUSION OF CONTRACTOR EMPLOYEES.— In this subsection, the term "employee" includes an employee of a contractor, subcontractor, grantee, subgrantee, or personal services contractor, of an agency. With respect to such employees, the term "employing agency" shall be deemed to be the contracting agency.

SEC. 3002. [50 U.S.C. 3343] SECURITY CLEARANCES; LIMITATIONS.

(a) DEFINITIONS.—In this section:

(1) CONTROLLED SUBSTANCE.— The term "controlled substance" has the meaning given that term in section 102 of the Controlled Substances Act (21 U.S.C. 802).

(2) COVERED PERSON.—The term "covered person" means—

(A) an officer or employee of a Federal agency;

(B) a member of the Army, Navy, Air Force, or Marine Corps who is on active duty or is in an active status; and

(C) an officer or employee of a contractor of a Federal agency.

(3) RESTRICTED DATA.— The term "Restricted Data" has the meaning given that term in section 11 of the Atomic Energy Act of 1954 (42 U.S.C. 2014).

(4) SPECIAL ACCESS PROGRAM.— The term "special access program" has the meaning given that term in section 4.1 of Executive Order No. 12958 (60 Fed. Reg. 19825).

(b) PROHIBITION.— After January 1, 2008, the head of a Federal agency may not grant or renew a security clearance for a covered person who is an unlawful user of a controlled substance or an addict (as defined in section 102(1) of the Controlled Substances Act (21 U.S.C. 802)).

(c) DISQUALIFICATION.—

(1) IN GENERAL.—After January 1, 2008, absent an express written waiver granted in accordance with paragraph (2), the head of a Federal agency may not grant or renew a security clearance described in paragraph (3) for a covered person who—

(A) has been convicted in any court of the United States of a crime, was sentenced to imprisonment for a term exceeding 1 year, and was incarcerated as a result of that sentence for not less than 1 year;

(B) has been discharged or dismissed from the Armed Forces under dishonorable conditions; or

(C) is mentally incompetent, as determined by an adjudicating authority, based on an evaluation by a duly qualified mental health professional employed by, or acceptable to and approved by, the United States Government and in accordance with the adjudicative guidelines required by subsection (d).

(2) WAIVER AUTHORITY.—In a meritorious case, an exception to the disqualification in this subsection may be authorized if there are mitigating factors. Any such waiver may be authorized only in accordance with—

(A) standards and procedures prescribed by, or under the authority of, an Executive order or other guidance issued by the President; or

(B) the adjudicative guidelines required by subsection (d).

(3) COVERED SECURITY CLEARANCES.—This subsection applies to security clearances that provide for access to—

(A) special access programs;

(B) Restricted Data; or

(C) any other information commonly referred to as "sensitive compartmented information".

(4) ANNUAL REPORT.—

(A) REQUIREMENT FOR REPORT.— Not later than February 1 of each year, the head of a Federal agency shall submit a report to the appropriate committees of Congress if such agency employs or employed a person for whom a waiver was granted in accordance with paragraph (2) during the preceding year. Such annual report shall not reveal the identity of such person, but shall include for each waiver issued the disqualifying factor under paragraph (1) and the reasons for the waiver of the disqualifying factor.

(B) DEFINITIONS.—In this paragraph:

(i) APPROPRIATE COMMITTEES OF CONGRESS.—The term "appropriate committees of Congress" means, with respect to a report submitted under subparagraph (A) by the head of a Federal agency—

(I) the congressional defense committees;

(II) the congressional intelligence committees;

(III) the Committee on Homeland Security and Governmental Affairs of the Senate;

(IV) the Committee on Oversight and Government Reform of the House of Representatives; and

(V) each Committee of the Senate or the House of Representatives with oversight authority over such Federal agency.

(ii) CONGRESSIONAL DEFENSE COMMITTEES.— The term "congressional defense committees" has the meaning given that term in section 101(a)(16) of title 10, United States Code.

(iii) CONGRESSIONAL INTELLIGENCE COMMITTEES.— The term "congressional intelligence committees" has the meaning given that term in section 3 of the National Security Act of 1947 (50 U.S.C. 401a).

(d) ADJUDICATIVE GUIDELINES.—

(1) REQUIREMENT TO ESTABLISH.— The President shall establish adjudicative

guidelines for determining eligibility for access to classified information.

(2) REQUIREMENTS RELATED TO MENTAL HEALTH.—The guidelines required by paragraph (1) shall—

(A) include procedures and standards under which a covered person is determined to be mentally incompetent and provide a means to appeal such a determination; and

(B) require that no negative inference concerning the standards in the guidelines may be raised solely on the basis of seeking mental health counseling.

* * * * * * *

TITLE VIII—OTHER MATTERS

Subtitle A—INTELLIGENCE MATTERS

SEC. 8101. [50 U.S.C. 3024 note] INTELLIGENCE COMMUNITY USE OF NATIONAL INFRASTRUCTURE SIMULATION AND ANALYSIS CENTER.

(a) IN GENERAL.— The Director of National Intelligence shall establish a formal relationship, including information sharing, between the elements of the intelligence community and the National Infrastructure Simulation and Analysis Center.

(b) PURPOSE.— The purpose of the relationship under subsection (a) shall be to permit the intelligence community to take full advantage of the capabilities of the National Infrastructure Simulation and Analysis Center, particularly vulnerability and consequence analysis, for real time response to reported threats and long term planning for projected threats.

* * * * * * *

CIA—Specific Authorities

Central Intelligence Agency Act of 1949

Central Intelligence Agency Retirement Act

Central Intelligence Agency Information Act

SELECTED PROVISIONS OF THE CENTRAL INTELLIGENCE AGENCY ACT OF 1949

CHAPTER 227
AS AMENDED THROUGH P.L. 118–159

CENTRAL INTELLIGENCE AGENCY ACT OF 1949

[Chapter 227; 63 Stat. 208; approved June 20, 1949]

[As Amended Through P.L. 118–159, Enacted December 23, 2024]

AN ACT To provide for the administration of the Central Intelligence Agency, established pursuant to section 102, National Security Act of 1947, and for other purposes.

Be it enacted by the Senate and House of Representatives of the United States of America in Congress assembled,

DEFINITIONS

SECTION 1. [50 U.S.C. 3501] That when used in this Act, the term—

(1) "Agency" means the Central Intelligence Agency;

(2) "Director" means the Director of the Central Intelligence Agency; and

(3) "Government agency" means any executive department, commission, council, independent establishment, corporation wholly or partly owned by the United States which is an instrumentality of the United States, board, bureau, division, service, office, officer, authority, administration, or other establishment, in the executive branch of the Government.

SEAL OF OFFICE

SEC. 2. [50 U.S.C. 3502] The Director shall cause a seal of office to be made for the Central Intelligence Agency, of such design as the President shall approve, and judicial notice shall be taken thereof.

PROCUREMENT AUTHORITIES

SEC. 3. [50 U.S.C. 3503] (a) In the performance of its functions the Central Intelligence Agency is authorized to exercise the authorities contained in sections 3201, 3203, 3204, 3206, 3207, 3302 through 3306, 3321 through 3323, 3801 through 3808, 3069, 3134, 3841, and 4752 of title 10, United States Code.

(b) In the exercise of the authorities granted in subsection (a) of this section, the term "Agency head" shall mean the Director, the Deputy Director, or the Executive of the Agency.

(c) The determinations and decisions provided in subsection (a) of this section to be made by the Agency head may be made with respect to individual purchases and contracts or with respect to classes of purchases or contracts, and shall be final. Except as provided in subsection (d) of this section, the Agency head is authorized to delegate his powers provided in this section, including the making of such determinations and decisions, in his discretion and subject to his direction, to any other officer or officers or officials of the Agency.

(d) The power of the Agency head to make the determinations or decisions specified in sections 3201 through 3204 of title 10, United States Code, shall not be delegable. Each determination or decision required by sections 3201 through 3204, 3321 through 3323, and 3841 of title 10, United States Code[1], shall be based upon written findings made by the official making such determinations, which findings shall be final and shall be available within the Agency for a period of at least six years following the date of the determination.

---

[1] Section 7332(2) of division G of Public Law 118–31 provides for an amendment to strike "in paragraphs" and all that follows through "1947". The amendment did not specify to which occurrence of "1947" to strike, however, it was carried out through the 2nd occurrence to reflect the probable intent of Congress.

[Original section 4 (50 U.S.C. 3504) was repealed by section 21(b)(2) of Public Law 85–507 (72 Stat. 337, July 7, 1958).]

TRAVEL, ALLOWANCES, AND RELATED EXPENSES

SEC. 4. [50 U.S.C. 3505] (a) Under such regulations as the Director may prescribe, the Agency, with respect to its officers and employees assigned to duty stations outside the several States of the United States of America, excluding Alaska and Hawaii, but including the District of Columbia, shall—

(1)(A) pay the travel expenses of officers and employees of the Agency, including expenses incurred while traveling pursuant to authorized home leave;

(B) pay the travel expenses of members of the family of an officer or employee of the Agency when proceeding to or returning from his post of duty; accompanying him on authorized home leave; or otherwise traveling in accordance with authority granted pursuant to the terms of this or any other Act;

(C) pay the cost of transporting the furniture and household and personal effects of an officer or employee of the Agency to his successive posts of duty and, on the termination of his services, to his residence at time of appointment or to a point not more distant, or, upon retirement, to the place where he will reside;

(D) pay the cost of packing and unpacking, transporting to and from a place of storage, and storing the furniture and household and personal effects of an officer or employee of the Agency, when he is absent from his post of assignment under orders, or when he is assigned to a post to which he cannot take or at which he is unable to use such furniture and household and personal effects, or when it is in the public interest or more economical to authorize storage; but in no instance shall the weight or volume of the effects stored together with the weight or volume of the effects transported exceed the maximum limitations fixed by regulations, when not otherwise fixed by law;

(E) pay the cost of packing and unpacking, transporting to and from a place of storage, and storing the furniture and household and personal effects of an officer or employee of the Agency in connection with assignment or transfer to a new post, from the date of his departure from his last post or from the date of his departure from his place of residence in the case of a new officer or employee and for not to exceed three months after arrival at the new post, or until the establishment of residence quarters, whichever shall be shorter; and in connection with separation of an officer or employee of the Agency, the cost of packing and unpacking, transporting to and from a place of storage, and storing for a period not to exceed three months, his furniture and household and personal effects; but in no instance shall the weight or volume of the effects stored together with the weight or volume of the effects transported exceed the maximum limitations fixed by regulations, when not otherwise fixed by law; and

(F) pay the travel expenses and transportation costs incident to the removal of the members of the family of an officer or employee of the Agency and his furniture and household and personal effects, including automobiles, from a post at which, because of the prevalence of disturbed conditions, there is imminent danger to life and property, and the return of such persons, furniture, and effects to such post upon the cessation of such conditions; or to such other post as may in the meantime have become the post to which such officer or employee has been assigned.

(2) Charge expenses in connection with travel of personnel, their dependents, and transportation of their household goods and personal effects, involving a change of permanent station, to the appropriation for the fiscal year current when any part of either the travel or transportation pertaining to the transfer begins pursuant to previously issued travel and transfer orders, notwithstanding the fact that such travel or transportation may not all be effected during such fiscal year, or the travel and transfer orders may have been issued during the prior fiscal year.

(3)(A) Order to any of the several States of the United States of America (including the District of Columbia, the Commonwealth of Puerto Rico, and any territory or possession of the United States) on leave of absence each officer or employee of the Agency who was a resident of the United States (as described above) at time of employment, upon completion of two years' continuous service abroad, or as soon as possible thereafter.

(B) While in the United States (as described in paragraph (3)(A) of this section) on leave, the service of any officer or employee shall be available for work or duties in the Agency or elsewhere as the Director may prescribe; and the time of such work or duty shall not be counted as leave.

(C) Where an officer or employee on leave returns to the United States (as described in paragraph (3)(A) of this section), leave of absence granted shall be exclusive of the time actually and necessarily occupied in going to and from the United States (as so described) and such time as may be necessarily occupied in awaiting transportation.

(4) Notwithstanding the provisions of any other law, transport for or on behalf of

an officer or employee of the Agency, a privately owned motor vehicle in any case in which it shall be determined that water, rail, or air transportation of the motor vehicle is necessary or expedient for all or any part of the distance between points of origin and destination, and pay the costs of such transportation. Not more than one motor vehicle of any officer or employee of the Agency may be transported under authority of this paragraph during any four-year period, except that, as replacement for such motor vehicle, one additional motor vehicle of any such officer or employee may be so transported during such period upon approval, in advance, by the Director and upon a determination, in advance, by the Director that such replacement is necessary for reasons beyond the control of the officer or employee and is in the interest of the Government. After the expiration of a period of four years following the date of transportation under authority of this paragraph of a privately owned motor vehicle of any officer or employee who has remained in continuous service outside the several States of the United States of America, excluding Alaska and Hawaii, but including the District of Columbia, during such period, the transportation of a replacement for such motor vehicle for such officer or employee may be authorized by the Director in accordance with this paragraph.

(5)(A) In the event of illness or injury requiring the hospitalization of an officer or full time employee of the Agency, incurred while on assignment abroad, in a locality where there does not exist a suitable hospital or clinic, pay the travel expenses of such officer or employee by whatever means the Director deems appropriate and without regard to the Standardized Government Travel Regulations and section 5731 of title 5, United States Code, to the nearest locality where a suitable hospital or clinic exists and on the recovery of such officer or employee pay for the travel expenses of the return to the post of duty of such officer or employee of duty. If the officer or employee is too ill to travel unattended, the Director may also pay the travel expenses of an attendant;

(B) Establish a first-aid station and provide for the services of a nurse at a post at which, in the opinion of the Director, sufficient personnel is employed to warrant such a station: *Provided,* That, in the opinion of the Director, it is not feasible to utilize an existing facility;

(C) In the event of illness or injury requiring hospitalization of an officer or full time employee of the Agency incurred in the line of duty while such person is assigned abroad, pay for the cost of the treatment of such illnesss or injury at a suitable hospital or clinic;

(D) Provide for the periodic physical examination of officers and employees of the Agency and for the cost of administering inoculations or vaccinations to such officers or employees.

(6) Pay the costs of preparing and transporting the remains of an officer or employee of the Agency or a member of his family who may die while in travel status or abroad, to his home or official station, or to such other place as the Director may determine to be the appropriate place of interment, provided that in no case shall the expense payable be greater than the amount which would have been payable had the destination been the home or official station.

(7) Pay the costs of travel of new appointees and their dependents, and the transportation of their household goods and personal effects, from places of actual

residence in foreign countries at time of appointment to places of employment and return to their actual residences at the time of appointment or a point not more distant: *Provided,* That such appointees agree in writing to remain with the United States Government for a period of not less than twelve months from the time of appointment.

Violation of such agreement for personal convenience of an employee or because of separation for misconduct will bar such return payments and, if determined by the Director or his designee to be in the best interests of the United States, any money expended by the United States on account of such travel and transportation shall be considered as a debt due by the individual concerned to the United States.

(b)(1) The Director may pay to officers and employees of the Agency, and to persons detailed or assigned to the Agency from other agencies of the Government or from the Armed Forces, allowances and benefits comparable to the allowances and benefits authorized to be paid to members of the Foreign Service under chapter 9 of title I of the Foreign Service Act of 1980 (22 U.S.C. 4081 et seq.) or any other provision of law.

(2) The Director may pay allowances and benefits related to officially authorized travel, personnel and physical security activities, operational activities, and cover-related activities (whether or not such allowances and benefits are otherwise authorized under this section or any other provision of law) when payment of such allowances and benefits is necessary to meet the special requirements of work related to such activities. Payment of allowances and benefits under this paragraph shall be in accordance with regulations prescribed by the Director. Rates for allowances and benefits under this paragraph may not be set at rates in excess of those authorized by sections 5724 and 5724a of title 5, United States Code, when reimbursement is provided for relocation attributable, in whole or in part, to relocation within the United States.

(3) Notwithstanding any other provision of this section or any other provision of law relating to the officially authorized travel of Government employees, the Director, in order to reflect Agency requirements not taken into account in the formulation of Government-wide travel procedures, may by regulation—

(A) authorize the travel of officers and employees of the Agency, and of persons detailed or assigned to the Agency from other agencies of the Government or from the Armed Forces who are engaged in the performance of intelligence functions, and

(B) provide for payment for such travel, in classes of cases, as determined by the Director, in which such travel is important to the performance of intelligence functions.

(4) Members of the Armed Forces may not receive benefits under both this section and title 37, United States Code, for the same purpose. The Director and Secretary of Defense shall prescribe joint regulations to carry out the preceding sentence.

(5) Regulations, other than regulations under paragraph (1), issued pursuant to this subsection shall be submitted to the Permanent Select Committee on Intelligence of the House of Representatives and the Select Committee on

Intelligence of the Senate before such regulations take effect.

GENERAL AUTHORITIES

SEC. 5. [50 U.S.C. 3506] (a) IN GENERAL.—In the performance of its functions, the Central Intelligence Agency is authorized to—

(1) Transfer to and receive from other Government agencies such sums as may be approved by the Office of Management and Budget, for the performance of any of the functions or activities authorized under section 104A of the National Security Act of 1947 (50 U.S.C. 403–4a), and any other Government agency is authorized to transfer to or receive from the Agency such sums without regard to any provisions of law limiting or prohibiting transfers between appropriations. Sums transferred to the Agency in accordance with this paragraph may be expended for the purposes and under the authority of this Act without regard to limitations of appropriations from which transferred;

(2) Exchange funds without regard to section 3651 Revised Statutes (31 U.S.C. 543);

(3) Reimburse other Government agencies for services of personnel assigned to the Agency, and such other Government agencies are hereby authorized, without regard to provisions of law to the contrary, so to assign or detail any officer or employee for duty with the Agency;

(4) Authorize personnel designated by the Director to carry firearms to the extent necessary for the performance of the Agency's authorized functions, except that, within the United States, such authority shall be limited to the purposes of—

(A) the training of Agency personnel and other authorized persons in the use of firearms;

(B) the protection of classified materials and information;

(C) the protection of installations and property of the Agency;

(D) the protection of—

(i) current and former Agency personnel and their immediate families;

(ii) individuals nominated by the President to the position of Director (including with respect to an individual whom a President-elect (as defined in section 3(c) of the Presidential Transition Act of 1963 (3 U.S.C. 102 note) has declared an intent to nominate) and their immediate families; and

(iii) defectors and their immediate families, and other persons in the United States under Agency auspices; and

(E) with respect to the Office of the Director of National Intelligence, the protection of—

(i) installations and property of the Office of the Director of National Intelligence;

(ii) the Director of National Intelligence and the immediate family of the Director;

(iii) current and former personnel of the Office of the Director of National Intelligence and their immediate families as the Director of National Intelligence may designate; and

(iv) individuals nominated by the President to the position of Director of National Intelligence (including with respect to an individual whom a President-elect has declared an intent to nominate) and their immediate families;

(5) Make alterations, improvements, and repairs on premises rented by the Agency, and pay rent therefor;

(6) Determine and fix the minimum and maximum limits of age within which an original appointment may be made to an operational position within the Agency, notwithstanding the provision of any other law, in accordance with such criteria as the Director, in his discretion, may prescribe;

(7) Notwithstanding section 1341(a)(1) of title 31, United States Code, enter into multiyear leases for up to 15 years; and

(8) Upon the approval of the Director, provide, during any fiscal year, with or without reimbursement, subsistence to any personnel assigned to an overseas location designated by the Agency as an austere location.

(b) Scope of Authority for Expenditure.—(1) The authority to enter into a multiyear lease under subsection (a)(7) shall be subject to appropriations provided in advance for—

(A) the entire lease; or

(B) the first 12 months of the lease and the Government's estimated termination liability.

(2) In the case of any such lease entered into under subparagraph (B) of paragraph (1)—

(A) such lease shall include a clause that provides that the contract shall be terminated if budget authority (as defined by section 3(2) of the Congressional Budget and Impoundment Control Act of 1974 (2 U.S.C. 622(2))) is not provided specifically for that project in an appropriations Act in advance of an obligation of funds in respect thereto;

(B) notwithstanding section 1552 of title 31, United States Code, amounts obligated for paying termination costs with respect to such lease shall remain available until the costs associated with termination of such lease are paid;

(C) funds available for termination liability shall remain available to satisfy rental obligations with respect to such lease in subsequent fiscal years in the event such lease is not terminated early, but only to the extent those funds are in excess of the amount of termination liability at the time of their use to satisfy such rental obligations; and

(D) funds appropriated for a fiscal year may be used to make payments on such lease, for a maximum of 12 months, beginning any time during such fiscal year.

(c) Transfers for Acquisition of Land.—(1) Sums appropriated or otherwise made available to the Agency for the acquisition of land that are transferred to another department or agency for that purpose shall remain available for 3 years.

(2) The Director shall submit to the Select Committee on Intelligence of the Senate and the Permanent Select Committee on Intelligence of the House of

Representatives a report on the transfer of sums described in paragraph (1) each time that authority is exercised.

SEC. 6. [50 U.S.C. 3507] In the interests of the security of the foreign intelligence activities of the United States and in order further to implement section 102A(i) of the National Security Act of 1947 that the Director of National Intelligence shall be responsible for protecting intelligence sources and methods from unauthorized disclosure, the Agency shall be exempted from the provisions of sections 1 and 2, chapter 795 of the Act of August 28, 1935[2] (49 Stat. 956, 957; 5 U.S.C. 654), and the provisions of any other laws which require the publication or disclosure of the organization or functions of the Agency, or of the names, official titles, salaries, or numbers of personnel employed by the Agency: *Provided,* That in furtherance of this section, the Director of the Office of Management and Budget shall make no reports to the Congress in connection with the Agency under section 607, title VI, chapter 212 of the Act of June 30, 1945, as amended[3] (5 U.S.C. 947(b)).

[2] The cited Act of August 28, 1935, was repealed by the Independent Offices Appropriation Act, 1961 (Public Law 86–626, 74 Stat. 427).

[3] Section 607 of the Act of June 30, 1945, was repealed by section 301(85) of the Budget and Accounting Procedures Act of 1950 (64 Stat. 843).

SEC. 7. [50 U.S.C. 3508] Whenever the Director, the Attorney General and the Commissioner of Immigration shall determine that the admission of a particular alien into the United States for permanent residence is in the interest of national security or essential to the furtherance of the national intelligence mission, such alien and his immediate family shall be admitted to the United States for permanent residence without regard to their inadmissibility under the immigration or any other laws and regulations, or to the failure to comply with such laws and regulations pertaining to admissibility: *Provided,* That the number of aliens and members of their immediate families admitted to the United States under the authority of this section shall in no case exceed one hundred persons in any one fiscal year.

APPROPRIATIONS

SEC. 8. [50 U.S.C. 3510] (a) Notwithstanding any other provisions of law, sums made available to the Agency by appropriation or otherwise may be expended for purposes necessary to carry out its functions, including—

(1) personal services, including personal services without regard to limitations on types of persons to be employed, and rent at the seat of government and elsewhere; health-service program as authorized by law (5 U.S.C. 150);[4]payment of death benefits in cases in which the circumstances of the death of an employee of the Agency, a detailee of the Agency or other employee of another department or agency of the Federal Government assigned to the Agency, or an individual affiliated with the Agency (as determined by the Director), is not covered by section 11, other similar provisions of Federal law, or any regulation issued by the Director providing death benefits, but that the Director determines such payment appropriate; rental of news-reporting services; purchase or rental and operation

of photographic, reproduction, cryptographic, duplication and printing machines, equipment and devices, and radio-receiving and radio-sending equipment and devices, including telegraph and teletype equipment; purchase, maintenance, operation, repair, and hire of passenger motor vehicles, and aircraft, and vessels of all kinds; subject to policies established by the Director, transportation of officers and employees of the Agency in Government-owned automotive equipment between their domiciles and places of employment, where such personnel are engaged in work which makes such transportation necessary, and transportation in such equipment, to and from school, of children of Agency personnel who have quarters for themselves and their families at isolated stations outside the continental United States where adequate public or private transportation is not available; printing and binding; purchase, maintenance, and cleaning of firearms, including purchase, storage, and maintenance of ammunition; subject to policies established by the Director, expenses of travel in connection with, and expenses incident to attendance at meetings of professional, technical, scientific, and other similar organizations when such attendance would be a benefit in the conduct of the work of the Agency; association and library dues; payment of premiums or costs of surety bonds for officers or employees without regard to the provisions of 61 Stat. 646; 6 U.S.C. 14;[5] payment of claims pursuant to 28 U.S.C.; acquisition of necessary land and the clearing of such land; construction of buildings and facilities without regard to 36 Stat. 699; 40 U.S.C. 259, 267;[6] repair, rental, operation, and maintenance of buildings, utilities, facilities, and appurtenances; and

[4] The law codified to section 150 of title 5 before the enactment of that title was replaced by section 7901 of title 5 upon the enactment of that title by Public Law 89–544 (Sept. 6, 1966, 80 Stat. 378).

[5] Section 14 of title 6, United States Code, relating to the purchase of bonds to cover Government employees, was repealed by section 203(1) of Public Law 92–310 (Act of June 6, 1972, 86 Stat. 202).

[6] Section 3734 of the Revised Statutes of the United States, formerly classified to sections 259 and 267 of title 40, was repealed by section 17(12) of the Public Buildings Act of 1959 (Public Law 86–249, 73 Stat. 485). That Act is shown in the United States Code as chapter 12 of title 40 (40 U.S.C. 601 et seq.).

(2) supplies, equipment, and personnel and contractual services otherwise authorized by law and regulations, when approved by the Director.

(b) The sums made available to the Agency may be expended without regard to the provisions of law and regulations relating to the expenditure of Government funds; and for objects of a confidential, extraordinary, or emergency nature, such expenditures to be accounted for solely on the certificate of the Director and every such certificate shall be deemed a sufficient voucher for the amount therein certified.

(c) NOTIFICATION.— Not later than 30 days after the date on which the Director makes a novel and significant expenditure pursuant to subsection (a), the Director shall notify the Permanent Select Committee on Intelligence of the House of Representatives, the Select Committee on Intelligence of the Senate, the Subcommittee on Defense of the Committee on Appropriations of the Senate, and the Subcommittee on Defense of the Committee on Appropriations of the House of Representatives of such expenditure.

[Original section 9 (50 U.S.C. 3509) was repealed by section 601(b) of Public Law 763,

68 Stat. 1115; September 1, 1954.]

SEPARABILITY OF PROVISIONS

SEC. 9. [50 U.S.C. 3501 note] If any provision of this Act, or the application of such provision to any person or circumstances, is held invalid, the remainder of this Act or the application of such provision to persons or circumstances other than these as to which it is held invalid, shall not be affected thereby.

SHORT TITLE

SEC. 10. [50 U.S.C. 3501 note] This Act may be cited as the "Central Intelligence Agency Act of 1949".

BENEFITS AVAILABLE IN EVENT OF THE DEATH OF PERSONNEL

SEC. 11. (a) AUTHORITY.— The Director may pay death benefits substantially similar to those authorized for members of the Foreign Service pursuant to the Foreign Service Act of 1980 (22 U.S.C. 3901 et seq.) or any other provision of law. The Director may adjust the eligibility for death benefits as necessary to meet the unique requirements of the mission of the Agency.

(b) REGULATIONS.— Regulations issued pursuant to this section shall be submitted to the Select Committee on Intelligence of the Senate and the Permanent Select Committee on Intelligence of the House of Representatives before such regulations take effect.

GIFTS, DEVISES, AND BEQUESTS

SEC. 12. [50 U.S.C. 3512] (a)(1) Subject to the provisions of this section, the Director may accept, hold, administer, and use gifts of money, securities, or other property whenever the Director determines it would be in the interest of the United States to do so.

(2) Any gift accepted by the Director as a gift to the Agency under this subsection (and any income produced by any such gift)—

(A) may be used only for—

(i) artistic display;

(ii) purposes relating to the general welfare, education, or recreation of employees or dependents of employees of the Agency or for similar purposes; or

(iii) purposes relating to the welfare, education, or recreation of an individual described in paragraph (3); and

(B) under no circumstances may such a gift (or any income produced by any such gift) be used for operational purposes.

(3) An individual described in this paragraph is an individual who—

(A) is an employee or a former employee of the Agency who suffered injury or illness while employed by the Agency that—

(i) resulted from hostile or terrorist activities;

(ii) occurred in connection with an intelligence activity having a significant element of risk; or

(iii) occurred under other circumstances determined by the Director to be analogous to the circumstances described in clause (i) or (ii);

(B) is a family member of such an employee or former employee; or

(C) is a surviving family member of an employee of the Agency who died in circumstances described in clause (i), (ii), or (iii) of subparagraph (A).

(4) The Director may not accept any gift under this section that is expressly conditioned upon any expenditure not to be met from the gift itself or from income produced by the gift unless such expenditure has been authorized by law.

(5) The Director may, in the Director's discretion, determine that an individual described in subparagraph (A) or (B) of paragraph (3) may accept a gift for the purposes described in paragraph (2)(A)(iii).

(b) Unless otherwise restricted by the terms of the gift, the Director may sell or exchange, or invest or reinvest, any property which is accepted under subsection (a), but any such investment may only be in interest-bearing obligations of the United States or in obligations guaranteed as to both principal and interest by the United States.

(c) There is hereby created on the books of the Treasury of the United States a fund into which gifts of money, securities, and other intangible property accepted under the authority of subsection (a), and the earnings and proceeds thereof, shall be deposited. The assets of such fund shall be disbursed upon the order of the Director for the purposes specified in subsection (a) or (b).

(d) For purposes of Federal income, estate, and gift taxes, gifts accepted by the Director under subsection (a) shall be considered to be to or for the use of the United States.

(e) For the purposes of this section, the term "gift" includes a bequest or devise.

(f)(1) The Director may engage in fundraising in an official capacity for the benefit of nonprofit organizations that provide support to surviving family members of deceased Agency employees or that otherwise provide support for the welfare, education, or recreation of Agency employees, former Agency employees, or their family members.

(2) In this subsection, the term "fundraising" means the raising of funds through the active participation in the promotion, production, or presentation of an event designed to raise funds and does not include the direct solicitation of money by any other means.

(3) Not later than the date that is 7 days after the date the Director engages in fundraising authorized by this subsection or at the time the decision is made to participate in such fundraising, the Director shall notify the Select Committee on Intelligence of the Senate and the Permanent Select Committee on Intelligence of the House of Representatives of the fundraising.

(g) The Director, in consultation with the Director of the Office of Government Ethics, shall issue regulations to carry out the authority provided in this section. Such regulations shall ensure that such authority is exercised consistent with all relevant ethical constraints and principles, including—

(1) the avoidance of any prohibited conflict of interest or appearance of impropriety; and

(2) a prohibition against the acceptance of a gift from a foreign government or an agent of a foreign government.

MISUSE OF AGENCY NAME, INITIALS OR SEAL

SEC. 13. [50 U.S.C. 3513] (a) No person may, except with the written permission of the Director, knowingly use the words "Central Intelligence Agency", the initials "CIA", the seal of the Central Intelligence Agency, or any colorable imitation of such words, initials, or seal in connection with any merchandise, impersonation, solicitation, or commercial activity in a manner reasonably calculated to convey the impression that such use is approved, endorsed, or authorized by the Central Intelligence Agency.

(b) Whenever it appears to the Attorney General that any person is engaged or is about to engage in an act or practice which constitutes or will constitute conduct prohibited by subsection (a), the Attorney General may initiate a civil proceeding in a district court of the United States to enjoin such act or practice. Such court shall proceed as soon as practicable to the hearing and determination of such action and may, at any time before final determination, enter such restraining orders or prohibitions, or take such other action as is warranted, to prevent injury to the United States or to any person or class of persons for whose protection the action is brought.

RETIREMENT EQUITY FOR SPOUSES OF CERTAIN EMPLOYEES

SEC. 14. [50 U.S.C. 3514] (a) The provisions of sections 102, 221(b) (1)–(3), 221(f), 221(g), 221(i)(2), 221(j), 221(m), 222, 223, 224, 225, 232(b), 241(b), 241(d), and 264(b) of the Central Intelligence Agency Retirement Act (50 U.S.C. 403 note) establishing certain requirements, limitations, rights, entitlements, and benefits relating to retirement annuities, survivor benefits, and lump-sum payments for a spouse or former spouse of an Agency employee who is a participant in the Central Intelligence Agency Retirement and Disability System shall apply in the same manner and to the same extent in the case of an Agency employee who is a participant in the Civil Service Retirement and Disability System.

(b) The Director of the Office of Personnel Management, in consultation with the Director of the Central Intelligence Agency, shall prescribe such regulations as may be necessary to implement the provisions of this section.

SECURITY PERSONNEL AT AGENCY INSTALLATIONS

SEC. 15. [50 U.S.C. 3515] (a)(1) The Director may authorize Agency personnel within the United States to perform the same functions as officers and agents of the Department of Homeland Security, as provided in section 1315(b)(2) of title 40, United States Code, with the powers set forth in that section, except that such personnel shall perform such functions and exercise such powers—

(A) within the Agency Headquarters Compound and the property controlled and occupied by the Federal Highway Administration located immediately adjacent to such Compound;

(B) in the streets, sidewalks, and the open areas within the zone beginning at the outside boundary of such Compound and property and extending outward 500 yards;

(C) within any other Agency installation and protected property;

(D) within an installation owned, or contracted to be occupied for a period of one year or longer, by the Office of the Director of National Intelligence; and

(E) in the streets, sidewalks, and open areas within the zone beginning at the outside boundary of any installation or property referred to in subparagraph (C) or (D) and extending outward 500 yards.

(2) The performance of functions and exercise of powers under subparagraph (B) or (E) of paragraph (1) shall be limited to those circumstances where such personnel can identify specific and articulable facts giving such personnel reason to believe that the performance of such functions and exercise of such powers is reasonable to protect against physical damage or injury, or threats of physical damage or injury, to Agency installations, property, or employees.

(3) Nothing in this subsection shall be construed to preclude, or limit in any way, the authority of any Federal, State, or local law enforcement agency, or any other Federal police or Federal protective service.

(4) The rules and regulations enforced by such personnel shall be the rules and regulations prescribed by the Director and shall only be applicable to the areas referred to in subparagraph (A), (C), or (D) of paragraph (1).

(b) The Director is authorized to establish penalties for violations of the rules or regulations promulgated by the Director under subsection (a) of this section. Such penalties shall not exceed the maximum penalty authorized for a Class B misdemeanor under section 3559 of title 18, United States Code.

(c) Agency personnel designated by the Director under subsection (a) of this section shall be clearly identifiable as United States Government security personnel while engaged in the performance of the functions to which subsection (a) of this section refers.

(d)(1) Notwithstanding any other provision of law, any Agency personnel designated by the Director under subsection (a), or designated by the Director to carry firearms under subparagraph (D) or (E) of section 5(a)(4), shall be considered for purposes of chapter 171 of title 28, United States Code, or any other provision of law relating to tort liability, to be acting within the scope of their office or employment when such Agency personnel take reasonable action, which may include the use of force, to—

(A) protect an individual in the presence of such Agency personnel from a crime of violence;

(B) provide immediate assistance to an individual who has suffered or who is threatened with bodily harm; or

(C) prevent the escape of any individual whom such Agency personnel reasonably believe to have committed a crime of violence in the presence of such Agency personnel.

(2) Paragraph (1) shall not affect the authorities of the Attorney General under section 2679 of title 28, United States Code.

(3) In this subsection, the term "crime of violence" has the meaning given that term in section 16 of title 18, United States Code.

HEALTH BENEFITS FOR CERTAIN FORMER SPOUSES OF CENTRAL INTELLIGENCE AGENCY EMPLOYEES

SEC. 16. [50 U.S.C. 3516] (a) Except as provided in subsection (e), any individual—

(1) formerly married to an employee or former employee of the Agency, whose marriage was dissolved by divorce or annulment before May 7, 1985;

(2) who, at any time during the eighteen-month period before the divorce or annulment became final, was covered under a health benefits plan as a member of the family of such employee or former employee; and

(3) who was married to such employee for not less than ten years during periods of service by such employee with the Agency, at least five years of which were spent outside the United States by both the employee and the former spouse,

is eligible for coverage under a health benefits plan in accordance with the provisions of this section.

(b)(1) Any individual eligible for coverage under subsection (a) may enroll in a health benefits plan for self alone or for self and family if, before the expiration of the six-month period beginning on the effective date of this section, and in accordance with such procedures as the Director of the Office of Personnel Management shall by regulation prescribe, such individual—

(A) files an election for such enrollment; and

(B) arranges to pay currently into the Employees Health Benefits Fund under section 8909 of title 5, United States Code, an amount equal to the sum of the employee and agency contributions payable in the case of an employee enrolled under chapter 89 of such title in the same health benefits plan and with the same level of benefits.

(2) The Director of the Central Intelligence Agency shall, as soon as possible, take all steps practicable—

(A) to determine the identity and current address of each former spouse eligible for coverage under subsection (a); and

(B) to notify each such former spouse of that individual's rights under this section.

(3) The Director of the Office of Personnel Management, upon notification by the Director of the Central Intelligence Agency, shall waive the six-month limitation set forth in paragraph (1) in any case in which the Director of the Central Intelligence Agency determines that the circumstances so warrant.

(c) Eligibility of Former Wives or Husbands.—(1) Notwithstanding subsections (a) and (b) and except as provided in subsections (d), (e), and (f), an individual—

(A) who was divorced on or before December 4, 1991, from a participant or retired participant in the Central Intelligence Agency Retirement and Disability System or the Federal Employees Retirement System Special Category;

(B) who was married to such participant for not less than ten years during the participant's creditable service, at least five years of which were spent by the participant during the participant's service as an employee of the Agency outside the United States, or otherwise in a position the duties of which qualified the participant for designation by the Director as a participant under section 203 of the Central Intelligence Agency Retirement Act (50 U.S.C. 2013); and

(C) who was enrolled in a health benefits plan as a family member at any time during the 18-month period before the date of dissolution of the marriage to such participant;

is eligible for coverage under a health benefits plan.

(2) A former spouse eligible for coverage under paragraph (1) may enroll in a health benefits plan in accordance with subsection (b)(1), except that the election for such enrollment must be submitted within 60 days after the date on which the Director notifies the former spouse of such individual's eligibility for health insurance coverage under this subsection.

(d) CONTINUATION OF ELIGIBILITY.— Notwithstanding subsections (a), (b), and (c) and except as provided in subsections (e) and (f), an individual divorced on or before December 4, 1991, from a participant or retired participant in the Central Intelligence Agency Retirement and Disability System or Federal Employees' Retirement System Special Category who enrolled in a health benefits plan following the dissolution of the marriage to such participant may continue enrollment following the death of such participant notwithstanding the termination of the retirement annuity of such individual.

(e)(1) Any former spouse who remarries before age fifty-five is not eligible to make an election under subsection (b)(1).

(2) Any former spouse enrolled in a health benefits plan pursuant to an election under subsection (b)(1) or to subsection (d) may continue the enrollment under the conditions of eligibility which the Director of the Office of Personnel Management shall by regulation prescribe, except that any former spouse who remarries before age fifty-five shall not be eligible for continued enrollment under this section after the end of the thirty-one-day period beginning on the date of remarriage.

(3)(A) A former spouse who is not eligible to enroll or to continue enrollment in a health benefits plan under this section solely because of remarriage before age fifty-five shall be restored to such eligibility on the date such remarriage is dissolved by death, annulment, or divorce.

(B) A former spouse whose eligibility is restored under subparagraph (A) may, under regulations which the Director of the Office of Personnel Management shall prescribe, enroll in a health benefits plan if such former spouse—

(i) was an individual referred to in paragraph (1) and was an individual covered under a benefits plan as a family member at any time during the 18-month period before the date of dissolution of the marriage to the Agency employee or annuitant; or

(ii) was an individual referred to in paragraph (2) and was an individual covered under a benefits plan immediately before the remarriage ended the enrollment.

(f) No individual may be covered by a health benefits plan under this section during any period in which such individual is enrolled in a health benefits plan under any other authority, nor may any individual be covered under more than one enrollment under this section.

(g) For purposes of this section the term "health benefits plan" means an approved health benefits plan under chapter 89 of title 5, United States Code.

SEC. 17. [50 U.S.C. 3517] INSPECTOR GENERAL FOR THE AGENCY.

(a) PURPOSE; ESTABLISHMENT.—In order to—

(1) create an objective and effective office, appropriately accountable to Congress, to initiate and conduct independently inspections, investigations, and audits relating to programs and operations of the Agency;

(2) provide leadership and recommend policies designed to promote economy, efficiency, and effectiveness in the administration of such programs and operations, and detect fraud and abuse in such programs and operations;

(3) provide a means for keeping the Director fully and currently informed about problems and deficiencies relating to the administration of such programs and operations, and the necessity for and the progress of corrective actions; and

(4) in the manner prescribed by this section, ensure that the Senate Select Committee on Intelligence and the House Permanent Select Committee on Intelligence (hereafter in this section referred to collectively as the "intelligence committees") are kept similarly informed of significant problems and deficiencies as well as the necessity for and the progress of corrective actions,

there is hereby established in the Agency an Office of Inspector General (hereafter in this section referred to as the "Office").

(b) APPOINTMENT; SUPERVISION; REMOVAL.—(1) There shall be at the head of the Office an Inspector General who shall be appointed by the President, by and with the advice and consent of the Senate. This appointment shall be made without regard to political affiliation and shall be on the basis of integrity and demonstrated ability in accounting, auditing, financial analysis, law, management analysis, public administration, or investigation. Such appointment shall also be made on the basis of compliance with the security standards of the Agency and prior experience in the field of foreign intelligence.

(2) The Inspector General shall report directly to and be under the general supervision of the Director.

(3) The Director may prohibit the Inspector General from initiating, carrying out, or completing any audit, inspection, or investigation if the Director determines that such prohibition is necessary to protect vital national security interests of the United States.

(4) If the Director exercises any power under paragraph (3), he shall submit an appropriately classified statement of the reasons for the exercise of such power within seven days to the intelligence committees. The Director shall advise the Inspector General at the time such report is submitted, and, to the extent consistent with the protection of intelligence sources and methods, provide the Inspector General with a copy of any such report. In such cases, the Inspector General may submit such comments to the intelligence committees that he considers appropriate.

(5) In accordance with section 535 of title 28, United States Code, the Inspector General shall report to the Attorney General any information, allegation, or complaint received by the Inspector General relating to violations of Federal criminal law that involve a program or operation of the Agency, consistent with such guidelines as may be issued by the Attorney General pursuant to subsection (b)(2) of such section. A copy of all such reports shall be furnished to the Director.

(6)(A) The Inspector General may be removed from office only by the President. The President shall communicate in writing to the intelligence committees the substantive rationale, including detailed and case-specific reasons, for any such removal not later than 30 days prior to the effective date of such removal. Nothing in this paragraph shall be construed to prohibit a personnel action otherwise authorized by law, other than transfer or removal.

(B)[7] If there is an open or completed inquiry into the Inspector General that relates to the removal or transfer of the Inspector General under subparagraph (A), the written communication required under that subparagraph shall—

(i) identify each entity that is conducting, or that conducted, the inquiry; and

(ii) in the case of a completed inquiry, contain the findings made during the inquiry.

---

[7] Margins of paragraphs (6)(B) and (7)

---

(7)(A) Subject to the other provisions of this paragraph, only the President may place the Inspector General on nonduty status.

(B) If the President places the Inspector General on nonduty status, the President shall communicate in writing the substantive rationale, including detailed and case-specific reasons, for the change in status to the congressional intelligence committees not later than 15 days before the date on which the change in status takes effect, except that the President may submit that communication not later than the date on which the change in status takes effect if—

(i) the President has made a determination that the continued presence of the Inspector General in the workplace poses a threat described in any of clauses (i) through (iv) of section 6329b(b)(2)(A) of title 5, United States Code; and

(ii) in the communication, the President includes a report on the determination described in clause (i), which shall include—

(I) a specification of which clause of section 6329b(b)(2)(A) of title 5, United States Code, the President has determined applies under clause (i);

(II) the substantive rationale, including detailed and case-specific reasons, for the determination made under clause (i);

(III) an identification of each entity that is conducting, or that conducted, any inquiry upon which the determination under clause (i) was made; and

(IV) in the case of an inquiry described in subclause (III) that is completed, the findings made during that inquiry.

(C) The President may not place the Inspector General on non-duty status during the 30-day period preceding the date on which the Inspector General is removed or transferred under paragraph (6)(A) unless the President—

(i) has made a determination that the continued presence of the Inspector

General in the workplace poses a threat described in any of clauses (i) through (iv) of section 6329b(b)(2)(A) of title 5, United States Code; and

(ii) not later than the date on which the change in status takes effect, submits to the congressional intelligence committees a written communication that contains the information required under subparagraph (B), including the report required under clause (ii) of that subparagraph.

(8)(A)[8] In this subsection, the term "first assistant to the position of Inspector General" has the meaning given in section 3 of the Inspector General Act of 1978 (5 U.S.C. App.).

[8] Margin of paragraph (8) is so in law.

(B) If the Inspector General dies, resigns, or is otherwise unable to perform the functions and duties of the position—

(i) section 3345(a) of title 5, United States Code shall not apply;

(ii) subject to subparagraph (D), the first assistant to the position of Inspector General shall perform the functions and duties of the Inspector General temporarily in an acting capacity subject to the time limitations of section 3346 of title 5, United States Code; and

(iii) notwithstanding clause (ii), and subject to subparagraphs (D) and (E), the President (and only the President) may direct an officer or employee of any Office of an Inspector General to perform the functions and duties of the Inspector General temporarily in an acting capacity subject to the time limitations of section 3346 of title 5, United States Code, only if—

(I) during the 365-day period preceding the date of death, resignation, or beginning of inability to serve of the Inspector General, the officer or employee served in a position in an Office of an Inspector General for not less than 90 days, except that—

(aa) the requirement under this subclause shall not apply if the officer is an Inspector General; and

(bb) for the purposes of this clause, performing the functions and duties of an Inspector General temporarily in an acting capacity does not qualify as service in a position in an Office of an Inspector General;

(II) the rate of pay for the position of the officer or employee described in subclause (I) is equal to or greater than the minimum rate of pay payable for a position at GS–15 of the General Schedule;

(III) the officer or employee has demonstrated ability in accounting, auditing, financial analysis, law, management analysis, public administration, or investigations; and

(IV) not later than 30 days before the date on which the direction takes effect, the President communicates in writing to the congressional intelligence committees the substantive rationale, including the detailed and case-specific reasons, for such direction, including the reason for the direction that someone other than the individual who is performing the functions and duties of the Inspector General temporarily in an acting capacity (as of the date on which the President issues that direction) perform those functions and duties temporarily in an acting capacity.

(C) Notwithstanding section 3345(a) of title 5, United States Code and clauses (ii) and (iii) of subparagraph (B), and subject to subparagraph (D), during any period in which the Inspector General is on nonduty status—

(i) the first assistant to the position of Inspector General shall perform the functions and duties of the position temporarily in an acting capacity subject to the time limitations of section 3346 of title 5, United States Code; and

(ii) if the first assistant described in clause (i) dies, resigns, or becomes otherwise unable to perform those functions and duties, the President (and only the President) may direct an officer or employee in the Office of Inspector General to perform those functions and duties temporarily in an acting capacity, subject to the time limitations of section 3346 of title 5, United States Code, if—

(I) that direction satisfies the requirements under subclauses (II), (III), and (IV) of subparagraph (B)(iii); and

(II) that officer or employee served in a position in that Office of Inspector General for not fewer than 90 of the 365 days preceding the date on which the President makes that direction.

(D) An individual may perform the functions and duties of the Inspector General temporarily and in an acting capacity under clause (ii) or (iii) of subparagraph (B), or under subparagraph (C), with respect to only 1 Inspector General position at any given time.

(E) If the President makes a direction under subparagraph (B)(iii), during the 30-day period preceding the date on which the direction of the President takes effect, the functions and duties of the position of the Inspector General shall be performed by—

(i) the first assistant to the position of Inspector General; or

(ii) the individual performing those functions and duties temporarily in an acting capacity, as of the date on which the President issues that direction, if that individual is an individual other than the first assistant to the position of Inspector General.

(c) Duties and Responsibilities.—It shall be the duty and responsibility of the Inspector General appointed under this section—

(1) to provide policy direction for, and to plan, conduct, supervise, and coordinate independently, the inspections, investigations, and audits relating to the programs and operations of the Agency to ensure they are conducted efficiently and in accordance with applicable law and regulations;

(2) to keep the Director fully and currently informed concerning violations of law and regulations, fraud and other serious problems, abuses and deficiencies that may occur in such programs and operations, and to report the progress made in implementing corrective action;

(3) to take due regard for the protection of intelligence sources and methods in the preparation of all reports issued by the Office, and, to the extent consistent with

the purpose and objective of such reports, take such measures as may be appropriate to minimize the disclosure of intelligence sources and methods described in such reports; and

(4) in the execution of his responsibilities, to comply with generally accepted government auditing standards.

(d) SEMIANNUAL REPORTS; IMMEDIATE REPORTS OF SERIOUS OR FLAGRANT PROBLEMS; REPORTS OF FUNCTIONAL PROBLEMS; REPORTS TO CONGRESS ON URGENT CONCERNS.—(1) The Inspector General shall, not later than October 31 and April 30 of each year, prepare and submit to the Director a classified semiannual report summarizing the activities of the Office during the immediately preceding six-month periods ending September 30 and March 31, respectively. Not later than 30 days after the date of the receipt of such reports, the Director shall transmit such reports to the intelligence committees with any comments he may deem appropriate. Such reports shall, at a minimum, include a list of the title or subject of each inspection, investigation, review, or audit conducted during the reporting period and—

(A) a description of significant problems, abuses, and deficiencies relating to the administration of programs and operations of the Agency identified by the Office during the reporting period;

(B) a description of the recommendations for corrective action made by the Office during the reporting period with respect to significant problems, abuses, or deficiencies identified in subparagraph (A);

(C) a statement of whether corrective action has been completed on each significant recommendation described in previous semiannual reports, and, in a case where corrective action has been completed, a description of such corrective action;

(D) a certification that the Inspector General has had full and direct access to all information relevant to the performance of his functions;

(E) a description of the exercise of the subpoena authority under subsection (e)(5) by the Inspector General during the reporting period; and

(F) such recommendations as the Inspector General may wish to make concerning legislation to promote economy and efficiency in the administration of programs and operations undertaken by the Agency, and to detect and eliminate fraud and abuse in such programs and operations.

(2) The Inspector General shall report immediately to the Director whenever he becomes aware of particularly serious or flagrant problems, abuses, or deficiencies relating to the administration of programs or operations. The Director shall transmit such report to the intelligence committees within seven calendar days, together with any comments he considers appropriate.

(3) In the event that—

(A) the Inspector General is unable to resolve any differences with the Director affecting the execution of the Inspector General's duties or responsibilities;

(B) an investigation, inspection, or audit carried out by the Inspector General should focus on any current or former Agency official who—

(i) holds or held a position in the Agency that is subject to appointment by the President, by and with the advice and consent of the Senate, including such a position held on an acting basis; or

(ii) holds or held the position in the Agency, including such a position held on an acting basis, of—

(I) Deputy Director;

(II) Associate Deputy Director;

(III) Director of the National Clandestine Service;

(IV) Director of Intelligence;

(V) Director of Support; or

(VI) Director of Science and Technology.

(C) a matter requires a report by the Inspector General to the Department of Justice on possible criminal conduct by a current or former Agency official described or referred to in subparagraph (B);

(D) the Inspector General receives notice from the Department of Justice declining or approving prosecution of possible criminal conduct of any of the officials described in subparagraph (B); or

(E) the Inspector General, after exhausting all possible alternatives, is unable to obtain significant documentary information in the course of an investigation, inspection, or audit,

the Inspector General shall immediately notify and submit a report on such matter to the intelligence committees.

(4) Pursuant to Title V of the National Security Act of 1947, the Director shall submit to the intelligence committees any report or findings and recommendations of an inspection, investigation, or audit conducted by the office which has been requested by the Chairman or Ranking Minority Member of either committee.

(5)(A)(i) An employee of the Agency, or of a contractor to the Agency, who intends to report to Congress a complaint or information with respect to an urgent concern may report such complaint or information in writing to the Inspector General.

(ii) The Inspector General shall—

(I) provide reasonable support necessary to ensure that an employee can report a complaint or information under this subparagraph in writing; and

(II) if such submission is not feasible, create a written record of the employee's verbal complaint or information and treat such written record as a written submission.

(B)(i) In accordance with clause (ii), the Inspector General shall determine whether a complaint or information reported under subparagraph (A) appears credible. Upon making such a determination, the Inspector General shall transmit to the Director a notice of that determination, together with the complaint or information.

(ii) The Inspector General shall make the determination under clause (i) with respect to a complaint or information under subparagraph (A) by not later than the end of the 14-calendar-day period beginning on the date on which the employee who reported the complaint or information confirms to the Inspector General the intent of the employee to report to Congress that complaint or information.

(iii) If the Director determines that a complaint or information transmitted under subparagraph (A) would create a conflict of interest for the Director, the Director shall return the complaint or information to the Inspector General with that determination and the Inspector General shall make the transmission to the Director of National Intelligence. In such a case, the requirements of this subsection for the Director of the Central Intelligence Agency apply to the Director of National Intelligence.

(C) Upon receipt of a transmittal from the Inspector General under subparagraph (B), the Director shall, within 7 calendar days of such receipt, forward such transmittal to the intelligence committees, together with any comments the Director considers appropriate.

(D)(i) If the Inspector General does not find credible under subparagraph (B) a complaint or information submitted under subparagraph (A), or does not transmit the complaint or information to the Director in accurate form under subparagraph (B), the employee (subject to clause (ii)) may submit the complaint or information to Congress by contacting either or both of the intelligence committees directly.

(ii) The employee may contact the intelligence committees directly as described in clause (i) only if the employee—

(I) before making such a contact, furnishes to the Director, through the Inspector General, a statement of the employee's complaint or information and notice of the employee's intent to contact the intelligence committees directly; and

(II) obtains and follows from the Director, through the Inspector General, direction on how to contact the intelligence committees in accordance with appropriate security practices.

(iii) A member or employee of one of the intelligence committees who receives a complaint or information under clause (i) does so in that member or employee's official capacity as a member or employee of that committee.

(E) The Inspector General shall notify an employee who reports a complaint or information to the Inspector General under this paragraph of each action taken under this paragraph with respect to the complaint or information. Such notice shall be provided not later than 3 days after any such action is taken.

(F) An action taken by the Director or the Inspector General under this paragraph shall not be subject to judicial review.

(G)(i) In this paragraph:

(I) The term "urgent concern" means any of the following:

(aa) A serious or flagrant problem, abuse, violation of law or Executive order, or deficiency relating to the funding, administration, or operations of an intelligence activity of the Federal Government that is—

(AA)[9] a matter of national security; and

---

[9] The margin of subitems (AA) and (BB) are so in law.

(BB) not a difference of opinion concerning public policy matters.

(bb) A false statement to Congress, or a willful withholding from Congress, on an issue of material fact relating to the funding, administration, or operation of an intelligence activity.

(cc) An action, including a personnel action described in section 2302(a)(2)(A) of title 5, United States Code, constituting reprisal or threat of reprisal prohibited under subsection (e)(3)(B) in response to an employee's reporting an urgent concern in accordance with this paragraph.

(II) The term "intelligence committees" means the Permanent Select Committee on Intelligence of the House of Representatives and the Select Committee on Intelligence of the Senate.

(III) The term "employee" includes a former employee or former contractor, if the complaint or information reported under subparagraph (A) arises from or relates to the period during which the former employee or former contractor was an employee or contractor, as the case may be.

(ii) Within the executive branch, the Inspector General shall have sole authority to determine whether any complaint or information reported to the Inspector General is a matter of urgent concern under this paragraph.

(H) An individual who has submitted a complaint or information to the Inspector General under this section may notify any member of the Permanent Select Committee on Intelligence of the House of Representatives or the Select Committee on Intelligence of the Senate, or a staff member of either such Committee, of the fact that such individual has made a submission to the Inspector General, and of the date on which such submission was made.

(e) AUTHORITIES OF THE INSPECTOR GENERAL.—(1) The Inspector General shall have direct and prompt access to the Director when necessary for any purpose pertaining to the performance of his duties.

(2) The Inspector General shall have access to any employee or any employee of a contractor of the Agency whose testimony is needed for the performance of his duties. In addition, he shall have direct access to all records, reports, audits, reviews, documents, papers, recommendations, or other material which relate to the programs and operations with respect to which the Inspector General has responsibilities under this section. Failure on the part of any employee or contractor to cooperate with the Inspector General shall be grounds for appropriate administrative actions by the Director, to include loss of employment or the termination of an existing contractual relationship.

(3)(A) The Inspector General is authorized to receive and investigate complaints or information from any person concerning the existence of an activity constituting a violation of laws, rules, or regulations, or mismanagement, gross waste of funds, abuse of authority, or a substantial and specific danger to the public health and safety. Once such complaint or information has been received from an employee of the Agency—

(i) the Inspector General shall not disclose the identity of the employee without the consent of the employee, unless the Inspector General determines that such disclosure is unavoidable during the course of the investigation or the disclosure is made to an official of the Department of Justice responsible for determining whether a prosecution should be undertaken; and

(ii) no action constituting a reprisal, or threat of reprisal, for making such complaint or providing such information may be taken by any employee of the Agency in a position to take such actions, unless the complaint was made or the information was disclosed with the knowledge that it was false or with willful disregard for its truth or falsity.

(B)(i) An individual may disclose classified information to the Inspector General in accordance with the applicable security standards and procedures established under section 102A or 803 of the National Security Act of 1947 (50 U.S.C. 3024, 3162a), chapter 12 of the Atomic Energy Act of 1954 (42 U.S.C. 2161 et seq.), Executive Order 13526 (50 U.S.C. 3161 note; relating to Classified National Security Information), or any applicable provision of law.

(ii) A disclosure under clause (i) of classified information made by an individual without appropriate clearance or authority to access such classified information at the time of the disclosure, but that is otherwise made in accordance with applicable security standards and procedures, shall be treated as an authorized disclosure that does not violate a covered provision.

(iii) Nothing in clause (ii) may be construed to limit or modify the obligation of an individual to appropriately store, handle, or disseminate classified information in accordance with applicable security guidance and procedures, including with respect to the removal or retention of classified information.

(iv) In this subparagraph, the term "covered provision" means—

(I) any otherwise applicable nondisclosure agreement;

(II) any otherwise applicable regulation or order issued under the authority of chapter 18 of the Atomic Energy Act of 1954 (42 U.S.C. 2271 et seq.) or Executive Order 13526;

(III) section 798 of title 18, United States Code; or

(IV) any other provision of law with respect to the unauthorized disclosure of national security information.

(4) The Inspector General shall have authority to administer to or take from any person an oath, affirmation, or affidavit, whenever necessary in the performance of his duties, which oath, affirmation, or affidavit when administered or taken by or before an employee of the Office designated by the Inspector General shall have the same force and effect as if administered or taken by or before an officer having a seal.

(5)(A) Except as provided in subparagraph (B), the Inspector General is authorized to require by subpoena the production of all information, documents, reports, answers, records, accounts, papers, and other data in any medium (including electronically stored information or any tangible thing) and documentary evidence necessary in the performance of the duties and responsibilities of the Inspector

General.

(B) In the case of Government agencies, the Inspector General shall obtain information, documents, reports, answers, records, accounts, papers, and other data and evidence for the purpose specified in subparagraph (A) using procedures other than by subpoenas.

(C) The Inspector General may not issue a subpoena for or on behalf of any other element or component of the Agency.

(D) In the case of contumacy or refusal to obey a subpoena issued under this paragraph, the subpoena shall be enforceable by order of any appropriate district court of the United States.

(6) The Inspector General shall be provided with appropriate and adequate office space at central and field office locations, together with such equipment, office supplies, maintenance services, and communications facilities and services as may be necessary for the operation of such offices.

(7)(A) Subject to applicable law and the policies of the Director, the Inspector General shall select, appoint and employ such officers and employees as may be necessary to carry out his functions. In making such selections, the Inspector General shall ensure that such officers and employees have the requisite training and experience to enable him to carry out his duties effectively. In this regard, the Inspector General shall create within his organization a career cadre of sufficient size to provide appropriate continuity and objectivity needed for the effective performance of his duties.

(B) Consistent with budgetary and personnel resources allocated by the Director, the Inspector General has final approval of—

(i) the selection of internal and external candidates for employment with the Office of Inspector General; and

(ii) all other personnel decisions concerning personnel permanently assigned to the Office of Inspector General, including selection and appointment to the Senior Intelligence Service, but excluding all security-based determinations that are not within the authority of a head of other Central Intelligence Agency offices.

(C)(i) The Inspector General may designate an officer or employee appointed in accordance with subparagraph (A) as a law enforcement officer solely for purposes of subchapter III of chapter 83 or chapter 84 of title 5, United States Code, if such officer or employee is appointed to a position with responsibility for investigating suspected offenses against the criminal laws of the United States.

(ii) In carrying out clause (i), the Inspector General shall ensure that any authority under such clause is exercised in a manner consistent with section 3307 of title 5, United States Code, as it relates to law enforcement officers.

(iii) For purposes of applying sections 3307(d), 8335(b), and 8425(b) of title 5, United States Code, the Inspector General may exercise the functions, powers, and duties of an agency head or appointing authority with respect to the Office.

(8)(A) The Inspector General shall—

(i) appoint a Counsel to the Inspector General who shall report to the Inspector General; or

(ii) obtain the services of a counsel appointed by and directly reporting to another Inspector General or the Council of the Inspectors General on Integrity and Efficiency on a reimbursable basis.

(B) The counsel appointed or obtained under subparagraph (A) shall perform such functions as the Inspector General may prescribe.

(9)(A) The Inspector General may request such information or assistance as may be necessary for carrying out the duties and responsibilities of the Inspector General provided by this section from any Federal, State, or local governmental agency or unit thereof.

(B) Upon request of the Inspector General for information or assistance from a department or agency of the Federal Government, the head of the department or agency involved, insofar as practicable and not in contravention of any existing statutory restriction or regulation of such department or agency, shall furnish to the Inspector General, or to an authorized designee, such information or assistance.

(C) Nothing in this paragraph may be construed to provide any new authority to the Central Intelligence Agency to conduct intelligence activity in the United States.

(D) In this paragraph, the term "State" means each of the several States, the District of Columbia, the Commonwealth of Puerto Rico, the Commonwealth of the Northern Mariana Islands, and any territory or possession of the United States.

(f) SEPARATE BUDGET ACCOUNT.—(1) Beginning with fiscal year 1991, and in accordance with procedures to be issued by the Director of National Intelligence in consultation with the intelligence committees, the Director of National Intelligence shall include in the National Intelligence Program budget a separate account for the Office of Inspector General established pursuant to this section.

(2) For each fiscal year, the Inspector General shall transmit a budget estimate and request through the Director to the Director of National Intelligence that specifies for such fiscal year—

(A) the aggregate amount requested for the operations of the Inspector General;

(B) the amount requested for all training requirements of the Inspector General, including a certification from the Inspector General that the amount requested is sufficient to fund all training requirements for the Office; and

(C) the amount requested to support the Council of the Inspectors General on Integrity and Efficiency, including a justification for such amount.

(3) In transmitting a proposed budget to the President for a fiscal year, the Director of National Intelligence shall include for such fiscal year—

(A) the aggregate amount requested for the Inspector General of the Central Intelligence Agency;

(B) the amount requested for Inspector General training;

(C) the amount requested to support the Council of the Inspectors General on Integrity and Efficiency; and

(D) the comments of the Inspector General, if any, with respect to such proposed budget.

(4) The Director of National Intelligence shall submit to the Committee on Appropriations and the Select Committee on Intelligence of the Senate and the Committee on Appropriations and the Permanent Select Committee on Intelligence of the House of Representatives for each fiscal year—

(A) a separate statement of the budget estimate transmitted pursuant to paragraph (2);

(B) the amount requested by the Director of National Intelligence for the Inspector General pursuant to paragraph (3)(A);

(C) the amount requested by the Director of National Intelligence for training of personnel of the Office of the Inspector General pursuant to paragraph (3)(B);

(D) the amount requested by the Director of National Intelligence for support for the Council of the Inspectors General on Integrity and Efficiency pursuant to paragraph (3)(C); and

(E) the comments of the Inspector General under paragraph (3)(D), if any, on the amounts requested pursuant to paragraph (3), including whether such amounts would substantially inhibit the Inspector General from performing the duties of the Office.

(g) TRANSFER.— There shall be transferred to the Office the office of the Agency referred to as the "Office of Inspector General." The personnel, assets, liabilities, contracts, property, records, and unexpended balances of appropriations, authorizations, allocations, and other funds employed, held, used, arising from, or available to such "Office of Inspector General" are hereby transferred to the Office established pursuant to this section.

(h) INFORMATION ON WEBSITE.—(1) The Director of the Central Intelligence Agency shall establish and maintain on the homepage of the Agency's publicly accessible website information relating to the Office of the Inspector General including methods to contact the Inspector General.

(2) The information referred to in paragraph (1) shall be obvious and facilitate accessibility to the information related to the Office of the Inspector General.

SPECIAL ANNUITY COMPUTATION RULES FOR CERTAIN EMPLOYEES' SERVICE ABROAD

SEC. 18. [50 U.S.C. 3518] (a) Notwithstanding any provision of chapter 83 of title 5, United States Code, the annuity under subchapter III of such chapter of an officer or employee of the Central Intelligence Agency who retires on or after October 1, 1989, is not designated under section 203 of the Central Intelligence Agency Retirement Act, and has served abroad as an officer or employee of the Agency on or after January 1, 1987, shall be computed as provided in subsection (b).

(b)(1) The portion of the annuity relating to such service abroad that is actually performed at any time during the officer's or employee's first ten years of total service shall be computed at the rate and using the percent of average pay specified in section 8339(a)(3) of title 5, United States Code, that is normally applicable only to so much of an employee's total service as exceeds ten years.

(2) The portion of the annuity relating to service abroad as described in subsection (a) but that is actually performed at any time after the officer's or employee's first ten years of total service shall be computed as provided in section 8339(a)(3) of title 5, United States Code; but, in addition, the officer or employee shall be deemed for annuity computation purposes to have actually performed an equivalent period of service abroad during his or her first ten years of total service, and in calculating the portion of the officer's or employee's annuity for his or her first ten years of total service, the computation rate and percent of average pay specified in paragraph (1) shall also be applied to the period of such deemed or equivalent service abroad.

(3) The portion of the annuity relating to other service by an officer or employee as described in subsection (a) shall be computed as provided in the provisions of section 8339(a) of title 5, United States Code, that would otherwise be applicable to such service.

(4) For purposes of this subsection, the term "total service" has the meaning given such term under chapter 83 of title 5, United States Code.

(c) For purposes of subsections (f) through (m) of section 8339 of title 5, United States Code, an annuity computed under this section shall be deemed to be an annuity computed under subsections (a) and (o) of section 8339 of title 5, United States Code.

(d) The provisions of subsection (a) of this section shall not apply to an officer or employee of the Central Intelligence Agency who would otherwise be entitled to a greater annuity computed under an otherwise applicable subsection of section 8339 of title 5, United States Code.

SPECIAL RULES FOR DISABILITY RETIREMENT AND DEATH-IN-SERVICE BENEFITS WITH RESPECT TO CERTAIN EMPLOYEES

SEC. 19. [50 U.S.C. 3519] (a) OFFICERS AND EMPLOYEES TO WHOM CIARDS SECTION 231 RULES APPLY.—Notwithstanding any other provision of law, an officer or employee of the Central Intelligence Agency subject to retirement system coverage under subchapter III of chapter 83 of title 5, United States Code, who—

(1) has five years of civilian service credit toward retirement under such subchapter III of chapter 83, title 5, United States Code;

(2) has not been designated under section 203 of the Central Intelligence Agency Retirement Act (50 U.S.C. 403 note)as a participant in the Central Intelligence Agency Retirement and Disability System;

(3) has become disabled during a period of assignment to the performance of duties that are qualifying toward such designation under such section 203; and

(4) satisfies the requirements for disability retirement under section 8337 of title 5, United States Code—

shall, upon his own application or upon order of the Director, be retired on an annuity computed in accordance with the rules prescribed in section 231 of such Act, in lieu of an annuity computed as provided by section 8337 of title 5, United States Code.

(b) SURVIVORS OF OFFICERS AND EMPLOYEES TO WHOM CIARDS SECTION 232 RULES APPLY.—Notwithstanding any other provision of law, in the case of an officer or employee of the Central Intelligence Agency subject to retirement system coverage under subchapter III of chapter 83, title 5, United States Code, who—

(1) has at least eighteen months of civilian service credit toward retirement under such subchapter III of chapter 83, title 5, United States Code;

(2) has not been designated under section 203 of the Central Intelligence Agency Retirement Act (50 U.S.C. 2013), as a participant in the Central Intelligence Agency Retirement and Disability System;

(3) prior to separation or retirement from the Agency, dies during a period of assignment to the performance of duties that are qualifying toward such designation under such section 203; and

(4) is survived by a widow or widower, former spouse, and/or a child or children as defined in section 204 and section 232 of the Central Intelligence Agency Retirement Act of 1964 for Certain Employees[10], who would otherwise be entitled to an annuity under section 8341 of title 5, United States Code—

[10] The amendment made by section 803(a)(3)(B)(iii) of P.L. 102–496 (106 Stat. 3252) was not executable. The amendment strikes "widow or widower, former spouse, and/or child or children as defined in section 204 and section 232 of such the Central Intelligence Agency Retirement Act of 1964 for Certain Employees" and inserts "surviving spouse, former spouse, or child as defined in section 102 of the Central Intelligence Agency Retirement Act".

such surviving spouse, former spouse, or child of such officer or employee shall be entitled to an annuity computed in accordance with section 232 of such Act, in lieu of an annuity computed in accordance with section 8341 of title 5, United States Code.

(c) Annuities Under This Section Deemed Annuities Under CSRS.— The annuities provided under subsections (a) and (b) of this section shall be deemed to be annuities under chapter 83 of title 5, United States Code, for purposes of the other provisions of such chapter and other laws (including the Internal Revenue Code of 1986) relating to such annuities, and shall be payable from the Central Intelligence Agency Retirement and Disability Fund maintained pursuant to section 202 of the Central Intelligence Agency Retirement Act.

SEC. 19A. [50 U.S.C. 3519b] SPECIAL RULES FOR CERTAIN INDIVIDUALS INJURED BY REASON OF WAR, INSURGENCY, HOSTILE ACT, TERRORIST ACTIVITIES, OR INCIDENTS DESIGNATED BY THE DIRECTOR.

(a) Definitions.—In this section:

(1) Covered dependent.—The term "covered dependent" means a family member (as defined by the Director) of a covered employee who, on or after September 11, 2001—

(A) accompanies the covered employee to an assigned duty station in a foreign country; and

(B) becomes injured by reason of a qualifying injury.

(2) Covered employee.— The term "covered employee" means an officer or employee of the Central Intelligence Agency who, on or after September 11, 2001, becomes injured by reason of a qualifying injury.

(3) Covered individual.—The term "covered individual" means an individual

who—

(A)(i) is detailed to the Central Intelligence Agency from other agencies of the United States Government or from the Armed Forces; or

(ii) is affiliated with the Central Intelligence Agency, as determined by the Director; and

(B) who, on or after September 11, 2001, becomes injured by reason of a qualifying injury.

(4) QUALIFYING INJURY.—The term "qualifying injury" means the following:

(A) With respect to a covered dependent, an injury incurred—

(i) during a period in which the covered dependent is accompanying the covered employee to an assigned duty station in a foreign country;

(ii) in connection with war, insurgency, hostile act, terrorist activity, or an incident designated for purposes of this section by the Director; and

(iii) that was not the result of the willful misconduct of the covered dependent.

(B) With respect to a covered employee or a covered individual—

(i) an injury incurred—

(I) during a period of assignment to a duty station in a foreign country;

(II) in connection with war, insurgency, hostile act, or terrorist activity; and

(III) that was not the result of the willful misconduct of the covered employee or the covered individual; or

(ii) an injury incurred—

(I) in connection with an incident designated for purposes of this section by the Director; and

(II) that was not the result of the willful misconduct of the covered employee or the covered individual.

(b) ADJUSTMENT OF COMPENSATION FOR TOTAL DISABILITY RESULTING FROM CERTAIN INJURIES.—

(1) INCREASE.—The Director may increase the amount of monthly compensation paid to a covered employee under section 8105 of title 5, United States Code. Subject to paragraph (2), the Director may determine the amount of each such increase by taking into account—

(A) the severity of the qualifying injury;

(B) the circumstances by which the covered employee became injured; and

(C) the seniority of the covered employee.

(2) MAXIMUM.— Notwithstanding chapter 81 of title 5, United States Code, the total amount of monthly compensation increased under paragraph (1) may not exceed the monthly pay of the maximum rate of basic pay for GS–15 of the General Schedule under section 5332 of such title.

(c) COSTS FOR TREATING QUALIFYING INJURIES.— The Director may pay the costs of treating a qualifying injury of a covered employee, a covered individual, or a covered dependent, or may reimburse a covered employee, a covered individual, or a covered dependent for such costs, that are not otherwise covered by chapter 81 of title 5, United States Code, or other provision of Federal law.

(d) AUTHORITY TO MAKE PAYMENTS FOR QUALIFYING INJURIES TO THE BRAIN.—

(1) DEFINITIONS.—In this subsection:

(A) COVERED DEPENDENT.— The term "covered dependent" has the meaning given such term in subsection (a), except that the assigned duty station need not be in a foreign country.

(B) QUALIFYING INJURY.— The term "qualifying injury" has the meaning given such term in subsection (a), except that the assigned duty station need not be in a foreign country.

(2) AUTHORITY.— Notwithstanding any other provision of law but subject to paragraph (3), the Director may provide payment to a covered dependent, a covered employee, and a covered individual for a qualifying injury to the brain.

(3) FUNDING.—

(A) IN GENERAL.—Payment under paragraph (2) in a fiscal year may be made using any funds—

(i) appropriated specifically for payments under such paragraph; or

(ii) reprogrammed in accordance with section 504 of the National Security Act of 1947 (50 U.S.C. 3094).

(B) BUDGET.— For each fiscal year, the Director shall include with the budget justification materials submitted to Congress in support of the budget of the President for that fiscal year pursuant to section 1105(a) of title 31, United States Code, an estimate of the funds required in that fiscal year to make payments under paragraph (2).

(4) REGULATIONS.—

(A) IN GENERAL.— The Director shall prescribe regulations to carry out this subsection.

(B) ELEMENTS.— The regulations prescribed under subparagraph (A) shall include regulations detailing fair and equitable criteria for payment under paragraph (2).

(5) NO EFFECT ON OTHER BENEFITS.—

(A) IN GENERAL.— Payments made under paragraph (2) are supplemental to any other benefit furnished by the United States Government for which a covered dependent, covered employee, or covered individual is entitled, and the receipt of such payments may not affect the eligibility of such a person to any other benefit furnished by the United States Government.

(B) RELATION TO CERTAIN FEDERAL WORKERS COMPENSATION LAWS.— Without regard to the requirements in sections (b) and (c), covered employees need not first seek benefits provided under chapter 81 of title 5, United States Code, to be eligible solely for payment authorized under paragraph (2) of this subsection.

GENERAL COUNSEL OF THE CENTRAL INTELLIGENCE AGENCY

SEC. 20. [50 U.S.C. 3520] (a) There is a General Counsel of the Central Intelligence Agency, appointed from civilian life by the President, by and with the advice and consent of the Senate.

(b) The General Counsel is the chief legal officer of the Central Intelligence Agency.

(c) The General Counsel of the Central Intelligence Agency shall perform such functions as the Director may prescribe.

CENTRAL SERVICES PROGRAM

SEC. 21. [50 U.S.C. 3521] (a) IN GENERAL.— The Director may carry out a program under which elements of the Agency provide items and services on a reimbursable basis to other elements of the Agency, nonappropriated fund entities or instrumentalities associated or affiliated with the Agency, and other Government agencies. The Director shall carry out the program in accordance with the provisions of this section.

(b) PARTICIPATION OF AGENCY ELEMENTS.—(1) In order to carry out the program, the Director shall—

(A) designate the elements of the Agency that are to provide items or services under the program (in this section referred to as "central service providers");

(B) specify the items or services to be provided under the program by such providers;

(C) assign to such providers for purposes of the program such inventories, equipment, and other assets (including equipment on order) as the Director determines necessary to permit such providers to provide items or services under the program; and

(D) authorize such providers to make known their services to the entities specified in subsection (a) through Government communication channels.

(2) The designation of elements and the specification of items and services under paragraph (1) shall be subject to the approval of the Director of the Office of Management and Budget.

(3) The authority in paragraph (1)(D) does not include the authority to distribute gifts or promotional items.

(c) CENTRAL SERVICES WORKING CAPITAL FUND.—(1) There is established a fund to be known as the Central Services Working Capital Fund (in this section referred to as the "Fund"). The purpose of the Fund is to provide sums for activities under the program.

(2) There shall be deposited in the Fund the following:

(A) Amounts appropriated to the Fund.

(B) Amounts credited to the Fund from payments received by central service providers under subsection (e).

(C) Fees imposed and collected under subsection (f)(1).

(D) Amounts received in payment for loss or damage to equipment or property of a central service provider as a result of activities under the program.

(E) Other receipts from the sale or exchange of equipment, recyclable materials, or property of a central service provider as a result of activities under the program.

(F) Receipts from individuals in reimbursement for utility services and meals provided under the program.

(G) Receipts from individuals for the rental of property and equipment under the program.

(H) Such other amounts as the Director is authorized to deposit in or transfer to the Fund.

(3) Amounts in the Fund shall be available, without fiscal year limitation, for the following purposes:

(A) To pay the costs of providing items or services under the program.

(B) To pay the costs of carrying out activities under subsections (b)(1)(D) and (f)(2).

(d) Limitation on Amount of Orders.— The total value of all orders for items or services to be provided under the program in any fiscal year may not exceed an amount specified in advance by the Director of the Office of Management and Budget.

(e) Payment for Items and Services.—(1) A Government agency provided items or services under the program shall pay the central service provider concerned for such items or services an amount equal to the costs incurred by the provider in providing such items or services plus any fee imposed under subsection (f). In calculating such costs, the Director shall take into account personnel costs (including costs associated with salaries, annual leave, and workers' compensation), plant and equipment costs (including depreciation of plant and equipment other than structures owned by the Agency), operation and maintenance expenses, amortized costs, and other expenses.

(2) Payment for items or services under paragraph (1) may take the form of an advanced payment by an agency from appropriations available to such agency for the procurement of such items or services.

(f) Fees.—(1) The Director may permit a central service provider to impose and collect a fee with respect to the provision of an item or service under the program. The amount of the fee may not exceed an amount equal to four percent of the payment received by the provider for the item or service.

(2) The Director may obligate and expend amounts in the Fund that are attributable to the fees imposed and collected under paragraph (1) to acquire equipment or systems for, or to improve the equipment or systems of, central service providers and any elements of the Agency that are not designated for participation in the program in order to facilitate the designation of such elements for future participation in the program.

(g) Termination.—(1) Subject to paragraph (2), the Director of the Central Intelligence Agency and the Director of the Office of Management and Budget, acting jointly—

(A) may terminate the program under this section and the Fund at any time; and

(B) upon such termination, shall provide for the disposition of the personnel, assets, liabilities, grants, contracts, property, records, and unexpended balances of appropriations, authorizations, allocations, and other funds held, used, arising from, available to, or to be made available in connection with the program or the Fund.

(2) The Director of the Central Intelligence Agency and the Director of the

Office of Management and Budget may not undertake any action under paragraph (1) until 60 days after the date on which the Directors jointly submit notice of such action to the Permanent Select Committee on Intelligence of the House of Representatives and the Select Committee on Intelligence of the Senate.

DETAIL OF EMPLOYEES

SEC. 22. [50 U.S.C. 3522] The Director may—

(1) detail any personnel of the Agency on a reimbursable basis indefinitely to the National Reconnaissance Office without regard to any limitation under law on the duration of details of Federal Government personnel; and

(2) hire personnel for the purpose of any detail under paragraph (1).

INTELLIGENCE OPERATIONS AND COVER ENHANCEMENT AUTHORITY

SEC. 23. [50 U.S.C. 3523] (a) DEFINITIONS.—In this section—

(1) the term "designated employee" means an employee designated by the Director of the Central Intelligence Agency under subsection (b); and

(2) the term "Federal retirement system" includes the Central Intelligence Agency Retirement and Disability System, and the Federal Employees' Retirement System (including the Thrift Savings Plan).

(b) IN GENERAL.—

(1) AUTHORITY.—Notwithstanding any other provision of law, the Director of the Central Intelligence Agency may exercise the authorities under this section in order to—

(A) protect from unauthorized disclosure—

(i) intelligence operations;

(ii) the identities of undercover intelligence officers;

(iii) intelligence sources and methods; or

(iv) intelligence cover mechanisms; or

(B) meet the special requirements of work related to collection of foreign intelligence or other authorized activities of the Agency.

(2) DESIGNATION OF EMPLOYEES.— The Director of the Central Intelligence Agency may designate any employee of the Agency who is under nonofficial cover to be an employee to whom this section applies. Such designation may be made with respect to any or all authorities exercised under this section.

(c) COMPENSATION.— The Director of the Central Intelligence Agency may pay a designated employee salary, allowances, and other benefits in an amount and in a manner consistent with the nonofficial cover of that employee, without regard to any limitation that is otherwise applicable to a Federal employee. A designated employee may accept, utilize, and, to the extent authorized by regulations prescribed under subsection (i), retain any salary, allowances, and other benefits provided under this section.

(d) RETIREMENT BENEFITS.—

(1) IN GENERAL.— The Director of the Central Intelligence Agency may establish

and administer a nonofficial cover employee retirement system for designated employees (and the spouse, former spouses, and survivors of such designated employees). A designated employee may not participate in the retirement system established under this paragraph and another Federal retirement system at the same time.

(2) CONVERSION TO OTHER FEDERAL RETIREMENT SYSTEM.—

(A) IN GENERAL.—A designated employee participating in the retirement system established under paragraph (1) may convert to coverage under the Federal retirement system which would otherwise apply to that employee at any appropriate time determined by the Director of the Central Intelligence Agency (including at the time of separation of service by reason of retirement), if the Director of the Central Intelligence Agency determines that the employee's participation in the retirement system established under this subsection is no longer necessary to protect from unauthorized disclosure—

(i) intelligence operations;

(ii) the identities of undercover intelligence officers;

(iii) intelligence sources and methods; or

(iv) intelligence cover mechanisms.

(B) CONVERSION TREATMENT.—Upon a conversion under this paragraph—

(i) all periods of service under the retirement system established under this subsection shall be deemed periods of creditable service under the applicable Federal retirement system;

(ii) the Director of the Central Intelligence Agency shall transmit an amount for deposit in any applicable fund of that Federal retirement system that—

(I) is necessary to cover all employee and agency contributions including—

(aa) interest as determined by the head of the agency administering the Federal retirement system into which the employee is converting; or

(bb) in the case of an employee converting into the Federal Employees' Retirement System, interest as determined under section 8334(e) of title 5, United States Code; and

(II) ensures that such conversion does not result in any unfunded liability to that fund; and

(iii) in the case of a designated employee who participated in an employee investment retirement system established under paragraph (1) and is converted to coverage under subchapter III of chapter 84 of title 5, United States Code, the Director of the Central Intelligence Agency may transmit any or all amounts of that designated employee in that employee investment retirement system (or similar part of that retirement system) to the Thrift Savings Fund.

(C) TRANSMITTED AMOUNTS.—

(i) IN GENERAL.— Amounts described under subparagraph (B)(ii) shall be paid from the fund or appropriation used to pay the designated employee.

(ii) Offset.— The Director of the Central Intelligence Agency may use amounts contributed by the designated employee to a retirement system established under paragraph (1) to offset amounts paid under clause (i).

(D) Records.— The Director of the Central Intelligence Agency shall transmit all necessary records relating to a designated employee who converts to a Federal retirement system under this paragraph (including records relating to periods of service which are deemed to be periods of creditable service under subparagraph (B)) to the head of the agency administering that Federal retirement system.

(e) Health Insurance Benefits.—

(1) In general.— The Director of the Central Intelligence Agency may establish and administer a nonofficial cover employee health insurance program for designated employees (and the family of such designated employees). A designated employee may not participate in the health insurance program established under this paragraph and the program under chapter 89 of title 5, United States Code, at the same time.

(2) Conversion to federal employees health benefits program.—

(A) In general.—A designated employee participating in the health insurance program established under paragraph (1) may convert to coverage under the program under chapter 89 of title 5, United States Code, at any appropriate time determined by the Director of the Central Intelligence Agency (including at the time of separation of service by reason of retirement), if the Director of the Central Intelligence Agency determines that the employee's participation in the health insurance program established under this subsection is no longer necessary to protect from unauthorized disclosure—

(i) intelligence operations;

(ii) the identities of undercover intelligence officers;

(iii) intelligence sources and methods; or

(iv) intelligence cover mechanisms.

(B) Conversion treatment.—Upon a conversion under this paragraph—

(i) the employee (and family, if applicable) shall be entitled to immediate enrollment and coverage under chapter 89 of title 5, United States Code;

(ii) any requirement of prior enrollment in a health benefits plan under chapter 89 of that title for continuation of coverage purposes shall not apply;

(iii) the employee shall be deemed to have had coverage under chapter 89 of that title from the first opportunity to enroll for purposes of continuing coverage as an annuitant; and

(iv) the Director of the Central Intelligence Agency shall transmit an amount for deposit in the Employees' Health Benefits Fund that is necessary to cover any costs of such conversion.

(C) Transmitted amounts.— Any amount described under subparagraph (B)(iv) shall be paid from the fund or appropriation used to pay the designated employee.

(f) Life Insurance Benefits.—

(1) In general.— The Director of the Central Intelligence Agency may establish and administer a nonofficial cover employee life insurance program for designated employees (and the family of such designated employees). A designated employee may not participate in the life insurance program established under this paragraph and the program under chapter 87 of title 5, United States Code, at the same time.

(2) Conversion to federal employees group life insurance program.—

(A) In general.—A designated employee participating in the life insurance program established under paragraph (1) may convert to coverage under the program under chapter 87 of title 5, United States Code, at any appropriate time determined by the Director of the Central Intelligence Agency (including at the time of separation of service by reason of retirement), if the Director of the Central Intelligence Agency determines that the employee's participation in the life insurance program established under this subsection is no longer necessary to protect from unauthorized disclosure—

(i) intelligence operations;

(ii) the identities of undercover intelligence officers;

(iii) intelligence sources and methods; or

(iv) intelligence cover mechanisms.

(B) Conversion treatment.—Upon a conversion under this paragraph—

(i) the employee (and family, if applicable) shall be entitled to immediate coverage under chapter 87 of title 5, United States Code;

(ii) any requirement of prior enrollment in a life insurance program under chapter 87 of that title for continuation of coverage purposes shall not apply;

(iii) the employee shall be deemed to have had coverage under chapter 87 of that title for the full period of service during which the employee would have been entitled to be insured for purposes of continuing coverage as an annuitant; and

(iv) the Director of the Central Intelligence Agency shall transmit an amount for deposit in the Employees' Life Insurance Fund that is necessary to cover any costs of such conversion.

(C) Transmitted amounts.— Any amount described under subparagraph (B)(iv) shall be paid from the fund or appropriation used to pay the designated employee.

(g) Exemption From Certain Requirements.—The Director of the Central Intelligence Agency may exempt a designated employee from mandatory compliance with any Federal regulation, rule, standardized administrative policy, process, or procedure that the Director of the Central Intelligence Agency determines—

(1) would be inconsistent with the nonofficial cover of that employee; and

(2) could expose that employee to detection as a Federal employee.

(h) Taxation and Social Security.—

(1) In general.—Notwithstanding any other provision of law, a designated

employee—

(A) shall file a Federal or State tax return as if that employee is not a Federal employee and may claim and receive the benefit of any exclusion, deduction, tax credit, or other tax treatment that would otherwise apply if that employee was not a Federal employee, if the Director of the Central Intelligence Agency determines that taking any action under this paragraph is necessary to—

(i) protect from unauthorized disclosure—

(I) intelligence operations;

(II) the identities of undercover intelligence officers;

(III) intelligence sources and methods; or

(IV) intelligence cover mechanisms; and

(ii) meet the special requirements of work related to collection of foreign intelligence or other authorized activities of the Agency; and

(B) shall receive social security benefits based on the social security contributions made.

(2) INTERNAL REVENUE SERVICE REVIEW.— The Director of the Central Intelligence Agency shall establish procedures to carry out this subsection. The procedures shall be subject to periodic review by the Internal Revenue Service.

(i) REGULATIONS.— The Director of the Central Intelligence Agency shall prescribe regulations to carry out this section. The regulations shall ensure that the combination of salary, allowances, and benefits that an employee designated under this section may retain does not significantly exceed, except to the extent determined by the Director of the Central Intelligence Agency to be necessary to exercise the authority in subsection (b), the combination of salary, allowances, and benefits otherwise received by Federal employees not designated under this section.

(j) FINALITY OF DECISIONS.— Any determinations authorized by this section to be made by the Director of the Central Intelligence Agency or the Director's designee shall be final and conclusive and shall not be subject to review by any court.

(k) SUBSEQUENTLY ENACTED LAWS.— No law enacted after the effective date of this section shall affect the authorities and provisions of this section unless such law specifically refers to this section.

SEC. 24. [50 U.S.C. 3525] OFFICE OF THE OMBUDSMAN FOR ANALYTIC OBJECTIVITY.

(a) ESTABLISHMENT.—

(1) IN GENERAL.— There is established in the Agency an Office of the Ombudsman for Analytic Objectivity (in this section referred to as the "Office").

(2) APPOINTMENT OF OMBUDSMAN.— The Office shall be headed by an Ombudsman, who shall be appointed by the Director from among current or former senior staff officers of the Agency.

(b) DUTIES AND RESPONSIBILITIES.—The Ombudsman shall—

(1) on an annual basis, conduct a survey of analytic objectivity among officers and employees of the Agency;

(2) implement a procedure by which any officer or employee of the Agency may submit to the Office a complaint alleging politicization, bias, lack of objectivity, or

other issues relating to a failure of tradecraft in analysis conducted by the Agency;

(3) except as provided in paragraph (4), upon receiving a complaint submitted pursuant to paragraph (2), take reasonable action to investigate the complaint, make a determination as to whether the incident described in the complaint involved politicization, bias, or lack of objectivity, and prepare a report that—

(A) summarizes the facts relevant to the complaint;

(B) documents the determination of the Ombudsman with respect to the complaint; and

(C) contains a recommendation for remedial action;

(4) if a complaint submitted pursuant to paragraph (2) alleges politicization, bias, or lack of objectivity in the collection of intelligence information, refer the complaint to the official responsible for supervising collection operations of the Agency; and

(5) continuously monitor changes in areas of analysis that the Ombudsman determines involve a heightened risk of politicization, bias, or lack of objectivity, to ensure that any change in the analytic line arises from proper application of analytic tradecraft and not as a result of politicization, bias, or lack of objectivity.

(c) Reports.—(1) On an annual basis, the Ombudsman shall submit to the intelligence committees a report on the results of the survey conducted pursuant to subsection (b)(1) with respect to the most recent fiscal year.

(2) On an annual basis, the Ombudsman shall submit to the intelligence committees a report that includes—

(A) the number of complaints of submitted pursuant to subsection (b)(2) during the most recent fiscal year; and

(B) a description of the nature of such complaints, the actions taken by the Office or any other relevant element or component of the Agency with respect to such complaints, and the resolution of such complaints.

(3) On a quarterly basis, the Ombudsman shall submit to the intelligence committees a report that includes—

(A) a list of the areas of analysis monitored during the most recent calendar quarter pursuant to subsection (b)(5); and

(B) a brief description of the methods by which the Office has conducted such monitoring.

(d) Intelligence Committees Defined.— In this section, the term "intelligence committees" means the Permanent Select Committee on Intelligence of the House of Representatives and the Select Committee on Intelligence of the Senate.

SEC. 25. [50 U.S.C. 3526] IMPROVEMENT OF EDUCATION IN SCIENCE, TECHNOLOGY, ENGINEERING, ARTS, AND MATHEMATICS.

(a) Definitions.—In this section:

(1) Eligible entity.— The term "eligible entity" includes a department or agency of the Federal Government, a State, a political subdivision of a State, an individual, and a not-for-profit or other organization in the private sector.

(2) Educational institution.— The term "educational institution" includes

any public or private elementary school or secondary school, institution of higher education, college, university, or any other profit or nonprofit institution that is dedicated to improving science, technology, engineering, the arts, mathematics, business, law, medicine, or other fields that promote development and education relating to science, technology, engineering, the arts, or mathematics.

(3) STATE.— The term "State" means each of the several States, the District of Columbia, the Commonwealth of Puerto Rico, the Commonwealth of the Northern Mariana Islands, and any other territory or possession of the United States.

(b) REQUIREMENTS.—The Director shall, on a continuing basis—

(1) identify actions that the Director may take to improve education in the scientific, technology, engineering, arts, and mathematics (known as "STEAM") skills necessary to meet the long-term national security needs of the United States for personnel proficient in such skills; and

(2) establish and conduct programs to carry out such actions.

(c) AUTHORITIES.—

(1) IN GENERAL.—The Director, in support of educational programs in science, technology, engineering, the arts, and mathematics, may—

(A) award grants to eligible entities;

(B) provide cash awards and other items to eligible entities;

(C) accept voluntary services from eligible entities;

(D) support national competition judging, other educational event activities, and associated award ceremonies in connection with such educational programs; and

(E) enter into one or more education partnership agreements with educational institutions in the United States for the purpose of encouraging and enhancing study in science, technology, engineering, the arts, and mathematics disciplines at all levels of education.

(2) EDUCATION PARTNERSHIP AGREEMENTS.—

(A) NATURE OF ASSISTANCE PROVIDED.—Under an education partnership agreement entered into with an educational institution under paragraph (1)(E), the Director may provide assistance to the educational institution by—

(i) loaning equipment to the educational institution for any purpose and duration in support of such agreement that the Director considers appropriate;

(ii) making personnel available to teach science courses or to assist in the development of science courses and materials for the educational institution;

(iii) providing sabbatical opportunities for faculty and internship opportunities for students;

(iv) involving faculty and students of the educational institution in Agency projects, including research and technology transfer or transition projects;

(v) cooperating with the educational institution in developing a program under which students may be given academic credit for work on Agency projects, including research and technology transfer for transition projects; and

(vi) providing academic and career advice and assistance to students of the educational institution.

(B) PRIORITIES.—In entering into education partnership agreements under paragraph (1)(E), the Director shall prioritize entering into education partnership agreements with the following:

(i) Historically Black colleges and universities and other minority-serving institutions, as described in section 371(a) of the Higher Education Act of 1965 (20 U.S.C. 1067q(a)).

(ii) Educational institutions serving women, members of minority groups, and other groups of individuals who traditionally are involved in the science, technology, engineering, arts, and mathematics professions in disproportionately low numbers.

(d) DESIGNATION OF ADVISOR.— The Director shall designate one or more individuals within the Agency to advise and assist the Director regarding matters relating to science, technology, engineering, the arts, and mathematics education and training.

SEC. 26. [50 U.S.C. 3527] CHAPLAIN CORPS AND CHIEF OF CHAPLAINS.

(a) ESTABLISHMENT OF CHAPLAIN CORPS.— There is in the Agency a Chaplain Corps for the provision of spiritual or religious pastoral services.

(b) CHIEF OF CHAPLAINS.— The head of the Chaplain Corps shall be the Chief of Chaplains, who shall be appointed by the Director.

(c) STAFF AND ADMINISTRATION.—

(1) STAFF.—The Director may appoint and fix the compensation of such staff of the Chaplain Corps as the Director considers appropriate, except that the Director may not—

(A) appoint more than 10 full-time equivalent positions; or

(B) provide basic pay to any member of the staff of the Chaplain Corps at an annual rate of basic pay in excess of the maximum rate of basic pay for grade GS–15 as provided in section 5332 of title 5, United States Code.

(2) ADMINISTRATION.—The Director may—

(A) reimburse members of the staff of the Chaplain Corps for work-related travel expenses;

(B) provide security clearances to such members;

(C) furnish such physical workspace at the headquarters building of the Agency as the Director considers appropriate; and

(D) certify that all Chaplains meet common standards for professional chaplaincy and board certification by a national chaplaincy and pastoral care organization or equivalent.

SEC. 27. [50 U.S.C. 3528] COMPENSATION AND PROFESSIONAL STANDARDS FOR CERTAIN MEDICAL OFFICERS.

(a) Office of Medical Services.— There is in the Agency an Office of Medical Services.

(b) Compensation.— Beginning not later than 1 year after the date of the enactment of the Intelligence Authorization Act for Fiscal Year 2022, each medical officer of the Office of Medical Services who meets the qualifications under subsection (c) shall be compensated during a pay period pursuant to a pay range that is equal to the pay range published in the Federal Register pursuant to section 7431(e)(1)(C) of title 38, United States Code (for the corresponding pay period), for a physician in the Veterans Health Administration in the District of Columbia region with a medical subspecialty that is the equivalent of the medical subspecialty of the officer.

(c) Clinical Practice Qualifications.—A medical officer meets the qualifications under this subsection if the officer provides direct care services to patients in connection with the official duties of the officer and—

(1) maintains current, active, full, and unrestricted licensure or registration as a physician from a State, the District of Columbia, or a commonwealth or territory of the United States;

(2) holds active board certification and maintains accreditation in an American Board of Medical Specialties direct care clinical specialty; and

(3) except as provided in subsection (d), maintains a minimum of 96 hours per year of clinical practice in an accredited clinic or hospital facility that is not affiliated with the Central Intelligence Agency.

(d) Exception for Overseas Service.— If a medical officer is a medical officer located in a duty station outside of the United States pursuant to a permanent change of station and greater than 50 percent of the official duties of the officer in such duty station involve direct patient care, the officer, in lieu of performing the minimum hours under subsection (c)(3) on an annual basis, may count up to 480 hours of clinical practice performed as specified in such subsection prior to such change of station, to fulfill in advance the requirement under such subsection for up to 3 years.

(e) Clinical Practice Hours.— The head of the Office of Medical Services shall make available to medical officers excused absence time to allow for the maintenance of clinical practice hours in accordance with subsection (c)(3).

SEC. 28. [50 U.S.C. 3529] MEDICAL ADVISORY BOARD.

(a) Establishment.— The Director shall establish within the Agency a medical advisory board (in this section referred to as the "Board").

(b) Duties.—The Board shall—

(1) conduct a study on the Office of Medical Services of the Agency, and submit reports regarding such study, in accordance with subsection (c); and

(2) upon request, provide advice and guidance in connection with any independent review of the Office conducted by an inspector general.

(c) Study.—

(1) Objectives.—In conducting the study under subsection (b)(1), the Board shall seek to—

(A) contribute to the modernization and reform of the Office of Medical

Services;

(B) ensure that the activities of the Office are of the highest professional quality; and

(C) ensure that all medical care provided by the Office is provided in accordance with the highest professional medical standards.

(2) REPORTS.—The Board shall submit to the congressional intelligence committees, in writing—

(A) interim reports on the study; and

(B) a final report on the study, which shall—

(i) set forth in detail the findings of the study and the recommendations of the Board, based on such findings and taking into consideration the objectives under paragraph (1), regarding any changes to the activities of the Office of Medical Services; and

(ii) include, as applicable, any additional or dissenting views submitted by a member of the Board.

(d) MEMBERSHIP.—

(1) NUMBER AND APPOINTMENT.—The Board shall be composed of 9 members, appointed as follows:

(A) 1 member appointed by the Speaker of the House of Representatives.

(B) 1 member appointed by the minority leader of the House of Representatives.

(C) 1 member appointed by the majority leader of the Senate.

(D) 1 member appointed by the minority leader of the Senate.

(E) 1 member appointed by the Chairman of the Permanent Select Committee on Intelligence of the House of Representatives.

(F) 1 member appointed by the ranking minority member of the Permanent Select Committee on Intelligence of the House of Representatives.

(G) 1 member appointed by the Chairman of the Select Committee on Intelligence of the Senate.

(H) 1 member appointed by the Vice Chairman of the Select Committee on Intelligence of the Senate.

(I) 1 member appointed by the Director of National Intelligence.

(2) CHAIRPERSON.— During the first meeting under subsection (e)(1), the members of the Board shall elect a Chairperson of the Board. In addition to meeting the criteria under paragraph (3), the Chairperson may not be an employee, or former employee, of the Agency.

(3) CRITERIA.—The members appointed under paragraph (1) shall meet the following criteria:

(A) Each member shall be a recognized expert in at least 1 medical field, as demonstrated by appropriate credentials.

(B) Each member shall possess significant and diverse medical experience, including clinical experience.

(C) Each member shall be eligible to hold an appropriate security clearance.

(4) TERMS.—

(A) IN GENERAL.— Each member, including the Chairperson, shall be appointed or elected, as applicable, for the life of the Board.

(B) VACANCIES.— Any vacancy in the Board occurring prior to the expiration of the term under subparagraph (A) shall be filled in the manner in which the original appointment or election was made.

(5) COMPENSATION AND TRAVEL EXPENSES.—

(A) COMPENSATION.— Except as provided in subparagraph (B), each member of the Board, including the Chairperson, may be compensated at not to exceed the daily equivalent of the annual rate of basic pay in effect for a position at level IV of the Executive Schedule under section 5315 of title 5, United States Code, for each day during which that member is engaged in the actual performance of the duties under subsection (b).

(B) EXCEPTION FOR FEDERAL EMPLOYEES.— Members of the Board, including the Chairperson, who are officers or employees of the United States shall receive no additional pay by reason of the service of the member on the Board.

(C) TRAVEL EXPENSES.— Each member of the Board, including the Chairperson, while away from the home or regular places of business of the member in the performance of services for the Board, may be allowed travel expenses, including per diem in lieu of subsistence, in the same manner as persons employed intermittently in the Government service are allowed expenses under section 5703 of title 5, United States Code.

(6) DETAILEES.—

(A) IN GENERAL.— Upon request of the Board, the Director of National Intelligence may detail to the Board, without reimbursement from the Board, any of the personnel of the Office of the Director of National Intelligence to assist in carrying out the duties under subsection (b). Any such detailed personnel shall retain the rights, status, and privileges of the regular employment of the personnel without interruption.

(B) CLEARANCE.— Any personnel detailed to the Board under subparagraph (A) shall possess a security clearance in accordance with applicable laws and regulations concerning the handling of classified information.

(e) MEETINGS.—

(1) BOARD MEETINGS.— The Board shall meet not less frequently than on a quarterly basis.

(2) MEETINGS WITH CONGRESS.— The Board shall meet with the congressional intelligence committees on a biannual basis.

(f) INFORMATION ACCESS.—

(1) IN GENERAL.— Except as provided in paragraph (2), the Board may secure directly from any department or agency of the United States Government information necessary to enable it to carry out the duties under subsection (b) and, upon request of the Chairperson of the Board, the head of that department or agency shall furnish such information to the Board.

(2) Exception.— The Director (without delegation) may deny a request for information made by the Board pursuant to paragraph (1), regardless of the agency from which such information is requested.

(3) Notification requirement.— If the Director denies a request under paragraph (2), not later than 15 days after the date of such denial, the Director shall submit to the congressional intelligence committees a written notification of such denial.

(4) Briefings.— The Director shall ensure that the Board receives comprehensive briefings on all activities of the Office of Medical Services, including by promptly scheduling such briefings at the request of the Board.

(g) Termination.— The Board shall terminate on the date that is 5 years after the date of the first meeting of the Board.

(h) Definitions.— In this section, the terms "congressional intelligence committees" and "intelligence community" have the meanings given such terms in section 3 of the National Security Act of 1947 (50 U.S.C. 3003).

SEC. 29. [50 U.S.C. 3530] OFFICE OF WELLNESS AND WORKFORCE SUPPORT.

(a) Establishment.— The Director shall establish within the Agency an office (in this section referred to as the "Office") to provide support for the physical health, mental health, and wellbeing of eligible individuals under subsection (d).

(b) Chief Wellbeing Officer; Assigned Staff.—

(1) Chief wellbeing officer.— The head of the Office is the Chief Wellbeing Officer, who shall provide to the Director regular updates on the operations of the Office.

(2) Assigned staff.— To assist in performing the functions under subsection (c), the Director shall assign to the Office a sufficient number of individuals, who shall have no official duties other than duties related to the Office while so assigned.

(c) Functions of Office.—

(1) Functions.—The Director shall establish the functions and role of the Office, which shall include the following:

(A) Providing to eligible individuals under subsection (d) advice and assistance on health and wellbeing, including with respect to—

(i) physical health and access to physical health care;

(ii) mental health and access to mental health care; and

(iii) other related programs and benefits for which the individual may be eligible.

(B) In providing advice and assistance to individuals under subparagraph (A), assisting such individuals who are applying for, and navigating the process to obtain, benefits furnished by the United States Government for which the individual is eligible, including, at a minimum—

(i) health care and benefits described in such subparagraph; and

(ii) benefits furnished pursuant to section 19A.

(C) Maintaining, and making available to eligible individuals under subsection (d), the following:

(i) A list of physicians and mental health care providers (including from the private sector, as applicable), who have experience with the physical and mental health care needs of the Agency workforce.

(ii) A list of chaplains and religious counselors who have experience with the needs of the Agency workforce, including information regarding access to the Chaplain Corps established under section 26.

(iii) Information regarding how to select and retain private attorneys who have experience with the legal needs of the Agency workforce, including detailed information on the process for the appropriate sharing of information with retained private attorneys.

(D) Any other functions the Director determines appropriate.

(2) RULE OF CONSTRUCTION.— The inclusion of any person on a list maintained or made available pursuant to paragraph (1)(C) shall not be construed as an endorsement of such person (or any service furnished by such person), and the Director shall not be liable, as a result of such inclusion, for any portion of compensable injury, loss, or damage attributable to such person or service.

(3) CONFIDENTIALITY.—

(A) REQUIREMENT.— The Director shall ensure that, to the extent permitted by law, the advice and assistance provided by the Office to eligible individuals under subsection (d) is provided in a confidential manner.

(B) REGULATIONS.— The Director may prescribe regulations regarding the requirement for confidentiality under this paragraph. The Director shall submit to the congressional intelligence committees (as defined in section 3 of the National Security Act of 1947 (50 U.S.C. 3003)), the Subcommittee on Defense of the Committee on Appropriations of the Senate, and the Subcommittee on Defense of the Committee on Appropriations of the House of Representatives any such regulations not later than 30 days after prescribing such regulations.

(d) ELIGIBILITY.—

(1) IN GENERAL.— An individual described in paragraph (2) may receive a service under the Office at the election of the individual.

(2) INDIVIDUALS DESCRIBED.—An individual described in this paragraph is—

(A) a current or former officer or employee of the Agency; or

(B) an individual affiliated with the Agency, as determined by the Director.

SEC. 30. [50 U.S.C. 3531] SEXUAL ASSAULT AND SEXUAL HARASSMENT WITHIN THE AGENCY.

(a) RESPONSIBILITIES OF DIRECTOR.—The Director shall carry out the following responsibilities:

(1) Establishing professional and uniform training for employees assigned to working with all aspects of the response of the Agency to allegations of sexual assault and sexual harassment.

(2) Developing and implementing policies and procedures to protect the confidentiality of employees who report sexual assault or sexual harassment and to mitigate negative effects on the reputation or career of such an employee as a result of such a report.

(3) Developing and implementing documented standards for—

(A) appropriate mitigation and protection measures for individuals who make allegations of a sexual assault or sexual harassment to be put in place while an investigation proceeds;

(B) appropriate employee consequences to be imposed based on the findings of an inquiry or investigation into a substantiated allegation of sexual assault or sexual harassment;

(C) appropriate career path protection for all employees involved in an incident resulting in a reported allegation of sexual assault or sexual harassment while an administrative or criminal investigation or review of the allegation is pending; and

(D) mitigation measures to protect employees and mission execution while such allegations are being addressed.

(4) Articulating and enforcing norms, expectations, practices, and policies, including with respect to employee promotions and assignments, that are published for the workforce and designed to promote a healthy workplace culture that is inhospitable to sexual assault and sexual harassment.

(5) Developing and issuing workforce messaging to inform Agency employees of policies, procedures, resources, and points of contact to obtain information related to, or to report, sexual assault or sexual harassment globally.

(6) Developing and implementing sexual assault and sexual harassment training for all Agency employees that—

(A) is designed to strengthen individual knowledge, skills, and capacity to prevent and respond to sexual assault and sexual harassment;

(B) includes onboarding programs, annual refresher training, and specialized leadership training; and

(C) includes details of the definitions of sexual assault and sexual harassment, the distinction between such terms, and what does or does not constitute each.

(7) Developing and implementing processes and procedures applicable to personnel involved in providing the training referred to in paragraph (6) that—

(A) are designed to ensure seamless policy consistency and mechanisms for submitting reports of sexual assault and sexual harassment in all training environments; and

(B) include requirements for in-person training that—

(i) covers the reporting processes for sexual assault and sexual harassment that are specific to training environments for students and trainers; and

(ii) shall be provided at an appropriate time during the first 5 days of any extended or residential training course.

(8) Developing and implementing, in consultation with the Victim Advocacy Specialists of the Federal Bureau of Investigation, appropriate training requirements, policies, and procedures applicable to all employees whose professional responsibilities include interaction with people making reports alleging sexual

assault or sexual harassment.

(9) Developing and implementing procedures under which current and former employees of the Agency who have reported an allegation of sexual assault or sexual harassment may obtain documents and records related to such a report, as appropriate and upon request.

(10) Developing and implementing procedures under which an employee who makes a restricted or unrestricted report containing an allegation of a sexual assault or sexual harassment may transfer out of the current assignment or location of the employee, upon the request of the employee making the report. Such procedures shall be consistent with the privilege established in section 31.

(11) Developing policies and procedures for the Special Victim Investigator, as applicable, to facilitate outside engagement requests of employees reporting allegations of sexual assault or sexual harassment as described in sections 31 and 32.

(12) Coordinating the response of the Agency to allegations of sexual assault and sexual harassment.

(b) Semiannual Report.—Not less frequently than once every 180 days, the Director shall submit to the Select Committee on Intelligence of the Senate and the Permanent Select Committee on Intelligence of the House of Representatives a report on the activities of all Agency offices responsible for preventing, investigating, adjudicating, and addressing claims of sexual assault or sexual harassment. The Director shall personally review, approve, and submit each report under this subsection on a nondelegable basis. Each such report shall include—

(1) for the period covered by the report—

(A) the number of new allegations of sexual assault and sexual harassment reported to any Agency office, disaggregated by restricted and unrestricted reports;

(B) the number of new or ongoing cases in which the Sexual Harassment/Assault Response and Prevention Office has provided victim advocacy services;

(C) a description of all training activities related to sexual assault and sexual harassment carried out Agency-wide, and the number of such trainings conducted; and

(2) for the period beginning on the date of the enactment of the Intelligence Authorization Act for Fiscal Year 2024 and ending on the last day of the period covered by the report—

(A) the total number of allegations of sexual assault and sexual harassment;

(B) the disposition of each report of such an allegation;

(C) any corrective action taken in response to each such report;

(D) the number of such allegations that were not substantiated; and

(E) the number of employee reassignment and relocation requests, including—

(i) the number of such requests that were granted;

(ii) the number of such requests that were denied; and

(iii) for any such request that was denied, the position of the individual who denied the request and the reason for denial.

(c) APPLICABILITY.—

(1) IN GENERAL.—The policies developed pursuant to this section shall apply to each of the following:

(A) Any employee of the Agency.

(B) Any person other than an Agency employee who alleges they were sexually assaulted or harassed at a facility associated with the Agency or during the performance of a function associated with the Agency. If such person is an employee of an industrial contractor, the contracting officer for the relevant contract shall coordinate with the contractually identified representative for the prime contractor in a manner consistent with section 31.

(2) RELATION TO EXISTING REGULATIONS.— The policies developed pursuant to this section for handling allegations of sexual harassment shall be in addition to the requirements of part 1614 of title 29, Code of Federal Regulations, or successor regulations.

SEC. 31. [50 U.S.C. 3532] REPORTING AND INVESTIGATION OF ALLEGATIONS OF SEXUAL ASSAULT AND SEXUAL HARASSMENT.

(a) POLICIES RELATING TO RESTRICTED AND UNRESTRICTED REPORTING OF SEXUAL ASSAULT AND SEXUAL HARASSMENT.—

(1) IN GENERAL.— The Director shall develop and implement policies, regulations, personnel training, and workforce education to establish and provide information about restricted reports and unrestricted reports of allegations of sexual assault and sexual harassment within the Agency in accordance with this subsection.

(2) WORKFORCE EDUCATION.— Workforce education developed under paragraph (1) shall be designed to clearly inform Agency employees of the differences between restricted and unrestricted reporting of allegations of sexual assault and sexual harassment, and which individual or office within the Agency is responsible for receiving each type of report.

(3) RELATIONSHIP TO THE SEXUAL HARASSMENT/ASSAULT RESPONSE AND PREVENTION OFFICE.—To the extent consistent with preserving a victim's complete autonomy, the policies, regulations, training, and messaging described in this subsection shall—

(A) encourage Agency employees to make restricted or unrestricted reports of sexual assault and sexual harassment to the Sexual Harassment/Assault Response and Prevention Office;

(B) encourage Agency employees to use the Sexual Harassment/Assault Response and Prevention Office as the primary point of contact and entry point for Agency employees to make restricted or unrestricted reports of sexual assault and sexual harassment;

(C) encourage Agency employees to seek the victim advocacy services of the Sexual Harassment/Assault Response and Prevention Office after reporting an allegation of sexual assault or sexual harassment, to the extent consistent with the victim's election; and

(D) encourage Agency employees and individuals who receive disclosures of sexual assault and sexual harassment to provide the report to, and receive guidance from, the Sexual Harassment/Assault Response and Prevention Office.

(b) ELECTION.— Any person making a report containing an allegation of a sexual assault or sexual harassment shall elect whether to make a restricted report or an unrestricted report. Once an election is made to make an unrestricted report, such election may not be changed.

(c) UNRESTRICTED REPORTS.—

(1) ASSISTANCE.— A person who elects to make an unrestricted report containing an allegation of sexual assault or sexual harassment may seek the assistance of another employee of the Agency with taking the action required under paragraph (2).

(2) ACTION REQUIRED.—A person electing to make an unrestricted report containing an allegation of sexual assault or sexual harassment shall submit the report to the Sexual Harassment/Assault Response and Prevention Office. To the extent consistent with the person's election after consultation with the Sexual Harassment/Assault Response and Prevention Office, the Sexual Harassment/Assault Response and Prevention Office may facilitate the person's contact with any other appropriate Agency official or office, and make available to Agency employees the following:

(A) A list of physicians and mental health care providers (including from the private sector, as applicable) who have experience with the physical and mental health care needs of the Agency workforce.

(B) A list of chaplains and religious counselors who have experience with the needs of the Agency workforce, including information regarding access to the Chaplain Corps established under section 26.

(C) Information regarding how to select and retain private attorneys who have experience with the legal needs of the Agency workforce, including detailed information on the process for the appropriate sharing of information with retained private attorneys.

(3) RULE OF CONSTRUCTION.— The inclusion of any person on a list maintained or made available pursuant to subsection (c)(2) shall not be construed as an endorsement of such person (or any service furnished by such person), and neither the Sexual Harassment/Assault Response and Prevention Office nor the Agency shall be liable, as a result of such inclusion, for any portion of compensable injury, loss, or damage attributable to such person or service.

(d) RESTRICTED REPORTS.—

(1) PROCESS FOR MAKING REPORTS.— A person who elects to make a restricted report containing an allegation of sexual assault or sexual harassment shall submit the report to the Sexual Harassment/Assault Response and Prevention Office.

(2) ACTION REQUIRED.—A restricted report containing an allegation of sexual assault or sexual harassment—

(A) shall be treated by the person who receives the report in the same manner as a communication covered by the privilege set forth in this section;

(B) shall not result in a referral to law enforcement or commencement of a formal administrative investigation, unless the victim elects to change the report from a restricted report to an unrestricted report;

(C) in a case requiring an employee reassignment, relocation, or other mitigation or protective measures, shall result only in actions that are managed in a manner to limit, to the extent possible, the disclosure of any information contained in the report;

(D) shall be exempt from any Federal or, to the maximum extent permitted by the Constitution, State reporting requirements, including the requirements under section 535(b) of title 28, United States Code, section 17(b)(5) of this Act, relevant provisions of Executive Order 12333 (50 U.S.C. 3001 note; relating to United States intelligence activities), or successor order, Executive Order 13462 (50 U.S.C. 3001 note; relating to President's intelligence advisory board and intelligence oversight board), or successor order, title VII of the Civil Rights Act of 1964 (42 U.S.C. 2000e et seq.), the Age Discrimination in Employment Act of 1967 (29 U.S.C. 621 et seq.), title I of the Americans with Disabilities Act of 1990 (42 U.S.C. 12111 et seq.), and sections 501 and 505 of the Rehabilitation Act of 1973 (29 U.S.C. 791 and 794a), except when reporting is necessary to prevent or mitigate an imminent threat of serious bodily harm.

(3) Rule of construction.— The receipt of a restricted report submitted under subsection (d) shall not be construed as imputing actual or constructive knowledge of an alleged incident of sexual assault or sexual harassment to the Agency for the purpose of the Agency's responsibility to exercise reasonable care to take immediate and appropriate corrective action to prevent and correct harassing behavior.

(e) Privileged Communications With Agency Employees.—

(1) In general.— A victim shall be entitled to maintain and assert a privilege against disclosure of, and be able to prevent any other person from disclosing, any confidential communication made between the victim and any employee of the Sexual Harassment/Assault Response and Prevention Office, if such communication was made for the purpose of facilitating advice or assistance to the victim in accordance with this section. A victim may consent to additional disclosures.

(2) When a communication is confidential.— A communication is confidential for the purposes of this section if made in the course of the relationship between the victim and any employee of the Sexual Harassment/Assault Response and Prevention Office and not intended to be disclosed to third persons, other than those to whom disclosure is made in furtherance of the provision of advice or assistance to the victim or those reasonably necessary for such transmission of the communication.

(3) Maintenance of privilege.— The privilege is maintained by the victim. A victim may authorize the Sexual Harassment/Assault Response and Prevention Office employee who received the communication to assert the privilege on his or her behalf, with confidentiality. The Sexual Harassment/Assault Response and Prevention Office employee who received the communication may assert the privilege on behalf of the victim. The authority of such Sexual Harassment/Assault Response and Prevention Office employee to so assert the privilege is presumed in the absence of evidence to the contrary.

(4) Exceptions.—The privilege shall not apply to prevent limited disclosures necessary under the following circumstances:

(A) When the victim is deceased.

(B) When the Sexual Harassment/Assault Response and Prevention Office employee who received the communication has a reasonable belief that a victim's mental or emotional condition makes the victim a danger to any person, including the victim.

(C) When the otherwise privileged communication clearly contemplates the future commission of a crime or breach of national security, or aiding any individual to commit or plan to commit what the victim knew or reasonable should have known to be a crime or breach of national security.

(D) When disclosure of a communication is constitutionally required.

(5) Handling of exceptions.— When the Sexual Harassment/Assault Response and Prevention Office employee determines that information requires an exception to the privilege, the Sexual Harassment/Assault Response and Prevention Office employee who received the communication will protect information pertaining to the facts and circumstances surrounding the underlying sexual assault or sexual harassment allegations to the greatest extent possible.

(f) Incident Reports When Victim or Alleged Perpetrator is an Agency Employee.—

(1) Incident reporting policy.—The Director shall establish and maintain a policy under which—

(A) the head of the Sexual Harassment/Assault Response and Prevention Office is required to submit a written incident report not later than 8 days after receiving an unrestricted report containing an allegation of sexual assault or sexual harassment; and

(B) each such incident report required under subparagraph (A) shall be provided to—

(i) the Director of the Agency;

(ii) the Chief Operating Officer of the Agency;

(iii) the Special Victim Investigator; and

(iv) such other individuals as the Director determines appropriate.

(2) Purpose.—The purpose of an incident report required under paragraph (1) is—

(A) to record the details about actions taken or in progress to provide the necessary care and support to the victim of the alleged incident;

(B) to document the referral of the allegations to the appropriate investigatory or law enforcement agency; and

(C) to provide initial formal notification of the alleged incident.

(3) Elements.—Each incident report required under paragraph (1) shall include each of the following:

(A) The time, date, and location of the alleged sexual assault or sexual harassment.

(B) An identification of the type of offense or harassment alleged.

(C) An identification of the assigned office and location of the victim.

(D) An identification of the assigned office and location of the alleged perpetrator, including information regarding whether the alleged perpetrator has been temporarily transferred or removed from an assignment or otherwise restricted, if applicable.

(E) A description of any post-incident actions taken in connection with the incident, including—

(i) referral to any services available to victims, including the date of each referral;

(ii) notification of the incident to appropriate investigatory organizations, including the organizations notified and dates of notifications; and

(iii) issuance of any personal protection orders or steps taken to separate the victim and the alleged perpetrator within their place of employment.

(F) Such other elements as the Director determines appropriate.

(g) COMMON PERPETRATOR NOTICE REQUIREMENT.—

(1) UNRESTRICTED REPORTS.—Upon receipt of an incident report under subsection (f)(1) containing an allegation of sexual assault or sexual harassment against an individual known to be the subject of at least one allegation of sexual assault or sexual harassment by another reporter, the Special Victim Investigator shall notify each of the following of all existing allegations against the individual:

(A) The Director of the Agency.

(B) The Chief Operating Officer of the Agency.

(C) The Sexual Harassment/Assault Response and Prevention Office.

(D) If the individual is an Agency employee, the head of the directorate employing the individual and the first-level supervisor of the individual.

(E) If the individual is an Agency contractor, the Acquisition Group Chief and the contracting officer for the relevant contract. For industrial contractor personnel, the contracting officer shall notify the contractually identified representative for the prime contractor.

(F) The Inspector General of the Agency.

(G) Such other individuals as the Director determines appropriate.

(2) RESTRICTED REPORTS.— In the case of restricted reports under subsection (d), the Sexual Harassment/Assault Response and Prevention Office shall notify any victims known to have filed a restricted report against an individual known to be the subject of at least one unrestricted allegation of sexual assault or sexual harassment by another reporter that another allegation has been made against the same individual who is the alleged subject of the victim's report at the time of the victim's initial report or any time thereafter upon receipt of any subsequent unrestricted report under subsection (c) or a common perpetrator notice under paragraph (1) of this subsection.

(h) APPLICABILITY.—The policies developed pursuant to this section shall apply to each of the following:

(1) Any employee of the Agency.

(2) Any person other than an Agency employee who alleges they were sexually assaulted or harassed at a facility associated with the Agency or during the performance of a function associated with the Agency.

(i) RECORDS.—

(1) IN GENERAL.— The Director shall establish a system for the tracking and, in accordance with chapter 31 of title 44, United States Code (commonly known as the "Federal Records Act of 1950"), long-term temporary retention of all Agency records related to any investigation into an allegation of sexual assault or sexual harassment made in an unrestricted report, including any related medical documentation.

(2) RELATION TO PRIVILEGE.— Any Agency records created under the authority of this section are subject to the privileges described in this section. Routine records management activities conducted by authorized Agency personnel with respect to such records, including maintaining, searching, or dispositioning of records, shall not result in a waiver of those privileges.

(3) APPLICABILITY TO FOIA.— This section shall constitute a withholding statute pursuant to section 552(b)(3) of title 5, United States Code, with respect to any information that may reveal the identity of a victim of sexual assault or sexual harassment, or any information subject to the privileges described in this section.

(j) RELATIONSHIP TO THE OFFICE OF EQUAL EMPLOYMENT OPPORTUNITY.— In the case of a restricted report of sexual harassment, such report shall not result in a referral to the Office of Equal Employment Opportunity, unless the victim elects to change the report from a restricted report to an unrestricted report. In the case of an unrestricted report, the Special Victim Investigator, the Office of Equal Employment Opportunity, law enforcement, or any other appropriate investigative body, or any appropriate combination thereof, may investigate the unrestricted report, as appropriate. Policies and procedures developed pursuant to this section are intended to offer victims options in addition to the process described in part 1614 of title 29, Code of Federal Regulations, or successor regulations.

(k) DEFINITIONS.—In this section:

(1) REPORT.—The term "report" means a communication—

(A) by a victim;

(B) that describes information relating to an allegation of sexual assault or sexual harassment;

(C) to an individual eligible to document an unrestricted or restricted report; and

(D) that the victim intends to result in formal documentation of an unrestricted or restricted report.

(2) VICTIM.— The term "victim" means a person who alleges they have suffered direct physical or emotional harm because they were subjected to sexual assault or sexual harassment.

SEC. 32. [50 U.S.C. 3533] SPECIAL VICTIM INVESTIGATOR.

(a) ESTABLISHMENT.— The Director shall establish in the Office of Security a Special Victim Investigator, who shall be authorized to investigate or facilitate the investigation of unrestricted reports containing allegations of sexual assault and sexual harassment. The person appointed as the Special Victim Investigator shall be an appropriately credentialed Federal law enforcement officer and may be detailed or assigned from a Federal law enforcement entity. No individual appointed as the Special Victim Investigator may, at the time of such appointment, be a current employee of the Central Intelligence Agency.

(b) RESPONSIBILITIES.—The Investigator shall—

(1) at the election of a victim (as defined in section 31(k)), be authorized to conduct internal Agency inquiries, investigations, and other fact-finding activities related to allegations of sexual harassment, which may be separate and in addition to any inquiry or investigation conducted by the Office of Equal Employment Opportunity;

(2) conduct and manage internal Agency inquiries, investigations, and other fact-finding activities related to specific allegations of sexual assault;

(3) testify in a criminal prosecution in any venue, where appropriate;

(4) serve as the case agent for a criminal investigation in any venue, where appropriate;

(5) facilitate engagement with other law enforcement relating to such allegations, where appropriate, including coordinating on the matter and any related matters with other Federal, State, local, and Tribal law enforcement agencies, as necessary and appropriate, pursuant to regulations, requirements, and procedures developed in consultation with the Federal Bureau of Investigation, the Department of State's Diplomatic Security Service, or other Federal, State, local, or Tribal law enforcement authorities, for any such inquiries, investigations, or other fact-finding activities;

(6) develop and implement policies and procedures necessary for the Special Victim Investigator or any law enforcement partner to conduct effective investigations and also protect sensitive information;

(7) serve as the primary internal investigative body in the Agency for allegations of sexual assault, except that, in the case of an allegation of a sexual assault involving an employee of the Office of Security, the Special Victim Investigator shall coordinate with the Inspector General or appropriate criminal investigators employed by a Federal, State, local, or Tribal law enforcement entity, as necessary, to maintain the integrity of the investigation and mitigate potential conflicts of interest;

(8) establish and coordinate clear policies regarding which agency should take the lead on conducting, or be the lead in coordinating with local law enforcement when applicable, investigations of sexual assault and sexual harassment overseas; and

(9) sharing information with the Sexual Harassment/Assault Response and Prevention Office, including providing a copy of materials related to investigations with such redactions as deemed necessary, to facilitate the support and advocacy of such Office for victims of alleged sexual assault or sexual harassment.

(c) TIMEFRAME FOR INVESTIGATIONS.—The Special Victim Investigator shall—

(1) ensure that any Special Victim Investigator investigation into an allegation of

a sexual assault or sexual harassment contained in an unrestricted report submitted under section 31 is completed by not later than 60 days after the date on which the report is referred to the Special Victim Investigator; and

(2) if the Special Victim Investigator determines that the completion of an investigation will take longer than 60 days—

(A) not later than 60 days after the date on which the report is referred to the Special Victim Investigator, submit to the Director a request for an extension that contains a summary of the progress of the investigation, the reasons why the completion of the investigation requires additional time, and a plan for the completion of the investigation; and

(B) provide to the person who made the report and the person against whom the allegation in the report was made notice of the extension of the investigation.

CENTRAL INTELLIGENCE AGENCY RETIREMENT ACT

PUBLIC LAW 88–643

AS AMENDED THROUGH P.L. 118–31

CENTRAL INTELLIGENCE AGENCY RETIREMENT ACT

[(Public Law 88–643; 78 Stat. 1043; approved October 13, 1964)]

[As Amended Through P.L. 118–31, Enacted December 22, 2023]

AN ACT To provide for the establishment and maintenance of a Central Intelligence Agency Retirement and Disability System for a limited number of employees, and for other purposes.

Be it enacted by the Senate and House of Representatives of the United States of America in Congress assembled,

SECTION 1. [50 U.S.C. 2001 note] SHORT TITLE; TABLE OF CONTENTS.

(a) SHORT TITLE.— This Act may be cited as the "Central Intelligence Agency Retirement Act".

(b) TABLE OF CONTENTS.— The table of contents for this Act is as follows:

TITLE I—DEFINITIONS

SEC. 101. [50 U.S.C. 2001] DEFINITIONS RELATING TO THE SYSTEM.

When used in this Act:

(1) AGENCY.— The term "Agency" means the Central Intelligence Agency.

(2) DIRECTOR.— The term "Director" means the Director of the Central Intelligence Agency.

(3) QUALIFYING SERVICE.— The term "qualifying service" means service determined by the Director to have been performed in carrying out duties described in section 203.

(4) FUND BALANCE.—The term "fund balance" means the sum of—

(A) the investments of the fund calculated at par value; and

(B) the cash balance of the fund on the books of the Treasury.

(5) UNFUNDED LIABILITY.—The term "unfunded liability" means the estimated amount by which—

(A) the present value of all benefits payable from the fund exceeds

(B) the sum of—

(i) the present value of deductions to be withheld from the future basic pay of participants subject to title II and of future Agency contributions to be made on the behalf of such participants;

(ii) the present value of Government payments to the fund under sections 261(c) and 261(d); and

(iii) the fund balance as of the date on which the unfunded liability is determined.

(6) NORMAL COST.— The term "normal cost" means the level percentage of payroll required to be deposited in the fund to meet the cost of benefits payable under the system (computed in accordance with generally accepted actuarial practice on an entry-age basis) less the value of retirement benefits earned under another retirement system for government employees and less the cost of credit allowed for military service.

(7) LUMP-SUM CREDIT.— The term "lump-sum credit" means the unrefunded amount consisting of retirement deductions made from a participant's basic pay and

amounts deposited by a participant covering earlier service, including any amounts deposited under section 252(h).

(8) CONGRESSIONAL INTELLIGENCE COMMITTEES.— The term "congressional intelligence committees" means the Permanent Select Committee on Intelligence of the House of Representatives and the Select Committee on Intelligence of the Senate.

(9) EMPLOYEE.— The term "employee" includes an officer of the Agency.

SEC. 102. [50 U.S.C. 2002] DEFINITIONS RELATING TO PARTICIPANTS AND ANNUITANTS.

(a) GENERAL DEFINITIONS.—When used in title II:

(1) FORMER PARTICIPANT.—The term "former participant" means a person who—

(A) while an employee of the Agency was a participant in the system; and

(B) separates from the Agency without entitlement to immediate receipt of an annuity from the fund.

(2) RETIRED PARTICIPANT.—The term "retired participant" means a person who—

(A) while an employee of the Agency was a participant in the system; and

(B) is entitled to receive an annuity from the fund based upon such person's service as a participant.

(3) SURVIVING SPOUSE.—

(A) IN GENERAL.— The term "surviving spouse" means the surviving wife or husband of a participant or retired participant who (i) was married to the participant or retired participant for at least 9 months immediately preceding the participant's or retired participant's death, or (ii) who is the parent of a child born of the marriage.

(B) TREATMENT WHEN PARTICIPANT DIES LESS THAN 9 MONTHS AFTER MARRIAGE.—In a case in which the participant or retired participant dies within the 9-month period beginning on the date of the marriage, the requirement under subparagraph (A)(i) that a marriage have a duration of at least 9 months immediately preceding the death of the participant or retired participant shall be treated as having been met if—

(i) the death of the participant or retired participant was accidental; or

(ii) the surviving wife or husband had been previously married to the participant or retired participant (and subsequently divorced) and the aggregate time married is at least 9 months.

(4) FORMER SPOUSE.—The term "former spouse" means a former wife or husband of a participant, former participant, or retired participant as follows:

(A) DIVORCES ON OR BEFORE DECEMBER 4, 1991.— In the case of a divorce that became final on or before December 4, 1991, such term means a former wife or husband of a participant, former participant, or retired participant who was married to such participant for not less than 10 years during periods of the participant's creditable service, at least 5 years of which were spent outside the United States by both such participant and former wife or husband during the participant's service as an employee of the Agency.

(B) DIVORCES AFTER DECEMBER 4, 1991.— In the case of a divorce that becomes final after December 4, 1991, such term means a former wife or husband of a participant, former participant, or retired participant who was married to such participant for not less than 10 years during periods of the participant's creditable service, at least 5 years of which were spent by the participant during the participant's service as an employee of the Agency (i) outside the United States, or (ii) otherwise in a position the duties of which qualified the participant for designation by the Director as a participant under section 203.

(C) CREDITABLE SERVICE.— For purposes of subparagraphs (A) and (B), the term "creditable service" means all periods of a participant's service that are creditable under sections 251, 252, and 253.

(5) PREVIOUS SPOUSE.— The term "previous spouse" means an individual who was married for at least 9 months to a participant, former participant, or retired participant who had at least 18 months of service which are creditable under sections 251, 252, and 253.

(6) SPOUSAL AGREEMENT.—The term "spousal agreement" means an agreement between a participant, former participant, or retired participant and the participant, former participant, or retired participant's spouse or former spouse that—

(A) is in writing, is signed by the parties, and is notarized;

(B) has not been modified by court order; and

(C) has been authenticated by the Director.

(7) COURT ORDER.—The term "court order" means—

(A) a court decree of divorce, annulment, or legal separation; or

(B) a court order or court-approved property settlement agreement incident to such court decree of divorce, annulment, or legal separation.

(8) COURT.— The term "court" means a court of a State, the District of Columbia, the Commonwealth of Puerto Rico, Guam, the Northern Mariana Islands, or the Virgin Islands, and any Indian court.

(b) DEFINITION OF CHILD.—For purposes of sections 221 and 232:

(1) IN GENERAL.—The term "child" means any of the following:

(A) MINOR CHILDREN.—An unmarried dependent child under 18 years of age, including—

(i) an adopted child;

(ii) a stepchild, but only if the stepchild lived with the participant or retired participant in a regular parent-child relationship;

(iii) a recognized natural child; and

(iv) a child who lived with the participant, for whom a petition of adoption was filed by the participant or retired participant, and who is adopted by the surviving spouse after the death of the participant or retired participant.

(B) DISABLED ADULT CHILDREN.— An unmarried dependent child, regardless of age, who is incapable of self-support because of a physical or mental disability incurred before age 18.

(C) STUDENTS.— An unmarried dependent child between 18 and 22 years of age who is a student regularly pursuing a full-time course of study or training in residence in a high school, trade school, technical or vocational institute, junior college, college, university, or comparable recognized educational institution.

(2) SPECIAL RULES FOR STUDENTS.—

(A) Extension of age termination of status as "child".—For purposes of this subsection, a child whose 22nd birthday occurs before July 1 or after August 31 of a calendar year, and while regularly pursuing such a course of study or training, shall be treated as having attained the age of 22 on the first day of July following that birthday.

(B) TREATMENT OF INTERIM PERIOD BETWEEN SCHOOL YEARS.— A child who is a student is deemed not to have ceased to be a student during an interim between school years if the interim does not exceed 5 months and if the child shows to the satisfaction of the Director that the child has a bona fide intention of continuing to pursue a course of study or training in the same or different school during the school semester (or other period into which the school year is divided) immediately following the interim.

(3) DEPENDENT DEFINED.— For purposes of this subsection, the term "dependent", with respect to the child of a participant or retired participant, means that the participant or retired participant was, at the time of the death of the participant or retired participant, either living with or contributing to the support of the child, as determined in accordance with regulations prescribed under title II.

(4) EXCLUSION OF STEPCHILDREN FROM LUMP-SUM PAYMENT.— For purposes of section 241(c), the term "child" includes an adopted child and a natural child, but does not include a stepchild.

TITLE II—THE CENTRAL INTELLIGENCE AGENCY RETIREMENT AND DISABILITY SYSTEM

PART A—ESTABLISHMENT OF SYSTEM

SEC. 201. [50 U.S.C. 2011] THE CIARDS SYSTEM.

(a) IN GENERAL.—

(1) ESTABLISHMENT OF SYSTEM.— There is a retirement and disability system for certain employees of the Central Intelligence Agency known as the Central Intelligence Agency Retirement and Disability System (hereinafter in this Act referred to as the "system"), originally established pursuant to title II of the Central Intelligence Agency Retirement Act of 1964 for Certain Employees.

(2) DCI REGULATIONS.— The Director shall prescribe regulations for the system. The Director shall submit any proposed regulations for the system to the congressional intelligence committees not less than 14 days before they take effect.

(b) ADMINISTRATION OF SYSTEM.— The Director shall administer the system in accordance with regulations prescribed under this title and with the principles established by this title.

(c) FINALITY OF DECISIONS OF DCI.— In the interests of the security of the foreign intelligence activities of the United States and in order further to implement section

102A(i) of the National Security Act of 1947 (50 U.S.C. 403–3(c)(1)) that the Director of National Intelligence shall be responsible for protecting intelligence sources and methods from unauthorized disclosure, and notwithstanding the provisions of chapter 7 of title 5, United States Code, or any other provision of law (except section 305(b) of this Act), any determination by the Director authorized by this Act shall be final and conclusive and shall not be subject to review by any court.

SEC. 202. [50 U.S.C. 2012] CENTRAL INTELLIGENCE AGENCY RETIREMENT AND DISABILITY FUND.

The Director shall maintain the fund in the Treasury known as the "Central Intelligence Agency Retirement and Disability Fund" (hereinafter in this Act referred to as the "fund"), originally created pursuant to title II of the Central Intelligence Agency Retirement Act of 1964 for Certain Employees.

SEC. 203. [50 U.S.C. 2013] PARTICIPANTS IN THE CIARDS SYSTEM.

(a) Designation of Participants.— The Director may from time to time designate employees of the Agency who shall be entitled to participate in the system. Employees so designated who elect to participate in the system are referred to in this Act as "participants".

(b) Qualifying Service.—Designation of employees under this section may be made only from among employees of the Agency who have completed at least 5 years of qualifying service. For purposes of this Act, qualifying service is service performed by an Agency employee in carrying out duties that are determined by the Director—

(1) to be in support of intelligence activities abroad hazardous to life or health; or

(2) to be so specialized because of security requirements as to be clearly distinguishable from normal government employment.

(c) Election of Employee To Be a Participant.—

(1) Permanence of election.— An employee of the Agency who elects to accept designation as a participant in the system shall remain a participant of the system for the duration of that individual's employment with the Agency.

(2) Irrevocability of election.— Such an election shall be irrevocable except as and to the extent provided in section 301(d).

(3) Election not subject to approval.— An election under this section is not subject to review or approval by the Director.

SEC. 204. [50 U.S.C. 2014] ANNUITANTS.

Persons who are annuitants under the system are—

(1) those persons who, on the basis of their service in the Agency, have met all requirements for an annuity under this title or any other Act and are receiving an annuity from the fund; and

(2) those persons who, on the basis of someone else's service, meet all the requirements under this title or any other Act for an annuity payable from the fund.

Part B—Contributions

SEC. 211. [50 U.S.C. 2021] CONTRIBUTIONS TO FUND.

(a) In General.—

(1) Definition.—In this subsection, the term "revised annuity participant" means an individual who—

(A) on December 31, 2012—

(i) is not a participant;

(ii) is not performing qualifying service; and

(iii) has less than 5 years of qualifying service; and

(B) after December 31, 2012, becomes a participant performing qualifying service.

(2) Contributions.—

(A) In general.— Except as provided in subsection (d), 7 percent of the basic pay received by a participant other than a revised annuity participant for any pay period shall be deducted and withheld from the pay of that participant and contributed to the fund.

(B) Revised annuity participants.— Except as provided in subsection (d), 9.3 percent of the basic pay received by a revised annuity participant for any pay period shall be deducted and withheld from the pay of that revised annuity participant and contributed to the fund.

(3) Agency contributions.—

(A) In general.— An amount equal to 7 percent of the basic pay received by a participant other than a revised annuity participant shall be contributed to the fund for a pay period for the participant from the appropriation or fund which is used for payment of the participant's basic pay.

(B) Revised annuity participants.— An amount equal to 4.7 percent of the basic pay received by a revised annuity participant shall be contributed to the fund for a pay period for the revised annuity participant from the appropriation or fund which is used for payment of the revised annuity participant's basic pay.

(4) Deposits to the fund.— The amounts deducted and withheld from basic pay, together with the amounts so contributed from the appropriation or fund, shall be deposited by the Director to the credit of the fund.

(b) Consent of Participant To Deductions From Pay.— Each participant shall be deemed to consent and agree to such deductions from basic pay, and payment less such deductions shall be a full and complete discharge and acquittance of all claims and demands whatsoever for all regular services during the period covered by such payment, except the right to the benefits to which the participant is entitled under this title, notwithstanding any law, rule, or regulation affecting the individual's pay.

(c) Treatment of Contributions After 35 Years of Service.—

(1) Accrual of interest.— Amounts deducted and withheld from the basic pay of a participant under this section for pay periods after the first day of the first pay period beginning after the day on which the participant completes 35 years of creditable service computed under sections 251 and 252 (excluding service credit for unused sick leave under section 221(a)(2)) shall accrue interest. Such interest shall accrue at the rate of 3 percent a year through December 31, 1984, and thereafter

at the rate computed under section 8334(e) of title 5, United States Code, and shall be compounded annually from the date on which the amount is so deducted and withheld until the date of the participant's retirement or death.

(2) USE OF AMOUNTS WITHHELD AFTER 35 YEARS OF SERVICE.—

(A) USE FOR DEPOSITS DUE UNDER SECTION 252(B).— Amounts described in paragraph (1), including interest accrued on such amounts, shall be applied upon the participant's retirement or death toward any deposit due under section 252(b).

(B) LUMP-SUM PAYMENT.— Any balance of such amounts not so required for such a deposit shall be refunded to the participant in a lump sum after the participant's separation (or, in the event of a death in service, to a beneficiary in order of precedence specified in section 241(c)), subject to prior notification of a current spouse, if any, unless the participant establishes to the satisfaction of the Director, in accordance with regulations which the Director may prescribe, that the participant does not know, and has taken all reasonable steps to determine, the whereabouts of the current spouse.

(C) PURCHASES OF ADDITIONAL ELECTIVE BENEFITS.—In lieu of such a lump-sum payment, the participant may use such amounts—

(i) to purchase an additional annuity in accordance with section 281; or

(ii) provide any additional survivor benefit for a current or former spouse or spouses.

(d) OFFSET FOR SOCIAL SECURITY TAXES.—

(1) PERSONS COVERED.—In the case of a participant who was a participant subject to this title before January 1, 1984, and whose service—

(A) is employment for the purposes of title II of the Social Security Act and chapter 21 of the Internal Revenue Code of 1954, and

(B) is not creditable service for any purpose under title III of this Act or chapter 84 of title 5, United States Code,

there shall be deducted and withheld from the basic pay of the participant under this section during any pay period only the amount computed under paragraph (2).

(2) REDUCTION IN CONTRIBUTION.—The amount deducted and withheld from the basic pay of a participant during any pay period pursuant to paragraph (1) shall be the excess of—

(A) the amount determined by multiplying the percent applicable to the participant under subsection (a) by the basic pay payable to the participant for that pay period, over

(B) the amount of the taxes deducted and withheld from such basic pay under section 3101(a) of the Internal Revenue Code of 1954 (relating to old-age, survivors, and disability insurance) for that pay period.

PART C—COMPUTATION OF ANNUITIES

SEC. 221. [50 U.S.C. 2031] COMPUTATION OF ANNUITIES.

(a) ANNUITY OF PARTICIPANT.—

(1) COMPUTATION OF ANNUITY.—The annuity of a participant is the product of—

(A) the participant's high-3 average pay (as defined in paragraph (4)); and

(B) the number of years, not exceeding 35, of service credit (determined in accordance with sections 251 and 252) multiplied by 2 percent.

(2) CREDIT FOR UNUSED SICK LEAVE.— The total service of a participant who retires on an immediate annuity (except under section 231) or who dies leaving a survivor or survivors entitled to an annuity shall include (without regard to the 35-year limitation prescribed in paragraph (1)) the days of unused sick leave to the credit of the participant. Days of unused sick leave may not be counted in determining average basic pay or eligibility for an annuity under this title. A deposit shall not be required for days of unused sick leave credited under this paragraph.

(3) CREDITING OF PART-TIME SERVICE.—

(A) IN GENERAL.— In the case of a participant whose service includes service on a part-time basis performed after April 6, 1986, the participant's annuity shall be the sum of the amounts determined under subparagraphs (B) and (C).

(B) COMPUTATION OF PRE-APRIL 7, 1986, ANNUITY.— The portion of an annuity referred to in subparagraph (A) with respect to service before April 7, 1986, shall be the amount computed under paragraph (1) using the participant's length of service before that date (increased by the unused sick leave to the credit of the participant at the time of retirement) and the participant's high-3 average pay, as determined by using the annual rate of basic pay that would be payable for full-time service in that position.

(C) COMPUTATION OF POST-APRIL 6, 1986, ANNUITY.—The portion of an annuity referred to in subparagraph (A) with respect to service after April 6, 1986, shall be the product of—

(i) the amount computed under paragraph (1), using the participant's length of service after that date and the participant's high-3 average pay, as determined by using the annual rate of basic pay that would be payable for full-time service; and

(ii) the ratio which the participant's actual service after April 6, 1986 (as determined by prorating the participant's total service after that date to reflect the service that was performed on a part-time basis) bears to the total service after that date that would be creditable for the participant if all the service had been performed on a full-time basis.

(D) TREATMENT OF EMPLOYMENT ON TEMPORARY OR INTERMITTENT BASIS.— Employment on a temporary or intermittent basis shall not be considered to be service on a part-time basis for purposes of this paragraph.

(4) HIGH-3 AVERAGE PAY DEFINED.— For purposes of this subsection, a participant's high-3 average pay is the amount of the participant's average basic pay for the highest 3 consecutive years of the participant's service for which full contributions have been made to the fund.

(5) COMPUTATION OF SERVICE.— In determining the aggregate period of service upon which an annuity is to be based, any fractional part of a month shall not be counted.

(b) SPOUSE OR FORMER SPOUSE SURVIVOR ANNUITY.—

(1) REDUCTION IN PARTICIPANT'S ANNUITY TO PROVIDE SPOUSE OR FORMER SPOUSE

SURVIVOR ANNUITY.—

(A) GENERAL RULE.— Except to the extent provided otherwise under a written election under subparagraph (B) or (C), if at the time of retirement a participant or former participant is married (or has a former spouse who has not remarried before attaining age 55), the participant shall receive a reduced annuity and provide a survivor annuity for the participant's spouse under this subsection or former spouse under section 222(b), or a combination of such annuities, as the case may be.

(B) JOINT ELECTION FOR WAIVER OR REDUCTION OF SPOUSE SURVIVOR ANNUITY.— A married participant or former participant and the participant's spouse may jointly elect in writing at the time of retirement to waive a survivor annuity for that spouse under this section or to reduce such survivor annuity under this section by designating a portion of the annuity of the participant as the base for the survivor annuity. If the marriage is dissolved following an election for such a reduced annuity and the spouse qualifies as a former spouse, the base used in calculating any annuity of the former spouse under section 222(b) may not exceed the portion of the participant's annuity designated under this subparagraph.

(C) JOINT ELECTION OF PARTICIPANT AND FORMER SPOUSE.— If a participant or former participant has a former spouse, such participant and the participant's former spouse may jointly elect by spousal agreement under section 264(b) to waive, reduce, or increase a survivor annuity under section 222(b) for that former spouse. Any such election must be made (i) before the end of the 2-year period beginning on the date on which the divorce or annulment involving that former spouse becomes final, or (ii) at the time of retirement of the participant, whichever is later.

(D) UNILATERAL ELECTIONS IN ABSENCE OF SPOUSE OR FORMER SPOUSE.— The Director may prescribe regulations under which a participant or former participant may make an election under subparagraph (B) or (C) without the participant's spouse or former spouse if the participant establishes to the satisfaction of the Director that the participant does not know, and has taken all reasonable steps to determine, the whereabouts of the spouse or former spouse.

(2) AMOUNT OF REDUCTION IN PARTICIPANT'S ANNUITY.— The annuity of a participant or former participant providing a survivor annuity under this section (or section 222(b)), excluding any portion of the annuity not designated or committed as a base for any survivor annuity, shall be reduced by 2½ percent of the first $3,600 plus 10 percent of any amount over $3,600. The reduction under this paragraph shall be calculated before any reduction under section 222(a)(5).

(3) AMOUNT OF SURVIVING SPOUSE ANNUITY.—

(A) IN GENERAL.— If a retired participant receiving a reduced annuity under this subsection dies and is survived by a spouse, a survivor annuity shall be paid to the surviving spouse. The amount of the annuity shall be equal to 55 percent of (i) the full amount of the participant's annuity computed under subsection (a), or (ii) any lesser amount elected as the base for the survivor annuity under paragraph (1)(B).

(B) LIMITATION.— Notwithstanding subparagraph (A), the amount of the annuity calculated under subparagraph (A) for a surviving spouse in any case in which there is also a surviving former spouse of the retired participant who qualifies for an annuity under section 222(b) may not exceed 55 percent of the portion (if any) of the base for survivor annuities which remains available under section 222(b)(4)(B).

(C) EFFECTIVE DATE AND TERMINATION OF ANNUITY.— An annuity payable from the fund to a surviving spouse under this paragraph shall commence on the day after the retired participant dies and shall terminate on the last day of the month before the surviving spouse's death or remarriage before attaining age 55. If such survivor annuity is terminated because of remarriage, it shall be restored at the same rate commencing on the date such remarriage is dissolved by death, annulment, or divorce if any lump sum paid upon termination of the annuity is returned to the fund.

(c) 18–MONTH OPEN PERIOD AFTER RETIREMENT TO PROVIDE SPOUSE COVERAGE.—

(1) SURVIVOR ANNUITY ELECTIONS.—

(A) ELECTION WHEN SPOUSE COVERAGE WAIVED AT TIME OF RETIREMENT.—A participant or former participant who retires after March 31, 1992 and who—

(i) is married at the time of retirement; and

(ii) elects at that time (in accordance with subsection (b)) to waive a survivor annuity for the spouse,

may, during the 18-month period beginning on the date of the retirement of the participant, elect to have a reduction under subsection (b) made in the annuity of the participant (or in such portion thereof as the participant may designate) in order to provide a survivor annuity for the participant's spouse.

(B) ELECTION WHEN REDUCED SPOUSE ANNUITY ELECTED.—A participant or former participant who retires after March 31, 1992, and—

(i) who, at the time of retirement, is married, and

(ii) who, at that time designates (in accordance with subsection (b)) that a portion of the annuity of such participant is to be used as the base for a survivor annuity,

may, during the 18-month period beginning on the date of the retirement of such participant, elect to have a greater portion of the annuity of such participant so used.

(2) DEPOSIT REQUIRED.—

(A) REQUIREMENT.— An election under paragraph (1) shall not be effective unless the amount specified in subparagraph (B) is deposited into the fund before the end of that 18-month period.

(B) AMOUNT OF DEPOSIT.—The amount to be deposited with respect to an election under this subsection is the amount equal to the sum of the following:

(i) ADDITIONAL COST TO SYSTEM.—The additional cost to the system that is associated with providing a survivor annuity under subsection (b) and that results from such election, taking into account—

(I) the difference (for the period between the date on which the annuity of the participant or former participant commences and the date of the election) between the amount paid to such participant or former participant under this title and the amount which would have been paid if such election had been made at the time the participant or former participant applied for the annuity; and

(II) the costs associated with providing for the later election.

(ii) INTEREST.— Interest on the additional cost determined under clause (i), computed using the interest rate specified or determined under section 8334(e) of title 5, United States Code, for the calendar year in which the amount to be deposited is determined.

(3) VOIDING OF PREVIOUS ELECTIONS.— An election by a participant or former participant under this subsection voids prospectively any election previously made in the case of such participant under subsection (b).

(4) REDUCTIONS IN ANNUITY.— An annuity that is reduced in connection with an election under this subsection shall be reduced by the same percentage reductions as were in effect at the time of the retirement of the participant or former participant whose annuity is so reduced.

(5) RIGHTS AND OBLIGATIONS RESULTING FROM REDUCED ANNUITY ELECTION.— Rights and obligations resulting from the election of a reduced annuity under this subsection shall be the same as the rights and obligations that would have resulted had the participant involved elected such annuity at the time of retirement.

(d) ANNUITIES FOR SURVIVING CHILDREN.—

(1) PARTICIPANTS DYING BEFORE APRIL 1, 1992.—In the case of a retired participant who died before April 1, 1992, and who is survived by a child or children—

(A) if the retired participant was survived by a spouse, there shall be paid from the fund to or on behalf of each such surviving child an annuity determined under paragraph (3)(A); and

(B) if the retired participant was not survived by a spouse, there shall be paid from the fund to or on behalf of each such surviving child an annuity determined under paragraph (3)(B).

(2) PARTICIPANTS DYING ON OR AFTER APRIL 1, 1992.—In the case of a retired participant who dies on or after April 1, 1992, and who is survived by a child or children—

(A) if the retired participant is survived by a spouse or former spouse who is the natural or adoptive parent of a surviving child of the participant, there shall be paid from the fund to or on behalf of each such surviving child an annuity determined under paragraph (3)(A); and

(B) if the retired participant is not survived by a spouse or former spouse who is the natural or adoptive parent of a surviving child of the participant, there shall be paid to or on behalf of each such surviving child an annuity determined under paragraph (3)(B).

(3) AMOUNT OF ANNUITY.—

(A) The annual amount of an annuity for the surviving child of a participant covered by paragraph (1)(A) or (2)(A) of this subsection (or covered by paragraph (1)(A) or (2)(A) of section 232(c)) is the smallest of the following:

(i) 60 percent of the participant's high-3 average pay, as determined under subsection (a)(4), divided by the number of children.

(ii) $900, as adjusted under section 291.

(iii) $2,700, as adjusted under section 291, divided by the number of children.

(B) The amount of an annuity for the surviving child of a participant covered by paragraph (1)(B) or (2)(B) of this subsection (or covered by paragraph (1)(B) or (2)(B) of section 232(c)) is the smallest of the following:

(i) 75 percent of the participant's high-3 average pay, as determined under subsection (a)(4), divided by the number of children.

(ii) $1,080, as adjusted under section 291.

(iii) $3,240, as adjusted under section 291, divided by the number of children.

(4) Recomputation of child annuities.—

(A) In the case of a child annuity payable under paragraph (1), upon the death of a surviving spouse or the termination of the annuity of a child, the annuities of any remaining children shall be recomputed and paid as though the spouse or child had not survived the retired participant.

(B) In the case of a child annuity payable under paragraph (2), upon the death of a surviving spouse or former spouse or termination of the annuity of a child, the annuities of any remaining children shall be recomputed and paid as though the spouse, former spouse, or child had not survived the retired participant. If the annuity of a surviving child who has not been receiving an annuity is initiated or resumed, the annuities of any other children shall be recomputed and paid from that date as though the annuities of all currently eligible children were then being initiated.

(5) Definition of former spouse.— For purposes of this subsection, the term "former spouse" includes any former wife or husband of the retired participant, regardless of the length of marriage or the amount of creditable service completed by the participant.

(e) Commencement and Termination of Child Annuities.—

(1) Commencement.— An annuity payable to a child under subsection (d), or under section 232(c), shall begin on the day after the date on which the participant or retired participant dies or, in the case of an individual over the age of 18 who is not a child within the meaning of section 102(b), shall begin or resume on the first day of the month in which the individual later becomes or again becomes a student as described in section 102(b). Such annuity may not commence until any lump-sum that has been paid is returned to the fund.

(2) Termination.— Such an annuity shall terminate on the last day of the month before the month in which the recipient of the annuity dies or no longer qualifies as a child (as defined in section 102(b)).

(f) Participants Not Married at Time of Retirement.—

(1) Designation of persons with insurable interest.—

(A) Authority to make designation.— Subject to the rights of former spouses under sections 221(b) and 222, at the time of retirement an unmarried participant found by the Director to be in good health may elect to receive an annuity reduced in accordance with subparagraph (B) and designate in writing an individual having an insurable interest in the participant to receive an annuity under the system after the participant's death. The amount of such an annuity shall be equal to 55 percent of the participant's reduced annuity.

(B) Reduction in participant's annuity.— The annuity payable to the participant making such election shall be reduced by 10 percent of an annuity computed under subsection (a) and by an additional 5 percent for each full 5 years the designated individual is younger than the participant. The total reduction under this subparagraph may not exceed 40 percent.

(C) Commencement of survivor annuity.— The annuity payable to the designated individual shall begin on the day after the retired participant dies and terminate on the last day of the month before the designated individual dies.

(D) Recomputation of participant's annuity on death of designated individual.— An annuity which is reduced under this paragraph shall, effective the first day of the month following the death of the designated individual, be recomputed and paid as if the annuity had not been so reduced.

(2) Election of survivor annuity upon subsequent marriage.— A participant who is unmarried at the time of retirement and who later marries may irrevocably elect, in a signed writing received by the Director within two years after the marriage, to receive a reduced annuity as provided in section 221(b). Such election and reduction shall be effective on the first day of the month beginning 9 months after the date of marriage. The election voids prospectively any election previously made under paragraph (1).

(g) Effect of Divorce After Retirement.—

(1) Recomputation of retired participant's annuity upon divorce.— An annuity which is reduced under this section (or any similar prior provision of law) to provide a survivor annuity for a spouse shall, if the marriage of the retired participant to such spouse is dissolved, be recomputed and paid for each full month during which a retired participant is not married (or is remarried, if there is no election in effect under paragraph (2)) as if the annuity had not been so reduced, subject to any reduction required to provide a survivor annuity under subsection (b) or (c) of section 222 or under section 226.

(2) Election of survivor annuity upon subsequent remarriage.—

(A) In general.— Upon remarriage, the retired participant may irrevocably elect, by means of a signed writing received by the Director within two years after such remarriage, to receive a reduced annuity for the purpose of providing an annuity for the new spouse of the retired participant in the event such spouse survives the retired participant. Such reduction shall be equal to the reduction in effect immediately before the dissolution of the previous marriage (unless such reduction is adjusted under section 222(b)(5) or elected under subparagraph (B)).

(B) When annuity previously not (or not fully) reduced.—

(i) Election.— If the retired participant's annuity was not reduced (or was not fully reduced) to provide a survivor annuity for the participant's spouse or former spouse as of the time of retirement, the retired participant may make an election under the first sentence of subparagraph (A) upon remarriage to a spouse other than the spouse at the time of retirement. For any remarriage that occurred before August 14, 1991, the retired participant may make such an election within 2 years after such date.

(ii) DEPOSIT REQUIRED.—

(I) The retired participant shall, within two years after the date of the remarriage (or by August 14, 1993 for any remarriage that occurred before August 14, 1991), deposit in the fund an amount determined by the Director, as nearly as may be administratively feasible, to reflect the amount by which the retired participant's annuity would have been reduced if the election had been in effect since the date the annuity commenced, plus interest.

(II) The annual rate of interest for each year during which the retired participant's annuity would have been reduced if the election had been in effect since the date the annuity commenced shall be 6 percent.

(III) If the retired participant does not make the deposit, the Director shall collect such amount by offset against the participant's annuity, up to a maximum of 25 percent of the net annuity otherwise payable to the retired participant, and the retired participant is deemed to consent to such offset.

(IV) The deposit required by this subparagraph may be made by the surviving spouse of the retired participant.

(C) EFFECTS OF ELECTION.— An election under this paragraph and the reduction in the participant's annuity shall be effective on the first day of the month beginning 9 months after the date of remarriage. A survivor annuity elected under this paragraph shall be treated in all respects as a survivor annuity under subsection (b).

(h) CONDITIONAL ELECTION OF INSURABLE INTEREST SURVIVOR ANNUITY BY PARTICIPANTS MARRIED AT THE TIME OF RETIREMENT.—

(1) AUTHORITY TO MAKE DESIGNATION.— Subject to the rights of former spouses under subsection (b) and section 222, at the time of retirement a married participant found by the Director to be in good health may elect to receive an annuity reduced in accordance with subsection (f)(1)(B) and designate in writing an individual having an insurable interest in the participant to receive an annuity under the system after the participant's death, except that any such election to provide an insurable interest survivor annuity to the participant's spouse shall only be effective if the participant's spouse waives the spousal right to a survivor annuity under this Act. The amount of the annuity shall be equal to 55 percent of the participant's reduced annuity.

(2) REDUCTION IN PARTICIPANT'S ANNUITY.— The annuity payable to the participant making such election shall be reduced by 10 percent of an annuity computed under subsection (a) and by an additional 5 percent for each full 5 years the designated individual is younger than the participant. The total reduction under this subparagraph may not exceed 40 percent.

(3) COMMENCEMENT OF SURVIVOR ANNUITY.— The annuity payable to the designated individual shall begin on the day after the retired participant dies and

terminate on the last day of the month before the designated individual dies.

(4) RECOMPUTATION OF PARTICIPANT'S ANNUITY ON DEATH OF DESIGNATED INDIVIDUAL.— An annuity that is reduced under this subsection shall, effective the first day of the month following the death of the designated individual, be recomputed and paid as if the annuity had not been so reduced.

(i) COORDINATION OF ANNUITIES.—

(1) SURVIVING SPOUSE.— A surviving spouse whose survivor annuity was terminated because of remarriage before attaining age 55 shall not be entitled under subsection (b)(3)(C) to the restoration of that survivor annuity payable from the fund unless the surviving spouse elects to receive it instead of any other survivor annuity to which the surviving spouse may be entitled under the system or any other retirement system for Government employees by reason of the remarriage.

(2) FORMER SPOUSE.— A surviving former spouse of a participant or retired participant shall not become entitled under section 222(b) or 224 to a survivor annuity or to the restoration of a survivor annuity payable from the fund unless the surviving former spouse elects to receive it instead of any other survivor annuity to which the surviving former spouse may be entitled under this or any other retirement system for Government employees on the basis of a marriage to someone other than the participant.

(3) SURVIVING SPOUSE OF POST-RETIREMENT MARRIAGE.— A surviving spouse who married a participant after the participant's retirement shall be entitled to a survivor annuity payable from the fund only upon electing that annuity instead of any other survivor annuity to which the surviving spouse may be entitled under this or any other retirement system for Government employees on the basis of a marriage to someone other than the retired participant.

(j) SUPPLEMENTAL SURVIVOR ANNUITIES.—

(1) SPOUSE OF RECALLED ANNUITANT.— A married recalled annuitant who reverts to retired status with entitlement to a supplemental annuity under section 271(b) shall, unless the annuitant and the annuitant's spouse jointly elect in writing to the contrary at the time of reversion to retired status, have the supplemental annuity reduced by 10 percent to provide a supplemental survivor annuity for the annuitant's spouse. Such supplemental survivor annuity shall be equal to 55 percent of the supplemental annuity of the annuitant.

(2) REGULATIONS.— The Director shall prescribe regulations to provide for the application of paragraph (1) of this subsection and of subsection (b) of section 271 in any case in which an annuitant has a former spouse who was married to the recalled annuitant at any time during the period of recall service and who qualifies for an annuity under section 222(b).

(k) OFFSET OF ANNUITIES BY AMOUNT OF SOCIAL SECURITY BENEFIT.— Notwithstanding any other provision of this title, an annuity (including a disability annuity) payable under this title to an individual described in sections 211(d)(1) and 301(c)(1) and any survivor annuity payable under this title on the basis of the service of such individual shall be reduced in a manner consistent with section 8349 of title 5, United States Code, under conditions consistent with the conditions prescribed in that section.

(l) INFORMATION FROM OTHER AGENCIES.—

(1) OTHER AGENCIES.—For the purpose of ensuring the accuracy of the information used in the determination of eligibility for and the computation of annuities payable from the fund under this title, at the request of the Director—

(A) the Secretary of Defense shall provide information on retired or retainer pay paid under title 10, United States Code;

(B) the Secretary of Veterans Affairs shall provide information on pensions or compensation paid under title 38, United States Code;

(C) the Secretary of Health and Human Services shall provide information contained in the records of the Social Security Administration; and

(D) the Secretary of Labor shall provide information on benefits paid under subchapter I of chapter 81 of title 5, United States Code.

(2) LIMITATION ON INFORMATION REQUESTED.— The Director shall request only such information as the Director determines is necessary.

(3) LIMITATION ON USES OF INFORMATION.— The Director, in consultation with the officials from whom information is requested, shall ensure that information made available under this subsection is used only for the purposes authorized.

(m) INFORMATION ON RIGHTS UNDER THE SYSTEM.—The Director shall, on an annual basis—

(1) inform each retired participant of the participant's right of election under subsections (c), (f)(2), and (g); and

(2) to the maximum extent practicable, inform spouses and former spouses of participants, former participants, and retired participants of their rights under this Act.

SEC. 222. [50 U.S.C. 2032] ANNUITIES FOR FORMER SPOUSES.

(a) FORMER SPOUSE SHARE OF PARTICIPANT'S ANNUITY.—

(1) PRO RATA SHARE.—Unless otherwise expressly provided by a spousal agreement or court order under section 264(b), a former spouse of a participant, former participant, or retired participant is entitled to an annuity—

(A) if married to the participant, former participant, or retired participant throughout the creditable service of the participant, equal to 50 percent of the annuity of the participant; or

(B) if not married to the participant throughout such creditable service, equal to that proportion of 50 percent of such annuity that is the proportion that the number of days of the marriage of the former spouse to the participant during periods of creditable service of such participant under this title bears to the total number of days of such creditable service.

(2) DISQUALIFICATION UPON REMARRIAGE BEFORE AGE 55.— A former spouse is not qualified for an annuity under this subsection if before the commencement of that annuity the former spouse remarries before becoming 55 years of age.

(3) COMMENCEMENT OF ANNUITY.— The annuity of a former spouse under this subsection commences on the day the participant upon whose service the annuity is based becomes entitled to an annuity under this title or on the first day of the month

after the divorce or annulment involved becomes final, whichever is later.

(4) TERMINATION OF ANNUITY.—The annuity of such former spouse and the right thereto terminate on—

(A) the last day of the month before the month in which the former spouse dies or remarries before 55 years of age; or

(B) the date on which the annuity of the participant terminates (except in the case of an annuity subject to paragraph (5)(B)).

(5) TREATMENT OF PARTICIPANT'S ANNUITY.—

(A) REDUCTION IN PARTICIPANT'S ANNUITY.—The annuity payable to any participant shall be reduced by the amount of an annuity under this subsection paid to any former spouse based upon the service of that participant. Such reduction shall be disregarded in calculating—

(i) the survivor annuity for any spouse, former spouse, or other survivor under this title; and

(ii) any reduction in the annuity of the participant to provide survivor benefits under subsection (b) or under section 221(b).

(B) TREATMENT WHEN ANNUITANT RETURNS TO SERVICE.— If an annuitant whose annuity is reduced under subparagraph (A) is recalled to service under section 271, or reinstated or reappointed, in the case of a recovered disability annuitant, or if any annuitant is reemployed as provided for under sections 272 and 273, the pay of that annuitant shall be reduced by the same amount as the annuity would have been reduced if it had continued. Amounts equal to the reductions under this subparagraph shall be deposited in the Treasury of the United States to the credit of the fund.

(6) DISABILITY ANNUITANT.—Notwithstanding paragraph (3), in the case of a former spouse of a disability annuitant—

(A) the annuity of that former spouse shall commence on the date on which the participant would qualify on the basis of the participant's creditable service for an annuity under this title (other than a disability annuity) or the date on which the disability annuity begins, whichever is later, and

(B) the amount of the annuity of the former spouse shall be calculated on the basis of the annuity for which the participant would otherwise so qualify.

(7) ELECTION OF BENEFITS.— A former spouse of a participant, former participant, or retired participant shall not become entitled under this subsection to an annuity payable from the fund unless the former spouse elects to receive it instead of any survivor annuity to which the former spouse may be entitled under this or any other retirement system for Government employees on the basis of a marriage to someone other than the participant.

(8) LIMITATION IN CASE OF MULTIPLE FORMER SPOUSE ANNUITIES.— No spousal agreement or court order under section 264(b) involving a participant may provide for an annuity or a combination of annuities under this subsection that exceeds the annuity of the participant.

(b) FORMER SPOUSE SURVIVOR ANNUITY.—

(1) PRO RATA SHARE.—Subject to any election under section 221(b)(1)(B) and (C) and unless otherwise expressly provided by a spousal agreement or court order under

section 264(b), if an annuitant is survived by a former spouse, the former spouse shall be entitled—

(A) if married to the annuitant throughout the creditable service of the annuitant, to a survivor annuity equal to 55 percent of the unreduced amount of the annuitant's annuity, as computed under section 221(a); and

(B) if not married to the annuitant throughout such creditable service, to a survivor annuity equal to that proportion of 55 percent of the unreduced amount of such annuity that is the proportion that the number of days of the marriage of the former spouse to the participant during periods of creditable service of such participant under this title bears to the total number of days of such creditable service.

(2) DISQUALIFICATION UPON REMARRIAGE BEFORE AGE 55.— A former spouse shall not be qualified for an annuity under this subsection if before the commencement of that annuity the former spouse remarries before becoming 55 years of age.

(3) COMMENCEMENT, TERMINATION, AND RESTORATION OF ANNUITY.— An annuity payable from the fund under this title to a surviving former spouse under this subsection shall commence on the day after the annuitant dies and shall terminate on the last day of the month before the former spouse's death or remarriage before attaining age 55. If such a survivor annuity is terminated because of remarriage, it shall be restored at the same rate commencing on the date such remarriage is dissolved by death, annulment, or divorce if any lump sum paid upon termination of the annuity is returned to the fund.

(4) SURVIVOR ANNUITY AMOUNT.—

(A) MAXIMUM AMOUNT.— The maximum survivor annuity or combination of survivor annuities under this subsection (and section 221(b)(3)) with respect to any participant may not exceed 55 percent of the full amount of the participant's annuity, as calculated under section 221(a).

(B) LIMITATION ON OTHER SURVIVOR ANNUITIES BASED ON SERVICE OF SAME PARTICIPANT.— Once a survivor annuity has been provided under this subsection for any former spouse, a survivor annuity for another individual may thereafter be provided under this subsection (or section 221(b)(3)) with respect to the participant only for that portion (if any) of the maximum available which is not committed for survivor benefits for any former spouse whose prospective right to such annuity has not terminated by reason of death or remarriage.

(C) FINALITY OF COURT ORDER UPON DEATH OF PARTICIPANT.— After the death of a participant or retired participant, a court order under section 264(b) may not adjust the amount of the annuity of a former spouse of that participant or retired participant under this section.

(5) EFFECT OF TERMINATION OF FORMER SPOUSE ENTITLEMENT.—

(A) RECOMPUTATION OF PARTICIPANT'S ANNUITY.— If a former spouse of a retired participant dies or remarries before attaining age 55, the annuity of the retired participant, if reduced to provide a survivor annuity for that former spouse, shall be recomputed and paid, effective on the first day of the month beginning after such death or remarriage, as if the annuity had not been so reduced, unless an election is in effect under subparagraph (B).

(B) Election of spouse annuity.— Subject to paragraph (4)(B), the participant may elect in writing within two years after receipt of notice of the death or remarriage of the former spouse to continue the reduction in order to provide a higher survivor annuity under section 221(b)(3) for any spouse of the participant.

(c) Optional Additional Survivor Annuities for Other Former Spouse or Surviving Spouse.—

(1) In general.—In the case of any participant providing a survivor annuity under subsection (b) for a former spouse—

(A) such participant may elect, or

(B) a spousal agreement or court order under section 264(b) may provide for,

an additional survivor annuity under this subsection for any other former spouse or spouse surviving the participant, if the participant satisfactorily passes a physical examination as prescribed by the Director.

(2) Limitation.— Neither the total amount of survivor annuity or annuities under this subsection with respect to any participant, nor the survivor annuity or annuities for any one surviving spouse or former spouse of such participant under this section or section 221, may exceed 55 percent of the unreduced amount of the participant's annuity, as computed under section 221(a).

(3) Contribution for additional annuities.—

(A) Provision of additional survivor annuity.—In accordance with regulations which the Director shall prescribe, the participant involved may provide for any annuity under this subsection—

(i) by a reduction in the annuity or an allotment from the basic pay of the participant;

(ii) by a lump-sum payment or installment payments to the fund; or

(iii) by any combination thereof.

(B) Actuarial equivalence to benefit.— The present value of the total amount to accrue to the fund under subparagraph (A) to provide any annuity under this subsection shall be actuarially equivalent in value to such annuity, as calculated upon such tables of mortality as may from time to time be prescribed for this purpose by the Director.

(C) Effect of former spouse's death or disqualification.—If a former spouse predeceases the participant or remarries before attaining age 55 (or, in the case of a spouse, the spouse predeceases the participant or does not qualify as a former spouse upon dissolution of the marriage)—

(i) if an annuity reduction or pay allotment under subparagraph (A) is in effect for that spouse or former spouse, the annuity shall be recomputed and paid as if it had not been reduced or the pay allotment terminated, as the case may be; and

(ii) any amount accruing to the fund under subparagraph (A) shall be refunded, but only to the extent that such amount may have exceeded the actuarial cost of providing benefits under this subsection for the period such benefits were provided, as determined under regulations prescribed by the

Director.

(D) RECOMPUTATION UPON DEATH OR REMARRIAGE OF FORMER SPOUSE.— Under regulations prescribed by the Director, an annuity shall be recomputed (or a pay allotment terminated or adjusted), and a refund provided (if appropriate), in a manner comparable to that provided under subparagraph (C), in order to reflect a termination or reduction of future benefits under this subsection for a spouse in the event a former spouse of the participant dies or remarries before attaining age 55 and an increased annuity is provided for that spouse in accordance with this section.

(4) COMMENCEMENT AND TERMINATION OF ADDITIONAL SURVIVOR ANNUITY.— An annuity payable under this subsection to a spouse or former spouse shall commence on the day after the participant dies and shall terminate on the last day of the month before the spouse's or the former spouse's death or remarriage before attaining age 55.

(5) NONAPPLICABILITY OF COLA PROVISION.— Section 291 does not apply to an annuity under this subsection, unless authorized under regulations prescribed by the Director.

SEC. 223. [50 U.S.C. 2033] ELECTION OF SURVIVOR BENEFITS FOR CERTAIN FORMER SPOUSES DIVORCED AS OF NOVEMBER 15, 1982.

(a) FORMER SPOUSES AS OF NOVEMBER 15, 1982.— A participant, former participant, or retired participant in the system who on November 15, 1982, had a former spouse may, by a spousal agreement, elect to receive a reduced annuity and provide a survivor annuity for such former spouse under section 222(b).

(b) TIME FOR MAKING ELECTION.—

(1) If the participant or former participant has not retired under such system on or before November 15, 1982, an election under this section may be made at any time before retirement.

(2) If the participant or former participant has retired under such system on or before November 15, 1982, an election under this section may be made within such period after November 15, 1982, as the Director may prescribe.

(3) For the purposes of applying this title, any such election shall be treated in the same manner as if it were a spousal agreement under section 264(b).

(c) BASE FOR ANNUITY.— An election under this section may provide for a survivor annuity based on all or any portion of that part of the annuity of the participant which is not designated or committed as a base for a survivor annuity for a spouse or any other former spouse of the participant. The participant and the participant's spouse may make an election under section 221(b)(1)(B) before the time of retirement for the purpose of allowing an election to be made under this section.

(d) REDUCTION IN PARTICIPANT'S ANNUITY.—

(1) COMPUTATION.— The amount of the reduction in the participant's annuity shall be determined in accordance with section 221(b)(2).

(2) EFFECTIVE DATE OF REDUCTION.—Such reduction shall be effective as of—

(A) the commencing date of the participant's annuity, in the case of an election under subsection (b)(1); or

(B) November 15, 1982, in the case of an election under subsection (b)(2).

SEC. 224. [50 U.S.C. 2034] SURVIVOR ANNUITY FOR CERTAIN OTHER FORMER SPOUSES.

(a) SURVIVOR ANNUITY.—

(1) IN GENERAL.—An individual who was a former spouse of a participant or retired participant on November 15, 1982, shall be entitled, except to the extent such former spouse is disqualified under subsection (b), to a survivor annuity equal to 55 percent of the greater of—

(A) the unreduced amount of the participant's or retired participant's annuity, as computed under section 221(a); or

(B) the unreduced amount of what such annuity as so computed would be if the participant, former participant, or retired participant had not elected payment of the lump-sum credit under section 294.

(2) REDUCTION IN SURVIVOR ANNUITY.— A survivor annuity payable under this section shall be reduced by an amount equal to any survivor annuity payments made to the former spouse under section 223.

(b) LIMITATIONS.—A former spouse is not entitled to a survivor annuity under this section if—

(1) the former spouse remarries before age 55, except that the entitlement of the former spouse to such a survivor annuity shall be restored on the date such remarriage is dissolved by death, annulment, or divorce; or

(2) the former spouse is less than 50 years of age.

(c) COMMENCEMENT AND TERMINATION OF ANNUITY.—

(1) COMMENCEMENT OF ANNUITY.—The entitlement of a former spouse to a survivor annuity under this section shall commence—

(A) in the case of a former spouse of a participant or retired participant who is deceased as of October 1, 1986, beginning on the later of—

(i) the 60th day after such date; or

(ii) the date on which the former spouse reaches age 50; and

(B) in the case of any other former spouse, beginning on the latest of—

(i) the date on which the participant or retired participant to whom the former spouse was married dies;

(ii) the 60th day after October 1, 1986; or

(iii) the date on which the former spouse attains age 50.

(2) TERMINATION OF ANNUITY.— The entitlement of a former spouse to a survivor annuity under this section terminates on the last day of the month before the former spouse's death or remarriage before attaining age 55. The entitlement of a former spouse to such a survivor annuity shall be restored on the date such remarriage is dissolved by death, annulment, or divorce.

(d) APPLICATION.—

(1) TIME LIMIT; WAIVER.— A survivor annuity under this section shall not be payable unless appropriate written application is provided to the Director, complete with any supporting documentation which the Director may by regulation require. Any such application shall be submitted not later than April 1, 1989. The Director

may waive the application deadline under the preceding sentence in any case in which the Director determines that the circumstances warrant such a waiver.

(2) Retroactive benefits.— Upon approval of an application provided under paragraph (1), the appropriate survivor annuity shall be payable to the former spouse with respect to all periods before such approval during which the former spouse was entitled to such annuity under this section, but in no event shall a survivor annuity be payable under this section with respect to any period before October 1, 1986.

(e) Restoration of Annuity.— Notwithstanding subsection (d)(1), the deadline by which an application for a survivor annuity must be submitted shall not apply in cases in which a former spouse's entitlement to such a survivor annuity is restored under subsection (b)(1) or (c)(2).

SEC. 225. [50 U.S.C. 2035] RETIREMENT ANNUITY FOR CERTAIN FORMER SPOUSES.

(a) Retirement Annuity.—An individual who was a former spouse of a participant, former participant, or retired participant on November 15, 1982, and any former spouse divorced after November 15, 1982, from a participant or former participant who retired before November 15, 1982, shall be entitled, except to the extent such former spouse is disqualified under subsection (b), to an annuity—

(1) if married to the participant throughout the creditable service of the participant, equal to 50 percent of the annuity of the participant; or

(2) if not married to the participant throughout such creditable service, equal to that former spouse's pro rata share of 50 percent of such annuity.

(b) Limitations.—A former spouse is not entitled to an annuity under this section if—

(1) the former spouse remarries before age 55, except that the entitlement of the former spouse to an annuity under this section shall be restored on the date such remarriage is dissolved by death, annulment, or divorce; or

(2) the former spouse is less than 50 years of age.

(c) Commencement and Termination.—

(1) Retirement annuities.—The entitlement of a former spouse to an annuity under this section—

(A) shall commence on the later of—

(i) the day the participant upon whose service the right to the annuity is based becomes entitled to an annuity under this title;

(ii) the first day of the month in which the divorce or annulment involved becomes final; or

(iii) such former spouse's 50th birthday; and

(B) shall terminate on the earlier of—

(i) the last day of the month before the former spouse dies or remarries before 55 years of age, except that the entitlement of the former spouse to an annuity under this section shall be restored on the date such remarriage is dissolved by death, annulment, or divorce; or

(ii) the date on which the annuity of the participant terminates.

(2) Disability annuities.—Notwithstanding paragraph (1)(A)(i), in the case of a former spouse of a disability annuitant—

(A) the annuity of the former spouse shall commence on the date on which the participant would qualify on the basis of the participant's creditable service for an annuity under this title (other than disability annuity) or the date the disability annuity begins, whichever is later; and

(B) the amount of the annuity of the former spouse shall be calculated on the basis of the annuity for which the participant would otherwise so qualify.

(3) Election of benefits.— A former spouse of a participant or retired participant shall not become entitled under this section to an annuity or to the restoration of an annuity payable from the fund unless the former spouse elects to receive it instead of any survivor annuity to which the former spouse may be entitled under this or any other retirement system for Government employees on the basis of a marriage to someone other than the participant.

(4) Application.—

(A) Time limit; waiver.— An annuity under this section shall not be payable unless appropriate written application is provided to the Director, complete with any supporting documentation which the Director may by regulation require, not later than June 2, 1990. The Director may waive the application deadline under the preceding sentence in any case in which the Director determines that the circumstances warrant such a waiver.

(B) Retroactive benefits.— Upon approval of an application under subparagraph (A), the appropriate annuity shall be payable to the former spouse with respect to all periods before such approval during which the former spouse was entitled to an annuity under this section, but in no event shall an annuity be payable under this section with respect to any period before December 2, 1987.

(d) Restoration of Annuities.— Notwithstanding subsection (c)(4)(A), the deadline by which an application for a retirement annuity must be submitted shall not apply in cases in which a former spouse's entitlement to such annuity is restored under subsection (b)(1) or (c)(1)(B).

(e) Savings Provision.— Nothing in this section shall be construed to impair, reduce, or otherwise affect the annuity or the entitlement to an annuity of a participant or former participant under this title.

SEC. 226. [50 U.S.C. 2036] SURVIVOR ANNUITIES FOR PREVIOUS SPOUSES.

The Director shall prescribe regulations under which a previous spouse who is divorced after September 29, 1988, from a participant, former participant, or retired participant shall be eligible for a survivor annuity to the same extent and, to the greatest extent practicable, under the same conditions (including reductions to be made in the annuity of the participant) applicable to former spouses (as defined in section 8331(23) of title 5, United States Code) of participants in the Civil Service Retirement and Disability System (CSRS) as prescribed by the Civil Service Retirement Spouse Equity Act of 1984.

Part D—Benefits Accruing to Certain Participants

SEC. 231. [50 U.S.C. 2051] RETIREMENT FOR DISABILITY OR INCAPACITY—MEDICAL EXAMINATION—RECOVERY.

(a) Disability Retirement.—

(1) Eligibility.— A participant who has become disabled shall, upon the participant's own application or upon order of the Director, be retired on an annuity computed under subsection (b).

(2) Standard for disability determination.—A participant shall be considered to be disabled only if the participant—

(A) is found by the Director to be unable, because of disease or injury, to render useful and efficient service in the participant's position; and

(B) is not qualified for reassignment, under procedures prescribed by the Director, to a vacant position in the Agency at the same grade or level and in which the participant would be able to render useful and efficient service.

(3) Time limit for application.—

(A) One year requirement.— A claim may be allowed under this section only if the application is submitted before the participant is separated from the Agency or within one year thereafter.

(B) Waiver for mentally incompetent participant.— The time limitation may be waived by the Director for a participant who, at the date of separation from the Agency or within one year thereafter, is mentally incompetent, if the application is filed with the Agency within one year from the date of restoration of the participant to competency or the appointment of a fiduciary, whichever is earlier.

(b) Computation of Disability Annuity.—

(1) In general.— Except as provided in paragraph (2), an annuity payable under subsection (a) shall be computed under section 221(a). However, if the disabled or incapacitated participant has less than 20 years of service credit toward retirement under the system at the time of retirement, the annuity shall be computed on the assumption that the participant has had 20 years of service, but the additional service credit that may accrue to a participant under this paragraph may not exceed the difference between the participant's age at the time of retirement and age 60.

(2) Coordination with military retired pay and veterans' compensation and pension.— If a participant retiring under this section is receiving retired pay or retainer pay for military service (except that specified in section 252(e)(3)) or Department of Veterans Affairs compensation or pension in lieu of such retired or retainer pay, the annuity of that participant shall be computed under section 221(a), excluding credit for such military service from that computation. If the amount of the annuity so computed, plus the retired or retainer pay which is received, or which would be received but for the application of the limitation in section 5532 of title 5, United States Code, or the Department of Veterans Affairs compensation or pension in lieu of such retired or retainer pay, is less than the annuity that would be payable under this section in the absence of the previous sentence, an amount equal to the difference shall be added to the annuity payable under section 221(a).

(c) Medical Examinations.—

(1) Medical examination required for determination of disability.— In each case, the participant shall be given a medical examination by one or more duly qualified physicians or surgeons designated by the Director to conduct

examinations, and disability shall be determined by the Director on the basis of the advice of such physicians or surgeons.

(2) Annual reexaminations until age 60.— Unless the disability is permanent, like examinations shall be made annually until the annuitant becomes age 60. If the Director determines on the basis of the advice of one or more duly qualified physicians or surgeons conducting such examinations that an annuitant has recovered to the extent that the annuitant can return to duty, the annuitant may apply for reinstatement or reappointment in the Agency within one year from the date the annuitant's recovery is determined.

(3) Reinstatement.— Upon application, the Director may reinstate any such recovered disability annuitant in the grade held at time of retirement, or the Director may, taking into consideration the age, qualifications, and experience of such annuitant, and the present grade of the annuitant's contemporaries in the Agency, appoint the annuitant to a grade higher than the one held before retirement.

(4) Termination of disability annuity.— Payment of the annuity shall continue until a date one year after the date of examination showing recovery or until the date of reinstatement or reappointment in the Agency, whichever is earlier.

(5) Payment of fees.— Fees for examinations under this subsection, together with reasonable traveling and other expenses incurred in order to submit to examination, may be paid out of the fund.

(6) Suspension of annuity pending required examination.— If the annuitant fails to submit to examination as required under this section, payment of the annuity shall be suspended until continuance of the disability is satisfactorily established.

(7) Termination of annuity upon restoration of earning capacity.— If the annuitant receiving a disability retirement annuity is restored to earning capacity before becoming age 60, payment of the annuity terminates on reemployment by the Government or 180 days after the end of the calendar year in which earning capacity is restored, whichever is earlier. Earning capacity shall be considered to be restored if in any calendar year the income of the annuitant from wages or self-employment, or both, equals at least 80 percent of the current rate of pay for the grade and step the annuitant held at the time of retirement.

(d) Treatment of Recovered Disability Annuitant Who Is Not Reinstated.—

(1) Separation.— If a recovered or restored disability annuitant whose annuity is discontinued is for any reason not reinstated or reappointed in the Agency, the annuitant shall be considered, except for service credit, to have been separated within the meaning of section 234 as of the date of termination of the disability annuity.

(2) Retirement.— After such termination, the recovered or restored annuitant shall be entitled to the benefits of section 234 or 241(a), except that the annuitant may elect voluntary retirement under section 233, if qualified thereunder, or may be placed by the Director in an involuntary retirement status under section 235(a), if qualified thereunder. Retirement rights under this paragraph shall be based on the provisions of this title in effect as of the date on which the disability annuity is discontinued.

(3) Further disability before age 62.— If, based on a current medical

examination, the Director determines that a recovered annuitant has, before reaching age 62, again become totally disabled due to recurrence of the disability for which the annuitant was originally retired, the annuitant's terminated disability annuity (same type and rate) shall be reinstated from the date of such medical examination. If a restored-to-earning-capacity annuitant has not medically recovered from the disability for which retired and establishes to the Director's satisfaction that the annuitant's income from wages and self-employment in any calendar year before reaching age 62 was less than 80 percent of the rate of pay for the grade and step the annuitant held at the time of retirement, the annuitant's terminated disability annuity (same type and rate) shall be reinstated from the first of the next following year. If the annuitant has been allowed an involuntary or voluntary retirement annuity in the meantime, the annuitant's reinstated disability annuity shall be substituted for it unless the annuitant elects to retain the former benefit.

(e) COORDINATION OF BENEFITS.—

(1) WORKERS' COMPENSATION.—A participant is not entitled to receive for the same period of time—

(A) an annuity under this title, and

(B) compensation for injury to, or disability of, such participant under subchapter I of chapter 81 of title 5, United States Code, other than compensation payable under section 8107 of such title.

(2) SURVIVOR ANNUITIES.— An individual is not entitled to receive an annuity under this title and a concurrent benefit under subchapter I of chapter 81 of title 5, United States Code, on account of the death of the same person.

(3) GREATER BENEFIT.— Paragraphs (1) and (2) do not bar the right of a claimant to the greater benefit conferred by either this title or subchapter I of chapter 81 of title 5, United States Code.

(f) OFFSET FROM SURVIVOR ANNUITY FOR WORKERS' COMPENSATION PAYMENT.—

(1) REFUND TO DEPARTMENT OF LABOR.—If an individual is entitled to an annuity under this title and the individual receives a lump-sum payment for compensation under section 8135 of title 5, United States Code, based on the disability or death of the same person, so much of the compensation as has been paid for a period extended beyond the date payment of the annuity commences, as determined by the Secretary of Labor, shall be refunded to the Department for credit to the Employees' Compensation Fund. Before the individual may receive the annuity, the individual shall—

(A) refund to the Secretary of Labor the amount representing the commuted compensation payments for the extended period; or

(B) authorize the deduction of the amount from the annuity.

(2) SOURCE OF DEDUCTION.— Deductions from the annuity may be made from accrued or accruing payments. The amounts deducted and withheld from the annuity shall be transmitted to the Secretary for reimbursement to the Employees' Compensation Fund.

(3) PRORATING DEDUCTION.— If the Secretary finds that the financial circumstances of an individual entitled to an annuity under this title warrant deferred refunding, deductions from the annuity may be prorated against and paid from

accruing payments in such manner as the Secretary determines appropriate.

SEC. 232. [50 U.S.C. 2052] DEATH IN SERVICE.

(a) RETURN OF CONTRIBUTIONS WHEN NO ANNUITY PAYABLE.— If a participant dies and no claim for an annuity is payable under this title, the participant's lump-sum credit and any voluntary contributions made under section 281, with interest, shall be paid in the order of precedence shown in section 241(c).

(b) SURVIVOR ANNUITY FOR SURVIVING SPOUSE OR FORMER SPOUSE.—

(1) IN GENERAL.— If a participant dies before separation or retirement from the Agency and is survived by a spouse or by a former spouse qualifying for a survivor annuity under section 222(b), such surviving spouse shall be entitled to an annuity equal to 55 percent of the annuity computed in accordance with paragraphs (2) and (3) of this subsection and section 221(a), and any such surviving former spouse shall be entitled to an annuity computed in accordance with section 222(b) and paragraph (2) of this subsection as if the participant died after being entitled to an annuity under this title. The annuity of such surviving spouse or former spouse shall commence on the day after the participant dies and shall terminate on the last day of the month before the death or remarriage before attaining age 55 of the surviving spouse or former spouse (subject to the payment and restoration provisions of sections 221(b)(3)(C), 221(i), and 222(b)(3)).

(2) COMPUTATION.— The annuity payable under paragraph (1) shall be computed in accordance with section 221(a), except that the computation of the annuity of the participant under such section shall be at least the smaller of (A) 40 percent of the participant's high-3 average pay, or (B) the sum obtained under such section after increasing the participant's length of service by the difference between the participant's age at the time of death and age 60.

(3) LIMITATION.— Notwithstanding paragraph (1), if the participant had a former spouse qualifying for an annuity under section 222(b), the annuity of a surviving spouse under this section shall be subject to the limitation of section 221(b)(3)(B), and the annuity of a former spouse under this section shall be subject to the limitation of section 222(b)(4)(B).

(4) PRECEDENCE OF SECTION 224 SURVIVOR ANNUITY OVER DEATH-IN-SERVICE ANNUITY.— If a former spouse who is eligible for a death-in-service annuity under this section is or becomes eligible for an annuity under section 224, the annuity provided under this section shall not be payable and shall be superseded by the annuity under section 224.

(c) ANNUITIES FOR SURVIVING CHILDREN.—

(1) PARTICIPANTS DYING BEFORE APRIL 1, 1992.—In the case of a participant who before April 1, 1992, died before separation or retirement from the Agency and who was survived by a child or children—

(A) if the participant was survived by a spouse, there shall be paid from the fund to or on behalf of each such surviving child an annuity determined under section 221(d)(3)(A); and

(B) if the participant was not survived by a spouse, there shall be paid from the fund to or on behalf of each such surviving child an annuity determined under section 221(d)(3)(B).

(2) PARTICIPANTS DYING ON OR AFTER APRIL 1, 1992.—In the case of a participant who on or after April 1, 1992, dies before separation or retirement from the Agency and who is survived by a child or children—

(A) if the participant is survived by a spouse or former spouse who is the natural or adoptive parent of a surviving child of the participant, there shall be paid from the fund to or on behalf of each such surviving child an annuity determined under section 221(d)(3)(A); and

(B) if the participant is not survived by a spouse or former spouse who is the natural or adoptive parent of a surviving child of the participant, there shall be paid to or on behalf of each such surviving child an annuity determined under section 221(d)(3)(B).

(3) FORMER SPOUSE DEFINED.— For purposes of this subsection, the term "former spouse" includes any former wife or husband of a participant, regardless of the length of marriage or the amount of creditable service completed by the participant.

SEC. 233. [50 U.S.C. 2053] VOLUNTARY RETIREMENT.

(a) A participant who is at least 50 years of age and has completed 20 years of service may, on the participant's application and with the consent of the Director, be retired from the Agency and receive benefits in accordance with the provisions of section 221 if the participant has not less than 10 years of service with the Agency.

(b) A participant who has at least 25 years of service, ten years of which are with the Agency, may retire, with the consent of the Director, at any age and receive benefits in accordance with the provisions of section 221 if the Office of Personnel Management has authorized separation from service voluntarily for Agency employees under section 8336(d)(2) of title 5, United States Code, with respect to the Civil Service Retirement System or section 8414(b)(1)(B) of such title with respect to the Federal Employees' Retirement System.

SEC. 234. [50 U.S.C. 2054] DISCONTINUED SERVICE BENEFITS.

(a) DEFERRED ANNUITY.—A participant who separates from the Agency may, upon separation or at any time before the commencement of an annuity under this title, elect—

(1) to have the participant's contributions to the fund returned to the participant in accordance with section 241(a); or

(2) except in a case in which the Director determines that separation was based in whole or in part on the ground of disloyalty to the United States, to leave the contributions in the fund and receive an annuity, computed as prescribed in section 221, commencing at age 62.

(b) REFUND OF CONTRIBUTIONS IF FORMER PARTICIPANT DIES BEFORE AGE 62.— If a participant who qualifies under subsection (a) to receive a deferred annuity commencing at age 62 dies before reaching age 62, the participant's contributions to the fund, with interest, shall be paid in accordance with the provisions of section 241.

SEC. 235. [50 U.S.C. 2055] MANDATORY RETIREMENT.

(a) INVOLUNTARY RETIREMENT.—

(1) AUTHORITY OF DIRECTOR.— The Director may, in the Director's discretion, place in a retired status any participant in the system described in paragraph (2).

(2) Paragraph (1) applies with respect to any participant who has not less than 10 years of service with the Agency and who—

(A) has completed at least 25 years of service; or

(B) is at least 50 years of age and has completed at least 20 years of service.

(b) MANDATORY RETIREMENT FOR AGE.—

(1) IN GENERAL.—A participant in the system shall be automatically retired from the Agency—

(A) upon reaching age 65, in the case of a participant in the system who is at the Senior Intelligence Service rank of level 4 or above; and

(B) upon reaching age 60, in the case of any other participant in the system.

(2) EFFECTIVE DATE OF RETIREMENT.— Retirement under paragraph (1) shall be effective on the last day of the month in which the participant reaches the age applicable to that participant under that paragraph.

(3) AUTHORITY FOR EXTENSION.— In any case in which the Director determines it to be in the public interest, the Director may extend the mandatory retirement date for a participant under this subsection by a period of not to exceed 5 years.

(c) RETIREMENT BENEFITS.— A participant retired under this section shall receive retirement benefits in accordance with section 221.

SEC. 236. [50 U.S.C. 2056] ELIGIBILITY FOR ANNUITY.

(a) ONE-OUT-OF-TWO REQUIREMENT.— A participant must complete, within the last two years before any separation from service (except a separation because of death or disability) at least one year of creditable civilian service during which the participant is subject to this title and in a pay status before the participant or the participant's survivors are eligible for an annuity under this title based on that separation.

(b) REFUND OF CONTRIBUTIONS FOR TIME NOT ALLOWED FOR CREDIT.— If a participant (other than a participant separated from the service because of death or disability) fails to meet the service and pay status requirement of subsection (a), any amounts deducted from the participant's pay during the period for which no eligibility is established based on the separation shall be returned to the participant on the separation.

(c) EXCEPTION.— Failure to meet the service and pay status requirement of subsection (a) shall not deprive the participant or the participant's survivors of any annuity to which they may be entitled under this title based on a previous separation.

PART E—LUMP-SUM PAYMENTS

SEC. 241. [50 U.S.C. 2071] LUMP-SUM PAYMENTS.

(a) ENTITLEMENT TO LUMP-SUM CREDIT.—Subject to section 252(d) and subsection (b) of this section, a participant who—

(1) is separated from the Agency for at least 31 consecutive days and is not

transferred to employment covered by another retirement system for Government employees;

(2) files an application with the Director for payment of the lump-sum credit;

(3) is not reemployed in a position in which the participant is subject to this title at the time the participant files the application; and

(4) will not become eligible to receive an annuity under this title within 31 days after filing the application,

is entitled to be paid the lump-sum credit. Receipt of the payment of the lump-sum credit by the former participant voids all annuity rights under this title based on the service on which the lump-sum credit is based, until the former participant is reemployed in service subject to this title.

(b) CONDITIONS FOR PAYMENT OF LUMP-SUM CREDIT.—

(1) IN GENERAL.— Whenever a former participant becomes entitled to receive payment of the lump-sum credit under subsection (a), such lump-sum credit shall be paid to the former participant and to any former spouse or former wife or husband of the former participant in accordance with paragraphs (2) through (4). The former participant's lump-sum credit shall be reduced by the amount of the lump-sum credit payable to any former spouse or former wife or husband.

(2) PRO RATA SHARE FOR FORMER SPOUSE.—Unless otherwise expressly provided by any spousal agreement or court order under section 264(b), a former spouse of the former participant shall be entitled to receive a share of such participant's lump-sum credit—

(A) if married to the participant throughout the period of creditable service of the participant, equal to 50 percent of such lump-sum credit; or

(B) if not married to the participant throughout such creditable service, equal to a proportion of 50 percent of such lump-sum credit which is the proportion that the number of days of the marriage of the former spouse to the participant during periods of creditable service of such participant bears to the total number of days of such creditable service.

(3) SHARE FOR FORMER WIFE OR HUSBAND.—Payment of the former participant's lump-sum credit shall be subject to the terms of a court order under section 264(c) concerning any former wife or husband of the former participant if—

(A) the court order expressly relates to any portion of such lump-sum credit; and

(B) payment of the lump-sum credit would extinguish entitlement of such former wife or husband to a survivor annuity under section 226 or to any portion of the participant's annuity under section 264(c).

(4) NOTIFICATION.—A lump-sum credit may be paid to or for the benefit of a former participant—

(A) only upon written notification to (i) the current spouse, if any, (ii) any former spouse, and (iii) any former wife or husband who has a court order covered by paragraph (3); and

(B) only if the express written concurrence of the current spouse has been received by the Director.

This paragraph may be waived under circumstances described in section

221(b)(1)(D).

(c) ORDER OF PRECEDENCE OF PAYMENT.—A lump-sum payment authorized by subsection (d) or (e) of this section 281(d) and a payment of any accrued and unpaid annuity authorized by subsection (f) of this section shall be paid in the following order of precedence to individuals surviving the participant and alive on the date entitlement to the payment arises, upon establishment of a valid claim therefor, and such payment bars recovery by any other individual:

(1) To the beneficiary or beneficiaries designated by such participant in a signed and witnessed writing received by the Director before the participant's death. For this purpose, a designation, change, or cancellation of beneficiary in a will or other document not so executed and filed with the Director shall have no force or effect.

(2) If there is no designated beneficiary, to the surviving wife or husband of such participant.

(3) If none of the above, to the child or children of such participant and descendent of deceased children by representation.

(4) If none of the above, to the parents of such participant or the survivor of them.

(5) If none of the above, to the duly appointed executor or administrator of the estate of such participant.

(6) If none of the above, to such other next of kin of such participant as the Director determines to be legally entitled to such payment.

(d) DEATH OF FORMER PARTICIPANT BEFORE RETIREMENT.—

(1) IN GENERAL.— Except as provided in paragraph (2), if a former participant eligible for a deferred annuity under section 234 dies before reaching age 62, such former participant's lump-sum credit shall be paid in accordance with subsection (c).

(2) LIMITATION.— In any case where there is a surviving former spouse or surviving former wife or husband of such participant who is entitled to a share of such participant's lump-sum credit under paragraphs (2) and (3) of subsection (b), the lump-sum credit payable under paragraph (1) shall be reduced by the lump-sum credit payable to such former spouse or former wife or husband.

(e) TERMINATION OF ALL ANNUITY RIGHTS.— If all annuity rights under this title based on the service of a deceased participant or annuitant terminate before the total annuity paid equals the lump-sum credit, the difference shall be paid in accordance with subsection (c).

(f) PAYMENT OF ACCRUED AND UNPAID ANNUITY WHEN RETIRED PARTICIPANT DIES.— If a retired participant dies, any annuity accrued and unpaid shall be paid in accordance with subsection (c).

(g) TERMINATION OF SURVIVOR ANNUITY.—An annuity accrued and unpaid on the termination, except by death, of the annuity of a survivor annuitant shall be paid to that individual. An annuity accrued and unpaid on the death of a survivor annuitant shall be paid in the following order of precedence, and the payment bars recovery by any other individual:

(1) To the duly appointed executor or administrator of the estate of the survivor

annuitant.

(2) If there is no executor or administrator, to such next of kin of the survivor annuitant as the Director determines to be legally entitled to such payment, except that no payment shall be made under this paragraph until after the expiration of 30 days from the date of death of the survivor annuitant.

PART F—PERIOD OF SERVICE FOR ANNUITIES

SEC. 251. [50 U.S.C. 2081] COMPUTATION OF LENGTH OF SERVICE.

(a) IN GENERAL.—

(1) CREDITING SERVICE AS PARTICIPANT.— For the purposes of this title, the period of service of a participant shall be computed from the date on which the participant becomes a participant under this title.

(2) EXCLUSION OF CERTAIN PERIODS.— In computing the period of service of a participant, all periods of separation from the Agency and so much of any leave of absence without pay as may exceed six months in the aggregate in any calendar year shall be excluded, except leaves of absence while receiving benefits under chapter 81 of title 5, United States Code, and leaves of absence granted participants while performing active and honorable service in the Armed Forces.

(3) CREDITING CERTAIN PERIODS OF SEPARATION.— A participant or former participant who returns to Government duty after a period of separation shall have included in the participant or former participant's period of service that part of the period of separation in which the participant or former participant was receiving benefits under chapter 81 of title 5, United States Code.

(b) EXTRA CREDIT FOR PERIODS SERVED AT UNHEALTHFUL POSTS OVERSEAS.—

(1) CLASSIFICATION OF CERTAIN POSTS AS UNHEALTHFUL.— The Director may from time to time establish a list of places outside the United States that, by reason of climatic or other extreme conditions, are to be classed as unhealthful posts. Such list shall be established in consultation with the Secretary of State.

(2) EXTRA CREDIT.— Each year of duty at a post on the list established under paragraph (1), inclusive of regular leaves of absence, shall be counted as one and a half years in computing the length of service of a participant under this title for the purpose of retirement. In computing such service, any fractional month shall be treated as a full month.

(3) COORDINATION WITH BENEFITS UNDER TITLE 5.— Extra credit for service at an unhealthful post may not be credited to a participant who is paid a differential under section 5925 or 5928 of title 5, United States Code, for the same service.

SEC. 252. [50 U.S.C. 2082] PRIOR SERVICE CREDIT.

(a) IN GENERAL.—A participant may, subject to the provisions of this section, include in the participant's period of service—

(1) civilian service in the Government before becoming a participant that would be creditable toward retirement under subchapter III of chapter 83 of title 5, United States Code (as determined under section 8332(b) of such title); and

(2) honorable active service in the Armed Forces before the date of the

separation upon which eligibility for an annuity is based, or honorable active service in the Regular or Reserve Corps of the Public Health Service after June 30, 1960, or as a commissioned officer of the National Oceanic and Atmospheric Administration after June 30, 1961.

(b) LIMITATIONS.—

(1) IN GENERAL.—Except as provided in paragraphs (2) and (3), the total service of any participant shall exclude—

(A) any period of civilian service on or after October 1, 1982, for which retirement deductions or deposits have not been made,

(B) any period of service for which a refund of contributions has been made, or

(C) any period of service for which contributions were not transferred pursuant to subsection (c)(1);

unless the participant makes a deposit to the fund in an amount equal to the percentages of basic pay received for such service as specified in the table contained in section 8334(c) of title 5, United States Code, together with interest computed in accordance with section 8334(e) of such title. The deposit may be made in one or more installments (including by allotment from pay), as determined by the Director.

(2) EFFECT OF RETIREMENT DEDUCTIONS NOT MADE.— If a participant has not paid a deposit for civilian service performed before October 1, 1982, for which retirement deductions were not made, such participant's annuity shall be reduced by 10 percent of the deposit described in paragraph (1) remaining unpaid, unless the participant elects to eliminate the service involved for the purpose of the annuity computation.

(3) EFFECT OF REFUND OF RETIREMENT CONTRIBUTIONS.—A participant who received a refund of retirement contributions under this or any other retirement system for Government employees covering service for which the participant may be allowed credit under this title may deposit the amount received, with interest computed under paragraph (1). Credit may not be allowed for the service covered by the refund until the deposit is made, except that a participant who—

(A) separated from Government service before March 31, 1991, and received a refund of the participant's retirement contributions covering a period of service ending before March 31, 1991;

(B) is entitled to an annuity under this title (other than a disability annuity) which commences after December 1, 1992; and

(C) does not make the deposit required to receive credit for the service covered by the refund;

shall be entitled to an annuity actuarially reduced in accordance with section 8334(d)(2)(B) of title 5, United States Code.

(4) ENTITLEMENT UNDER ANOTHER SYSTEM.— Credit toward retirement under the system shall not be allowed for any period of civilian service on the basis of which the participant is receiving (or will in the future be entitled to receive) an annuity under another retirement system for Government employees, unless the right to such annuity is waived and a deposit is made under paragraph (1) covering that period of service, or a transfer is made pursuant to subsection (c).

(c) TRANSFER FROM OTHER GOVERNMENT RETIREMENT SYSTEMS.—

(1) IN GENERAL.— If an employee who is under another retirement system for Government employees becomes a participant in the system by direct transfer, the Government's contributions (including interest accrued thereon computed in accordance with section 8334(e) of title 5, United States Code) under such retirement system on behalf of the employee as well as such employee's total contributions and deposits (including interest accrued thereon), except voluntary contributions, shall be transferred to the employee's credit in the fund effective as of the date such employee becomes a participant in the system.

(2) CONSENT OF EMPLOYEE.— Each such employee shall be deemed to consent to the transfer of such funds, and such transfer shall be a complete discharge and acquittance of all claims and demands against the other Government retirement fund on account of service rendered before becoming a participant in the system.

(3) ADDITIONAL CONTRIBUTIONS; REFUNDS.— A participant whose contributions are transferred pursuant to paragraph (1) shall not be required to make additional contributions for periods of service for which full contributions were made to the other Government retirement fund, nor shall any refund be made to any such participant on account of contributions made during any period to the other Government retirement fund at a higher rate than that fixed for employees by section 8334(c) of title 5, United States Code, for contributions to the fund.

(d) TRANSFER TO OTHER GOVERNMENT RETIREMENT SYSTEMS.—

(1) IN GENERAL.— If a participant in the system becomes an employee under another Government retirement system by direct transfer to employment covered by such system, the Government's contributions (including interest accrued thereon computed in accordance with section 8334(e) of title 5, United States Code) to the fund on the participant's behalf as well as the participant's total contributions and deposits (including interest accrued thereon), except voluntary contributions, shall be transferred to the participant's credit in the fund of such other retirement system effective as of the date on which the participant becomes eligible to participate in such other retirement system.

(2) CONSENT OF EMPLOYEE.— Each such employee shall be deemed to consent to the transfer of such funds, and such transfer shall be a complete discharge and acquittance of all claims and demands against the fund on account of service rendered before the participant's becoming eligible for participation in that other system.

(e) PRIOR MILITARY SERVICE CREDIT.—

(1) APPLICATION TO OBTAIN CREDIT.— If a deposit required to obtain credit for prior military service described in subsection (a)(2) was not made to another Government retirement fund and transferred under subsection (c)(1), the participant may obtain credit for such military service, subject to the provisions of this subsection and subsections (f) through (h), by applying for it to the Director before retirement or separation from the Agency.

(2) EMPLOYMENT STARTING BEFORE, ON, OR AFTER OCTOBER 1, 1982.—Except as provided in paragraph (3)—

(A) the service of a participant who first became a Federal employee before October 1, 1982, shall include credit for each period of military service performed before the date of separation on which entitlement to an annuity under this title is based, subject to section 252(f); and

(B) the service of a participant who first becomes a Federal employee on or after October 1, 1982, shall include credit for—

(i) each period of military service performed before January 1, 1957, and

(ii) each period of military service performed after December 31, 1956, and before the separation on which entitlement to an annuity under this title is based, only if a deposit (with interest, if any) is made with respect to that period, as provided in subsection (h).

(3) EFFECT OF RECEIPT OF MILITARY RETIRED PAY.—In the case of a participant who is entitled to retired pay based on a period of military service, the participant's service may not include credit for such period of military service unless the retired pay is paid—

(A) on account of a service-connected disability—

(i) incurred in combat with an enemy of the United States; or

(ii) caused by an instrumentality of war and incurred in the line of duty during a period of war (as defined in section 1101 of title 38, United States Code); or

(B) under chapter 67 of title 10, United States Code.

(4) SURVIVOR ANNUITY.—Notwithstanding paragraph (3), the survivor annuity of a survivor of a participant—

(A) who was awarded retired pay based on any period of military service, and

(B) whose death occurs before separation from the Agency,

shall be computed in accordance with section 8332(c)(3) of title 5, United States Code.

(f) EFFECT OF ENTITLEMENT TO SOCIAL SECURITY BENEFITS.—

(1) IN GENERAL.— Notwithstanding any other provision of this section (except paragraph (3) of this subsection) or section 253, any military service (other than military service covered by military leave with pay from a civilian position) performed by a participant after December 1956 shall be excluded in determining the aggregate period of service on which an annuity payable under this title to such participant or to the participant's spouse, former spouse, previous spouse, or child is based, if such participant, spouse, former spouse, previous spouse, or child is entitled (or would upon proper application be entitled), at the time of such determination, to monthly old-age or survivors' insurance benefits under section 202 of the Social Security Act (42 U.S.C. 402), based on such participant's wages and self-employment income. If the military service is not excluded under the preceding sentence, but upon attaining age 62, the participant or spouse, former spouse, or previous spouse becomes entitled (or would upon proper application be entitled) to such benefits, the aggregate period of service on which the annuity is based shall be redetermined, effective as of the first day of the month in which the participant or spouse, former spouse, or previous spouse attains age 62, so as to exclude such service.

(2) LIMITATION.—The provisions of paragraph (1) relating to credit for military

service do not apply to—

(A) any period of military service of a participant with respect to which the participant has made a deposit with interest, if any, under subsection (h); or

(B) the military service of any participant described in subsection (e)(2)(B).

(3) Effect of entitlement before september 8, 1982.—(A) The annuity recomputation required by paragraph (1) shall not apply to any participant who was entitled to an annuity under this title on or before September 8, 1982, or who is entitled to a deferred annuity based on separation from the Agency occurring on or before such date. Instead of an annuity recomputation, the annuity of such participant shall be reduced at age 62 by an amount equal to a fraction of the participant's old-age or survivors' insurance benefits under section 202 of the Social Security Act. The reduction shall be determined by multiplying the participant's monthly Social Security benefit by a fraction, the numerator of which is the participant's total military wages and deemed additional wages (within the meaning of section 229 of the Social Security Act (42 U.S.C. 429)) that were subject to Social Security deductions and the denominator of which is the total of all the participant's wages, including military wages, and all self-employment income that were subject to Social Security deductions before the calendar year in which the determination month occurs.

(B) The reduction determined in accordance with subparagraph (A) shall not be greater than the reduction that would be required under paragraph (1) if such paragraph applied to the participant. The new formula shall be applicable to any annuity payment payable after October 1, 1982, including annuity payments to participants who had previously reached age 62 and whose annuities had already been recomputed.

(C) For purposes of this paragraph, the term “determination month” means—

(i) the first month for which the participant is entitled to old-age or survivors' insurance benefits (or would be entitled to such benefits upon application therefor); or

(ii) October 1982, in the case of any participant entitled to such benefits for that month.

(g) Deposits Paid by Survivors.— For the purpose of survivor annuities, deposits authorized by subsections (b) and (h) may also be made by the survivor of a participant.

(h)(1)(A) Each participant who has performed military service before the date of separation on which entitlement to an annuity under this title is based may pay to the Agency an amount equal to 7 percent of the amount of basic pay paid under section 204 of title 37, United States Code, to the participant for each period of military service after December 1956; except, the amount to be paid for military service performed beginning on January 1, 1999, through December 31, 2000, shall be as follows:

7.25 percent of basic pay January 1, 1999, to December 31, 1999. 7.4 percent of basic pay January 1, 2000, to December 31, 2000.

(B) The amount of such payments shall be based on such evidence of basic pay for military service as the participant may provide or, if the Director determines sufficient evidence has not been provided to adequately determine basic pay for military service, such payment shall be based upon estimates of such basic pay provided to the Director under paragraph (4).

(2) Any deposit made under paragraph (1) more than two years after the later of—

(A) October 1, 1983, or

(B) the date on which the participant making the deposit first becomes an employee of the Federal Government,

shall include interest on such amount computed and compounded annually beginning on the date of expiration of the two-year period. The interest rate that is applicable in computing interest in any year under this paragraph shall be equal to the interest rate that is applicable for such year under section 8334(e) of title 5, United States Code.

(3) Any payment received by the Director under this subsection shall be deposited in the Treasury of the United States to the credit of the fund.

(4) The provisions of section 221(l) shall apply with respect to such information as the Director determines to be necessary for the administration of this subsection in the same manner that such section applies concerning information described in that section.

SEC. 253. [50 U.S.C. 2083] CREDIT FOR SERVICE WHILE ON MILITARY LEAVE.

(a) General Rule.— A participant who, during the period of any war or of any national emergency as proclaimed by the President or declared by the Congress, leaves the participant's position in the Agency to enter military service shall not be considered, for purposes of this title, as separated from the participant's position in the Agency by reason of such military service, unless the participant applies for and receives a refund of contributions under this title. Such a participant may not be considered as retaining such position in the Agency after December 31, 1956, or upon the expiration of five years of such military service, whichever is later.

(b) Waiver of Contributions.— Except to the extent provided under section 252(e) or 252(h), contributions shall not be required covering periods of leave of absence from the Agency granted a participant while performing active service in the Armed Forces.

Part G—Moneys

SEC. 261. [50 U.S.C. 2091] ESTIMATE OF APPROPRIATIONS NEEDED.

(a) Estimates of Annual Appropriations.— The Director shall prepare the estimates of the annual appropriations required to be made to the fund.

(b) Actuarial Valuations.— The Director shall cause to be made actuarial valuations of the fund at such intervals as the Director determines to be necessary, but not less often than every five years.

(c) Changes in Law Affecting Actuarial Status of Fund.—Any statute which authorizes—

(1) new or increased benefits payable from the fund under this title, including annuity increases other than under section 291;

(2) extension of the coverage of this title to new groups of employees; or

(3) increases in pay on which benefits are computed;

is deemed to authorize appropriations to the fund in order to provide funding for the unfunded liability created by that statute, in 30 equal annual installments with interest computed at the rate used in the then most recent valuation of the system and with the first payment thereof due as of the end of the fiscal year in which such new or liberalized benefit, extension of coverage, or increase in pay is effective.

(d) AUTHORIZATION.— There is hereby authorized to be appropriated to the fund for each fiscal year such amounts as may be necessary to meet the amount of normal cost for each year that is not met by contributions under section 211(a).

(e) UNFUNDED LIABILITY; CREDIT ALLOWED FOR MILITARY SERVICE.—There is hereby authorized to be appropriated to the fund for each fiscal year such sums as may be necessary to provide the amount equivalent to—

(1) interest on the unfunded liability computed for that year at the interest rate used in the then most recent valuation of the system; and

(2) that portion of disbursement for annuities for that year that the Director estimates is attributable to credit allowed for military service,

less an amount determined by the Director to be appropriate to reflect the value of the deposits made to the credit of the fund under section 252(h).

SEC. 262. [50 U.S.C. 2092] INVESTMENT OF MONEYS IN THE FUND.

The Director may, with the approval of the Secretary of the Treasury, invest from time to time in interest-bearing securities of the United States such portions of the fund as in the Director's judgment may not be immediately required for the payment of annuities, cash benefits, refunds, and allowances from the fund. The income derived from such investments shall be credited to and constitute a part of the fund.

SEC. 263. [50 U.S.C. 2093] PAYMENT OF BENEFITS.

(a) ANNUITIES STATED AS ANNUAL AMOUNTS.— Each annuity is stated as an annual amount, 1/12 of which, rounded to the next lowest dollar, constitutes the monthly rate payable on the first business day of the month after the month or other period for which it has accrued.

(b) COMMENCEMENT OF ANNUITY.—

(1) COMMENCEMENT OF ANNUITY FOR PARTICIPANTS GENERALLY.— Except as otherwise provided in paragraph (2), the annuity of a participant who has met the eligibility requirements for an annuity shall commence on the first day of the month after separation from the Agency or after pay ceases and the service and age requirements for title to an annuity are met.

(2) EXCEPTIONS.—The annuity of—

(A) a participant involuntarily separated from the Agency;

(B) a participant retiring under section 231 due to a disability; and

(C) a participant who serves 3 days or less in the month of retirement;

shall commence on the day after separation from the Agency or the day after pay ceases and the service and age or disability requirements for title to annuity are met.

(3) Other annuities.— Any other annuity payable from the fund commences on the first day of the month after the occurrence of the event on which payment thereof is based.

(c) Termination of Annuity.—An annuity payable from the fund shall terminate—

(1) in the case of a retired participant, on the day death or any other terminating event provided by this title occurs; or

(2) in the case of a former spouse or a survivor, on the last day of the month before death or any other terminating event occurs.

(d) Application for Survivor Annuities.— The annuity to a survivor shall become effective as otherwise specified but shall not be paid until the survivor submits an application for such annuity, supported by such proof of eligibility as the Director may require. If such application or proof of eligibility is not submitted during the lifetime of an otherwise eligible individual, no annuity shall be due or payable to the individual's estate.

(e) Waiver of Annuity.— An individual entitled to an annuity from the fund may decline to accept all or any part of the annuity by submitting a signed waiver to the Director. The waiver may be revoked in writing at any time. Payment of the annuity waived may not be made for the period during which the waiver is in effect.

(f) Limitations.—

(1) Application before 115th anniversary.— No payment shall be made from the fund unless an application for benefits based on the service of the participant is received by the Director before the 115th anniversary of the participant's birth.

(2) Application within 30 years.— Notwithstanding paragraph (1), after the death of a participant or retired participant, no benefit based on that participant's service may be paid from the fund unless an application for the benefit is received by the Director within 30 years after the death or other event which gives rise to eligibility for the benefit.

(g) Withholding of State Income Tax From Annuities.—

(1) Agreements with states.— The Director shall, in accordance with this subsection, enter into an agreement with any State within 120 days of a request for agreement from the proper State official. The agreement shall provide that the Director shall withhold State income tax in the case of the monthly annuity of any annuitant who voluntarily requests, in writing, such withholding. The amounts withheld during any calendar quarter shall be held in the fund and disbursed to the States during the month following that calendar quarter.

(2) Limitation on multiple requests.— An annuitant may have in effect at any time only one request for withholding under this subsection, and an annuitant may not have more than two such requests during any one calendar year.

(3) Change in state designation.— Subject to paragraph (2), an annuitant may change the State designated by that annuitant for purposes of having withholdings made, and may request that the withholdings be remitted in accordance with such change. An annuitant also may revoke any request of that annuitant for withholding. Any change in the State designated or revocation is effective on the first day of the month after the month in which the request or the revocation is processed by the Director, but in no event later than on the first day of the second month beginning

after the day on which such request or revocation is received by the Director.

(4) General provisions.— This subsection does not give the consent of the United States to the application of a statute which imposes more burdensome requirements of the United States than on employers generally, or which subjects the United States or any annuitant to a penalty or liability because of this subsection. The Director may not accept pay from a State for services performed in withholding State income taxes from annuities. Any amount erroneously withheld from an annuity and paid to a State by the Director shall be repaid by the State in accordance with regulations prescribed by the Director.

(5) Definition.— For the purpose of this subsection, the term "State" includes the District of Columbia and any territory or possession of the United States.

SEC. 264. [50 U.S.C. 2094] ATTACHMENT OF MONEYS.

(a) Exemption From Legal Process.— Except as provided in subsections (b), (c), and (e), none of the moneys mentioned in this title shall be assignable either in law or equity, or be subject to execution, levy, attachment, garnishment, or other legal process, except as otherwise may be provided by Federal laws.

(b) Payment to Former Spouses Under Court Order or Spousal Agreement.—In the case of any participant, former participant, or retired participant who has a former spouse who is covered by a court order or who is a party to a spousal agreement—

(1) any right of the former spouse to any annuity under section 222(a) in connection with any retirement or disability annuity of the participant, and the amount of any such annuity;

(2) any right of the former spouse of a participant or retired participant to a survivor annuity under section 222(b) or 222(c), and the amount of any such annuity; and

(3) any right of the former spouse of a former participant to any payment of a lump-sum credit under section 241(b), and the amount of any such payment;

shall be determined in accordance with that spousal agreement or court order, if and to the extent expressly provided for in the terms of the spousal agreement or court order that are not inconsistent with the requirements of this title.

(c) Other Payments Under Court Orders.— Payments under this title that would otherwise be made to a participant, former participant, or retired participant based upon that participant's service shall be paid, in whole or in part, by the Director to another individual if and to the extent expressly provided for in the terms of any court decree of divorce, annulment, or legal separation, or the terms of any court order or court-approved property settlement agreement incident to any court decree of divorce, annulment, or legal separation.

(d) Prospective Payments; Bar To Recovery.—

(1) Subsections (b) and (c) apply only to payments made under this title for periods beginning after the date of receipt by the Director of written notice of such decree, order, or agreement and such additional information and documentation as the Director may require.

(2) Any payment under subsection (b) or (c) to an individual bars recovery by

any other individual.

(e) Allotments.— An individual entitled to an annuity from the fund may make allotments or assignments of amounts from such annuity for such purposes as the Director considers appropriate.

SEC. 265. [50 U.S.C. 2095] RECOVERY OF PAYMENTS.

Recovery of payments under this title may not be made from an individual when, in the judgment of the Director, the individual is without fault and recovery would be against equity and good conscience. Withholding or recovery of money payable pursuant to this title on account of a certification or payment made by a former employee of the Agency in the discharge of the former employee's official duties may be made if the Director certifies that the certification or payment involved fraud on the part of the former employee.

Part H—Retired Participants Recalled, Reinstated, or Reappointed in the Agency or Reemployed in the Government

SEC. 271. [50 U.S.C. 2111] RECALL.

(a) Authority To Recall.— The Director may, with the consent of a retired participant, recall that participant to service in the Agency whenever the Director determines that such recall is in the public interest.

(b) Pay of Retired Participant While Serving.— A retired participant recalled to duty in the Agency under subsection (a) or reinstated or reappointed in accordance with section 231(c) shall, while so serving, be entitled, in lieu of the retired participant's annuity, to the full basic pay of the grade in which the retired participant is serving. During such service, the retired participant shall make contributions to the fund in accordance with section 211.

(c) Recomputation of Annuity.— When the retired participant reverts to retired status, the annuity of the retired participant shall be redetermined in accordance with section 221.

SEC. 272. [50 U.S.C. 2112] REEMPLOYMENT.

A participant retired under this title shall not, by reason of that retired status, be barred from employment in Federal Government service in any appointive position for which the participant is qualified.

SEC. 273. [50 U.S.C. 2113] REEMPLOYMENT COMPENSATION.

(a) Deduction From Basic Pay.— An annuitant who has retired under this title and who is reemployed in the Federal Government service in any appointive position (either on a part-time or full-time basis) shall be entitled to receive the annuity payable under this title, but there shall be deducted from the annuitant's basic pay a sum equal to the annuity allocable to the period of actual employment.

(b) Part-Time Reemployed Annuitants.— The Director shall have the authority to reemploy an annuitant on a part-time basis in accordance with section 8344(l) of title 5, United States Code.

(c) Recovery of Overpayments.— In the event of an overpayment under this section, the amount of the overpayment shall be recovered by withholding the amount involved from the basic pay payable to such reemployed annuitant or from any other moneys, including the annuitant's annuity, payable in accordance with this title.

(d) DEPOSIT IN THE FUND.— Sums deducted from the basic pay of a reemployed annuitant under this section shall be deposited in the Treasury of the United States to the credit of the fund.

PART I—VOLUNTARY CONTRIBUTIONS

SEC. 281. [50 U.S.C. 2121] VOLUNTARY CONTRIBUTIONS.

(a) AUTHORITY FOR VOLUNTARY CONTRIBUTIONS.—

(1) IN GENERAL.— Under such regulations as may be prescribed by the Director, a participant may voluntarily contribute additional sums in multiples of one percent of the participant's basic pay, but not in excess of 10 percent of such basic pay.

(2) INTEREST.—The voluntary contribution account in each case is the sum of unrefunded contributions, plus interest—

(A) for periods before January 1, 1985, at 3 percent a year; and

(B) for periods on or after January 1, 1985, at the rate computed under section 8334(e) of title 5, United States Code,

compounded annually to the date of election under subsection (b) or the date of payment under subsection (d).

(b) TREATMENT OF VOLUNTARY CONTRIBUTIONS.—Effective on the date of retirement and at the election of the participant, the participant's account shall be—

(1) returned in a lump sum;

(2) used to purchase an additional life annuity;

(3) used to purchase an additional life annuity for the participant and to provide for a cash payment on the participant's death to a beneficiary; or

(4) used to purchase an additional life annuity for the participant and a life annuity commencing on the participant's death payable to a beneficiary, with a guaranteed return to the beneficiary or the beneficiary's legal representative of an amount equal to the cash payment referred to in paragraph (3).

In the case of a benefit provided under paragraph (3) or (4), the participant shall notify the Director in writing of the name of the beneficiary of the cash payment or life annuity to be paid upon the participant's death.

(c) VALUE OF BENEFITS.— The benefits provided by subsection (b) (2), (3), or (4) shall be actuarially equivalent in value to the payment provided for in subsection (b)(1) and shall be calculated upon such tables of mortality as may be from time to time prescribed for this purpose by the Director.

(d) LUMP-SUM PAYMENT.— A voluntary contribution account shall be paid in a lump sum at such time as the participant dies or separates from the Agency without entitlement to an annuity. In the case of death, the account shall be paid in the order of precedence specified in section 241(c).

(e) BENEFITS IN ADDITION TO OTHER BENEFITS.— Any benefit payable to a participant or to the participant's beneficiary with respect to the additional contributions provided under this section shall be in addition to benefits otherwise provided under this title.

PART J—COST-OF-LIVING ADJUSTMENT OF ANNUITIES

SEC. 291. [50 U.S.C. 2131] COST-OF-LIVING ADJUSTMENT OF ANNUITIES.

(a) IN GENERAL.—Each annuity payable from the fund shall be adjusted as follows:

(1) Each cost-of-living annuity increase under this section shall be identical to the corresponding percentage increase under section 8340(b) of title 5, United States Code.

(2) A cost-of-living increase made under paragraph (1) shall become effective under this section on the effective date of each such increase under section 8340(b) of title 5, United States Code. Except as provided in subsection (b), each such increase shall be applied to each annuity payable from the fund which has a commencing date not later than the effective date of the increase.

(b) ELIGIBILITY.—Eligibility for an annuity increase under this section shall be governed by the commencing date of each annuity payable from the fund as of the effective date of an increase, except as follows:

(1) The first cost-of-living increase (if any) made under subsection (a) to an annuity which is payable from the fund to a participant who retires, to the surviving spouse, former spouse, or previous spouse of a participant who dies in service, or to the surviving spouse, former spouse, previous spouse, or insurable interest designee of a deceased annuitant whose annuity has not been increased under this subsection or subsection (a), shall be equal to the product (adjusted to the nearest 1/10 of one percent) of—

(A) 1/12 of the applicable percent change computed under subsection (a), multiplied by

(B) the number of months (not to exceed 12 months, counting any portion of a month as a month)—

(i) for which the annuity was payable from the fund before the effective date of the increase, or

(ii) in the case of a surviving spouse, former spouse, previous spouse, or insurable interest designee of a deceased annuitant whose annuity has not been so increased, since the annuity was first payable to the deceased annuitant.

(2) Effective from its commencing date, an annuity payable from the fund to an annuitant's survivor (other than a child entitled to an annuity under section 221(d)) shall be increased by the total percentage increase the annuitant was receiving under this section at death.

(3) For purposes of computing the annuity of a child under section 221(d) that commences after October 31, 1969, the dollar amounts specified in section 221(d)(3) shall each be increased by the total percentage increases allowed and in force under this section on or after such day and, in the case of a deceased annuitant, the percentages specified in that section shall be increased by the total percent allowed and in force to the annuitant under this section on or after such day.

(c) LIMITATION.— An annuity increase provided by this section may not be computed on any additional annuity purchased at retirement by voluntary contributions.

(d) ROUNDING TO NEXT LOWER DOLLAR.— The monthly annuity installment, after adjustment under this section, shall be rounded to the next lowest dollar, except that such installment shall, after adjustment, reflect an increase of at least $1.

(e) LIMITATION ON MAXIMUM AMOUNT OF ANNUITY.—

(1) IN GENERAL.—An annuity shall not be increased by reason of an adjustment under this section to an amount which exceeds the greater of—

(A) the maximum pay payable for GS–15 30 days before the effective date of the adjustment under this section; or

(B) the final pay (or average pay, if higher) of the participant with respect to whom the annuity is paid, increased by the overall annual average percentage adjustments (compounded) in the rates of pay of the General Schedule under subchapter I of chapter 53 of title 5, United States Code, during the period—

(i) beginning on the date on which the annuity commenced (or, in the case of a survivor of the retired participant, the date on which the participant's annuity commenced), and

(ii) ending on the effective date of the adjustment under this section.

(2) PAY DEFINED.— For purposes of paragraph (1), the term “pay” means the rate of salary or basic pay as payable under any provision of law, including any provision of law limiting the expenditure of appropriated funds.

PART K—CONFORMITY WITH CIVIL SERVICE RETIREMENT SYSTEM

SEC. 292. [50 U.S.C. 2141] AUTHORITY TO MAINTAIN EXISTING AREAS OF CONFORMITY BETWEEN CIVIL SERVICE AND CENTRAL INTELLIGENCE AGENCY RETIREMENT AND DISABILITY SYSTEMS.

(a) PRESIDENTIAL AUTHORITY.—

(1) CONFORMITY TO CSRS BY EXECUTIVE ORDER.—Whenever the President determines that it would be appropriate for the purpose of maintaining existing conformity between the Civil Service Retirement and Disability System and the Central Intelligence Agency Retirement and Disability System with respect to substantially identical provisions, the President may, by Executive order, extend to current or former participants in the Central Intelligence Agency Retirement and Disability System, or to their survivors, a provision of law enacted after January 1, 1975, which—

(A) amends subchapter III of chapter 83 of title 5, United States Code, and is applicable to civil service employees generally; or

(B) otherwise affects current or former participants in the Civil Service Retirement and Disability System, or their survivors.

(2) EXTENSION TO CIARDS.— Any such order shall extend such provision of law so that it applies in like manner with respect to such Central Intelligence Agency Retirement and Disability System participants, former participants, or survivors.

(3) LEGAL STATUS.— Any such order shall have the force and effect of law.

(4) EFFECTIVE DATE.— Any such order may be given retroactive effect to a date not earlier than the effective date of the corresponding provision of law applicable to employees under the Civil Service Retirement System.

(b) EFFECT OF EXECUTIVE ORDER.—Provisions of an Executive order issued pursuant to this section shall modify, supersede, or render inapplicable, as the case may be, to the extent inconsistent therewith—

(1) provisions of law enacted before the effective date of the Executive order; and

(2) any prior provision of an Executive order issued under this section.

SEC. 293. [50 U.S.C. 2142] THRIFT SAVINGS PLAN PARTICIPATION.

(a) ELIGIBILITY FOR THRIFT SAVINGS PLAN.— Participants in the system shall be deemed to be employees for the purposes of section 8351 of title 5, United States Code.

(b) MANAGEMENT OF THRIFT SAVINGS PLAN ACCOUNTS BY DIRECTOR.— Subsections (k) and (m) of section 8461 of title 5, United States Code, shall apply with respect to contributions made by participants to the Thrift Savings Fund under section 8351 of such title and to earnings attributable to the investment of such contributions.

SEC. 294. [50 U.S.C. 2143] ALTERNATIVE FORMS OF ANNUITIES.

(a) AUTHORITY FOR ALTERNATIVE FORM OF ANNUITY.— The Director shall prescribe regulations under which any participant who has a life-threatening affliction or other critical medical condition may, at the time of retiring under this title (other than under section 231), elect annuity benefits under this section instead of any other benefits under this title (including any survivor benefits under this title) based on the service of the participant creditable under this title.

(b) BASIS FOR ALTERNATIVE FORMS OF ANNUITY.— The regulations and alternative forms of annuity shall, to the maximum extent practicable, meet the requirements prescribed in section 8343a of title 5, United States Code.

(c) LUMP-SUM CREDIT.— Any lump-sum credit provided pursuant to an election under subsection (a) shall not preclude an individual from receiving other benefits provided under that subsection.

(d) SUBMISSION OF REGULATIONS TO CONGRESSIONAL INTELLIGENCE COMMITTEES.— The Director shall submit the regulations prescribed under subsection (a) to the congressional intelligence committees before the regulations take effect.

SEC. 295. [50 U.S.C. 2144] PAYMENTS FROM CIARDS FUND FOR PORTIONS OF CERTAIN CIVIL SERVICE RETIREMENT SYSTEM ANNUITIES.

The amount of the increase in any annuity that results from the application of section 18 of the Central Intelligence Agency Act of 1949, if and when such increase is based on an individual's overseas service as an employee of the Central Intelligence Agency, shall be paid from the fund.

TITLE III—PARTICIPATION IN THE FEDERAL EMPLOYEES' RETIREMENT SYSTEM

SEC. 301. [50 U.S.C. 2151] APPLICATION OF FEDERAL EMPLOYEES' RETIREMENT SYSTEM TO AGENCY EMPLOYEES.

(a) General Rule.— Except as provided in subsections (b) and (c), all employees of the Agency, any of whose service after December 31, 1983, is employment for the purpose of title II of the Social Security Act and chapter 21 of the Internal Revenue Code of 1954, shall be subject to chapter 84 of title 5, United States Code.

(b) Exception for Pre-1984 Employees.— Participants in the Central Intelligence Agency Retirement and Disability System who were participants in such system on or before December 31, 1983, and who have not had a break in service in excess of one year since that date, are not subject to chapter 84 of title 5, United States Code, without regard to whether they are subject to title II of the Social Security Act.

(c) Nonapplicability of FERS to Certain Employees.—

(1) The provisions of chapter 84 of title 5, United States Code, shall not apply with respect to—

(A) any individual who separates, or who has separated, from Federal Government service after having been an employee of the Agency subject to title II of this Act; and

(B) any employee of the Agency having at least 5 years of civilian service which was performed before January 1, 1987, and is creditable under title II of this Act (determined without regard to any deposit or redeposit requirement under subchapter III of chapter 83 of title 5, United States Code, or under title II of this Act, or any requirement that the individual become subject to such subchapter or to title II of this Act after performing the service involved).

(2) Paragraph (1) shall not apply with respect to an individual who has elected under regulations prescribed under section 307 to become subject to chapter 84 of title 5, United States Code, to the extent provided in such regulations.

(3) An individual described in paragraph (1) shall be deemed to be an individual excluded under section 8402(b)(2) of title 5, United States Code.

(d) Election To Become Subject to FERS.—An employee who is designated as a participant in the Central Intelligence Agency Retirement and Disability System after December 31, 1987, pursuant to section 203 may elect to become subject to chapter 84 of title 5, United States Code. Such election—

(1) shall not be effective unless it is made during the six-month period beginning on the date on which the employee is so designated;

(2) shall take effect beginning with the first pay period beginning after the date of the election; and

(3) shall be irrevocable.

(e) Special Rules.— The application of the provisions of chapter 84 of title 5, United States Code, to an employee referred to in subsection (a) shall be subject to the exceptions and special rules provided in this title. Any provision of that chapter which is inconsistent with a special rule provided in this title shall not apply to such employees.

SEC. 302. [50 U.S.C. 2152] SPECIAL RULES RELATING TO SECTION 203 CRITERIA EMPLOYEES.

(a) In General.— Except as otherwise provided in this section, in the application of chapter 84 of title 5, United States Code, to an employee of the Agency who is subject to such chapter and is designated by the Director under the criteria prescribed in section 203, such employee shall be treated for purposes of determining such employee's retirement benefits and obligations under such chapter as if the employee were a law enforcement officer (as defined in section 8401(17) of title 5, United States Code).

(b) Voluntary and Mandatory Retirement.— The provisions of sections 233 and 235 shall apply to employees referred to in subsection (a), except that the retirement benefits shall be determined under chapter 84 of title 5, United States Code.

(c) Recall.—

(1) Except as provided in paragraph (2), section 271 shall apply to an employee referred to in subsection (a).

(2) Contributions during recall service shall be made as provided in section 8422 of title 5, United States Code.

(3) When an employee recalled under this subsection reverts to a retired status, the annuity of such employee shall be redetermined under the provisions of chapter 84 of title 5, United States Code.

(d) Employees Disabled on Duty.—

(1) Definitions.—In this subsection—

(A) the term "affected employee" means an employee of the Agency covered under subchapter II of chapter 84 of title 5, United States Code, who—

(i) is performing service in a position designated under subsection (a);

(ii) while on duty in the position designated under subsection (a), becomes ill or is injured as a direct result of the performance of such duties before the date on which the employee becomes entitled to an annuity under section 233 of this Act or section 8412(d)(1) of title 5, United States Code;

(iii) because of the illness or injury described in clause (ii), is permanently unable to render useful and efficient service in the employee's covered position, as determined by the Director; and

(iv) is appointed to a position in the civil service that is not a covered position but is within the Agency; and

(B) the term "covered position" means a position as—

(i) a law enforcement officer described in section 8331(20) or 8401(17) of title 5, United States Code;

(ii) a customs and border protection officer described in section 8331(31) or 8401(36) of title 5, United States Code;

(iii) a firefighter described in section 8331(21) or 8401(14) of title 5, United States Code;

(iv) an air traffic controller described in section 8331(30) or 8401(35) of title 5, United States Code;

(v) a nuclear materials courier described in section 8331(27) or 8401(33) of title 5, United States Code;

(vi) a member of the United States Capitol Police;

(vii) a member of the Supreme Court Police;

(viii) an affected employee; or

(ix) a special agent described in section 804(15) of the Foreign Service Act of 1980 (22 U.S.C. 4044(15)).

(2) TREATMENT OF SERVICE AFTER DISABILITY.— Unless an affected employee files an election described in paragraph (3), creditable service by the affected employee in a position described in paragraph (1)(A)(iv) shall be treated as creditable service in a covered position for purposes of this Act and chapter 84 of title 5, United States Code, including eligibility for an annuity under section 233 of this Act or 8412(d)(1) of title 5, United States Code, and determining the amount to be deducted and withheld from the pay of the affected employee under section 8422 of title 5, United States Code.

(3) BREAK IN SERVICE.— Paragraph (2) shall only apply if the affected employee transitions to a position described in paragraph (1)(A)(iv) without a break in service exceeding 3 days.

(4) LIMITATION ON TREATMENT OF SERVICE.— The service of an affected employee shall no longer be eligible for treatment under paragraph (2) if such service occurs after the employee is transferred to a supervisory or administrative position related to the activities of the former covered position of the employee.

(5) OPT OUT.— An affected employee may file an election to have any creditable service performed by the affected employee treated in accordance with chapter 84 of title 5, United States Code, without regard to paragraph (2).

SEC. 303. [50 U.S.C. 2153] SPECIAL RULES FOR OTHER EMPLOYEES FOR SERVICE ABROAD.

(a) SPECIAL COMPUTATION RULE.— Notwithstanding any provision of chapter 84 of title 5, United States Code, the annuity under subchapter II of such chapter of a retired employee of the Agency who is not designated under section 302(a) and who has served abroad as an employee of the Agency after December 31, 1986, shall be computed as provided in subsection (b).

(b) COMPUTATION.—

(1) SERVICE ABROAD.— The portion of the annuity relating to such service abroad shall be computed as provided in section 8415(e) of title 5, United States Code.

(2) OTHER SERVICE.— The portions of the annuity relating to other creditable service shall be computed as provided in section 8415 of such title that is applicable to such service under the conditions prescribed in chapter 84 of such title.

SEC. 304. [50 U.S.C. 2154] SPECIAL RULES FOR FORMER SPOUSES.

(a) GENERAL RULE.— Except as otherwise specifically provided in this section, the provisions of chapter 84 of title 5, United States Code, shall apply in the case of an employee of the Agency who is subject to chapter 84 of title 5, United States Code, and who has a former spouse (as defined in section 8401(12) of title 5, United States Code) or a qualified former spouse.

(b) DEFINITIONS.—For purposes of this section:

(1) EMPLOYEE.— The term "employee" means an employee of the Agency who is subject to chapter 84 of title 5, United States Code, including an employee referred to in section 302(a).

(2) QUALIFIED FORMER SPOUSE.—The term "qualified former spouse" means a former spouse of an employee or retired employee who—

(A) in the case of a former spouse whose divorce from such employee became final on or before December 4, 1991, was married to such employee for not less than 10 years during periods of the employee's service which are creditable under section 8411 of title 5, United States Code, at least 5 years of which were spent outside the United States by both the employee and the former spouse during the employee's service with the Agency; and

(B) in the case of a former spouse whose divorce from such employee becomes final after December 4, 1991, was married to such employee for not less than 10 years during periods of the employee's service which are creditable under section 8411 of title 5, United States Code, at least 5 years of which were spent by the employee outside the United States during the employee's service with the Agency or otherwise in a position the duties of which qualified the employee for designation by the Director under the criteria prescribed in section 203.

(3) PRO RATA SHARE.— The term "pro rata share" means the percentage that is equal to (A) the number of days of the marriage of the qualified former spouse to the employee during the employee's periods of creditable service under chapter 84 of title 5, United States Code, divided by (B) the total number of days of the employee's creditable service.

(4) SPOUSAL AGREEMENT.—The term "spousal agreement" means an agreement between an employee, former employee, or retired employee and such employee's spouse or qualified former spouse that—

(A) is in writing, is signed by the parties, and is notarized;

(B) has not been modified by court order; and

(C) has been authenticated by the Director.

(5) COURT ORDER.— The term "court order" means any court decree of divorce, annulment or legal separation, or any court order or court-approved property settlement agreement incident to such court decree of divorce, annulment, or legal separation.

(c) ENTITLEMENT OF QUALIFIED FORMER SPOUSE TO RETIREMENT BENEFITS.—

(1) ENTITLEMENT.—

(A) IN GENERAL.— Unless otherwise expressly provided by a spousal agreement or court order governing disposition of benefits payable under subchapter II or V of chapter 84 of title 5, United States Code, a qualified former spouse of an employee is entitled to a share (determined under subparagraph (B)) of all benefits otherwise payable to such employee under subchapter II or V of chapter 84 of title 5, United States Code.

(B) AMOUNT OF SHARE.—The share referred to in subparagraph (A) equals—

(i) 50 percent, if the qualified former spouse was married to the employee throughout the entire period of the employee's service which is creditable under chapter 84 of title 5, United States Code; or

(ii) a pro rata share of 50 percent, if the qualified former spouse was not married to the employee throughout such creditable service.

(2) Annuity supplement.— The benefits payable to an employee under subchapter II of chapter 84 of title 5, United States Code, shall include, for purposes of this subsection, any annuity supplement payable to such employee under sections 8421 and 8421a of such title.

(3) Disqualification upon remarriage before age 55.— A qualified former spouse shall not be entitled to any benefit under this subsection if, before the commencement of any benefit, the qualified former spouse remarries before becoming 55 years of age.

(4) Commencement and termination.—

(A) Commencement.—The benefits of a qualified former spouse under this subsection commence on the later of—

(i) the day on which the employee upon whose service the benefits are based becomes entitled to the benefits; or

(ii) the first day of the second month beginning after the date on which the Director receives written notice of the court order or spousal agreement, together with such additional information or documentation as the Director may prescribe.

(B) Termination.—The benefits of the qualified former spouse and the right thereto terminate on—

(i) the last day of the month before the qualified former spouse remarries before 55 years of age or dies; or

(ii) the date on which the retired employee's benefits terminate (except in the case of benefits subject to paragraph (5)(B)).

(5) Payments to retired employees.—

(A) Calculation of survivor annuity.—Any reduction in payments to a retired employee as a result of payments to a qualified former spouse under this subsection shall be disregarded in calculating—

(i) the survivor annuity for any spouse, former spouse (qualified or otherwise), or other survivor under chapter 84 of title 5, United States Code, and

(ii) any reduction in the annuity of the retired employee to provide survivor benefits under subsection (d) of this section or under section 8442 or 8445 of title 5, United States Code.

(B) Reduction in basic pay upon recall to service.— If a retired employee whose annuity is reduced under paragraph (1) is recalled to service under section 302(c), the basic pay of that annuitant shall be reduced by the same amount as the annuity would have been reduced if it had continued. Amounts equal to the reductions under this subparagraph shall be deposited in the Treasury of the United States to the credit of the Civil Service Retirement and Disability Fund.

(6) Special rules for disability annuitants.—Notwithstanding paragraphs (1) and (4), in the case of any qualified former spouse of a disability annuitant—

(A) the annuity of such former spouse shall commence on the date on which the employee would qualify, on the basis of the employee's creditable service, for benefits under subchapter II of chapter 84 of title 5, United States Code, or on the date on which the disability annuity begins, whichever is later; and

(B) the amount of the annuity of the qualified former spouse shall be calculated on the basis of the benefits for which the employee would otherwise qualify under subchapter II of chapter 84 of such title.

(7) PRO RATA SHARE IN CASE OF EMPLOYEES TRANSFERRED TO FERS.—Notwithstanding paragraph (1)(B), in the case of an employee who has elected to become subject to chapter 84 of title 5, United States Code, the share of such employee's qualified former spouse shall equal the sum of—

(A) 50 percent of the employee's annuity under subchapter III of chapter 83 of title 5, United States Code, or under title II of this Act (computed in accordance with section 302(a) of the Federal Employees' Retirement System Act of 1986 or section 307 of this Act), multiplied by the proportion that the number of days of marriage during the period of the employee's creditable service before the effective date of the election to transfer bears to the employee's total creditable service before such effective date; and

(B) if applicable, 50 percent of the employee's benefits under chapter 84 of title 5, United States Code, or section 302(a) of this Act (computed in accordance with section 302(a) of the Federal Employees' Retirement System Act of 1986 or section 307 of this Act), multiplied by the proportion that the number of days of marriage during the period of the employee's creditable service on and after the effective date of the election to transfer bears to the employee's total creditable service after such effective date.

(8) TREATMENT OF PRO RATA SHARE UNDER INTERNAL REVENUE CODE.— For purposes of the Internal Revenue Code of 1986, payments to a qualified former spouse under this subsection shall be treated as income to the qualified former spouse and not to the employee.

(d) QUALIFIED FORMER SPOUSE SURVIVOR BENEFITS.—

(1) ENTITLEMENT.—

(A) IN GENERAL.— Subject to an election under section 8416(a) of title 5, United States Code, and unless otherwise expressly provided by any spousal agreement or court order governing survivor benefits payable under this subsection to a qualified former spouse, such former spouse is entitled to a share, determined under subparagraph (B), of all survivor benefits that would otherwise be payable under subchapter IV of chapter 84 of title 5, United States Code, to an eligible surviving spouse of the employee.

(B) AMOUNT OF SHARE.—The share referred to in subparagraph (A) equals—

(i) 100 percent, if the qualified former spouse was married to the employee throughout the entire period of the employee's service which is creditable under chapter 84 of title 5, United States Code; or

(ii) a pro rata share of 100 percent, if the qualified former spouse was not married to the employee throughout such creditable service.

(2) SURVIVOR BENEFITS.—

(A) The survivor benefits payable under this subsection to a qualified former spouse shall include the amount payable under section 8442(b)(1)(A) of title 5, United States Code, and any supplementary annuity under section 8442(f) of such title that would be payable if such former spouse were a widow or widower entitled to an annuity under such section.

(B) Any calculation under section 8442(f) of title 5, United States Code, of the supplementary annuity payable to a widow or widower of an employee referred to in section 302(a) shall be based on an "assumed CIARDS annuity" rather than an "assumed CSRS annuity" as stated in section 8442(f) of such title. For the purpose of this subparagraph, the term "assumed CIARDS annuity" means the amount of the survivor annuity to which the widow or widower would be entitled under title II of this Act based on the service of the deceased annuitant determined under section 8442(f)(5) of such title.

(3) Disqualification upon remarriage before age 55.— A qualified former spouse shall not be entitled to any benefit under this subsection if, before commencement of any benefit, the qualified former spouse remarries before becoming 55 years of age.

(4) Restoration.—If the survivor annuity payable under this subsection to a surviving qualified former spouse is terminated because of remarriage before becoming age 55, the annuity shall be restored at the same rate commencing on the date such remarriage is dissolved by death, divorce, or annulment, if—

(A) such former spouse elects to receive this survivor annuity instead of any other survivor benefit to which such former spouse may be entitled under subchapter IV of chapter 84 of title 5, United States Code, or under another retirement system for Government employees by reason of the remarriage; and

(B) any lump sum paid on termination of the annuity is returned to the Civil Service Retirement and Disability Fund.

(5) Modification of court order or spousal agreement.— A modification in a court order or spousal agreement to adjust a qualified former spouse's share of the survivor benefits shall not be effective if issued after the retirement or death of the employee, former employee, or annuitant, whichever occurs first.

(6) Effect of termination of qualified former spouse's entitlement.— After a qualified former spouse of a retired employee remarries before becoming age 55 or dies, the reduction in the retired employee's annuity for the purpose of providing a survivor annuity for such former spouse shall be terminated. The annuitant may elect, in a signed writing received by the Director within 2 years after the qualified former spouse's remarriage or death, to continue the reduction in order to provide or increase the survivor annuity for such annuitant's spouse. The annuitant making such election shall pay a deposit in accordance with the provisions of section 8418 of title 5, United States Code.

(7) Pro rata share in case of employees transferred to FERS.—Notwithstanding paragraph (1)(B), in the case of an employee who has elected to become subject to chapter 84 of title 5, United States Code, the share of such employee's qualified former spouse to survivor benefits shall equal the sum of—

(A) 50 percent of the employee's annuity under subchapter III of chapter 83 of title 5, United States Code, or under title II of this Act (computed in accordance with section 302(a) of the Federal Employees' Retirement System Act of 1986 or section 307 of this Act), multiplied by the proportion that the number of days of marriage during the period of the employee's creditable service before the effective date of the election to transfer bears to the employee's total creditable service before such effective date; and

(B) if applicable—

(i) 50 percent of the employee's annuity under chapter 84 of title 5, United States Code, or section 302(a) of this Act (computed in accordance with section 302(a) of the Federal Employees' Retirement System Act of 1986 or section 307 of this Act), plus

(ii) the survivor benefits referred to in subsection (d)(2)(A),

multiplied by the proportion that the number of days of marriage during the period of the employee's creditable service on and after the effective date of the election to transfer bears to the employee's total creditable service after such effective date.

(e) QUALIFIED FORMER SPOUSE THRIFT SAVINGS PLAN BENEFIT.—

(1) ENTITLEMENT.—

(A) IN GENERAL.— Unless otherwise expressly provided by a spousal agreement or court order governing disposition of the balance of an account in the Thrift Savings Fund under subchapter III of chapter 84 of title 5, United States Code, a qualified former spouse of an employee is entitled to a share (determined under subparagraph (B)) of the balance in the employee's account in the Thrift Savings Fund on the date the divorce of the qualified former spouse and employee becomes final.

(B) AMOUNT OF SHARE.— The share referred to in subparagraph (A) equals 50 percent of the employee's account balance in the Thrift Savings Fund that accrued during the period of marriage. For purposes of this subsection, the employee's account balance shall not include the amount of any outstanding loan.

(2) PAYMENT OF BENEFIT.—

(A) TIME OF PAYMENT.— The entitlement of a qualified former spouse under paragraph (1) shall be effective on the date the divorce of the qualified former spouse and employee becomes final. The qualified former spouse's benefit shall be payable after the date on which the Director receives the divorce decree or any applicable court order or spousal agreement, together with such additional information or documentation as the Director may require.

(B) METHOD OF PAYMENT.— The qualified former spouse's benefit under this subsection shall be paid in a lump sum.

(C) LIMITATION.— A spousal agreement or court order may not provide for payment to a qualified former spouse under this subsection of an amount that exceeds the employee's account balance in the Thrift Savings Fund.

(D) DEATH OF QUALIFIED FORMER SPOUSE.— If the qualified former spouse dies before payment of the benefit provided under this subsection, such payment shall be made to the estate of the qualified former spouse.

(E) BAR TO RECOVERY.— Any payment under this subsection to an individual bars recovery by any other individual.

(3) CLOSED ACCOUNT.— No payment under this subsection may be made by the

Director if the date on which the divorce becomes final is after the date on which the total amount of the employee's account balance has been withdrawn or transferred, or the date on which an annuity contract has been purchased, in accordance with section 8433 of title 5, United States Code.

(f) PRESERVATION OF RIGHTS OF QUALIFIED FORMER SPOUSES.— An employee may not make an election or modification of election under section 8417 or 8418 of title 5, United States Code, or other section relating to the employee's annuity under subchapter II of chapter 84 of title 5, United States Code, that would diminish the entitlement of a qualified former spouse to any benefit granted to such former spouse by this section or by court order or spousal agreement.

(g) PAYMENT OF SHARE OF LUMP-SUM CREDIT.— Whenever an employee or former employee becomes entitled to receive the lump-sum credit under section 8424(a) of title 5, United States Code, a share (determined under subsection (c)(1)(B) of this section) of that lump-sum credit shall be paid to any qualified former spouse of such employee, unless otherwise expressly provided by any spousal agreement or court order governing disposition of the lump-sum credit involved.

(h) PAYMENT TO QUALIFIED FORMER SPOUSES UNDER COURT ORDER OR SPOUSAL AGREEMENT.—In the case of any employee or retired employee who has a qualified former spouse who is covered by a court order or who is a party to a spousal agreement—

(1) any right of the qualified former spouse to any retirement benefits under subsection (c) and to any survivor benefits under subsection (d), and the amount of any such benefits;

(2) any right of the qualified former spouse to any Thrift Savings Plan benefit under subsection (e), and the amount of any such benefit; and

(3) any right of the qualified former spouse to any payment of a lump-sum credit under subsection (g), and the amount of any such payment;

shall be determined in accordance with that spousal agreement or court order, if and to the extent expressly provided for in the terms of the spousal agreement or court order that are not inconsistent with the requirements of this section.

(i) APPLICABILITY OF CIARDS FORMER SPOUSE BENEFITS.—

(1) Except as provided in paragraph (2), in the case of an employee who has elected to become subject to chapter 84 of title 5, United States Code, the provisions of sections 224 and 225 shall apply to such employee's former spouse (as defined in section 102(a)(4)) who would otherwise be eligible for benefits under sections 224 and 225 but for the employee having elected to become subject to such chapter.

(2) For the purposes of computing such former spouse's benefits under sections 224 and 225—

(A) the retirement benefits shall be equal to the amount determined under subsection (c)(7)(A); and

(B) the survivor benefits shall be equal to 55 percent of the full amount of the employee's annuity computed in accordance with section 302(a) of the Federal Employees' Retirement System Act of 1986 or regulations prescribed under section 307 of this Act.

(3) Benefits provided pursuant to this subsection shall be payable from the

Central Intelligence Agency Retirement and Disability Fund.

SEC. 305. [50 U.S.C. 2155] ADMINISTRATIVE PROVISIONS.

(a) FINALITY OF DECISIONS OF DIRECTOR.— Section 201(c) of this Act shall apply in the administration of chapter 84 of title 5, United States Code, with respect to employees of the Agency.

(b) EXCEPTION.— Notwithstanding subsection (a), section 8461(e) of title 5, United States Code, shall apply with respect to employees of the Agency who are not participants in the Central Intelligence Agency Retirement and Disability System and are not designated under section 302(a).

SEC. 306. [50 U.S.C. 2156] REGULATIONS.

(a) REQUIREMENT.— The Director shall prescribe in regulations appropriate procedures to carry out this title. Such regulations shall be prescribed in consultation with the Director of the Office of Personnel Management and the Executive Director of the Federal Retirement Thrift Investment Board.

(b) CONGRESSIONAL REVIEW.— The Director shall submit regulations prescribed under subsection (a) to the congressional intelligence committees before they take effect.

SEC. 307. [50 U.S.C. 2157] TRANSITION REGULATIONS.

(a) REGULATIONS.— The Director shall prescribe regulations providing for the transition from the Central Intelligence Agency Retirement and Disability System to the Federal Employees' Retirement System provided in chapter 84 of title 5, United States Code, in a manner consistent with sections 301 through 304 of the Federal Employees' Retirement System Act of 1986.

(b) CONGRESSIONAL REVIEW.— The Director shall submit regulations prescribed under subsection (a) to the congressional intelligence committees before they take effect.

Selected Provisions of the Central Intelligence Agency Information Act

Public Law 98–477

CENTRAL INTELLIGENCE AGENCY INFORMATION ACT

[(Public Law 98–477; 98 Stat. 2209; approved October 15, 1984)]

AN ACT To amend the National Security Act of 1947 to regulate public disclosure of information held by the Central Intelligence Agency, and for other purposes.

Be it enacted by the Senate and House of Representatives of the United States of America in Congress assembled,

That this Act may be cited as the "Central Intelligence Agency Information Act". [50 U.S.C. 3001 note]

SEC. 2. [Subsections (a) and (b) added title VII to the National Security Act of 1947.]

(c) Subsection (q) of section 552a of title 5, United States Code, is amended—

(1) by inserting "(1)" after "(q)"; and

(2) by adding at the end thereof the following:

"(2) No agency shall rely on any exemption in this section to withhold from an individual any record which is otherwise accessible to such individual under the provisions of section 552 of this title.".

SEC. 3. (a) The Director of Central Intelligence, in consultation with the Archivist of the United States, the Librarian of Congress, and appropriate representatives of the historical discipline selected by the Archivist, shall prepare and submit by June 1, 1985, a report on the feasibility of conducting systematic review for declassification and release of Central Intelligence Agency information of historical value.

(b)(1) The Director shall, once each six months, prepare and submit an unclassified report which includes—

(A) a description of the specific measures established by the Director to improve the processing of requests under section 552 of title 5, United States Code;

(B) the current budgetary and personnel allocations for such processing;

(C) the number of such requests (i) received and processed during the preceding six months, and (ii) pending at the time of submission of such report; and

(D) an estimate of the current average response time for completing the processing of such requests.

(2) The first report required by paragraph (1) shall be submitted by a date which

is six months after the date of enactment of this Act. The requirements of such paragraph shall cease to apply after the submission of the fourth such report.

(c) Each of the reports required by subsections (a) and (b) shall be submitted to the Permanent Select Committee on Intelligence and the Committee on Government Operations[1] of the House of Representatives and the Select Committee on Intelligence and the Committee on the Judiciary of the Senate.

[1] The Committee on Government Operations was renamed to the Committee on Government Reform and Oversight by H. Res. 6 in the 104th Congress, and renamed the Committee on Government Reform by H. Res. 5 in the 106th Congress.

SEC. 4. [50 U.S.C. 3141 nt] The amendments made by subsections (a) and (b) of section 2 shall be effective upon enactment of this Act and shall apply with respect to any requests for records, whether or not such request was made prior to such enactment, and shall apply to all civil actions not commenced prior to February 7, 1984.

Foundational National Security Framework

- **National Security Act of 1947**
- **National Security Agency Act of 1959**
- **Intelligence Reform and Terrorism Prevention Act of 2004**

CIA—Specific Authorities

- **Central Intelligence Agency Act of 1949**
- **Central Intelligence Agency Retirement Act**
- **Central Intelligence Agency Information Act**

www.ingramcontent.com/pod-product-compliance
Lightning Source LLC
Chambersburg PA
CBHW070047030426
42335CB00016B/1821

* 9 7 8 1 9 6 2 9 7 8 3 2 3 *